12 November 2021

The Last Great War of Antiquity

For my stepdaughter and her sons

The Last Great War of Antiquity

JAMES HOWARD-JOHNSTON

Great Clarendon Street, Oxford, OX2 6DP,
United Kingdom

Oxford University Press is a department of the University of Oxford.
It furthers the University's objective of excellence in research, scholarship,
and education by publishing worldwide. Oxford is a registered trade mark of
Oxford University Press in the UK and in certain other countries

© James Howard-Johnston 2021

The moral rights of the author have been asserted

First Edition published in 2021

Impression: 1

All rights reserved. No part of this publication may be reproduced, stored in
a retrieval system, or transmitted, in any form or by any means, without the
prior permission in writing of Oxford University Press, or as expressly permitted
by law, by licence or under terms agreed with the appropriate reprographics
rights organization. Enquiries concerning reproduction outside the scope of the
above should be sent to the Rights Department, Oxford University Press, at the
address above

You must not circulate this work in any other form
and you must impose this same condition on any acquirer

Published in the United States of America by Oxford University Press
198 Madison Avenue, New York, NY 10016, United States of America

British Library Cataloguing in Publication Data

Data available

Library of Congress Control Number: 2021932105

ISBN 978–0–19–883019–1

DOI: 10.1093/oso/9780198830191.001.0001

Printed and bound by
CPI Group (UK) Ltd, Croydon, CR0 4YY

Links to third party websites are provided by Oxford in good faith and
for information only. Oxford disclaims any responsibility for the materials
contained in any third party website referenced in this work.

Preface

East-West conflict has been of perennial interest to historians, from the westernmost thrust of Persian power in the fifth century BC, when Xerxes attempted to conquer Greece, to the Cold War and the current rivalry between the old Western and the rising Eastern great power. All but one of the episodes of open warfare have had their historians, operating in the manner of Herodotus, but normally without his omnivorous curiosity. Politics being the prime subject matter of history in the classical period and violent action by discrete political entities its most intense manifestation, contemporary and near-contemporary historians gave plenty of space in their works to the many wars fought by Romans against the loose-knit Parthian empire and its more militarized Sasanian successor. The roll call of historians runs from Tacitus in the heyday of the Principate and Ammianus Marcellinus in the fourth century to Procopius and his three successors (Agathias, Menander Protector, and Theophylact Simocatta), who, between them, covered the four wars fought in the sixth century. Then, after a gap which this book is designed to fill, came the earliest Islamic historians, who, from the eighth century, pieced together narratives out of antecedent material about the Arab conquests, beginning with a victory over Roman forces not far from Gaza in 634. Their successors and their Christian counterparts covered the confrontations of Islam with Byzantium and Latin Christendom and the outward drive of the Ottomans.

The gap extends from 602 to 630. The grisly end of the Emperor Maurice and five of his six sons in November 602, after a military coup mounted by the Balkan field army and its new commander Phocas, provided the Sasanian king Khusro II with the pretext he needed to go to war to reassert the traditional parity of Persians with Romans. For Maurice was Khusro's benefactor, having restored him to the Sasanian throne, but he had demanded large, damaging territorial concessions. The war broke out in spring 603 and was only brought to an end two years after the overthrow and execution of Khusro, when a durable peace was negotiated by his daughter Boran with Phocas' nemesis and successor Heraclius in summer 630.

There *is* evidence about the war, but it is fragmentary and scattered across different types of source in different languages. It is a painstaking and time-consuming process to extract, vet, and piece together the bits of information into some sort of coherent story. That may partly explain why there is no full, solidly founded critical history of the last war between the two established great powers of western Eurasia at the end of antiquity. Learned articles have been written on individual episodes and on ideological aspects of the conflict. Many wider-ranging works, from Gibbon's *Decline and Fall* to that recent worldwide sensation, Peter Frankopan's *Silk Roads*, include outline accounts of the fighting, but they view it primarily as a precursor to the rise of Islam. Only two connected accounts of the whole war have been published, neither of which is grounded in comprehensive critical analysis of the primary material. One, the first volume of Andreas Stratos's *Byzantium in the Seventh Century*, simply recycles what is chronicled by the sources, while the other, Walter Kaegi's *Heraclius Emperor of Byzantium*, covers the fighting but is primarily concerned with the feats of one important participant.

A great deal of time has been consumed in research for this book. A prophecy of my wife's, that it would take as long to write as the events took to unfold, has, I fear, come true. Serious work began in autumn 1990, when I started a year's sabbatical leave. I am topping and tailing the eleven chapters, none very skimpy, into which it is divided, nearly twenty-seven years later and deep into *defunctitude* (aka retirement from university teaching, dubbed *The Twilight of the Scholar* by the young graduate students who enliven my existence). It is, I must confess, even worse than that. For the original inception of the project dates back to the early 1980s and took the form of a skeleton chronology handed out to undergraduate takers of an optional course in sixth- and seventh-century Middle Eastern history at Oxford. So what faces the reader is the product of *nearly forty years' work* at the coal face of knowledge. That (as well as convenience) explains the old-fashioned terminology (Monophysite and Nestorian) used for non-Chalcedonian confessions (Miaphysite and Church of the East are now preferred). There were, I am glad to say, some by-products—learned papers delivered at conferences (cited in the bibliography) and a book, *Witnesses to a World Crisis*, which laid down the historiographical foundations. The structure which rises from those foundations has acquired considerable bulk, despite unrelenting effort to keep footnotes short and to limit references to primary sources and a necessary minimum of secondary works. I hope that the bulk will not be too off-putting.

I have benefited from scholarly company of all sorts over these forty years, above all from my undergraduate pupils with whom I discussed the last great war of antiquity in tutorials from the 1980s to 2009. They have been replaced since 2009 by a small number of young scholars with whom I have been meeting weekly in term to read texts in Ethiopic, Arabic, and Syriac. I am immensely grateful to Phil Booth, Marek Jankowiak, Ed Zychovicz-Coghill (a fine Arabist whom I cannot help but call Professor), and Simon Ford, not merely for helping me to plug shameful gaps in linguistic competence but also for innumerable discussions of historical issues. There are many, many other debts—to Faculty and College colleagues, to the graduate students with whom I like to hobnob in these declining days, to participants in several conferences on Sasanian history and archaeology held since the 1990s, to the conference on the reign of the

Emperor Heraclius organized by Gerrit Reinink and Bernard Stolte at Gröningen in 2001, to the Seventh-Century Syrian Numismatic Round Table, which meets at intervals of two to three years, and to travelling companions on journeys to Iran, Tunisia, Armenia, and Algeria over the last two decades (for the ideas and banter exchanged).

Although it may be invidious to single them out and there is always the danger that someone who should be mentioned may be omitted, let me thank in particular the following for their contributions of information and ideas: (1) on the Sasanians, Richard Payne, the late Zeev Rubin, and Josef Wiesehöfer: (2) on pre-Islamic Arabia, Michael Macdonald; (3) on numismatics, Tony Goodwin, Rika Gyselen, Cécile Morrisson, and Susan Tyler-Smith; (4) on archaeology, the late Judith Mackenzie, Jodi Magness, the late Boris Marshak, Eberhard Sauer, St.John Simpson, and Alan Walmsley; and (5) on texts, Michael Jackson Bonner, Tim Greenwood, David Gyllenhaal, the late Cyril Mango, and Mary Whitby. Finally there are three scholars to whom I owe a particularly large debt: Phil Booth, with whom I have analysed the text of John of Nikiu and who has read and helped to improve several chapters; Marek Jankowiak, first leader of our Arabic reading group, with whom I have been wrestling over certain historical cruxes since we first met ten years ago; and Constantin Zuckerman, Marek's former supervisor, whom I regard as a peerless scholar of this period and a formidable antagonist when we disagree (as we do from time to time).

In addition, I am most grateful to the Oxford University Committee for Byzantine Studies for allowing me to keep an office in the Ioannou Centre for Classical and Byzantine Studies, for all these years of defunctitude.

JH-J

Temple House, Temple End, Harbury
November 2017

Postscript. Three and a half years have passed by since I wrote about the magnificent deformation of history in Corneille's *Héraclius* at the end of this book. Scholars of Late Antiquity and Byzantium have been as active as ever in adding to knowledge and understanding. I have cited a few recent publications of particular importance, none more so than T.B. Mitford, *East of Asia Minor: Rome's Hidden Frontier*, 2 vols. (Oxford, 2018), a gripping exploration of the Euphrates *limes*. Otherwise the text is unchanged. Finally, I am indebted to Callan Meynell for adding that vital component of any work of history, the index.

Brighton
February 2021

Contents

List of Abbreviations   xi
List of Maps   xv
List of Figures   xv
Table of Events   xvii

Introduction   1

1. Khusro's War of Revenge   8
   1.1 Phocas' Seizure of Power   12
   1.2 Persian Preparations for War   18
   1.3 Opening Campaigns   22
   1.4 Second Persian Offensive   29

2. The Heraclian Revolution   37
   2.1 Rebellion in the West, Disaffection in the East   39
   2.2 Battle for Egypt   49
   2.3 Fall of Phocas   61

3. Persian Breakthrough   72
   3.1 Theodore of Syceon and the War   73
   3.2 Persian Advance into Syria and Asia Minor, 610–13   78
   3.3 The Jerusalem Episode, 614   87
   3.4 Aftermath   96

4. Khusro's Fateful Decision   103
   4.1 The Senate's Letter   105
   4.2 Iran and Turan   113
   4.3 Further Persian Advances   120

5. The Middle East in the 620s   134
   5.1 The Roman Empire   136
   5.2 The Middle East under Persian Occupation   153
   5.3 The Sasanian Empire   173

6. Opening of the Battle for Survival   191
   6.1 Heraclius Takes Command in Asia Minor in 622   192
   6.2 Crisis in the Balkans   200
   6.3 The Avar Surprise   207

7. Heraclius' First Counteroffensive   214
   7.1 Heraclius' Opening Moves   217
   7.2 Invasion of Persian Territory   224
   7.3 The Persian Hunt for Heraclius   233

- 8. Climax of the War — 246
  - 8.1 Pursuit of Heraclius — 251
  - 8.2 Information, Confusion, and Disinformation in the Chronicle of Theophanes — 257
  - 8.3 Siege of Constantinople — 268
  - 8.4 Persian Reverses — 284
- 9. Heraclius' Second Counteroffensive — 293
  - 9.1 Turkish-Roman Alliance — 295
  - 9.2 Invasion of Mesopotamia — 304
  - 9.3 March on Ctesiphon — 310
  - 9.4 Fall of Khusro — 314
- 10. The Difficult Road to Peace — 321
  - 10.1 First Round of Negotiations — 322
  - 10.2 Celebration of Victory at Constantinople — 328
  - 10.3 Second Round of Negotiations — 336
  - 10.4 Celebration of Victory at Jerusalem — 346
  - 10.5 The Final Settlement — 353
- 11. Conclusion — 360
  - 11.1 Explanations — 362
  - 11.2 Consequences — 372

Afterword — 389

Appendix 1. *Dramatis Personae* — 395
Appendix 2. *Scene* — 399
Appendix 3. *Sources* — 403

Bibliography — 413
Index — 435

List of Abbreviations

Periodicals and Series

AMI	Archäologische Mitteilungen aus Iran
An. Boll.	Analecta Bollandiana
AT	Antiquité tardive
BAR	British Archaeological Reports
BASOR	Bulletin of the American Schools of Oriental Research
BMGS	Byzantine and Modern Greek Studies
BSOAS	Bulletin of the School of Oriental and African Studies
Byz.	Byzantion
BZ	Byzantinische Zeitschrift
CAH	Cambridge Ancient History
CFHB	Corpus Fontium Historiae Byzantinae
CRAI	Comptes rendus de l'Académie des inscriptions et belles-lettres
CSCO	Corpus Scriptorum Christianorum Orientalium
CSHB	Corpus Scriptorum Historiae Byzantinae
DOP	Dumbarton Oaks Papers
EHR	English Historical Review
EIr	Encyclopaedia Iranica
GRBS	Greek, Roman and Byzantine Studies
Ist.Mitt.	Istanbuler Mitteilungen
JA	Journal asiatique
JHS	Journal of Hellenic Studies
JÖB	Jahrbuch der Österreichischen Byzantinistik
JRA	Journal of Roman Archaeology
JRAS	Journal of the Royal Asiatic Society
JRS	Journal of Roman Studies
JTS	Journal of Theological Studies
MGH	Monumenta Germanicae Historiae
NC	Numismatic Chronicle
ODB	Oxford Dictionary of Byzantium, 3 vols. (New York, 1991)
PG	Patrologia Graeca
PL	Patrologia Latina
PO	Patrologia Orientalis
REB	Revue des études byzantines
RN	Revue numismatique
SNS	Sylloge Nummorum Sasanidarum
TIB	Tabula Imperii Byzantini
TM	Travaux et mémoires
TTH	Translated Texts for Historians
VV	Vizantiskij Vremmenik

Primary sources

Agap.	A. A. Vasiliev, ed. and trans., *Kitab al-'Unvan, histoire universelle écrite par Agapius (Mahboub) de Menbidj*, PO 7.4 and 8.3
Bal.	al-Baladhuri, *Kitab futuh al-buldan*, ed. M.J. de Goeje, *Liber expugnationis regionum* (Leiden, 1866), trans. P. K. Hitti, *The Origins of the Islamic State* (New York, 1916) and F.C. Murgotten, *The Origins of the Islamic State, Part II* (New York, 1924)
Chron.1234	*Chronicon ad annum Christi 1234 pertinens*, ed. J. B. Chabot, CSCO, Scriptores Syri, 3.ser., 14 (Paris, 1920), partial trans. A. Palmer, *The Seventh Century in the West-Syrian Chronicles*, TTH 15 (Liverpool, 1993), 111–221
Chron.724	*Chronicon miscellaneum ad annum Domini 724 pertinens*, ed. E. W. Brooks, CSCO, Scriptores Syri 3, Chronica Minora II (Louvain, 1960), 77–154, partial trans. Palmer, *Seventh Century*, 13–23
Chron.Pasch.	*Chronicon Paschale*, ed. L. Dindorf, CSHB (Bonn, 1832), partial trans. M. and M. Whitby, *Chronicon Paschale 284-628 AD*, TTH 7 (Liverpool, 1989)
Geo.Pis.	Georgius Pisides: A. Pertusi, ed. and trans., *Giorgio di Pisidia poemi: I panegirici epici* (Ettal, 1959); L. Tartaglia, ed. and trans., *Carmi di Giorgio di Pisidia* (Turin, 1998)
HNov	J. Konidaris, ed. and trans., *Die Novellen des Kaisers Herakleios*, Fontes Minores 5.3 (Frankfurt, 1982)
H.Patr.Alex.	*History of the Patriarchs of the Coptic Church of Alexandria (St. Mark to Benjamin I)*, ed. and trans. B. Evetts, PO 1.2 and 4, 5.1, 10.5
JA (John of Antioch)	Ioannes Antiochenus: U. Roberto, ed. and trans., *Ioannis Antiocheni fragmenta ex historia chronica*, Berlin-Brandenburgische Ak. Wiss., Texte und Untersuchungen zur Geschichte der altchristlichen Literatur 154 (Berlin, 2005)
JN (John of Nikiu)	H. Zotenberg, ed. and trans., *Chronique de Jean, évêque de Nikiou* (Paris, 1883)
Khuz.Chron.	(*Khuzistan Chronicle*) *Chronicon anonymum*, ed. I. Guidi, CSCO, Scriptores Syri 1, Chronica Minora I (Paris, 1903), 15–39, trans. T. Nöldeke, 'Die von Guidi herausgegebene syrische Chronik übersetzt und commentiert', *Sitzungsberichte der kais. Ak. Wiss., Phil.-hist. Cl.*, 128 (Vienna, 1893), partial trans. Greatrex and Lieu, *Roman Eastern Frontier*, 229–37
MD	Movses Daskhurants'i (or Kałankatuats'i), ed. V. Arak'eljan, *Movses Kałankatuats'i: Patmut'iwn Ałuanits'* (Erevan, 1983), trans. C. J. F. Dowsett,

	Moses Dasxuranc'i's History of the Caucasian Albanians (London, 1961)
Mich.Syr. (Michael the Syrian)	J. B. Chabot, ed. and trans., *Chronique de Michel le Syrien, Patriarche Jacobite d'Antioche (1166–1199)*, 5 vols. (Paris, 1899–1924)
Mir.Dem. (*Miracula S. Demetrii*)	P. Lemerle, *Les Plus Anciens Recueils des miracles de saint Démétrius*, I *Le Texte* (Paris, 1979), II *Commentaire* (Paris, 1981)
Nic.	Nicephorus, *Breviarium*, ed. and trans. C. Mango, *Nikephoros Patriarch of Constantinople, Short History*, CFHB 13 (Washington DC, 1990)
Paul D (Paul the Deacon)	*Pauli historia Langobardorum*, ed. L. Bethmann and G. Waitz (Hanover, 1878), trans. W. D Foulke, *Paul the Deacon, History of the Lombards* (Philadelphia, PA, 1907), trans. F. Bougard, *Paul Diacre, Histoire des Lombards* (Turnhout, 1994)
ps.S (ps.Sebeos)	*Patmut'iwn Sebeosi*, ed. G. V. Abgaryan (Erevan, 1979), trans. R. W. Thomson in R. W. Thomson and J. Howard-Johnston, *The Armenian History Attributed to Sebeos*, TTH 31, 2 vols. (Liverpool, 1999), I *Translation and Notes*, II *Historical Commentary*
Seert Chron.	*Seert Chronicle*: ed. A. Scher, trans. A. Scher, R. Griveau, et al., *Histoire nestorienne (Chronique de Séert)*, PO 4.3, 5.2, 7.2, 13.4
Sim.	Theophylactus Simocatta, *Historiae*, ed. C. de Boor, rev. P. Wirth (Stuttgart, 1972), trans. Michael and Mary Whitby, *The History of Theophylact Simocatta* (Oxford, 1986)
Strategicon	Mauricius, *Strategicon*, ed. G. T. Dennis and trans. (German) E. Gamillscheg, CFHB 17 (Vienna, 1981), trans. (English) G. T. Dennis, *Maurice's Strategikon: Handbook of Byzantine Military Strategy* (Philadelphia, PA, 1984)
TA	T'ovma Artsruni *Patmut'iwn Tann Artsruneats'*, ed. K. Patkanean (St Petersburg, 1887), 2.3 (89.20–1), trans. R. W. Thomson, *Thomas Artsruni: History of the House of the Artsrunik'* (Detroit, MI, 1985)
Tab. (al-Tabari)	ed. M. J. de Goeje et al., *Annales quos scripsit Abu Djafar Mohammed ibn Djarir at-Tabari*, 15 vols. (Leiden, 1879–1901), partial trans. C. E. Bosworth, *The Sasanids, the Byzantines, the Lakhmids, and Yemen: The History of al-Tabari* V (pp. 813–1072), K. Y. Blankinship, *The Challenge to the Empires*, H of Tab. XI (pp. 2016–212), and Y. Friedmann, *The Battle of al-Qadisiyyah and the Conquest of Syria and Palestine*, H of Tab. XII (pp. 2212–418) (Albany, NY, 1999, 1993, 1992)

Theod.Sync., *Hom.* I	Theodorus Syncellus, *Homily* I, ed. L. Sternbach, *Analecta Avarica*, Rozprawy Akademii Umiejętności, Wydział Filologiczny, ser.2, 15 (Kraków, 1900), 298–320
Theod.Sync., *Hom.* II	Theodorus Syncellus, *Homily* II, ed. C. Loparev, 'Staroe svidetelstvo o polozhenii rizy Bogorodnitsy vo Vlakherniakh . . .', *VV* 2 (1895), 581–628, at 592–612, trans. Averil Cameron, 'The Virgin's Robe: An Episode in the History of Early Seventh-Century Constantinople', *Byz.* 49 (1979), 42–56, repr. in Cameron, *Continuity and Change in Sixth-Century Byzantium* (London, 1981), no. XVII
Theoph.	Theophanes, *Chronographia*, ed. C. de Boor, 2 vols. (Leipzig, 1883–5), trans. C. Mango and R. Scott, *The Chronicle of Theophanes Confessor: Byzantine and Near Eastern History AD 284–813* (Oxford, 1997)
V.Anast. (*Vita S. Anastasii*)	*Vita S. Anastasii*, ed. and trans. B. Flusin, *Saint Anastase le Perse et l'histoire de la Palestine au début du VIIe siècle*, I *Les Textes* (Paris, 1992)
V.Georg. (*Vita S. Georgii*)	ed. C. Houze, 'Vita S. Georgii Chozebitae . . .', *An. Boll.* 7 (1888), 97–144, 336–70
V.Ioannis (epit.)	ed. E. Lappa-Zizicas, 'Un Épitomé de la Vie de S. Jean l'Aumônier par Jean et Sophronios', *An.Boll.* 88 (1970), 265–78
V.Theod. (*Vita S. Theodori*)	A.-J. Festugière, ed. and trans., *Vie de Théodore de Sykéôn*, 2 vols (Brussels, 1970)

List of Maps

1. Western Eurasia — xx
2. Armenia and neighbouring lands — xxii
3. Fertile Crescent — xxiv
4. Sasanian empire — xxvi
5. Egypt — xxvii
6. Alexandria and its hinterland — xxviii
7. Constantinople and environs — xxix
8. Asia Minor — xxx
9. Balkans — xxxii

List of Figures

1. Constantinople (a) land walls (b) gate
2. Royal palace at Ctesiphon (Taq-i Kisra): façade
3. Royal palace at Ctesiphon (Taq-i Kisra): side view
4. Taq-i Kisra: ground plan
5. Coins of Heraclius: silver hexagram (615–38)
6. Seal of Wistaxm, Ērān-spāhbed of the West (under Khusro I [531–79])
7. Coins of Khusro II: ceremonial dinar of year 33
8. Coins of Khusro II: ceremonial dinar of year 21
9. Taq-i Bustan: lake
10. Taq-i Bustan: grotto
11. Taq-i Bustan: investiture of Khusro II
12. Taq-i Bustan: Khusro's *fravashi*
13. Taq-i Bustan: boar hunt
14. Taq-i Bustan: deer hunt
15. Bisutun: blank screen prepared for Khusro II monumental relief

16. Naqsh-i Rustam: general view
17. Naqsh-i Rustam: blank screen
18. Constantinople: St. Sophia
19. Takht-i Sulaiman: defences
20. Takht-i Sulaiman: lake
21. David Plates: David's first audience with Saul
22. David Plates: David and Goliath
23. Mren, relief over north portal: Heraclius, dismounted, outside Jerusalem
24. Jerusalem: Golden Gate
25. Joshua Roll (folio VII): two spies report back to Joshua—the Israelites are repulsed from the city of Ai
26. Joshua Roll (folio X): Joshua is promised that Ai will fall; denuded of defenders, lured out by a feigned retreat, Ai is taken and fired (above right); the men of Ai are slaughtered in a pincer attack (below right)
27. Joshua Roll (folio XII): Joshua receives the submission of the Gibeonites
28. Joshua Roll (folio XIII): the Amorites are routed and their five kings take refuge in a cave
29. Jerusalem: Dome of the Rock
30. Coins of Heraclius: solidus (629–31)
31. Rostock, Klosterkirche 'Zu den Heiligen Kreuz', Nonnenaltar: thirteenth-century cycle of scenes from the Legenda Aurea: Khusro II captures the True Cross; Heraclius restores the True Cross
32. Battle of Nineveh, by Piero della Francesca

Table of Events

591	restoration of Khusro II
594/5–601/2	rebellion of Bistam
602	mutiny of Balkan field army, election of Phocas as leader, march on Constantinople, coronation of Phocas (23 November), and entry into the city (25 November) 602–3 winter: rebellion of Narses, commander of Roman forces in the south-east
603	Persian victory south of the Armenian Taurus, Persian reverse in Armenia
604	fall of Dara, victorious Persian campaign in Armenia
605	Persian victory in Bagrewand, and advance to the Araxes-Euphrates watershed
606	pause in Persian military operations
607	Persian victory in Armenia, dispatch of raiding forays west and south-west, capitulation of Theodosiopolis, siege of Cepha
608	victory of Shahen in Armenia
	rebellion of Heraclius Exarch of North Africa
	fall of Cepha (on the eve of winter)
609	fall of Mardin, Persian occupation of Tur Abdin (spring)
	invasion of Egypt by Heraclian forces, entry into Alexandria (spring–summer)
	capitulation of Edessa, Amida, Theodosiopolis (Resaena), and Constantia (summer)
	Bonosus' attack on Alexandria repulsed (23 November)
610	Persian crossing of the Euphrates and capture of Zenobia (7 August)
	arrival of rebel fleet at Constantinople (3 October)
	coronation of Heraclius (5 October)
	fall of Antioch (8 October), Apamea (15 October), Emesa (a few days later in October)
611	Shahen's invasion of Asia Minor and occupation of Caesarea
	victory of Nicetas outside Emesa
612	Shahen's breakout from Caesarea
613	Persian defeat of Heraclius near Antioch, and subsequent capture of Damascus
614	pogrom in Jerusalem, Persian siege, fall of the city (17 May)
615	Persian advance to Chalcedon
	diversionary campaign of Philippicus into Armenia
	Roman Senate's letter to Khusro
	Turkish invasion of Iran
616	victorious campaign of Smbat Bagratuni in the north-east
	occupation of Palestine

617	raiding expeditions of Shahrbaraz and Shahen into Asia Minor
619	fall of Alexandria (June)
620	Slav attack on Thessalonica
622	blockade of cities in or near the Pontic region by Persians
	Heraclius' army exercises in Bithynia (spring), and victory over shadowing Persian army (summer)
	thirty-three-day Avar-Slav siege of Thessalonica
	emigration (*hijra*) of Muhammad and followers from Mecca to Medina
623	surprise Avar attack before scheduled summit meeting (5 June)
624	dispatch of Roman ambassador to Turks
	HERACLIUS' FIRST COUNTEROFFENSIVE
	assembly of Roman expeditionary army at Caesarea (Cappadocia), march across Armenia, invasion of Atropatene, flight of Khusro from Ganzak (April–July)
	destruction of fire-temple at Thebarmais, devastation of Media and west Atropatene (summer)
	withdrawal north to winter near P'artaw in Caucasian Albania
625	march south, victories over three pursuing Persian armies, devastation of eastern Atropatene, withdrawal north towards Caucasus
	arrival of Turkish embassy (autumn)
	departure of Laz and Abasgian contingents, march south-west to winter near Lake Van
	midwinter raid on Shahrbaraz's headquarters
626	Heraclius' withdrawal and Persian pursuit, through northern Syria and Cilicia (spring)
	arrival of Shahrbaraz at Chalcedon (June)
	crossing of Long Wall by Avar vanguard (29 June)
	Avar siege of Constantinople (29 July–7 August)
	defeat of Shahen in northern Asia Minor (autumn)
	Turkish attack across the Caucasus, exchange of diplomatic notes between the *shad* and Khusro
627	Turkish invasion in force across the Caucasus, fall of Derbend (guarding Caspian Gates) and P'artaw (summer)
	HERACLIUS' SECOND COUNTEROFFENSIVE
	Roman invasion of Lazica (summer)
	invasion of Iberia from east and west, summit meeting of Heraclius and the *yabghu khagan* outside Tiflis, joint Roman-Turkish siege of Tiflis (autumn)
	Heraclius' march across the Zagros range to the Great Zab river (16 October–1 December)
627	victory over scratch Persian force commanded by Rahzadh near Nineveh (Saturday 12 December), followed by victorious advance south
	flight of Khusro from palace at Dastagerd to Ctesiphon (23 December)
628	arrival of Roman army at Nahrawan canal (10 January)
	devastation of Shahrazur region (February)
628	overthrow of Khusro II (24 February)

	coronation of Kavad Shiroe (25 February)
	execution of Khusro II (28 February)
	Turkish occupation of Albania, formal submission of Albania by delegation headed by Catholicos Viroy
629	Turkish victory over Arab force in Armenia
	Persian evacuation of Alexandria (June)
	summit meeting between Heraclius and Shahrbaraz (July)
	crisis in central Asia and Turkish withdrawal
630	ceremonial restoration of True Cross in Jerusalem (21 March)
	conclusion of peace between Persians and Romans
	Muslim takeover of Mecca
632	death of Muhammad

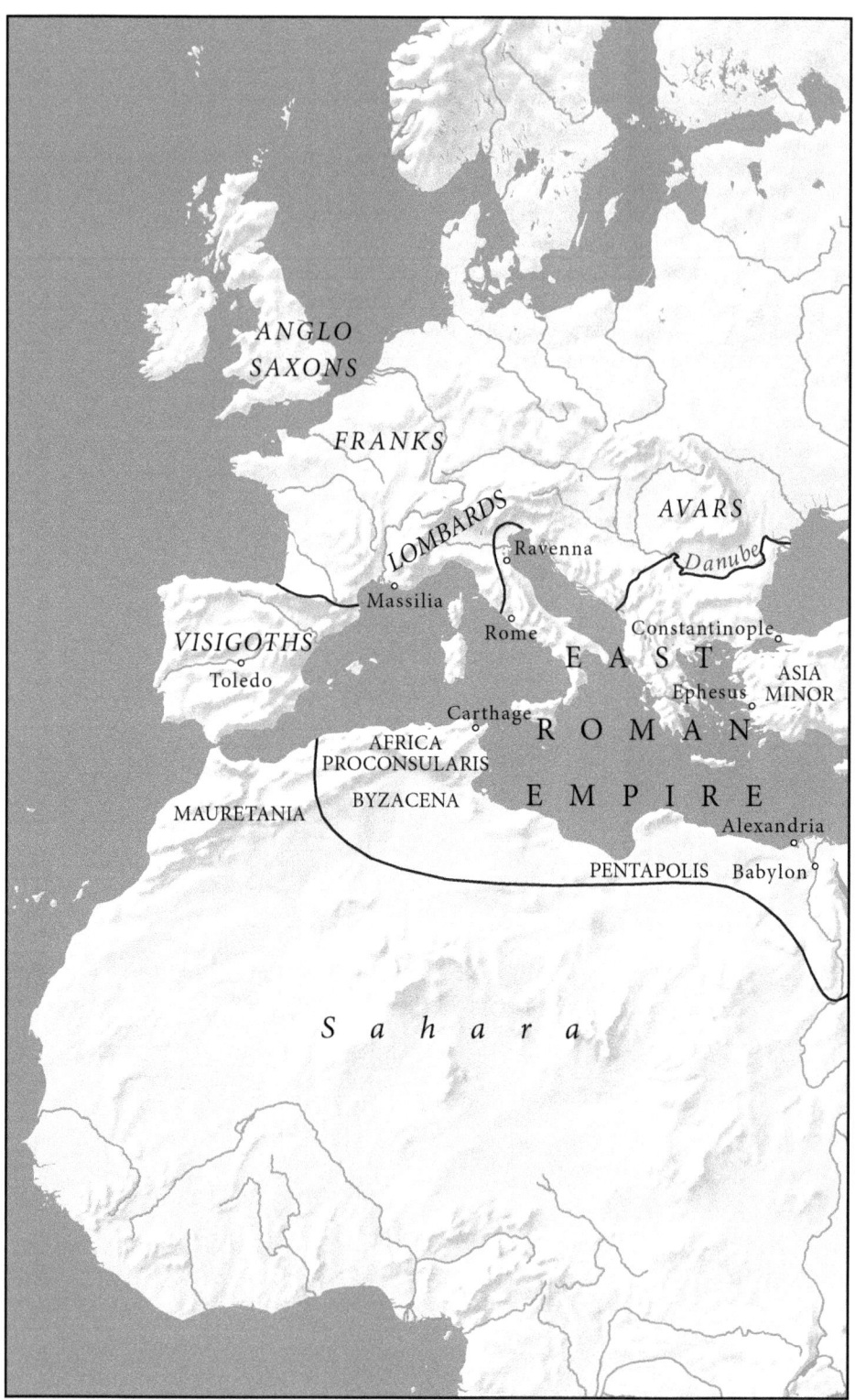

Map 1 Western Eurasia

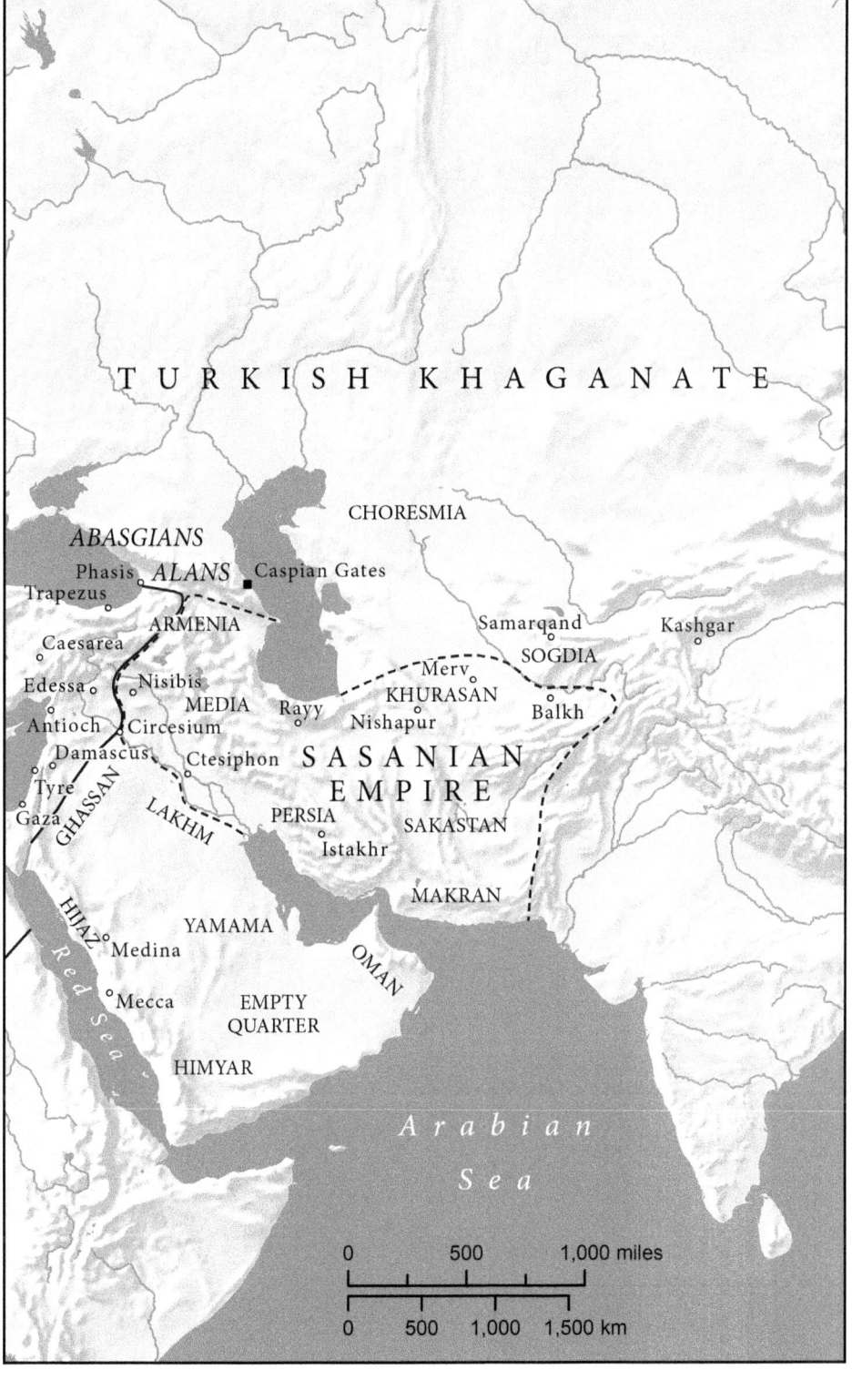

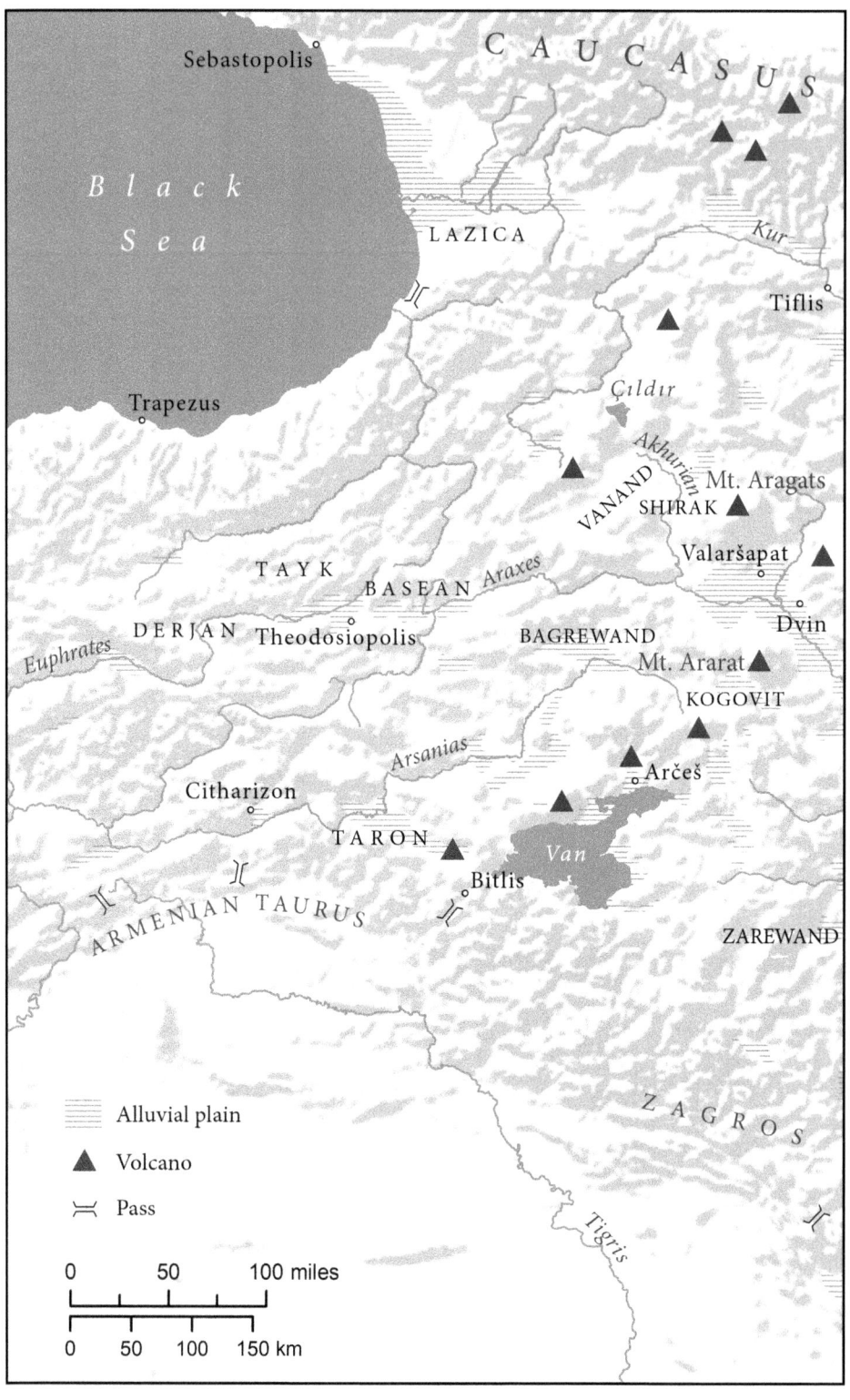

Map 2 Armenia and neighbouring lands

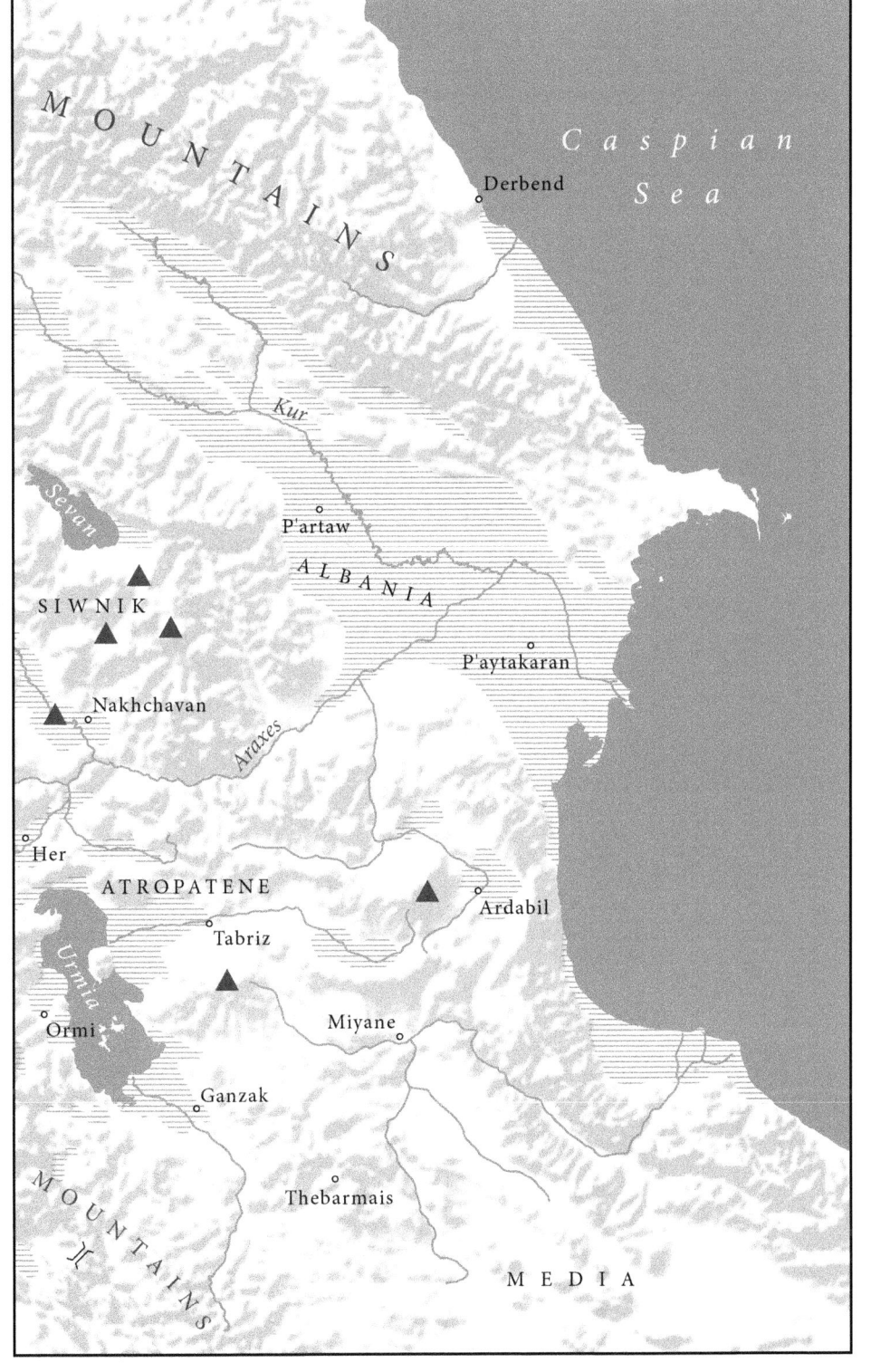

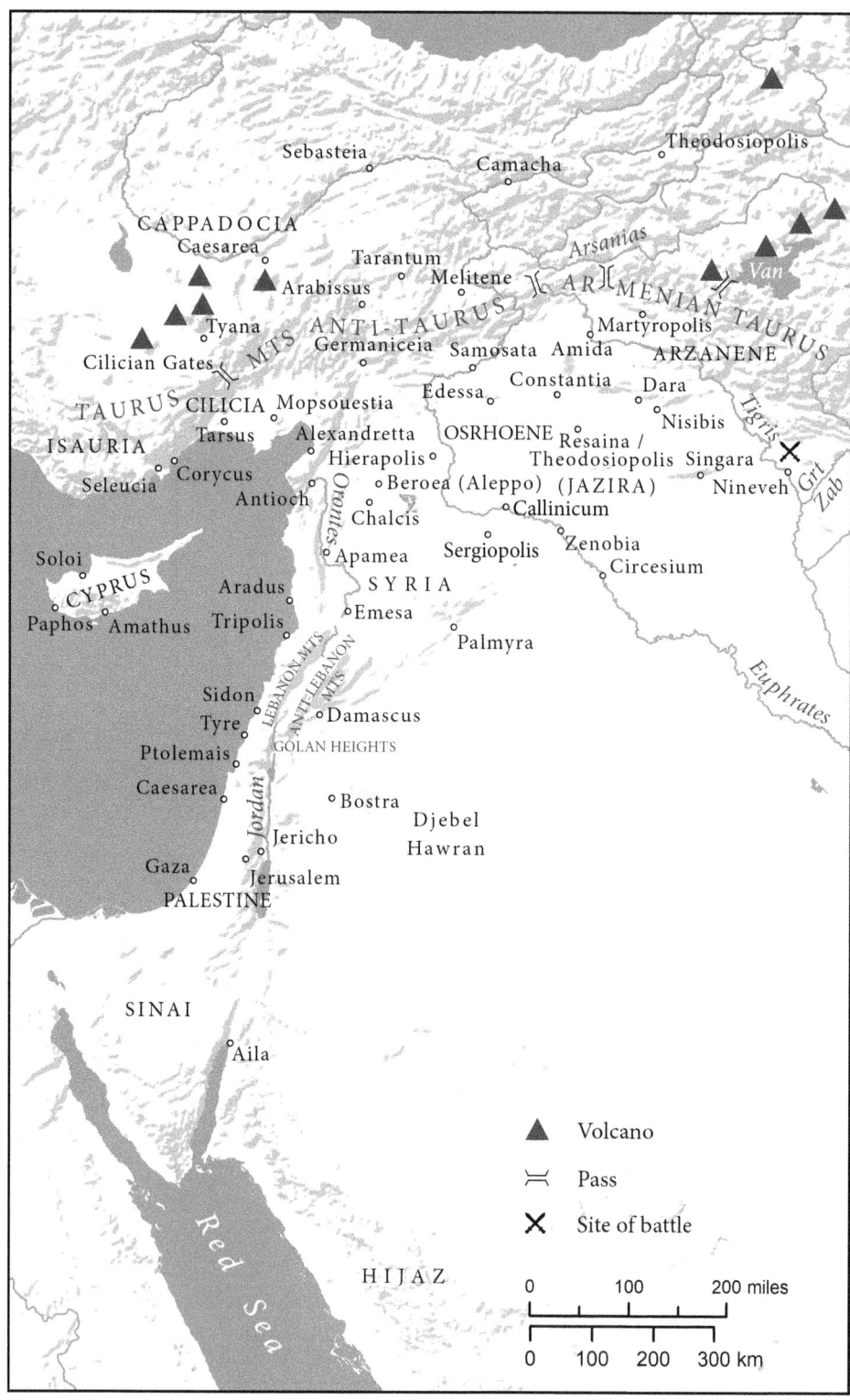

Map 3 Fertile Crescent

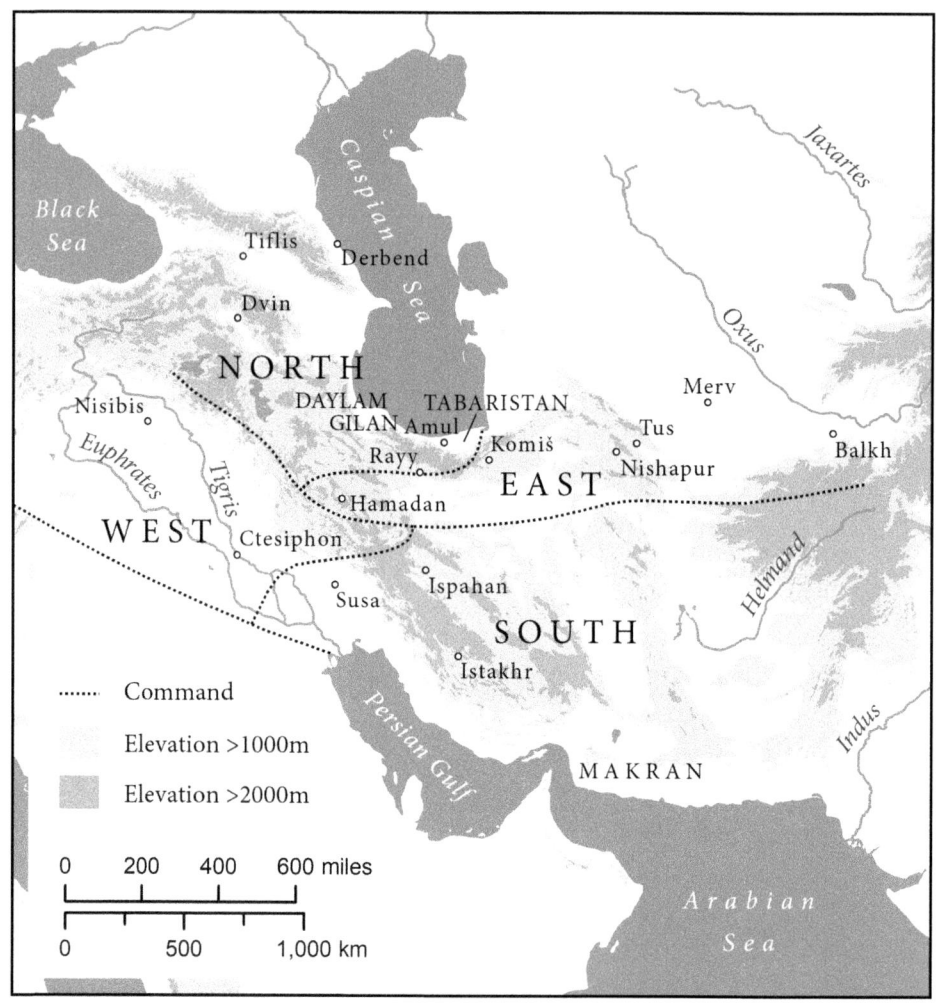

Map 4 Sasanian empire

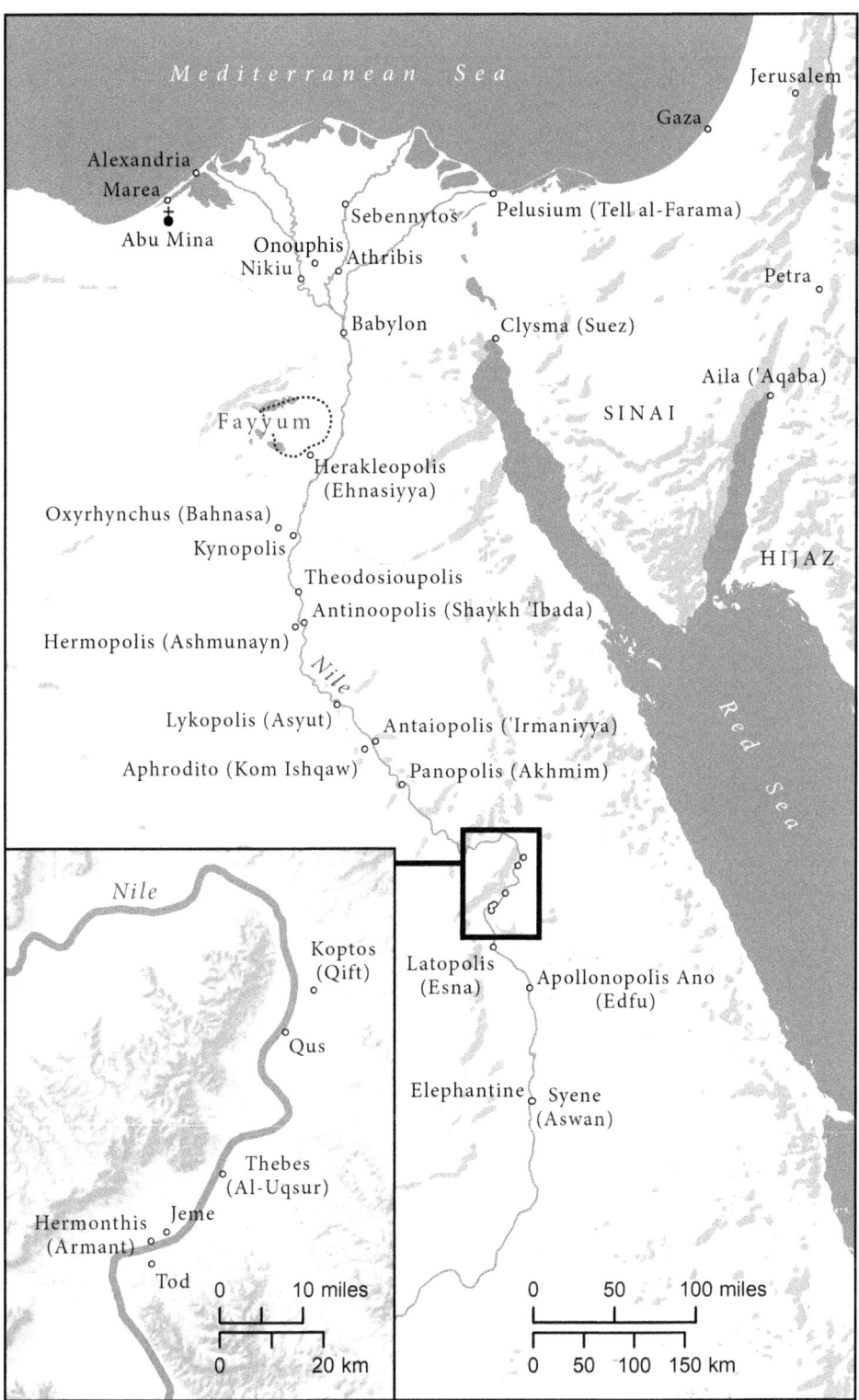

Map 5 Egypt

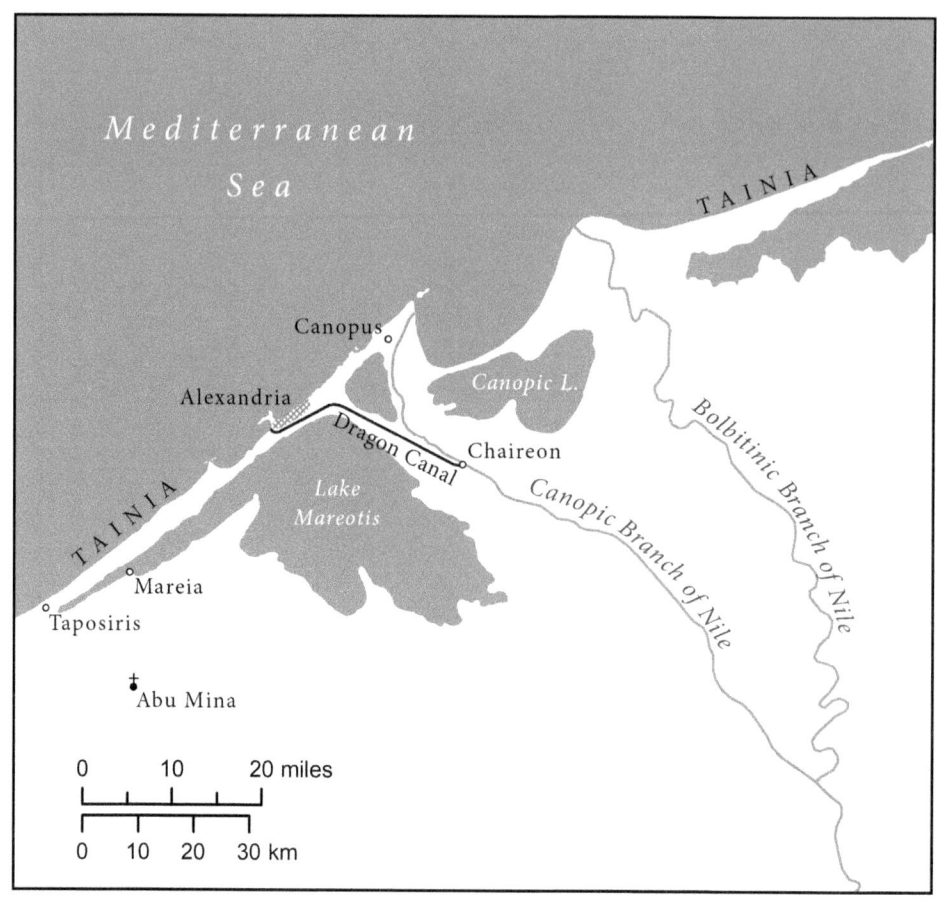

Map 6 Alexandria and its hinterland

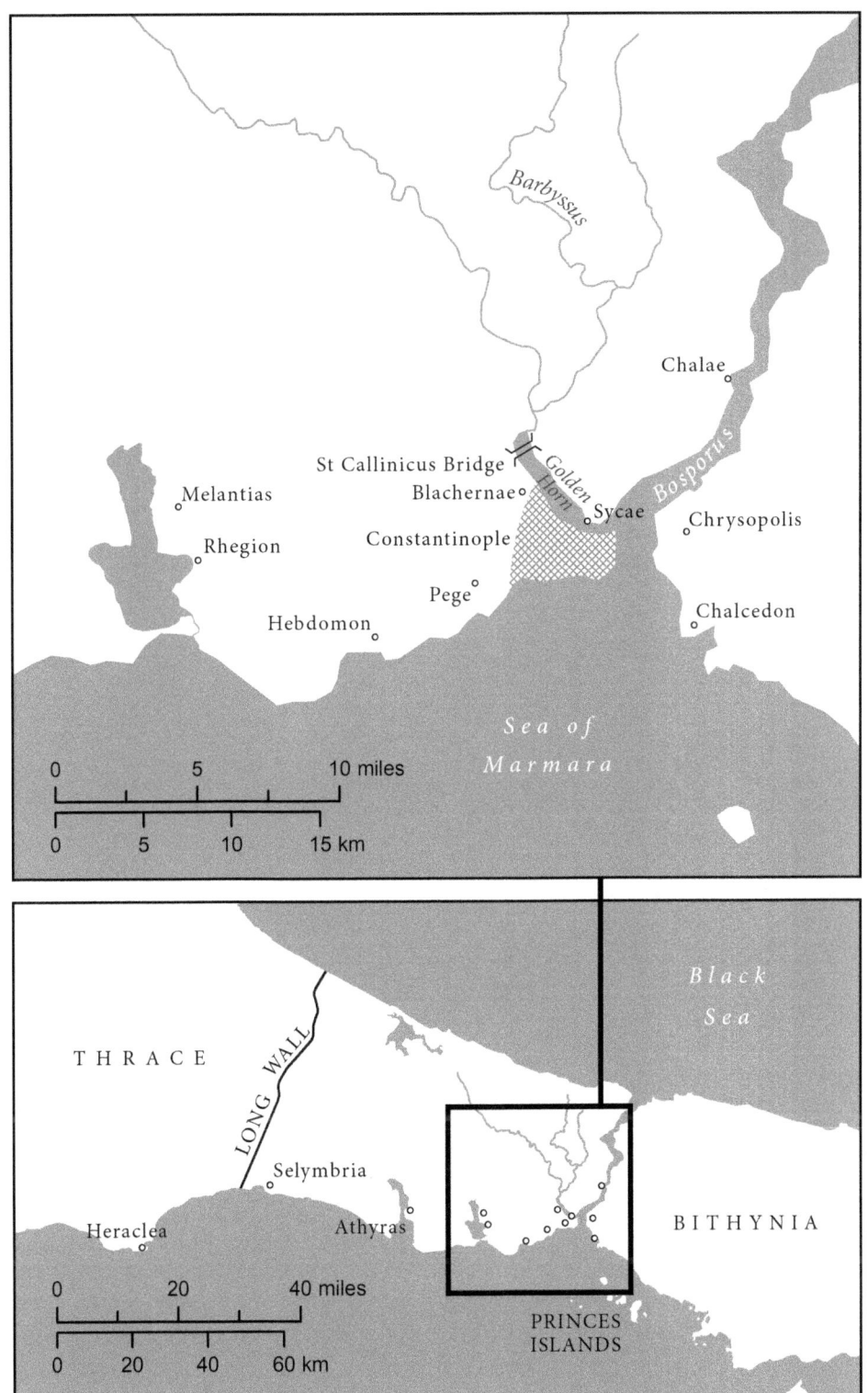

Map 7 Constantinople and environs

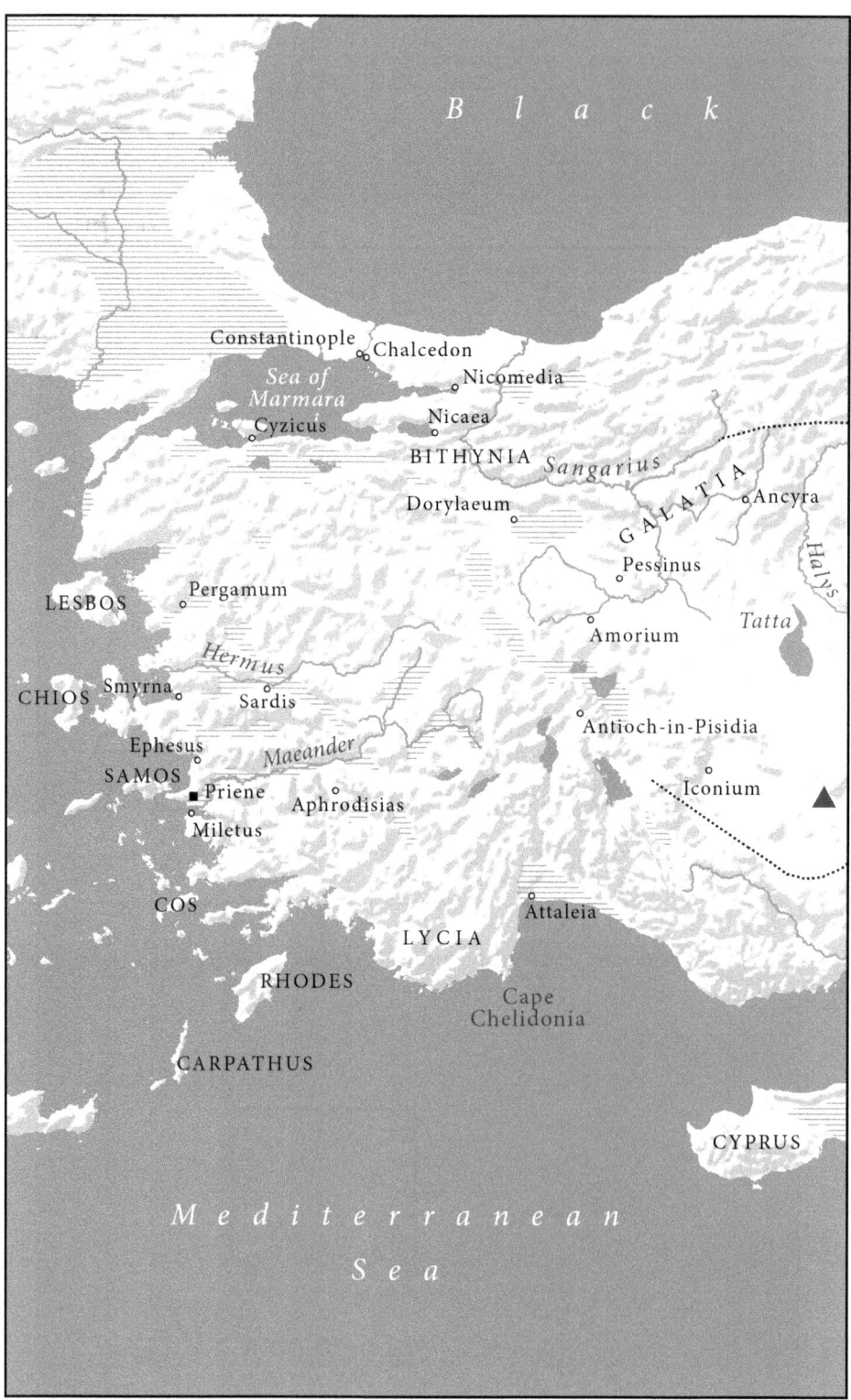

Map 8 Asia Minor

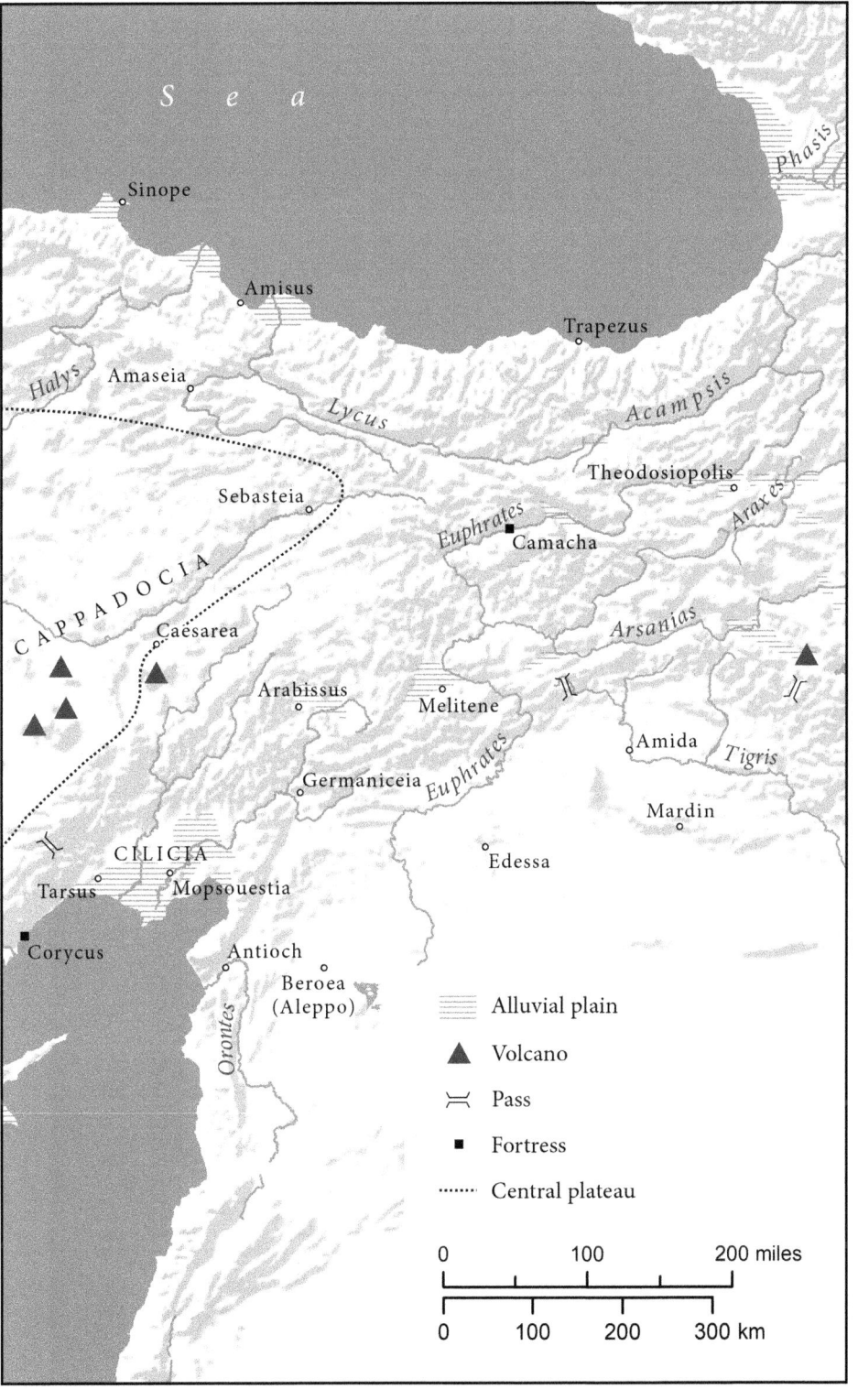

Map 9 Balkans

Introduction

It was not a war to end all wars. It was not a war to destroy or truncate the Roman Empire in the east. The Persian aim at the outset was not even regime change, merely restoration of an ousted regime. But the fighting went on and on. There was a steady escalation in its scope and intensity with the passing years. After a decade of conflict, foreboding came upon contemporaries. The saints were plainly withdrawing their favour from mankind. God was turning his face from the present generation. The world and all things in it were being troubled because of man's sinfulness, and those few who strove to squeeze out desire, ambition, envy, and other human feelings from their lives should withdraw and pray for a softening of God's anger. For one distant observer, far to the south of the Fertile Crescent, where the two belligerent great powers were engaged in combat, the war presaged the end of time. The last days were at hand, when the earth would shake and the seas boil, when the sky would be torn apart and the stars scattered, when men would come face to face with the creator and manager of all things.[1]

The last and longest war of classical antiquity was fought in the early seventh century. It opened in summer 603, when Persian armies launched coordinated attacks across the Roman frontier, taking advantage of a violent change of regime in Constantinople. Twenty-five years later the fighting stopped after a bold—almost insanely bold—Roman thrust into the Persians' Mesopotamian heartland. This triggered a virtually bloodless putsch against a king, Khusro II Parvez, whose achievements up to 626 had surpassed those of all his ancestors. Two years of tortuous negotiations followed before the Romans were able to reach a durable peace agreement in 630 with the third of three ephemeral Persian regimes.[2]

It was a conflict of more than passing significance, given the scale and intensity of the fighting. The two long-established empires of western Eurasia, the east Roman and the Sasanian, committed all available resources to the struggle.[3]

Military operations took place along the full length of the frontier, from Transcaucasia in the north to the *badiya*, the swathe of grazing land fringing the

---

[1] *Vita Theodori*, c.127.15–20, ed. and trans. A.-J. Festugière, *Vie de Théodore de Sykeôn*, 2 vols (Brussels, 1970)—cited henceforth as *V. Theod.*; *Vita S. Georgii*, c.18, ed. C. Houze, 'Vita S. Georgii Chozebitae...', *An.Boll.* 7 (1888), 97–144, 336–70—cited henceforth as *V.Georg.*; Qur'an, suras 81, 82, 99.
[2] J. Howard-Johnston, *Witnesses to a World Crisis: Historians and Histories of the Middle East in the Seventh Century* (Oxford, 2009), 436–45.
[3] Appendix 1, Dramatis Personae.

Arabian Desert, in the south. The great powers of the outer steppe world were drawn in. The Turks, who, in the 550s and 560s, had founded the first transcontinental empire, stretching eventually from the inner Asian frontiers of China to the Crimea, intervened first on their own initiative in 615, when they raided deep into Iran, and then, at Roman invitation, in the last years of the war (626–9), when they tipped the balance decisively in the Romans' favour. The nomad ally courted by the Persians was the Avar khaganate, which, from the 560s, was able to project its power outward from a core territory in the Carpathian basin. The Avars were no match for the Turks, from whom they had fled to the west, but they could apply pressure on the Balkans, either using the Slavs as surrogates (from before 620, as previously in the 570s and 580s) or launching direct attacks on Thessalonica and Constantinople (as they did in 622, 623, and 626).[4]

The war was raised onto a high ideological plane. The Romans exploited religion to an unprecedented degree. For them it was a head-on conflict between faiths, of Christians, who worshipped the true God and were led by God's vicegerent on earth, against impious Zoroastrians, whose king delighted in bloodshed and sacrilege. The sacking of Jerusalem in 614 and the removal of the fragments of the True Cross provided rich veins for propaganda. Later, Roman troops, at least those serving on the bold counteroffensive campaigns of 624–6 and 627–8, were offered the rewards of paradise, if they laid down their lives for the cause. The Persians could not respond in kind, given that they had long accepted the religious pluralism of their subjects. But they could take inspiration from the mythical version of the deep past which was recorded in the official dynastic history, the *Khwadaynamag* ('Book of Lords'). They could strive to emulate the Kayanid rulers of Iran, whose feats surpassed those of the Sasanians' real but forgotten Achaemenid predecessors.[5] There was, therefore, no reason for them to shy away from the prospect of reasserting Iran's position as the sole great power of the sedentary world, after they had broken into the Roman Levant and had divided the empire in two. Hence Khusro's fateful decision, to eradicate Roman rule from the Middle East, which shaped the second half of the war.

---

[4] J. Howard-Johnston, 'The Sasanians' Strategic Dilemma', in H. Börm and J. Wiesehöfer, eds., *Commutatio et contentio: Studies in the Late Roman, Sasanian, and Early Islamic Near East, in Memory of Zeev Rubin* (Düsseldorf, 2010), 37–70; W. Pohl, 'A Non-Roman Empire in Central Europe: The Avars', in H.-W. Goetz, J. Jarnut, and W. Pohl, eds., *Regna et Gentes: The Relationship between Late Antique and Early Medieval Peoples and Kingdoms in the Transformation of the Roman World* (Leiden, 2003), 571–95.

[5] Y. Stoyanov, *Defenders and Enemies of the True Cross: The Sasanian Conquest of Jerusalem in 614 and Byzantine Ideology of Anti-Persian Warfare*, Österr. Ak. Wiss., Phil.-hist. Kl., Sitzungsberichte 819 (Vienna, 2011); J. Howard-Johnston, 'Heraclius' Persian Campaigns and the Revival of the East Roman Empire, 622–630', *War in History*, 6 (1999), 1–44, at 36–40, repr. in J. Howard-Johnston, *East Rome, Sasanian Persia and the End of Antiquity: Historiographical and Historical Studies* (Aldershot, 2006), no.VIII; E. Yarshater, 'Iranian National History', *Cambridge History of Iran*, III.1 (1983), 359–477.

Ambition was the driving force behind the escalation evident from winter 615–16. It was an ambition on the point of realization as the war entered its final climactic phase in the early 620s. The whole Roman Middle East was under Persian rule, including the breadbasket of the east Mediterranean (Egypt) and the empire's main commercial and manufacturing centres (in the Levant and Egypt). Persian forces were poised to invade Asia Minor, the last remaining substantial land mass under Roman control.

Apart from regular annual pauses in winter, traditionally the season when belligerents consolidated their positions, engaged in diplomacy, and devised plans for future action, there was no interruption to the campaigning. Towards the end, even winter was being eroded, as the last army which could be put into the field by the Romans and which was commanded by the Emperor Heraclius in person showed itself adept at continuing operations well beyond the end of autumn. The resources of both sides, in terms of ideology, finance, manpower, and materiel, were exploited to an unprecedented extent. The stamina of both was being tested as never before.

It is a war which demands attention as the final episode in classical history, forming a pendant to the great war between the free cities of Greece and the Achaemenid Empire fought over a millennium earlier. The drama was great, as one empire gradually bludgeoned the other to death, but then, in a remarkable reversal of fortune, the defeated and doomed Roman Empire struck back and dealt a series of mortal blows to the prestige and domestic political standing of the victorious Persian king. The war was also the prelude to a yet more dramatic episode in the history of the world, an episode which was the analogue, on the plane of human affairs, to the Big Bang—namely the rise of Islam, the definitive destruction of the ancient world order as the Arabs conquered three of the four power centres of the Middle East, and a decisive shift of the economic centre of gravity of western Eurasia from Egypt and the eastern Mediterranean to Iraq and Iran.[6]

Narrative history now has an old-fashioned air about it, although the historian's first and fundamental task has always been to scour the sources for evidence and to piece together chronologically ordered accounts of events. For Europe and China from antiquity, for the Middle East and the lands conquered by Islam from the eighth century, for the Americas, Africa, and the Antipodes in the colonial period, the creation of a history of events was the collective achievement of successive generations of scholars, antiquarians, and historians, especially those at work in Europe in the eighteenth, nineteenth, and early twentieth centuries. It was, therefore, not unreasonable for the *Annales* school in France at the end of the Second World War and their many foreign admirers to be blasé about *histoire*

---

[6] Howard-Johnston, *Witnesses*, 445–501.

événementielle. The historian's task, in their view, was to understand and to explain historical phenomena, most of which were well established. They turned their attention to the analysis of structures, economic, social, institutional, and cultural. They have spread out to tackle innumerable specific topics. There has been an extraordinary proliferation of learned publications, daunting in the extreme to the lay reader.

But blank or largely blank areas remain, some very large, like the history of India and its cultural dependencies in Southeast Asia before the first inroads of Islam (which brought with it the history writing habit), some small and caused either by temporary failings in contemporaries' coverage of events in historically mature societies or because of a dearth of modern research in particular fields of inquiry. In such cases the first duty of the historian is to trace out a sequence of events through time, to arrange them into successive episodes, and to observe possible causal connections. The last great war of antiquity is one such case, because no one has hitherto set out to tell the story of what happened with proper attention to the full range of preserved data. It has been covered fleetingly in general histories of the classical and medieval Mediterranean and Middle East, as well as the many outline histories of Byzantium which have been hitting university bookshelves over the last two decades. Even the conference on the reign of Heraclius held in Gröningen in 2001 shied away from military and diplomatic history.[7] Individual episodes have been subjected to minute scrutiny. They include the siege and sack of Jerusalem in 614, the subsequent establishment of Persian control over the Roman Levant, perilous moments in the history of Thessalonica (620 and 622), Heraclius' narrow escape from capture at the hands of the Avars (623), the joint Avar-Persian attack on Constantinople (626), Heraclius' Persian campaigns (624–6, 627–8), the identity of the bride promised to the Turkish khagan at his summit meeting with Heraclius, and negotiations between Heraclius and the great Persian general Shahrbaraz during and after the war.[8]

The sources have been probed and examined thoroughly in the recent past, which has rendered them usable to the historian, but only three historians have ventured to write histories combining a broad sweep with a close grip on particulars. All three have viewed the war from the Roman perspective and have had difficulty in achieving a balance between military and diplomatic narrative,

---

[7] G. J. Reinink and B. H. Stolte, ed., *The Reign of Heraclius (610-641): Crisis and Confrontation* (Leuven, 2002).

[8] B. Flusin, *Saint Anastase le Perse et l'histoire de la Palestine au début du VIIe siècle* (Paris, 1992), II, 129–64; C. Foss, 'The Persians in the Roman Near East (602–630 AD)', *JRAS*, ser.3, 13 (2003), 149–70; P. Lemerle, *Les Plus Anciens Recueils des miracles de saint Démétrius*, II *Commentaire* (Paris, 1981), 85–103; N. H. Baynes, 'The Date of the Avar Surprise: A Chronological Study', *BZ* 21 (1912), 110–28; E. Gerland, 'Die persischen Feldzüge des Kaisers Herakleios', *BZ* 3 (1894), 330–73; C. Zuckerman, 'La Petite Augusta et le Turc: Epiphania-Eudocie sur les monnaies d'Héraclius', *RN* 150 (1995), 113–26; C. Mango, 'Deux Études sur Byzance et la Perse sassanide', *TM* 9 (1985), 91–118.

on the one hand, and analysis of causes, motivations, aims, and outcomes, on the other. *Byzantium in the Seventh Century, I 602–634* (Amsterdam, 1968), written by the late Andreas Stratos, is a lineal descendant of medieval Byzantine historical compilations, like those of Theophanes and his many successors in which notices were pieced together out of earlier sources. Stratos was able to draw on a much larger pool of information, but, like them, he restricted himself to the arrangement of the raw material into a linear sequence. His is naked narrative history, stripped of much of the commentary and interpretation necessary to make sense of it. It is also innocent, since Stratos takes on trust much of the tendentious material put into circulation at the time. John Haldon's, *Byzantium in the Seventh Century: The Transformation of a Culture* (Cambridge, 1990), veers to the opposite extreme. Narrative is reduced to a bare minimum to leave as much space as possible for analysis of institutions, social developments, and ideological changes. Finally there is Walter Kaegi's *Heraclius Emperor of Byzantium* (Cambridge, 2003). He does allocate plenty of space to military operations. He has taken note of topographical features and picks out the tactical rationale behind army movements. But, like Stratos, he is liable to be taken in by contemporary black propaganda and unreliable anecdotal material, and struggles at times to sort out chronology. The biographical format also works to the disadvantage of diplomatic as well as military history, since he is more concerned to track Heraclius (if necessary, with much conjecture) than to place the war in its wider west Eurasian context.

There is much disentangling of chronology to be done as well as much vetting of the information transmitted to us before events can be put into their proper chronological order and a first attempt can be made to see their patterning.[9] The geography of the Middle East, above all that of the fortified zones on either side of the frontier, must also be surveyed and its articulation understood, before individual campaigns can be interpreted.[10] The military historian must strive to see the ground as it was seen at the time by the generals in command. This means an appreciation of the general configuration of the land—the alignments of the major mountain chains and great rivers which defined regions, and the disposition of important resource bases, agricultural or pastoral, which determined the distribution of population. Major through routes must be traced, that is, routes feasible for large, organized bodies of men accompanied by wheeled transport carrying supplies and equipment. Narrow passages and mountain passes, where armies on the march would be especially vulnerable to attack, must be identified and their defences, if any, located and appraised. There is much else to attend to—the location, size, and defensive strength of major cities, the density and effectiveness of purpose-built military installations, internal communications

---

[9] Appendix 3, Sources.   [10] Appendix 2, Scene.

and assembly places necessary for the mobilization of large armies, highland regions with reservoirs of fighting manpower, etc.

With knowledge of terrain and monuments of many sorts put up by man, military operations can at last be followed on the ground, with the help of precise data extracted from the sources—about commanders, troop strengths, times and places, routes and distances, cities and forts, marches and manoeuvres, engagements and sieges, etc. Individual operations can be linked together to form campaigns, each with its own rationale, and individual campaigns can then be viewed as component parts of larger strategies. In almost all cases, however, motivation and intention—the immediate driving forces behind operations—have to be teased out from actions carefully tabulated in space and time. The evidence is indirect, rather than coming from records of debate and decision-making. We know that governments and high commands on both sides paused occasionally to take stock and to plan ahead—the Persians after the initial battles and victories of 603–5 and again in winter 615–16 after the arrival of a grovelling plea for peace from the Roman Senate, the Romans almost certainly once Heraclius had seized power in October 610 and some eleven years later, after the loss of Egypt. This last round of planning is reported by George of Pisidia, who tells us that Heraclius and his entourage spent much of the winter of 621–2 considering their options, caught as they were between western and eastern adversaries. He simply notes the final decision which was to take to the offensive in Asia Minor.[11] How one longs for even a few fragments of papers produced for those meetings, distant precursors of the invaluable documentation generated by Churchill's entourage in the run-up to summit meetings in the Second World War. Instead we have to fumble around, hoping to pick up key strands in the thinking of the small elites who devised the plans and attempted to direct the operations of large groups of men at a distance.

Military campaigns must be placed in the wider context of international relations at the time—what was happening on other fronts, what diplomatic initiatives were being launched, whether relations were improving or deteriorating with other powers. War must never be dissociated from its accompanying diplomacy. In the case of the Persian-Roman war of 603–30, examination of the diplomatic context helps to explain the outcome of individual campaigns and the war as a whole. The various diplomatic documents reproduced and summarized in the sources also provide vital insights into Persian and Roman motivations. But we must be careful. For there is always the danger of mistaking bluff for underlying policy and negotiating position for serious aim, not to mention the many traps laid by the propaganda broadcast by both sides.

---

[11] Georgius Pisides (cited henceforth as Geo.Pis.), *Heraclias*, ed. and trans. A. Pertusi, *Giorgio di Pisidia poemi: I panegirici epici* (Ettal, 1959), 240–61, at ii.98–143.

It is no easy task to write the history of the last great war of antiquity. Innocence is the great enemy, closely followed by an excess of suspicion which may result in overingenious interpretation. Gaps in the narrative can only be filled by conjecture, which must be kept in hand. Attitudes and aims are all too often out of reach. But given the importance of the war, it is worth making the effort to describe its course and to identify some of the factors which influenced its course and outcome.

1
Khusro's War of Revenge

After nearly twenty years of unremitting military effort by the Emperor Maurice, the strain was beginning to show in 602. His achievements were far from negligible. Civil war in Persia had been successfully exploited to bring the conflict initiated by Justin II to a close on highly advantageous terms. In the second half of the reign, free to concentrate his forces in Europe, Maurice had succeeded in cowing the Avars and had begun the painstaking process of pacifying the Slavs who had settled in the Balkans. In Italy, making the most of the resources to hand, he had striven to pen the Lombards back into the central Po Valley and the mountain territories which they had seized. It was plain, though, that Roman authority could not be reimposed within former Roman territory without a continuing military commitment on a large scale. The gains would be undramatic. The costs were already obvious and keenly felt. Resentment was growing against Maurice's regime.

The Slavs were loosely organized and elusive in their forest lairs. Impressive displays of Roman military power might be laid on, as they were in the years 593–5. Expeditionary forces, as long as they took due precautions, were able in those years to cut at will through Slav tribal territories on either side of the lower and middle Danube, while other units intercepted raiding bands. Tribes in those relatively accessible areas could be brought under military control in a relatively short time, but years of patient and delicate administrative effort backed by localized military action and propaganda would be required to imbue them with Roman culture and to extend Roman authority further afield, into the remoter uplands. Every available interlude of peace or comparative peace would have to be devoted to this task, building on the successes achieved during a short-lived treaty with the Avars (late 595–mid 596) and a later lull in Roman-Avar fighting in 600–1. Only then would such cities as survived in the northern and inner provinces of the Balkans be able to re-establish control over their hinterlands. Only then would those provinces be effectively reintegrated into the empire.

The second decade of Maurice's reign provided sobering experience of how little could be achieved even when there were no serious distractions elsewhere. The Avars, although on the defensive for much of the time, remained a formidable adversary, as they demonstrated in 597–8, when they made a surprise attack, trapped and blockaded one Roman general in Tomi on the Black Sea, routed a second as he came to his colleague's relief, and then advanced south towards

Constantinople. The consequences for Roman prestige among their recently acquired Slav subjects and for the maintenance of Roman control over them would have been catastrophic but for an outbreak of plague which halted the invading army in its tracks and forced the khagan to negotiate a renewal of the lapsed peace (on improved terms for him). Even though the Roman field army pressed home its temporary advantage in 599 and invaded Pannonia, even though Roman diplomats then managed to win over the Antae (Gothic-influenced Slavs living beyond the lower Danube) and through them triggered revolts among other Avar subjects in 601, the Avar khaganate was too well organized and resilient to be in danger of imminent collapse. It was to remain a major, menacing power on the edge of Roman territory in Europe for many years to come.[1]

In autumn 602, substantial field forces were deployed in the Danube region. The troops, who had probably not forgotten a previous attempt of Maurice's to improve cost-efficiency (in winter 593/4), were far from content at the prospect of more years of campaigning in inhospitable terrain and often unpleasant weather. Now came an order that they were not to return to winter quarters and enjoy a respite from fighting. Instead, they were to remain north of the Danube and to keep up the pressure on the belt of Slavs adjoining Roman territory. For the Slavs would be at their most vulnerable in winter, when the deciduous forests provided thinner cover. When the order was announced, there was an outcry in the ranks and soon deep reluctance to obey developed into open mutiny.[2]

In Italy, Maurice's drive to reassert effective Roman authority over the Lombards came to naught for lack of the necessary military force. Italy plainly ranked third after the east and the Balkans in east Roman priorities, as it had done for all but four years (551–4) since its initial recovery in 540. The regional supremo, the exarch based in Ravenna, had to magnify the limited military power which he could bring to bear, by diplomacy and subversion. There was no hope of reasserting Roman authority unless direct action by the exarch's forces was supplemented by Frankish military intervention on a large scale and by coordinated rebellions on the part of suborned Lombard dukes, as happened in 590. There were some subsequent successes, notably the recovery of Perugia, a vital strategic position on the trans-Apennine route between the exarchate and Rome. The Roman authorities held onto several key cities (Padua, Cremona, and Mantua) from which they could keep the core territory of the Lombards in the central plain north of the Po under surveillance. The Lombards of Spoleto were also deterred from pressing against Rome itself from their Apennine redoubts. But

---

[1] Michael Whitby, *The Emperor Maurice and His Historian: Theophylact Simocatta on Persian and Balkan Warfare* (Oxford, 1988), 80–6, 158–65, 178–83, 292–304.

[2] Theophylactus Simocatta, *Historiae*, ed. C. de Boor, rev. P. Wirth (Stuttgart, 1972), trans. M. and M. Whitby, *The History of Theophylact Simocatta* (Oxford, 1986), viii.6.2—cited henceforth as Sim.; cf. Whitby, *Emperor Maurice*, 165–8.

overall Roman operations proved counterproductive.[3] King Agilulf (590–616) was antagonized by the capture and detention of his daughter and son-in-law in 599 and set about changing the balance of power on the ground. He attacked key fortified cities in the Po Valley and negotiated an alliance with the Avar khaganate. Padua fell after a long siege in 601. Istria was subjected to concerted attack by Lombards and Avars in 602, after which the refractory Lombard dukes of Trento and Cividale were won over by Agilulf (603). It was only after Maurice's fall in November 602 and the loss of Cremona (20 August) and Mantua (13 September) in 604, that a new exarch agreed a truce with Agilulf, and, finally, after threatening Lombard moves in northern Umbria, negotiated a full peace treaty. This came into force in November 605 and was to last for many years. The price was considerable: the release of grand hostages with their children and possessions, and a payment of 12,000 solidi.[4]

A crisis was also developing in Armenia. Roman attempts to sponsor the Chalcedonian rite, including the appointment of a Chalcedonian Catholicos, had caused widespread resentment in a region where the rival Monophysite confession was deeply entrenched. The new Catholicos, who was installed at Theodosiopolis, capital of the old Roman sector of Armenia, where his safety could be guaranteed, did not smooth matters when he appropriated the plate and other movable property of his Monophysite rival, who continued to reside at Dvin just over the frontier. The Armenian nobility and fighting classes were being antagonized at the same time by the strenuous efforts of Maurice's regime to transform Armenia into a recruiting ground and to send the troops raised there to the Balkans. The losses suffered and also doubtless the unpleasant conditions encountered were alienating the loyalties of Armenians at home as well as in the field.

The problems engendered by these policies were compounded by a mood of heightened national awareness dating from 572, when, with covert Roman support, disaffected elements in Persarmenia organized a general uprising. Hopes raised then had been dashed, but not forgotten, when the Sasanians reimposed their authority (by 578). They were reawoken when much of Armenia was prised loose from Sasanian control in 591, and manifested themselves thereafter in sporadic anti-Roman agitation. It was, of course, quite natural for Armenians to vent their disgruntlement and frustration on the currently dominant power in the

---

[3] C. Wickham, *Early Medieval Italy: Central Power and Local Society* (London, 1981), 30–3; N. Christie, *The Lombards: The Ancient Longobards* (Oxford, 1995), 84–91.

[4] *Pauli historia Langobardorum*, ed. L. Bethmann and G. Waitz (Hanover, 1878), iv.20, 23–8, 32, trans. W. D Foulke, *Paul the Deacon, History of the Lombards* (Philadelphia, PA, 1907), trans. F. Bougard, *Paul Diacre, Histoire des Lombards* (Turnhout, 1994)—cited henceforth as Paul D. The chronological precision of these notices points to use of a contemporary source written by Secundus Bishop of Trento. The territories remaining under Roman control are enumerated by A. Guillou, 'L'Italia bizantina dall'invasione longobarda alla caduta di Ravenna', *Storia d'Italia*, I *longobardi e bizantini*, ed. P. Delogu, A. Guillou, and G. Ortalli (Turin, 1980), 217–338, at 220–7.

region, irrespective of that power's specific policies towards them. But there was all too sharp a contrast between the heroic battles on the fringes of the steppe fought by Armenian forces recruited from the Persian sector, battles from which their general, Smbat Bagratuni, accumulated unrivalled prestige at home, and the hard slog in the cold and wet of the Balkans endured by those recruited by the Romans from their sector.

A rebellion was nipped in the bud late in 601, when a hitherto loyal Armenian commander slipped across the Dardanelles and rode with a small body of companions back to Armenia. The *magister militum* there had been alerted and moved quickly to arrest the rebels, going so far as to pursue them onto Sasanian territory and to besiege them in Nakhchawan until a Persian army approached. Now, in 602, came news that the emperor was planning to transplant 30,000 cavalrymen and their families permanently to Thrace. Priscus, one of Maurice's four senior and most trusted commanders, was detailed to organize the delicate operation and was on his way to Armenia.[5]

There were ominous signs of increasing disaffection elsewhere in the empire. Egypt, the richest of all the empire's provinces, had been disturbed by two rebellions earlier in Maurice's reign. One originated in factional rivalries in three cities near Alexandria. It escalated rapidly. The rebel leaders, four notables belonging to the same family, were able to mobilize support against the provincial authorities on a scale large enough to disrupt Alexandria's communications up the Nile and across the Mediterranean as well as to encourage insurrection elsewhere in Egypt. The authorities had to draw on all available military resources, including those of Nubia, to suppress it. The second was little more than a grand act of brigandage involving the seizure of provincial tax revenues. At the approach of loyalist troops the rebel leader and his band of lawless men and Ethiopian slaves fled to a natural stronghold where they managed to hold out for a while.[6] The underlying cause is probably to be found in the financial strain caused by the inflated military budget needed to fund the heroic enterprise of restoring Roman rule in the Balkans. Certainly, the main target of the opposition was the empire's chief financial officer, Constantine Lardys, praetorian prefect of the East, as was made plain when his Constantinopolitan house was burned down on the night of rioting which drove Maurice from power.[7]

There was a worrying incident in Constantinople early in 602. The immediate cause was a food shortage. As the emperor was going barefoot through the city

---

[5] *Patmut'iwn Sebeosi*, ed. G. V. Abgaryan (Erevan, 1979), 104.22–105.15, 105.28–33, trans. R. W. Thomson in R. W. Thomson and J. Howard-Johnston, *The Armenian History Attributed to Sebeos*, TTH 31, 2 vols. (Liverpool, 1999), I *Translation and Notes*, with II *Historical Commentary*, nn. 22 and 24—cited henceforth as ps.S.

[6] H. Zotenberg, ed. and trans., *Chronique de Jean, évêque de Nikiou* (Paris, 1883),174.24–178.20 (trans. 409–13)—cited henceforth as JN. Cf. Whitby, *Emperor Maurice*, 24.

[7] Sim., viii.9.5–6.

in procession on the night of 1–2 February, stones were thrown at him. A feigned attack by his bodyguard brandishing iron clubs temporarily dispersed the crowd and enabled him, together with Theodosius, his eldest son, to proceed to Blachernae and celebrate the Purification of the Virgin Mother at her church there. But the crowd regrouped and demonstrated its opposition by guying the emperor. A bald man who looked like Maurice was put on a donkey, crowned with a wreath of garlic, and then taunted with various mocking shouts. The crowd likened him to a cock mounting a soft, sensuous heifer and fathering children like *xylokoukouda* (hard seed?), accused him of muzzling dissent, and asked God to strike him on the head.[8] By the autumn, Maurice's position had become much weaker. While he was able to extract declarations of loyalty from the partisans of both Blue and Green racing colours in the hippodrome before the mutinous Balkan expeditionary army reached the capital, and felt able to assign them roles in the defence of the city, their commitment was easily frayed as the political crisis developed. Both groups deserted him before the rebel army reached the suburbs.[9]

1.1 Phocas' Seizure of Power

In the Balkans the expeditionary force had completed an anti-Slav sweep on the north bank of the middle Danube and was withdrawing when the emperor's order arrived. The troops remonstrated with their commander-in-chief, the emperor's brother Peter, but he stood by the order. At this they mutinied, crossed the Danube back onto Roman territory at Palastolum, and marched downstream to Securisca. But their resolve was weakening. An offer of increased pay and rations to compensate them for the hazardous and unpleasant conditions which they faced probably helped to bring this about. Certainly, they agreed to construct the boats needed to ferry the army back across to the north bank, and were doing so when they got their first taste of the winter to come, furious storms and the onset of cold. Their opposition revived and they refused to cross the river. An eight-man deputation was sent to reason with Peter at his headquarters, which he had kept at a safe distance from the main camp since the

---

[8] Sim., viii.4.10–5.4; U. Roberto, ed. and trans., *Ioannis Antiocheni fragmenta ex historia chronica*, Berlin-Brandenburgische Ak. Wiss., Texte und Untersuchungen zur Geschichte der altchristlichen Literatur 154 (Berlin, 2005), fr.317—cited henceforth as JA; Theophanes, *Chronographia*, ed. C. de Boor, 2 vols. (Leipzig, 1883–5), 283.12–24, trans. C. Mango and R. Scott, *The Chronicle of Theophanes Confessor: Byzantine and Near Eastern History AD 284-813* (Oxford, 1997)—cited henceforth as Theoph. Simocatta misdates the episode a few days after rather than before Theodosius' wedding to Germanus' daughter (9 February 602 (*Chronicon Paschale*, ed. L. Dindorf, CSHB (Bonn, 1832), 693.3–5, trans. Michael Whitby and Mary Whitby, *Chronicon Paschale 284-628 AD*, TTH 7 (Liverpool, 1989)—cited henceforth as *Chron.Pasch.*)).

[9] Sim., viii.9.4.

beginning of the mutiny. He agreed to come and address the troops on the following day.[10]

He gave no ground, when he did so, and insisted that orders be obeyed. First he addressed a meeting of senior officers (*taxiarchai*), reading out the latest letter from the emperor. They were unmoved and came out firmly in the troops' favour. When he took the same adamant line in his speech to the full assembly of the army, there was an outcry and the meeting broke up. The troops then convened their own assembly, at which we may presume they reiterated their opposition. At a second assembly on the following day, they elected Phocas their leader and raised him on a shield, thereby proclaiming him their candidate for the throne.[11]

So bad was Phocas' subsequent reputation as a ruler, so eager was Heraclius to blacken his name both before and after his own seizure of power, that very little is reported in the extant sources about his background and previous career. The most informative is a contemporary chronicler, the continuator of John of Antioch. He notes that Phocas came from Thrace, that he was 55 years old, married (to Leontia) and with a daughter (named Domentzia after his mother). He gives the lie to Simocatta, who assigns him the lowly rank of centurion. For John's account of the deputation sent on an earlier occasion to lodge the army's complaints against Comentiolus, Peter's predecessor (in command until winter 600–1), makes it plain that Phocas was one of its leading members. It was Phocas who presented the deputation's case most forcefully at an imperial audience and who was the last to leave, thus giving an enraged patrician the opportunity to assault him. He represented the army again on the deputation sent to Peter at Securisca. There is, therefore, nothing inherently improbable in the claim made in the Egyptian chronicle of John of Nikiu and possibly derived from a lost part of the continuation of John of Antioch that Phocas was one of four senior commanders in Thrace in autumn 602.[12]

The army now prepared to march on Constantinople under Phocas' command. Two of his rivals for the rebel leadership, Alexander and Lilius, both likewise senior commanders, were sent ahead to Constantinople, presumably in the hope that they might be able to negotiate a peaceful transfer of power. Meanwhile Peter fled together with officers who had joined him from the main camp and sent a messenger ahead to inform the emperor of what was happening.[13]

Maurice's first action on hearing the grim news was to keep it secret for as long as possible and to hold special chariot races in the hippodrome as if nothing were amiss. When the news broke, he extracted public declarations of support from

---

[10] Sim., viii.5.5–7. Cf. Whitby, *Emperor Maurice*, 165–8.

[11] Sim., viii.7.4–7; JA, fr.318.1–8; JN, 183.10–17 (trans. 417–18). Cf. Whitby, *Emperor Maurice*, 25, 168.

[12] *Chron.Pasch.*, 693.9–11; Sim., viii.6.9, 7.7; JA, fr.316, 318.23–5; JN, 183.17–18 (trans. 418). Cf. Whitby, *Emperor Maurice*, 17, 122–4.

[13] Sim., viii.7.6–7; JA, fr.318.6–8.

both Blue and Green circus factions and organized the defence of the capital, allocating stations on the Theodosian walls to faction members (Figure 1). Phocas' emissaries were not admitted to the city when they arrived and were only able to make contact with one person who slipped out. All they could do was to go back to the rebel army as it was continuing its march. Maurice made no attempt to hold the Long Wall which ran from the Marmara to the Black Sea coast some 60–70 kilometres from Constantinople. The advance units of the rebel army crossed it unopposed. It was now Maurice's turn to try to negotiate, but without success. Phocas evidently insisted that Maurice must abdicate. The defences of the city were activated and put in the hands of Germanus, a magnate with an extraordinarily distinguished lineage who could be trusted because of a double marriage link (he and Maurice had married sisters, daughters of the Emperor Tiberius (578–82), and he had recently become Theodosius' father-in-law).[14]

A breach was achieved before the full rebel army arrived, by what appears to have been a highly successful piece of disinformation on the part of the rebels.[15] They had let it be known that they would support the candidature of Maurice's eldest son Theodosius or of his father-in-law Germanus, if either were willing to join in the attempt to oust Maurice. A letter expressing this view was rumoured to have been received by Theodosius when he was out hunting with Germanus before the rebels made the approaches to the city unsafe. Credence was given to the story when a rebel foray raided the horses grazing outside the city and carefully spared those belonging to Germanus. Soon the story reached the emperor's ears and led him, as intended, to suspect Germanus of treason. On the following day (21 November) he dismissed him from his command, replacing him with Comentiolus, an appointment which was not calculated to appease the rebel army. Then, on 22 November, he summoned Germanus and confronted him with the evidence of his treason. Although Germanus defended himself vigorously and was allowed to leave the audience, it was evident that the emperor was not convinced of his innocence.[16]

Germanus made his way home along the Mese, the main east-west street. A natural anxiety about his own safety had been sharpened by a whispered warning from Theodosius as he left the emperor's presence. That afternoon, accompanied by his armed retinue, he took refuge in a nearby church. Events now began to move fast. When the news of Germanus' action reached Maurice at dusk, he sent a high-ranking palace official, the eunuch Stephen, Theodosius' tutor, to

---

[14] Sim., viii.7.8–8.2; Theoph., 287.9–23. R. Pfeilschifter, *Der Kaiser und Konstantinopel: Kommunikation und Konfliktaustrag in einer spätantike Metropole*, Millennium-Studien 44 (Berlin, 2013), 277–9 argues that he was also a blood relative of Justinian's.

[15] Pfeilschifter, *Der Kaiser und Konstantinopel*, 261–93, who takes the army's offer to Theodosius and Germanus to be genuine, gives the leading role in events to Germanus and the Greens.

[16] Sim., viii.8.3–9, who accepts the story (and is followed in doing so by Whitby, *Emperor Maurice*, 25–6, 168).

persuade him to come out. In this he failed completely. He was manhandled out of the church and abused by Germanus' bodyguard. It was now dark. Escorted by his retinue, Germanus moved to the centre of the city, where he sought sanctuary in St Sophia. News of his presence there must have spread quickly. For a crowd had gathered in the forecourt when a force of Excubitors arrived to persuade him to leave the church. Whatever it was they had to say swayed Germanus. He was on his way out when he heard a loud shout from one of the clergy of St Sophia warning him that death lay in store for him. He turned back.[17]

At this the crowd began to shout slogans against the emperor. The commotion grew. The members of the circus factions abandoned their stations on the Theodosian walls and joined in. The trouble spread out from St Sophia and developed into a riot, in the course of which the house of the unpopular praetorian prefect of the East, Constantine Lardys, was burned down. Maurice had lost control of the city at a critical moment, when the rebel army was close at hand (it was making a forced march that very night). Realizing that his cause was doomed, Maurice together with his immediate family slipped away in the small hours before dawn on 23 November. They were accompanied by Constantine Lardys and Theodosius' tutor, Stephen.[18]

Meanwhile representatives of the Green faction also slipped out of the city and made contact with the rebel army, evidently to pledge Phocas their support. Inside the city Germanus made a feeble bid for power, apparently with the backing of the Blues, of whom he was patron. He quickly abandoned it when his emissary to the Greens met with a rebuff (because of his known connection with the Blues), and gave Phocas his support.[19]

Hence, Phocas encountered no resistance as he approached on 23 November. At Rhegium on the Marmara coast, he was acclaimed by the Greens and formally invited to the military parade ground in the Hebdomon outside the city walls. He responded by sending an emissary to St Sophia to issue a public invitation for the people, the patriarch, and the Senate to attend on him. They met him in the Hebdomon, where the factions, acting as representatives of the people, raised him on a shield in the Tribunal of the parade ground and acclaimed him emperor in the presence of the senators and the other spectators. This secular election was then followed by a ceremony in the church of St John the Baptist nearby: first the Patriarch Cyriacus extracted a solemn declaration of orthodox faith from Phocas and an undertaking that he would leave the church undisturbed; then Phocas made a show of reluctance by offering the throne to Germanus, which Germanus declined; finally, the patriarch crowned him.[20]

---

[17] Sim., viii.8.3.
[18] *Chron.Pasch.*, 693.11–16; Sim., viii.9.1, 3–7; JA, fr.318.10–11, 14–15; JN, 183.18–24 (trans. 418).
[19] Sim., viii.9.13–16; JA, fr.318.10.
[20] *Chron.Pasch.*, 693.16–19; Sim., viii.10.1–6; JA, fr.318.12–14; JN, 184.4–7 (trans. 418); Theoph., 289.8–22.

Two days later, on Sunday 25 November, Phocas made a ceremonial entry into the city, seated in a chariot and distributing gold as he went. Cheering crowds welcomed him as the procession came in through the Golden Gate and went along the Mese to the palace. Races were then held to celebrate his accession. The celebrations continued on the following day. A donative was distributed among the troops, Phocas' wife, Leontia, was crowned Augusta, and more races were held in her honour.[21]

The fugitive imperial family did not evade the new ruler's grasp. The ship on which they were travelling was forced by contrary winds to put in at Diadromoi, a port on the north side of Gulf of Nicomedia. From there Theodosius was sent off by land, accompanied by Constantine Lardys, to appeal to the *shahanshah* Khusro II for help. The emperor, with the rest of his family—his wife Constantina, his other five sons (Tiberius, Peter, Paul, Justin, and Justinian), and his three daughters (Anastasia, Theoctiste, and Cleopatra)—continued his voyage (perhaps to put the pursuers off Theodosius' scent) but got no farther than Praenetus on the opposite shore of the gulf of Nicomedia, where they stopped and sought sanctuary in the church of St Autonomus because of the emperor's gout. There they were arrested and brought back to Chalcedon on the Asian shore of Bosporus opposite Constantinople to await their fate.[22]

It was determined by Phocas at the races celebrating Leontia's coronation as Augusta. He was spurred on to order a round of executions by a commotion which arose when the Blues would not give up their customary prime position to the Greens. In the course of it, shouts were heard coming from the Blues referring to the fact that Maurice was still alive. On the following day, Tuesday 27 November, Phocas commanded that Maurice and his sons be executed. The order was carried out promptly in the harbour of Eutropius outside Chalcedon. A semi-legendary story soon grew up which gave a moving account of the occasion: Maurice watched as four of his sons were beheaded; then, when the nurse of the youngest, Justinian, substituted her own baby, he insisted that his own son be produced; and, after all those present had lamented when they saw milk as well as blood flow from the small corpse, he was beheaded himself.[23]

Four other executions were carried out, probably on the same day. Maurice's unpopular Balkan generals, his brother Peter (who had fled with the imperial family and had probably been arrested with them), and Comentiolus (executed near the church of St Conon on the north shore of the Golden Horn), were singled out, presumably as a sop to the army which had brought Phocas to power.

---

[21] Chron.Pasch., 693.19–23; Sim., viii.10.6–10 (mistakenly dating Phocas' entry only one day after his coronation); Theoph., 289.22–5 (mistakenly placing Leontia's coronation two days rather than one after the ceremonial entry, which is correctly dated).

[22] Chron.Pasch., 694.1–3; Sim., viii.9.7, 9–10; JA, fr.318.10–11, 14–17, 19–20; JN, 184.7–13 (trans. 418).

[23] Chron.Pasch., 694.3–5; Sim., viii.10.9–11.6; JA, fr.318.26–8; JN, 184.13–14 (trans. 418–19).

The other two were senior officers closely associated with the old regime, who may also have antagonized the Balkan troops—Peter's *domesticus* Praesentinus and the second-in-command to another of Maurice's generals, his brother-in-law Philippicus. Other leading figures in Maurice's regime who had been arrested were spared, including Philippicus and Germanus, who were allowed to retire and take holy orders the following year.[24]

A gruesome display of the severed heads of Maurice and his five sons posted up on the military parade ground in the Hebdomon suburb conveyed vividly and unequivocally the news that the old regime had fallen, to the army, to the population of the capital, and, through them, to the world at large.[25] One head, though, was missing, that of Theodosius, Maurice's eldest son. Speculation grew that he had been sent to get help from the Sasanian king, Khusro II, and that he had succeeded in escaping. Official Roman sources, which are, as usual, reflected in the *Chronicon Paschale*'s account, reported that he too had been caught and executed together with Constantine Lardys, who was accompanying him.[26] The place of their execution was named, Diadromoi, where they had been put ashore, but, uncharacteristically, the chronicler was unable to supply a precise date. This suggests that it was not given in the bulletin which he was using. This official version failed to quell rumours that Theodosius was alive and, later, that he had reached Persian territory and gained the support of the *shahanshah* for his claim to the imperial throne.

Within the east Roman Empire any suggestion that the son of the deposed and executed emperor was still alive and seeking to recover his throne was likely to increase disaffection at a time when the new regime was at its most vulnerable. Phocas' government denied categorically that Theodosius had escaped. The original version of his death was amended and elaborated: Theodosius had journeyed as far as Nicaea when he received an urgent summons to turn back from Maurice, authenticated by a ring brought by the messenger. Dutifully he went back to face execution, which was now said to have taken place at St Autonomus at the hands of Alexander, one of Phocas' two senior military allies. The official account is unlikely to have become more convincing with the addition of these rather implausible circumstantial details. A new and completely different version was also in circulation. It was admitted that Theodosius had got away, had reached the Black Sea, and had taken a ship to Lazica, planning to continue his journey overland. But it was claimed that he had died long before reaching Persian territory, either drowning during the voyage or collapsing as he travelled through desolate country beyond Lazica. John of Antioch noted the first of these stories,

---

[24] *Chron.Pasch.*, 694.5–12, 695.3–5; Sim., viii.13.1–2; JA, fr.318.20.
[25] Theoph., 291.2–4. Simocatta, who does not include this item, reports that the headless corpses were cast into the sea and that spectators gathered on the shore by Chalcedon to watch as they were carried to land or swept out again by the current (viii.12.1–2).
[26] Pfeilschifter, *Der Kaiser und Konstantinopel*, 269 accepts the official version.

but refrained from giving it his assent, reporting merely that Theodosius escaped initially and avoided execution at Phocas' hands. Theophylact Simocatta, writing in the 620s, noted the second story but rejected it, as any author who sought official patronage in Heraclius' reign would have had to. Public opinion, however, was probably still not won over, since there was still a glaring absence of proof that Theodosius had been executed and changes in the official line cast doubt on the truth of all the versions peddled.[27]

1.2 Persian Preparations for War

The news of the revolution in Constantinople reached Khusro II probably in his capital, Ctesiphon (Figures 2-4). He may have been genuinely saddened at the overthrow and murder of his benefactor Maurice. The arrival of Theodosius, if he did succeed in reaching Persia, may have aroused pity and a determination to wreak vengeance on the usurper. But apart from any moral or personal considerations, the opportunity was too good to miss. He decided to replay the events of 590–1, this time with the Persians intervening to restore the legitimate ruler, or a claimant masquerading as such, to the rival, partner empire of the Romans. The reward would be the recovery of the territory which Maurice had demanded as the price for his military and political support.

The fall of Maurice provided the best possible pretext for going to war. The timing was also miraculously fortunate from the Persian point of view. For Khusro had been preoccupied hitherto by other pressing political and military concerns. His restoration in 591 had not ended civil strife within Persia. The opposition, which was led by his uncle Bistam, had come out in open rebellion in 595–6. Defeat in battle had forced Bistam out of the open country of Media into the fastnesses of the Elburz mountains to the north. But he remained for many years a formidable foe, backed as he was by Dailamite highlanders and a disgruntled court party. He strengthened his position, winning over regular troops from his home region of Komiš and an Armenian force stationed at Ispahan, and gaining control of the whole length of the Elburz range. He thereby extended his reach perilously close to the north-eastern frontier, where it abutted onto the transcontinental empire of the Turks. At the same time there was no relaxation of the pressure which the Turks could apply on the outer defences of the sown lands of Persia in the 590s. The bulk of Khusro's field forces, which included an important Armenian component, were

---

[27] Official version: *Chron.Pasch.*, 694.7–10. Variant of official version: Sim., viii.9.11–12, 11.1–2 (Theodosius sent off to Khusro, but recalled in time for execution). Rumours: Sim., viii.13.3–6, followed by Theoph., 291.5–11; JA, fr.318.17–19. Persian version (successful flight): *Chronicon anonymum*, ed. I. Guidi, CSCO, Scriptores Syri 1, Chronica Minora I (Paris, 1903), 15–39, at 20.20–1, trans. Greatrex and Lieu, *Roman Eastern Frontier*, 229–37 (at 232)—cited henceforth as *Khuz.Chron.*

therefore committed to a long, demanding defensive war in the north and northeast. In 601–2, though, both the domestic and foreign problems were solved. Smbat Bagratuni, an Armenian general much lauded among his countrymen, crushed the last remnants of Bistam's rebel forces, while the Turks, apart from the perennial distraction of succession crises, were drawn east to intervene in China in those very years.[28]

By the end of 602 it was clear that there was an opportunity to set about redressing the strategic balance, so unfavourable to Persia. Cession of the eastern third of the Armenian Taurus had given the Romans control over the whole range, from the Euphrates gorges in the west to Lake Van in the east, and over all three strategic passes across the mountains. This brought with it a decisive advantage of inner lines. For command of all the passes and their denial to the enemy would, at times of war, enable the Romans to transfer troops between the Armenian and Mesopotamian theatres of war with a speed which could not be matched by the Persians using the circuitous and more difficult passes across the Zagros, well to the rear of the frontier. The resulting superior capacity of the Romans to mobilize and concentrate their military resources, whether for defensive or offensive purposes, was in danger of relegating Persia to the status of an inferior power. No *shahanshah* could ignore the chance of altering arrangements which amounted to the military castration of Persia in the west.

The territorial adjustments made in Armenia and Iberia were militarily of less significance, but were likely to inflict considerable political damage in the longer term. For it was the steady encroachment of Roman power and influence which posed the greatest threat to the security of the Sasanian Empire. Since its first appearance in these northern lands, Christianity had acted as a corrosive agent, breaking down the traditional cultural connections between the local nobilities of the region and those of the Iranian plateau and its fringing mountains. Behind the advance of the new faith, Roman authority had been pushed outwards step by step towards the main Persian dependencies in Transcaucasia. The definitive annexation of Lazica, agreed under the terms of the 562 treaty, was a serious setback.[29] Further damage was done to Persian interests by the territorial concessions extracted from Khusro II in 590. Roman rule was extended deep into two of Persia's three north-western dependencies. Both Persarmenia and Iberia lost their western territories. The two provincial capitals, Dvin and Tiflis, were left exposed, perilously close to the new frontier. Beyond, the open valleys of the Araxes and

---

[28] Ps.S, 94.27–95.15, 96.3–97.6, 97.15–98.17, 99.14–19, with *Hist.Com.*, nn.18, 19 (dates emended to accord with redating of Khusro II's accession to 590–1 [(S. Tyler-Smith, 'Calendars and Coronations: The Literary and Numismatic Evidence for the Accession of Khusrau II', *BMGS* 28 (2004), 33–65)); T. J. Barfield, *The Perilous Frontier: Nomadic Empires and China* (Oxford, 1989), 137–9; Howard-Johnston, 'The Sasanians' Strategic Dilemma', 56–61.
[29] Menander Protector, ed. and trans. R. C. Blockley, *The History of Menander the Guardsman* (Liverpool, 1985), 54–87 (fr.6.1).

Kura rivers led into the plains of Albania, the third dependency, and Atropatene, the westernmost region in the Persian heartlands. Khusro had little choice but to go to war with the aim of recovering some or all of the lost territories, and thus improving the security of Iran. Had he failed to act in 603 or very soon afterwards, his position would assuredly have come under threat at home.[30]

Finally Khusro cannot have been unaffected by a general souring of relations between the two great powers. That sense of shared interest in the face of the outer peoples, of being engaged in a common endeavour of protecting the civilized world from attack by northern barbarians, had been destroyed or, at any rate, seriously weakened in the course of the sixth century. Successive acts of aggression by each side shook the faith of the other in the existing world order. Each round of warfare thickened the atmosphere of suspicion and fear left by the previous one. Justin II's decision to ally with the Turks, whereby the Roman Empire abandoned its old commitment to coexistence, administered the *coup de grâce*. Beneath the superficial restoration of the old order brought about when Maurice agreed to give Khusro his political and military support, old resentments festered and new wrongs demanded to be righted.

Considerations such as these impelled Khusro to seize the extraordinary opportunity proffered in the winter of 602–3. He instituted a period of national mourning for the death of Maurice and insisted on its ostentatious observance by the army, thereby preparing public opinion for war. He gave orders for the mobilization of Persian forces. A northern army was to move forward and take up winter quarters at Dvin, capital of Persarmenia.[31] There, it was placed close to the Roman frontier, ready to invade in the following spring. To the south of the Armenian Taurus, in Mesopotamia, Khusro probably supervised preparations himself, since he took personal command when operations began. There too Persian forces were probably concentrated close to the frontier, in Nisibis, the main forward base. Finally, either Theodosius or a convincing impostor was produced and portrayed in Persian propaganda as the rightful ruler of the Roman Empire, thus softening up the exposed frontier provinces before the start of offensive operations.[32]

News of Maurice's overthrow was received calmly in most Roman provinces. There was no disturbance in Egypt. Some advance intelligence came from a calligrapher who had dined well at a merchant's house. His informants were statues which, he claimed, descended stealthily from their pedestals and accosted him as he made his way home in the small hours. They gave him the hot news, nine days before the arrival of official confirmation. Simocatta, the source for this story, was probably well informed about conditions in the province, since the Augustalis (governor) at the time was a relative of his.[33] Armenia too did not stir.

[30] Sim., iv.13.24; ps.S, 76.8–18, 84.23–31, with *Hist.Com.*, n.10. Cf. Whitby, *Emperor Maurice*, 303–4.
[31] Ps.S, 107.31–108.2. [32] Ps.S, 106.15–17. [33] Sim., viii.13.7–14.

Disenchantment with Maurice's military and ecclesiastical policies had a delayed effect which only showed itself in 605 in the form of fraying loyalty in the high command. The only recorded reaction among Armenian leaders to the news of Maurice's death at the time was on the part of Atat Khorkhoruni, the bold commander who had attempted to rouse armed insurrection against Maurice in 601. He now planned to slip away from the Persian court at Ctesiphon and to offer his services to the new Roman emperor, but his plan was discovered and he was executed on Khusro's orders.[34]

Events in Syria and northern Mesopotamia, however, did provide Khusro with some encouragement. Narses, commander-in-chief of the armies of Oriens (the Levant), a distinguished general of Maurice's, refused to recognize the usurper, left Antioch when news of the putsch reached him, and seized Edessa. Edessa was a powerfully defended city in the heavily militarized forward zone, on the far bank of the Euphrates. As such it could act as a secure base for his rebel forces. It was also within striking distance of the Persian frontier, giving Narses the option of calling on the Persians for assistance. This he proceeded to do, writing to Khusro and inviting him to assemble his forces and make war upon the Romans.[35] Khusro now had formal, legal justification for intervening in the internal affairs of the Roman Empire. The prospects of military success were also greatly enhanced, since the rebels would be able to disrupt the mobilization of Roman forces and any efforts they made to reinforce the defences of the principal cities and bases close to the frontier—Dara, Theodosiopolis, Constantia, and Amida.

The new government of Phocas moved fast to snuff out the rebellion. Germanus, a senior regional commander (to be distinguished from Theodosius' father-in-law, who was in Constantinople), was ordered to move against Narses.[36] It was probably well before the start of spring and the completion of Persian preparations for war that Germanus' forces dug themselves in round Edessa and began siege operations. Narses, however, remained quiet inside the city, confident that the Persians would send assistance before long and that the fortifications would keep the besiegers at bay in the meantime.[37]

The revolt was a serious challenge to Phocas' regime. For the moment the trouble was contained and the prospects of suppressing it in the near future looked good until news came of Persian military preparations. There was no sense of urgency initially as Phocas prepared to dispatch an embassy to inform Khusro

---

[34] Ps.S, 105.17–20.
[35] Ps.S, 106.30–2; Theoph., 291.27–292.1; *Chronicon ad annum Christi 1234 pertinens*, ed. J. B Chabot, CSCO, Scriptores Syri, 3.ser., 14 (Paris, 1920), 219.31–220.6, trans. A. Palmer, *The Seventh Century in the West-Syrian Chronicles*, TTH 15 (Liverpool, 1993), 120—cited henceforth as Chron.1234.
[36] J. R. Martindale, *Prosopography of the Later Roman Empire*, III (Cambridge, 1992), Germanus 11 (the father-in-law) and Germanus 13 (the general).
[37] Ps.S, 106.30–3; Theoph., 291.27–292.1.

of his accession, in accordance with the tradition which required each great power to communicate with the other on such occasions.[38] Several months passed before the ambassador, Lilius, set off in March 603, travelling along the main diagonal road across Asia Minor, then through the Mesopotamian military zone to Dara, where he was entertained by Germanus. From Dara he crossed the frontier and proceeded to the royal court at Ctesiphon. His reception there was anything but welcoming. The Persians refused to recognize the new regime and sent back a blunt note expressing Khusro's regard for Maurice and declaring war. Lilius was detained at Ctesiphon, where he remained, apparently until his death. By this act, which flouted the conventions governing diplomatic exchanges, Khusro made yet plainer his determination to dispose of the upstart emperor who had ousted and murdered his benefactor.[39]

1.3 Opening Campaigns

Several months were spent in preparations for the Persian offensive before attacks in force were launched across the frontier both in the north, into that part of Persarmenia which had been annexed by the Romans in 591, and into the forward defensive zone in northern Mesopotamia south of the Armenian Taurus.

Dzuan Veh, who had spent the winter in Dvin, faced a substantial Roman force which had taken up a position very close to the frontier, atEłivard.Ełivard, a small town (*kałakagiwł*, *komopolis*), lay some 50 kilometres from Dvin, midway between two northern tributaries of the Araxes. There the Roman troops were well placed to counter a Persian attempt to invade along the obvious, easy route up the Araxes valley, either by swooping down against its northern flank or by making a diversionary attack on the exposed plain of Dvin in its rear. Dzuan Veh, however, did not take the easy line of advance, but turned north to engage the Romans in the plain ofEłivard. He was defeated in the ensuing battle. The Persians suffered heavy losses, including Dzuan Veh himself, who was killed. Their camp was captured and rich booty gathered from inside it. The sector of the plain bordering the river was called Meadow of the Romans.

This northern campaign was, however, as much a diversionary action designed to detain the regional Roman field army in the Armenian theatre as an attempt to win a victory or gain territory there or influence Armenian opinion. For it was essential for the Persians to secure the southern invasion army from the danger of a flank attack launched across one of the three main Armenian Taurus passes. Despite the disastrous end of the campaign, this purpose was achieved. No

---

[38] M. P. Canepa, *The Two Eyes of the Earth: Art and Ritual of Kingship between Rome and Sasanian Iran* (Berkeley and Los Angeles, 2009), 123–30.
[39] Sim., viii.15.2–7; Theoph., 291.11–14.

threatening move from the north distracted the Persian forces in Mesopotamia from their objectives.[40]

Khusro took personal charge of operations in the south, a sign of the greater importance attached to them. Germanus was in a relatively weak position, caught between the besieged rebel forces in Edessa and a Persian field army bearing down on him from the south-east. He retreated towards the Euphrates, apparently taking the road north to Samosata rather than the main road west towards the crossing at Zeugma and hoping thereby to avoid combat with Khusro's army. Khusro meanwhile marched against Dara without encountering serious resistance. Leaving a general there to organize siege operations, he advanced deeper into Roman territory, seeking to bring Germanus to battle. This he did, catching the Roman army on the nearer, left bank of the Euphrates and winning a decisive victory. Germanus was mortally wounded and taken off by his bodyguards to Constantia (the nearest secure Roman base), where he died eleven days later. Khusro could now proceed at his leisure to Edessa.[41]

The main gate of the city was opened when he arrived. This was the first Roman city entered by the Persians in the course of the war. It provided the setting for the assertion of the claims of the pretender Theodosius before a Roman audience. A full coronation ceremony was laid on. It was carefully stage-managed to maximize its impact on those present and on public opinion elsewhere. The leading role was assigned to Narses, the general who had demonstrated his devotion to Maurice and his family by his open opposition to the new regime. After the young man, who wore imperial robes, was crowned, Narses formally placed him under the protection of the *shahanshah*, asking him to show the same compassion as he had been shown by Maurice. The ceremony made a considerable impression, despite strenuous efforts by Phocas' government to discredit the pretender and to portray the whole event as Narses' idea.[42]

It is impossible for us to be certain whether or not the pretender was Maurice's son. Too much obfuscation has been cast by the propaganda spewed out by both great powers in the opening engagements of the war. Was he a stooge of Khusro's who was brought in state by the Persian army and introduced by Khusro to Narses at Edessa? Was he an impostor whom Narses presented to Khusro on the occasion of his visit to Edessa? Or were his claims genuine? Was he the Theodosius, whose birth on 4 August 583 was celebrated by Evagrius in an encomium? Was it to him that the future Pope Gregory the Great stood godfather when he was baptized at Epiphany 584, an occasion commemorated by massive 12-solidi gold

---

[40] Ps.S, 107.4–6, 107.31–108.9, with *Hist.Com.*, n.28.
[41] Ps.S, 107.1–4, 6–11, with *Hist.Com.*, n.27; Theoph., 292.6–11.
[42] Ps.S, 107.11–16 (swallowing the official Roman line about the pretender), with *Hist.Com.*, n.27. *Khuz.Chron.*, 20.20–4, trans. Greatrex, 232 accepts the pretender's claims, but relocates his coronation to a Nestorian church where the Catholicos Sabrisho officiates and places the ceremony before the start of military operations.

medallions distributed by the Emperor Maurice. Was it the young man destined to reign as Theodosius III who was crowned in a solemn ceremony at Edessa in the presence of the *shahanshah*?[43] Whatever the truth, the coronation and the formal public appeal for Persian aid issued by Narses had the desired effect. There can be little doubt that it undermined to a significant extent the will to resist of the frontier provinces, and thus helped the Persians to break through the forward defences and to reach the Euphrates by 610. Clear, direct evidence of this came a few years later in 607 at Theodosiopolis, on the edge of the Roman sector of Armenia. The city capitulated promptly after a deputation met Theodosius and was convinced of his identity.[44] In Constantinople, the key surviving members of Theodosius' family, his mother, three sisters, wife, and father-in-law Germanus, are reported to have believed that he was the pretender sponsored by Khusro, and to have taken part in a broad-based but unsuccessful conspiracy to dethrone Phocas in 604–5. For this they paid with their lives.[45]

After the ceremony at Edessa, Khusro concentrated on the siege of Dara, establishing his headquarters at Nisibis, just across the frontier. Narses seems to have been left to carry on defending Edessa with his own forces against whatever new armies the emperor might send against him. The presence of a Persian field army within striking distance was likely to deter all but the most formidable of armies from renewing the siege. In the event, Phocas was able to deploy a large relieving force in the 604 campaigning season, after negotiating a new treaty with the Avars (with a substantial increase in the cash subvention) which freed up large numbers of Balkan troops for service in the east. A similar treaty agreed with the Lombards a year later ensured that there would be no distractions from the west for more than a decade.[46]

Khusro was prevented from repeating the tactics of 603, when the commanding general, Leontius, a eunuch, followed Phocas' orders and divided his army, sending half towards Dara to mask his own attack on Edessa. This risky move paid off at first. Narses was unable to hold out in Edessa and fled to Hierapolis. But Khusro was able to engage the other force as it approached Dara. This second battle, fought on the Arzamon river (modern Zergan Su, which flows south from the Tur Abdin plateau to the Khabur river, a few kilometres west of Dara), resulted in a crushing victory, with large numbers of Roman troops taken prisoner. The strategic initiative had been regained and would not be relinquished for many years to come. Khusro could delegate the rest of the siege to a subordinate, now that Dara's fate was sealed, and return triumphant to his capital. On

---

[43] Whitby, *Emperor Maurice*, 18, 21; J. P. C. Kent and K. S. Painter, eds. *Wealth of the Roman World AD 300–700* (London, 1977), 115 (cat.no.192).
[44] Ps.S, 111.17–24, with *Hist.Com.*, n.30 (dating to be brought one year forward).
[45] *Chron.Pasch.*, 696.6–697.3; Theoph., 294.27–295.13.
[46] Avars: Theoph., 292.11–14. For the Lombards, see n. 4 of this chapter.

the Roman side, Leontius was dismissed and replaced by the emperor's nephew Domnitziolus, who persuaded Narses to give himself up with the promise of a fair trial (although what awaited him on arrival in Constantinople was death at the stake). Dara continued to hold out, but eventually, after a year and a half, the powerful defences of this hardest of hard-point fortresses succumbed to Persian mining operations.[47]

The news from the northern, Armenian front was also encouraging. The defeat of 603 was avenged in the 604 campaigning season. Doubtless, larger forces were deployed. The account, in the *History of Khosrov*, is rather fuller than of that of 603 (perhaps reflecting the balance of an official Sasanian source which was inclined to elaborate on success rather than failure). In the course of the narrative it becomes plain that the strains engendered by internal conflict within the Roman Empire were affecting army morale in 604, and that by 605 there was disaffection on the part of the Armenian element in its high command and in the ranks, a first manifestation perhaps of disenchantment with Roman rule generated by Maurice's military and, to a lesser extent, religious policies.

The Persian invasion force was commanded by a certain Datoyean in 604. The Romans were encamped at the village of Şirakavan on the eastern edge of Vanand (the Kars plain).[48] As in 603, they were holding the line of a major tributary of the Araxes, this time the Akhurian, which flows from north to south, farther back in Roman territory, to the north-west rather than the south of Mount Aragats. No explanation is given for this withdrawal deeper into Roman territory. Unreported Persian raids or forays may have preceded the main attack and forced the Romans back. Or it may have been a deliberate tactical retreat to a stronger position (Şirakavan commanded the only easy ford over the Akhurian) in the face of a more powerful enemy. If the latter was the case, it was a move which failed. For the Romans were surprised by the speed of the Persian advance and hurriedly

---

[47] Ps.S, 107.17–25, with *Hist.Com.*, n.27; Theoph., 292.11–25, 292.28–293.5; *Chronicon miscellaneum ad annum Domini 724 pertinens*, ed. E. W. Brooks, CSCO, Scriptores Syri 3, Chronica Minora II (Louvain, 1960), 145.29–30, trans. Palmer, *Seventh Century*, 17—cited henceforth as *Chron.724*; A. A. Vasiliev, ed. (and trans.), *Kitab al-'Unvan, histoire universelle écrite par Agapius (Mahboub) de Menbidj*, part 2.2, PO 8 (1912), 399–547, at 436.9–10—cited henceforth as Agap.; J. B. Chabot, ed. (and trans.), *Chronique de Michel le Syrien, Patriarche Jacobite d'Antioche (1166–1199)*, 5 vols. (Paris, 1899–1924), IV, 390—cited henceforth as Mich.Syr.; and *Chron.1234*, 221.14–17 (these last three texts, which have a common source, are translated by R. G. Hoyland, *Theophilus of Edessa's Chronicle and the Circulation of Historical Knowledge in Late Antiquity and Early Islam*, TTH 57 (Liverpool, 2011), 56–7). *Khuz.Chron.*, 20.24–21.15, trans. Greatrex, 232 has Khusro only take charge of the campaign in winter 603-4, after an army commanded by the pretender was defeated, going on to start siege operations against Dara (involving construction of earthworks as well as mining) after defeating the Romans in a hard-fought battle.

[48] T. A. Sinclair, *Eastern Turkey: An Architectural and Archaeological Survey*, 4 vols. (London, 1987–90), I, 423, 425 for the site of Şirakavan which he identifies with Başsüregel on the western, Turkish bank of the Arpa Çay. The Roman camp in 604 was evidently on the eastern side, since the Romans retreated across the river.

withdrew across the river to a new position a few kilometres to the north-west, at the village of Getik near the fortress of Erginay.[49] The fortress was packed with refugees from thirty-three villages. The Persians followed and launched an attack. Although the able-bodied young men among the refugees inside the fortress sallied out in force and inflicted considerable losses on them, the Persians were not distracted from their main task. They engaged the Roman army, put it to flight, and pursued the fugitives, slaughtering all whom they caught. After gathering the booty and returning to their camp, they turned their attention to Erginay. Mounting a full-scale assault, they stormed it and captured the refugees inside. No attempt was made to garrison Erginay and turn it into a Persian bridgehead on the edge of the plain of Kars, nor even to hold the territory farther east which the Romans had not defended in 604. Instead the victorious Persian army withdrew to its base in Atropatene with its rich haul of prisoners and booty. The defeat of 603 had been avenged. Persian prestige had been restored.[50]

The Persians concentrated on the Armenian front in 605. There is no report of fighting in Mesopotamia. They seem to have been content to consolidate their position in and around Dara, ready to defend the city if the Roman field army made an effort to recover it. Since the military initiative lay with them, this pause must reflect a deliberate change of strategy on their part. The forces in the south were being given a secondary, supporting role, that of detaining the main body of Roman troops and preventing them intervening north of the Taurus.

It is tempting, with hindsight, to suggest that political considerations also exercised some influence. For it was in 604–5 that a broad alliance of dissident elements in the governing circles of Constantinople set about organizing a counter-coup against Phocas.[51] In Armenia too, treason was in the air and, in the event, acting in apparent collusion with the Persian forces, Armenians serving with the Roman field army ensured that it suffered a second serious defeat in open battle. It would not have been unreasonable for the Persians to suppose that the shock of a double defeat in the east might weaken the position of Phocas' government and prepare the ground for a counter-coup. They might also have hoped that discontent either in the army, evidently fighting a losing war, or in the rich provinces of the Levant and Asia Minor which would be exposed if the forward defensive zone in Mesopotamia suffered further serious damage would lead to a second and more dangerous uprising in support of the Persian-backed pretender. Khusro, from his vantage point at Ctesiphon, may, therefore, have decided on relative inaction in the southern theatre, biding his time and waiting on events which ought to favour the Persian cause and might enable victory to be achieved without several more years of wearing conflict.

---

[49] Sinclair, *Eastern Turkey*, I, 423, 425 for the location of modern Argina, with which Erginay should be identified.
[50] Ps.S, 108.10–109.2, with *Hist.Com.*, n.28.   [51] See n. 45 of this chapter.

Senitam Khusro was appointed *spahbed* (regional military commander) of the West and took over the supreme command relinquished by the *shahanshah* after the fall of Dara.[52] His presence in Armenia is a sure indication of the priority accorded to operations there.[53] Aware that the Romans would expect him to renew the offensive on the easiest sector of the front, the upper Araxes valley and the relatively open country to the north, where the flattened mass of the Aragats volcano leads into the upland plain of Kars, he chose instead to attack south of Mount Ararat, crossing an easy pass and descending into the elongated plain of Bagrewand, where the Arsanias river gathers its headwaters. A Roman force was stationed in the eastern sector of the plain, where it was well placed both to march north and attack the Persians in the rear if they advanced up the Araxes and to bar access to the Arsanias valley. It included a considerable number of Armenian troops. The commanding general was also Armenian, T'eodos Khorkhoruni. He had created a well-fortified encampment at a village close to the Arsanias, demolishing a second village on the opposite bank (presumably to prevent the Persian army from taking it over). From this strong defensive position as well as the large fortress of Angł nearby, which he garrisoned, he would be able to send out harassing forays or to strike in greater force against the Persian army, confident in the strength of the two mutually supporting positions.

Senitam Khusro succeeded in circling round and establishing a camp of his own to the rear of Romans. The Romans were offered an opportunity to withdraw, before they decided, after some hesitation, to stay put and fight. A dawn attack then achieved complete surprise. Continuous arrow fire by massed archers caused mayhem in the Roman camp, where both men (unarmed) and mounts (tethered by the tents) were exposed. The wounded horses broke free and trampled over the tents and other parts of the camp. Confusion was compounded by the actions of the retainers of the Armenian princes serving in the army. They attacked the soldiers as they armed themselves and cut the girths of the horses as they were being saddled. In all the confusion, the Persians were able to breach the fortified perimeter and pour into the camp. The defenders then made their own breach and took flight on foot and horseback, apart from the many who had been caught and killed. There does not seem to have been a pursuit. The Persians stayed in the Roman camp overnight and, the next day, sent a note demanding the evacuation of the Roman garrison from Angł. The Romans duly departed within the three days which had been stipulated, taking their baggage and equipment with them, while T'eodos Khorkhoruni was detained and sent to Khusro with a

---

[52] Ps.S, 109.3. *Spahbeds*: R. Gyselen, *The Four Generals of the Sasanian Empire: Some Sigillographic Evidence* (Rome, 2001).

[53] The *History of Khosrov* does not refer automatically to the passing of winter or coming of spring to mark off one campaigning season from the next. But whenever a change of command is reported, we may infer and are probably intended to infer that the operations undertaken by the new general take place in a new campaigning season.

recommendation that he be treated well. Whether he really had helped the Persians, as was publicly stated, or the story was a piece of black propaganda issued to encourage disaffection among the Armenian nobility is an unanswerable question.[54]

Senitam Khusro then resumed his advance. His route took him across Bagrevand, north over the mountains and into the Araxes valley well to the west of the farthest point reached in 604. In the great plain of Basean, he met a second, probably larger Roman army, won a second victory, and threw the Romans back across the pre-591 frontier on the Araxes-Euphrates watershed. The campaign narrative ends with a list of the chief gains of the year (here all classified as cities), three in Armenia—Angł (a local commander was installed), Gayłatukh (commanding a strategic pass on the Bagrewand-Basean route taken by Senitam Khusro), and Erginay (in Vanand), which was presumably now garrisoned, a year after its initial capture in 604—and one in the Mesopotamian theatre, Tsnakhert near Dara.[55]

At the end of the campaigning season Senitam Khusro received orders to withdraw to Persian territory. The achievements of the year were considerable. Roman authority had been peeled off the territories ceded in a moment of extraordinary political weakness at the start of Khusro's reign. The advantage of inner lines given by control of the central Armenian lands as well as all three Armenian Taurus passes had been seized from the Romans. Senitam Khusro had complemented the successes achieved south of the Armenian Taurus, where Khusro had, by the capture of Dara, made the first vital breach in the outer defences of Mesopotamia and, no less important, had shaken the confidence of the great adversary of Sasanian Persia.

Much, of course, remained to be done in both theatres of war if Khusro's intention was to force an equitable peace treaty out of the Romans and to impose his own candidate on them. The systems of defence elaborated by the Roman military authorities at great cost to the imperial exchequer over many generations would now have to be assaulted in a laborious, slow-moving, unrelenting offensive, the strategic equivalent of street fighting, which would put great strain on Persian resources and morale.[56] It would be a war of attrition, chipping away at key points in the nexus of Roman fortifications. A decisive superiority in manpower and materiel would be needed, together with steely determination. Khusro, therefore, ordered a halt to the advance in the 606. A year's breathing space would allow his forces in both theatres to recuperate and would enable him to institute a recruiting drive throughout his empire.

---

[54] Ps.S, 109.3–110.3, with *Hist.Com.*, n.29 (which takes the story on trust).
[55] Ps.S, 110.4–11, with *Hist.Com.*, n.29 (with a different interpretation of Persian strategy).
[56] J. Howard-Johnston, 'Military Infrastructure in the Roman Provinces North and South of the Armenian Taurus in Late Antiquity', in A. Sarantis and N. Christie, eds., *War and Warfare in Late Antiquity: Current Perspectives*, Late Antique Archaeology 8.2 (Leiden, 2013), 853–91.

1.4 Second Persian Offensive

No major operations are recorded for 606. The Persians were preparing the ground for a second offensive on a grander scale, almost certainly with a barrage of propaganda supporting the claims of the pretender and denouncing the regime of Phocas. Hitherto, they had responded to events with the resources to hand, exploiting the opportunities offered in both theatres by the open rebellion of Narses and the covert treachery of T'eodos Khorkhoruni. They had made substantial gains, but they still faced powerful Roman armies which could be expected to put up a stubborn fight. The main purpose of the year's pause was to enlist and train the additional troops required to negate the marginal advantage enjoyed by the Romans. For they still controlled the most direct lines of north-south communication both within Armenia, linking the Euphrates and Arsanias valleys, and between the Armenian and Mesopotamian fronts.[57]

The strategy which was adopted and implemented in 607 involved major attacks on both fronts. The two Roman regional armies were to be engaged on a large enough scale to prevent troop transfers between fronts, save for those dictated by the Persians so as to draw off reserves before decisive blows were struck. Each attack marked the first step in an offensive which would be sustained for several campaigning seasons. The Armenian *History of Khosrov*, the best source for operations in this first phase of the war, gives summary accounts of the main stages of the Persian advance to 610, when a second temporary halt seems to have been called. The narrative of events is consolidated into two separate notices, dealing respectively with the southern and northern fronts.[58]

Meagre information is supplied about operations in the south. They were marginal to the history of Armenia. It is fortunate that the *History*'s account can be supplemented by a number of notices in Syrian sources, of which the most trustworthy is the *Chronicle to 724*. Patchy though the coverage is, it is evident that the Persian advance was painfully slow to begin with and that it only gathered momentum in 609. This is at odds with the impression given by the telescoping of several campaigns into the *History*'s single notice that the conquest was easy and rapid.

Khoream Erazman, *spahbed* of the East, was brought west (presumably with a body of troops) and given the southern command. His orders were to invade Roman Mesopotamia and to treat well all those who submitted voluntarily. A certain amount of wishful thinking lay behind the second of these orders. There is no evidence that the provincials, despite their adherence to the Monophysite confession, were ready to collaborate with the invaders. Instead Khoream had to fight hard to achieve his first objective, the conquest of the Tur Abdin massif. Then and

---

[57] Ps.S, 110.23.   [58] Ps.S, 110.23–111.31, with *Hist.Com.*, n.30.

only then was there a perceptible faltering in the resistance put up by Roman troops and civilians.[59]

The start of Khoream's operations is reported before the renewal of action on the Armenian front, which is dated to the eighteenth year of Khusro's reign (June 607–June 608).[60] If the southern offensive was intended to draw reserves away from the northern theatre, it was launched between one and two months earlier, probably in late spring or early summer 607. The Tur Abdin had to be the Persians' first objective since it formed a heavily defended outer bastion in the complex nexus of fortifications of Mesopotamia. As long as the forts with which Anastasius and his immediate successor Justin I had endowed the Tur Abdin hills remained in Roman hands, any gains made by the Persians in the upper Tigris basin to the north or immediately to the south and south-west would be threatened, as would be their lines of supply.[61] Khoream, therefore, concentrated his forces against the Tur Abdin. His principal target was Cepha, which controlled a strategic bridge over the Tigris and guarded the approaches to the north-east end of the Tur Abdin. Stubborn resistance by the garrison assuredly encouraged the defenders elsewhere. The fall of Cepha, on the eve of a particularly severe winter in 608–9, triggered a first strategic withdrawal by Roman forces. They evacuated all the forts which they still held and fell back on the great fortresses of the plains and the inner defensive line on the Euphrates.[62]

Not that this was the end of resistance in the Tur Abdin. At Mardin civilians continued the fight after the departure of Roman regulars. Monophysite monks joined in, after asking for and probably obtaining their bishop's permission to take up arms. However frayed their political loyalty to the East Roman regime, however deep their resentment of the authorities' repeated attempts to repress or at least contain Monophysitism in the eastern provinces, there was no question of their abandoning the struggle when the enemy was the dualist Persian state which harboured within it the Nestorians, the most hated of all the Monophysites' rivals among the Christian sects. The monks are portrayed as taking a leading role in the defence of the city, in effect as shock troops of Christendom in battle with the agents of the Devil. They kept up the resistance for an appreciable time (six months or so)—probably until early spring 609. It was only then, when Mardin fell, that the Persians were able to occupy the whole of the Tur Abdin and to inaugurate the second phase of their offensive.[63]

They now brought intense pressure to bear on the main Roman cities of Mesopotamia, which could, with their powerful fortifications, double as major

---

[59] Ps.S, 110.23–8.   [60] Ps.S, 111.11–12.
[61] M. Whitby, 'Procopius and the Development of Roman Defences in Upper Mesopotamia', in P. Freeman and D. Kennedy, eds., *The Defence of the Roman and Byzantine East* (Oxford, 1986), 717–35.
[62] Mich.Syr., IV. 390 (trans. Chabot, II, 378).
[63] *Chron.724*, 146.1–7 (trans. 17); Mich.Syr., IV.390–1 (trans. Chabot, II, 378); *Chron.1234*, 221.19–22 (trans. Palmer, 122).

military bases and formed the nodal points of the regional defensive system. The first to yield was not among those most exposed to Persian attack. For it was Edessa, lying a considerable distance to the south-west of Amida, the great Roman redoubt in the rich, rolling plains of the upper Tigris, and well to the rear of the chief military centres of the lands fringing the desert to the south and south-west of the Tur Abdin. Edessa capitulated in summer 609 and, in so doing, fatally undermined the defence of the forward military zone. For the main cities which remained in Roman hands were now cut off from the interior of the empire, since Edessa commanded the routes leading to them from Roman positions on the Euphrates. Their fate sealed, Amida surrendered, together with the southern Theodosiopolis (formerly Resaena) and Constantia, which had probably resumed their old fourth- and fifth-century roles as the two main forward bases of the Romans south of the Tur Abdin after the loss of Dara. Persian power was now coming close to the Romans' last effective line of defence, the Euphrates *limes* dating from the Principate.[64]

Carrhae, lying to the south of Edessa, where the cultivable plain of Osrhoene shades into semi-desert, now felt the full force of Persian military power. So too did the two main Roman bases on the east bank of the Euphrates, Circesium, near the traditional frontier, and Callinicum, due south of Carrhae, both of which had been lynchpins of the defensive system designed both to impede Persian advance up the Euphrates valley and to control the Beduin of the north-west desert since its development by Diocletian. They were all in Persian hands before the end of the campaigning season. The following winter (609–10) the Euphrates was the frontier between the two empires.[65] The patient strategy of Khoream had gradually worn down the material defences of Mesopotamia and eroded the resolve of the Roman forces deployed there. The conquest of the whole region, thereby depriving the rich provinces beyond of their apparently impregnable shield, was a signal military achievement. It was only outshone by the first ferocious attacks on the Roman Empire of Shapur I in the initial dynamic expansion of Sasanian power in the third century. It was surely in recognition of these services that Khusro designated Khoream Shahrbaraz 'Panther of the Realm'.[66]

The Persians waited on events in 610. The long-expected revolution was gathering momentum inside the east Roman Empire. Shahrbaraz contented himself that summer with a single operation of significance—an attack across the Euphrates at the southern end of the front. With his capture of Zenobia, which fell on 7 August, he secured a bridgehead midway between Circesium and

---

[64] *Chron.Pasch.*, 699.7; ps.S, 110.31–111.7; Mich.Syr., IV, 391 (tr. Chabot, II, 378); *Chron.1234*, 221.22–5 (trans. Palmer, 122). T.B. Mitford, *East of Asia Minor: Rome's Hidden Frontier*, 2 vols. (Oxford, 2018).

[65] *Chron.724*, 146.8–11 (trans. 17); Mich.Syr., IV, 391 (trans. Chabot, II, 378).

[66] Mich. Syr., IV, 390 (trans. Chabot, II, 377–8) and *Chron.1234*, 221.2–14 (trans. Palmer, 121–2) date the bestowal of the honorific implausibly early, before the start of operations in 603.

Callinicum from which to launch attacks deep into Syria. He also succeeded in distracting the attention of the Roman defenders from what was almost certainly his main objective that year, the Euphrates crossing much farther upstream on the direct road to Antioch.[67]

In the north, two decisive victories in the field opened the way for a sequence of wide-ranging campaigns which brought the Persians to the Anatolian plateau by 611 and enabled them to impose their authority on much of Roman Armenia. The first of these victories was won by Astat Yeztayar in 607 over a Roman army which was counterattacking towards Basean, the westernmost district occupied by the Persians. Astat and his expeditionary force were intercepted at Du and Ordru just below the watershed between the Euphrates and Araxes catchment areas.[68] The ensuing battle ended in bloody defeat for the Romans. The fleeing remnants of their army were pursued as far as Satala in north-east Anatolia, while the main body of the Persians advanced without encountering further opposition over the pass and closed in on Theodosiopolis. Theodosiopolis was the key military base in this northern sector of Roman Armenia. Since the beginning of the fifth century, it had been both the chief city of the region, from which Roman influence gradually percolated into the surrounding highlands, and had housed the garrison which secured the eastern end of the natural invasion route formed by the upper Euphrates valley.

The siege did not go well at first. The Roman defenders put up stout resistance and inflicted considerable losses. Astat then decided to deploy his secret weapon, the pretender Theodosius, who had been assigned to the northern theatre for this first year of the second Persian offensive. He was brought up to the front line. A deputation of dignitaries from the city was invited to meet him. The audience with him convinced them that he was Maurice's son, and on their return to the city they convinced their fellow citizens. The gates were opened. The city formally submitted. Astat thus gained a great prize at minimal expense, thanks to the psychological impact of the apparently legitimate pretender's claims on his adversaries. He left a garrison in the city, doubtless a very powerful one, given the strategic importance of Theodosiopolis, and continued operations.

These operations are best construed as consisting of distinct raids carried out by separate forays deep into Roman territory.[69] Astat's role was presumably to direct and coordinate from the rear the actions of the independent detachments which he sent ahead. One foray was dispatched before the capitulation of Theodosiopolis, immediately after the battle. Its original task was to pursue the routed Roman forces as they fled west, but after a time the nature of the operation changed. What had begun as an urgent pursuit turned into a deep-penetrating raid along the Romans' main northern support road, which took this foray into

---

[67] *Chron.724*, 146.11–13 (trans. 17).
[68] Hewsen, *Armenia: A Historical Atlas*, 89–91 (map 69). [69] Ps.S, 111.24–6.

the north-east corner of the Anatolian plateau. There, two Roman bases, Satala and Nicopolis, which dated from the Principate and acted as major buttresses of the northern sector of the Euphrates *limes*, came under attack.

Another foray operated south of the northern support road, entering the fertile plain of Derjan (modern Erzincan), a region of especial importance in Armenian eyes into which the Roman military authorities had refrained from intruding. The chief centre of the region, Eriza, was attacked. A third foray raided far to the south-west, advancing beyond the plain of Taron, where the Persians had established a presence in 605, into the district of Asthianene, which was still in Roman hands. Asthianene was the next large plain in the Arsanias valley downstream from Taron and commanded the northern approach to the easiest central pass over the Armenian Taurus. The Persians' objective there was the fortress of Citharizon, which had been built in the early sixth century with the triple function of securing the northern access to the pass, controlling the southern invasion route along the Arsanias valley, and intensifying Roman authority over the hill country to the north.[70]

All three forays were successful. The *History of Khosrov* reports that all four of the named places which they attacked were taken, but makes no mention of their being garrisoned. It seems safe to infer from this silence that no attempt was made to occupy them and turn them into forward bases for harassing the surrounding areas, but that as winter drew near, the forays returned to the main army under Astat's command. The whole army then withdrew to Persian-held territory.[71]

The fall of Theodosiopolis was a serious blow to the Romans and must have lowered Roman prestige throughout Armenia, as well as depressing morale and increasing dissidence in the other provinces of the east. The subsequent raids extended the material and psychological damage and were an earnest of what the northern Persian command had in store for the lands north of the Taurus in the near future. They may also have set a pattern which was to be followed in the operations of the next few years, a main Persian force advancing in good order to deal with major centres of population behind a screen of raiding forays.

Despite these striking achievements, Astat was replaced by a new general. Shahen Patgosapan, who was to have an extraordinarily distinguished career in Khusro's service, now (spring 608 presumably) made his first appearance on the historical stage. He marched across the Araxes-Euphrates watershed into the

---

[70] Ps.S, 111.24–6. Eriza: A. Bryer and D. Winfield, *The Byzantine Monuments and Topography of the Pontos* (Washington DC, 1985), 32–3. Citharizon: J. Howard-Johnston, 'Procopius, Roman Defences North of the Taurus and the New Fortress of Citharizon', in D. H. French and C. S. Lightfoot, eds., *The Eastern Frontier of the Roman Empire*, BAR Int.Ser. 553 (Oxford, 1989), 203–29, repr. in Howard-Johnston, *East Rome*, no.II.

[71] Three of the campaign's main successes—the victory on the edge of Basean and the capture of Citharizon and Theodosiopolis—are noted in the *Narratio de rebus Armeniae*, c.112, ed. and trans. G. Garitte, CSCO 132, Subsidia 4 (Louvain, 1952). The date is given both as 606–7 (Phocas' fifth regnal year) and 609–10 (Khusro's twentieth).

district of Theodosiopolis, bypassing the city itself, and engaged the latest and last effective fighting force fielded by the Romans in Armenia. He won a decisive victory and drove the defeated Roman troops out of the country.[72] Roman defence of their lands east of the Euphrates seems now to have collapsed.

At his leisure, in the following campaigning season, Shahen advanced westwards across Armenia. The start of operations is dated to the twentieth year of Khusro's reign (June 609–June 610). No details are given about specific actions in 609–10, probably because there were no notable battles to record, but by the winter of 610–11 Shahen's forces had reached the Romans' inner line of defence on the Euphrates, where the river turns south and forces its way against the grain of the relief towards the Taurus and, beyond, Syria and Mesopotamia. For he was able, in spring 611, to strike deep into Anatolia and to seize the city of Caesarea in Cappadocia.[73]

Doubtless, Shahen's advance along the two great river valleys which provide relatively easy access to eastern Anatolia was slowed by local pockets of Roman resistance and by the organizational task of setting up local military administrations. But his principal concern in these two years was probably to get a firm military grip on the mountainous spine of western Armenia separating the river valleys[74] and to establish a degree of Persian authority on the outer fringes of the formidable highland regions flanking this central Armenian causeway. For it was essential to discourage the highlanders from resorting to insurgency tactics, which would very rapidly affect Persian communications and the security of smaller, isolated outposts, by a formidable display of military might right at the start of the period of Persian occupation. The process of pacification would be a long and laborious one, and it had to be initiated on a grand scale in these years. It is, however, almost entirely concealed from our gaze, save for one dramatic episode. This involved the deportation of population from Theodosiopolis, the chief city of Roman Armenia, to Hamadan, the chief city of Media. It was ordered by Khusro himself in 610–11, the year in which the initial conquest of Roman Armenia was completed. It was presumably a security measure designed to remove dissident elements from the city, notably the Roman-sponsored Chalcedonian Catholicos John. He was deported along with all the treasure of his catholicosate, which included a great deal of plate purloined not long before from the Monophysite catholicosate.[75]

Much of the foregoing reconstruction is speculative. But fixed chronological points are supplied by the *History of Khosrov*, which leaves little doubt about the

---

[72] Ps.S, 111.27–31. [73] Ps.S, 112.9–11.

[74] The following ranges separate the Euphrates from the Arsanias valleys: in the east, the vast, spreading mass of the Bingöl Dağ, a long extinct and flattened volcano; in the centre, the Şeytan Dağları, a virtually impassable range which has earned its name as the mountains of Satan; and in the west the formidable but just surmountable high ridge of the Munzur Dağ.

[75] Ps.S, 111.32–112.8.

main stages of Shahen's western advance in the northern theatre of war. First, there was his decisive victory in the field in 608, which followed up that won by Astat Yeztayar in the previous year, then a phase lasting two years in which his forces overran and occupied western Armenia, and finally, in 611, the first major breach in the northern sector of the Romans' Euphrates *limes*.

The Emperor Phocas (602–10) has been given a bad press. His image is that of a tyrant at home who disposed ruthlessly of opponents and a disastrous war leader abroad.[76] Hard-fought campaigns dissolve into swift Persian advances in the course of which successive chunks of Roman territory are taken and city after city falls into enemy hands. The Persians not only break through the Romans' inner defences by the end of his reign, but push on through the Levant to Egypt and cross Asia Minor to the Bosporus. In the Balkans too the Roman position collapses as the Avars are reactivated and ravage widely. Such was the record of his reign current a century or so later when Theophilus of Edessa, at work in the Caliphate, was piecing together a history of the demise of the ancient world and the rise of Islam. It was picked up from him half a century or so later and recycled by the Byzantine historian Theophanes.

In reality, Phocas was a more than competent general. It is hard otherwise to explain his election by officers and men of the Balkan expeditionary force as their leader, or the intelligence displayed in his seizure of power. As emperor, he faced grave problems. The troops who had brought him to power were weary of fighting. The Avars, temporarily disabled by defeat, must be cajoled into agreeing to make peace on terms which would secure the gains made by the Romans in recent years but which were attractive enough to ensure their quiescence for the foreseeable future. In the east, war loomed and the Roman position was fatally weakened by the rebellion of Narses, commander-in-chief in the Levant.

The response of the new regime was swift and effective. Loyal troops were mobilized to isolate and besiege Narses in Edessa. By the middle of summer 603, when the Persians attacked in force, the field armies of Oriens and Armenia were ready to meet them in open battle. The prospect for the southern commander, Germanus, was grim, caught as he was between a rebel to his rear and a full Persian invasion force ahead. The opening battle went against him, but the Romans managed to strengthen their position over the following year or so, while Khusro concentrated on the siege of Dara. Narses was driven from Edessa and forced to surrender. Dara eventually fell, but the rest of the forward defensive system—the network of fortified places which turned the Tur Abdin into a massive redoubt, the great city of Amida to the north, and the three well-defended cities behind Dara (Theodosiopolis (Resaena), Constantia, and Edessa)—was activated and ready to withstand assault. North of the Armenian Taurus, an

---

[76] Cf. M. Meier, 'Kaiser Phocas (602–610) als Erinnerungsproblem', *BZ* 107 (2014), 139–74.

unnamed general inflicted a serious defeat on the invading army. It took another two years of hard campaigning for the Persians to redress the balance and to push forward to the old pre-591 frontier in Armenia.

For three years (603–5), Phocas thus succeeded in stemming the Persian advance. Of the strongholds lying inside the traditional boundaries of the empire, only Dara had fallen. Otherwise the defensive system built up over many centuries and completed in the sixth century was intact. His real coup, though, took place in the Balkans and Italy, where the Avars and Lombards agreed peace treaties which were to hold good for many years and which made it possible to redeploy troops to the east. It should cause little surprise, then, that an honorific statue was erected in 608 on a pre-existing column (the tallest) in the Roman Forum by the Exarch Smaragdus (who had signed the peace treaty with the Lombards three years earlier) in recognition of Phocas' pious benefactions and the peace which he brought to Italy.[77] His armies did, in effect, fight the Persians to a standstill by 606. Khusro was forced to increase the forces which he could put into the field before resuming what turned out to be a battle of attrition lasting three and half years (607–10). He owed his success ultimately to superior numbers and the opportunity which they gave his generals to strike where and when they chose, thus negating the Romans' advantage of inner lines or even turning it against them if feints succeeded in drawing away reserves from targeted sectors of front.

Khusro could be confident of the outcome from 607, but not of the length of time which it would take to break the will of the Roman armies. His confidence must have been strengthened by news from within the east Roman Empire. A rebellion initiated in North Africa by the governor Heraclius in 608 developed into an empire-wide revolutionary movement in the course of 609 and 610. Political uncertainty was bound to have an effect on the morale and fighting ability of the armies in the field. With a bridgehead across the Euphrates at Zenobia from which attacks might be launched into Syria and with troops poised to cross the Euphrates at other places, it would only require a temporary abatement in Roman military effort for the breakthrough to be achieved and for Persian forces to drive west to Antioch, the greatest city of the Levant, and to the Mediterranean coast beyond.

---

[77] R. Krautheimer, *Rome: Profile of a City, 312–1308* (Princeton, NJ, 1980), 67; A. Claridge, *Rome: An Oxford Archaeological Guide* (rev. ed., Oxford, 2010), 87–8; G. Kalas, 'The Divisive Politics of Phocas (602-610) and the Last Imperial Monument of Rome', *AT* 25 (2017), 173–90, at 177–80, 184.

2
The Heraclian Revolution

Danger threatened the east Roman Empire from within as well as without in the last years of Phocas' reign. Several opposition groups came out into the open. The targets of their attacks were various—the state itself, the regime in power, local city establishments, and rival local organizations. The gathering crisis reached a climax in autumn 610 and the following winter, when a new emperor took over at the centre and, in the face of considerable opposition, imposed his authority on the provinces. It was prolonged into the first years of the new reign, despite the menacing advance of Persian power deep into the Levant, only abating after 614 when Persian occupation forces were entrenched in Syria and the north of Palestine.

It is reported that in 609 or 610 the Jews of the Levant were suspected of planning a general uprising, which, by diverting forces away from the eastern front, would have provided invaluable aid to the Persians as they fought their way through the defences of Roman Mesopotamia or sought an opportunity to establish a bridgehead across the Euphrates.[1] When trouble erupted on the streets of Antioch and many of the city's political bosses were slaughtered, one rumour, picked up by a later source, had it masterminded by Jews, holding them responsible for the murder of the Patriarch Anastasius and for the mutilation of his corpse. Later, in 614, those of Jerusalem were charged with being an enemy fifth column, responsible for urging the Persian high command to besiege the city and subsequently exploiting the fall of the city to launch a ferocious attack on their Christian fellow citizens and to desecrate the holy places.[2]

The open political challenge to Phocas' regime originated in the west. The beginning of the rebellion is datable to 608. The leaders were the elder Heraclius, exarch of Africa, his brother Gregory, and their sons Heraclius and Nicetas. Their first moves took place after assurances of support were received from several quarters in neighbouring provinces. At the time or soon afterwards, a story began to circulate which put rather a different construction on the rebellion, suggesting

---

[1] Agap., 449.1–3; Eutychius, *Annals*, ed. and trans. M. Breydy, *Das Annalenwerk des Eutychios von Alexandrien: Ausgewählte Geschichten und Legenden kompiliert von Sa'id ibn Batriq um 935 AD*, CSCO 471–2 (Leuven, 1985), 121.10–13 (trans. 101).

[2] These reports, which are discussed below (pp. 47, 64, 87, 88–9, 92), have been taken seriously by historians—see, for example, W. H. C. Frend, *The Rise of the Monophysite Movement* (Cambridge, 1972), 335, A. N. Stratos, *Byzantium in the Seventh Century*, I 602–634 (Amsterdam, 1968), 75, 77.

that its mainspring was a party in the Senate in Constantinople. It is, however, plain that, from the first, the political initiative lay with the African provincial leadership, that it acted as the catalyst for the opposition elsewhere with its swift and successful attack on Alexandria, and that it never relinquished its directing role in the events which were to bring about Phocas' downfall. It is unclear how long the battle for Egypt lasted after the intervention of Bonosus, the regime's hard man, or how large were the forces deployed by the two sides. The fullest account, that of the Egyptian chronicler John of Nikiu, is, alas, rather blinkered, and seems to concertina time.[3] It is, therefore, hard to tell how many troops were withdrawn from the eastern front and what the impact was on the Roman war effort.

The established social order within the localities was being subjected to stress. Brief but highly coloured reports in the extant sources suggest that the traditional rivalry and propensity to violence of the circus factions burst out into rioting and gang warfare on the streets of the great cities of the Middle East. This appears to have spread rapidly, a successful insurrection in one city inspiring the youth of others to emulate it, so that by the end of Phocas' reign the crisis was so intense and widespread that it was registered by a distant observer in the far west, Isidore of Seville.[4] There is also clear evidence of political polarization between the factions—from Antioch in 609, where Blues feared the consequences of their association with Phocas, and later that year from Egypt, where Blues were ready to back the regime of Phocas in one city (Manuf/Onouphis) before the arrival of Bonosus with loyalist forces, and were attacked by Greens after his defeat.[5] Rival loyalist and pro-rebel parties within the governing elites of some Egyptian cities may have helped stir up the local circus/youth organizations against each other. But factional allegiances were determined primarily by common political stances, transcending city and provincial boundaries.[6] Once activated, the young men soon escaped from external control. The familiar

---

[3] Cf. Z. Borkowski, *Inscriptions des factions à Alexandrie, Alexandrie* II (Warsaw, 1981), 33–6, who, however, may slow down the action too much.

[4] Isidorus iunior, *Chronica*, ed. T. Mommsen MGH, Auctores antiquissimi XI, Chronica minora II.2 (Berlin, 1894), 478.412, a notice picked up and reused by Paul D, iv.36 (p.128.16–17). Cf. Alan Cameron, *Circus Factions: Blues and Greens at Rome and Byzantium* (Oxford, 1976), especially 280–5; C. Roueché, *Performers and Partisans at Aphrodisias in the Roman and Late Roman Periods*, JRS Monographs 6 (London, 1993), 129–56; W. Liebeschuetz, 'The Circus Factions', in *Convegno per Santo Mazzarino* (Rome, 1998), 163–85; M. Whitby, 'The Violence of the Circus Factions', in K. Hopwood, ed., *Organised Crime in Antiquity* (London, 1999), 229–53.

[5] JN, cc.104 (p.185.1–2, trans. 419), 107 (p.188.28–30, trans. 424), 109 (p.194.26–8, trans. 430). Full discussion in P. Booth, 'Shades of Blues and Greens in the *Chronicle* of John of Nikiou', *BZ* 104 (2011), 555–601, at 575–9, 582–5, 588–93. Manuf = Onouphis (strictly speaking, Upper Onouphis, some 8 km. north-east of Nikiu, rather than Lower Onouphis, some 35 km to the south-west of Sebennytos [Samnud]): S. Timm, *Das christlich-koptische Ägypten in arabischer Zeit*, Beihefte zum Tübinger Atlas des vorderen Orients, Reihe B, no.41, 7 vols. (Wiesbaden, 1984–2007), IV, 1575–85.

[6] Booth, 'Shades of Blues and Greens', 581–2, 596–7.

dynamics of a segmentary system took over, pitting gang against gang in an escalating series of violent clashes.

The picture thus pieced together is a gloomy one, the only element missing being the hostility of the Monophysite majority among the Christians of the Middle Eastern provinces towards the Chalcedonian orthodoxy of the imperial regime and the local Chalcedonian communities and church hierarchies who benefited from its protection.[7]

Historians have, on the whole, agreed in concluding that the crisis was grave, that the defence effort was fatally weakened at a critical juncture, and that the urban basis of Roman civilization was increasingly disturbed. If they are right, much of the credit for the extraordinary success achieved by Persian arms over the following decade or so must be attributed not to the strategy devised and relentlessly pursued by the Persian high command but rather to the internal divisions of the east Roman Empire. Sociological and cultural explanations, therefore, come to the fore, while the successful application of brute force, which historians are often reluctant to view as a determining factor, is relegated to a subsidiary role.

If the future course of the war is to be understood, it is essential to examine this body of evidence and the modern consensus resting upon it with a critical eye. The first step is to handle the polemical material about Phocas with care. The second is to see which, if any, of the three major problems said to have faced the East Roman authorities (Jewish fifth column, empire-wide conspiracy leading to open rebellion on the periphery, and widespread urban disorder) is securely documented. The third is to assess the extent to which the war effort was hampered by these domestic difficulties and the countermeasures taken by Phocas' regime.[8]

2.1 Rebellion in the West, Disaffection in the East

The sources are remarkably uninformative about the ancestry and origins of Heraclius. George of Pisidia simply presents him as a true Christian who was driven by his faith to take action to save the Roman state. He has nothing whatsoever to say about his family or connections. Simocatta, despite making extensive

---

[7] Apart from one enigmatic reference at JN, c.110 (p.197.21–2, trans. 433).
[8] See D. M. Olster, *The Politics of Usurpation in the Seventh Century: Rhetoric and Revolution in Byzantium* (Amsterdam, 1993) for the extensive literature on these topics. Olster's reconstruction (cc.6–7) differs from mine both in chronology and on some crucial issues (notably the degree of disinformation affecting extant sources and the causes of disaffection in Antioch), but he agrees (1) in stressing the scale of the urban disturbances in the cities of the Levant in 609 and (2) in viewing the Heraclian revolution as self-generated rather than inspired from the centre. Pfeilschifter, *Der Kaiser und Konstantinopel*, 584–604 has the rebellion triggered by a démarche from Priscus, who, she suggests, may have gone to North Africa.

use of a memoir about his father, the elder Heraclius, lets nothing slip about his background or previous career.[9] The few crumbs of information which have been left are provided in an extended edition of the universal history of John of Antioch (its first continuation). But it is not always easy to interpret them. Although arguments from silence are never very safe, there is one obvious conclusion to be drawn from the reticence of Heraclius' contemporaries about his family, namely that it was not a distinguished one and could not claim a place among the great senatorial houses. A connection with Cappadocia is attested towards the end of Phocas' reign. Heraclius' wife Eudocia daughter of one Rogas from Africa, was living there, together with his mother Epiphania and another relative, the young, nubile Favia, when Phocas had them brought to Constantinople and installed in a convent.[10] Contraindications pointing to the west are to be found in the names borne by three of his close relatives, his illegitimate son Athalaric, his niece Martina, and a son Martin by Martina, Athalaric perhaps being the issue of an affair with a Gothic girl.

Heraclius' father was probably a self-made man, a career officer in the army, who achieved senior command by the later 580s. Simocatta includes long accounts of a number of subsidiary operations conducted by him in his narrative of the Mesopotamian campaigns of 586, 587, and 589, giving the impression that his contribution was rather more important than it was in reality and masking one partial failure. It is plain, though, that the elder Heraclius was a bold commander who was highly regarded and belonged to the second tier of Maurice's corps of talented generals.[11]

Nothing is heard of him in the 590s. He was not involved in counter-Slav operations in the Balkans. He reappears in 608 as exarch of Africa, that is, as holder of a senior governorship roughly akin to the Augustalis in Egypt, with combined authority over the military and civilian administrations. It is unclear whether he was an appointee of Maurice's who was left in post by Phocas or was promoted to this senior command by Phocas. One explanation for the presence of his wife, daughter-in-law, and Favia (whoever she was) in Cappadocia when the rebellion was being planned (so in 607–8), is that they had been detained as guarantors of his loyalty, probably from the time of his appointment.

---

[9] Geo.Pis., *In Heraclium ex Africa redeuntem*, ed. and trans. Pertusi, *Giorgio di Pisidia*, 77–83, at lines 39–55; Whitby, *Emperor Maurice*, 230–3 for Simocatta's material on the elder Heraclius, which he could conceivably have pieced together out of orally transmitted information. The city to which Simocatta (iii.1.1) has him ordered to return in winter 587–8 was probably his headquarters rather than his home city (*pace* C. Mango, 'Deux Études sur Byzance et la Perse sassanide', *TM* 9 (1985), 91–118, at 114).

[10] JN, c.106 (p.186.1–5,7–12, trans. 421) only names Favia, who has somehow become Eudocia's daughter; see Theoph., 298.21–6 for the presence of Eudocia (taken to be betrothed rather than married to Heraclius) and Epiphania later in Constantinople. Heraclius is called 'the Cappadocian' at JN, c.109 (p.196.1, trans. 431).

[11] Whitby, *Emperor Maurice*, 230–3, 280–4, and 286–90.

The scale and ferocity of a purge following the betrayal of a conspiracy to assassinate Phocas in the imperial box at the Hippodrome in 604–5—Maurice's widow, daughters, and son-in-law Germanus were executed among others—may have shaken the loyalty of the elder Heraclius and his immediate relatives in Africa, but they remained quiet until 608. Their motives for taking action then can only be guessed at. But their comparative safety, on the periphery of the empire, and the increasingly grim news from the eastern front must have been important factors. The prime mover, one suspects, was the younger Heraclius, who was, from the first, designated leader of the rebellion.

They declared their hand in two ways in 608, probably in the middle of the year. They began to enlarge the basis of the rebellion by winning over allies in the provinces between Africa and Egypt and by making contact with disaffected elements in the governing classes of Egypt itself. The disbursement of large sums of money secured the active support of the Berbers of Tripolis and Pentapolis, who were to remain to the end a key military component in the coalition gradually built up by the rebels. This opened the way to the western land approaches to Egypt. Beyond, in Egypt itself, the governor of Mareotis, the district fronting the capital Alexandria, was won over to the rebel cause by another large payment, despite being an appointee of Phocas', while a dissident party inside Alexandria secretly promised to help depose Phocas and to support Heraclius. They included two retired senior officials, one a former governor of Alexandria from the reign of Maurice who claimed to be able to bring out thousands of supporters in Constantinople.[12] Out of these various bilateral deals a plan of action began to take shape, with the objective of seizing Alexandria and the ultimate aim of bringing down Phocas' government. At the same time it appears that a propaganda campaign was launched which questioned the legitimacy of Phocas' rule and put forward the claims of the younger Heraclius. The main medium for its dissemination was probably word of mouth, although it is possible that an effort was made to glamorize the family and win support among the literate, thinking classes by writing and distributing a memoir about some notable achievements of the elder Heraclius.[13]

Their political stance was also conveyed, in a very abbreviated form, in the legends and designs of gold coins issued in their names in the course of the 607–8 financial year. The issue of these coins, which was the rebels' first open move and therefore of great political significance, was probably occasioned by the need to provide cash for distribution among potential allies outside the exarchate. The

---

[12] JN, c.107 (p.186.15–27, trans. 421–2). The Berbers were singled out alongside the African provincials as a key component in Heraclius' forces by John of Antioch, fr.321.23–4 describing the arrival of the rebel fleet before Constantinople in October 610.

[13] However, Whitby, *Emperor Maurice*, 232–3 views the putative memoir as a celebratory work, written *after* one of two family successes, either Heraclius senior's appointment as exarch or Heraclius junior's seizure of power.

first series of what look like unofficial issues of poor workmanship (so probably bypassing the official mint organization) was probably produced for an initial round of disbursement before the rebel leadership declared itself within the exarchate. Once the rebellion was announced (before the end of August 608), the Carthage mint could be used to produce coins for general distribution (so with the normal fabric of solidi) in 607–8 and the two following years, and for circulation within the exarchate (with the thick fabric characteristic of Carthage).[14] Phocas' name and image were removed from the gold solidi and replaced by busts of Heraclius and his son, both wearing consular dress. Although there is some variation in the accompanying legend, which may refer to Heraclius Consul in the singular or in the plural, it seems plain from the design of the busts that both Heraclii assumed the consulship and that the son, whose bust occupies the position of priority on the spectator's left, was the senior of the two. The regime of Phocas was thus openly challenged and the claims of the younger Heraclius put forward in a delicate, deliberately ambiguous way.[15]

Assumption of the consulship implied a bid for imperial power, since the ancient office had become a prerogative of the imperial family and was customarily assumed in the inaugural year of an emperor or co-emperor. On the other hand, by introducing the fiction of consular office, the rebels indicated a concern for the dignity of the Senate, tacitly acknowledged its right to designate or at least to play a major part in the election of the next emperor, and thus increased

[14] P. Grierson, 'Dated Solidi of Maurice, Phocas, and Heraclius', *NC*, ser.6, 10 (1950), 49–70, at 57–9 and 67–8; Grierson, 'The Consular Coinage of "Heraclius" and the Revolt against Phocas of 608–610', *NC*, ser.6, 10 (1950), 71–93; Grierson, *Byzantine Coins in the Dumbarton Oaks Collection and in the Whittemore Collection*, II.1 (Washington DC, 1968), 43–4, 207–15. The solidi, with two consular busts on the obverse, are of three types: (a) coins of crude workmanship, dated 607–8, in which the obverse type is outlined in high relief on a flat surface, and the reverse is derived either (i) from an old die of Tiberius II (578–82) or (ii) from a new die with a legend invoking victory for the consuls (*DOC*, II.1, nos.10 and 11, pp.212–13); (b) good quality coins of the same type as (a) (ii), issued in 607–8, 608–9, and 609–10 (*DOC*, II.1, nos.12–14, pp.213–14); and (c) small, stubby coins of characteristic Carthaginian fabric (16–17 mm. in diameter), dated to the same three years (607–8, 608–9, and 609–10) and of the same design, except for the reverse legend which reads 'consul' in the singular (*DOC*, II.1, nos.1–3, p.210). The difference in the size of the module is surely to the explained by the different destinations of the issues, type (c) being intended for circulation within the exarchate, types (a) and (b) for circulation farther afield (i.e. Egypt and the western approaches to Egypt). Once Alexandria fell to the rebels, minting of type (b) was presumably transferred there, along with some mint workers (Grierson, 'Consular Coinage', 81–2). I place its fall in the 608–9 fiscal year (twelfth indiction, 1 September 608—31 August 609), rather than before the end of the previous fiscal year (Grierson's view). See also C. Morrisson, *Catalogue des monnaies byzantines de la Bibliothèque Nationale*, II (Paris, 1970), 245–7 and W. Hahn, *Moneta imperii Byzantini von Justinus II. bis Phocas (565–610)* (Vienna, 1975), 84–6 and table XIII.

[15] There are two consular busts on the obverse of all these coins. Types (a) (ii) and (b) have legends on the reverse which wish the consuls (plural) victory. The apparently contradictory reference to Heraclius Consul in the singular in all the obverse legends, as well as on the reverse of type (c), surely refers to the senior of the two figures on the obverse, the younger Heraclius (*contra* Grierson, 'Dated Solidi', 58–9 and 'Consular Coinage', 79–81). Presumably the single bust which appears on the obverse of one silver denomination and four of bronze, all struck at Carthage and undated, is that of Heraclius the younger (*contra* Grierson, 'Consular Coinage', 84–5). See also G. Rösch, 'Der Aufstand der Herakleioi gegen Phokas (608–610) im Spiegel numismatischer Quellen', *JÖB* 28 (1979), 51–62.

their chances of gaining its backing. By refraining from presenting the younger Heraclius in full imperial regalia, they also avoided alienating the support of other potential claimants to the throne, notably Priscus, one of Maurice's front-rank generals who had risen even higher under Phocas, marrying into his family. It was a carefully judged stance which gave the rebels a chance of finessing rivals who might be better placed by virtue of grander status or by presence at the centre, where the final outcome of the rebellion would be determined. By enlisting their support, they would maximize the rebellion's chances of success and by refraining from pressing their own claims until the last moment, they might succeed in making their own cause unstoppable when finally it was openly declared.

John of Nikiu wrote the only detailed account of the next stage in the rebellion.[16] Most of his material deals with Egypt and evidently comes from a local source or sources written in Nikiu. But he includes information about events occurring well outside Egypt which appears to have been taken from a Constantinopolitan source identifiable as the first continuation of John of Antioch.[17] Of course, John of Nikiu may have made mistakes in combining material from different sources, thus potentially muddling the chronological order of events. There are evident gaps in his political narrative, perhaps because he chose to leap over episodes with no bearing on Egyptian history.[18] Errors (affecting particularly the spelling of proper names) have entered the text in the course of its transmission over nearly a millennium and its passage across two and, in the case of Greek sources used by John, three language frontiers (Coptic, Arabic, and Ethiopic). It is hard to differentiate between many of the urban and provincial postholders mentioned in the text, on the basis of their designation in Ethiopic.[19] It is hazardous, therefore, to place too much weight on the precise wording of any individual passage, to read too much between the lines, when the sense conveyed by the lines in their present form may be misleading, and to construct a chronology which relies entirely on that indicated by the arrangement of material in the chronicle. Nevertheless it is

---

[16] The work, written originally in Coptic in the second half of the seventh century, survives in the form of an Ethiopic translation (dating from 1602) of a slightly abridged Arabic version of the original text. Citations are to Zotenberg's critical edition and translation (cited in ch. 1, n. 6). Cf. J.-M. Carrié, 'Jean de Nikiou et sa Chronique: une écriture "égyptienne" de l'histoire?', in N. Grimel and M. Baud, eds., *Événement, récit, histoire officielle: l'écriture de l'histoire dans les monarchies antiques* (Paris, 2003), 155–72, and Booth, 'Shades of Blues and Greens', 555–7. I am very grateful to Phil Booth for allowing me to make use of his new and much improved translation, which will be published in Corpus Scriptorum Christianorum Orientalium.

[17] Cf. Howard-Johnston, *Witnesses*, 181–5.

[18] There are gaps in coverage between chapters 103 and 104, 106 and 107, and 110 and 111.

[19] Three Ethiopic terms are used, apparently interchangeably, for civilian authorities—*šayyum*, *masfən* and *makwannən*. Garrison commanders, however, are distinguished from other postholders (the word used is *apellon*). Cf. Booth, 'Shades of Blues and Greens', 559, 589, n.115.

worthwhile taking some risks, so rich is the material preserved, in the hope of gaining a closer view of key events.

Events moved fast once news of the rebellion was broadcast. Neither the rebel leadership nor the government of Phocas could afford to dawdle. It was vital for the rebels to encourage disaffection as widely as possible as well as hastening preparations for their next move, an attack on Egypt. The government, for its part, had to move swiftly to contain the rebellion, broadcasting propaganda of its own, shoring up support by carefully targeted payments, and taking measures to oppose it militarily.[20]

There is no reason to suppose that the rebels confined their secret contacts to Egypt and its western approaches. Support from any quarter in the east Mediterranean would further their cause, which from the first had to rely as much on political declarations as military action for ultimate success. It is, therefore, tempting to see the hand of the rebels behind an open demonstration of opposition to the regime which took place in Antioch and which seems to have triggered disturbances in other cities of the Middle East. John of Nikiu's silence about contacts between the two parties is not conclusive, since any such contacts would have been kept secret. However, if his arrangement of material—events in Antioch are reported before the start of the rebellion in Africa—corresponds to reality, it was the Antiochene dissidents who made the first move and, far from benefiting initially from a distraction elsewhere, provided the African rebels with the ideal circumstances for initiating their political challenge to the regime. Whatever the truth, whichever group acted first (with or without collusion), it is likely that the other followed suit soon afterwards.

The issue which provoked the demonstration was the regime's insistence that no clerical elections take place anywhere in the empire without official imperial sanction. This was almost certainly directed against religious dissidents who would not accept ministration by clergy who accepted the Chalcedonian confession.[21]

It is likely, then, that there was a core of committed Monophysites in the crowds which assembled in Antioch. The phrase used by John of Nikiu for the demonstrators, 'the people of the East', implies both that they assembled in large numbers and that many of them had come into the city from outside. What then happened transformed peaceful protest in one locality into a grave challenge to the authority of the regime in the Levant. Troops intervened in force to break up the demonstration. The scale of the bloodshed which followed was

---

[20] JN, c.107 (p.187.3–15, trans. 422). The full range of government responses is discussed below, pp. 46–8.

[21] Phocas is reported to have expelled Monophysite bishops from their sees, replacing them with Chalcedonians—Cyriacus of Amida, *Translation of the Relics of James*, ed. and trans. E. W. Brooks, PO 19, 268.10–11.

doubtlessly exaggerated as the news was transmitted farther afield (John of Nikiu has every place in the city, including the cathedral, awash with the blood of the slain), but it is plain that the troops who came in on horseback were making an example of the demonstrators and were not restrained in their use of force.[22]

It is possible that members of one or both circus factions played a leading role in the demonstration. For John of Nikiu prefaces his brief account with a remark about the apprehension felt by leaders of the Blue faction on account of the regime's bloody record.[23] He was referring, presumably, to the draconian punishment of Greens for the extensive damage to Constantinople caused in a riot in 603, punishment which assuredly cowed them into submission for several years.[24] If there is a connection between the sentence about the Blues and the following passage, the Blues were, it may be inferred, taking part in the Antioch demonstration (along with Greens, presumably) so as to dissociate themselves from Phocas' regime. There may, however, be no connection, since the note about the Blues stands on its own in the text and may well refer to a passage dealing with the factions under Phocas which has dropped out of the text. There is nothing positive in the short account of the Antioch episode to indicate that the factions were the principal driving force behind the opposition or the principal victims of the crackdown which followed.[25] The stress is on the brutal behaviour of the security forces, the notice ending with the observation that the killing was extended to Palestine and Egypt.[26]

The scale and character of the disturbances which followed is hard to document. Accounts in sources written at a considerable distance, whether in Armenia, the far west, or even the Balkans, which give the impression that the disturbances enveloped the whole Middle East and led to a general breakdown of law and order in the cities, should be discounted to some extent. It was all too easy for rumour to magnify the scale of the problem facing the government as news was transmitted to distant observers, and all too easy for the government to distort it in its own interests. News management was an important part of ancient statecraft. It is plain, though, from the general reports which have come down to us that the imperial countermeasures worked and that the opposition was

---

[22] JN, c.104 (p.185.2–8, trans. 419–20).

[23] JN, c.104 (p.185.1–2, trans. 419), with the revised translation of Booth, 'Shades of Blues and Greens', 575.

[24] Riot and punishment: *Chron.Pasch.*, 695.5–696.2; JA, fr.319.8–10; Theoph., 296.25–297.5 (misdated).

[25] But see Booth, 'Shades of Blues and Greens', 561–3, 575, 579, who accepts that there is a connection and is inclined to take the word 'ahzāb (a calque on the Greek *demoi*, meaning either people or factions) used of the many killed in the church (JN, cc.104, 105 (p.185.7 and 26, trans. 420)) to refer to partisans of the factions.

[26] JN, c.104 (p.185.8–9, trans. 420); ps.S, 106.23–7. Cf. Booth, 'Shades of Blues and Greens', 579–80.

suppressed successfully by force, until the intervention of a countervailing military and political power, that of the Heraclian rebels.

There is very little concrete information about such troubles as occurred in Palestine and Syria, or about the stage when the factions divided and began to riot against each other. Strategius, who lays much of the blame for the sack of Jerusalem in 614 on the factions, is unforthcoming about the spread of disorder in Palestine in the brief cast-back which he introduces on the background to factional disturbances at Jerusalem. The only piece of information he gives comes in connection with the actions of the loyalist forces sent to reimpose imperial authority on the rebellious cities, in the course of which he refers to Laodicea as well as Antioch. He thus implies that at least one other large city followed the example of Antioch, came out openly against the regime, and eventually paid a heavy price in blood. In general, however, he imposes his own interpretation on his material. He places the blame for the factional violence against persons and property which troubled the Middle East onto the factions themselves and onto Phocas' regime in the form of Bonosus, who was sent out to restore order. He passes over the disturbances initiated by rebels and portrays Bonosus as a malign figure responsible for indiscriminate slaughter.[27]

At the time, Phocas' government had every incentive to underplay the extent of political disaffection, to exaggerate the scale of factional fighting, and to misrepresent the insurrections as destructive and criminal acts of largely hooligan groups. This predictable line of imperial propaganda corresponds to the main thrust of the brief accounts of this time of troubles given by sources written at a distance from the events. The Armenian *History of Khosrov* identifies gang warfare between the factions as the prime cause of the urban disturbances which were suppressed by Bonosus, and incidentally gives the lie to Strategius' version of events by naming Jerusalem alongside Antioch and Egypt as a centre of disturbances. It appears that the author was as usual faithful to his sources, although in this instance he may act as a conduit for the government version. The same view, again probably originating in government propaganda, resurfaces at the western end of the Mediterranean in the brief chronicle compiled by Isidore of Seville. Even the first author of the *Miracula S. Demetrii*, Archbishop John of Thessalonica, who was a contemporary but distant witness of these events, was not immune. He writes about urban violence in rather melodramatic terms. Violent crime spread from the streets into private houses. Women and children, old and young who were unable to escape were slaughtered and thrown out of

---

[27] Strategius, 2.2–4 and 6–7, 3.9–12, 4.6–8: Georgian version, trans. G. Garitte, *La Prise de Jérusalem par les Perses en 614*, CSCO 203 (Louvain, 1960); Arabic versions, ed. and trans. G. Garitte, *Expugnationis Hierosolymae AD 614 recensiones Arabicae*, 2 vols., CSCO 340, 347 (Louvain, 1973, 1974).

upstairs windows. Friends and relatives turned against each other. Murder and looting were rampant. Much of this rather tabloid stuff was, I suspect, lifted from accounts of the troubles in the east which had been carefully doctored by the government.[28]

On the other hand, Archbishop John seems to show independence when he defines the geographical extent of the disturbances. He locates the epicentre in Oriens, north of Palestine. He refers to adjoining regions which were affected—Cilicia and Asia Minor to the west, as well as Palestine to the south—before describing how it reached Constantinople and caused tension, though no actual outbreak of violence, in the Balkans. Egypt is conspicuous by its absence. The archbishop, who might well have thrown in a casual reference to Egypt, refrained from doing so and thereby exaggerating the scale of the problem. This tacit acknowledgement that Egypt remained calm at this stage inspires confidence. The *Miracula*, therefore, probably gives a fair idea of the geographical incidence of urban violence, although it magnifies its intensity.[29]

Such is the evidence about the outbreak of urban violence in the Middle East which was set off by a demonstration in Antioch. There is very little to be gleaned from other sources. No inference should be drawn from a story that a Jewish activist was involved in many of the troubles until his conversion to Christianity and his adoption of a new role as a Christian apologist, which is written up in an artfully composed text, the *Doctrina Jacobi nuper baptizati*. The protagonist, Jacob, is portrayed as an extremist, who, masquerading alternatively as Blue and Green, exploited factional antagonisms to set Christians fighting each other. It looks like a fiction contrived to discredit Jews at a time, in the 630s, when the government was sponsoring a campaign of forced baptism.[30]

The failure of those who came out in open opposition in the Levant requires explanation, given the evidence that Phocas' regime was unpopular and that the rebellion of a whole region of the empire in the west was compounding the problems facing the government. Two main reasons can be suggested. First, the very gravity of the empire's crisis at this time, when Roman forces were being pushed back towards the Euphrates and were being worn down remorselessly, may have artificially prolonged the life of Phocas' government. Resentful, restless, anxious elements in the population at large as well as the clergy and the secular urban elites may have been deterred by patriotism from answering the call to challenge the regime issued at Antioch. But the swift and decisive action taken by Phocas'

---

[28] Ps.S, 106.17–27; Isidorus, *Chronica*, 478.412; *Miracula S. Demetrii*, i.10.82–3, ed. P. Lemerle, *Les Plus Anciens Recueils des miracles de saint Démétrius*, I *Le Texte* (Paris, 1979), 112.15–113.10—cited henceforth as *Mir.Dem.*
[29] *Mir.Dem.*, i.10.82 (p.112.11–15).
[30] *Doctrina Jacobi nuper baptizati*, ed. and trans. V. Déroche, *TM* 11 (1991), 70–219, at i.40.5–18, v.20.13–16.

government to contain the crisis must have played a very important part in scotching what might have turned into a general insurrection.

As has been noted, the crackdown was directed by Bonosus, who is portrayed as the hard man of the regime. First mentioned shortly before Phocas' seizure of power as the officer sent with ships to ferry the Balkan field army across to the north bank of the Danube, he reappears now in Constantinople, where he was a well-known partisan or patron of the Blue circus faction. He was appointed *Comes Orientis* and was given special powers to purge local officialdom of suspect elements.[31] The appointment was made when, in addition to the news of trouble at Antioch, a disturbing report arrived from Pentapolis to the effect that the cadre of local administrators had risen up and killed the governor appointed by Phocas (in what was almost certainly a coup engineered from without by the Heraclian rebels) and local dissidents had seized five cities in Lower Egypt.[32] Bonosus' first act was one of psychological warfare. He sent off the wild beasts with which he would celebrate victory when he arrived in Alexandria, together with instruments of torture to be used on his defeated opponents.[33] He himself set sail for Cilicia, where he assembled loyalist troops and prepared to deal with whatever opposition showed itself from Antioch in the north to Egypt. He marched on Antioch, and followed up the initial military action with a purge of the local apparatus of government, directed presumably at officials suspected of helping or sympathizing with the dissidents. Members of the factions may also have been targeted. It was a savage purge involving many executions and, for those spared death, exile for life.[34] He then continued his grim progress through the Levant, on his way to Egypt.

Speed and judicious use of terror as a political weapon seem to have been the key to his success, although the brevity of the accounts of his actions may give a misleading impression both of the time which it took and of the severity of the countermeasures (opponents of Phocas, in the first place the Heraclian party, had every interest in exaggerating the savagery of Bonosus and magnifying the numbers of his victims). If the rising at Antioch was roughly contemporary with the beginnings of the African rebellion (summer 608), the loyalist forces were probably firmly in control of Antioch by the end of 608 at the latest, and Bonosus was on his way south.

---

[31] JN, c.105 (p.185.17–20, trans.420); Theoph., 296.21–2 (appointment as *Comes Orientis*). PLRE III, 'Bonosus 2'; Booth, 'Shades of Blues and Greens', 482–5.

[32] JN, c.105 (p.185.11–16, trans. 420). Booth, 'Shades of Blues and Greens', 582, n.95. The connection made between the two episodes (p.185.15–16) results probably from a mistaken assumption—on the part of one or other translator—that the five named cities were the cities from which the Pentapolis got its name. A passage making the transition from the murder in Pentapolis to events in Lower Egypt may consequently have dropped out of the text.

[33] JN, c.107 (p.187.10–15, trans. 422).

[34] JN, cc.104, 105 (p.185.5–8 and 20–8, trans. 420), with Booth, 'Shades of Blues and Greens', 586–8.

2.2 Battle for Egypt

It was at this stage (to judge by the order of John of Nikiu's narrative) that detailed information from authoritative sources in Alexandria reached Phocas about the African rebels' plan to attack Alexandria. Steps were immediately taken to strengthen the regime's hold on the city. Troops were sent out from Constantinople under a commander who was required to swear loyalty to the regime. Troops used against opposition activists in Antioch were ordered to proceed to Egypt, some by land from Antioch, others by sea from Palestine under Bonosus' command. The loyalty of the garrison commanders at two strategic points in the Delta, Onouphis and Athribis, was secured by large payments from the centre. A propaganda barrage was also laid down, playing down the significance of the threat by mocking Heraclius.[35] The rebels, however, were not deterred from attacking. They continued the work of undermining the will to resist of troops, civilian population, and authorities on the western approaches to Egypt and in the Delta.

The attack was launched in 609, a date given by the chronologically reliable *Chronicon Paschale*. In a note of his own composition introduced to plug a serious hole in the coverage of the documentary material available to him, the chronicler reports that in that (calendar) year Africa and Alexandria rebelled. He thus juxtaposes in a single short sentence events which he evidently connects together in his mind and which were probably interconnected in reality, namely the first armed acts of rebellion on the part of the Africans, their invasion of Egypt, and the almost bloodless capture of Alexandria. The next phase, the first phase of serious fighting, saw the city join the Heraclian cause and become the solid bastion from which rebel power began to reach out over lower Egypt.[36] The date within the year can only be fixed approximately by reference to that of the decisive battle before the walls of Alexandria which saw the effective end of Bonosus' attempt to drive the rebels from Egypt, after what appears to have been a violent and fast-moving counteroffensive campaign. Since this decisive battle was fought in November 609 (as will be shown below, pp. 56–7), the initial rebel attack should be placed in the first half of the year, probably around the beginning of spring.[37]

---

[35] JN, c.107 (p.187.2–15, trans. 422). Atrib (Athribis): Timm, *Ägypten*, I, 257–65.

[36] *Chron.Pasch.*, 699.3.

[37] Little can be inferred from the absence of Phocas' name in the dating formulae in two Oxyrhynchus papyri, of 8 May and 11 June 609 (*contra* Borkowski, *Inscriptions*, 33–4), since all but one of the Oxyrhynchus documents drafted between 598 and 610 omit the emperor's name (R. S. Bagnall, review of Borkowski, *Inscriptions*, in *Bulletin of the American Society of Papyrologists*, 20 (1983), 75–80, at 77–80). Phocas is mentioned on an Arsinoite papyrus dated 29 May 609 (Borkowski, *Inscriptions*, 34).

50 THE LAST GREAT WAR OF ANTIQUITY

The first step was to seize Pentapolis as a forward base for launching the attack. This was achieved quickly with the aid of local officials who rose up and killed the governor with his staff.[38] It was from there that Heraclius' cousin Nicetas conducted successful negotiations with dissident elements inside Egypt. He was joined there by the military commander, Ioannicius, who advanced from the exarchate of Africa with a force of 3,000 regular troops and a large number of Berber auxiliaries.[39] The main operation then began. It went remarkably smoothly. As they moved east, the rebel forces received various forms of assistance from their opponents. The governor of Mareotis came over, presumably when the rebel army crossed the border between Pentapolis and Egypt. The notables of a city on their route (surely Taposiris,[40] commanding the western end of Lake Mareotis), known collectively as the *Protectores*, opened the gates and were not harmed. Inmates released from the prisons there joined the rebels' ranks. Agents from the city were sent ahead to promote rebellion in the district of the Dragon Canal.[41] This linked the emporium of Chaireon on the Canopic branch of the Nile to Alexandria, skirting Lake Mareotis and then running first west, along the south side of the city, before turning north to cut across a narrow neck of land to reach the sea, immediately west of the city. It thus formed the city's outer line of defence to an army approaching from the west along the narrow spit of land which separates Lake Mareotis from the sea.[42] The rebel army was able to cross the canal without difficulty. With its western perimeter breached and disaffection rife inside the city, Alexandria fell an easy prey to the rebels. The only determined opposition is reported to have come from a senior officer or official (probably the Augustalis himself), who emerged and fought the rebels before the city. Once he was killed, resistance collapsed and many in the loyalist forces changed sides.[43]

John of Nikiu's account of the rebels' subsequent takeover of Alexandria makes it clear that they enjoyed the support of an overwhelming majority of the

---

[38] JN, c.105 (p.185.11–16, trans. 420). See n. 32 of this chapter for the problematic equation of Pentapolis with five cities in Augustamnica I and II.

[39] JN, c.107 (p.186.17–22, trans. 421). Ioannicius' name has been mangled in transmission, to Konākis and Yuhannes at its first two appearances (186.18, 187.15), later normally to Bonākis (Zotenberg's reading). I owe the correct reading to Phil Booth.

[40] Something has gone seriously wrong in the text of John of Nikiu, where the name is given as *Kabsen* (probably Kabasa, capital of a nome in the heart of the lower Delta, far to the east)—JN, c.107 (p.187.19, trans. 423).

[41] JN, c.107 (p.187.15–24, trans. 422–3).

[42] J. McKenzie, *The Architecture of Alexandria and Egypt c.300 BC to AD 700* (New Haven, CT, 2007), 36 (fig.37) and 254; P. Wilson, 'Waterways, Settlements and Shifting Power in the North-Western Nile Delta', *Water History*, 4 (2012), 95–117, at 103–5.

[43] JN, c.107 (pp.187.25–188.6, trans. 423). If it was indeed the Augustalis who came out, fought, and was killed (187.25, 188.18, 20, 25), something has again gone seriously awry in the Ethiopic text, where the title has been deformed into *balalun*. The killing which caused division throughout Egypt (189.12–13) was presumably his. If so, the title is subject to further mutations, becoming successively *aysāylilun* (189.13), *aysālelān* (189.16), *aysāylelān* (189.27), and *aylelus* (190.8). He is named earlier as John and described as governor of the city, who was both head of the *qasr* (palace, administrative headquarters) and commander of the troops in Alexandria (186.29–187.1).

population and that their allies inside had made preparations for a swift and orderly seizure of the main government buildings. The dispatch to Alexandria of wild beasts for circus displays and of instruments of torture by Phocas, intended to remind the population of the perils of rebellion, proved counterproductive.[44] The entry of elements from the rebel army bringing with them the dead governor's head impaled on a lance was the signal for them to act. A formal city assembly comprising magistrates and full citizens agreed unanimously to declare support for the rebels. In their denunciations of Phocas' regime, they concentrated their diatribes on its hard man, the hated figure of Bonosus. Then they seized hold of the provincial treasury (literally 'the emperor's taxes'), as well as the headquarters of the provincial administration. They also took possession of the precious items (gold and silver plate and fine garments) previously sent to the Augustalis, apparently by Heraclius as inducements to rebel.[45]

With the city and the local apparatus of government in their hands, the rebels had the severed head of Phocas' dead governor displayed at the city gate in a public declaration of rebellion against Phocas. Meanwhile the emperor's main supporters in the city—the head of a key part of the fiscal administration (the superintendent of the *annona*) and the military governor of the city—fled and sought sanctuary in the church of St Theodore on the east side of the city. The Chalcedonian patriarch, who had joined them in appealing to Phocas for help when they first got wind of the rebels' plan, did likewise but chose a different church (St Athanasius) by the seashore. John of Nikiu does not report their ultimate fate, but it seems likely that all three were extracted and executed.[46]

It looks as if the takeover of Alexandria was stage-managed to give the appearance of being a spontaneous insurrection of the people against the ruling regime, with the rebel army carefully refraining from taking any part, aside from sending in a token force with the governor's head, until the city had been secured by the opposition inside and it could invite the rebels in. The invitation was first extended to the younger Heraclius, the senior of the two self-proclaimed consuls, who, by this stage, had joined the expeditionary force led by Ioannicius. He was received with great honour by the citizens, who thereby committed themselves to the rebel cause and his leadership. Heraclius then sent one message to his troops outside the city, presumably to keep them informed of what was going on, and another to the island of Pharos, where he had the loyalist forces who had already arrived by sea arrested and held under strong guard. The exarchate's naval forces

---

[44] See n. 33 of this chapter.

[45] JN, c.107 (p.188.4–5 and 13–20, trans. 423–4), with Booth, 'Shades of Blues and Greens', 589 and n.116, who is surely right to take Ethiopic *həzbāwyān* as a translation of Greek/Coptic *demotai*—just as Ethiopic *shəyyūmān* ('officials') derives from Greek/Coptic *archontes*.

[46] JN, c.107 (p.188.6–13 and 18–19, trans. 423–4). Cf. McKenzie, *Architecture*, 255. The death of the patriarch 'at the hands of his opponents' is reported at *Chron.Pasch.*, 699.3–4, immediately after the rebellion of Africa and Alexandria. It is left unclear—perhaps deliberately so—whether Monophysites were responsible for his death or troops acting under Heraclius' orders.

could now be reinforced by the vessels which had brought the loyalist troops.[47] The constitutional niceties of the takeover of Alexandria, which are noted by John of Nikiu, were of considerable importance. For it would greatly strengthen the rebels' cause in the next crucial phase, the political battle for the support of the rest of Egypt, if the change of allegiance of the provincial capital could be presented as an independent rebellion leading to a voluntary alliance with the African rebels rather than the result of a successful armed attack on the city. The rebels were apparently successful in this, to judge by the impression which these events made on an Armenian observer in the next generation, who portrayed Heraclius as the leader of an Egyptian rebellion.[48]

Heraclius, who is not mentioned again, seems to have left the task of consolidation in Egypt to his cousin Nicetas and the general Ioannicius. Ioannicius commanded the rebel forces when they had to face Bonosus in the field. Nicetas, who had probably gone into Egypt with Ioannicius after the successful conclusion of his negotiations with the governor of Mareotis, was probably in overall charge, responsible for the general conduct of policy and for the political effort to win city authorities over to the rebels' side. Only when Ioannicius was killed did he take over direct command of military operations.[49] Heraclius' departure is surprising, given that the rebels' position was far from secure. Whatever the assignment which took him away, it must have been at least as important as that of extending the rebels' authority over the Delta and ultimately over Middle and Upper Egypt.

Over the next few months the rebels strove to persuade the provincial authorities and city notables in the hinterland of Alexandria to commit themselves to their cause. It was probably an uphill struggle, in spite of their striking initial success at Alexandria. For the news that the emperor had dispatched Bonosus to Egypt, which was doubtless broadcast widely, must have dampened the ardour of dissident elements. The reputation for cold-blooded brutality which Bonosus had acquired in the Levant cannot but have helped the government cause.

The battle for control of Egypt took place on several planes simultaneously. Militarily, the rebels had a clear advantage at first, until Bonosus arrived, probably in early summer 609.[50] His troops were to prove more than a match for the rebel army in the field. The rebels were, therefore, initially in a position to back up whatever political pressure they could bring to bear on provincial governors and city elites with military force or threatening shows of force. But on the

---

[47] JN, c.107 (p.188.16–17 and 20–3, trans. 423–4). Cf. Borkowski, *Inscriptions des factions*, 24–31. Note the presence of Heraclius at this important moment of transfer of authority to the rebels. He is not mentioned subsequently, since he left the task of consolidating the rebels' position in Egypt to Ioannicius.

[48] Ps.S, 106.28–30.   [49] JN, c.107 (pp.186.20–1, 190.11–14, 191.8–13, trans. 421, 425, 426–7).

[50] *Contra* Borkowski, *Inscriptions des factions*, 34–6, who believes that Bonosus spent approximately a year and a half in Egypt.

political level, they had to reckon with formidable opponents within the ranks of local officialdom who owed their preferment to Phocas and whose fates were going to be inextricably intertwined with that of the regime. A popular local official, like Paul at Samnud (Sebennytos), could bring the whole population out in opposition to the rebels.[51] The most important loyalist, though, was a local notable, Cosmas, son of Samuel, evidently disabled, since he had to be carried about by two men. He was arrested initially but was released later and set about organizing loyalist resistance among local cadres.[52] The main battle was fought in words, in propaganda salvos. The loyalists enjoyed an innate advantage since they were defending the status quo, with the regime still controlling all the levers of power at the centre. Strong though the rebels' political case was, it was hard for them to undermine the credibility of the regime, especially as Phocas, although a usurper, had been duly appointed emperor by those constitutionally empowered to do so. However fierce their attacks on his record at home and abroad, however much they made of the violent end of the previous dynasty, they were unlikely to win over many waverers. The prudent course was to wait and see. So they were probably forced to rely more than usual on the chief weapon of propagandists, exaggeration of their own success, in the hope of creating a bandwagon effect which would overcome the natural inertia of holders of local power.

It is impossible to follow the course of the battle for hearts and minds in Egypt in any detail, since John of Nikiu leaps forward from the rebellion and occupation of Alexandria to the next, military phase of the conflict, which began with Bonosus' arrival. He does, however, provide some illuminating details about the state of affairs on the eve of the loyalist counteroffensive, as well as a rough guide to the line-up of supporters of the two sides.[53] As might have been expected, the divisions between supporters of the rebels, loyalists, and those maintaining a studied neutrality ran along geographical lines. The rebels, who claimed the support of cities throughout Egypt, seem only to have imposed their authority effectively on the western Delta. The loyalists kept control of the eastern two-thirds of the Delta, which was obviously first in Bonosus' line of fire. The rest of Egypt, including Babylon at the apex of the Delta, the whole length of the Nile valley, and the Fayyum, seems to have stayed aloof at this stage and throughout the subsequent fighting.[54] It may be that the rebels contented themselves with promises of neutrality from the authorities outside the likely arena of conflict in the Delta, a course which they had urged in vain earlier on the military governor of

---

[51] JN, c.107 (p.189.2–5, 10–12, trans. 424). Samnud (Sebennytos): Timm, *Ägypten*, V, 2254–62.
[52] JN, c.107 (p.189.6–10, trans. 424), with Booth, 'Shades of Blues and Greens', 591, n.122 for his possible Blue affiliation.
[53] JN, c.107 (pp.188–90, trans. 424–5).
[54] *Contra* Borkowski, *Inscriptions*, 35, who attributes John of Nikiu's silence about Babylon to blinkered parochialism.

Alexandria. If so, there may have been a certain tenuous basis to their claim of widespread support in Egypt.

John of Nikiu provides a vignette of what was happening on the eve of Bonosus' intervention in the southern Delta. Nikiu was firmly on the rebel side.[55] Onouphis, a mere 8 km away, had gone over to the regime after partisans of the Blues rose up against the local notables and stripped them of their properties, as well as taking over those which had belonged to a close friend of Maurice's, Aristomachus.[56] Athribis, some 25 km to the east, was the main loyalist centre in the south. Efforts by the bishop of Nikiu (Theodore) and a senior lay official (Menas, 'the secretary') to persuade Marcian, governor of Athribis, and Christodora, sister of the late Augustalis,[57] who had taken refuge there after his death, to declare themselves for Heraclius were firmly rebuffed.[58] The stationing nearby of a rebel unit, under two officers, Plato the senior rebel commander in the area (described as a close friend of the former emperor Maurice), and his deputy Theodore, kept up the pressure. There it could act as a picket watching over the two eastern branches of the Nile, the Pelusiac and Bousiritic, which a loyalist army would use.[59] The centre of loyalist resistance in the north, in the heart of the Delta, was Sebennytos (Samnud), which had taken the lead in opposing the rebels after their success at Alexandria.[60]

Bonosus was in Caesarea of Palestine when he heard that Alexandria was in Heraclius' hands. It was only after he had restored order to the streets of Jerusalem and elsewhere that he was able to take action against the rebels in Egypt. At the time that he initiated operations, he was in Judaea, at Bethlehem. By then it was probably early summer.[61]

He moved his main force by sea to Pelusium at the mouth of the eastern branch of the Nile.[62] His immediate objective was to relieve Athribis, which, as has been seen, was under pressure, military and political, from the rebels. He and his seaborne force sailed up the eastern—Pelusiac—branch of the Nile, which came within ten kilometres of Athribis (on the next Bousiritic branch). At Athribis he joined forces with local troops under the command of Marcian from Athribis, and with two forces brought down from the north by Cosmas (a private army?) and Paul (the militia of Sebennytos). Ioannicius came to Nikiu in response to an

---

[55] JN, c.107 (p.189.1–2, trans.424). Nikiu: Timm, *Ägypten*, III, 1132–40.
[56] JN, c.107 (p.188.28–30, trans. 424), with commentary of Booth, 'Shades of Blues and Greens', 589–91. Onouphis: n. 5 in this chapter.
[57] See n. 43 of this chapter.   [58] JN, c.107 (pp.189.13–14, 16–18, 24–190.1, trans. 424–5).
[59] JN, c.107 (p.189.21–3, trans. 425).   [60] JN, c.107 (p.189.2–5, trans. 424).
[61] JN, c.107 (pp.188.23–6, 189.14–16, trans. 424, 425). The garbled placename (*Beta* ['House of'] '*Aptlemā*) surely stands for Bethlehem, rather than Ptolemais, as tentatively suggested by Zotenberg. It is highly unlikely that Bonosus would have moved north up the coast from Caesarea, farther away from Egypt, after hearing of the rebellion in Egypt.
[62] JN, c.107 (p.190.1–5, trans. 425). Phil Booth derives Ethiopic *Fermā* (190.5) from Arabic *Faramā* (Pelusium).

appeal from Plato, and marched east past Onouphis, hoping perhaps to instigate a rising by the defeated pro-rebel faction in the city. The battle between the two armies was fought to the east of Onouphis close to a river, which must be the Sebennytic branch of the Nile, which leaves the Bousiritic some 15 km upstream from Athribis. The troops commanded by Cosmas played a decisive role in the battle. The rebel army was defeated. Ioannicius was killed, as were two other named senior officers. Plato and Theodore fled. Many prisoners were taken.[63]

Bonosus now consolidated his position. At Onouphis the leaders of the defeated faction in the city's establishment (Isidore, John, and Julian) paid for the support which they had given the rebels in the past. Bonosus had them arrested and brought to Nikiu, along with the two commanders of the forward rebel force (Plato and his deputy Theodore) who had sought sanctuary in a monastery. Nikiu had submitted immediately after the battle. The two leading local allies of the rebels, the bishop and the secretary, had gone out to meet Bonosus and had pleaded for mercy. Installed in Nikiu, Bonosus dealt out summary justice. The bishop, who could justly be charged with flagrant treason (he had taken down Phocas' insignia from the city's gate and urged Athribis to do likewise), was executed. The secretary, Menas, was dealt with more leniently, being sentenced to scourging and released after disgorging 3,000 solidi (presumably from the city treasury). He died soon afterwards. The leaders of the pro-rebel faction at Onouphis, together with the military commanders Plato and Theodore, were scourged and then beheaded.[64] An inquiry was instituted into the service records of the rebel troops who had been captured. Any shown to have deserted from Phocas—presumably from among the troops sent out to reinforce local defences in response to the original appeal from loyalists in Alexandria—were executed. Others whose service went back to the reign of Maurice were sent into exile.[65]

The defeated remnants of the rebel army fell back on Alexandria. There they were joined by all those Egyptian notables who had come out in support of Heraclius and were therefore marked men. Nicetas, Heraclius' cousin, took charge of defensive preparations. The city had to be held at all costs. For if Bonosus were to succeed in recapturing it (and this was his obvious next move), the rebellion would be in danger of collapsing. Nicetas mobilized all available resources, regular troops, Berber auxiliaries, sailors, archers, and civilians. The Greens are singled out for special mention among the last.[66] Nicetas' plan was to fight Bonosus outside the city, rather than allowing him to attack the walls directly. But he would introduce a new element, massed rapid-firing artillery, to surprise and disorganize the enemy before he could come to close quarters. The plan, probably

---

[63] JN, c.107 (pp.189.14–16, 190.2–18, trans. 425–6).
[64] JN, c.107 (pp.189.24–190.1, 190.18–191.4, trans. 425–6).
[65] JN, c.107 (p.191.4–7, trans. 426). Cf. Borkowski, *Inscriptions*, 34–5.
[66] JN, c.107 (p.191.7–13, trans. 426–7), with Booth, 'Shades of Blues and Greens', 591–2.

improvised at the time, was a brilliant one, a harbinger of a style of warfare which was to become the norm many centuries later.

Bonosus, for his part, decided to use the waterways of the Delta to attack Alexandria.[67] The advantages of speed and easy penetration to the city itself outweighed any restriction which river transport would impose on the number of men he could deploy. A detachment was placed under the command of Paul, governor of Sebennytos, and detailed to make a preliminary assault. It was to use the Dragon Canal ('the river of Alexandria'), which approached from the south-east and ran along the southern wall. The attack was probably intended to soften up the defences and to divert attention before the main blow was delivered by Bonosus and the main force by land. He planned to move his men by water (down the Canopic branch of the Nile, presumably) until they were within striking distance of Alexandria, but to make the final approach by land, down the neck of land between the canal and the lagoon to the south of Canopus.[68]

His plan may have been betrayed. At any rate, Nicetas was well prepared and succeeded in preventing the two enemy forces from coordinating their attacks. As Paul of Sebennytos' fleet was approaching, it came under artillery fire. The artillery (*manganiqāt*) was probably of a new type, the rope-pulled traction trebuchet which had been developed centuries earlier in China but which had only reached the Mediterranean world a little over twenty years earlier. Although it was less accurate than the traditional Graeco-Roman torsion artillery, it had two great advantages—a rapid rate of fire and a higher calibre of stone projectile.[69] The projectiles hurled by the defenders kept Bonosus at a distance and forced Paul to beat a hasty retreat, probably because they threatened to hole or disable the rivercraft.[70]

Bonosus retreated a safe distance to Chaireon, on the canal 28 km to the southeast. Some reorganization and reinvigoration of his forces was probably needed, as well as a new plan of attack. This was formulated, we are told, just before the end of Phocas' seventh regnal year (Saturday 22 November 609). The attack was scheduled

---

[67] P. Wilson, 'Settlement Connections in the Canopic Region', in D. Robinson and A. Wilson, eds., *Alexandria and the North-Western Delta* (Oxford, 2010), 111–26.

[68] The plan can be inferred from John of Nikiu's account of operations, which went smoothly enough until each attacking force came near the city (cc.107, 108 (pp.191.13–22, 192.7–21, trans. 427, 427–8)).

[69] The first recorded use of the traction trebuchet in western Eurasia was by the Avars against Thessalonica in 586 (*Mir.Dem.*, i.14.150–4, pp.154.6–155.22). See K. Huuri, *Zur Geschichte des mittelalterlichen Geschützwesens aus orientalischen Quellen*, Studia Orientalia 9.3 (Helsinki, 1941), 79–93, 127–153 for its use in Byzantium and the Caliphate; see P. E. Chevedden, Z. Schiller, S. R. Gilbert, and D. J. Kagay, 'The Traction Trebuchet: A Triumph of Four Civilizations', *Viator*, 31 (2000), 433–86, at 436–41, 444–55 for its Chinese origin, performance, and design. See also L. I. R. Petersen, *Siege Warfare and Military Organization in the Successor States (400–800 AD): Byzantium, the West and Islam*, History of Warfare 91 (Leiden, 2013), 406–24, who places its arrival earlier and dissociates it from the Avars.

[70] JN, c.107 (p.191.15–18, trans. 427).

for Sunday, presumably the first day of his eighth regnal year, Sunday 23 November.[71] Again Nicetas organized the defence around the artillery. He positioned it before the main eastern gate, trebuchets being too large to place on the walls. They were guarded by some of his regular troops. Others, together with the Berber auxiliaries, were kept in reserve, behind a second gate to the north.[72] Morale was boosted when it became known, as it surely did, that Nicetas had had an audience with Theophilus the Confessor, a highly esteemed holy man who had spent thirty years on top of a pillar nearby. The saint, it was reported, had prophesied that the rebel forces would be victorious and that Phocas would fall from power within a year. When the attack was launched, the artillery barrage had a devastating effect on the attackers. They formed an easy target as they advanced on a relatively narrow front, between the canal to the south and reed beds to the north. The psychological impact of the large projectiles was probably as important as the hits which they scored in turning the battle in the defenders' favour. As soon as Bonosus' men began to break ranks, Nicetas attacked with his reserves and turned retreat into rout. Only a small part of the attacking army succeeded in escaping with Bonosus back to Chaireon.[73]

The loyalist position was fatally weakened by this defeat. Key allies, including Marcian, the governor of Athribis, were among the many men of distinction killed in the battle. Another, Paul of Sebennytos, now wavered. His contingent took no further part in the conflict. The most striking defection, though, was that of those aligned with the Blues in Alexandria, whether of high or low status, since they had previously backed the regime. Nicetas sought to profit from his victory and the evident swing of opinion in his favour, and sent out emissaries to raise funds and troops from other cities (and presumably to receive assurances of political support).[74] Bonosus withdrew to Nikiu and made a last, vain effort to attack Alexandria with what remained of his main force. Once again he made use of the many waterways of the Delta to attack the rich agricultural hinterlands of Alexandria, south and west of Lake Mareotis.[75] It is just possible to discern the outlines of his strategy from the account in John of Nikiu, which is apparently abbreviated and, at one point, garbled.

The initial raiding led to the death of many Alexandrians, and, we may infer, caused extensive damage to crops and agricultural installations on the southern Mareotis shore.[76] Bonosus' troops probably established themselves there and

---

[71] JN, c.107 (p.191.18–22, trans. 427). Chaireon appears as *Karyun* (192.28) and *Demqāruni*, i.e. Qaruni Village (from Coptic *tme*, 'village'—191.20). The chronology proposed follows the order of John of Nikiu's notices—(1) retreat to Chaireon in two stages, the first to Miphamonis, also called New Šabra (191.19-20), (2) plan to capture the city on Sunday, (3) end of Phocas' seventh regnal year.
[72] East wall: McKenzie, *Architecture*, 27–9.
[73] JN, c.108 (pp.191.24–192.28, trans. 427–8). Cf. McKenzie, *Architecture*, 254–5.
[74] JN, c.108 (pp.192.28–193.10, trans. 428). Cf. Booth, 'Shades of Blues and Greens', 592.
[75] JN, c.109 (p.193.12–15, trans. 429). Waterways: see n. 67 of this chapter.
[76] JN, c.109 (p.193.13–14, trans. 429). South Mareotis sites: see L. Blue and E. Khalil, *A Multidisciplinary Approach to Alexandria's Economic Past: The Lake Mareotis Resarch Project*, BAR, Int. Ser. 2285 (Oxford, 2011), 17–26, 291–300; M. Kenawi, *Alexandria's Hinterland: Archaeology of the Western Nile Delta, Egypt* (Oxford, 2014), 28–72, 223–5.

faced the task of crossing the Mareotis to attack the city from the south or the west. A raid was made on the Dragon Canal where it ran along the west wall of Alexandria, but the insurrection which it was meant to spark did not occur.[77] Next, Bonosus planned to march west to the great causeway across the long narrow western arm of Lake Mareotis which led to the artificial harbour of Taposiris (Dafusir). However he was anticipated by Nicetas, who cut the bridge linking the harbour's southern levee and the city, thus leaving the deep-water channel running east-west through the harbour as an impassable barrier.[78] Frustrated, Bonosus planned to have Nicetas assassinated, but the plan was betrayed.[79] Finally Bonosus led an assault—by boat, as the bridge had been cut—on Taposiris, the key position guarding the western approach to Alexandria along the Abusir Ridge (ancient Tainia) between Lake Mareotis and the sea. There was heavy fighting, but the arrival of reinforcements under Nicetas prompted Bonosus to abandon the attack and to withdraw once more to Nikiu.[80] Nicetas took control of the whole Mareotis district before marching south, recovering Onouphis by force, and capturing the leading members of the loyalist party there. At this Bonosus gave up the hopeless task and left Egypt, making first for Palestine and, then, when he encountered opposition there, leaving for Constantinople.[81]

All the cities of Egypt now submitted to the rebels. Phocas' name was excised from the dating formulae in all extant documents of 610.[82] Nicetas moved carefully and showed considerable tact in his handling of the leading loyalists (Paul of Sebennytos and Cosmas, son of Samuel). They were arrested and sent for detention in Alexandria for as long as Bonosus remained alive. His response was equally delicate when the Greens seized the opportunity of Bonosus' defeat to attack his Blue supporters, initiating a round of inter-factional fighting and widespread disorder. Nicetas brokered peace between the factions, insisted that they cease their violence and looting, appointed new city officials, and restored law and order.[83] Other policies won him and the rebel cause positive support throughout Egypt. He maintained good relations with the Monophysite hierarchy. It was probably on his recommendation that Heraclius, soon after his coronation, appointed an emollient, undoctrinaire Chalcedonian patriarch, John the Almsgiver (610-20), who could be trusted not to antagonize the Monophysite majority. In the event he lifted a ban on the construction and

---

[77] JN, c.109 (p.193.15-16, trans. 429).
[78] JN, c.109 (p.193.17-19, trans. 429). Causeway and Taposiris bridge, some 15 km to the west of Mareia (*contra* JN, ibid.): see A. de Cosson, *Mareotis* (London, 1935), 95, 109-11; Blue and Khalil, *Alexandria's Economic Past*, 22-4.
[79] JN, c.109 (pp.193.20-194.6, trans. 429).
[80] JN, c.109 (p.194.6-9, trans. 429).   [81] JN, c.109 (p.194.9-20, trans. 429-30).
[82] JN, c.109 (p.194.15-16, 20-3, trans. 430). Cf. Bagnall, review of Borkowski in *BASP*, 20 (1984), 78.
[83] JN, c.109 (pp.194.26-195.3, trans. 430). Cf. Booth, 'Shades of Blues and Greens', 593.

repair of Monophysite churches in the city and allowed in the Monophysite patriarch.[84] He also reduced taxes for the next three years. John of Nikiu concludes his account with the remark that 'the Egyptians were very much attached to him'.[85]

The battle for Egypt was over. The rebels could now use it as the platform for an attack on the imperial capital. The acquisition of its immense resources of manpower, finance, and shipping magnified their power many times and dealt a damaging blow to the standing of Phocas in the empire at large. Success in Egypt helped the rebels towards victory in the wider political battle for support in the Levant.

But at what price had it been won? Had the war effort slackened with the launching of the loyalist counterstrike on the rebel positions in Egypt? Were significant numbers of troops withdrawn from the Mesopotamian front to serve under Bonosus in Egypt? Did what amounted to a civil war in the Delta erode the foundations of the old urban order there? Did the factional fighting with which it ended accelerate a decline in the economic level and social cohesion of the cities which was already under way?

There is nothing to indicate that the war effort was significantly impaired either during the initial phase of the rebellion or during the fighting in Egypt. Nor does there seem to have been a general breakdown in law and order in the course of 608 and 609. In Egypt, as previously in the Levant, Bonosus relied on a small force of reliable troops and sought, by acting with speed and boldness, to make a surgical counterstrike against the rebels while the great majority of the provincial and city authorities of Egypt were still maintaining a careful and prudent neutrality. He achieved the strategic mobility upon which, along with his reputation, rested his hopes of success by transporting his main force to Egypt by sea and then, after receiving substantial reinforcements from loyalists in the Delta, by using the inland waterways to cut through the densely populated countryside, aiming straight for the rebel nerve centre at Alexandria. This dependence on shipping would have severely restricted the size of his strike force, given the limited capacity of ancient ships, even if another consideration, the need for absolute reliability in his troops, had not already determined this. There was also another advantage in limiting the size of the loyalist force in the field: the smaller and swifter-moving it was, the less damage its passage and provisioning would cause to the civilian population for whose support Bonosus and the rebels were competing.

Both sides showed considerable flair in devising their strategies. In the event, Bonosus' audacity and adoption of a Viking-like plan of campaign paid off

---

[84] Borkowski, *Inscriptions*, 54–8; P. Booth, *Crisis of Empire: Doctrine and Dissent at the End of Late Antiquity* (Berkeley, CA, 2014), 50–4, 101, n.49.

[85] JN, c.109 (p.195.3, trans. 430).

handsomely when he achieved strategic surprise and destroyed a large part of the rebel army in the central Delta. Nicetas, however, proved ultimately more than a match for him when, with a brilliant piece of improvisation, he deployed traction trebuchets in battle. The dockyard workers of Alexandria were probably responsible for their construction (they had the necessary skills in carpentry and rigging), while it is likely that the task of firing them was entrusted to crews of oarsmen (used as they were to rhythmic, collective pulling). The shock of the bombardment which they unleashed surprised and fatally disrupted the loyalists' advance. Mere weight of numbers played little or no part in this fast-moving campaign. As for the psychological impact of the Egyptian rebellion on the Persian war, it was probably much less than that of the insurrections and government countermeasures in the Levant in the second half of 608 and early 609, chiefly because of the distance between Egypt and the war front.

As for the economic and social health of the cities of the Egypt, the evidence of John of Nikiu is unequivocal: the old order was still firmly in place. Cities were effectively managed by the provincial authorities working together with each city's local establishment, and most of them were successfully kept out of the conflict. Those which were involved because of their geographical position remained under the control of the authorities until the civil war was over or almost over. In some cases (Nikiu, Athribis, and Sebennytos), probably representative of the majority, the authorities succeeded in bringing the whole city out in support of one side or the other. In others (Alexandria and Onouphis), probably representative of a minority, there were sharp divisions in the local elite which broke out into the open in the course of the battle for hegemony in Egypt. But even in such cases of fission at the apex of a city, the opposing parties in the elite remained in control of events. It was only probably towards the end of the civil war and in the following transitional period between Bonosus' departure and the imposition of the new rebel regime's authority that the factions escaped briefly from the control of the authorities. John of Nikiu, who is probably repeating the official line, blames the Greens for starting the troubles, points to a common pattern in the disturbances—inter-factional fighting sparking off local crime waves—and indicates, without giving any details, that they were widespread.[86] Whatever their incidence, whether or not the Greens took the lead in every outbreak, and whether or not local political influences were at work behind the scenes (none of which can be determined from John of Nikiu's short notice), the disturbances should not be regarded as manifestations of a deep-seated economic and social malaise, nor as marking a deterioration in the long-established local political order—for one simple reason: they were suppressed without apparent difficulty by the new rebel regime as it established its authority in the interior.

---

[86] JN, c.109 (pp.194.26–195.2, trans. 430). Cf. Booth, 'Shades of Blues and Greens', 593.

2.3 Fall of Phocas

One figure was conspicuous by his absence from the battle for Egypt—Heraclius. After being formally recognized as rebel leader in Alexandria and securing control of the harbour and the loyalist troops there, he disappeared from the scene.[87] The war which followed was fought in his name, but there is no evidence at any stage of his participation. Given the scope and apparent reliability of John of Nikiu's account, this silence cannot be ignored, and it must be concluded that Heraclius was elsewhere while Ioannicius and Nicetas confronted Bonosus.

There are only two pieces of written evidence, one of them questionable, about Heraclius' movements between the seizure of Alexandria (probably spring 609) and his arrival with a fleet at the Dardanelles in autumn 610. John of Nikiu reports that he touched at the islands and the various stations on the sea coast on his way but gives no information about his route or about his actions before his arrival there.[88] More can be inferred from the story of the race for Constantinople between Heraclius and Nicetas, according to which the first to arrive would win the imperial crown. While it contains demonstrably fictional elements (Heraclius was designated leader of the rebellion from the first and, since he was moving by sea, would win the race hands down), there was probably a kernel of truth to it. Otherwise it is hard to explain how it managed to gain such wide currency in east and west and lodged so soon in the first continuation of John of Antioch's chronicle, which was completed in Constantinople only a generation later and was later recycled by the Patriarch Nicephorus.[89] The kernel of truth was probably that Heraclius took charge of all naval operations, and probably a whole range of associated political activities.[90]

This was indeed an obvious course of action to take once the government's grip on Egypt had been prised loose. Besides consolidating and extending their authority in Egypt, the rebels had to maintain, if not increase, the momentum of their revolution, and with command of the seas they were in a position to extend the political battle over the whole east Mediterranean and the Aegean approaches to Constantinople. A secure base was required for this second phase of rebel activity, which would involve the dissemination of anti-government propaganda and the promotion of subversion in the Levant. The most convenient such base was Cyprus, which lay within easy reach of a fleet setting out from Alexandria.

---

[87] JN, c.107 (p.188.21–3, trans. 424).   [88] JN, c.109 (p.195.24–6, trans. 431).

[89] Nicephorus, *Breviarium*, c.1.7–20 (London version, c.1, 6–18), ed. and trans. C. Mango, *Nikephoros Patriarch of Constantinople, Short History*, CFHB 13 (Washington DC, 1990)—cited henceforth as Nic.; Theoph., 297.5–10; Agap., 449.6–9, Mich.Syr., x.25 (p.391), *Chron.1234*, 225.10–28, trans. Hoyland, *Theophilus*, 60–1; *Chronica Byzantia-Arabica*, c.6.5–11, recycled in *Chronica Muzarabica*, c.1.5–10, ed. J. Gil, Corpus Scriptorum Muzarabicorum, I (Madrid, 1973).

[90] See A. J. Butler, *The Arab Conquest of Egypt and the Last Thirty Years of the Roman Domination*, rev. edn, P. M. Fraser (Oxford,1978), 4–5, and Borkowski, *Inscriptions*, 39–41 for the conclusion that Heraclius was in charge of naval operations and the associated political campaign.

Commanding the much-trafficked sea lanes between Egypt and the Levant, on the one hand, and the Levant and Aegean, on the other, Cyprus was, as it still is, the most attractive base for a naval power wishing to exercise influence in the Middle East. It is, therefore, perhaps not unwarranted to conjecture that Cyprus was the rebels' second principal objective after Alexandria and that Heraclius sailed there *as soon as the rebel position in Egypt seemed secure.*

Corroboration comes in the form of bronze coins in two denominations, the follis of 40 nummia and the 10-nummia piece, minted on the island in the financial year which ended on 31 August 610. In the course of 610, the rebels seem to have gained a foothold on the mainland, at Alexandretta on the far side of the Amanus mountains from Antioch, to judge by the issue there of folles of a similar type together with half-folles. At first the busts of Heraclius, son and father, on the coins from both mints wear consular dress, but, then, before the end of August 610 on Cyprus and after the beginning of September at Alexandretta, in a gesture bespeaking confidence about the outcome of the rebellion, they both begin to sport crowns and pendilia.[91]

This hypothesis seems rather more seductive than such rival ones as can be advanced. Heraclius might have chosen to advance port by port up the Palestinian and Phoenician coasts, but risks would have been involved and considerable time would have passed before he could bring direct pressure to bear on the key centres of the Levant (Caesarea and Antioch). The impact on opinion would be swifter and greater if he made the bold, headline-catching move of establishing a base of operations on Cyprus. Another suggestion (advanced by Butler on the flimsiest possible evidence, that of Eutychius, the most fanciful of the extant sources), that Heraclius sailed north and established himself at Thessalonica, not only makes less political sense (Thessalonica being marginal to the crucial political battle for mastery in the richer lands of the Middle East and Asia Minor) but flies in the face of a rich store of contemporary local information in the *Miracula S. Demetrii*, which breathes not a word about Heraclius' hypothetical residence in the city.[92]

There is no reason to suppose that Heraclius encountered any serious opposition at sea either on the voyage to Cyprus or once he was established there. His fleet, bringing together, as it probably did, Egyptian and African shipping, assuredly outnumbered any force which could have been assembled against it by a determined opponent. Even Bonosus seems to have taken care to avoid it. He

---

[91] The design of the obverse is modelled on that of the solidi with two consular busts struck at Carthage. The same hand probably designed the coins issued at the two mints, which are dated to thirteenth and fourteenth indictions. Grierson, 'Consular Coinage', 82–4, 90–1; Grierson, *DOC* II.1, 208, 214–15; Morrisson, *Catalogue*, 251–2; Hahn, *Moneta*, 86–7, table XIII (who questions Grierson's attribution of those marked ALEXAND to Alexandretta (Alexandria ad Issum) and reassigns them to Alexandria).

[92] Butler, *Arab Conquest*, 5–6, whom both Borkowski, *Inscriptions*, 41–43 and Kaegi, *Heraclius*, 45–6 seem inclined to follow.

probably launched his attack on Egypt when Heraclius was already well to the north. After slipping south along the coast, he quickly dived into the inland waterways of Egypt, where he would be safe from a naval counterstrike.[93] The principal functions of the rebel fleet were, therefore, two: to interdict seaborne movement by loyalist forces and to secure the island base from which Heraclius could open up communications with the whole littoral of the Levant and could conduct a political campaign to impress public opinion with the power of the rebels. Although the fleet would later perform the all-important function of conveying rebel forces to threaten Constantinople, there is no evidence that Heraclius made any attempt to impose rebel authority by force on the coastal cities at this stage. Apart from being hazardous, it would probably have been counterproductive.

The battle for sympathy and support was probably fought at a distance and confined largely to propaganda. With the fall of Alexandria, the regime's position was significantly weakened and rendered vulnerable to the charges of incompetence in foreign affairs and brutality at home brought against it by the rebels and picked up by several extant sources.[94] The arguments were, one may suppose, backed up with displays of naval power offshore and the dispatch of deputations to negotiate with notables in important cities and with key figures in the local apparatuses of imperial government. While the means used remain a matter of speculation, there can be no doubt that the rebels were making headway by the end of 609. For support for the regime in Palestine was ebbing away, when Bonosus reappeared there after being driven from Egypt. The opposition caused him to leave and make his way directly to Constantinople.[95]

It does not follow, however, that the rebels received much open support, even though claims were made to that effect and were believed by some contemporaries.[96] As had happened in Egypt, a large majority of postholders in the Levant, and later in the Aegean, probably refrained from committing themselves until the final, decisive battle for control of the imperial city and the throne was engaged and decided. A small minority of cities were probably divided, with rival parties in the local establishment taking up different political positions. Such was the case at Ephesus, the greatest city on the west coast of Asia Minor. Blues asked God to help Phocas, described as 'God-crowned', and themselves. Two inscriptions recording this prayer, with minor differences of wording, have been found on columns in the Doric colonnade fronting the street running south from the theatre (Eutropius Street), which seems to have been the designated place for Blue inscriptions. Both suffered damage, presumably at the

---

[93] JN, c.107 (p.189.14–16 and 18–21, trans. 425).
[94] Nic., c.1.3–6 (L, c.1.3–6); Theoph., 296.10–12; Mich.Syr., x.25 (p.391) and *Chron.1234*, 224.22–6, 225.10–12, trans. Hoyland, *Theophilus*, 58, 60–1. Cf. JN, c.109 (p.195.3–5, trans. 430).
[95] JN, c.109 (p.194.16–20, trans. 430). [96] JN, c.109 (pp.195.22–196.1, trans. 431).

hands of Greens.[97] The Greens (and their patrons probably) not only failed to match these Blue-led expressions of loyalty, but refrained from putting up any inscriptions in Phocas' reign in their main display area, the arch at the north end of the street, and elsewhere in the city.[98] After Phocas' fall, there is evidence of tension between the factions (and hence probably also between whatever backers they had in the city's governing classes). Greens defaced a Blue inscription in honour of their Christian emperors, substituting themselves for Blues. They also added their good wishes for a long life to two acclamations, one of which named the emperors as Heraclius and his baby son, Heraclius the New Constantine (to be dated probably soon after the latter's coronation as co-emperor on 22 January 613).[99]

There is no evidence that the loyalist party in Ephesus actively opposed Heraclius' forces nor that the tensions within the city led to serious disturbances. Elsewhere, though, there were probably pockets of determined resistance. The only documented case is that of Antioch, where the authorities, or a diehard party among them, formed one such centre of opposition. The city was the scene of fighting as late as September 610, and the Chalcedonian patriarch was among those killed by troops, probably those sent in by the rebels to secure the city.[100] There was no truth in the accusation that the Jews of the city killed him in the course of anti-Christian riots which they had started, a charge which surfaces in Theophanes' text and originates with Theophilus of Edessa. This was an anti-Semitic canard, made particularly horrific by the addition of gruesome and fictitious details about the subsequent mutilation and public display of the patriarch's body.[101]

With Egypt firmly controlled by Nicetas and with Bonosus back in Constantinople, the balance of the public argument began to swing against Phocas' government. Heraclius made preparations for a direct attack on the capital. An invasion fleet was massed and began its long voyage to the Dardanelles, sailing along the south coast of Asia Minor, then north through the Aegean.

---

[97] H. Grégoire, *Recueil des inscriptions grecques chrétiennes d'Asie Mineure*, I (Paris, 1922), nos.113 (2) and 113 (3). C. Foss, *Ephesus after Antiquity: A Late Antique, Byzantine and Turkish City* (Cambridge, 1979), 17 and 61–3 for their location. Cf. Cameron, *Circus Factions*, 146–9.

[98] The Greens seem to have preferred formulae which did not name particular emperors, on one occasion styling themselves orthodox (Grégoire, *Recueil*, nos.114 [2], 114 [3a], and 114 [5], with Foss, *Ephesus*, 17, 61–3). Since Phocas had no colleague, these inscriptions must, if they belong to this period, date either from 590–602, when Maurice reigned with his eldest son Theodosius, or after 22 January 613, when Heraclius crowned his son Heraclius the New Constantine co-emperor (*Chron. Pasch.*, 691.13–17 and 703.16–704.2).

[99] Grégoire, *Recueil*, nos.114.5 (substitution), 114.3a (the addition is evident on the photograph at Foss, *Ephesus*, 18, fig.2), and 114.1 (two lines added, emperors named).

[100] The news of the patriarch's death reached Constantinople at the end of September and was noted at *Chron.Pasch.*, 699.16–18.

[101] Theoph., 296.17–21, a notice tacked inappropriately onto another taken probably from the first continuation of John of Antioch about the repression of the insurrection of 608 by Bonosus (296.21–25).

Propaganda that volunteers were flocking to join it was put out to demoralize the loyalists in its path. The Greens of Constantinople seem to have been particularly targeted (hence the spotlight on the Greens who joined the rebel cause). For if only they could be prised loose from the emperor whom they had helped to make, even perhaps turned against him, the rebels would find it much easier to break through the capital's defences.[102]

No attempt seems to have been made to blockade the metropolitan region or even to halt the annual shipments of Egyptian grain to the capital. The rebels must have calculated that short rations or starvation would alienate rather than win over public opinion and that subversion would be easier if communications remained open. Such indeed turned out to be the case. For it was Phocas who eventually severed communications and impounded the Alexandrian grain fleet, probably after receiving the 610 shipments.[103]

The rebels had made contact earlier with dissident elements inside Constantinople. A plan of action was prepared before Heraclius arrived at the Dardanelles. To judge by the roles assigned to them in the well-executed operation to remove Phocas from power, the key figures were three high-ranking senators. Priscus, who had married Phocas' daughter and belonged to his inner circle, commanded a crack guards regiment, the Excubitors, and also possessed an armed retinue of his own *bucellarii*. At some stage (the exact point cannot be determined for lack of precise information) before the rebel fleet arrived at the Dardanelles, he made contact with them or they with him, and it was agreed that the two parties would work together to bring about the fall of Phocas. The carefully judged political stance of the rebels must have smoothed the way for this alliance.[104] The other key figures, whose task was to deliver the *coup de grâce* to the regime by entering the palace and arresting Phocas, were Photius, curator of the Palace of Placidia, who bore a personal grudge against the emperor but, like Priscus, appears successfully to have concealed his disaffection, and Probus, who held the high rank of *patricius*.[105]

Heraclius' fleet approached the Sea of Marmara towards the end of the sailing season. At the Dardanelles he received the Count of Abydus, to whom fell the task of supervising the movement of shipping and goods through the straits. The count was able to inform Heraclius of what was afoot in the capital. A ceremony was now staged in which Heraclius received in audience Phocas' most important

---

[102] JN, c.109, 110 (pp.195.24–6, 196.17–19, trans. 431, 432). It is evident from the vital role assigned to them in the defence of Constantinople in 610 that, despite their occasionally stormy relations, the Greens of the city had not lost Phocas' trust (*contra* Cameron, *Circus Factions*, 146–9).

[103] JN, c.109 (p.196.5–8, trans. 431).

[104] See Whitby, *Emperor Maurice*, 15–16 for a summary of Priscus' career.

[105] *Chron.Pasch.*, 700.14–18. Phocas had had designs on Photius' wife (JA, fr.321.31; Nic., c.1.35–6(L, c.1.31–2)) or, according to the racier version of JN, c.110 (p.197.4–7, trans. 432) (which has dropped Photius' name), raped her although she had become a nun.

political opponents (all probably members of the Senate), who had been punished with exile.[106]

From Abydus, he sailed north to Heraclea, on the European shore of the Sea of Marmara, within striking distance of Constantinople. There he paid a visit, accompanied by his train of exiled senators, to the shrine of the martyr St Glyceria. This was undoubtedly a carefully choreographed event, designed to impress public opinion in the metropolitan region. The rebel leader, acting with the stately decorum of an emperor, was seeking the active support of one of the earliest martyrs, who *was the daughter of a consul*. As such, she was the ideal supernatural patron for the rebel leader who had assumed the consulship and was relying for ultimate success on the support of the Senate. She had other credentials too. As an acknowledged martyr, she had real influence in the court of heaven and could do much to help her earthly client: for this the miraculous oil exuded by her relics was living proof. Her cult was also associated with the Emperor Maurice, the brutal murder of whose family Heraclius was seeking to avenge. Maurice too had visited her shrine, in autumn 590, to inspect the damage done to it by the Avars, and had supplied funds for repair and restoration work. By his visit, Heraclius was, therefore, associating himself ostentatiously with Phocas' predecessor and reiterating as publicly as possible one of the central themes of his propaganda. That the shrine stood near the city of *Heraclea* must surely have made the saint's patronage of Heraclius all the more natural.[107]

Heraclius, we may infer, proceeded *by land* from Heraclea to Selymbria, close to the Long Wall, since it was at Selymbria that he again took to the sea. Phocas' brother, the Magistros Domnitziolus who had been sent to hold the Long Wall, withdrew on hearing that the rebel fleet had entered the Sea of Marmara and was, therefore, in a position to make a landing to his rear. It was, therefore, safe for Heraclius and his senatorial entourage to make this short progress and thereby to rub home the increasing weakness of a regime now cowering inside the inner defences of the capital. It must have fostered a sense of impending doom for Phocas and his supporters.[108]

The final scene in this programme of public ceremonial acts by the rebels took place on the main Princes Island, Calonymus, within sight of Constantinople. Heraclius sailed there from Selymbria. A ceremony was staged, in which the metropolitan of Cyzicus offered Heraclius a crown, taken from the church of the Mother of God at Artake, an offer which it appears he neither accepted nor

---

[106] JA, fr.321.3–5, 6–7; Theoph., 298.26–8, 299.1–2, who gives the count's name, Theodore, which is missing from the condensed fragment. JN, c.109 (pp.195.26–196.1, trans. 431) reports that a large number of soldiers came over with a certain Theodore, described as a grandee, at some unspecified place on his voyage north.

[107] JA, fr.321.7–8; Theoph., 299.2–3, noting that the exiles accompanied Heraclius. See R. Aubert, 'Glyceria', *Dictionnaire d'histoire et de géographie ecclésiastiques*, XXI (Paris, 1986), 230–1 for the cult; see Sim., vi.1.1–3 for Maurice's visit, dated by Whitby, *Emperor Maurice*, 156–8.

[108] JA, fr.321.5–6 and 8–9; Theoph., 298.28–299.1.

refused.[109] Here too he received his wife and mother, who had been released from their convent and spirited out of the city by members of the Green faction. The Greens had evidently responded to the propaganda and political pressure which had been brought to bear upon them. They were probably acting on instructions from Priscus, the leading conspirator inside the city, who had spent the preceding days, as tension grew in the city, taking a cure at the shrine of the Mother of God in the suburb of Blachernae. This policy of lying low worked, in spite of arousing the suspicion of Bonosus, who vainly urged Phocas to have him executed. The conveyance to Heraclius of his womenfolk not only provided tangible proof of the good faith of the conspirators inside the city but also enabled them to communicate their plan in its final form to the rebel high command outside.[110]

On Saturday 3 October, Heraclius made a first appearance. That evening, Phocas, who had gone out to see the rebel fleet from a small port a little beyond the Hebdomon suburb on the Marmara shore, returned to the palace and made his dispositions for the defence of the city. Both factions were allotted key sectors of the sea walls, Blues being stationed in the quarter of Hormisdas at the eastern apex of the city, Greens guarding the harbours of Caesarius (or Theodosius) and Sophia (or Julian) on the south side, where a landing was likely. Priscus, who had returned to the city from Blachernae, also made his dispositions. He gave orders for the Excubitors under his command and his own retinue of *bucellarii* to assemble in the hippodrome of what must have been a palatial residence of his own.[111]

The following day (4 October), Heraclius deployed his whole fleet before the city. He propitiated the Mother of God, chief among the supernatural defenders of the city, against whose opposition St Glyceria would have been powerless to help the rebels, by attaching caskets and icons depicting her to the masts of his ships. He then launched an attack against the harbour of Sophia (Julian), the smaller of the two harbours guarded by Greens. There was some fighting, but the assault seems to have been a feint, intended to distract attention from the landing of an easily recognized Green, the charioteer Calliopas, at the end of a mole near the Green positions in the harbour of Caesarius (Theodosius). Calliopas had been assigned the vital task, first of triggering a rebellion of Greens against Phocas and then of making contact with Priscus.[112]

Calliopas came ashore disguised as a soldier and gave the signal for which the Greens were waiting by removing his helmet and identifying himself. The Greens

---

[109] JA, fr.321.9–11; Theoph., 299.3–5.
[110] JA, fr.321.11–16. Cf. Nic., c.1.20–9 (L, c.1.18–26) for Priscus' double game.
[111] *Chron.Pasch.*, 699.19–700.3, with Whitby and Whitby, nn. 271 and 423 (topography); JA, fr.321.17–23.
[112] *Chron.Pasch.*, 700.3–4 (date); Theoph., 298.15–19 (date, caskets, and icons), citing George of Pisidia, and 299.5–7 (fighting in harbour of Sophia); JA, fr.321.23–7 (landing of Calliopas); JN, c.110 (p. 196.14, trans. 432) (fighting on the seashore).

now set fire to the quarter behind the harbour of Caesarius. The fire, which was intended to cause maximum disruption to the defence, drew Bonosus and the reserves under his command to that sector. There the Greens engaged him in heavy fighting. The Greens held their own throughout the day, eventually forcing back the government troops. Bonosus himself slipped away by boat to the harbour of Sophia, from where he presumably intended to make his way to the palace. But he was spotted before he had got far. He attempted to swim away but was caught and killed by an Excubitor. His body was then dragged to the Forum Bovis, behind the harbour of Caesarius, where it was publicly burned. By this stage, therefore, the rebel forces and their Green allies had not only established a bridge-head in the harbour of Caesarius but had extended their control over the whole quarter, at least as far as the main ceremonial street, the Mese.[113]

While this was going on, Calliopas made his way to Priscus, whom he presumably briefed about Heraclius' latest plans. Priscus sent him on, probably under cover of darkness, when the rebel forces were already firmly entrenched in the city, to deliver his orders to the Excubitors and his own *bucellarii*. Calliopas would also be able to give them a first-hand report about his meeting with Heraclius on the Princes Island and thus convince them that Heraclius and Priscus were acting in concert.

The fighting probably continued through the night, since it was at dawn on Monday 5 October that Priscus' men moved into the palace under the command of Photius and Probus. They arrested Phocas in the chapel of the Archangel Michael, stripped him of his imperial garb, put a black tunic on him instead, and tied his hands behind his back. He was then taken by boat to be shown to the fleet and brought before Heraclius. The penultimate act in the revolution was the ceremonial *calcatio* performed by Heraclius, when Phocas bent his neck beneath Heraclius' heel. Phocas was then executed on the boat, by decapitation, and had his right arm cut off. Right hand and head were later paraded down the Mese from the Forum of Constantine to the Hippodrome, held aloft on a sword and a spear. The headless and one-armed corpse was dragged along behind, as was the unmutilated and still breathing figure of Leontius, one of his senior ministers. Leontius was clubbed to death at the end of the parade. Both bodies were taken to the Forum Bovis for incineration, along with those of two other hated figures (the race starter at the Hippodrome and the sergeant of the City Prefect).[114]

Heraclius now came ashore. He made a seemly show of reluctance about taking power, insisting that Priscus should be preferred to him and claiming

---

[113] JA, fr.321.24-9; *Chron.Pasch.*, 700.3-13 (transferring the blame for the fire to Bonosus—cf. Whitby and Whitby, n.423); Nic., c.1.29-35 (L, c.1.26-31); JN, c.110 (p.196.14-15, trans. 132).

[114] *Chron.Pasch.*, 700.14-701.10 (giving the date as 6 October rather than 5 October), with Whitby and Whitby, nn.316 and 424 (for topography), 425 (identifications); JA, fr.321.31-40 and Nic., c.1.35-51 (L, c.1.31-44), who add that Domnitziolus' corpse, like Bonosus', was also dragged down the Mese and burnt.

that his sole aim had been to avenge the murder of Maurice and his children. Only when Priscus refused, was he proclaimed emperor. Such at least was the official version which has lodged in the sources, put out partly for the benefit of the Persian king. It probably masked some serious negotiations between Heraclius and Priscus, the two principal contenders for power, which ended with Priscus agreeing to give way in return for the Asia Minor army command. Heraclius was crowned by the Patriarch Sergius in St Sophia before the day was out. The next day (6 October) he held celebratory races in the Hippodrome to enable the people at large to participate in the victory and to witness the burning of Leontius' head together with the picture of Phocas customarily brought to the races during his reign and the flag of the Blues (who had signally failed to rise up against him).[115]

Phocas could now be vilified as the very type of the bad ruler, as bloodthirsty, brutal, and the bringer of disaster on his people, while the new emperor was praised as his antithesis. Heraclius had need of such propaganda, both negative (damning his predecessor) and positive (lauding his own character and achievements), to bolster his political position. While it was secure in the short term, resting as it did on the armed might of the land and sea forces which he had brought with him, he needed to win the active support of his subjects by bringing the war with Persia to an end on acceptable terms. So hopes of peace were proclaimed by the most eloquent of his panegyrists, the great poet George of Pisidia. Such hopes of peace were surely not unrealistic. It was not unreasonable to expect an end to hostilities and to the flow of blood on battlefields which had more than matched that at home, now that Heraclius had achieved for the Persians their announced war aim.[116]

George refrained from describing the military feats of the African rebels (other panegyrists had done so), preferring to concentrate on Heraclius' motives and character. As was to be expected of an author who was probably acting as the mouthpiece of the patriarchate, he stressed that Heraclius was fired by the love of God to take action and that God had forwarded his cause and had made the Romans his subjects. He praised him for not being deterred by the long sea journey nor by pity for his mother held hostage in Constantinople.[117] He hoped that peace, which had gone prudently into hiding during Phocas' reign so as not to see the slaughter, would come out again. With God as his colleague, Heraclius would surely succeed for the second time in realizing his hopes. He introduced an apt comparison with Phineas. For Phineas too had acted boldly and decisively to deal with a general problem, the widespread philandering of the Israelites with the daughters of Moab and participation in their pagan rites. By stabbing one of the

---

[115] Nic., c.2.1–10 (L, c.2.1–9); JN, c.110 (p.196.17–21, trans. 432); *Chron.Pasch.*, 700.11–18; Theoph., 299.8–14.
[116] Geo.Pis., *In Heraclium*, 33–8, 67–9.   [117] Geo.Pis, *In Heraclium*, 1–55.

philanderers and his Midianite paramour, whom he caught in flagrante, Phineas saved the Israelites from the general punishment of all offenders which the Lord was demanding. George hoped that now too the main obstacle in the way of peace, namely God's anger against his people, had been removed and that mere human difficulties would be overcome.[118]

The bold decision of the African provincial leadership to challenge Phocas' rule can only be understood against the background of the Persian war. Africa was the ideal base for a rebel movement when the empire's field forces were concentrated on the eastern fronts, because of its peripheral position in the west, shielded by the waters of the Mediterranean and often unpredictable weather. This had been amply demonstrated by the Vandals in the fifth century, when they chose it as their settlement area and held out for several generations against the greatly superior power of the eastern empire. Conditions within Africa in the early seventh century also conspired to help the rebels. The usual checks and balances used by the centre to enhance its power in the localities had been removed when power, military, civil, and judicial, was centralized in the hands of a single figure, the exarch. The Berbers, who had troubled the provinces of the region on an off since their reconquest by Justinian, were temporarily quiescent after a defeat near Carthage in 595.[119] A foreign adventure, in this case a rebellion which would entail campaigning against Egypt and ultimately the centre, would help to maintain this rare, unnatural harmony within Africa, while the temporary redirection outwards and fusion of the energies of Berbers and provincials would give the rebellion great initial impetus.

Even so, but for the Persian war, the rebels would have had little hope of succeeding in the face of the inevitable counterattack from the centre, which could take many forms—propaganda offensive, subversion, reactivation of local enmities, and sponsorship of disaffection, as well as direct naval and military action. It was the war which gave them the hope of ultimate success, itself a precondition for initiating the rebellion. The plan of action devised reveals a sound appreciation of strategic and political conditions in the empire at large in the latter part of Phocas' reign. Phocas could not withdraw substantial forces from the eastern fronts without outraging military and civilian opinion in the outer reaches of the empire and provoking opposition at the centre. As has already been seen, the only forces he deployed against the rebels relied for success on speed of movement, strategic surprise, and the terror induced by the reputation of their commander. Phocas was trapped by the war, his dispositions fixed by external demands. The rebels could, therefore, choose their objectives with a view to their future use as platforms for subverting the regime and, eventually, for

---

[118] Geo.Pis., *In Heraclium*, 56–89; *Numbers*, 25:1–15.
[119] Sim., vii.6.6–7. Cf. R. D. Pringle, *The Defence of Byzantine Africa from Justinian to the Arab Conquest*, BAR Int. Ser. 99 (Oxford, 2001), 41–4.

attacking the centre. It was not unreasonable to think that they would be able to overcome such resistance as might be offered and fend off any counterattack.

The momentum of their advance was maintained by Heraclius at sea. Once Bonosus and his expeditionary force had been driven from Egypt, Phocas faced almost certain doom. All he could do was to concentrate the remaining loyalist forces in the capital and to call on paramilitary elements in the population to help defend the walls. With his main field forces committed to the Persian war, he could only watch, like a man paralysed, as Heraclius undermined his regime in the Levant and then delivered his swift blow to the centre. Heraclius had achieved something akin to strategic surprise. Although Phocas had the time to react, he did not have the wherewithal to do so effectively. Heraclius was able to cut across the inner maritime heart of the empire unimpeded until he reached Constantinople, and, with the aid of the conspirators within, to dispose of Phocas.

The breadth of vision and boldness evident from its inception in the rebels' plan and the resolution and brilliance with which it was executed augured well for the future. The young Heraclius showed that he had the makings of a great general, displaying, as he did, decisive leadership and politically astute generalship. These and other qualities, above all resilience in the face of adversity and effectiveness in managing public opinion and inspiring soldiers, would play a vital part in saving the empire and defeating Persia in the long run.

The immediate future, though, looked grim, since the Persians had managed at last to breach the Romans' inner line of defence on the Euphrates in early August 610, when they captured Zenobia on the right bank of the river. The domestic crisis undoubtedly had some effect on the fighting capability of the empire. There were no reserves left to shore up the defences at a vulnerable point, and news of warfare in the interior is likely to have unsettled the troops engaged at the front. These effects, however, were probably marginal. Even without distractions, the defending forces were being steadily ground down by the Persians' attritional strategy. The most that Bonosus' troops could have done would have been to delay the Persian breakthrough by a few months. Persian attrition was finally working. After two sustained offensives, the first lasting three years, the second four, the two field armies had mastered their Roman opponents on the Armenian and the Syrian fronts. They were poised to break into the soft interior of the empire and to divide it in two.

3
Persian Breakthrough

The quickened pace of Persian advance evident towards the end of Phocas' reign continued after Heraclius' seizure of power. Blow after blow was struck, alternating between the northern and southern fronts. The new regime in Constantinople made Herculean but vain efforts to halt the forward movement of Persian armies. Successes were gained but the strategic initiative remained with the Persians, and at no stage in the second phase of the war, from autumn 610 to winter 621–2, did their general offensive lose momentum. This second phase witnessed their entry into two interior provinces of the empire, Syria and Cappadocia (the subject of this chapter) and then the successive conquests of Palestine and Egypt (the subject of Chapter 4). Shorn of the Levant, economically the most developed of Roman regions, and of Egypt, home of the greatest commercial entrepôt of the Mediterranean as well as its breadbasket, the rump of the empire in Asia Minor and the Balkans was seemingly doomed to destruction at the end of this phase.

The fault did not lie with the soldiers fighting the war, nor indeed with Phocas. At no stage during his reign was there any significant weakening of the frontier armies. Instead of seconding units to shore up his rule, Phocas remained a true Roman emperor, committed to the defence of the territories bequeathed to him by his predecessors. Nor was there a serious deterioration in the fighting spirit of Roman forces. Their morale held up remarkably well in spite of the long, losing, attritional war they were waging. They were ready to move onto the offensive, once the new emperor had secured his position and had decided on a new strategy of bold counterstrikes.

It was the political dislocation of the empire resulting from the forced change of regime, the temporary hiatus affecting the command at the centre, which presented the Persians with an opportunity to exploit the bridgehead established at Zenobia in early August 610 and to strike deep into Roman territory beyond the Euphrates. But before we turn to the military operations of 610–13, when first Syria and then Asia Minor came under attack, it will be worth glancing into one part of the empire's prosperous, highly urbanized interior, looking out through the eyes of two contemporaries, a great holy man and his biographer.

3.1 Theodore of Syceon and the War

Only one component of Roman Empire in the east survived the stresses and strains of the late sixth century and the disasters of the first decade of the seventh largely unscathed. Asia Minor had not been directly affected by the fighting against Persia since 576, when Khusro I made an unsuccessful thrust across the Euphrates. It also seems to have remained calm during the two years (608–10) of empire-wide revolutionary activity and local urban troubles preceding Heraclius' seizure of power. This was in marked contrast to the fortunes of the other major components of the empire in the east. Northern Mesopotamia and Armenia had suffered badly from the war of attrition waged by the Persians and had been overrun. The rich provinces of Syria and Palestine had been scarred by isolated but violent insurrections. Egypt had seen full-scale civil war in 609.

The war did not impinge upon the lives of Asia Minor provincials except for those living on or near the main roads leading to the east. They witnessed the passage of troops and high-ranking generals on their way to and from the fronts. Living in the Siberis valley, on the northern edge of a swathe of rich plains and low hills in the north-west angle of the Anatolian plateau, the monks at Syceon, who had gathered around a famous holy man, Theodore, were well placed to observe the comings and goings on the main road to Ancyra which passed nearby.[1] The most frequent visitor was Phocas' nephew and designated heir, Domnitziolus. He called in for the first time when he was travelling east to take command of the field army and to campaign against the Persians, not long after Phocas' accession. On receiving news of a Laz raid into Cappadocia—the only recorded direct attack on Asia Minor in Phocas' reign—and of the death of Phocas' stepfather Sergius, he was nervous of continuing his journey and went to consult Theodore. Theodore reassured him, telling him that the Laz would not block his route and commending him to God and St George. St George, Theodore's patron saint, would save him from danger during the campaign. Impressed by the accuracy of these prophecies (the Laz *did* withdraw, and Domnitziolus *did* escape by hiding in a reed bed after his army was defeated in an ambush), he called in again on his return journey to give thanks to God and to the holy man who had interceded on his behalf. Thereafter, he never wavered in his devotion to Theodore, whom he visited unfailingly whenever he passed by. He became one of the monastery's chief benefactors.[2]

---

[1] *Vita S. Theodori*, ed. and trans., A.-J. Festugière, *Vie de Théodore de Sykéôn*, 2 vols (Brussels, 1970), cc.3, 40–1. Cf. S. Mitchell, *Anatolia: Land, Men, and Gods*, II *The Rise of the Church* (Oxford, 1993), 122–6.

[2] *V. Theod.*, c.120. Domnitziolus paid, inter alia, for lead roof tiles for the church of St George (c.120.49–51); later he commissioned a gold reliquary cross which incorporated several precious fragmentary relics donated by the Patriarch Thomas (c.128.1–14). A later visit: c.148.25–35.

Bonosus was the other notable visitor during Phocas' reign. His interview with Theodore was witnessed by Theodore's young disciple and future biographer, George, and must therefore date from 607 or later when George, aged 12, was put in his charge.[3] Bonosus sent his compliments to the holy man and, pleading lack of time because of the urgency of his journey to the east, asked to be received at a chapel near the post station on the road. Theodore obliged and began to pray. Bonosus remained standing with his head up, at which, to the horror of those present, Theodore seized hold of the hair above his forehead, pulled it, and made him bow. Bonosus' reaction was to kiss the holy man's hands, then to hold them to his chest because of a pain which troubled him, and to ask him to pray for its cure. Theodore tapped him gently on the chest and told him that first Bonosus too must pray. The inner man had to repent if the outer man were to be healthy. His own prayer would only work if Bonosus committed himself to good and feared God. He then admonished him—fruitlessly, his biographer observes—to show mercy to those placed under his authority, and to avoid arbitrary and brutal punishments for minor offences. When Bonosus thrust fifty gold tremisses into his hand for distribution among the monks, he remarked immediately that there were not enough to go around. Bonosus was impressed by his correct calculation of the total and promised to send more from his baggage (a promise which he kept).[4]

Of political troubles, as Phocas' regime came under increasing threat, of insurrections, and of local factional disturbances, there is little trace in Theodore's relatively large sphere of activity in north-west Galatia and its surrounds (plus Bithynia, to which he paid one memorable visit). His Life, unmatched as a source of detailed social information for the late sixth and early seventh century (to his death in 613), only registers the tremors of serious disturbance in one relatively small Galatian city, Germia, where, at a time of heightened tension (in 613), the city notables found themselves openly challenged by those of more modest means and their own young.[5] Elsewhere, in great cities like Amorium and Ancyra, the old elites remained firmly entrenched and were not involved in serious political quarrels with each other.[6] Apart from the ailments of individuals, the only problem encountered by the urban notables with whom Theodore dealt was a disease affecting herds of cattle at Ancyra and a drought at Pessinus.[7] There was more evidence of social stress in the country, which took the form of trouble

---

[3] *V.Theod.*, cc.142.14–18 (eyewitness account of meeting with Bonosus), 165.8–24, and 170.1–23 (autobiographical notes).

[4] *V. Theod.*, c.142.   [5] *V.Theod.*, c.161.

[6] *V. Theod.*, cc.25.1–7, 45.1–15 *protectores* of Ancyra, presumably including the *ktetor* mentioned at 162.81–2); 58.1–6, 78.21–33, 169.41–7 (*ktetores* of Anastasiopolis, including a *protector* who is named (76.1–5)); 101.3–11 (*domestici* of Pessinus);107.6–9, 20–4, 28–33, 109.9–12 (two named *illustres* of Amorium); 161.11–14, 176–7 (*eleutheroi*, freemen, of Germia, also called *proteuontes*, leading men, and *ktetores* at 163–5 and 169–72). Cf. Mitchell, *Anatolia*, II, 127.

[7] *V. Theod.*, cc.45.1–15, 101.1–11, 33–50.

between *georgoi*, poor peasants who worked others' lands, and rich peasant landlords resident in the villages. The incidents picked out in the Life look like early manifestations of a gradual change in intra-village social relations, a process which was ultimately to result in the emancipation of the poorer majority of the peasantry. The few outbreaks of violence, which caused considerable damage to property (grain stores and houses) and some threats to life and limb, were attributed to demonic possession, like the great public demonstration at Germia. Theodore was called in to expel the demons from village rioters just as he was from urban protesters. These collective exorcisms were recognized as his greatest miraculous feats. The social and economic causes which may be substituted for the contemporary explanation had nothing to do with high politics or indeed with any grim news from the fronts in the east, except in the case of the Germia episode, which occurred at a time of gathering anxiety early in Heraclius' reign. The rural crises all date before Maurice's fall.[8]

The only clear reference to the political and factional troubles of Phocas' last years comes when another visitor called on Theodore. A certain George, a powerfully built man from Cappadocia, who was accused of rebelling against Phocas, was being taken under armed guard to Constantinople. When he asked to go up and receive Theodore's blessing, his escort readily agreed, as they wanted it too. After praying for them and urging the prisoner to accept his fate in this life submissively, Theodore gave him, at his request, the Eucharist. Nervous that he might escape, his escort refused to release him from his chains and later rushed to secure the door of the chapel when the locks opened and the chains fell off the prisoner at a sigh from Theodore as he lifted up the chalice. Theodore assured them that there was no cause for alarm, and, indeed, after he completed the liturgy and provided both escort and prisoner with food, they had no difficulty in putting the chains back on him.[9]

There are many more such vignettes to be found in the last part of the Life of Theodore of Syceon. He hobnobbed with the great, from intimates of the emperor to local urban magnates, from the patriarch of Constantinople to the bishops of neighbouring cities. But he also answered many calls for help from villagers (especially when they were leading villagers) and was always ready to intervene on behalf of the underdog and to cure the ailments of the humblest. He was the very type of the active, interventionist, extrovert holy man. His period of withdrawal from the world, of brutal mortification of the flesh (at first confined

---

[8] *V.Theod.*, cc.114.1–115.43, 116.1–118.19, where three of the four outbreaks of violence are dated to Euphrantas' tenure as governor of Galatia I, and are recorded immediately before the death of Maurice (c.119.3–4). There had been one earlier incident, described in c.43. Germia episode: c.161. Cf. P. R. L. Brown, 'The Rise and Function of the Holy Man in Late Antiquity', in P. R. L. Brown, *Society and the Holy in Late Antiquity* (London, 1982), 103–52, at 123–6; Mitchell, *Anatolia*, II, 133, 139–41.

[9] *V. Theod.*, c.125.

within a cave, later manacled and clad in mail in an iron cage), and of prolonged solitary combat against demons had endowed him with extraordinary authority among men and exceptional influence in heaven, powers which he used to the full on his re-entry into the world. He could foresee the future (as in the case of Domnitziolus). He could work miraculous cures (but was ready to refer patients, where appropriate, to doctors or spas) and could manage the forces of nature so as to protect those who sought his help. Refractory animals became submissive at a word from him.[10]

But his *askesis* had given him a particular expertise in fighting the Devil's agents on earth. Latent demons could not escape detection by him, and, once detected, none could resist him (although the farther they lived from his native Galatia, the more refractory they proved). Faced by him, they were unable to cling onto the human beings whom they had made their *plasmata*, their malleable matter. Bands of demons could put up stiffer resistance, but even they were compelled eventually to yield to Theodore's authority and the heavenly firepower which he could bring down upon them—through nightlong prayers and hymn-singing, solemn processions of whole communities, reading of Scripture, and the sign of the cross. His skill as an anti-demon specialist was highly prized in what was still, below the surface of monotheism, a thoroughly dualist world. His many feats in exorcizing individuals and communities, prey at all times to demonic attack, secured him a starring role among contemporary holy men.[11] They brought him to the attention of successive emperors and ensured that he was lionized by the cities which he visited in the course of his occasional travels. He would be treated like the greatest of secular magnates or victorious generals. The whole population would turn out to welcome him and escort him to the main church, where his prayers were eagerly sought, to provide prophylactic protection against whatever troubles the future might hold.[12]

With his ramified connections within and beyond his home province of Galatia, Theodore was well placed to gauge the mood of the times and the impact of the war in the east on those living deep in the empire's interior. Its impact seems to have been slight in the early years. It is not registered even as a distant rumbling in his Life before 609, when the Persians were nearing the Euphrates. It was at this point that confidence in the power of Roman arms was first dented and anxiety roused in the inner, civilian core of the empire. Some unusual occurrences caught the attention of Theodore and his contemporaries and became the foci of apprehension. There was the case of the hot Eucharistic bread handed to a future exarch of Italy during a service in the monastic church at

---

[10] *V.Theod.*, cc.145–7. Cf. Brown, 'Holy Man', 130–48; Mitchell, *Anatolia*, II, 134–7.

[11] Mass exorcisms: references in note 8 of this chapter; Mitchell, *Anatolia*, II, 139–50. Cf. P. R. L. Brown, *The Cult of the Saint: Its Rise and Function in Late Antiquity* (Chicago, 1981), 106–13.

[12] *V.Theod.*, cc.101.28–34 (Pessinus), 107.1–3 (Amorium), 130.16–17 (Dorylaeum), 156.1–7 (Nicomedia).

Syceon. A little later came the swaying of processional crosses witnessed by a large crowd of townsmen and countrymen taking part in a religious ceremony. Both incidents were taken by Theodore to point to future tribulation and suffering. His prophecy was brief and to the point on the second occasion, but he was more forthcoming to the future exarch, explaining that the favour of the saints was being withdrawn and that they should pray that God's love for mankind might temper the execution of his commands.[13]

When news of the swaying crosses reached Constantinople, Theodore was invited there by the Patriarch Thomas, who clearly shared Theodore's foreboding. It was winter, not long before Christmas. He was summoned to an audience with Phocas, whose hands and feet were hurting. He asked the holy man, who was prepared to speak his mind with astonishing frankness, to ease the pain in his limbs—which Theodore did—and to pray for him and his empire. This Theodore refused to do, saying that his prayers would do no good if Phocas did not reform and give up the executing of his opponents at home. He left the audience unharmed, despite the offence which he had given. Later, at his meeting with the patriarch he listed the evils coming upon the Romans—apostasy, barbarian invasions, bloodshed on a large scale, general ruin and captivity, abandonment of churches, cessation of the liturgy, the fall of the empire, and the imminent arrival of the Antichrist. The patriarch's response, far from unnatural, was to ask Theodore to pray for his release from this life—a request which was granted a few months later. Theodore was only given permission to return to his monastery after the installation of the new patriarch, Sergius, who had asked for and received his blessing, and after a visit to Domnitziolus' house to bless the family and exorcize a demon from a slave girl. It was at Syceon that he heard the news of Phocas' death on 7 October. There was no crowing on Theodore's part. His sense of impending doom was not lightened. There is not a glimmer of the optimism which shines through George of Pisidia's poem welcoming Heraclius' accession. His only reaction was to petition Heraclius (successfully) for the life of the monastery's benefactor, Domnitziolus.[14]

Reality was already living up to foreboding. The Roman position on both fronts deteriorated during the last months of Phocas' reign and the first of the new regime. Heraclius was in a weak diplomatic position when he sent off an embassy to present his credentials to his partner ruler of the civilized world, Khusro II. When the embassy was rebuffed, initial hopes of negotiating an end to the war faded away. There would be no halt to operations in the near future. Soon, in summer 611, the fighting would reach deep into Asia Minor and cause panic among the monks of Theodore's monastery at Syceon.

---

[13] *V.Theod.*, c.127.   [14] *V.Theod.*, cc.128.14–22, 133–6, 140, 152.1–18.

3.2 Persian Advance into Syria and Asia Minor, 610–13

The Persians waited on events in summer 610. Shahen's armies were probably pressing on with the laborious process (far from newsworthy) of pacifying western Armenia. As they did so, they were extending effective Persian authority down the valley of the upper Euphrates and beginning to threaten Satala, while, on the second natural east-west line of advance along the river Arsanias (south of the Munzur Dağ), they were coming closer and closer to the key Roman base of Melitene and the Euphrates crossing which it guarded. Meanwhile, Shahrbaraz made no move to break out of his bridgehead at Zenobia, neither marching up the Euphrates against other riverine garrison cities nor targeting Sergiopolis to the south. No action was required on his part to weaken his opponents. Merely by maintaining a Persian military presence on the far side of the Euphrates, thereby turning the south-east flank of the Romans' inner line of defence on the river, he forced them to disperse their troops. He thereby weakened, without effort, the forces facing him across the central sector of the Euphrates frontier farther upstream, where the river described a great curve and where depth was added to the defence by a network of forts around Chalcis and Hierapolis.

Encouraging news came from the Syrian interior. The transfer of power to the Heraclian rebels did not go smoothly everywhere. Troops sent from Egypt to take over key centres encountered resistance at Antioch. Fighting broke out, instigated perhaps by hard-line Chalcedonians who had had strong backing against their local sectarian rivals (the Monophysites) from Phocas' government. It was in September during the fighting that the Chalcedonian patriarch, Anastasius, was killed.[15] Instability in the capital of the Levant, commanding the north Syrian hinterland of the frontier zone, could not but distract Roman commanders from the military task at hand, that of countering whatever offensive move the Persians might make.

Shahrbaraz launched his attack toward the end of September or at the very beginning of October, when the Heraclian forces were closing in on Constantinople. The timing was surely deliberate. As the internal revolution approached its final crisis at the centre, there was little danger that reserves would be dispatched promptly to shore up a threatened sector of the frontier or to contain any breakthrough. The Syrian sources which alone report the direction of the attack and the initial gains made are laconic in the extreme. It is uncertain whether the troops at Zenobia were involved in a flank attack on the fortified zones around Chalcis and Hierapolis or whether the seizure of Zenobia was used as a feint. However it was done, by frontal attack across the central Euphrates sector with or without support from Zenobia, the vital breach was made in

---

[15] See Chapter 2, n. 100.

Roman defences. Shahrbaraz was able to push west in such force that no open resistance was offered. He advanced swiftly to the Orontes, capturing Antioch on 8 October. He then turned south and took control of the whole Orontes valley in not much more than a week. Apamea fell on 15 October, Emesa a few days later. Emesa, which was filled with refugees from elsewhere in the Levant, put up no resistance.[16]

By this well-executed thrust, Shahrbaraz captured a strategically vital east-west corridor across the open country between the Euphrates and Antioch, together with the belt of hills separating Antioch from its port of Seleucia. He thus split the empire in two, leaving each of its two parts—Asia Minor fronted by Cilicia to the west, the Levant backed by Egypt to the south—exposed to attack. The strategic initiative now lay with the Persians. The advantage of inner lines previously enjoyed by the Romans was not only negated, but decisively reversed. It would be much quicker and easier to shift troops in large numbers the short distance between fronts by land than for the Romans to transport them by sea. Shahrbaraz was also in a position to project Persian power over the whole of northern Syria. It is highly likely that all the region's rich cities submitted forthwith, just as those to the east of Euphrates had done once the main military bases had fallen. Finally, with the seizure of the full length of the Orontes valley, a dagger pressing into the heart of the Levant, Persian forces were well placed to push on into Lebanon, southern Syria, and Palestine, as well as interdicting any attack from the south on the east-west corridor in the north. Hoards of gold and copper coins concealed over the following few years (610–14) testify to widespread apprehension on the part of provincials in Palestine.[17]

News of the Persians' advance to the coast must have reached Heraclius only a few days after his coronation on 5 October. Euphoria at his political victory doubtlessly evaporated as the grim reality that the war was being lost was impressed forcibly on the consciousness of his subjects. A second blow, which was felt soon afterwards, confirmed the sombre warnings of Theodore.

It might have been expected that resistance to the new regime would have subsided completely once Phocas himself had been deposed and executed. His brother Comentiolus, however, refused to recognize Heraclius and claimed the throne for himself. Since he was the general responsible for guarding the eastern approaches to Asia Minor (so probably holding the command of *Magister Militum per Armeniam*), his rebellion seriously weakened Roman defences on the northern front—fatally as it turned out. For Shahen it was an extraordinary stroke of luck when much of the Armenian field army he was facing withdrew with

---

[16] *Chron.724*, 146.14–15, trans. Palmer, 17; Agap., 450.2–5, Mich.Syr., xi.1 (403), *Chron.1234*, 226.13–17, trans. Hoyland, 62–3.

[17] G. I. Bijovsky, *Gold Coin and Small Change: Monetary Circulation in Fifth–Seventh Century Byzantine Palestine* (Trieste, 2012), 423–8.

Comentiolus and took up winter quarters far to the west, at Ancyra. There the rebel forces were within striking distance of the metropolitan region, but much farther removed from eastern front.

The Life of Theodore, our only source of information about the rebellion, is vague on the chronology, but gives the impression that the crisis lasted most of the winter. There was time for the new regime to make two attempts to negotiate an end to the crisis. The two emissaries, one a certain Herodianus, a holy man famed for his clairvoyance, the other Philippicus, Maurice's son-in-law, who had been in holy orders from early in Phocas' reign, both called on Theodore on their way to Ancyra. Herodianus went on his way with Theodore's blessing. Philippicus came as a prisoner, having been captured in Bithynia by a raiding foray sent out by Comentiolus, and was assured that he would not come to harm. There was time too for opposition to surface among Comentiolus' senior commanders, some of whom made contact with Theodore. The worst of winter was over when the denouement came. Comentiolus was preparing to march on Constantinople when the highest-ranking of the dissidents in his army, Justin Patrician of the Armenians, assassinated him at night. By then, though, the damage had been done. The northern front had been stripped of many of its defenders on the eve of a campaigning season, when there was every reason to expect Shahen's army to attempt to emulate the achievements of Shahrbaraz on the southern front in the previous year.[18]

It was perhaps the news of continuing domestic problems in the empire which hardened Khusro II's attitude in that first winter after Heraclius' coup. Something of the sort is needed to explain his extraordinary reaction to the Roman embassy which came, with unusually magnificent presents, to announce the fall of Phocas and the accession of Heraclius in accordance with the long-established convention that each great power informed the other of changes of regime. The letter which presented Heraclius' credentials also contained a proposal that the two sides should negotiate peace.[19] It was not unreasonable to hope that negotiations would then start, since the Persians' stated war aim, the avenging of the murdered Maurice, had been achieved by Heraclius. At a similar moment late in 531, four years into Justinian's first Persian war, Khusro I's accession provided the occasion for both sides to step back and to negotiate a treaty without time limit.[20] George of Pisidia was optimistic when he wrote his poem celebrating the start of the reign. The embassy, he believed, would succeed. With God's help, Heraclius' hopes would be realized for the second time. The gates leading to peace would be opened. Heraclius himself was portrayed as a mounted archer eager to hunt down the wrongdoing which caused quarrels. The honey-steeped words which he shot

---

[18] V.Theod., c.152.19–67. Cf. Kaegi, 'New Evidence', 308–22.
[19] Ps.S., 113.3–5; Agap., 450.1; Mich.Syr., xi.1 (403); Chron.1234, 226.6–12, trans. Palmer, 127.
[20] G. Greatrex, *Rome and Persia at War, 502–532* (Leeds, 1998), 210–18.

would cause pleasurable wounds. The wildness of the Persians would be tamed by the quality of his argument. Peace would be coaxed out her hiding place.[21]

Khusro, though, was not softened by the message from Heraclius. He reiterated his support for Theodosius, whom, he declared, he had installed as king. He refused to recognize Heraclius, since he had acted without authorization from him, Khusro. He did not consider the presents sent to be presents, but his own by right. He simply appropriated them, without incurring any obligation. By insisting that candidates for the Roman throne should first seek his approval, he was claiming suzerainty over the Roman Empire, casting aside the long-standing view, accepted by both great powers, of their ideological parity. As for the Roman ambassadors, he gave orders for their execution. By this act, in violation of diplomatic protocol, he not only prevented negotiations from starting but completely severed diplomatic relations. There was no prospect of either side sending off an embassy for the foreseeable future, for fear of reprisals and more executions.[22]

Instead of the reply which they were awaiting from Persia, Heraclius and his advisers received a note from heaven. A violent earthquake struck Constantinople on Tuesday 20 April 611, at the seventh hour. It was plain then that the Romans had offended God and that he was punishing them. They did what they could to assuage his anger. Two days later, on the Thursday before Pentecost, Heraclius led a procession to the Campus Martius at Hebdomon outside the city wall. There, emperor and people pleaded with God to have mercy on his people. A sense of foreboding about the immediate future was undoubtedly deepened.[23]

The Persian offensive on the northern front was almost certainly launched early in the 611 campaigning season, while the Roman forces in Asia Minor were still disorganized. Shahen made rapid progress, penetrating deep into Cappadocia and capturing Caesarea, the provincial capital. He broke with the strategy hitherto followed. Instead of concentrating on major defended centres of population and pushing forward step by step, he delivered a bold stroke which caught the Roman defenders unprepared as well as disorganized. This is probably why Caesarea does not appear to have put up much of a fight, despite its formidable fortifications, upgraded in the early sixth century as part of Anastasius' and Justinian's military building programmes. After expelling much of the population, Shahen turned the city's defences against the Romans, using it first as a secure base from which to send out raiding forays, and then, if intention may be judged by outcome, as bait to draw the northern field army, once it had regrouped, to him and to wear it down in counterattacks against the walls.[24] This was a strategy akin to that

---

[21] Geo.Pis., *In Heraclium*, 14–38, 63–71. [22] Ps.S., 113.5–11.
[23] *Chron.Pasch.*, 702.7–10.
[24] Ps.S., 112.9–13; Nic., c.2.9–22 (L, c.2.8–20); Theoph., 299.31–2; Agap., 450.5–6. The Persian general is misidentified as Bahram by Mich.Syr., xi.1 (403) and *Chron.1234*, 226.20–2, trans. Palmer, 127. Fortifications: Procopius, *De aedificiis*, v.4.7–14.

developed by Belisarius in Italy, when he leapfrogged deep into Goth-held territory and seized key strongholds which he knew the Goths would try to recover. Offensive momentum against a numerically superior adversary was maintained by a series of defensive actions fought from carefully selected forward emplacements.[25]

Shahen made no attempt to secure communications to his rear. The powerful fortress of Melitene does not appear to have been attacked. It remained in Roman hands for several years to come.[26] This was probably also true of other fortified places on his line of advance. Then, with Caesarea in his hands, he concentrated on plundering the interior of Asia Minor, thereby both causing serious economic damage and striking a severe blow to the prestige of the new emperor, whose family may well have come from Cappadocia.[27] Fear swept through the provinces. Although Galatia was beyond the reach of the boldest of forays, the monks at Syceon were nervous that they might be attacked and asked Theodore for permission to evacuate the monastery. He refused, telling them that God had listened to him and would not countenance any attack during his lifetime.[28]

Priscus, who had been given command of the northern field army under the terms of his compact with Heraclius, could only take it up after the death of Comentiolus. When he did so, he conducted a successful campaign of damage limitation. He drove the raiding forays back to their base at Caesarea and eventually, in the course of the summer, instituted a blockade. Shahen was now trapped. The blockade should, as the months went by, have a depressing effect on the morale of his troops as well as debilitating them physically. In the end, faced with starvation, they would have the choice either of surrendering or of sallying out in a weakened state to virtually certain defeat. Back in Syceon, the monks were relieved at the news of the blockade, only to hear a new disheartening pronouncement from Theodore. The Persians would escape, he told them, and, unless the Romans repented, they would return in great force and would ravage the whole country as far as the sea—but after his death.[29]

Far away to the south, Heraclius' cousin Nicetas, who had been left in charge of the Heraclian forces in Egypt and had subsequently become de facto viceroy of the Roman Middle East, mobilized his forces and attacked the Persian salient in the Orontes valley. He too was successful. He won a victory outside Emesa in summer 611. The battle was hard-fought, and both sides suffered heavy losses.[30] Nicetas probably then concentrated on shoring up Roman defences in central

---

[25] Procopius, *Bella*, ed. and trans. H. B. Dewing, 5 vols. (Cambridge, MA, 1914–28), v.14–vi.13, 16–22. Cf. E. Stein, *Histoire du Bas Empire*, II (Paris, 1949), 339–68; P. Heather, *The Goths* (Oxford, 1996), 263–7.
[26] Ps.S., 113.23–7, with *Hist.Com.*, n.32. for its fall, probably in 617.   [27] See Chapter 2, p. 40.
[28] *V.Theod.*, c.153.1–11.
[29] *V.Theod.*, c.153.11–24; ps.S., 113.12–17; Nic., c.2.9–10 (L, c.2.8–9).
[30] *Chron.724*, 146.16–18, trans. Palmer, 17; Agap., 450.8–9.

Syria and northern Palestine. Damascus in the interior, controlling the desert frontage, and Caesarea, commanding the rich coastal plain of Palestine, were key forward positions. Later, in the winter of 611–12, he journeyed to Constantinople, confident presumably that the Persians would make no serious effort to seize back the initiative in the south, while Shahen remained beleaguered in Caesarea of Cappadocia. He was feted as the first general to defeat the Persians in open battle since the victory at Ełivard in 603. A gilded statue was commissioned in his honour. He stayed in the city for several months because of a serious illness which seemed likely to prevent him from returning to his command. He was there when Theodore arrived in May. Theodore restored Nicetas to health, in time for him to ride out to meet Heraclius on his return to the city, after an expedition to inspect the forces deployed around Caesarea.[31]

The blockade of Caesarea went on and on. The Persian army proved remarkably resilient, largely, one suspects, because most of the civilian population which would have worsened the supply problem had been extruded and foodstuffs had been gathered along with other plunder before the start of the blockade. Heraclius was confident enough of the outcome to pay this formal, probably choreographed visit to Priscus outside the city in late April–early May 612. He might thereby be able to siphon off much of the credit for the forthcoming victory.[32] He then returned to Constantinople at the news of the birth of Heraclius the New Constantine, his eldest son and heir, and summoned Theodore of Syceon to bless the baby. Theodore, who had been invited to dine with Nicetas after the latter's recovery, was then allowed to return to his monastery.[33] Nicetas too probably departed at roughly the same time, in May or early June, to resume the southern command. But then misfortune struck. Shahen's troops, despite a year's confinement within the walls of Caesarea, set fire to the city, sallied out and cut their way through the encircling Roman forces, withdrawing thereafter to Armenia. It was a notable Persian victory which could not but diminish the new emperor's standing. Hence, perhaps a canard was put into circulation which implied that Priscus had rejected guidance from Heraclius. He was said to have resented Heraclius' visit, refusing initially to see him, and then, when he did so, feigning illness and receiving him lying down.[34]

Shahen's escape from Caesarea was a significant military reverse but no disaster. For, as in the case of the counterattack in the south, the prime objective was attained. The Persians were driven out of Cappadocia and back across the Euphrates. This, in conjunction with Nicetas' victory in 611 which halted the Persians' advance up the Orontes valley, ensured that the Roman Empire

---

[31] *V.Theod.*, c.154.1–9, 28–56; Nic., c.2.24–8 (L, c.2.22–6). See note 38 of this chapter for the dedication of the statue.
[32] *V.Theod.*, c.154.5–7; Nic., c.2.10–14 (L, c.2.9–12). Cf. ps.S, 113.12–15.
[33] *V.Theod.*, c.155.1–8; Nic., c.2.22–6 (L, c.2.20–4).
[34] *V.Theod.*, c.153.11–24; ps.S., 113.16–22; Nic., c.2.14–22 (L, c.2.12–20).

remained intact, except for the narrow salient driven west from the Euphrates to the sea. The political consequences, however, were graver. The new regime had failed its first serious test. One of Heraclius' responses was to blame Priscus, with the result that relations between them deteriorated, despite an effort to keep up the appearance of continuing harmony between the emperor and the leading senator who had backed the revolution. Another was to make full use of the imperial office and the associated ceremonial apparatus to enhance his position as God's vicegerent at the head of the earthly hierarchy of rule. When his wife Eudocia died on 13 August 612, a full state funeral was laid on. Her body, sumptuously dressed, was taken in an open coffin from the palace of Blachernae just outside the walls on the Golden Horn to the church of the Holy Apostles in the heart of the city, the traditional burial place of emperors. A large crowd watched the funeral cortège. The sympathy and awe aroused were reawakened a month and half later, on 4 October, when her small daughter, Epiphania, was crowned Augusta in her place, and taken, seated in a chariot and escorted by court dignitaries, in procession for the short distance between the Great Palace, where the coronation took place, and St Sophia.[35]

Another two months passed. The political ground was prepared. More ceremonies were planned to project Heraclius as founder of a new dynasty. The decisive move against Priscus was made on 5 December. He was lured into the palace by an invitation to be godfather to the young Heraclius the New Constantine. There he found himself facing a formal gathering of senators together with representatives of the people and the patriarch, who formed a de facto court of law with unquestionable authority. Heraclius accused Priscus of offensive behaviour at the time of his visit to Cappadocia, recalled his treachery to his father-in-law Phocas, and ordered that he be stripped of all his posts and be ordained forthwith. The assembly signalled at least tacit consent by remaining silent and the patriarch carried out the ordination. Heraclius then went out to inform Priscus' military retinue (his *bucellarii*) of the fait accompli. He announced that they had been transferred to his personal command, that they would continue to be treated as elite soldiers, and that they would receive forthwith the allowances due to regular soldiers. This bold act, that of a born commander, won them over, and they acclaimed him, thereby committing themselves to his service. He followed this up by reassigning Priscus' command (the northern field army), apparently jointly, to his brother Theodore and the Emperor Maurice's brother-in-law, Philippicus, who came out of monastic retirement. Priscus himself spent the remaining year of his life in the monastery of Chora in Constantinople.[36]

Heraclius sealed his position with more ceremonies—the baptism of his baby son, Heraclius the New Constantine, by the patriarch, which was followed by his

---

[35] *Chron.Pasch.*, 702.19–703.8; Nic., c.3.1–8 (L, c.3.1–6).
[36] *Chron.Pasch.*, 703.9–12; ps.S, 114.1–8; Nic., c.2.28–64 (L, c.2.26–56).

coronation as co-emperor on 22 January 613, the beginning of the consular year. The coronation took place privately in the Great Palace, but was followed by two public ceremonies which secured the backing of men and God for this second member of the Heraclian dynasty. The baby, wearing his crown, was taken first into the Hippodrome to receive the obeisance of the Senate and the acclamations of the circus factions, and then to St Sophia (for a patriarchal blessing, presumably).[37] Finally came the dedication of Nicetas' statue in the Forum of Constantine. Two inscriptions commemorated his achievements against the Persians, one, in the name of emperor, army, cities, and people, hailing his 'great Mede-slaughtering labours', the other, put up by the Greens, calling Nicetas 'great in battles, a leader who trembles not'. It was rather feeble praise, especially if it is compared to the long poetic encomia of Heraclius penned in the 620s by George of Pisidia.[38]

His position secure after the fall of Priscus, Heraclius prepared to take charge of military operations in 613, overseeing and coordinating the movements of the two field armies. Theodore and Nicetas would serve as army commanders under his command. This was a bold move at so critical a juncture. Two centuries had passed since the last time an emperor had taken to the field and that emperor, Theodosius I, had not had to confront Rome's great adversary in the east. Heraclius would be investing his prestige in a very direct and public way, taking on a risk from which even emperors with plenty of military experience, like Zeno and Maurice, had shied away. The campaign was to intended to halt the Persian advance and to begin the process of driving the Persians off Roman territory. Shahrbaraz was the target. Just as Shahen had been driven from Caesarea, Shahrbaraz was to be confronted in open battle and forced back from his forward position around Antioch, thus reopening the vital land bridge between Asia Minor and the Levant.

There is, alas, all too little information about the campaign. It is passed over in silence by contemporary and later Syrian sources. A single notice in the Armenian *History of Khosrov* summarizes what happened. There is also a passing reference in the Life of Theodore, which notes that Heraclius journeyed at high speed towards the front during Lent (26 February–6 April). En route he visited Theodore and obtained his blessing, going up to the monastery (unlike Bonosus in 609) in spite of his hurry.[39]

The battle he sought was fought in the vicinity of Antioch. Nicetas took part as well as Heraclius and his brother Theodore. It follows that the army of the Levant

---

[37] Chron.Pasch., 703.17–704.2; Nic., c.5.1–6 (L, c.5.1–3).
[38] Nic., c.5.8–10 (L, c.5.4–6); *Anthologia Graeca*, xvi.46 and 47, ed. and trans. R. Aubreton and F. Buffière, *Anthologie grecque, 2ème partie, Anthologie de Planude*, XIII (Paris, 1980), 100, with commentary of C. Mango, 'Épigrammes honorifiques, statues et portraits à Byzance', *Aphieroma ston Niko Svorono* (Rethymno, 1986), I, 23–35, at 30–1.
[39] V.Theod., c.166.1–22.

(Oriens) was not restricted to a diversionary role but made a successful flank attack and pushed north to the plain of Antioch at the head of the Orontes valley. The battle was evenly balanced. Both sides suffered heavy losses. Then came a pause during which the Persians 'gained strength', presumably in the form of reinforcements. This tipped the balance in their favour. The Romans were defeated but were able to retreat in good order. They made a successful stand on the pass leading to Cilicia across the Amanus range, but were soon forced to resume the retreat. The way was open for the Persians to occupy Cilicia and Tarsus, menacingly close to the main pass leading up through the Taurus into southern Cappadocia.[40]

Theodore of Syceon had had a presentiment of the outcome when Heraclius, whom he had embraced and commended to God, was unable to stay for the refreshments (bread, apples, and wine) which he had blessed. This augured ill for the campaign, he told his future biographer, George, but he left a ray of hope by predicting that Heraclius would reign for thirty years.[41] A few weeks later, after playing his usual part in the Easter celebrations of the monastery and the surrounding country, he died in the early hours of Sunday 22 April.[42]

Heraclius did indeed live on and fight on. He survived his defeat outside Antioch and the series of losses which lay ahead. Times were grim, but already perhaps soldiers and civilians were aware of his flair as a military commander—the campaign had, after all, come close to success—and were impressed by his willingness to share the hardships and dangers of his men (of which much would be made later by his panegyrist, George of Pisidia).

The Persians, though, were the clear victors in 613. They retained the strategic initiative. They enlarged their north Syrian salient, and deprived the Romans of an important resource base, in the form of the large, highly urbanized plain of Cilicia. Cilicia could also act a forward assembly zone for expeditions into Asia Minor, relatively secure behind the formidable barrier of the Taurus Mountains. Before the year was out, they also broke out of the southern Orontes valley, pushing east over the Anti-Lebanon to Damascus. From Damascus they could project their power for a considerable distance south over the *badiya*, the fertile zone on the edge of the desert which had prospered in late antiquity. At this stage, the Golan Heights, the Jebel Druze, and the intervening lava fields of the Trachonitis probably marked the southern limit of their zone of authority, forming as they did a significant barrier to north-south movement along the *badiya*.[43]

---

[40] V.Theod., c.166.22–4; ps.S., 114.29–115.4.   [41] V.Theod., c.166.11–22, 24–35.
[42] V.Theod., c.167–8.
[43] Damascus: V.Georg., 127.19–128.1; Chron.724, 146.19–20, trans. Palmer, 17; Theoph., 300.20–1, Mich.Syr., xi.1 (403), Chron.1234, 226.22–4, trans. Hoyland, 64. Caesarea was under firm Persian control in the early months of 614, when the Jerusalem crisis broke (see next section).

But tempting prospects were offered by the roads which ran south and southwest from Damascus. One transected the Trachonitis to reach the large, fertile, urbanized plain of the Hawran, dominated by Bostra with its impressive Justinianic churches. Another ran south-south-west to Galilee and the Jordan valley, which then offered an easy route south to Jericho and the Judaean desert to the east of Jerusalem. A third road ran west over the south end of the Anti-Lebanon to Tyre on the coast. The Phoenician and Palestinian provinces, the most highly urbanized and commercially developed in the Roman Empire, thus lay within easy striking distance, as did the Holy City itself, venerated by Jews and Christians all over the Roman, sub-Roman, and Persian worlds.[44]

3.3 The Jerusalem Episode, 614

The capture of Jerusalem by Shahrbaraz's army in the first half of 614 was the most sensational item of news to come out of the Middle East in the whole course of the last and greatest of Roman-Persian wars, with a single possible exception—Heraclius' victory at the Battle of Nineveh in December 627 and his subsequent advance on Ctesiphon, which precipitated a successful coup against Khusro II towards the end of February 628.[45] It was one of very few episodes of the war occurring away from the capital to be recorded in the *Chronicon Paschale*. It caught the attention of western observers whose horizons reached the Mediterranean, and was duly registered in the chronicles of Isidore of Seville and Paul the Deacon.[46] Sophronius, the future patriarch of Jerusalem, who was in Alexandria at the time with his friend and spiritual guide John Moschus, wrote a moving verse lamentation. He noted in passing that Jews took part in the attack, but did not indulge in the sort of anti-Semitic diatribes which surface in other sources, Theophanes, for example, and the history written in Arabic by Eutychius, the Melkite (Chalcedonian) patriarch of Alexandria in the tenth century.[47]

The fall of the city made no less of an impression on Christians living under Persian rule, in Armenia and Mesopotamia. The fullest account of the

---

[44] Cf. Isaac, *Limits of Empire*, 62–6, 134–40, maps III and IV.
[45] Recent studies: B. Flusin, *Saint Anastase le Perse et l'histoire de la Palestine au début du VIIe siècle*, II Commentaire (Paris, 1992), 129–81; Y. Stoyanov, *Defenders and Enemies of the True Cross: The Sasanian Conquest of Jerusalem in 614 and Byzantine Ideology of Anti-Persian Warfare*, Österr. Ak. Wiss., Phil.-hist. Kl., Sitzungsberichte 819 (Vienna, 2011), 11–23; Booth, *Crisis of Empire*, 94–100.
[46] *Chron.Pasch.*, 704.13–705.2; Isidorus, *Chronica*, 413 (p.478); Paul D, iv.36.
[47] Sophronius, *Anacreontica*, ed. and trans. M. Gigante (Rome, 1957), no.14 (lines 61–4 for the remark about Jews); Theoph., 300.30–301.3; Eutychius, *Annals*, ed. and trans. M. Breydy, *Das Annalenwerk des Eutychios von Alexandrien: Ausgewählte Geschichten und Legenden kompiliert von Sa'id ibn Batriq um 935 A.D.*, CSCO 471-2, Scriptores Arabici 44–5 (Louvain, 1985), I, 128.9–13, II (trans.), 108.13–20. Sophronius' travels: H. Chadwick, 'John Moschus and His Friend Sophronius the Sophist', *JTS* n.s.25 (1974), 41–74, at 49–53; Booth, *Crisis of Empire*, 44–6, 49–50, 97–101, 108–111, 231–3.

circumstances which led to the siege is given in the *History of Khosrov*, while the *Khuzistan Chronicle* makes it a central episode in its brief history of the war.[48] One non-Christian born into a Zoroastrian priestly family whose service as a cavalryman in the army was coming to an end was jolted into contemplating a change of faith.[49] For monks living in Judaea, the disaster had more direct consequences—because of the Beduin raids which took place at the same time and led to at least one mass killing. Antiochus, the archimandrite of the Laura of St Sabas, the most famous monastery in the Judaean desert, included a brief history of his community at the time of the Persian conquest in the covering letter which he sent to the abbot of a monastery near Ancyra with a copy of his *Pandect*s, a collection of 130 short sermons on virtues and vices with supporting scriptural quotations. The authorship of another, much fuller account of the siege and its aftermath is attributed to Strategius, a colleague of Antiochus' at St Sabas. When note is taken both of the character of the text (based in large part on the testimony of eyewitnesses and presenting a full version of a long homily given by the Patriarch Zacharias on the Mount of Olives) and of its completion within a year of the siege, high hopes may be entertained of the reliability of the information which it provides. Finally, to complete this roll call of primary evidence, there are important references in the Life of George, the holiest of the monks at the monastery of Choziba, who had to go into hiding when Beduin raiders came, while useful dating information can be culled from liturgical calendars in several early lectionaries.[50]

It should, then, be an easy task to piece together a detailed narrative of the events and then to probe behind them for explanations. But the sources are remarkably discordant as well as highly tendentious. While the length of the siege (either 19 or 20 days) is not at issue, there is a fundamental disagreement over the date of the city's capture: the contemporary account of Strategius has the siege start on 15 April and end on the twenty-first day (5 May); but the notice in the usually reliable *History of Khosrov* puts the city's fall a fortnight later, on 19 May (ten days after a church festival, mistakenly identified as Easter (30 March) rather than Ascension (8 May)).[51] Much too is made of the casualties and material damage inevitably caused when a city was captured by force. All the extant accounts have a strong anti-Persian bias. The worst possible construction is put

---

[48] Ps.S., 115.5–23; *Khuz.Chron.*, 25.4–17, trans. Nöldeke, 24–5.

[49] *Vita S. Anastasii* (cited henceforth as *V.Anast.*), cc.6–7, ed. and trans. B. Flusin, *Saint Anastase le Perse et l'histoire de la Palestine au début du VIIe siècle*, I *Les textes* (Paris, 1992), with II *Commentaire*, 221–6.

[50] Antiochus monachus S. Sabae, *Epistula ad Eustathium*, PG 89, cols.1421–8, with Flusin, *Saint Anastase*, II, 51–2 (on *Pandects*) and 177–9 (partial trans.); Strategius, ed. and trans. G. Garitte, *La Prise de Jérusalem par les Perses en 614*, CSCO 202–3, Scriptores Iberici 11–2 (Louvain, 1960) and *Expugnationis Hierosolymae AD 614 recensiones Arabicae*, CSCO 340–1 and 347–8, Scriptores Arabici 26–9 (Louvain, 1973–4); *V. Georg.*; Flusin, *Saint Anastase*, II, 155–6 for liturgical calendars.

[51] Strategius, c.8.5; ps.S, 115.28–31.

on Persian actions, as also on the role of Jews as collaborators. Given this prejudice and exaggeration, there is much sifting to be done of the materials which have been transmitted. This is absolutely essential in the case of Strategius' narrative. This has the hallmarks of propaganda, probably officially sponsored, produced for broadcasting as widely as possible, in the hope of outraging Christian opinion at home and, even more important, among Christians throughout the Sasanian Empire. Authentic material, such as the text of Zacharias' valedictory sermon and an eyewitness account of the deportation of some of the population to Mesopotamia, was combined with highly charged hagiographical material and an immensely inflated figure for the number killed, for which spurious documentation is adduced.[52]

The balance of the evidence supports the later dating of the *History of Khosrov*. The author of the *Chronicon Paschale* introduced a short lament of his own about the fall of the city, relying almost certainly on memory at the time of writing some fifteen years later. He could only give a vague date in June, presumably recalling that that was when the news reached Constantinople.[53] The date of the annual commemoration of the martyrdom of the monks of St Sabas, 16 May, is a better guide. For the death of the monks is placed a few days after the initial Beduin attack on the monastery, which was itself dated a week before the capture of Jerusalem. It follows that Jerusalem fell a day or two after 16 May.[54] Finally, there is documentary evidence from early liturgical calendars. They commemorate the Fire of Jerusalem on 17 May (the date presumably when the Persians broke in) and the Devastation of Jerusalem on 20 May (marking, it may be conjectured, the end of three days of pillaging).[55] These dates do not correspond exactly with either of those recorded in Armenia nearly two generations later in the *History of Khosrov* (18 and 19 May). If these latter dates were not already attached to different versions of the siege and sack when they went into circulation, they probably emerged in the course of oral transmission and the crossing of language frontiers. As for Strategius' earlier dating, that is very hard to explain, save as evidence of an extraordinarily cavalier attitude to the truth on the part of those who concocted the text.[56]

It is the *History of Khosrov* which again comes to the historian's rescue when confronted with the bias of the texts. It is the only source to outline the context of the siege, and thus to explain why the Persians embarked on the fraught process of attacking a city which meant so much to their Christian and Jewish subjects. The horrors of the sack can also be offset against the texts which it reproduces of

---

[52] Howard-Johnston, *Witnesses*, 164–7.   [53] *Chron.Pasch.*, 704.13–15.
[54] H. Delehaye, ed., *Synaxarium ecclesiae Constantinopolitanae, Propylaeum ad Acta Sanctorum Novembris* (Brussels, 1902), 689.7–8. Antiochus, however, puts their martyrdom a day earlier, on 15 May (cols.1424 B–C, 1425 D).
[55] Flusin, *Saint Anastase*, 155–6.   [56] Cf. Flusin, *Saint Anastase*, II, 154–8.

two letters, one an appeal for funds sent by Modestus, the acting head of the Jerusalem church, the other a polite refusal by Komitas, the Catholicos of the Armenian church. The letters, written within two or three years of the sack, give the lie to the stories of wholesale destruction and atrocities transmitted by most other sources.[57]

The real history of the Jerusalem episode is just visible, despite so much deliberate obfuscation. The circumstances are discernible. The chronology is recoverable. The sacrilegious destruction of churches can be questioned with the help of documentary sources which cast light on a Persian-sponsored programme of reconstruction. The mass slaughter, with tens of thousands killed, in the course of three days of mayhem cannot be wiped away completely, given the bloodlust likely to affect troops at the moment of triumph. But the imputation that it was encouraged by the Persian high command can be shown to be false.

Perhaps the best way to approach this dramatic episode in the war is to go to the monastery of Choziba, located just off the Jordan valley, not far from Jericho, where George, the monastery's revered holy man, and Antony, his disciple and biographer, were living as Persian armies pushed south in 613.[58]

George was one of the great men of the early seventh century—a true holy man who shunned the world and worldly praise. He immersed himself in the worship of God throughout his life, never ceasing to regard himself as polluted by sin. He was the antithesis of the activist, interventionist Theodore of Syceon, being a contemplative who spent his life mortifying the flesh and pleading with God to show mercy to his creatures. Man, he warned his fellow monks, was under insidious attack through the emotions activated from the moment that the *protoplasts* tasted of the fruit of knowledge. Thereafter no-one could rid themselves entirely of sin, even the smallest slither of which was far more dangerous than assault from without. He singled out three sins in particular: first *pleonexia*, whether appetite for food, drink, and women, or the selfish drive for gain, which might be directed at wealth, power, or fame, or the striving for achievement in the spiritual sphere; it was *pleonexia*, he said, which was the prime cause of the disputes, slanders, and violent conflicts which scarred the secular world; second, *kenodoxia*, the vainglory of monks who prided themselves on sinlessness; and, third, *aphobia*, a careless indifference to the power of God, who could, by a mere look, make the world melt away and everything upon it. Men played on earth, George said, oppressing one another, making a theatre of the church of God, and disturbing the liturgy, while all the powers of heaven were standing near and singing God's praises.[59]

---

[57] Ps.S, 116.8–121.2.
[58] D. J. Chitty, *The Desert a City* (London, 1977), 150–2; Y. Hirschfeld, *The Judean Desert Monasteries in the Byzantine Period* (New Haven, CT, 1992), 36–8, 135–6, 166–8, 207–11.
[59] V.Georg., 137.14–141.18 (c.39), 337.14–355.16 (cc.44–56).

He lived as a recluse in a cell outside the monastery. He would come in once a week, on Sunday.[60] Only the most determined of lay petitioners succeeded in penetrating the double protective shell of the monastery and his own seclusion and gained access to his spiritual guidance. Only the grimmest events in the outer world disturbed the regular rhythm of his private contemplative existence.

His first presentiments of doom probably surfaced soon after the Persians reached the Mediterranean coast toward the end of 610. He told his fellow monks of his fear and trembling at the evil coming fast upon the civilized world.[61] With the Persians established in Damascus and disturbances in the country around the monastery, he received a clearer warning. He was sitting on a rock and warming his thin frame in the sun when a voice told him to go to Jericho. He and the monks with him had reached the gardens outside the city when he stopped and stared up at the sky. There he saw Indians (south Arabians) fighting, at the same time feeling the ground shake beneath his feet. The rest of the party, unaware of this, turned back when they saw regular troops, cavalry, and infantry, and a militia armed with daggers and spears issue forth from the city. The next morning, sitting on the same rock, he saw a column of fire travel across the sky from Jerusalem to Bostra.[62]

As in the case of the lavra of St Sabas, it was not Persian military operations but the concomitant raiding by Beduin tribesmen which disrupted life at Choziba. The monks abandoned the monastery, the majority following the abbot, who sought safety in the province of Arabia, a minority going into hiding either in caves nearby or in a ravine near the monastery of Calamon. George was in this last group, which was caught by the Beduin. He alone was freed. They had seen how poor and emaciated he was and had recognized his holiness. The other monks, most of whom evaded the Beduin and only one of whom was killed, thus fared much better than the oldest and most venerable of the monks of St Sabas, who had stayed put rather than take their abbot's advice and withdraw south into the province of Arabia. The Beduin, after looting the holy vessels, were convinced that there was concealed treasure. They tortured the monks for several days and, frustrated when no one talked, slaughtered all forty-four of them.[63]

Two years later, after Beduin raiding had abated and the monks had returned to Choziba, he had a yet more terrifying vision, so grim that he dared not tell his disciple Antony about it. He never revealed what he had seen, but a clear sense of imminent doom lay behind the long sermon about the sins vitiating the spiritual efforts of monks which forms the chilling climax of Antony's biography. He died not long afterwards, thus escaping the worst of the subsequent troubles.[64]

---

[60] *V.Georg.*, 107.19–108.15 (c.12).   [61] *V.Georg.*, 116.15–118.6 (c.18).
[62] *V.Georg.*, 127.19–129.13 (c.30).
[63] *V.Georg.*, 129.14–130.11 (c.31); Antiochus, col.1424 B–C.
[64] *V.Georg.*, 134.17–136.7 (c.35–6).

By the time George was warming himself, probably in the wan winter sun, on a rock near Choziba, Heraclius' offensive had been beaten back and Persian forces had occupied Damascus. There is nothing to indicate any subsequent pause in Persian operations, which involved an advance first south to Galilee, then west to the coast at Ptolemais. The Jews of Tiberias, the hills of Galilee, and the environs of Jerusalem are reported by Eutychius (citing what Heraclius was told in 630, highly tendentious but probably not entirely fictitious) to have come out openly on their side and to have attacked local Christians and their churches. Christian refugees crowded into Ptolemais, where the Jewish community is said to have seized the opportunity to strike a blow against their Christian neighbours as well as the refugees. Again the source is suspect but unlikely to have made up the story entirely. Many Christians were killed, it reports. Churches were burned down. Abandoned Christian property was looted. The bishop's palace was broken into. Three details, perhaps embellished for propaganda purposes, made this last incident particularly shocking: an apostate priest took part in the raid, a copy of the New Testament was torn up, and six famous patristic texts were read out to mocking laughter.[65]

From Ptolemais, the Persians could extend their authority north up the coast of Phoenicia and south to Caesarea, the chief city of the Palestinian provinces. There is no record of their encountering any resistance. Caesarea was occupied and the whole of Palestine offered to submit. Shahrbaraz's army camped at Caesarea.[66]

Shahrbaraz then made contact with the local authorities in Palestine. The plan was to manage affairs from a distance, the army under his command providing any backing which might be needed in negotiation. It is only possible to follow his dealings with the authorities of Jerusalem. More delicacy may have been required than in handling other cities, but the arrangements made are unlikely to have been unique. Shahrbaraz offered to maintain the peace and prosperity of the city if the authorities would formally confirm their acceptance of Persian authority. This they did without hesitation, led by the Patriarch Zacharias. Their formal submission was accompanied by fine presents for Shahrbaraz and his senior commanders. They also invited him, assuredly not without prompting, to send in a political mission, in effect a control commission. The Persian representatives duly arrived and installed themselves.[67] Other such missions may have been dispatched to other cities, although not throughout Palestine. Jericho remained out of reach. The troops garrisoned there, some of whom came out and frightened the party of Choziba monks accompanying George that winter, were

---

[65] Eutychius, 128.9–13 (trans.108.13–20); *Doctrina Jacobi*, iv.5.16–26, v.12.12–25.
[66] Ps.S., 115.5–10; Strategius, c.3.1–3.
[67] Ps.S., 115.11–17. Cf. Strategius, c.5.8–15 who telescopes events, so that Zacharias' conciliatory stance is opposed immediately and successfully by the faction leaders.

Roman. It was also to Jericho that the Patriarch Zacharias was to appeal for help when the local agreement made by Jerusalem with the Persians broke down in spring and Shahrbaraz's army was advancing on the city.[68] The approaches to Egypt in southern Palestine and the adjoining province of Arabia were probably also outside the Persian sphere at this stage. Nicetas himself was not far away when Jerusalem fell.[69]

All was calm at first. The agreement seemed to be working. Its first serious test came soon after Easter, which fell on 30 March in 614. Easter must always have occasioned some intercommunal tension between the Christian majority and the Jews, who could be denounced as crucifiers of Christ. That year it provoked serious violence on the streets. The local factions of Blues and Greens, which had been fighting each other since the start of Zacharias' patriarchate in 609, buried their differences and joined forces to attack the Persian control commission and the Jews who had supposedly welcomed its arrival. They did so, it seems, on a formal ceremonial occasion before an assembly of the people, denouncing the agreement made with the Persians and destroying it by a single violent act, a murderous attack on the members of the Persian mission who were present. Many in the watching crowd threw in their lot with the factions. Christian feelings, already roused by stories of Jewish violence brought by refugees from Galilee and further increased by the annual reminder of the ancient antagonism between the two related faiths, burst out into the open. In the riots which followed, the Christians gained the upper hand and began a pogrom. Some Jews escaped and hastened to Caesarea to appeal for help.[70]

Shahrbaraz lost no time in mobilizing his army and advanced swiftly against Jerusalem. While Zacharias was filled with foreboding and bewailed what he saw lying in store for his flock and the holy places, the fervour of the crowd sustained spirits among the defenders. Hope even flickered in some outside observers that the Persians might be so impressed by the strength of the city's defences that they would be ready to negotiate rather than press on with a siege. Zacharias, his policy of accommodation in ruins, did what he could and sent off an emissary, Modestus, the abbot of St Theodosius, to ask the Roman force at Jericho to launch a diversionary attack.[71]

The siege began at the very end of April when the Persians surrounded the city and began to construct siege towers and artillery pieces. Inevitably, damage was caused to sites in the vicinity. The size of the Persian army deterred the Roman

---

[68] *V.Georg.*, 128.17–20; Strategius, cc.5.19–20, 7.2–3.

[69] *Chron.Pasch*, 705.3–14 for the receipt by Nicetas of two relics of the Passion, the Sponge and the Lance, and their onward dispatch to Constantinople, where they arrived in autumn 614. But see H. A. Klein, 'Niketas und das wahre Kreuz', *BZ* 94 (2001), 580–7, who redates the episode to 629 and identifies the Nicetas in question as son of the Persian general Shahrbaraz (see Nic., c.17.16–17, with Mango, 'Héraclius', 105–6, 110–12).

[70] Ps.S., 115.17–23; Strategius, cc.2.2–4, 3.6–7.   [71] Ps.S., 115.23–5; Strategius, c.5.1–20.

force summoned from Jericho, which promptly withdrew, probably south to join Nicetas. Their departure allowed the Beduin to intervene and to raid widely, which prompted a general evacuation of the monasteries in the Judaean desert immediately to the east of Jerusalem. The mood plummeted inside Jerusalem. There were premonitions of disaster outside. A monk of St Sabas had a vision first of Christ on the Cross at Golgotha, turning away from the entreaties of the faithful, and then of the church of the Holy Sepulchre awash with mud. He was killed a few days later. Two prisoners, monks from Phoenicia, were watching the city when they saw its protective angels leave under orders from above, sixteen or seventeen days into the siege. Three days later, probably on 17 May, the walls were breached by mining, by the Damascus Gate on the north-east side, and the Persians fought their way into the city.[72]

There followed three days of continuing armed action before Shahrbaraz ordered a ceasefire and issued a proclamation inviting the population to come out of hiding and guaranteeing their safety. The defenders had scattered, concealing themselves in caves and cisterns, from which they had fought on. Persian forces were undoubtedly responsible for atrocities, for starting fires which caused extensive damage, and for indiscriminate killing, as, with emotions running high, they sought out and destroyed the last pockets of resistance.[73] Most of the casualties were probably caused when they forced their way into churches, suspecting, not unreasonably, that there might be soldiers and paramilitaries among the civilian refugees crowding into them. Christian sources did everything they could to magnify the tribulations of the city—with troops running amok, wholesale destruction of monuments, and very large numbers killed—but they only documented one episode—the rape of thirty-nine nuns and the execution of one after Persian troops broke into a nunnery on the Mount of Olives.[74] The final body count is reported to have reached a horrific total—17,000 according to the *History of Khosrov* (inflated to 57,000 in the version given by Thomas Artsruni), a figure at least double that, possibly over 60,000, according to Strategius, or 90,000

---

[72] Ps.S., 115.25–31; Strategius, cc.5.21–8.6. Cf. J. Magness, 'Archaeological Evidence for the Sasanian Persian Invasion of Jerusalem', in K. G. Holum and H. Lapin, *Shaping the Middle East: Jews, Christians, and Muslims in an Age of Transition 400–800 CE* (Bethesda, MD, 2011), 85–98, at 88–94.

[73] A mass burial in a cave by the pool of Mamilla (or Maqella) outside the Jaffa Gate corroborates the massacre there reported by Strategius, c.11.2. Several hundred skeletons were found piled up in a cave which is fronted by a funerary chapel, with a mosaic inscription praying for the salvation and succour 'of those whose names the Lord knows'. The latest of the 130 coins found in the cave was a gold solidus of the Emperor Phocas (602–10). See R. Reich, '"God Knows Their Names": Mass Christian Grave Revealed in Jerusalem', *Biblical Archaeology Review*, 22.2 (1996), 26–33, 60; *Corpus inscriptionum Iudaeae/Palaestinae*, ed. H. M. Cotton et al., I.2 (Berlin, 2012), 245–6 (no.869). G. Avni, 'The Persian Conquest of Jerusalem (614 C.E.)—An Archaeological Assessment', *BASOR* 357 (2010), 35–48, at 36–40, associates six other mass burials, two north of the Damascus Gate, two on Mount Zion inside the southern wall, and two others outside the west wall in the general vicinity of the Mamilla pool, with the Persian sack of the city.

[74] Strategius, cc 8.7–9.4, 12.1–15.

according to the west Syrian historical tradition.[75] As for the churches in the city, they undoubtedly suffered considerable fire damage, but there was no question of systematic and wholesale destruction. Modestus, the acting head of the local church, was able to carry out the necessary repair and restoration work over the next few years.[76]

Shahrbaraz's troops spent twenty-one days at Jerusalem. Their principal assignment, apart from clearing up some of the damage and restoring law and order to the streets, was to screen the population. The leaders of the city, foremost among them the patriarch, and those with useful trades were selected for deportation. When the screening was completed, the whole Christian population was evacuated temporarily, the two groups, deportees and those allowed to stay, being kept separate. The latter, far more numerous than the deportees, were held at the Mamilla pool, just outside the city wall. It was a hot day and many in the tight-packed crowd were suffering from the heat, when the ringleaders of the pogrom were picked out by Jews and taken away for execution. The deportees, meanwhile, were joined by the patriarch, who later on the Mount of Olives gave a long and tearful address and then bade Jerusalem farewell. He counselled his flock against the despairing view that they had been abandoned by God, asserting rather that they were being accompanied by the full array of heavenly powers and that their suffering would give them the chance to atone for past sins.[77]

The deportees then began the long journey into exile under armed guard, initially along the direct route north past the monastery of Choziba and Jericho to Damascus. The journey seems to have been uneventful. Strategius was hard put to find evidence of brutality on the part of the military escort, apart from two incidents involving children, the 8- and 10-year-old daughters of a deacon of the church of the Anastasis (killed as was the deacon), and twin boys aged 11 (forcibly parted). The main worry of the deportees concerned their fate at the other end. Zacharias did what he could to keep up their spirits when they arrived outside Ctesiphon-Veh Ardashir and were threatened with execution if they did not trample on the cross. He organized a grand ceremony at which young boys (up to the age of 7) interceded on behalf of their sinful elders, while he prayed aloud, pleading with God to mitigate the punishment of his people, who put their hope in him. He then gave a short morale-boosting sermon, stressing God's power and

---

[75] Ps.S., 115.31–116.2; T'ovma Artsruni *Patmut'iwn Tann Artsruneats'*, ed. K. Patkanean (St Petersburg, 1887), ii.3 (89.20–1), trans. R. W. Thomson, *Thomas Artsruni: History of the House of the Artsrunik'* (Detroit, MI, 1985); Strategius, c.23 (Flusin, *Saint Anastase*, II, 160 tabulates the different body counts given in the manuscripts, which range from 33,067 to 66,509 (totals) and from 33,867 to 66,466 (calculated from breakdown by location)); Theoph., 300.31–301.1, Mich.Syr., xi.1 (403), Chron.1234, 226.25–8, trans. Hoyland, 64–5. Discussion: Flusin, *Saint Anastase*, II, 159–61.

[76] Ps.S., 116.8–13, 117.10–16, with *Hist.Com.*, n.35; Antiochus, col.1428 A–B. Cf. Flusin, *Saint Anastase*, II, 174–7; Avni, 'Persian Conquest', 41–3; Stoyanov, *Defenders and Enemies of the True Cross*, 17–21.

[77] Ps.S., 115.32–116.7; Strategius, cc.9.5–10.8 and cc.13–14 with Flusin, *Saint Anastase*, II, 161–4.

urging his listeners to show fortitude. In the event nothing untoward happened to the patriarch and the other deported leaders. They were received politely by the king and were taken under the protection of his Christian wife. The other deportees were probably resettled and put to work in Mesopotamia.[78]

3.4 Aftermath

The movements of the main body of Shahrbaraz's army are not recorded after the screening of the population (and the resulting selections) and the departure of the deportees. It seems likely, though, that it withdrew to Caesarea, its base of operations, where it would be well placed to watch over Palestine and to sustain Persian authority over the coming months. Certainly, Caesarea retained its pre-eminent position in the region during the Persian occupation. There was much to be gained from building on its existing role as a provincial capital and making it the military and administrative headquarters for the whole of the southern Levant. It was indeed in Caesarea that the *marzban*, the military governor with supreme authority, was based in the closing stages of the war, when Anastasius, a Christian convert who had served in the Persian army, set out to court martyrdom. The Persian authorities had come to stay, as was shown by the new administrative building under construction nearby. Anastasius, inspired by reading stories of the early Christian martyrs, flaunted his faith, was arrested and jailed, confronted the *marzban* in head-on disputation, refused to compromise in any way, and eventually left the authorities with no choice but to order his repatriation for trial and execution in Mesopotamia.[79]

Jerusalem seems to have been left to fend for itself. None of the extant sources reports the installation of a garrison immediately after the siege—a collective silence of some significance which is backed by a telltale reference to the 'passage' of the Persians in the Life of George and by scattered references to a period of disturbance inside and outside the city. An unusual issue of copper coins (folles), with a Jerusalem mint mark, should probably be dated to this period when the city was in limbo. The same is probably true of the hoard of 264 gold coins (solidi) found in the south wing of an administrative building in the city. All were in mint condition and struck from a pair of dies engraved with an unusual variant of the design on Heraclius' first series. Most were slightly underweight, a few overweight. It is tempting then to suppose that the mint was in Jerusalem and that it was not subject to the normal strict oversight of the empire.[80]

---

[78] Strategius, cc.15–21. Cf. Flusin, *Saint Anastase*, II, 164–72.
[79] V.Anast., cc.15–30, with commentary of Flusin, *Saint Anastase*, II, 231–43.
[80] V.Georg., c.31 (130.8–11); S. Mansfield, 'Heraclean Folles of Jerusalem', in A. Oddy, ed., *Coinage and History in the Seventh Century Near East*, 2 (Exeter, 2010), 49–55; G. Bijovsky, 'A Single Die Solidi Hoard of Heraclius from Jerusalem', *TM* 16 (2010), 55–92.

The Jews of the city staked a claim to the Temple Mount. A small sanctuary is reported to have been built on the esplanade, for the renewal of religious rites on this most sacred site—but for a few months only.[81] It was dismantled in the face of opposition from the Christian majority, backed perhaps by threats that Nicetas and the troops under his command might intervene. Outside Beduin marauders continued to prey on the settled lands fringing the desert near Jericho and Bethlehem, preventing the monks of St Sabas and Choziba from returning to their monasteries. Two months after the initial attack, hearing of more trouble, the survivors of the St Sabas community migrated in a body to the monastery of St Anastasius, just outside Jerusalem, which had been abandoned by its own monks. There they stayed for *two years*.[82] The monks of Choziba faced a double threat, from local Jews as well as Beduin raiders. Two of the three groups of refugees weathered the initial storm (those who had taken refuge in the province of Arabia and those, including George's biographer Antony, who had hidden in nearby caves). They made their way to Jericho, where they stayed for the duration of the disturbances. George, the only member of the third group to have been released after being taken prisoner near the monastery of Calamon, sat out the troubles in Jerusalem.[83]

Meanwhile an emergency aid programme was organized in Egypt, apparently on the initiative of the Chalcedonian patriarch of Alexandria, John, known as the Almsgiver. Generous funding of charitable works is the leitmotiv of his biography. A church official, Ctesippus, the supervisor of the monasteries of Ennaton, was sent out to assess the scale of the crisis and to take charge of the distribution of relief supplies. Gold (for purchases on site), bread, grain, pulses, olive oil, clothing (for monks and laity), and special foods for the sick were shipped out along with the pack animals needed to move them overland to Jerusalem and its environs. A sum of money was earmarked for the relief and rehousing of a thousand nuns, allegedly violated by the Persians. Subsidiary missions, including two led by bishops, took relief to other cities and ransomed prisoners from Beduin raiders (Ma'add).[84] The mood in Jerusalem was, not unnaturally, sombre, to judge by the prayer appended by Antiochus to the copy of his *Pandects* which he sent to his correspondent Eustathius in Galatia. He begged God to have mercy on the people of Jerusalem now that their sins had been punished and to spare them from annihilation. They were but few, like scattered leaves or mud, but they were God's handiwork, his people, and they relied on his protection.[85]

---

[81] G. Dagron and V. Déroche, 'Juifs et chrétiens dans l'Orient du VIIe siècle', *TM* 11 (1991), 17–273, at 26–8.
[82] Antiochus, col.1425 A-B.   [83] *V.Georg.*, c.31 (129.14–130.11).
[84] *Vita S. Ioannis (epitome)*, ed. E. Lappa-Zizicas, 'Un épitomé de la Vie de S. Jean l'Aumônier par Jean et Sophronios', *An.Boll.* 88 (1970), 265–78, at c.9.7–26.
[85] Antiochus, cols.1849–56.

It seems that Shahrbaraz had a strictly limited purpose when he intervened—to stop the pogrom and to cleanse the city of its political leadership and the refractory elements which had caused the trouble. His withdrawal is intelligible, given the problem of the Beduin. The old Roman system of client management, which had been reinstated in the late sixth century and which channelled favours of several sorts to a limited number of tribal leaders, had broken down by late 613. Before Palestine could be occupied, security had to be re-established in the *badiya*, with the aid of one or more tribal leaders picked out as prime clients by the Persian authorities. There was also a political advantage in returning to a policy of watching and waiting. A time of troubles would concentrate minds in a province which could no longer look to the Roman authorities for law and order in the cities and for defence against the Beduin. Such antagonism as was felt by urban notables and people towards the Persians would diminish when the only realistic hope of a return to normality was offered by Shahrbaraz's army.

In the course of the months which followed, the Persians prepared the ground for a peaceful takeover. Nothing is known of the negotiations which went on with Beduin leaders, and virtually nothing of the new system of client management put in place, save that it involved the rehabilitation of the Jafnid-led Ghassan, who had fallen foul of the Roman authorities in the 570s and 580s.[86] A year, possibly two years elapsed before the Persians returned to Jerusalem, took control of Palestine, and restored law and order. Only after this had been achieved, was it safe for the monks to return to their monasteries in the Judaean desert, a move sanctioned by the Zacharias' deputy, Modestus, two years and two months after the fall of Jerusalem (so in July 616).[87]

The whole of Christendom took note of events in Palestine. Chroniclers, contemporary and near-contemporary, from Spain in the far west to lower Mesopotamia and Armenia in the Sasanian Empire, recorded the capture of Jerusalem. Their notices were, on the whole, short and to the point. But before long, the bare narrative was embellished, as a result both of a natural process of elaboration in the course of transmission and of a conscious effort by the Roman authorities to blacken their enemies. It took time, however, for anecdotes to attach themselves to the main story. Shocked at the news from Palestine and aware of the complex and discreditable circumstances surrounding the attack on Jerusalem, officialdom first responded by striving to raise morale in and near Constantinople, at a time when a renewed assault on Asia Minor was awaited with foreboding. A notice about the most notable of these efforts is included in the *Chronicon Paschale*. At the beginning of Lent 615, a new chant was introduced into the liturgy of St Sophia to accompany the entry of the presanctified offerings. The congregation proclaimed that the powers of heaven were present and were

---

[86] See Chapter 6.   [87] Antiochus, col.1425 A–B.

joining in the liturgy. This encapsulated one of the themes of the Patriarch Zacharias' sermon to the deportees from Jerusalem, that their supernatural protectors would accompany them wherever they were taken. For the congregation in Constantinople the effect was probably no less heartening.[88]

The first tentative move to make propaganda out of the fall of Jerusalem was made around the same time. A new silver coin, the hexagram, was issued, bearing on the reverse the image of a cross on a globe on steps, together with an appeal to God for help ('Deus adiuta Romanis') (Figure 5). The new iconography had a mundane function, to justify an austerity measure introduced at the time, the halving of all state salaries, by emphasizing to the recipients the gravity of the crisis facing the Christian empire. But it conveyed a clear propaganda message too. The cross as the symbol of Christian victory was to inspire Romans in the dark times which lay ahead, like the new chant and two additions to the capital's celestial armoury, the Sponge and Lance which had apparently been smuggled out of Jerusalem and were sent on by Nicetas, arriving in autumn 614.[89] It also carried a double reference, to the great bejewelled cross at Golgotha standing on the Calvary steps and to the *globus cruciger*, which symbolized imperial rule.[90] The image of the cross thus simultaneously affirmed the faith and the political claims of the Roman Empire. It also referred indirectly to the True Cross itself, the fragments of which the Persians had removed together with other treasures from Jerusalem, and thereby broached a theme which was later to dominate Roman propaganda as the war approached its climax—namely that Romans fought primarily as Christians, that they would avenge the sacking of their holy city, and that they would recover the fragments of the True Cross which they treasured above all other relics.

The reaction in Jerusalem and its environs took a rather different form, to judge by the main body of Strategius' text, composed probably in the hiatus between the fall of the city and the Persians' occupation of Palestine. Attention was concentrated on the sufferings of the inhabitants of the city and of its buildings, frontal attacks being launched on Persian behaviour. The removal of church plate from the city and the transfer of the fragments of the True Cross to the care of devout—albeit Nestorian—Christians in Mesopotamia was of little concern. Loss of the Cross only became a central element in the tragic story of Jerusalem in 614 after several years of sustained propaganda from the centre—in the 620s, when the metropolitan and Palestinian themes coalesced, with an additional detail about the use of torture to discover where the True Cross was hidden, and were picked up in Mesopotamian church circles.[91]

---

[88] *Chron.Pasch.*, 705.18–706.8 (with an erroneous indiction date).
[89] *Chron.Pasch.*, 705.3–14. Cf. note 69 of this chapter.
[90] *Chron.Pasch.*, 706.9–11; Grierson, *DOC* II.1, 17–18, 95–9, 225, 270–4.
[91] *Khuz.Chron.*, 25.8–10, trans. Nöldeke, 24.

Four years after their initial breakthrough, the Persians had consolidated their position of strategic and political dominance in the Middle East. North of the Taurus, they had pushed on across the Euphrates and, in a dramatic move (probably intended to shock and demoralize their adversaries), had seized Caesarea in Cappadocia. Their year-long blockade there (611–12) need not have been construed as a setback. For Caesarea drew Roman attention away from western Armenia, where they could establish firm control of the formidable mountain ranges separating the Euphrates and Arsanias catchment areas and the adjoining hills and plains. To the south, the thin salient stretching west to the lower Orontes and the coast beyond Antioch seized in 610–11 was enlarged. The Roman counteroffensive in 613 failed. Despite the commitment of all available troops, the personal involvement of the two leading figures in the new regime, the emperor himself and his cousin Nicetas, and a well-worked strategy of coordinated attacks from west and south, Shahrbaraz's army was able to stand its ground and to drive the Romans back. By the end of the year, Persian control reached the southern foothills of the Taurus in the north-west and northern Palestine in the south. The salient had grown and taken over half of the Roman Levant, giving Persian forces the necessary depth of terrain for effective defence, should the Romans return to the attack by land or sea.

The strategic advantage of inner lines which the Romans had enjoyed between 591 and 602, with their command of the full length of the Armenian Taurus, had been seized by the Persians. The broad swathe of territory which they held, stretching from the great curve of the Euphrates to the Jebel Hawran, divided the Roman Empire in two. It provided Persian forces with a large platform from which to launch attacks either north-west, across the Taurus, into Asia Minor, or south into Palestine, with Egypt lurking beyond as a temptingly rich target. The initiative in choosing where to strike lay with them. For while they could make use of the Roman road network to transfer troops swiftly between fronts, the Romans would have to rely on sea transport, which was slower, less efficient, because of the limited capacity of shipping, and not entirely free of hazard.

Whatever his plans may have been for 614, Shahrbaraz's hand was forced when trouble erupted in Jerusalem. After dealing with it, he went back to Caesarea, presumably to take stock of the situation in the Levant and to seek instructions from Khusro's government in Ctesiphon. For he was confronted by a very serious problem—open hostility between Christians and Jews in Palestine. This had shown itself not just on the streets of Jerusalem, but also in Galilee, where Persian forces were welcomed by the Jews, and on the Phoenician coast, where a planned assault under cover of darkness on the Christians of Tyre was discovered and thwarted.[92] The government had to be consulted on policy in Palestine and

---

[92] Eutychius, 121.10–122.8 (trans.101–2).

Phoenicia, because of the inevitable repercussions on the large and influential Jewish and Christian communities in Mesopotamia. It was absolutely vital to foster good relations between the two monotheist faiths in what was the administrative and economic heartland of the Sasanian Empire. The government could not afford to alienate the large, tight-knit community of Babylonian Jewry, but at the same time it needed to attend to Christian public opinion in the Roman Levant. Stability in the occupied territories and hopes of further gains depended to a large extent on the Persian authorities obtaining the tacit consent of Christians to their presence, actual or prospective. Any action which might flaunt their alien religious as well as political system or which might be construed as serving Jewish interests would damage their position in provinces already under their control and would harden resistance in those which they planned to attack in future. It would also cause all Christian sects to close ranks and thus deprive them of their principal hope for securing their support in the medium term, which was to cultivate support among Monophysites.[93]

The second half of 614 passed by without further notable action on the part of Persian forces in the Middle East. This gave the Romans an opportunity to begin the process of shoring up public opinion at home and of bolstering Roman prestige abroad. The latter was by far the harder task. There was no disguising the scale of the disaster suffered in the Holy Land in 614. The damage done in the ideological sphere was virtually irreparable. The Roman Empire, with its wealth and centuries of hegemony over the Mediterranean world and its north European hinterland, had been pulled down for a while from the higher plane of earthly rule on which it had operated hitherto. Its special position as God's single authorized agent for regulating earthly affairs came into serious question.[94] The rulers of the Germanic peoples who had established themselves on Roman territory and had co-opted local sub-Roman elites into their governing systems could begin to emancipate themselves from a world view which had them gaze up at imperial Roman power. The consequences of this ideological shift involved changes of political attitude and brought into question the status quo on the ground. Yet graver were the consequences for the Balkans. The Avars, restrained merely by the terms of the treaty made with Phocas rather than by respect for a divinely sanctioned empire, began to stir up the Slav tribes already settled in the Balkans and thus to initiate a new phase of migration and disturbance.[95]

Persian military success thus gravely weakened the geopolitical position of the Roman Empire, both in the Middle East, where it was cut in two, and in the west, where its standing was undermined. The only offsetting gains for the Romans

---

[93] See Chapter 5.2.
[94] G. Fowden, *Empire to Commonwealth: Consequences of Monotheism in Late Antiquity* (Princeton, NJ, 1993), 86–93.
[95] See Chapter 6.2.

came in the ideological sphere. Defeat, death, loss of territory, deportation, economic degradation, etc. could be taken as evidence that God was punishing his people for their sins and that, with expiation close at hand, not only would the way to salvation open up but also defeat would yield place to victory in this world.[96] Much too could be made of Roman suffering, especially that of the population of Jerusalem. On a higher literary plane, the great poet George of Pisidia strove in the 620s to transform the great power conflict into a war of religion, between good and evil empires, between Christians who identified and worshipped the true God and idolatrous, blaspheming dualists.[97]

The Roman authorities could hope to inflame Christian opinion everywhere—in the west, in the occupied Roman provinces, inside the Sasanian Empire, and, of course, at home—by portraying the Persians as brutal oppressors of Christians and desecrators of the holy places. Divisive propaganda of this sort could be pumped out and the Persians would not be able to reply in kind. For theirs was not a confessional state. Performance of Zoroastrian rites was vital for its security and welfare, but was not conditional on the suppression of other religions. Zoroastrianism was the established religion, but it was not exclusive. Christianity, in its Nestorian and Monophysite forms, and Judaism were accepted as licit faiths, the leaders of which had direct contact with the secular authorities and were indeed appointed by the king in the case of Nestorian and Monophysite catholicoi.[98]

So the Sasanian authorities could not counter this barrage of propaganda with diatribes of their own. Nor could they set about denying or discrediting the lies and canards issuing forth from Roman sources. If they did so, they were all too likely to contribute to their dissemination yet farther afield. They simply had to endure their enemy's verbal fire and to respond quietly with deeds. A policy of even-handed treatment of Christians and Jews and of respect for sacred places and revered objects of other faiths was the only feasible option. It might well take time to work.

---

[96] Cf. the reassuring sermon of the Patriarch Zacharias to the deportees outside Jerusalem (Strategius, c.13).

[97] Mary Whitby, 'A New Image for a New Age: George of Pisidia on the Emperor Heraclius', in E. Dąbrowa, ed., *The Roman and Byzantine Army in the East* (Cracow, 1994), 197–225, at 212–18.

[98] J. Wiesehöfer, *Ancient Persia from 550 BC to 650 AD* (London, 1996), 199–216; S. Shaked, *Dualism in Transformation: Varieties of Religion in Sasanian Iran* (London, 1994), 99–115.

4
Khusro's Fateful Decision

Gloom, unrelieved gloom must have settled upon Heraclius' government during the lull in operations over the winter of 614–15. Immense damage had been inflicted on the morale, manpower, and financial resources of the empire. In spite of the change of regime, in spite of Heraclius' skills as a military commander, the roll call of successive defeats had not come to an end. Future defensive operations, even where aided by the Taurus Mountains and the desert, would only slow the steady encroachment of Persia on the territories still controlled by Constantinople. Indeed, as the empire's resource base was reduced with each successive advance, the strain of sustaining the war effort would grow and grow.

The financial crisis was in danger of escalating out of control. The cost of shoring up a vulnerable position in the Balkans might well become insupportable if the Avars were to decide to intervene in force. In Italy too, where relations had soured after the failed offensives of Maurice, the temptation for the Lombards to take advantage of patent Roman weakness must have been growing year by year. So far the danger had been averted. In the Balkans, the Avars had continued to observe the peace agreed with Phocas in 603. Small groups of Slavs may have been percolating south, but there was no large-scale movement into hitherto uncolonized Roman territory. In Italy too, the Lombards did not break the treaty of 605, despite the weakness of local Roman forces. But the deterrent effect of imperial status could not but diminish in the light of news from the east. The delicate balance between Roman authorities and both main Lombard groupings (in the Po valley and in the central Apennines) was unlikely to last much longer, just as Avar restraint was liable to lapse.

Only one course of action offered hope for Heraclius' government. A deal must be struck with the Persians. Large concessions would have to be offered, larger ones still agreed, to achieve an armistice or peace of some sort in the east. But almost any price would be worth paying to avert an event which almost certainly would doom the empire to extinction. If Egypt were to go the way of western Armenia, northern Mesopotamia, and Syria, if its immense resources were to be transferred from the Roman to the Persian side, all would be lost. Roman authority would begin to collapse in the Balkans. The Lombards would set about establishing their hegemony throughout Italy. Asia Minor would come under attack, forced to rely on its own steadily diminishing resources and what could be extracted from Africa and the Mediterranean islands. The defenders would be forced back and back until, eventually, Constantinople would be isolated and ready for the taking.

But peace appeared to be out of reach. It was impossible to communicate with the Persian government by conventional diplomatic means. The execution of the ambassadors who had brought news of Heraclius' accession had made it clear that death was the fate awaiting any new Roman delegation. The Romans could only cling to forlorn hopes—that a victory, small or large, might be won and miraculously might begin to shift the balance of advantage, that the Persians might become bogged down in a long battle for Egypt, that faith might raise the morale and fighting capacity of the defenders of Egypt and Asia Minor, or that insurrection in the occupied territories might distract Persian forces and give some relief. In short, they must pray for God to intervene in earthly affairs and to aid his people.

Meanwhile, economy measures were needed, if the war was to be carried on for the foreseeable future. The empire's reduced resources must be eked out. Early in 615, probably in Lent, when minds were more amenable to austerity, it was announced that imperial salaries would be halved. They were to be paid, at least in part, in heavy silver coins, hexagrams weighing six scruples (6.82 g) and worth two siliquae or a twelfth of a solidus on the traditional gold:silver ratio of 1:18.[1] Introduction of the hexagram served several purposes: it provided a valuable supplement to the gold coinage, enabling the state to fund part of its expenditure out of hitherto untapped stocks of silver bullion; it softened the blow of the salary cuts, since the recipients now received six coins in place of one on that portion of their salaries paid in silver; and it justified the cuts by the messages carried on the coins, alluding as they did to the gravity of the crisis.[2]

The hexagram not only demonstrates, by its entry into the monetary system, the extent of the fiscal strain affecting the empire, but also points, by its fabric, to bureaucratic stress. Traditional high standards of craftsmanship were abandoned in its production. The flans were usually irregular in shape. The striking was slovenly, so that inscriptions might run off the flan or fail to register properly.[3] A similar slackening of standards can be discerned in the minting of copper. Overstriking of earlier issues became the norm in the early years of Heraclius (it was, of course, cheaper than making fresh flans), to be followed, from 616, by a steady decline in the weight of the follis.[4]

What military and naval preparations were made for 615 can only be guessed at. Recent experience, over the last two campaigning seasons, might suggest that the Persians would concentrate their main effort in the south. So too would

---

[1] *Chron.Pasch.*, 706.9–11; P. Yannopoulos, *l'Hexagramme. Un Monnayage byzantin en argent du VIIe siècle* (Louvain, 1978); Grierson, *DOC*, II. 1, 17–18.
[2] Grierson, *Catalogue*, 10–11, 221–3, 225.   [3] Grierson, *Catalogue*, 17–18, 98–9, 115–16, 225.
[4] From an average 11 g, maintained until 615, down to 5.8 g, by the later 620s (Grierson, *Catalogue*, 22–4, 225–8).

knowledge of the comparative vulnerability of Egypt, lacking as it did a continuous mountain or water frontage which could act as a forward line of defence.

4.1 The Senate's Letter

In the event, the Persians struck in the north and caught the Romans somewhat off guard. Asia Minor was invaded from an unexpected quarter, not over the relatively easy Armenian approaches but from northern Syria across the strongest sector of the natural mountain rampart fronting the interior plateau. The obvious objective would have been to establish a bridgehead beyond the Taurus Mountains, close to firmly held territory in Cilicia and therefore relatively easy to resupply and reinforce. This would have provided the Persians with a base from which to begin the systematic, step-by-step conquest of the plateau, its fringing mountains, and the plains beyond. But that was not Shahen's objective. His plan of campaign was to cut diagonally across Asia Minor (probably using the Romans' main military road, as it were reversing its thrust) and to take control of the Asian shore of the Bosporus within sight of Constantinople itself.

Of the two great generals who had led the victorious Persian armies in previous campaigns, it was Shahen, with more experience than his colleague Shahrbaraz of the northern theatre of war, who was appointed to command the expeditionary force in 615.[5] While his movements leave little doubt about his immediate objective, questions can and should be asked about the underlying aims of the campaign. For the appearance of a Persian army on the Bosporus could not, of itself, bring about the fall of the Roman capital. For that to be a realistic aim, a large fleet must be mobilized to ferry the army across the straits and to provision it over the many months which it would take to force the city into submission. But of ships serving the Persian cause there was no sign in 615, when Shahen reached the Bosporus. His prime aim, if it were not to make a military gain within Asia Minor, was surely political—to administer a violent shock to the Roman body politic by demonstrating its weakness in the most visible way possible, in the hope of precipitating a putsch against Heraclius and his regime. A spectacular attack on Asia Minor would serve an additional strategic purpose: it would draw Roman attention to the north and act as a diversionary operation on a grand scale before the invasion of Egypt.

Nothing is said in the sources about the timing of Shahen's invasion or the date at which he arrived within sight of Constantinople. Much, though, is reported of

---

[5] *Chron.Pasch.*, 706.11–13; *V.Anast.*, c.8.1–3; Nic., c.6.1–3, 7–9 (L c.6.1–3, 6–7); Theoph., 301.15–16. *Contra* ps.S., 122.9–11, who here conflates into a single account two Persian advances to the Bosporus, that of Shahen in 615 and that of Shahrbaraz in 626, and makes the latter the commander of the combined episode.

his dealings with the Roman authorities once his forces were safely installed in and around the city of Chalcedon. For there were some unusual occurrences. The emperor went to extraordinary lengths to conciliate the invaders. Rich presents were sent across to Shahen and his senior commanders. The financially stricken treasury yielded up substantial cash sums for Heraclius to distribute as *roga* (pay) to the Persian troops (consisting perhaps mainly of hexagrams, since the Persians were used to silver currency). The whole army, officers and men, was then entertained to a series of feasts spread over seven days.[6] Then Heraclius took a bold step, one fraught with danger, because it entailed a public admission of Roman weakness. He crossed over and engaged Shahen in direct talks. Desperate measures were needed to reopen communications. None could be more desperate than for the emperor to plead for peace in person.

The summit meeting took place in the harbour of Chalcedon. Heraclius stayed on board the boat which had brought him across, accompanied by representatives of the Senate and a large armed escort on other vessels. Some clear water was left between the emperor's boat and the shore, but not so much as to impede the exchanges between the two principals.[7] This encounter, the first of three such striking meetings to occur in the second half of the great war, impressed contemporary and later writers. One of the longer notices in the last section of the *Chronicon Paschale* is devoted to the episode, most of it taken up by the verbatim reproduction of the formal document drafted after the negotiations by the Roman side. The *History of Khosrov* too was well aware of the importance of the episode, of which it gives a relatively full account. The Roman negotiating position is outlined in a speech delivered by Heraclius from the boat. Although the speech may be a historiographical construct, a convenient, conventional medium for summarizing what was said, the text of the document preserved in the *Chronicon Paschale* provides ample confirmation that its general thrust accurately represents the Roman negotiating position. The episode is also reported, less accurately, by Nicephorus.[8]

What could Heraclius offer the Persians to entice them into opening negotiations? His argument that God could halt their offensive whenever he chose and that he would eventually choose to do so, once he had punished the Romans enough for their sins, would not cut much ice in the light of recent experience, especially as Zoroastrians reckoned that it was they, not monotheist Christians, who had a true understanding of the disposition of powers in the cosmos and better access to supernatural forces.[9] A second (historical) argument, citing the forbearance shown by Maurice when he restored Khusro II to the Sasanian throne, was unlikely to be much more persuasive, since the Romans had

---

[6] Ps.S., 122.12–16; TA, 89.35–90.7.
[7] *Chron.Pasch.*, 706.13–17; ps.S., 122.17–18; TA, 90.7–8; Nic., c.6.9–15 (L c.6.7–12).
[8] Ps.S., 122.18–123.6; TA, 90.8–91.9; Nic., cc.6.15–7.4 (L cc.6.13–7.1).   [9] Ps.S., 122.19–24.

exacted a heavy price for their services at that time, one which had been much resented by the Persians.[10] Territorial concessions, involving the transfer of great walled cities, and open-ended offers of treasure (which might be taken as indicating a willingness to pay over large sums as regular tribute) were more attractive, but something more would have to be offered, since land and booty were there for the taking and the military effort involved in doing so was unlikely to induce the food shortages and fiscal strain in Sasanian lands envisaged by Heraclius.

The concessions made by Heraclius to induce Khusro to talk in the hope of halting the fighting, if only for a limited period, have to be disinterred from the wordy prose of a letter drafted for the Senate after the summit meeting. It is a quite extraordinary document, obsequious and pleading, which deserves to be quoted in full.[11] We have to pinch ourselves to remember that it was the *Roman Senate* which was making this grovelling plea for peace, the Senate which, centuries earlier, had presided over the conquest of the Mediterranean world and which, in the centuries of imperial rule, had counted all the great and the good of the Roman world among its members. Let us listen then to what the Senate said:

> God, who fashioned all things and sustains them with his power, bestowed upon mankind as a gift worthy of his goodness the providence of empire, by means of which we are deemed worthy of an undisturbed existence or, if we encounter difficulties, find a remedy. Looking to this divine thing, namely imperial providence, and, above all else, to Your Superabundant Clemency, we beseech you to deem us worth of pardon for daring to have recourse to Your Might in this manner, contrary to the arrangement formerly in place. For we are familiar with the custom prevailing in the past, which, when some dispute sprang up between the two states, encouraged both their rulers to resolve the points of dispute through diplomatic communications with each other. But that conspirator against the Roman state, Phocas, flouted this procedure. For, after his covert corruption of the Roman army in Thrace, he suddenly attacked our imperial city and *killed our pious emperor Maurice, and his wife, and in addition his children, relatives, and several high officials.* And he was not satisfied with all these evil deeds, but did not even show the respect due to Your Superabundant Clemency, so that thereafter, driven to take action by our sins, *You brought the affairs of the Roman state to this great diminution.*
>
> Observing what was done by that destructive figure, he who now reigns piously over us and his father of eternal memory planned to liberate the Roman state from the distress caused by that man. This they achieved, although they

---

[10] Ps.S., 122.34–123.2.
[11] *Chron.Pasch.*, 707.1–709.23. The translation given here is freer than that of Michael and Mary Whitby, *Chronicon Paschale 284–628 AD*, 160–2. The italics are mine.

found the state humbled by Your Might. Once the usurper was dead, our emperor wished to take his relatives and return to his own father in Africa, urging us to select whom we wanted as emperor. He was with difficulty induced by our pleas to accept the imperial power. *He had no opportunity to do what ought to have been done, namely to send an embassy to pay due respect to the Superabundant Might of Your Serenity, because of the disturbance prevailing in the two states, as well as civil war.*

That is the reason why we decided to disregard the custom which we mentioned above and, although insignificant men, to petition a high king of such stature, by dispatching some from among us who should be judged worthy of coming into Your Presence. We did not dare do this until now, *because of the intervening events.* When, however, Shahen, the most glorious *babmanzadago*, commander of the Persian army, came to the region of Chalcedon, met our most pious emperor and ourselves, and was asked by all for peace talks, he said that he did not have the authority himself, but that he would refer the request to Your Philanthropy. He has now sent us a reply by the hand of the *spadavar, promising on oath that Your Superabundant Might will receive those dispatched by us in the proper manner and will release them unharmed to return to us*, and that the order for this to be done came from Your Philanthropy. Putting our trust in what has thus transpired and, above all, in God and Your Majesty, we, in our turn, have sent off your slaves Olympius the most glorious former consul, patrician, and praetorian prefect, Leontius the most glorious former consul, patrician, and city prefect, and Anastasius the most God-loved presbyter and *syncellus. We plead that they be received as is proper by Your Superabundant Might, and that they return speedily to us*, securing for us the peace which is pleasing to God and appropriate to Your Peace-Loving Might.

We beg too of Your Clemency to accept Heraclius, our most pious emperor, as a true son, one who is eager to perform the service of Your Serenity in all things. For if you do this, you will procure a twofold glory for yourself, both from your valour in war and from your gift of peace. It will be through your ever-remembered gifts that we shall enjoy tranquillity henceforth. We will seize every opportunity to offer prayers to God for your long-lasting prosperity and will ensure that your benefaction is saved from oblivion for as long as the eternal Roman state endures.

The stream of submissive forms of address makes this a shamefully ingratiating letter. The purpose was presumably similar to that of the individual, who, by repeatedly dropping a first name into a conversation, suggests a considerable degree of intimacy and hopes to engender it. Care was taken to avoid raising awkward matters, as can be seen in the italicized passages. So the claims of Theodosius backed by the Sasanians are neither accepted nor denied. The phrasing—the reference to the death of Maurice's sons, not *all* his sons—leaves the question open. The Romans also had to skirt around the fate of the ambassadors who had been sent off to announce Heraclius' accession late in 610 and had been executed by the Persians. No excuse must be given for Khusro to cut off diplomatic contact again. Hence the vague reference to disturbances which impeded communication between the two states at the time of Heraclius' accession, and the insistence that the three high-ranking ambassadors who were setting off in 615 be treated properly and be allowed to return home. No attempt was made to disguise the scale of Roman defeat, although it is expressed in rather abstract terms ('this great diminution').

The last of the italicized passages touches delicately on the large, substantive concession which the Romans were ready to make. Khusro was being told that his principal war aim was achievable by negotiation. The Senate did, of course, argue that Heraclius had avenged the deaths of Khusro's benefactor and his family and that he should be allowed to remain on the throne. But it did not preclude the installation of Maurice's eldest son, Theodosius, whether genuine claimant or impostor, as Roman emperor. For they acknowledged the right of Khusro to place whomsoever he would on the imperial throne. They simply advocated Heraclius' candidacy and made it plain that he would look up to Khusro, from a position of inferiority (as son to father) and would do his bidding. In effect, the Senate, acting as mouthpiece for the emperor, was agreeing at the outset of negotiations that the diminished Roman Empire should be subordinated to the Sasanian Empire and that the Persian king should be able to install an emperor of his choice. The political shock delivered by Shahen had evidently been extreme. There was no need for a putsch, since the emperor was ready to resign his power and allow the Persian king to transform what remained of the Roman Empire into a client state. The Romans had been brought very low. Humiliating terms had to be offered in order to open negotiations. Worse still would be required of them were those negotiations to result in an agreement.[12]

At the time of their meeting, Shahen neither accepted nor rejected Heraclius' proposal that peace negotiations should begin. He explained that he did not have authority to deal with a matter of this importance and must refer it to Khusro. This he did, leaving the Romans to wait for weeks, perhaps months, to discover whether or not Heraclius' self-abasement would have its intended effect and communications would be restored.[13] Since clear indications of the timing of subsequent events cannot be extracted from the sources, a fair amount of guesswork is involved in piecing the story together.

Another of those saints' lives which convey the feel of the past rather better than most historical texts, the Life of Anastasius the Persian, supplies a vital piece

---

[12] Cf. Ps.S., 122.28–9; TA, 90.21–4.
[13] *Chron.Pasch.*, 708.18–709.1; TA, 91.9–12. *Contra* Nic., c.6.43–53 (L c.6.18–22), who has Shahen invite Heraclius to send the embassy straight away.

of information. In 615 Anastasius was serving in the cavalry under Shahen when news came that a Roman army was operating far to the rear of the Persian expeditionary force. The Roman general, Philippicus, had been brought out of retirement in 612 at the time of Priscus' dismissal and had been assigned, jointly with Heraclius' brother Theodore, the command of the army of Oriens. Some details about his movements are given by the *History of Khosrov* in a passage which has become detached from the account of the summit meeting but should follow on from it. Philippicus' base of operations was Caesarea of Cappadocia. He marched into the heart of Persarmenia, to the plain of Vałarshapat within easy striking distance of Dvin. There he encamped, waiting for the news of his presence (and of any damage that his troops were doing) to have the desired effect on the Persian high command.

We are not told how long this took, but as soon as Khusro heard of this Roman counter-thrust, he sent orders by high-speed couriers for Shahen to return and intercept Philippicus. Shahen therefore had no choice but to leave Chalcedon forthwith, whether or not he had received a reply about Heraclius' proposal. He marched east, driving his troops hard. Philippicus stayed provocatively still until Shahen entered the same province of Ayrarat and camped on the banks of the Araxes. Then, with Shahen within a day's march of the Roman camp, Philippicus set off at high speed, taking a route which first curved north behind Mount Aragats and then ran west through the districts of Shirak and Vanand, passing not far from Persian-held Theodosiopolis. The Persian army, depleted and exhausted by its long route march east, was in no condition to set off in pursuit. Instead Shahen halted a number of days, allowing his men to recuperate, and then marched south to Syria, to his base camp. This was the end of the campaign. The army dispersed. Presumably winter was not far off.[14]

Philippicus' diversionary campaign was well executed and succeeded in relieving the pressure on the metropolitan region of the Roman Empire. But certain risks were entailed. A demonstration of the military capability still possessed by the Romans might strengthen their bargaining position in peace negotiations, but only if such negotiations were set in train. There was a danger that Khusro might change his mind, if he had been inclined to negotiate, or might rescind a decision to that effect, if it had been taken. In the event, there was no untoward side-effect and a message was conveyed to the Romans that Khusro would entertain peace proposals. Shahen, remained the intermediary, and sent the *spadadavar* to Constantinople. There was evidently one precondition. Khusro refused to negotiate with Heraclius. He would only deal with the Senate, which had been represented at the summit meeting with Shahen.

---

[14] *V.Anast.*, c.8.3–4; ps.S., 114.1–26; TA, 91.12–13; Nic., c.2.55–61 (L c.2.52–4). Cf. Flusin, *Saint Anastase*, 88–93; *PLRE*, III, 'Philippicus 3'.

Winter may already have been approaching when the three senior figures chosen to represent the Senate, the praetorian prefect Olympius, the prefect of the city Leontius, and Anastasius, the church official responsible for relations with the secular authorities, set off, doubtlessly with some trepidation. Shahen was, it appears, responsible for ensuring that the ambassadors were conveyed safely to the Sasanian court. His emissary, the *spadadavar*, was probably charged with escorting them. They arrived in due course and handed over the presents which they had brought.[15]

At this point the thin stream of reliable information gives out. Nothing is said about the course of negotiations—how long they lasted, what the Roman tactics were, what were the sticking points on each side, or why they broke down. But break down sooner or later they did, and, in spite of the guarantees given by the Persians and the insistent pleas of the Senate that they be honoured, the ambassadors were not released and allowed to return to Constantinople. Nicephorus gives a little more detail about what lay in store for them. They were better treated than their immediate predecessors, but their fate was still a grim one. They were arrested and sent to separate prisons, where they were detained for the rest of their lives. Leontius, the prefect of the city, died of natural causes before the end of the war. Olympius, the praetorian prefect, and Anastasius, the patriarch's *syncellus*, lived longer but were put to death as the war reached its final climax in December 627–January 628.[16] Their executions took the brutal form of crucifixion, which had hitherto been reserved for use against Nestorian Christians accused of public disturbances or apostasy.[17]

So Heraclius' second attempt to open a channel of communication to the Persian court came to nought. The peace for which he and the Senate were ready to pay almost any price was removed from their grasp and was to remain out of reach for the rest of the war. Heraclius had shown clearly that he was willing to resign the throne if that would end the war. The Senate had reiterated that offer in expressing its readiness to accept a client ruler of Khusro's choice (and refrained from claiming divine sanction for Heraclius' seizure of power).[18] Territory and treasure, both in large quantities, were plainly on offer.[19] Khusro was, therefore, in a position to realize all his war aims: recognition of Sasanian suzerainty; the appointment of Maurice's eldest son, Theodosius, as Roman emperor; regular, large annual tributary payments by way of war reparations; material acknowledgement of Roman subjection; and massive territorial gains, both north and south of the Taurus. Quite how extensive these might have been can only be conjectured, but it seems not unreasonable to suppose that the Senate was

---

[15] *Chron.Pasch.*, 709.1–14; Nic., c.7.1–12 (L c.7.1–6); Theoph., 301.21–2.
[16] Ps.S., 123.5–9; TA, 91.14–16; Nic., cc.7.12–15, 20–2 (L c.7.8–9, 14–15), and 15.25–9.
[17] Flusin, *Saint Anastase*, 120–6.   [18] *Chron.Pasch.*, 707.22–708.9.
[19] TA, 90.26–31.

prepared to offer something along the following lines: all those provinces already held by the Persians—western Armenia, northern Mesopotamia, and northern Syria; and some additional forward positions which would act as bridgeheads for watching and controlling what remained of the empire—say Lazica (giving access to the Black Sea), Satala and Nicopolis (key positions on the northern support road), Melitene (controlling a strategic Euphrates crossing and opening the way to Cappadocia), Cilicia and perhaps the Cilician Gates (giving direct access to the interior plateau), and southern Syria and Palestine (from which Egypt could be monitored).

The Romans had to offer concessions as large as these if there were to be any realistic chance of reaching an agreement. To backtrack at all from their initial negotiating position, as outlined by Heraclius and indicated in the Senate's letter, would inevitably lead to the breakdown of talks, which would in turn doom the Roman Empire to gradual dismemberment over the next few years. Proposals along these lines presented Khusro with gains exceeding anything he could have dreamed of in 603. His prestige within the Sasanian Empire would be immeasurably enhanced by the Romans' open acknowledgement of his suzerainty and by annual inflows of tribute, some of which he might recycle as gold and silver plate and give out in donatives to the leading personnel of his realms. The territorial gains should ensure that the new relationship would last, since the Roman Empire would remain easy prey if ever it gave cause for displeasure. The strategic advantages which the Persians would now enjoy far outstripped those which Maurice had gained for the Romans in 591: divided in two, with Persian bridgeheads threatening both Asia Minor and Egypt, the Roman Empire would be impossible to defend against an adversary who could concentrate his forces at will against one or other of its major components.

Khusro's decision, taken in the winter of 615–16, to make no response at all and to incarcerate the Roman ambassadors was tantamount to a decision to liquidate the Roman Empire. His subsequent actions make it plain that this was indeed his intention. But what, the historian must ask, were his reasons for setting about the destruction of the long-established international order when hegemony over it was already within his grasp? Why on earth was the de facto ruler of the western world determined to press on with the war, a decision which, it turned out, quite unexpectedly, was fraught with danger? Did he really think that the whole of western Eurasia could be governed effectively by a single monarch? Did he think of himself as a Persian analogue to Alexander the Great who would dispose of his long-established adversary and then take control of the whole of Europe? Did he choose war simply because he was confident of winning? Was he perhaps a mere plaything of fortune, in that he was simply responding to circumstance and taking advantage mindlessly of an extraordinary advantage?[20] Or were there sound reasons for his decision?

[20] Cf. Sim., iv.13.11.

4.2 Iran and Turan

Only speculative answers can be offered. One thing was certain: the Romans would resent bitterly their new weakened, subordinate position, as Khusro would know from his own experience in the 590s; memories of past greatness and a set of interlocking ideologies would act as coiled springs within the minds of the governing elite for many generations to come, driving them to seize any and every opportunity to recover what they had lost or, at the very least, to strike wounding blows against their Sasanian suzerain. No one could expect a political entity which had dominated the affairs of western Eurasia for over six hundred years swiftly to relinquish its accustomed position of pre-eminence within its traditional sphere.

As events were to show, ideology imparted extraordinary resilience to the Roman state when it was dismembered for a second time by the Arabs in the initial ultra-dynamic phase of Muslim expansion in the 630s and early 640s. In Roman eyes the Caliphate's hegemony was a mere contingency, a fleeting reality, which would be reversed before long. Several generations were to pass before Romans could conceive of the Islamic state as a great power, there to stay, before they acknowledged that the old binary world order had been destroyed. It was only in the 720s and 730s, after the third and most dangerous Arab attack on Constantinople, when the empire had been reduced to the rump state known to us as Byzantium, that emperors and their advisers reconciled themselves to brute reality and abandoned their efforts to recover their lost territories and to resuscitate Roman imperial rule. Even so, claims to parity of status, however at variance with reality, were never entirely relinquished, and there is evidence of a continuing determination to recover at least a minimal part of what had been lost.[21]

Then there was the problem of Christianity, which had been eroding the traditional ties of Transcaucasian peoples with Iran for many generations. Christianity spread slowly but ineluctably and, as it did so, could not but strengthen the diplomatic position of the Christian Roman Empire in the region. To the south, in Mesopotamia, the political and economic heartland of the Sasanian Empire, there were large and important Christian communities, and some even in Iran proper. It was true that rival brands of Christianity took hold in different regions—Nestorianism (followed later by Monophysitism) in Mesopotamia, Monophysitism in Armenia, and the Chalcedonian compromise in Iberia, and that relations between the different confessions could be fraught.[22] But the direction of movement was, in general, one-way. Christianity was a

---

[21] Howard-Johnston, *Witnesses*, 507–11.
[22] L. Pietri, ed., *Les Églises d'Orient et d'Occident, Histoire du christianisme des origines à nos jours* III (Paris, 1998), 1103–239.

proselytizing faith. It only retreated under intense pressure, and that could not be maintained for long in a polyethnic society with diverse beliefs. Religious tolerance had to be the norm.[23]

The spread of Christianity threatened the well-being of the Sasanian Empire in the long run. The proper ordering of earthly affairs depended on the continuing performance of Zoroastrian rites by the official priesthood in fire temples, great and small, and by individuals in their daily lives. The sacred fires must burn in their small, secluded, pollution-free chambers. The purity of the four vital elements must be maintained, the Holy Immortals must be venerated, if evil and disorder were to be kept at bay.[24] But Zoroastrianism, in essence a religion of rites, was fraying in the face of a religion with moral grip, which also argued for an even greater degree of divine engagement in earthly affairs. A cosmic explanation of the problem of evil was matched by Christians who tempered their monotheism with acknowledgement of the ubiquitous activity of demons. Instead of being a governing principle of the universe, evil was to be found at all times in the localities, waging guerrilla rather than cosmic war on humanity, and had to be fought with holy weapons, above all those wielded by monks and holy men.[25] The political and military governing class of Iran could not be inoculated against this monotheist faith, and the harsh treatment meted out to members of the elite who converted could not entirely stem the flow.[26] The day would, therefore, come when the rites performed by a reduced priestly establishment and a small proportion of the laity would no longer be able to activate the supernatural forces of good on behalf of the Sasanian state, unless a decisive counterblow were struck against the ultimate source of the subversive faith, the state-sponsored church of the Roman Empire.

The Roman Empire was unlikely to abandon, of its own accord, its self-appointed role as patron and protector of Christians wherever they were to be found, or its inclination to interfere in Persian internal affairs on behalf of Christian communities. This had naturally been resented by the Sasanian authorities in the past. Any understandings reached between the two sides had had to be tacit, in the sense of not being included in formal treaties. At times of crisis, aspersions had been cast on the loyalty of Christian communities. Fanned by the Zoroastrian priesthood, suspicion could grow and lead to persecution, thereby both justifying Roman concern and exacerbating Persian anxiety. The obvious Roman tactic of issuing anti-Zoroastrian propaganda and striving to alienate Persian Christians from the Sasanian state only made things worse.[27]

---

[23] Wiesehöfer, *Ancient Persia*, 199–216.
[24] M. Boyce, *Zoroastrians: Their Religious Beliefs and Practices* (London, 1979), 18–27, 30–8, 43–6, 85–8, 123–5.
[25] P. Brown, *The World of Late Antiquity: AD 150–750* (London, 1971), 96–104.
[26] Flusin, *Saint Anastase*, II, 118–27.
[27] S. P. Brock, 'Christians in the Sasanian Empire: A Case of Divided Loyalties', *Studies in Church History*, 18 (1982), 1–19; Blockley, *East Roman Foreign Policy*, 139–45, 160–1.

Thus, the continued existence of a Christian power, even one cowed into submission, posed a potential threat to the internal stability of the Sasanian Empire. For it would remain capable of disturbing good relations between different faiths, in particular between Christianity and the established religion of the Persians, and of encouraging, if not actively supporting, Christian dissidence and, possibly, open rebellion.

But there was probably one overriding argument. The security of the Sasanian Empire could not be guaranteed as long as a potential adversary continued to threaten its western borders and to distract it from its main historical mission, the defence of the settled lands of Iran and its dependencies from nomadic Turan. Now at long last the opportunity had come to deal once and for all with the western danger.

Iran was a continental power with well-defined frontiers beyond which lay several very different worlds—steppes to the north and east, desiccated and sparsely populated borderlands to the south-east, the desert to the south, and finally, in the west, Transcaucasia and the Mediterranean world. The peoples of Iran could not but be aware of their relatively exposed position, of the need to band together and, if need be, to fight for their continued independence. Their world view was shaped by knowledge of the relative weakness of their natural defences in the east and of the military power which nomad peoples could generate. Impressed deeply on their collective memory, as manifest in the *Khwadaynamag* commissioned by Khusro II's grandfather, Khusro I Anushirwan (531–79), was a sense of the fundamental difference between Iran and Turan, between a familiar organized world, where crops were planted and harvested, where villages and towns were fixed places in the landscape, where peasants and gentry and aristocrats had defined places in a social order over which presided a hereditary monarch, on the one hand, and a steppe world of pastoral nomads, where clans and tribes jostled for power, where political structures were fluid, and where charismatic leaders could, from time to time, construct large federations and bring immense military power to bear against their adversaries. The earthly antithesis between the sown and the steppe, between the settled and the nomadic, between a society where order prevailed and one where it did not mirrored that between good and evil at the cosmic level.[28]

This world view, manifest in the officially sponsored account of the remote, mythical past, had been reinforced by the experiences of the Sasanian state in the remembered, historical past. Turan impinged forcefully on Iran from the middle of the fourth century, when large numbers of nomads from the eastern steppes

---

[28] M. Boyce, *A Persian Stronghold of Zoroastrianism* (Oxford, 1977), 16–22, 29–52, 92–138, 236–40; E. Yarshater, 'Iranian Common Beliefs and World-View', *Cambridge History of Iran*, III.1 (1983), 343–58 and 'Iranian National History', *Cambridge History of Iran*, III.1 (1983), 359–477; J. Wiesehöfer, *Iraniens, grecs et romains*, Studia Iranica, Cahier 32 (Paris, 2005), 138–47.

fronting China crossed the diagonal mountain spine of central Asia and entered the Sasanian sphere of influence. These nomads, the Xiongnu, brought with them an impressive organizational capability and advanced statecraft, both developed over centuries of political dialogue with China. To the feared military capability of the nomad was now added a political strength and diplomatic acumen hitherto monopolized by the settled peoples in western Eurasia. Luckily for the Sasanians, the Xiongnu (called Chionites/Huns in western sources), who had forced them to turn east for most of the 350s, soon posed an equally serious threat to the Romans as they extended their authority westward and stirred up the Goths of Ukraine, driving them in the 370s towards and over the Danube. The Romans were, therefore, ready to make a permanent peace agreement in the later 380s, despite their failure to recover territory lost to the Sasanians after the defeat and death of the Emperor Julian in 363. It was an agreement to which both sides were firmly committed. So it freed both of them to deal with enemies on other fronts.[29]

For the Sasanians, this meant that they could concentrate their considerable military forces and exercise all their diplomatic skills on the Xiongnu and the two Hunnic dynasties, Kidarites and Hephthalites, who subsequently took control of the steppe lands bordering Iran. A series of wars were fought in which Sasanian kings, principally Bahram V Gor (421–39) and Peroz (459–84), strove to emulate the feats of their Kayanid forebears in the mythical past, until Peroz overreached himself in 484 and led his forces to disaster.[30] He was killed. Sasanian military power was temporarily broken. Sasanian prestige plummeted. The new king, Balash, was forced to make a hurried compromise peace with rebel forces in Armenia and to pay a large annual tribute to the Hephthalites. For the next fifty years or so, the Sasanian Empire was reduced to the status of a Hephthalite satellite. The Hephthalites were able to place their candidate Kavad I on the throne after the deposition and execution of Balash in 477–8 and to restore him in 501–2 after he in turn had been deposed in 497–8 (he managed to escape from prison and make his way to the Hephthalite court). Kavad was undoubtedly conscious of his inferior position as a Hephthalite client ruler. His unprovoked attack on the

---

[29] Principal source: Ammianus Marcellinus, *Historiae*, ed. and trans. É. Galletier, J. Fontaine, M.-A. Marié, and G. Sabbah, 6 vols. (Paris, 1968–99), at xiv.3.1, xvi.9.3–4, xvii.5.1, xxxi.3. Secondary works: J. Matthews, *The Roman Empire of Ammianus* (London, 1989), 61–3: Blockley, *East Roman Foreign Policy*, 37–45; É. de La Vaissière, *Histoire des marchands sogdiens* (Paris, 2002), 48–52, 102–9; H. J. Kim, *The Huns* (Abingdon, 2016), 12–77. Cf. P. Heather, *Empires and Barbarians: The Fall of Rome and the Birth of Europe* (Oxford, 2010), 153–73, 208–21.

[30] Principal sources: Łazar P'arpets'i, *Patmut'iwn Hayots'*, ed. G. Ter-Mkrtch'ean and S. Malkhasean (Tiflis, 1904), 154–6, trans. R. W. Thomson, *The History of Łazar P'arpec'i* (Atlanta, GA, 1991), 213–15; Procopius, *Bella*, i.4.1–16, 32–5; M. J. de Goeje et al., *Annales quos scripsit Abu Djafar Mohammed ibn Djarir at-Tabari*, 15 vols. (Leiden, 1879–1901), 873, 876–9, trans. C. E. Bosworth, *The Sasanids, the Byzantines, the Lakhmids, and Yemen, The History of al-Tabari* V (Albany, NY, 1999), 110–111, 115–119—cited henceforth as Tab. Secondary works: T. Daryaee, *Sasanian Persia: The Rise and Fall of an Empire* (London, 2009), 17–18, 22–5; Kim, *Huns*, 48–54; K. Rezakhani, *ReOrienting the Sasanians* (Edinburgh, 2017), 93–103, 125–8, 134–40.

Romans in autumn 502 should probably be seen, at least in part, as an attempt to garner much-needed prestige and boost his position in the eyes of his greatest subjects.[31]

Kavad's son and successor Khusro I may have been the candidate of the anti-Hephthalite faction at court, but he too needed to avoid antagonizing them and to extract credit from a successful foreign war on another frontier. This he did in spectacular fashion in 540, when he broke a supposedly endless peace and invaded the Roman Levant in force.[32] It was only with the rise of the Turks, who established their hegemony over the inner Asian frontiers of China in the 550s and then extended their authority into the western steppes, that Khusro was able finally to liberate Iran from Hephthalite tutelage. However, the successful joint attack on the Hephthalites by Turks and Persians (the latter very much the junior partners), which probably took place in 563, simply substituted for a declining nomad neighbour a greater one with a transcontinental reach, stretching by 576 as far west as the Crimea.[33]

It was the lowering presence of the Turks which probably exercised the strongest influence on Khusro II's thinking in 615, when he received the Roman embassy and took note of the Roman offer of submission, which was even more humiliating for them than that forced on the Persians in 484. It is highly unlikely that either he or his advisers would have forgotten the supreme crisis of 573, when, on a diplomatic initiative of the Turks, Iran came under simultaneous attack from both neighbouring great powers at the same time as facing a general rising of the Armenians. The danger diminished subsequently. A delayed Persian counteroffensive in the late 580s achieved considerable success.[34] There followed a period of Turkish disengagement in the west, after the intervention of the western khagan Tardu in the eastern steppes in 601–2 and his death in 603. A continuing Turkish preoccupation with China in the early seventh century gave Khusro his opportunity to go to war in the west and to press on with offensive operations, with only one pause for recruiting, for thirteen years.[35]

---

[31] Principal source: P. Martin, ed. and trans., *Chronique de Josué le Stylite, écrite vers l'an 515*, Abhandlungen für die Kunde des Morgenlandes 6.1 (Leipzig, 1878), cc. 8–12, 19–25, 49–101; F. R. Trombley and J. W. Watt, *The Chronicle of Pseudo-Joshua the Stylite*, TTH 32 (Liverpool, 2000), 8–11, 16–22, 50–118. Secondary works: G. Greatrex, *Rome and Persia at War, 502–532* (Leeds, 1998), 73–119; M. R. J. Bonner, *Al-Dinawari's* Kitab al-Ahbar al-Tiwal: *An Historiographical Study of Sasanian Iran*, Res Orientales 23 (Bures-sur-Yvette, 2015), 84–6.

[32] Principal source: Procopius, *Bella*, ii.4.13–14.7. Commentary: G. Greatrex and S. N. C. Lieu, *The Roman Eastern Frontier and the Persian Wars, Part II* AD *363–630: A Narrative Sourcebook* (London, 2002), 102–8; Bonner, *Al-Dinawari*, 98–103.

[33] Principal sources: R. C. Blockley, ed. and trans., *The History of Menander the Guardsman* (Liverpool, 1985), fr.4.2–3; Tab., 895–6, 899, trans. 152–3, 160. Secondary works: Barfield, *Perilous Frontier*, 131–3; La Vaissière, *Marchands sogdiens*, 197–8, 230–3; Bonner, *Al-Dinawari*, 107–112.

[34] Sources: Sim., iii.6.9–14; ps.S, 73.16–23, with *Hist.Com.*, n.8; al-Tabari., 991–3, trans. Bosworth, 298–303. Commentary: Howard-Johnston, 'Strategic Dilemma', 48–57.

[35] Barfield, *Perilous Frontier*, 134–8; Howard-Johnston, 'Sasanians' Strategic Dilemma', 60–1.

But in the very year of the Senate's embassy, he was given a forceful reminder of Turkish power. Intelligence arrived of stirrings among the Kushans, the inhabitants of the eastern borderlands. This was the territory (up to the left bank of the Oxus) annexed by the Sasanians after the destruction and partition of the Hephthalite khaganate in 563. Khusro recalled a distinguished Armenian general, Smbat Bagratuni, to active service and put him in charge of Sasanian forces in the east. They included a 2,000-strong Armenian contingent stationed in Gurgan. When the trouble materialized, it took the form of widespread raiding by what is described as a Kushan army. Smbat had little trouble dealing with it. The Kushans retreated at the news of his approach and were defeated when caught and forced to fight. At this point they appealed for help to 'the great khagan, king of the regions of the north', identifiable as Shegui, older brother and predecessor of Tong Khagan (618–28), like him ruling over the western territories of the Turks. The appeal was perhaps not unexpected. For it may well be that the crisis was engineered by the Turks so as to create circumstances in which they could legitimately invade the Sasanian Empire.[36]

The Turks intervened towards the end of 615. They achieved complete surprise. Persian forces withdrew to their bases. Smbat managed to escape with a small escort from the walled village not far from Tus in Khurasan where he had established his headquarters, but the rest of the headquarters troops were trapped and subsequently routed when they sallied out. The Turkish expedition was a punitive raid on a very large scale. Smbat's orders, disobeyed in the case of the headquarters troops, were for Persian forces to withdraw (into their bases). Unopposed, the Turks were able to pass Nishapur and range as far afield as Ray and Ispahan. The whole Iranian interior was thus shown to be vulnerable to attack if too much of Persian fighting strength was concentrated in the west. The old dilemma of the Sasanian Empire, caught between the great powers of the steppes and the Mediterranean, had manifested itself all too clearly and at considerable cost.[37]

Order was restored and the frontier resealed in the following year. Smbat, exonerated by the commission of inquiry sent out by Khusro after 615, received reinforcements and launched a punitive attack of his own on the Kushans. He routed the main Kushan army, which was fighting alone, without Turkish aid, and sent his cavalry on plundering raids through the Kushan lands up to and including Bactria. Much booty was gathered. Fortresses were taken and destroyed. Sasanian authority was thus reimposed as forcefully as possible on the whole frontier region annexed a generation earlier. Smbat himself was invited to Ctesiphon, for a triumphal reception laid on in large part, it may be supposed, to impress the

---

[36] Ps.S., 100.27–101.27, with *Hist.Com.*, n.21; É. de La Vaissière, 'Oncles et frères: Les Qaghans Ashinas et le vocabulaire turc de la parenté', *Turcica*, 42 (2010), 267–77, at 272–3.

[37] Ps.S., 101.27–102.20, with *Hist.Com.*, n.21.

public and to reassure the governing classes about the future security of Iran. He stayed at court until his death soon afterwards (in 617–18). His body was taken back to Armenia for burial in his family mausoleum.[38]

If proper account is taken of the Iranian world view and of the historical experiences of the Sasanians, Khusro's decision to fight on and eradicate the Roman Empire takes on a more rational character. The latter-day historian's surprise diminishes. Nonetheless, much debate and argumentation were probably required before the governing elite managed to break free of the notion that the Roman Empire was a fixed element in the world order, one with which Iran had to reach an accommodation. It is a great pity that our principal source for events in the east at this stage, the Armenian *History of Khosrov*, restricts itself to retelling the final stage in the career of Smbat Bagratuni and says nothing about any debate about grand strategy provoked by the Turkish invasion in 615.

A steady escalation in the scale of warfare between the two great sedentary powers since the beginning of the sixth century had undoubtedly soured relations between them and weakened their commitment to the binary world order in western Eurasia. Yet more damage was done to the ideological status quo by the decision of Justin II's regime, taken within clear historical memory, to break the traditional alliance of the great settled powers against the steppe nomads and to respond positively to Turkish proposals for a joint assault on Iran. Other factors already mentioned came into play if attention switched from the past to the future—the likely ideological resilience of any rump Roman state and the pernicious advance of Christian monotheism if sponsored by an outside power. The fateful step which was taken over the course of the winter months in 615–16 is explicable on lines such as these.

It should be noted too that it was not the ultra-radical step of demolishing the binary world order. It was simply a matter of recognizing that the second great power, Iran's principal rival, was now to be found where it was to be expected, to the east rather than to the west. This was a brute fact. A Turkish world empire had materialized, militarily more than a match for Iran and, in addition, with a well-developed economy and effective governmental system. This was run by non-Sasanian Iranians recruited from the governing elites of the mercantile cities of Sogdia and its colonial diaspora in central Asia, which had been co-opted as junior partners in the Turkish imperial project.[39] The Sasanian Empire had to adjust to changed circumstances, had to reorient itself to the east. Consequently, the Roman problem needed to be dealt with once and for all. The military drive to the west which had dominated the first century of Sasanian rule must be resumed and pushed on to completion.

---

[38] Ps.S., 102.21–104.9, with *Hist.Com.*, n.21.
[39] La Vaissière, *Marchands sogdiens*, 196–207; S. Stark, *Die Alttürkenzeit in Mittel- und Zentralasien: Archäologische und historische Studien* (Wiesbaden, 2008), 287–314.

To judge by subsequent Persian actions, Khusro now determined to extend the zone of Persian control to the whole of the Levant, Egypt, and Asia Minor. Constantinople presumably lay within his sights, since it was the nerve centre of the old rival power and would, if left alone, sustain imperial pretensions. A Sasanian garrison in Constantinople should be able to keep watch over the Balkan interior, from the most secure of advance bases beyond the most defensible of waterway frontiers. From Constantinople, with the aid of a fleet, Sasanian power could be projected over the islands of the Aegean and farther afield into the central Mediterranean, thereby securing the rich maritime facades of Asia Minor and the Levant from naval attack. In the south, Egypt too would need to be shielded from attack from the west, by forward bases in the Pentapolis.

If these speculative suggestions about Khusro's aims do not stray too far from the truth, the new version of the binary world order envisaged by him would have involved a great unitary settled power centred on Iran and a great central Asian power, the Turkish khaganate with its distinct eastern and western component parts.[40] The Sasanian Empire would have been greatly strengthened, its strategic position transformed after the elimination of its traditional western adversary and the annexation of territory much more extensive than its share of the former Hephthalite khaganate in the east. It would also have gained direct access to a still commercially active Mediterranean basin.

Whatever his aims may have been, whatever hopes he may have entertained, whatever the issues raised in discussion, in the course winter months of 615–16, Khusro made a conscious, public decision to reconstruct the world order on new lines. His war with the Romans was thenceforth to be a war to the death. His decision marked a final stage in its escalation. All controls were removed from the conflict. It was a decision taken by an individual which changed the course of history.

4.3 Further Persian Advances

Very little is known about the six years following Khusro's fateful decision to reject the Senate's peace proposal and to press the war to its conclusion with the removal of the Roman Empire from the face of the earth. Apart from good but fragmentary information about the principal Sasanian offensive, the invasion of Egypt in 619, only two faint signals can be picked up from this period of radio silence. We must listen to them with the utmost attention, locate where they come from, and try to work out what has been blanked out by time.

---

[40] La Vaissière, 'Oncles et frères', 272–4; Stark, *Die Alttürkenzeit*, 16–17.

One signal has already been noted, coming from Palestine in July or August 616. Modestus, the acting head of the church during the Patriarch Zacharias' detention in Ctesiphon, authorized the monks of the Judaean desert to return to their houses.[41] Conditions had improved. The troubles afflicting Palestine since the fall of Jerusalem and the withdrawal of Persian forces to Caesarea had been dissipated. The local authorities might have been able to restore law and order after a temporary hiatus, but the widespread Beduin raiding which had begun at the time of the siege in 614 could only have been halted by military intervention on a considerable scale. It is virtually certain then that the Persians renewed their drive south in the first half of 616 and imposed direct rule on the whole of Palestine. Corroboration comes from a sudden drop in the inflow of newly minted Roman copper folles from 616–17.[42] This imposition of direct rule on Palestine should be viewed as one of the first consequences of the new policy adopted by Khusro in winter 615–16.

The display of force involved had to be massive if the bishops and notables of the cities of Palestine and the flourishing townships of the *badiya* were to be induced to submit without a fight and if Nicetas, in command of the southern Roman army based in Egypt, was to be deterred from intervening in support of whatever forces he had deployed in Palestine. Units may well have been seconded from Shahen's northern army to ensure that the takeover proceeded without incident and that Persian authority was extended to Egypt's eastern Sinai approaches without encountering resistance. Reinforcements were also needed to overawe the Beduin and force them into accepting a new Persian system of client management. In addition there was the delicate task of achieving all of this without exacerbating intercommunal relations in Palestine. Clashes between Jews and Christians, especially if there were deaths which could be written up as atrocities, would have serious repercussions on public opinion and intercommunal relations in Mesopotamia.

Nothing is known about the strategy pursued by Shahrbaraz, whether he relied on a single overwhelming display of force at the outset to obtain the submission of the whole province at a stroke or imposed Persian authority district by district through negotiation with local leaders who would have been susceptible to local displays of force, given that their prized orchards and gardens were defenceless in city suburbs. The troubles of the two preceding years undoubtedly prepared the way, whichever strategy was chosen. As for the fraught business of dealing with Christians and Jews without antagonizing either side, Shahrbaraz had to refrain from tampering with traditional arrangements, leaning, if anything, slightly towards the Christian side. For his intervention in 614 on the side of the Jews had disturbed the existing balance. Jews had taken advantage of the temporary hiatus

---

[41] Antiochus, cols.1425 A-1428 A, with Flusin, *Saint Anastase*, II, 177–80.
[42] Bijovsky, *Gold Coin and Small Change*, 419–20.

which followed to enter the holy city and boost the size of the community there. Christian opinion in Mesopotamia mollified by the arrival of the fragments of the True Cross might be inflamed if there were a new outbreak of communal violence in Jerusalem.

The solution adopted was a return to the status quo before the pogrom in 614. Jews who had come to the city since then were not allowed to stay. The Roman regulation forbidding Jewish immigration was reinstated and given retrospective force (back to 614). The effect was probably to remove the activists most likely to cause trouble in future, thus balancing the execution of the ringleaders of the pogrom and deportation of Christian leaders two years earlier.[43] The Persian authorities did what they could to encourage reconstruction, sponsoring a fundraising drive led by Modestus, the acting head of the Jerusalem church, for the repair and restoration of churches damaged when the city was sacked. Yazdin, Khusro's leading Christian minister, made a large donation. Letters, doubtless carefully vetted by the Persian authorities, were sent by Modestus to church leaders elsewhere. They documented the work of reconstruction sponsored by the Persians and helped thereby to counter the propaganda broadcast by the Romans. Three churches were singled out by Modestus, presumably because they had suffered the worst damage—the Holy Sepulchre, the church of the Ascension on the Mount of Olives, and Holy Zion.[44]

By putting an end to Beduin raiding, the Persians were likely to gain the approbation of both Christian and Jewish communities. This was, however, no easy task. Good intelligence, real understanding of tribal conditions, and a great deal of tact and patience would be required if order were to be restored to the *badiya*. How long the Persians took to achieve this and to begin to project their power over the north-western quadrant of the desert is not known, but the main features of the new system of client management may be inferred from the case of the Ghassan. They were probably one of a few leading tribes on the desert frontages of north Mesopotamia, Syria, and Palestine who were picked out and given favoured client status. Their power enhanced by the bestowal of dignities on their ruling dynasties and by monetary subvention, they could be used to subordinate neighbouring tribes and to organize them into networks responsive to Persian policy. This had long been the policy of both great powers, as indeed of Himyar in central Arabia, the Persians managing the tribes on the desert

---

[43] Ps.S., 116.10–11 for a brief reference to Khusro's command to remove Jews from the city. R. E. Payne, *A State of Mixture: Christians, Zoroastrians, and Iranian Political Culture in Late Antiquity* (Oakland, CA, 2015), 183–4 takes it literally and envisages the expulsion of the whole Jewish community. Cf. H. Sivan, 'Palestine between Byzantium and Persia (CE 614-618)', in *La Persia e Bisanzio*, Atti dei Convegni Lincei 201 (Rome, 2004), 77–92, at 91–2.

[44] Ps.S., 116.8–118.6, with *Hist.Com.*, n.35; Antiochus, col.1428 A–B; *Khuz.Chron.*, 27.2–6. Cf. A. Ovadiah, *Corpus of the Byzantine Churches in the Holy Land* (Bonn, 1970), 89–90; V. Shalev-Hurvitz, *Holy Sites Encircled: The Early Byzantine Concentric Churches of Jerusalem* (Oxford, 2015), 55–87, 106–16.

approaches to Mesopotamia through the Nasrid kings of Hira and their tribe of Lakhm.[45]

That fundamental change was in the offing became plain during the first phase of the war, when, at some point between 603 and 610, the Lakhm nexus of tribal alliances on the desert approaches to Mesopotamia was dissolved by Khusro.[46] They were replaced as leading clients on the north-eastern margins of the desert by the Banu Tayyi', who succeeded, despite serious opposition, in imposing their authority and developing their own network of alliances.[47] Khusro's act opened the way for a general reform some years later, for a shift from a unipolar to a multipolar system of client management—the only effective way of projecting authority across a much longer desert frontage into northern and central Arabia. We do not know upon whom their choice fell in the north and north-west, But in the south-west, on the desert approaches to Palestine, it was the Ghassan who were picked out. The Ghassan were not inexperienced in the role. For they had exercised supratribal authority for a half century or so, between 529, when Justinian raised their ruling dynasty, the Jafnids, to royal status, and the 570s and 580s, when their power was broken by the efforts sustained over ten years of Justin II, Tiberius, and Maurice.[48] Restored to favour under the Sasanians, the Ghassan were able to establish their hegemony over north-west Arabia and were consequently held in considerable awe by the Meccans, Medinans, and the nascent Muslim community in the 620s.[49]

The long gap in John of Nikiu's history from 610 to 641 leaves us in the dark about any measures taken by Nicetas to secure the eastern approaches to Egypt across the Sinai peninsula once the Persians had taken control of Palestine. The best potential defensive line ran between the head of the Red Sea and the Mediterranean coast. This relatively narrow land passage might be held if the fortifications of Clysma and Pelusium at either end were strengthened and their garrisons were boosted with units capable of operating in the open. The threat which could then be posed to the lines of communications of an invading army would act as a serious deterrent. Both fortresses would have to be taken before it was safe to advance into Egypt. The Romans could then fall back on the eastern

---

[45] C. Robin, 'Le Royaume hujride, dit "royaume de Kinda", entre Himyar et Byzance', *CRAI* (1996), 665–714.

[46] *Seert Chronicle*, ed. A. Scher, trans. A. Scher, R. Griveau, et al., *Histoire nestorienne (Chronique de Séert)*, PO 4.3, 5.2, 7.2, 13.4, 539.8–540.2—cited henceforth as *Seert Chron*. See also pp. 166–70.

[47] F. M. Donner, 'The Bakr b. Wa'il Tribes and Politics in Northeastern Arabia on the Eve of Islam', *Studia Islamica*, 51 (1980), 5–38.

[48] Whitby, *Emperor Maurice*, 210–11, 256–8, 272–4, 276, 280; M. Whittow 'Rome and the Jafnids: Writing the History of a Sixth-Century Tribal Dynasty', in J. H. Humphrey, ed., *The Roman and Byzantine Near East*, II *Some Recent Archaeological Research*, JRA Suppl. Ser. 31 (Portsmouth, RI, 1999), 207–24; J. Howard-Johnston, 'Al-Tabari on the Last Great War of Antiquity', in Howard-Johnston, *East Rome*, no.VI, 20–2; Howard-Johnston, *Witnesses*, 437–9.

[49] See pp. 170–1.

branch of the Nile and seek to hold the line of the river along the flank of the Delta. All of this, however, is pure speculation.

Something can be said with rather more assurance about the strategy adopted for the defence of Asia Minor, the other large land mass in the east still under Roman control. A key element was the counterstrike. This could be very effective, as was shown by Philippicus' campaign into Armenia in 615. It would be developed by Heraclius in the 620s into a sustained counteroffensive on an unprecedented scale. A secure forward base was needed for launching such an attack to replace the inner basin of the Anti-Taurus, the principal marshalling area for mobile field troops to the rear of the Euphrates since the third century.[50] For this was no longer safe with the Persians in control of the Cilician plain not far to the south. An alternative assembly ground shielded by mountainous terrain and with difficult routes of access had to be found, and there was one obvious place to look—in the adjacent segment of the Taurus consisting of (1) Rough Cilicia fronted by Seleucia, where the Taurus meets the coastline, and (2) Isauria to the west. The presence of troops may be inferred from the establishment of a temporary mint in this area in 616. Copper coins of rough workmanship were issued at Seleucia, a few folles in 615–16, folles in large quantities and some half-folles in 616–17, and then folles in 617–18 at Isauria (modern Zengibar Kalesi), a safer site inland in the mountains. The principal function of the mint was presumably to serve military units in its vicinity, issuing small change in the form of copper coins minted on site and, almost certainly, precious metal specie, either silver hexagrams or gold solidi or both, shipped out from the main Constantinopolitan mint.[51]

There were several good reasons for basing a defending force in Rough Cilicia and Isauria. Apart from the security provided by the mountainous terrain, there was the formidable fighting capacity of the local highlanders, who had long caused considerable trouble to the imperial authorities.[52] Guerrilla resistance backed by regular forces might well transform this traditionally refractory region into a virtually impregnable redoubt which the Persians would enter at their peril. It was also well placed for both offensive and defensive operations. If the Persians concentrated their forces in southern Palestine in preparation for an invasion of Egypt, the Cilician plain and the region of Antioch beyond the Amanus range

---

[50] J. Howard-Johnston, 'Military Infrastructure in the Roman Provinces North and South of the Armenian Taurus in Late Antiquity', in A. Sarantis and N. Christie, eds., *War and Warfare in Late Antiquity: Current Perspectives*, Late Antique Archaeology 8.2 (Leiden, 2013), 853–91, at 865–7.

[51] P. Grierson, 'The Isaurian Coins of Heraclius', *NC*, ser.6, 11 (1951), 56–67; Grierson, *Catalogue*, 39, 327–30; F. R. Trombley, 'The Coinage of the Seleucia Isauriae and Isaura Mints under Herakleios (ca. 615-619) and Related Issues', in W. Oddy, I. Schulze, and W. Schulze, eds., *Coinage and History in the Seventh Century Near East 4* (London, 2015), 251–72.

[52] K. Hopwood, 'Consent and Control: How the Peace was Kept in Rough Cilicia', in D. H. French and C. S. Lightfoot, eds., *The Eastern Frontier of the Roman Empire*, BAR, Int. Ser.553 (Oxford, 1989), I, 191–201.

would be exposed to attack. If, on the other hand, an offensive was mounted against Asia Minor, a field force stationed in Isauria-Rough Cilicia would be able to threaten the invasion force's flank and rear as it advanced west across the plateau. Faced with the possibility of a pincer attack from front and rear, and with their communications menaced, the Persians were likely to hesitate before pressing on.

In the event, this strategy failed when put to the test. We know this thanks to the second faint signal picked up by our sources. It comes from Armenia, in the form of a piece of information recorded over a generation later by the author of the *History of Khosrov*.[53] It concerns Asia Minor, which is portrayed as under Persian attack. Both Khusro's leading generals, Shahrbaraz and Shahen, were involved. Whereas Shahen in 615 had aimed to administer a powerful shock to the Roman governing elite, and, if possible, to force them to abandon the war by attacking the metropolitan region, the co-ordinated operations of the two armies on this later occasion were targeted on western and southern Asia Minor.

Shahrbaraz comes into view in Pisidia, the lake district in the south-west, towards the end of the campaigning season.[54] He was presumably in command of the Persians' southern army. Only conjectures can be offered about his objective or objectives this year. The most tempting targets lay in the far west, in the Aegean coastlands, studded as they were with fine cities and filled with fertile agricultural land. That was where the worst damage could be done to the Roman economy by raiding the country and the intensively cultivated zones in the immediate surroundings of the cities. Although arguments from silence are always perilous, it is hard to believe that he could have taken an important city, like Sardis or Ephesus without leaving some trace of the event in at least one of the extant sources. It follows that Shahrbaraz was probably not responsible for the fire, datable to 616, which destroyed a complex of gymnasium, baths, lecture hall, synagogue, and shopping arcade at Sardis nor for the destruction of an apartment block at Ephesus at roughly the same time.[55] It was probably after this raiding activity in the west and on his return march that Shahrbaraz passed through Pisidia. He had probably taken a different route out, crossing the Anti-Taurus to

---

[53] Ps.S., 113.23–8, with *Hist.Com.*, n.32. [54] Ps.S., 113.27–8.

[55] Cf. M. Whittow, 'Recent Research on the Late-Antique City in Asia Minor: The Second Half of the 6th-C Revisited', in L. Lavan, ed., *Recent Research in Late-Antique Urbanism*, JRA, Suppl. Ser. 42 (Portsmouth, RI, 2001), 137–53. Contra C. Foss, 'The Persians in Asia Minor and the End of Antiquity', *EHR* 90 (1975), 721–47, at 736–9. On the fire at Sardis, see J. Russell, 'The Persian Invasions of Syria/Palestine and Asia Minor in the Reign of Heraclius: Archaeological, Numismatic and Epigraphic Evidence', in *The Dark Centuries of Byzantium (7th–9th c.)*, National Hellenic Research Foundation, Institute for Byzantine Research, International Symposium 9 (Athens, 2001), 41–71, at 62–68, and J. Drauschke, 'Bemerkungen zu den Auswirkungen der Perser- und Arabereinfälle des 7. Jahrhunderts in Kleinasien', in O. Heinrich-Tamaska, ed., *Rauben, Plündern, Morden: Nachweis von Zerstörung und kreigerischer Gewalt im archäologischen Befund* (Hamburg, 2013), 117–59, at 128–33, who note that it may have been started accidentally in a workshop and dissociate the demise of the city from Persian attack.

enter the interior plateau of Asia Minor and then aiming for the Aegean coast. By taking different routes in and out and by dispatching raiding forays to the side of the main force, he could maximize the swathe of destruction. Pisidia, which lay behind the coast and on the northern edge of the Taurus, was certainly worth targeting as he withdrew, not just for the fertile basins to be found around the lakes and in the Taurus foothills, but also because, like Isauria to the east, it was a natural reservoir of fighting manpower.

More detail is given about the movements of the northern army commanded by Shahen. Theodosiopolis was its forward base of operations.[56] With the arrival of summer, Shahen advanced on Melitene, probably taking the route across the central mountain spine of western Armenia which rounded the west flank of the Bingöl Dağ. Melitene was a fortress of great strategic importance, commanding a vital sector of the inner lines of defence immediately north of the Anti-Taurus, where the Arsanias valley and the adjacent open rolling country to the north debouch from the east into a large plain transected by the Euphrates. It was a crucial component of a defensive system which dated back to the first century AD. It was still in Roman hands at this date, isolated and vulnerable, but capable of interdicting Persian communications across the western sector of the Armenian Taurus (via the Ergani Pass) as well as controlling access to the major route southwest through the Anti-Taurus to northern Syria and Cilicia.[57] After capturing and occupying the city, Shahen continued his march, probably following the Roman military road through the Anti-Taurus which snaked up onto the plateau to the east of Caesarea (back in Roman hands). He continued his march west until he met Shahrbaraz in Pisidia.[58]

Nothing is reported about the actions of the two generals after their junction. If, as is likely, the campaigning season was well advanced by that stage, they were probably content with the principal permanent gain of the campaign (Melitene and firm control over south-western Armenia), the extensive damage done to important Roman resource bases, and the massive display of force which they had laid on and its moral effect. The Roman authorities, in particular the policymaking coterie around the emperor, would have witnessed two damaging invasions deep into south-west Asia Minor, which the Roman forces based in the highlands of Rough Cilicia or Isauria were powerless to stop. Coming on top of Shahen's advance in 615 to the north-western edge of Asia Minor, these operations could not fail to shake Roman morale, not only at the centre but throughout the provinces, diminishing any hope of recovery which might be entertained by the population at large and local notables.

---

[56] Ps.S., 113.24–6.   [57] Howard-Johnston, 'Military Infrastructure', 864–7, 878.
[58] Ps.S., 113.26–7.

The two armies may be conjectured to have withdrawn in a coordinated operation along the most direct route to the nearest safe region, so through the Cilician Gates to the plain of Cilicia. As for the date of the campaign, there is some circumstantial evidence which helps to narrow it to one of two years. It must have followed the victory won by the Persians over the full Roman field army near Antioch in 613. For that was the decisive battle which opened up Asia Minor to invasion through Cilicia as well as from western Armenia. It cannot have taken place in a year when either Shahrbaraz or Shahen or both are known to have been active elsewhere. So the three campaigning seasons following 613 can be eliminated: 614, when Shahrbaraz had to respond to the pogrom in Jerusalem; 615, when Shahen invaded Asia Minor but marched north-west to Chalcedon rather than to Pisidia in the south-west; and 616, when the two tasks of imposing direct rule on all of Palestine without provoking resistance and of overawing the Beduin required massive shows of force, and, as has been suggested above, units were probably seconded from Shahen's army to support Shahrbaraz's forces. The year 619 is ruled out because both generals were involved in the Egyptian campaign, and the following years were taken up with the consolidation of Persian rule in Egypt and with preparations for the final phase of the war, the battle for Asia Minor. That then leaves two possible years, 617 and 618.

It follows that something has gone wrong with the placing of the brief notice about the campaign in the *History of Khosrov*, where it comes immediately after one summarizing Shahen's earlier seizure of Caesarea in Cappadocia (in 611), his escape (in 612), and his subsequent summons to court. His departure for Theodosiopolis and the attack on Melitene in 617 or 618 seem to have been conflated with an earlier departure from the court in 613, when he probably took part in the defence of Antioch and northern Syria from Heraclius' counterattack. Of the two years which have not been eliminated, 617 is the more likely, since it would have left more time to mobilize, provision, and train the large forces required for the Egyptian campaign in 619. A Persian attack that year would also provide a reason for the relocation of the temporary mint to a safer place in the interior of Isauria in 617–18. The cessation of minting in Isauria in 618 and the departure of troops which it signalled would then mark the moment when the Roman authorities realized that Egypt would be the Persians' main target in 619.

A vital precautionary measure was taken in Constantinople in 618. The official citizens of the city, descendants of the original inhabitants at the time of its foundation, who were entitled to a share of the civic *annona* (free distribution of bread), were first charged for the privilege and then denied it when the *annona* was suspended.[59] This bespeaks anxiety on the part of the authorities, fearful lest there were to be an interruption in the provisioning of the city. Grain from Egypt

---

[59] *Chron.Pasch.*, 711.11–15, with Whitby, n.449; C. Zuckerman, 'Le Cirque, l'argent et le peuple: À propos d'une inscription du Bas-Empire', *REB* 58 (2000), 69–96, at 81–7.

extracted in lieu of money taxes could now be stockpiled for the future rather than being dissipated forthwith, leaving it for grain merchants to make good the shortfall from other sources, both close at hand in Thrace and Bithynia and farther afield, in North Africa. The consequent increase in prices would have the beneficial effect of attracting additional suppliers to the market and reducing consumption in the city. Something was also done to bolster the emperor's authority and to maintain the commitment of officialdom and people to the struggle in the dark years when the war was being lost. Mental resilience was no less important than bodily nourishment. At some point between Heraclius' negotiations with Shahen (615) and the halting of the grain supply from Egypt (619), it was rumoured that Heraclius was planning to leave Constantinople and to direct the war from North Africa. The rumour, almost certainly officially inspired, had the intended effect. There were vociferous declarations of support for Heraclius and pleas that he stay put and fight on from his capital.[60]

Apprehension was growing in Egypt. Refugees from the occupied provinces had brought home the reality of war.[61] So too did such accounts as came back from the aid workers who had been sent to Palestine in the interlude between the sack of Jerusalem and the Persian takeover of Palestine.[62] Some of the refugees now began making their way farther west, to the greater safety of North Africa.[63] Throughout Egypt the better-off seem to have been transforming capital into the portable form of gold solidi, thereby pushing up the price of gold by 50 per cent between 614 and 618.[64] The notables and senior churchmen of Alexandria made contingency plans for escape, should the city come under attack. Ships were made ready to carry them and their movable wealth to safety.[65] Whereas the Monophysite Patriarch Andronicus (616–22) and his predecessor were preoccupied with church affairs, in particular with the restoration of communion with the Monophysites of Antioch (achieved in 617 with the backing of the secular authorities), the Chalcedonian Patriarch John the Almsgiver is reported to have been concerned with secular affairs and to have wanted to discuss peace with the emperor. The phrasing (in his Life) is such as to suggest that he was going to urge that more concessions be made to the Persians. Whatever his plan (perhaps even the negotiated surrender of Egypt), nothing came of it, since the news leaked out and he was forced to stay put.[66]

The Persians attacked in 619. Nothing is known of the campaign until they approached Alexandria. Such sources as cover the invasion—they do not, alas, include the chronicle of John of Nikiu—concentrate on the great city. This was

---

[60] Nic., c.8. [61] *V.Ioannis (epit.)*, 6.1–4. [62] Cf. *V.Ioannis (epit.)*, c.9.7–26.
[63] Booth, *Crisis of Empire*, 110–11.
[64] *P Oxy* LVIII 3958 (614), lines 26–7 (p.111), and XVI 1904 (618), lines 2–3 (p.129), with comments of J. R. Rea (*P Oxy* LVIII, p.114).
[65] *Khuz.Chron.*, 26.6–8 (trans. Nöldeke, 25–6).
[66] *V.Ioannis (epit.)*, c.13.1–5. Cf. Booth, *Crisis of Empire*, 102, 104–5.

(a)

(b)

Figure 1. Constantinople (a) land walls. LizCoughlan/Shutterstock.com. (b) Gate Nejdet Duzen/Shutterstock.com.

Figure 2. Royal palace at Ctesiphon (Taq-i Kisra): façade. Courtesy of Dr. Marion-Isabell Hoffmann, Bavarian State Office for Monument Protection.

Figure 3. Royal palace at Ctesiphon (Taq-i Kisra): side view. Library of Congress Prints and Photographs Division Washington, D.C. 20540 USA.

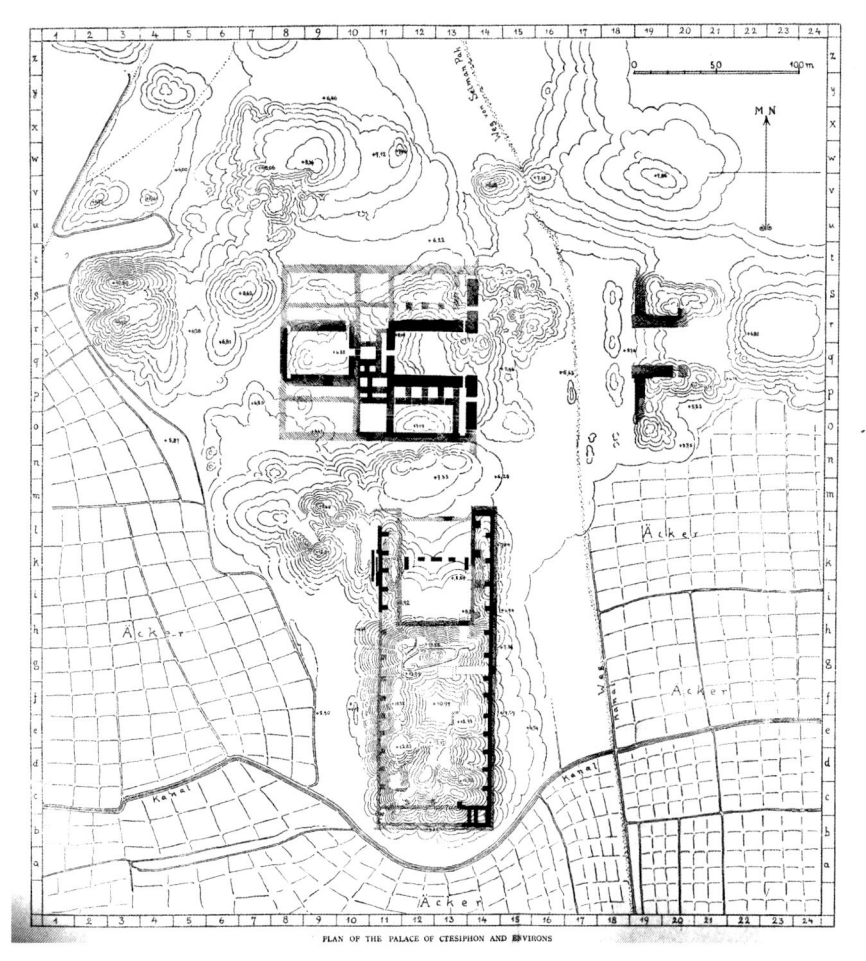

Figure 4. Taq-i Kisra: ground plan. Reproduced with permission from Reuther, O. (1929). *The German Excavations at Ctesiphon.* Antiquity 3(12), 434–451. DOI: https://doi.org/10.1017/S0003598X00003781. © Antiquity Publications Ltd 1929.

Figure 5. Coins of Heraclius: silver hexagram (615–38) – from DOC II.1, no.61.2. © Dumbarton Oaks, Byzantine Collection, Washington, DC.

Figure 6. Seal of Wistaxm, Ērān-spāhbed of the West (under Khusro I[531–79]). Reproduced with permission from Rika Gyselen, *The Four Generals of the Sasanian Empire: Some Sigillographic Evidence*. Conferenze 14, Roma: Istituto Italiano per l'Africa e l'Oriente, 2001, p. 42, Seal 3a.

Figure 7. Coins of Khusro II: ceremonial dinar of year 33. © Foto: Münzkabinett der Staatlichen Museen zu Berlin - Preußischer Kulturbesitz. Fotograf/in: Lutz-Jürgen Lübke (Lübke und Wiedemann).

Figure 8. Coins of Khusro II: ceremonial dinar of year 21. © Stephen Album Rare Coins Inc.

Figure 9. Taq-i Bustan: lake. Author's photograph.

Figure 10. Taq-i Bustan: grotto. Author's photograph.

Figure 11. Taq-i Bustan: investiture of Khusro II. Author's photograph.

Figure 12. Taq-i Bustan: Khusro's *fravashi*. Author's photograph.

Figure 13. Taq-i Bustan: boar hunt. Author's photograph.

Figure 14. Taq-i Bustan: deer hunt. Author's photograph.

not unreasonable, since the hegemony of Alexandria over Egypt was not matched by any other Roman regional capital. Power, both secular and ecclesiastical, was more centralized than elsewhere, and there was probably an unrivalled concentration of wealth there. Alexandria was not only the commercial hub of the east Mediterranean, but also the point at which the commerce of the Indian Ocean intersected with that of the Mediterranean.[67]

Shahrbaraz's was the leading role.[68] He advanced up to the city and began siege operations. They lasted for some time. The city was well defended, the Nile and its canals adding to the strength of the fortifications. Shahrbaraz took control of its immediate surroundings, including the Ennaton district with its concentration of monasteries on the spur of land running west to Taposiris. The famous shrine of St Menas and associated buildings, on the far side of Lake Mareotis, 45 kilometres from the city as the crow flies, seems to have been raided and to have suffered severe damage. News about the slaughter of monks and plundering of monastic buildings in the vicinity of Alexandria was put into circulation, which did not elicit much sympathy in the official history of the Coptic (Monophysite) church. The monks, it is implied, deserved their fate because they were insolent and without fear because of their wealth.[69] Shahen took up a position to the east, where he could intercept any attack from the east or from within the Delta on Shahrbaraz's rear. He is said to have protected the monasteries in his sector from depredation.[70] The two armies may have been accompanied by a fleet bringing supplies and equipment, but it did not include a maritime fighting capability. There had not been time to do more than requisition merchant ships from the ports of the Levant, and without warships and trained naval personnel it was impossible to launch an attack on the harbour, the city's weak point, or, probably, to sustain an effective blockade.

Instead of an open assault, like that staged by the Avars in 626 on the sea walls of Constantinople, the Persians resorted to subterfuge. They had been advised by a man from Qatar who knew the city well from his days as a philosophy student to seize the west gate. A small commando force slipped into the harbour under cover of darkness on small fishing boats and managed, in disguise, to enter the city just before dawn with the genuine fishermen returning from a night's fishing.

---

[67] A. H. M. Jones, *The Later Roman Empire 284-602* (Oxford, 1964), II, 857-8; J. Gascou, 'L'Égypte byzantine (284-641)', in C. Morrisson, ed., *Le Monde byzantin*, I *L'Empire romain d'Orient (330-641)* (Paris, 2004), 403-36, at 432-4.

[68] He is the unnamed *salar* of *History of the Patriarchs of the Coptic Church of Alexandria (St. Mark to Benjamin I)*, ed. and trans. B. Evetts, PO 1.2 and 4, 5.1, 10.5, at 485.9, 486.6 and 8—cited henceforth as *H.Patr.Alex*. Shahen, clearly the junior of the two, is named at *H.Patr.Alex.*, 487.5.

[69] J. Gascou, 'Enaton, the', in A. S. Atiya, ed., *The Coptic Encyclopedia*, 8 vols. (New York, 1991), III, 954-8; P. Grossmann, 'The Pilgrimage Center of Abû Mînâ', in D. Frankfurter, ed., *Pilgrimage and Holy Space in Late Antique Egypt* (Leiden, 1998), 281-302; N. Litinas, *Greek Ostraca from Abut Mina* (Berlin, 2008), ix-xi, 16-23. *H.Patr.Alex.*, 485.1-5.

[70] *H.Patr.Alex.*, 485.1-5, 487.4-6.

Once inside, they killed the troops guarding the west gate, opened it, and proclaimed Khusro's victory from the walls.[71] At this, panic spread through the city. The well-heeled, who had ships ready for their escape with their valuables on board, set sail—only for most of them to fall into Persian hands because the wind was blowing towards the Persian camp.[72] The besieging forces did not have to fight their way in, as the garrison commander, a certain Isaac, slipped away once he realized that the fight was lost.[73] This spared the city from being sacked, but Shahrbaraz temporarily evacuated the able-bodied men, aged 18-50, from the city, presumably with the same object as at Jerusalem—namely to identify those judged dangerous. The official Coptic church history transforms the episode into an atrocity on a huge scale, alleging that all the men, who numbered 80,000, were then executed.[74] John the Almsgiver, unlike Zacharias at Jerusalem, managed to escape. He left before the siege, fearing a plot against his life. He made his way to Cyprus, his place of origin, and, after surviving another plot, died there.[75] His Monophysite counterpart, Andronicus, seems to have stayed put.[76]

After taking control of the city—the date is securely established as June 619—and putting in hand the construction of new Persian headquarters, Shahrbaraz marched south to impose Persian authority first on the Delta and then down the Nile as far as Elephantine, immediately below the First Cataract. Shahen was perhaps charged with securing Alexandria and the western approaches until his return. The Coptic church history maintains its strong anti-Persian line, based probably on Roman propaganda issued at the time. Shahrbaraz is portrayed for a second time as a slayer of monks, on this occasion of 700 anchorites living in the vicinity of Nikiu.[77] There is no record of armed opposition. Indeed, the official classes throughout Egypt took note of the fall of Alexandria and forthwith altered the dating protocols to acknowledge the new Persian regime.[78]

However, many months were to pass before Egypt was brought under direct and effective Persian rule. Shahrbaraz's expedition to its southern frontier was but the first step in its subjugation. After this initial display of Persian military power, the army had to take control of all the component parts of Egypt. The bulk of the occupation forces were probably concentrated in Alexandria and Babylon because of their commanding strategic positions at the north-western corner and southern

---

[71] *Khuz.Chron.*,25.22-26.8 (trans. Nöldeke, 25-6).
[72] *Khuz.Chron.*, 26.8-11 (trans. Nöldeke, 25-6); *Vita S. Spyridonis*, ed. P. van den Ven, *La Légende de S. Spyridon évêque de Trimithonte*, Bibliothèque du Muséon 33 (Louvain, 1953), 81.14-83.7.
[73] *V.Ioannis (epit.)*, c.15.1-2; *H.Patr.Alex.*, 485.5-6. Cf. Booth, *Crisis of Empire*, 102-3.
[74] *H.Patr.Alex.*, 485.10-486.3.
[75] *V.Ioannis (epit.)*, cc.13.5-8, 15.2-11; *Vita S. Ioannis*, ed. H. Delehaye, 'Une Vie inédite de saint Jean l'Aumônier', *An. Boll.* 45 (1927), 5-74, at 67.22-69.22 (cc.47-8). Cf. Booth, *Crisis of Empire*, 101-3.
[76] *H.Patr.Alex.*, 486.8-11.   [77] *Chron.724*, 146.26-7, trans. 17-18; *H.Patr.Alex.*, 486.4-7.
[78] R. Altheim-Stiehl, 'Zur zeitlichen Bestimmung der sāsānidischen Eroberung Ägyptens', in O. Brehm and S. Klie, eds., ΜΟΥΣΙΚΟΣ ΑΝΗΡ. *Festschrift für Max Wegner zum 90. Geburtstag* (Bonn, 1992), 5-8.

head of the Delta. An effective, properly coordinated administration had to be installed, involving the military command and high civil officials, to oversee provincial administration and to take control of the most important branch of government, the fiscal system. An efficient logistics organization was also needed to requisition and distribute supplies to the occupation forces and, it may be conjectured, a network of reliable local informants to pick up early signs of dissidence in the localities.[79]

The first eleven years of Heraclius' reign were thus years of unmitigated disaster for the Romans. Once the empire was divided in two, a division confirmed with the repelling of Heraclius' counterattack in 613, and once it had suffered the terrible blow of the sacking of Jerusalem in 614, the task of the defenders was made very much more difficult. Leaving aside a plummeting of morale, inevitable in the circumstances, they could neither match nor anticipate Persian strategic deployment. With the failure of the Senate's peace initiative of 615, what remained of the empire was treated as a punchbag by Khusro's two great generals. Shahen's march to Chalcedon in 615 was followed by Shahrbaraz's 616 push south into Palestine up to the borders of Egypt. Then it was again the turn of Asia Minor, struck twice from the south-east, first by Shahrbaraz operating probably out of Cilicia, then by Shahen, whose army was well positioned to attack northern Asia Minor from Theodosiopolis but who chose to cut south-west, captured Melitene, a great Roman stopper at the western end of the Arsanias valley, and followed Shahrbaraz into southern Asia Minor.

The Romans probably had little difficulty in predicting that Egypt would be the next target once they realized that no major action was going to take place in 618, but in the event Nicetas, who had retained the southern command, was not able, as far as we can see, to put up serious resistance. With Alexandria in their hands, it was simply a matter of time before Persian forces took over Egypt and all its wealth. From June 619, Constantinople was cut off from its main source of grain. By winter 620–1, Egypt's massive agricultural and industrial output was contributing to the Persian war effort, as preparations began for the invasion of Asia Minor.

The scale of these conquests was breathtaking. Each successive gain weakened the Romans. It was a dynamic process, affecting their mental as well as their material resources. The land mass of Asia Minor was left as the outer bulwark of Constantinople and as the truncated empire's main resource base. The position was not quite as dire as it would become a little over twenty years later, when the Arabs, bearers of a new empowering faith, had succeeded in emulating the Persians. There was still hope, because the islands of the Aegean remained secure and in aggregate could make a significant contribution to the war effort.

---

[79] See Chapter 5.2.

The Balkan interior had not yet been flooded with Slav settlers, nor had the Lombards made the vital gain of Liguria which consolidated their hold on northern Italy. The most useful reserves, of money as well as grain, were to be found in North Africa. Of its wealth, there can be little doubt, given the importance of the Carthage mint and the steady increase in its output of gold coinage from Heraclius' accession to a peak in the years 622–5.[80] Rather than posing a threat to its security, the Berber tribes of the interior had been co-opted into the Heraclian cause and seem to have remained loyal to the Roman authorities throughout Heraclius' reign. There were no serious troubles akin to those of the decade 569–78 or the 587–8 crisis or the grand conspiracy of 595 which might have disrupted economic life.[81]

The principal advantage still enjoyed by the Romans was command of the sea. Without a naval capability, the Persians could not strike at Constantinople, the nerve centre of the empire. The rich Aegean coastlands of Asia Minor were relatively secure, as were the islands of the Aegean. The Balkans, Italy, and North Africa were out of reach. So there was little possibility of launching diversionary attacks which might weaken the defence of Asia Minor. The considerable forces which Romans could field would have to be confronted and broken in open battle in Asia Minor, with the inevitable risks that entailed.

First, though, the Persians had to consolidate their position in Egypt. Here, as earlier in Palestine and Syria, there was no incentive for the provincial authorities to organize armed resistance without the aid of a Roman field army. The cities of the Delta and the Nile valley could be defended, but all would eventually fall to blockade or assault. With no prospect of relief, there was little to be gained by holding out and much to be lost, as valuable assets in undefended suburbs (villas, gardens, orchards, etc.) would be destroyed. Not to mention the likelihood of reprisals against the leaders of the resistance. So Persian authority was recognized swiftly. Heraclius' name and regnal year were soon excised from the opening protocols of documents throughout Egypt. Already in January 620 clerks in Oxyrhynchus, well away from the Delta in Middle Egypt, were acknowledging the change of regime.[82]

Then preparations could begin for the conquest of Asia Minor—the planning of operations, the transfer of the main mobile fighting forces from Egypt to the two fronts facing Asia Minor (Cilicia and western Armenia), the assembly of supplies and the organization of logistics, etc. The opening attack was then

---

[80] C. Morrisson, 'L'Atelier de Carthage et la diffusion de la monnaie frappée dans l'Afrique vandale et byzantine (439–695)', *AT* 11 (2003), 65–84, at 74–84; H. Ben Slimène Ben Abbès, 'La Production de la monnaie d'or en Afrique byzantine', in J. González, P. Ruggeri, C. Vismara, and R. Zucca, eds., *Le ricchezze dell'Africa: risorse, produzioni, scambi*, L'Africa Romana 17, 4 vols. (Rome, 2008), II, 1151–64, at 1157–60.

[81] Y. Modéran, *Les Maures et l'Afrique romaine (IVe–VIIe siècle)*, Bibliothèque des Écoles Françaises d'Athènes et de Rome 314 (Rome, 2003), 668–81.

[82] Altheim-Stiehl, 'Zur zeitlichen Bestimmung', 5–8.

launched in spring 622 from western Armenia, targeting northern Asia Minor (in the hope, presumably, of disconcerting a defence expecting danger to materialize in the south-east, as in 617). It went well and resulted in a swift march west to Galatia and Phrygia. It was the first operation in the final phase of the war, a phase which was to be filled with drama and to culminate in a reversal of fortunes so extraordinary as to suggest supernatural intervention in human affairs. The story of what happened and why has to be pieced together from many different sources.

But before doing so, we should take stock. We should look at the geopolitical landscape of the Middle East, at this time of Sasanian hegemony, paying attention to social and economic conditions in the Roman and Persian heartlands as well as in the occupied territories.

5
The Middle East in the 620s

News travelled faster and farther than one might think in late antiquity, as it had in previous centuries and would continue to do even in the early Middle Ages. This was especially true of Arabia, where even trivial bits of news could pass from Beduin to Beduin and cross large swathes of desert at remarkable speed. The routes trafficked by caravans provided trunk lines of communication, above all between the Hijaz and the prosperous desert frontage of Palestine. Only in extreme circumstances could war bring about a complete breakdown in commercial relations. That did not happen in the course of the great war between Persians and Romans. Caravans continued to make their way to and fro in the 620s and kept the notables of the leading city state in the Hijaz well informed about what going on in the north. The only specific event picked out in the principal contemporary source, the Qur'an, was a great Roman defeat, probably that of 613 when Heraclius himself was in command and failed to break the Persian hold on the Antioch region. The sympathy of Muhammad lay, not unexpectedly, with the Romans qua monotheists. Their cause would, he assured his listeners, prevail in the end.[1]

More important, though, were the word pictures he painted of the End of Time, especially in his first halting prophetic utterances. Millenarian anxiety was infectious in an age of war, which did not cease but escalated with time. The words of the Prophet impressed themselves on his listeners, especially the young, those belonging to minor clans and the disadvantaged in Mecca, who formed the first band of his followers. News of his preaching also spread farther afield to other Hijaz cities. The grim prospect which he conjured up tallied with what Meccans and other Hijazis were hearing of the crisis flaring in the civilized world to the north and increased their susceptibility to his central message about the supreme God who governed all the affairs of heaven and earth without the aid of intermediaries, who took note of every deed, word, and thought of every single individual, and before whom each individual would be brought for judgement in the near future. Gripped by apocalyptic fear, under growing pressure from their fellow citizens, the nucleus of the future worldwide Muslim community, some seventy-strong, prepared to take the drastic step of exiling themselves from their native city, the main power centre of the sole independent region of Arabia. Once

---

[1] Qur'an, 30:1–5.

their destination was decided and formally agreed, they migrated in a body to Medina in 622 and embarked on a local gradually escalating war with Mecca.[2]

The speed of dissemination of news about the war is hard to gauge in the Mediterranean. The Sasanians had probably imposed an embargo on trade between the Middle Eastern provinces now under their control and the rump of the Roman Empire. With their invasion of Egypt and the capture of Alexandria in 619, they were able to cut Constantinople off from its main source of grain. It is highly unlikely that they would have allowed trade in other commodities to continue, thereby nourishing the many *emporia* which had grown up along the sea lanes leading to Constantinople and the west. Nonetheless, information about the course of events did percolate through to Italy, Burgundy, and Spain, and left its mark in the form of short notices in western chronicles.[3] The principal effect was corrosive, a gradual destruction of the residual ties linking the sub-Roman kingdoms established by Germanic peoples on former Roman territory to the empire in the east. It proved harder and harder to square its higher status as a superordinate, divinely ordained power charged with managing earthly affairs with the brute reality of successive defeats and steady loss of territory. While the Lombards continued to acknowledge Roman suzerainty by issuing coins bearing the emperor's name, the Visigoths, who had been issuing regal coins of their own since the 580s, were openly at odds with the authorities in what remained of the Roman enclave in south-east Spain. The Franks had likewise dispensed with formal acknowledgement of Roman suzerainty on their coinage from the 580s, but the important Marseilles mint took the more drastic step of issuing gold solidi (a known imperial prerogative) in the name of Dagobert II, probably from his accession in 613.[4]

The Avar khaganate was assuredly well informed about the course of the war, with its core territory lying within relatively easy reach of Roman outposts in the northern Balkans. The long period of quiescence originating when the Romans ceased to apply direct military pressure after their victorious campaign of 599 and cemented when Phocas negotiated peace (in 603–4) in order to transfer troops to the eastern front came to an end around 620. It is impossible to say whether it was news of the occupation of Palestine in 616 or the conquest of Egypt in 619 which stiffened Avar resolve to enter the war and take advantage of Roman weakness. Initially they acted through surrogates, Slav tribes established on both banks of the lower Danube. They were encouraged, covertly, to push south in the Balkans, raiding by land and by sea. Thessalonica, by this date the administrative capital of the Balkan provinces and the seat of the Praetorian Prefect of Illyricum, came

---

[2] Howard-Johnston, *Witnesses*, 445–56.   [3] Howard-Johnston, *Witnesses*, 431–4.
[4] P. Grierson and M. Blackburn, *Medieval European Coinage*, I *The Early Middle Ages (5th-10th centuries)* (Cambridge, 1986), 49–51, 58–9, 90–3.

under direct attack in 620. Within two years the Avars cast discretion aside and joined their Slav clients in a whole-hearted attempt to take out Thessalonica. Almost certainly, communications were established about that time with the Persians, whose influence would be detectable in future Avar actions.[5]

Information, true and false, played a central part not only in the arenas of combat but also in wider diplomatic spheres during the war. By the early 620s, with the final phase imminent, in which Persian forces would set about the conquest of Asia Minor, the empire looked increasingly doomed. Not unreasonably, its Turkic and Germanic neighbours in the north and west were changing their attitudes and behaviour, thereby making the demise of the empire more likely. More distant reaches of the world, like India and Sri Lanka (in regular touch by sea with the ports of the Persian Gulf and Red Sea), were not cut off. News of what was happening in the east Mediterranean—the collapse of an age-old trading partner and the growing power of another—could not but attract attention there and in their cultural colonies in Southeast Asia. But their attitudes could not affect, even indirectly, the course of events in the far north-west.[6]

It was very different in the case of central Asia. The notables of Sogdian city states with their ramified commercial networks extending from the Crimea in the west to Luoyang in north-east China would have had little difficulty in tracking Persian successes. As partners of the Turks in their imperial venture, they could keep them informed about developments in the west. The fortunes of the Tang, who started their rise to power very much as Turkish clients, might still be the Turks' primary concern around 620, but they had not lost interest in the west, both because of their past involvement there and because of the problems which an enlarged and strengthened Sasanian Empire might pose. Unlike Visigoths, Franks, Burgundians, Lombards, and the various powers of the Indian subcontinent, the Turks were capable of intervening directly and in great force in the great war being fought in western Eurasia. It was perhaps only a matter of time before they would do so.[7]

5.1 The Roman Empire

Half a millennium of imperial rule had generated large reserves of ideological assurance in Roman governing circles and the general population. Around 620 there were few signs, if any, of faint-heartedness despite the disastrous course of

---

[5] Theoph., 292.11–14; *Mir.Dem.*, ii.1–2.
[6] Cosmas Indicopleustes, *Topographia Christiana*, xi.13–16, ed. and trans. W. Wolska Conus, III, Sources chrétiennes 197 (Paris, 1973), 342–9. Cf. U. Singh, *A History of Ancient and Early Medieval India: From the Stone Age to the 12th Century* (Delhi, 2009), 408–18, 500–4; K. R. Hall, *A History of Early Southeast Asia: Maritime Trade and Societal Development* (Lanham, MD, 2011), 49–59, 109–14.
[7] La Vaissière, *Marchands sogdiens*, 118–23, 128–43, 198–207; Stark, *Alttürkenzeit*, 289–302.

the war—at any rate not enough to make their way into post-war narratives. Romans were ready to fight on in defence of their core territories in Europe and Asia, their sense of high status being reinforced by religion. Faith was fanned by propaganda, presenting the Romans as a special people on whom divine favour would be bestowed again, once their sins had been expiated through suffering.[8] Equally, if not more important were the material resources which they had accumulated over preceding centuries, in the age of revival after the third century. The inland sea at the heart of the empire fostered commercial life and individual enterprise on a scale which dwarfed the exchanges managed by the state. In the late antique heyday of the empire from the fourth to the middle of the sixth century, prosperity spread deep into the interior of the lands fringing the Mediterranean. Of this there can be no doubt, given the ubiquity of that invaluable tracer of modest affluence, red slipware from Africa and elsewhere, as well as the evidence of long-distance distribution of liquid comestibles (oil, wine, and fish sauce) provide by amphora sherds.[9]

The main form in which the accumulation of wealth manifested itself was the city, with its endowment of public buildings, squares, paved streets, cisterns, walls, and more or less opulent Christian basilicas. City life in the Balkans may have suffered from the impact of war and subversion, especially after the fatal decision taken by Justinian late in his reign to use the Avars to bring a final solution to his Balkan problems (Gepids foremost among them).[10] But many of the cities, large and small, which studded the landscape of Asia Minor away from its eastern and south-eastern margins, continued to flourish. There is, alas, no source which casts light on conditions in city and country in the 620s, but we may perhaps extrapolate from the detailed picture of north-west Galatia and coastal Bithynia in the Life of Theodore of Syceon, which becomes fuller as it approaches his death in 613.

The old social order was well entrenched. In constitutional terms cities had lost power with the withering away of their councils in the reign of Justinian, but this was more than counterbalanced by the leading role in civic affairs taken up by bishops and the informal authority wielded by city notables acting in concert.[11]

---

[8] Theodicy (God's punishment of sinners and the need for repentance) was a central theme of Patriarch Zacharias' farewell sermon outside Jerusalem: see Strategius, c.13.22–76 with Flusin, *Saint Anastase*, II, 164–70.

[9] B. Ward-Perkins, 'Specialized Production and Exchange', *CAH* XIV (Cambridge, 2000), 346–91; S. Kingsley and A. Decker, eds., *Economy and Exchange in the East Mediterranean during Late Antiquity* (Oxford, 2001).

[10] J. H. W. G. Liebeschuetz, 'The Lower Danube Region under Pressure: From Valens to Heraclius', in A. G. Poulter, ed., *The Transition to Late Antiquity on the Danube and Beyond* (Oxford, 2007), 101–34; J.-P. Sodini, 'The Transformation of Cities in Late Antiquity within the Provinces of Macedonia and Epirus', in Poulter, *Transition to Late Antiquity*, 311–36; A. Sarantis, 'War and Diplomacy in Pannonia and the Northwest Balkans during the Reign of Justinian: The Gepid Threat and Imperial Responses', *DOP* 63 (2009), 15–40; A. Sarantis, *Justinian's Balkan Wars: Campaigning, Diplomacy and Development in Illyricum, Thrace and the Northern World AD 527-65* (Prenton, 2016), 357–89.

[11] Mitchell, *Anatolia*, II, 127.

The governor of Galatia and his deputies were responsible for all aspects of provincial government. His power was extended down to the level of the village by his local deputies. In the event of serious disturbance in a locality, he might intervene directly as he did (not very effectively) in the case of the rioting, destruction of property, and threat to life which broke out in the village of Eukraon after an enterprising villager (designated a *georgos*, tenant) was suspected of unearthing buried treasure. Soon afterwards the governor was preparing to do so again in a nearby village (Sandos) where the troubles triggered by a member of the village elite set the main body of villagers (the *georgoi*) against the *oikodespotai* (landlords) until the latter called in Theodore and he managed to restore calm.[12]

The importance of the bishop is presupposed in the Life. Theodore's standing as a holy man was most assured when it was acknowledged by bishops—as it was in three smaller cities (Germia, Pessinus, a metropolitan see, and Sozopolis). The bishop was responsible for the spiritual welfare of the citizens, a responsibility which required him to organize rogation ceremonies in times of trouble, pleading with the Lord for remission of sins. That and the wealth of the church which enabled him to undertake public works for the benefit of a city (like the large cistern which the local bishop was excavating when the Germia crisis broke) underpinned his informal authority in secular matters.[13]

City notables are rather more to the fore in the Life of Theodore. It is they who normally invite Theodore to deal with grave problems affecting larger cities like Ancyra, Amorium, and distant Heraclia in Pontus, bypassing the episcopate (which plays no part in subsequent events). The use of honorific sobriquets—*Protectores* in the case of Ancyra, *Domestici* at Pessinus, *Illustres* at Amorium, and *Eleutheroi* (Freemen) at Germia—is perhaps the best indication of city elites' self-awareness, of their high status, and of their collective solidarity. They form the grand urban analogues to the landlords who preside over village affairs.[14] Their sense of special standing in their locality is best illustrated by their behaviour at the outbreak of trouble in Germia, when the *populus*, in the form of citizens of middling status, began denouncing the bishop and the established order. The Freemen took care to keep the members of their families, chiefly young, who were affected by such revolutionary sentiments, hidden from public view, at home or in hospital. Theodore, very much a defender of the traditional social order and, in this instance, sensitive to the feelings of the notables, did not insist on their relatives being brought out to take part in the public rite of exorcism.[15]

There is nothing to indicate impoverishment of significant sections of the population in rural and urban Galatia up to Theodore's death. Villages may have grown larger and more numerous in the hinterlands of cities, but at little cost to

---

[12] V.Theod., cc.114, 116.1–42, 151.1–21. Cf. Mitchell, Anatolia, II, 127–8, 133–4.
[13] V.Theod., cc.100, 101.33–56, 109.1–4, 161.4–8.
[14] V.Theod., cc.44, 45, 101.1–11, 107, 161.11, and 176.   [15] V.Theod., c.161.8–25, 146–81.

the cities. There were cases of ill-treatment of the peasantry, but they were exceptional. Theodore had a part to play as patron of humble countrymen and protector of their livelihoods, but indigence was not widespread.[16] Clearer positive evidence of continuing prosperity and active commercial life comes from Bithynia on the occasion of Theodore's visit on his return journey from Constantinople in 612. He stopped for a while in the outskirts of Nicomedia, keen to venerate the martyr Anthimus in his shrine, one of eight rural shrines which he visited in the region. He interrupted his stay with a journey to the monastery of St Autonomus, on the south shore of the Gulf of Nicomedia, on the road to Helenopolis.[17] Crowds greeted him wherever he went, growing larger the more news of his presence spread. People came from town and country, from lowlands and highlands, and, in the case of some, from a considerable distance—Pylae, for example, and Nicaea. On the journey back to Nicomedia, with an escort of monks and laymen carrying candles and censers, he was met by local people who asked him to bless their fields and wineries. Fishermen spread their nets over the road where he would pass. Eventually, he made his way through a jostling throng to a fishing vessel which took him across the head of the Gulf, from Diolkidon to Elaia, accompanied by a flotilla of small boats. There was no escaping the crowds, people running to see him as he passed, others following behind, on the way to Nicomedia, where large crowds were waiting on the approach to the city and in the suburb of Optatianae by the shrine of St Anthimus.[18]

The impression given of Theodore's visit is that of a guru passing through the late antique equivalent of a prosperous Indian district in the modern age. Bithynia was evidently highly developed and brimming with people. Trading ports (*emporia*), five of which are named, lined the coast.[19] Saints' shrines were to be found everywhere, on the coast and inland. It is noticeable that no appeals for help came from the poor. It may well be that only well-off petitioners caught the eye of the hagiographer, but there were many signs of prosperity, the fields producing crops (in some cases, not enough according to their owners), the vineyards wine (disappearing mysteriously from some wineries) for which the holy man's blessing was sought.[20] Trade and manufacturing were flourishing—to judge by the clientele seeking help, which was extensive and variegated. It included the owner of a fishing boat who is classified as a trader (at the *emporium* of Diolkidon), a camel driver (at the small town of Hebdomon on the road east from Nicomedia), a shopkeeper with a workshop in Nicomedia, a knife grinder,

---

[16] *V.Theod.*, cc.147.29–42, 148.1–13. Cf. Mitchell, *Anatolia*, II, 126–7.
[17] *V.Theod.*, cc.156.4, 157.16, 24–5, 34, 67–71, 158.26–7, 52, 160.19 (shrines of SS Anthimus, Theodore, George, Autonomus, Heraclius, Dionysius, and two of the Theotokos); cc.157–8 (visit to monastery of St Autonomus).
[18] *V.Theod.*, cc.156.1–7, 157.61–3, 158, 159.1–7.
[19] *V.Theod.*, cc.156.8 (Kalleon), 156.84 (Amareon), 157.10 (Eribolou), 157.23, and 51 (Herakleion), 158.12–13, and 26 (Diolkidon and others).
[20] *V.Theod.*, cc.158.16–18, 159.1–3.

the importunate manageress (a slave) of an inn on the road inland, and a Jew, clearly rich, since he brought a sick boy all the way from Nicaea.[21]

As happened when he visited other great provincial cities, Theodore seems to have been cold-shouldered by the metropolitan bishop. The nearest he came to an audience was with a future metropolitan bishop Tryphon, who held Theodore in high esteem.[22] But several of his clients belonged to the highest lay circles in Nicomedia—known as the *Scholarii*. They included a former Father of the City who had gone off his head and was brought to the saint by the three brothers of his first wife, who were *fabricenses* (arms manufacturers), and other leading citizens, and a leatherworker (presumably owner of a leather business).[23] The head and singing master of a poorhouse, known as *Happy Old Age*, in the vicinity of Nicomedia came, the latter put on a cart by his wife, the former taken by the registrar of the poorhouse and others to a house in the city.[24] The clergy too sought his help—an abbot, a deacon from the *emporium* of Kalleon, a priest nicknamed *Pepper* who was exorcized as he was coming out of a bathhouse in the *emporium* of Herakleion near the monastery of St Autonomus, and another priest suspected of sorcery and known as the *Goat of Bithynia*.[25] It was a world in which mischievous names could gain general currency, a world with its own culture and a streak of anticlericalism. It is a world which is likely to have survived largely unscathed into the 620s, since it was only touched once by war, when Shahen passed through with his expeditionary force on the way to and from the Bosporus in 615. Whatever destruction may have taken place on the way out was not replicated on the return journey, when the Roman offer of peace had been made and Shahen was marching at high speed.[26]

Similar scenarios of a well-populated and thoroughly Christianized landscape, with a thick scattering of villages, *emporia*, and cities, large and small, may be envisaged for other regions of Asia Minor at the beginning of the seventh century. This is highly likely to have been so along the highly developed coastal strip of Lycia in the south-west, where *emporia* with warehousing and flourishing townships (serving as gateway ports for the towns and villages of the interior) had spread out around every safe anchorage in late antiquity, feeding off the Alexandria-Constantinople trade route (before the Persian conquest of Egypt).[27] The broad river valleys of western Asia Minor likewise drew their vitality both from the sea lanes running south towards the strategic crossroads of the east Aegean around Rhodes, Cos, and the smaller neighbouring islands, and from the resources of their hinterlands. There is no reason to suppose that economic conditions there were worse than in Bithynia, that a severe economic depression

---

[21] *V.Theod.*, cc.156.21–2, 156a.1–4, and 21, 158.30–7, 160.20, and 49–52.
[22] *V.Theod.*, c.160.1–11.   [23] *V.Theod.*, cc.156.68, 159.9–11, and 38–61.
[24] *V.Theod.*, cc.156.26–53, 156a.31–9.   [25] *V.Theod.*, cc.156.8–9, 83–5, 157.51–9, 159.28–30.
[26] See pp. 109–10 above.
[27] C. Foss, 'The Lycian Coast in the Byzantine Age', *DOP* 48 (1994), 1–52.

had set in right at the start of the seventh century. The evidence rather points to a more gradual plague- and war-induced diminution in activity, which only gathered momentum in the middle decades of the seventh century with a precipitate decline in commercial traffic along the main axis of trade between Alexandria and Constantinople. The effects would have been greatest on coastal cities like Phocaea (the main east Mediterranean centre for the manufacture of fine crockery),[28] Smyrna, Ephesus, and Miletus, as well as the islands of the Aegean and the *emporia* strung out along the coast of the mainland. Cities within easy reach of the coast like Pergamum, Magnesia-on-the-Maeander, Sardis, and Aphrodisias would also have suffered, although perhaps not quite as badly, along with textile-manufacturing centres farther inland, like Philadelphia, Laodicea, and Hierapolis, which drew their raw material from flocks of sheep grazing on the hills around the Lycus and upper Maeander valleys and shipped their cloth out through the Aegean ports.[29]

It is not possible either to confirm or to confute this supposition from archaeological survey and excavation. For cities and towns in decline leave little hard material evidence of their condition, unlike their counterparts in eras of growth with new developments and large-scale refurbishment of existing structures. It is more difficult to detect dilapidation and impoverishment, and yet more difficult to distinguish between cities which collapsed and were abandoned and others which managed to carry on living with dramatically lower living standards. An urban population pushed down to a low, near-subsistence level, using mudbrick and timber for building rather than stone and brick, eating off perishable wooden platters rather than durable ceramic tableware, but still occupying the area defended by a powerful late antique wall would leave few detectable traces of its existence. The only secure archaeological evidence of decline is provided by construction of a reduced circuit of fortifications: this indicates (1) that there was a concentration of settlement worth defending at the

---

[28] J. W. Hayes, *Late Roman Pottery* (London, 1972), 323–70; L. E. Vaag, 'Phocaean Red Slip Ware: Main and Secondary Productions', in M. Berg Briese and L. E. Vaag, eds., *Trade Relations in the Eastern Mediterranean from the Late Hellenistic Period to Late Antiquity: The Ceramic Evidence* (Odense, 2005), 132–8.

[29] R. Naumann and K. Selahattin, 'Die Agora von Smyrna', in *Kleinasien und Byzanz: Gesammelte Aufsätze zur Altertumskunde und Kunstgeschichte*, Istanbuler Forschungen 17 (Berlin, 1950), 69–114; S. Ladstätter, 'Ephesos in byzantinischer Zeit: Das letzte Kapitel der Geschichte einer antiken Grossstadt', in F. Daim and J. Drauschke, eds., *Byzanz—das Römerreich im Mittelalter* (Mainz, 2010), II.2, 493–519; P. Niewöhner, 'Sind die Mauern die Stadt? Vorbericht über die siedlungsgeschichtlichen Ergebnisse neuer Grabungen im spätantiken und byzantinischen Milet', *Archäologischer Anzeiger* (2008),181–201; K. Rheidt, 'In the Shadow of Antiquity: Pergamon and the Byzantine Millennium', in H. Koester, ed., *Pergamon: Citadel of the Gods* (Harrisburg, PA, 1998), 395–423; C. Humann, *Magnesia am Maeander: Bericht über Ergebnisse der Ausgrabungen der Jahre 1891-1893* (Berlin, 1904); M. Rautman, 'Sardis in Late Antiquity', in O. Dally and C. Ratté, eds., *Archaeology and the Cities of Asia Minor in Late Antiquity* (Ann Arbor, MI, 2011), 1–26; C. Ratté, 'New Research on the Urban Development of Aphrodisias in Late Antiquity', in D. Parrish, ed., *Urbanism in Western Asia Minor*, JRA Suppl. Ser. 45 (Portsmouth, RI, 2001), 116–47; P. Thonemann, *The Maeander Valley: A Historical Geography from Antiquity to Byzantium* (Cambridge, 2011), 186–90.

time the new walls were built and (2) that the population had diminished and could be accommodated in a part of the old city.

A potentially useful indicator of decline is the number of stray finds of copper coins used in market transactions, which were lost *in situ* and not recovered: diminution over time, whether slow and steady or accelerating, may plausibly be taken as evidence of economic decline leading to one of three possible long-term outcomes—abandonment, shrinkage, or prolonged economic depression. There are problems, though, with such numismatic evidence. First, the centre of market exchange might move to an unexcavated area of a city—in which case a cessation of stray finds proves nothing.[30] Second, there were, we know, significant fluctuations in the volume of new folles issued—notably, an unusually high level of production in the early years of Heraclius' reign (610–16), and a steep drop under Constantine IV (669–85) to a low level which was to last until the second quarter of the ninth century—presumably because fewer were needed to top up the massive coin stocks inherited from the sixth and first half of the seventh century, given a general decrease in the level of commercial activity.[31] There were consequential increases and decreases in the number of folles reaching the localities. It follows (1) that the latest coins found on a particular urban site, dating, say, from the reign of Heraclius' grandson Constans II (641–69), may simply be the youngest coins in the ageing coin stock of the locality—and may have been lost many decades after the date of issue, and (2) that there were, in any case, fewer stray losses to be found in excavations, if, as seems likely, more effort than previously was put into retrieving lost folles when the local coin stock was not being replenished by plentiful new issues.

In the case of western Asia Minor, the archaeological record tends to place the main phase of urban decline after 600, in the second, not the first half of the seventh century. That is the currently accepted dating for a drastic contraction of the fortified perimeters of those cities where the late antique and early medieval phases have been investigated properly. In one case, Sardis, there is good circumstantial evidence—a sudden surge of coins dating from the reigns of Constans II (641–69) and Constantine IV (669–85) found in the city and associated with new roadworks which were almost certainly contemporary with the construction of powerful defences around the citadel.[32] It is then inferred, on the ground of similarity in masonry and general design—thick walls incorporating material quarried from ancient public buildings and monuments, with large

---

[30] See, for example, (on Sardis) Russell, 'Persian Invasions', 66–9.

[31] Drauschke, 'Bemerkungen zu den Auswirkungen der Perser- und Arabereinfälle', 135–7; C. Morrisson, 'Byzantine Money: Its Production and Circulation', in A. E. Laiou, ed., *The Economic History of Byzantium*, Dumbarton Oaks Studies 39, 3 vols. (Washington DC, 2002), III, 909–66, at 954–8, and fig.6.1–15.

[32] G. E. Bates, *Archaeological Exploration of Sardis: Byzantine Coins* (Cambridge, MA, 1971), 2–3, 12–13, 113–19; C. Foss, *Byzantine and Turkish Sardis* (Cambridge, MA, 1976), 53–60.

projecting towers, round, rectangular, or pentagonal, closely spaced along vulnerable sections of curtain wall—as well as circumstantial evidence, that improvements to the defences of other cities of the region were made at roughly the same time. The improvements might take the form of fortification of the central area— as at Ephesus, Miletus, and Magnesia-on-the-Maeander, where existing monumental structures were incorporated into formidable new circuits. Or a citadel might be transformed into a hard-point fortress, as at Pergamum, where it should not be assumed that the main urban area was abandoned, since it was protected by a strong outer circuit.[33] Cities similarly endowed with strongly fortified inner redoubts, but still relying on outer walls kept in good repair, were far from unknown well away from the west coast—cities such as Amorium, Ancyra, and Caesarea (where the outer circuit had been shortened under Justinian) in the interior plateau and Euchaita and Amastris in the Pontic region.[34] In one case, Smyrna, the citadel had already been rendered virtually impregnable under Arcadius, when the city was endowed with a new, slightly shortened set of defences. It may have been occupied twice by Arab forces, in the winters of 673–4 and 716–17, but probably suffered little damage. Certainly, it remained one of the two principal cities on the west coast of Asia Minor, continuing to rely on its late antique fortifications, which, to judge by one section on the south side still visible in the middle of the nineteenth century, were remodelled with the addition of closely spaced towers in the middle of the ninth century.[35]

It is to the middle or late seventh century that the dissolution of cities which did not survive through the age of crisis should probably be attributed. Phocaea probably dwindled away after it ceased to manufacture and export its ubiquitous red slip tableware in the seventh century.[36] Circumstantial evidence from coin finds which peter out after the reign of Heraclius, probably in that of his grandson Constans II, points to the demise of Aphrodisias at roughly the same time, a city which had flourished on its out-of-the-way plain in the heyday of the Roman Empire. The classical city was replaced by a small fortress around the theatre hill built probably in the middle or late seventh century to judge by the coins of

---

[33] C. Foss, *Ephesus after Antiquity: A Late Antique, Byzantine and Turkish City* (Cambridge, 1979), 103–7, 111–13; P. Niewöhner, 'The Riddle of the Market Gate: Miletus and the Character and Date of Earlier Byzantine Fortifications in Anatolia', in Dally and Ratté, *Archaeology and the Cities of Asia Minor in Late Antiquity*, 103–22; Humann, *Magnesia am Maeander*; K. Rheidt, *Die Stadtgrabung*, II *Die byzantinische Wohnstadt*, Altertümer von Pergamon 15.2 (Berlin, 1991), 171–2, with the review by U. Peschlow, *BZ* 86–7 (1993–4), 151–4, at 152–3; H. Voegtli, *Die Fundmünzen aus der Stadtgrabung von Pergamon*, Pergamenische Forschungen 8 (Berlin, 1993), 8–11 (C. Morrisson).

[34] P. Niewöhner, 'Archäologie und die "Dunklen Jahrhunderte" im byzantinischen Anatolien', in J. Henning, ed., *Post-Roman Towns, Trade and Settlement in Europe and Byzantium*, II *Byzantium, Piska, and the Balkans*, Millennium Studien 5.2 (Berlin, 2007), 119–57, at 128–34.

[35] W. Müller-Wiener, 'Die Stadtbefestigungen von Izmir, Sıgacık und Çandarlı', *Ist. Mitt.* 12 (1962), 59–114, at 61–4 and 81–2.

[36] See A. P. Kazhdan, 'Phokaia', *ODB* III, 1665 for its late Byzantine role in the alum trade.

Heraclius found in the debris of the theatre.[37] The evidence is much scantier from Hierapolis, which was still protected by high-grade fortifications built in late antiquity under Arcadius (395–408). Such indications as there are—a very few coins, small churches, and domestic housing—point to continuity of occupation by a reduced population within the walled circuit after serious damage was inflicted, probably by an earthquake, in the middle of the seventh century.[38]

It was not so much destruction caused by specific attacks as a steady erosion of cities' resources and a gradual diminution of their populations brought about by unrelenting warfare decade after decade which brought about urban decline in Asia Minor. Persian raiding expeditions into Asia Minor—in 610, when Caesarea was captured and occupied, in 615, when Shahen marched to the Bosporus, and in 617, when two raiding armies met up in Pisidia—doubtless caused considerable damage, but did not trigger collapse.[39] The contraction of Ancyra, for example, did not follow its capture in 623, since the formidable defences of the citadel, with close-set pentagonal towers, were almost certainly built later, probably when the pressure eased during the first Arab civil war (656–61).[40] What has been termed, in recent times, degradation of resources was not so much the outcome of Persian expeditions, which resumed as the war approached its climax in 626, as of sustained Arab military pressure from 661 to the 717–18 siege of Constantinople and beyond. Repeated devastation by raiding armies, with but few interludes during bouts of civil war, caused serious damage, compounded by the strenuous efforts of the Byzantine fiscal authorities to extract all available resources from the population. Aside from damage done to individual cities and their territories, there was a general effect—a marginal but persistent increase in mortality caused by plummeting living standards as well as enemy action. That is the context for ruralization and agricultural decline in Asia Minor from the second half of the seventh century.[41]

It was not unreasonable, therefore, well before this decline set in, for Heraclius and his advisers to continue the war into the 620s. The core territories of the rump Roman Empire in Asia Minor were capable of sustaining the war effort, in terms of both manpower and material resources. They could be supplemented from the islands of the eastern and southern Aegean islands, which were shielded from Slav sea raiders by islands closer to the Balkans and were only threatened by the Sasanians in the sailing season of 623. The only region likely to have suffered seriously was the south-west coast of Asia Minor. The damage there was *economic*

---

[37] Ratté, 'Aphrodisias in Late Antiquity', 138–40, 144–7.
[38] P. Arthur, 'Hierapolis of Phrygia: The Drawn-Out Demise of an Anatolian City', in N. Christie and A. Augenti, eds., *Urbes Extinctae: Archaeologies of Abandoned Classical Towns* (Farnham, 2012), 275–305, at 279–92.
[39] *Contra* Foss, 'Persians in Asia Minor'.
[40] C. Foss, 'Late Antique and Byzantine Ankara', *DOP* 31 (1977), 27–87.
[41] A. Izdebski, 'A Rural Economy in Transition: Asia Minor from Late Antiquity into the Early Middle Ages', *The Journal of Juristic Papyrology*, Suppl. 18 (Warsaw, 2013).

rather than the direct result of enemy action. It was occasioned by the loss of Egypt in 619 and the consequent halt in the regular convoying of grain across the eastern Mediterranean, and the embargo which the Persian authorities almost certainly put on trade with the rump Roman Empire.[42] But inland, the plethora of small cities which had sprung up with a full complement of public buildings in the highlands backing on to the coast, another thriving world (lit up for us by the sixth-century Life of Nicholas of Myra), was much less affected in the short term, while the coastal communities were still able to pay for the foodstuffs which they needed from accumulated savings.[43] A phase of widespread urban collapse in the interior of Lycia and the neighbouring regions of Pisidia and Caria can only be documented from the 660s. It is attributable to Arab raiding, forays penetrating into the Taurus highlands both from the interior plateau (starting in the 660s) and from the coastal districts where Arab fleets wintered (starting in the 670s). The scale of the collapse was as dramatic as it was because of the artificial overurbanization of the region under the early empire.[44]

Roman imperial pretensions were much more than ideological hot air. There were substantial financial and other material resources to hand in Asia Minor, relatively secure behind the Anti-Taurus and Taurus mountain ranges and shielded by the sea, which the Persians made no serious attempt to master, despite their capture of much shipping in the great ports of the Levant and Egypt. Of course, cuts had to be made after the retreat in 613, but the accumulated wealth of the cities of Asia Minor and the manpower available there, especially in the highlands fringing the plateau, formed a massive resource on which the state could continue to draw. The cuts, made in 615, were draconian—a halving of official salaries (noted in the *Chronicon Paschale* because of its direct effects in Constantinople), which was assuredly matched by an equally swingeing reduction in military pay. They enabled the state to continue to field armed forces commensurate with those of the Persians, from a resource base reduced perhaps by as much as two-thirds after the further loss of Egypt in 619. There was also, we may conjecture, an increase in taxation in the territories remaining under imperial control. It is a sign of the effectiveness of the propaganda pumped out by the authorities (in particular, their success in transforming the initial capture of Jerusalem into an act of sacrilege on an unprecedented scale and a series of wanton atrocities) that officers and men in the army and officialdom, high and low, seem to have accepted the financial blow without complaining vociferously or slackening their efforts on behalf of the beleaguered Roman state. Similarly, the sources are silent about reactions to the increased tax burden. The first evidence

---

[42] Foss, 'Lycian Coast', 3, 8–9, 11, 30–2, 40–2, 44–5, 48–50.
[43] I. Ševčenko and N. P. Ševčenko, eds. and trans., *The Life of Saint Nicholas of Sion* (Brookline, MA, 1984), cc.8, 9, 15–24, 27, 37–8, 52–8.
[44] M. Jankowiak, '*Notitia* I and the Impact of the Arab Invasions on Asia Minor', *Millennium*, 10 (2013), 435–61.

of resistance dates from May 626, when there were two demonstrations in St Sophia against the official in charge of bread supplies and the high prices charged, episodes which should probably be interpreted as as much a display of growing anxiety at the approach of Persian and Avar forces as of objections to fiscal policy.[45]

The Roman governmental system was highly developed—capable of administering far-flung provinces, tapping their resources, and channelling the resulting revenue to the main administrative centres (Constantinople, Thessalonica, Ravenna, and Carthage) from which the Praetorian Prefects of the East and Illyricum and the exarchs of Italy and Africa exercised general oversight over justice, administration, and expenditure in the provinces. The various arms of civil government, along with the organization and funding of armed forces, depended ultimately on an efficient and effective tax regime, reaching down through the various tiers of government, at the levels of region, province, and city, to individual villages. This, in turn, depended on the maintenance of an education system capable of producing literate officials in considerable numbers, on good communications, and on an ubiquitous monetary system, itself sustained by regular issues of coins. This governmental system had not been dislocated, save in localities directly affected by enemy action (i.e. on or close to the line of march of Persian armies in 615 and 617). The Romans retained in the 620s their traditional ability to project a high level of military power over long distances at targets of their choice.

This is not to say that war and the grave losses suffered in the second decade of the seventh century had had no effect on the governmental system. It is plain, for example, that the fiscal system was reshaped in the changed circumstances. It was only to be expected that the authorities in Constantinople would take over direct management of state finances at a time of war, when whole regions were being lopped off the empire. This is best exemplified by changes introduced to the system of mints, the issue of new coinage being increasingly concentrated in Constantinople. One of four mints issuing gold in the west—Catania—ceased to do so around 615, only resuming towards the end of Heraclius' reign.[46] The output of solidi at Rome and Ravenna dropped steeply. Only Carthage remained a major mint, its solidi thickening and assuming a globular form. There was no need for centralization in the east, where Constantinople had long enjoyed a monopoly over the minting of solidi and their fractions. This monopoly was extended to the new precious metal coinage, the silver hexagram, when it was

---

[45] *Chron.Pasch.*, 715.9–716.8.
[46] V. Prigent, 'Le Rôle des provinces d'Occident dans l'approvisionnement de Constantinople (618–717): témoignages numismatiques et sigillographiques', *Mélanges de l'École française de Rome, Moyen Âge*, 118 (2006), 269–99, at 277–8.

introduced in 615, primarily to supplement the output of solidi.[47] The most noticeable change, though, affected the copper coinage. There was a sharp reduction in the output from western mints (in Italy and at Carthage), and a virtual halt for five years at Thessalonica after the loss of Egypt. The two Bithynian mints were also closed down—Cyzicus from 614/15 to 625/6, Nicomedia from 617/18 to 625/6.[48] Permanent closure came at the end of the war, when the minting of folles and smaller denominations was centralized at Constantinople.[49] The only new mints brought on stream during the war were temporary, serving specific short-term needs—(1) a peripatetic military mint, operating from Seleucia (615/16–616/17) and Isaura (617/18), conveniently placed to supply copper coins minted on site (of poor design and crude workmanship) and gold solidi from Constantinople to a defensive force when it was stationed nearby, probably in the Anti-Taurus, in those years, and (2) a temporary mint established on Cyprus in the last years of the war (626/7–628/9), presumably to supply Roman forces as they moved back into the Levant.[50]

Centralization of financial management undoubtedly entailed institutional change, but it is impossible to define the nature of that change for lack of direct evidence. All one can do is to take account of the system as it is revealed in the rich material dating from the reign of Justinian (legislative, epigraphic, and literary) and to compare it with the organizational structure of the ninth-century successor state as revealed by Byzantine lists of rank. Between the late sixth and late ninth century the crown took control of all senior appointments, including those to financial bureaux, and allocated the task of coordinating the activities of government agencies to a financial supremo, the Sakellarios (Keeper of the Privy Purse). The old departments which handled revenue—Praetorian Prefectures, Sacrae Largitiones, Res Privata, and Patrimonium—disappeared, to be replaced by a single state revenue department, the Genikon headed by a Logothete, and Curatoriae managing imperial properties. Alongside a general civil expenditure department (the Sakelle or Sakellion, now headed by a Chartoularios rather than the Sakellarios himself), a set of three specialized military, naval, and equipment departments (Stratiotikon, Vestiarion, and Eidikon) was created, presumably to exercise closer control over expenditure within their defined spheres of activity than had been possible when most state expenditure was delegated to Praetorian Prefectures and exarchates.[51]

---

[47] Grierson, *Catalogue*, 17–18, 43, 46–7, 51, 234–5, 238–9, 270–4; Prigent, 'Rôle des provinces d'Occident', 277.
[48] Grierson, *Catalogue*, 36–8, 219–20, 230–1, 235–41, 308–27, 349–52, 358–65, 371–80.
[49] Grierson, *Catalogue*, 24–6, 219, 228, 295–7; Hahn, *Moneta*, 14–15, 101–4; Haldon, *Byzantium in the Seventh Century*, 186–90.
[50] Grierson, 'Isaurian Coins of Heraclius'; Grierson, *Catalogue*, 39, 220, 231–2, 327–31; Trombley, 'The Coinage of the Seleucia Isauriae'.
[51] N. Oikonomidès, *Les Listes de préséance byzantines des IXe et Xe siècles* (Paris, 1972), 312–18; Haldon, *Byzantium in the Seventh Century*, 173–83.

The principal influences on the new system were undoubtedly war and the principal consequence of war, loss of territory. For the apparatus of government of ninth-century Byzantium was geared to the prosecution of war and to the hoovering up of resources from the much reduced territory of the medieval successor state. It is hard, though, to define what changes were made by Phocas and Heraclius during the war against Persia, as against those introduced in different phases of the apparently everlasting war of defence against the Arabs. It is always hazardous to read much into silences of the sources, especially when they have thinned out as they have by the early seventh century, and to take chance references to the titles of individuals who happen to feature in important episodes as significant indicators of institutional change.

Some observations, however, can be made. In the first place, it is noticeable that there is no reference to any of the three old financial departments in the reign of Heraclius. The last of their chief officers to be mentioned was Athanasius Comes Sacrarum Largitionum, victim of a purge of Phocas' in June 605. This silence is of some significance, given the heightened importance of finance in time of war. The transfer of one function, the hallmarking of silver plate, from the Sacrae Largitiones to the City Prefecture in the first decade of the seventh century at the latest, shows that restructuring was under way early in the war.[52] In the second place, both Praetorian Prefectures were stripped of most of their circumscriptions during the war, the East being restricted to Asia Minor and the Aegean, Illyricum to Greece and a zone around Thessalonica once the Slavs resumed their raiding. This contraction of authority assuredly led to internal reorganization and, probably, to loss of functions. Both prefectures may well have continued to exist into the middle of the century, but probably as no more than residual husks of their old selves.[53] Third, Logothetes, plenipotentiary financial officials personally appointed by the emperor to carry out specific functions in the sixth century, are mentioned as senior figures in the regime in Constantinople, one (Constantine Lardys, described as ex-Praetorian prefect and curator of Hormisdas) being a casualty of Phocas' coup, another (Theodosius, Most Glorious Patrician and Logothete) serving on the high-ranking delegation sent out to the Avar Khagan during the siege of Constantinople.[54] It is tempting to view them as

---

[52] *Chron.Pasch.*, 696.11. Cf. W. Brandes, *Finanzverwaltung in Krisenzeiten: Untersuchungen zur byzantinischen Administration im 6.-9. Jahrhundert*, Forschungen zur byzantinischen Rechtsgeschichte 25 (Frankfurt am Main, 2002), 25-32, 34-9.

[53] PP per Orientem: *Chron.Pasch.*, 696.7 (Theodore, executed in the June 605 purge), 706.18, 709.8-9 (Olympius, a member of the embassy sent to Khusro in 615), 715.16-716.-8 (Alexander, listening and responding to vociferous complaints from Scholarioi in St Sophia on 15 May 626); J. Konidaris, ed. and trans., *Die Novellen des Kaisers Herakleios*, Fontes Minores 5.3 (Frankfurt am Main, 1982), 4.51-63 (pp.88-9) (cited henceforth as *H.Nov.*) for the existence of the post in 629. PP per Illyricum: *Mir.Dem.*, ii.4.231 and 5.290 (pp.208-9, 229), with the comments of Lemerle, *Les Plus Anciens Recueils*, II *Commentaire*, 76-8. Cf. Brandes, *Finanzverwaltung in Krisenzeiten*, 48-54.

[54] *Chron.Pasch.*, 694.8-9, 721.8. Cf. Brandes, *Finanzverwaltung in Krisenzeiten*, 81-2, 86-103.

carrying out some of the functions later distributed among departments under the control of permanent Logothetes.[55] Fourth and finally, the Sakellarios surfaced for the first time as a figure of real political importance in the reign of Phocas. Apart from Phocas, it was the fate of an ex-holder of the post, Leontius the Syrian, which was singled out in the account of Heraclius' seizure of power.[56]

What changes were made during the war remain largely a matter of guesswork. It would probably be wrong to try to trace a lineal descent of early medieval financial departments from component parts of the great departments of state of the sixth-century empire.[57] Powers (and staff) previously divided between Sacrae Largitiones and the Praetorian Prefecture of the East may have been combined in new ways in the Genikon, Stratiotikon, Eidikon, and Vestiarion, some of which may have grown out of others (the Stratiotikon, for example, from the Genikon).[58] All that can be asserted with confidence is (1) that the Roman state had to tighten up its financial management in the second phase of the war to have any hope of survival, (2) that the Sakellarios was the obvious senior minister through whom Heraclius could exercise oversight over state finances, (3) that the Logothete Theodore was probably included in the delegation sent out to negotiate with Avars during the siege of Constantinople because the issue of future financial payments might arise, and (4) that the department over which Theodore presided was something akin to the Genikon (the future revenue department, first clearly attested in 693–4), which perhaps also acted as a treasury.[59]

It was at the centre that reforms were first introduced, to adapt the apparatus of government to new circumstances in a war unprecedented in its scale and intensity. Phocas, an experienced military officer, probably introduced the first and most important change, the creation of a new centrally controlled revenue department headed by a Logothete. Heraclius followed this up not only by taking personal command of the army in the field but by assuming overall charge of financial matters, acting through his Sakellarios. The general coordinating function of the Sakellarios, only explicitly attested at the end of the ninth century,

---

[55] Genikon, Stratiotikon, or, conceivably, Dromos (in charge of diplomacy and internal communications)—the functions of which may be inferred from lists of subordinate officials in Philotheus, *Cletorologium*, ed. and trans. Oikonomidès, *Listes de préséance*, 113.26–115.4, 115.12–20, 117.10–18, 25–31.

[56] *Chron.Pasch.*, 701.3–8, 13–15.

[57] Brandes, *Finanzverwaltung in Krisenzeiten*, 498–9; *contra* Haldon, *Byzantium in the Seventh Century*, 180–1.

[58] Brandes, *Finanzverwaltung in Krisenzeiten*, 500–3.

[59] But see F. Montinaro, 'Les Premiers Commerciaires byzantins', in C. Zuckerman, ed., *Constructing the Seventh Century*, TM 17 (2013), 351–538, who, at 395–405, envisages a transitional phase in the middle decades of the seventh century between the demise of the old treasuries and the creation of the Genikon during which 'general' logothetes transferred taxes from the provinces to a single treasury at the centre, that of the Sakelle (Privy Purse).

probably originated with Heraclius' transformation of what had been a private domestic post (in the Cubiculum, Bedchamber) into a great office of state.[60]

Indirect corroboration for this scenario is provided by what seems at first sight to be a paradoxical increase, a doubling or more, in the volume of gold coins minted in Constantinople during the war. This cannot possibly reflect a doubling in the state's tax revenue, given the cumulative loss of over half its taxpayers in the rich provinces of Syria, Palestine, and Egypt now under Persian occupation. The numismatic evidence is solid, taking the form of an increase in the number of solidus dies used each year, and hence in the number of coins issued (conventionally assumed to be 20,000 per obverse die). The original number of dies used is calculated from the percentage of die links which can be identified in solidi of Phocas and Heraclius as well as preceding and succeeding emperors found in a large emergency hoard concealed at Nikertai, near Apamea, in northern Syria soon after 681. The hoard may be presumed to contain a cross-section of the gold in circulation at the time, since it was buried in a hurry. The number of obverse solidus dies used rose from what was probably an average of 30 per year in the sixth century (that was the approximate number under Justin I (518–27)) to 47.5 under Phocas and to a peak of 71.8 during the last two decades of the war under Heraclius. Thereafter, it dropped back to 37.4 in the last decade of his reign (632–41) and to 12.1 under Constans.[61] There is only one possible explanation: an unprecedentedly high percentage of the gold coinage in circulation in what remained of the empire was being recoined as it was recycled between taxpayers and state. Redirection of the whole annual tax revenue to a single department in Constantinople (the Genikon presumably) would explain this, on the assumption that a substantial proportion of the fiscal uptake from the main source of taxation, the land tax, had been retained in the past in the treasuries of regional Praetorian Prefectures, to be spent in the regions on projects, salaries, and wages in the form of old coin, minting being a prerogative of the Sacrae Largitiones in the capital.

A great increase in the amount of gold coined each year and the consequent strain on the trained workforce of the Constantinopolitan mint would go some way to explaining the haste, evident in slovenly workmanship, in the production of hexagrams and an even more dramatic lowering of traditional standards in the minting of copper folles. Most folles were no longer melted down to form blank flans to be struck and dated by new dies, but were simply overstruck or countermarked. One consequence of this was a greater variation in the weight of folles struck (resulting from different degrees of wear) and a steady decrease in

---

[60] Philotheus, *Cletorologium*, 113.23–5. Cf. Haldon, *Byzantium in the Seventh Century*, 183–6; contra Brandes, *Finanzverwaltung in Krisenzeiten*, 432–3, 441.

[61] C. Morrisson, 'Le Trésor byzantin de Nikertai', *Revue belge de numismatique et de sigillographie*, 118 (1972), 29–91, at 33–5, 37–43.

average weight from around 12 grams at Heraclius' accession to around 6 grams at the end of the war.[62]

The resources of Asia Minor, the Aegean, and the Balkans (despite extensive Slav settlement in the north and renewed raiding in the south) provided the wherewithal for the prosecution of the war against the victorious armies of Khusro II through the 620s. With its fiscal system streamlined and its outgoings deliberately reduced almost in line with the loss of revenue, the Roman state was capable not only of maintaining its resistance to Persian forces but also of seizing the initiative and striking back. From the early modern period, the costs of warfare have put serious strain on the economies of belligerents.[63] It would be easy to assume the same of the truncated Roman Empire after nearly twenty years of war. But evidence of this is hard to find.

It is true that the loss of the large annual shipments of Egyptian grain to Constantinople was a serious economic blow. But there were alternative, albeit more distant sources of supply in North Africa and Sicily, both generators of substantial grain surpluses and safe from external depredation. It is likely that arrangements were put in hand for procuring and transporting grain before the Persian invasion of Egypt and capture of Alexandria in 619. A government agent responsible for this was in post by 617-18.[64] Certainly measures were taken to reduce demand in Constantinople in 618, first with the imposition of a charge, and later with a halt in the free distribution of bread to those entitled by virtue of inherited official citizenship.[65] Once the Persians extended direct rule over Palestine (in 616) and Persian troops could move within striking distance of the Nile valley, it was only a matter of time before Egypt would be attacked, and the government in Constantinople could be under no illusion about the likely outcome.

There was no shortage of shipping, since there had been nothing, except for an adverse wind at Alexandria at the time of the final assault, to prevent merchant ships escaping from Middle Eastern ports at the approach of the Persians.[66] With the abolition of the free public distribution of bread, the cost of feeding a privileged part of the population of the city was transferred from the treasury to individuals. With respect to this staple, the effect of the loss of Egypt on state finances was probably neutral. Instead of being acquired in Egypt as tax in kind, grain was bought in the west, the state organizing its purchase and transport, and recouping the cost at the point of sale in Constantinople. The price which the

---

[62] Grierson, *Catalogue*, 18, 22-4, 52-60, 218-19.

[63] See, for example, R. I. Frost, *The Northern Wars: War, State and Society in Northeastern Europe, 1558-1721* (Harlow, 2000), 83, 148-52, 187, 192-3, 199-205, 324-5, and D. Parrott, *The Business of War: Military Enterprise and Military Revolution in Early Modern Europe* (Cambridge, 2012), 71-7.

[64] C. Morrisson and W. Seibt, 'Sceaux des commerciaires byzantins du VIIe siècle trouvés à Carthage', *Revue Numismatique*, ser.6, 24 (1982), 222-41, at 226-8.

[65] *Chron.Pasch.*, 711.11-15.

[66] *Khuz.Chron.*, 26.9-11 (trans. Greatrex and Lieu, 235); *Vita S.Spyridonis*, 81.14-83.7.

consumer paid for bread in Constantinople presumably covered the cost of purchase, shipment (in the form of freight charges) and baking.

Whether landowners in Africa received cash payment for grain sold or were granted remission of the equivalent amount of tax, they grew wealthy on the grain trade. This is evident from hoards of solidi concealed between 612 and 668 in the grain-growing provinces of Byzacena and Proconsularis.[67] In the case of Sicily, there is indirect evidence for cash payment. Sixth-century copper folles taken out of the eastern coin stock (over 95 per cent were minted in the metropolitan area) and countermarked specially for Sicily were sent out in large quantities. They should perhaps be viewed as tracers for large monetary transfers, folles being needed as a fractional coinage to accompany any solidi sent out. The first of the countermarks used—a bust of Heraclius with monogram to the right, carefully placed over the obverse figure, with the legend SCL below the line on the reverse—can be dated by the similarity of the bust to that on quarter-folles (decanummia) minted in Catania in 619–20. The start of monetary transfers to Sicily can thus be dated to the period immediately following the capture of Alexandria. This countermark remained in use until 628–9, after which new countermarks were introduced (evidently the new sources of supply in the west continued to be exploited).[68]

The best evidence that the strain of sustaining the war effort year after year was bearable after the cuts made in 615 is also provided by the coinage. The easiest way to eke out limited financial resources at a time of emergency would have been to tamper with the standard of the main high-value means of exchange, the gold solidus. But there is no evidence of debasement in the solidi with busts of Heraclius and his young son, Heraclius the New Constantine, issued from 613 to 626, when the latter attained his majority, and during the last three years of the war, 626–9.[69] Nor is there evidence of the state's resorting to the desperate measure of appropriating its ultimate reserve of precious metal held in the form of ecclesiastical plate and the revetment of church furniture and walls, save in 622, when war broke out in the west with the Avars, and it was plain that large sums would be needed to secure a renewal of peace in the Balkans. Even so, the measure was limited to charitable foundations run by the crown and the great church of St Sophia, with its close connection to the crown, and took the form of a forced loan.[70] Otherwise, the church was unscathed. No encroachment was made on the resources and internal decor of the sacred buildings in highlands and lowlands, in town and country, where clergy and laity assembled regularly to celebrate the liturgy and to pray to their all-powerful God.

---

[67] R. Guéry, C. Morrisson and H. Slim, *Recherches archéologiques franco-tunisiennes à Rougga*, III *Le Trésor de monnaies d'or byzantines*, Collection de l'École française de Rome 60 (Rome, 1982).
[68] Prigent, 'Rôle des provinces d'Occident', 273–90.   [69] Grierson, *Catalogue*, 10, 271.
[70] Theoph., 302.34–303.3.

5.2 The Middle East under Persian Occupation

The whole Roman Levant was occupied in 616. Egypt was under firm Persian control by 621. In little more than a decade after their first push across the Euphrates, the Persians had conquered the richest and commercially most active provinces of the Roman Empire, thereby adding greatly to the resource base of the Sasanian Empire. There was no loosening of their grip over the following years of intensifying warfare, thanks in part to a military presence large enough to deter potential rebels and in part to careful political management. The more alert the new authorities were to Roman sensibilities and needs and the greater their success in encouraging collaboration from leading provincials, the less need there was for large troop deployments. Given a continuing call for fighting manpower on the Anatolian front to press the Roman war to a final victorious conclusion, the balance in Persian policy came down firmly on the side of conciliation as against coercion.

The evidence about the Middle East in the years of Persian occupation is exiguous and scattered. Because of the preservation of documentary papyri emanating both from the provincials and the Persian authorities, a somewhat fuller picture can be presented for Egypt than other occupied provinces for which we have to rely on incidental references in literary sources. But even for Egypt the evidence is patchy. Most Greek and Coptic papyri are not dated, and only that minuscule proportion which either has precise dating formulae or makes explicit references to Persians can be confidently assigned to the period of occupation. No such problem arises in the case of papyri written in Pahlavi, of which over 350 have been edited with scrupulous care.[71]

The difficulty with the Persian papyri is their illegibility. Even the most expert of editorial eyes has trouble making out individual words in the cursive script which they use. Cryptographic skill of a high order is required to piece together their contents. Success has been greatest with the opening formulae of polite address.[72] Otherwise all that can be deciphered in the great majority of texts is the

---

[71] Main publications: A. G. Perikhanjan, 'Pekhlevijskie papirusy sobranija GMII imeni A.S. Pushkina', *Vestnik Drevnej Istorii*, 77.3 (1961), 78–93; D. Weber, ed. and trans., *Ostraca, Papyri und Pergamente*, Corpus Inscriptionum Iranicarum, III Pahlavi Inscriptions, vols. 4 and 5, Text I (London, 1992); D. Weber, ed. and trans., *Berliner Papyri, Pergamente und Leinenfragmente in mittelpersischer Sprache*, Corpus Inscriptionum Iranicarum, III Pahlavi Inscriptions, vols. 4 and 5, Text II (London, 2003). Unless otherwise specified, all references are to papyri published by Weber in Corpus Inscriptionum Iranicarum. Five hundred and seventy-six papyri in the Rainer collection of Vienna disappeared in the Second World War in Berlin, where they had been sent on loan in 1936, but they have reappeared in St Petersburg (D. Weber, 'The Vienna Collection of Pahlavi Papyri', in B. Palme, ed., *Akten des 23. Internationalen Papyrologenkongresses* (Vienna, 2007), 725–38, at 728–9).

[72] Opening formulae include 'to X endowed a thousand times with good fortune' (P 10, 20, 36), 'to X made worthy through inner peace, endowed with deathless good fortune' (P 25), 'to X made always fortunate by the gods, with deathless good fortune a thousandfold' (P 70). Others are 'god-remembered' (P 16, 75), 'made always fortunate by the gods' (P 76). The only letter to a woman begins

odd word—*nāmag*, 'letter' for example, or *drustīh/drōd ud rāmišn*, 'health and peace', or *sālār/gundsālār*, 'officer'—and snatches of correspondence—a kindness requested, a commercial transaction of some sort in progress, references to ships, day-by-day records of deliveries of foodstuffs, presents, an expression of thanks, a mention of Alexandria, etc.[73] A fair number of the correspondents are named, but in most cases without any indication of posts held. Much of the content, though, is irretrievable, leaving most of the official instructions and reports and private correspondence which officials and officers were sending each other tantalizingly out of reach. Odd bits of information can be picked up: the escape of an expensive slave; the swearing of a written affidavit that someone is innocent of a charge; various items of news sent by an unnamed person stationed at Memphis; news from home about difficulties on his estate received by an officer or official stationed at Oxyrhynchus; the issuing of a public notice; the manumission of a slave girl in the deep south, at Elephantine; security for a loan.[74] Only occasionally can something of the process of government be picked out, of which more below.[75]

Leaving aside the introduction of a superior military authority, which inevitably redrew traditional lines of accountability, the Persians did not disturb the established structures of Roman government.[76] It was not in their interest to do so. If they were to economize on the resources, military and administrative, which they committed to the occupied provinces, they had to work within the existing system. Of course, garrison troops were required, but there was no need for a ubiquitous military presence. Concentration at major centres from which the road network would allow rapid deployment was the most cost-effective way of underpinning Persian authority. Above all, it was vital that they should win over the active cooperation of city notables who traditionally ran local government and that they should do everything possible not to antagonize the population at large.

General considerations of this sort do seem to have shaped Persian policy, to judge by the scanty available evidence. Old provincial capitals, such as Edessa in Osrhoene and Caesarea in Palestine, remained seats of government. There is no evidence of any change to provincial boundaries or functions beneath the

---

'To her who has been blessed with all good fortune and peace by the gods' and ends by wishing her respect, peace, and safety (P 18).

[73] Letter: P 2, 4, 8, 13, 15, 44–6, 60, 68–9, 81, 94. Health and peace: P 44, 59, 68, 74, 109. Officer/general: P 17, 19, 23, 109, 136. Odd references: kindness (P 3); transaction (P 4, 63); ships (P 7, 29, 73); foodstuffs (P 140); presents (P 44, 46, 52); thanks (P 6); Alexandria (P 159).

[74] Runaway slave: Perikhanjan, P 8. Affidavit: P 52. News from Memphis: P 44. Bad news from home (written on parchment): P 19. Notice: P 138. Manumission: Perikhanjan, P 1. Loan security: Perikhanjan, P 7.

[75] Pp. 155–7, 162–3.

[76] Hence the *marzban* at Caesarea (capital of Palestine I) had authority over the governor of Palestine II: see C. Foss, 'The Persians in the Roman Near East (602–630 AD)', *JRAS*, ser.3, 13 (2003), 149–70, at 162. See also P. Sänger, 'The Administration of Sasanian Egypt: New Masters and Byzantine Continuity', *GRBS* 51 (2011), 653–65, at 661–5.

Sasanian regional command in Egypt. A wholesale remodelling of Syria and Palestine was to come in the seventh century, but only after the Arabs had swept over their desert frontage and sought to subordinate the rich settled urbanized lands to durable Beduin control.[77] Troop deployments were not obtrusive, to judge by the dearth of evidence. All we can say is that the numbers were large, since the operation to evacuate them, first from Egypt, then from Palestine and Syria, at the end of the war took many months.[78] It may be presumed that the troops at Caesarea (attested in a reliable source) formed a substantial force, but they were based in a special fortified compound, perhaps the theatre fortress at the south end of the city, to minimize friction with the local population. At Edessa, likewise, it is probably because he could call on nearby Persian forces under the command of a *marzban* (regional governor) that the authority of the city governor, a local notable, was imposed effectively.[79]

Alexandria was secured by a garrison housed in a fortified compound or citadel like that at Caesarea. Persian officialdom was present throughout Egypt. In the far south the old fort at Thebes seems to have been garrisoned and some controls on movement introduced.[80] What appears to have been a special unit of Egyptian auxiliaries serving under a certain Sherag included men recruited from Elephantine as well as ten cities in the central Nile valley.[81] Such references as there are to soldiers and senior officers are remarkably uninformative. We simply know that there were *gundsālārān* (regimental officers), *āzād-mardān* (gentry), *aswārān* (cavalry troopers), and a *kanārang* of cavalry.[82] The locations of their bases, their numbers, and the command structure are not known. What can be seen is their effect on the local economy. Procurement of foodstuffs and the issuing of rations are recurring themes in the Pahlavi papyri. There is no evidence

---

[77] The system of *ajnād* (plural of *jund*), military provinces introduced by the Arabs divided Palestine and Syria into horizontal zones plugged at their base into the north-western desert and running west to the Mediterranean coast. Cf. J. Haldon, 'Seventh-Century Continuities: The *Ajnād* and the "Thematic Myth"', in Cameron, *States, Resources and Armies*, 379–423 (with maps on pp. xii–xiv), who conjectures (409–14)—rather too speculatively to my mind—that one of the new military provinces, Jordan (al-Urdunn), was created by Heraclius after the end of the war to control its Jewish population.

[78] Chron.724, 146.28–30, 147.18–24 (trans. 17–18).

[79] V.Anast., cc.15–20, with commentary of Flusin in *Saint Anastase*, II, 231–5, Foss, 'Persians in the Roman Near East', 162, and J. Patrich, *Studies in the Archaeology and History of Caesarea Maritima, Caput Judaeae, Metropolis Palaestinae* (Leiden, 2011), 141–9 and fig.77; Mich.Syr., IV, 403–4, 408 (trans. II, 402–3, 411); Chron.1234, 230.17–231.13 (trans. Palmer, 133–5).

[80] H.Patr.Alex., 485.9–10, with A. Gariboldi, 'Social Conditions in Egypt under the Sasanian Occupation (619–629 AD)', *La Parola del Passato: Rivista di Studi Antichi*, 64 (2009), 321–350, at 7. H. E. Winlock and W. E. Crum, *The Monastery of Epiphanius at Thebes*, 2 vols. (New York, 1926), I, 98–103, II, 81, 239 (Coptic ostracon 324: a correspondent of the holy man Epiphanius, the dominant figure in a loose complex of monastic cells just to the north of the town, tells him that he has got permission from the local Persian commander to travel south on business and asks for his prayers).

[81] P 55. Commentaries: J. de Menasce, 'Recherches de papyrologie pehlevie', *JA* 241 (1953), 185–96, at 188–92; Perikhanjan, 'Pekhlevskie papyrusy', 91; J. Harmatta, 'Two Economic Documents from the Sasanian Age', *Oikumene*, 1 (1976), 225–37, at 226–8; Weber ad P 55.

[82] P 23, 109, 136, 172, 305.

of forcible requisitioning. It appears that staples such as meat (lamb and pork), grain, hens, eggs, and wine as well as delicacies such as quail, lark, and pigeon were purchased on the open market.[83] Some also came as gifts from local notables anxious to keep in with the Persian authorities.[84] Special warrants were issued for their transport.[85]

The upper echelons of provincial government were, we may be sure, taken over by Persian officials. Outside Egypt, all that can be seen is the presence of governors, but it is plain that they exercised effective power in the localities. Thus, at Edessa, a city which had put up sterling resistance before capitulating in 609, the head of one of the principal local families, evidently identified as a leader of an anti-Persian party, was deported together with his widowed mother and detained for a time in Ctesiphon. Tough measures could be taken which might affect a whole city, for example the appropriation of a massive amount of silver revetment from the cathedral of Edessa (reported to have weighed 112,000 (or 120,000) pounds) as a reprisal, it is said, for intrigues against the city governor.[86] It may be inferred that the main levers of local power, administrative and fiscal, were taken over and that revenues which had hitherto flowed into Roman coffers were diverted and now helped fund the Persian war effort.

Effective management of local affairs and appropriation of tax revenues are documented for Egypt. By a fortunate chance, a senior Persian official, a certain Shahralanozyan, figures in several papyri, Greek as well as Persian, and his reported activities provide invaluable glimpses of Persian administration in action. His area of responsibility covered the Fayyum, where he was based, and much of the Nile valley, from Arcadia if not farther north to the Upper Thebaid in the south. He appears to have had plenipotentiary powers. A senior Persian tax official who dealt with the fiscal authorities of Oxyrhynchus and Cynopolis was answerable to him. He carried out tours of inspection, to judge by one letter announcing his imminent arrival in a country district, and authorized the issue of transport warrants. The *dadwar* or legal official responsible for drafting and sealing the warrants was another of his subordinates, as, presumably, were the *ostvars* and *vidarbads* responsible for controlling movements up and down the

---

[83] See, for example, the itemized lists on Berlin papyri P 21, 48, 139–41. P 139 and 140 are re-edited along with a long Greek list by P. Sänger and D. Weber, 'Der Lebensmittelhaushalt des Herrn Saralaneozan/Šahr-Ālānyōzān . . .', *Archiv für Papyrusforschung*, 58 (2012), 81–96.

[84] *The Oxyrhynchus Papyri*, 80 vols. (London, 1898–2014): *P Oxy* LVIII 3960 (ed. J. R. Rea), a long account, dated 620–1, reveals that the wine steward responsible for a cluster of some thirteen to fourteen vineyards disbursed 7,281 *knidia* of wine (each roughly equivalent to 4.5 litres), out of a total of 33,289, to Persians according to a list kept in the *chartoularion* (estate office). This was a slightly smaller amount than the consignments sent to (1) churches, hostels, and martyrs' shrine, extramural as well as intramural (8,458 *knidia*) and (2) free contract workers (8,906 *knidia*)

[85] J. Harmatta, 'Laisser-passer en Égypte à la fin de l'antiquité', *Studia Aegyptiaca*, 1 (1974), 165–75; Weber, P 81. Cf. Gariboldi, 'Social Conditions in Egypt', 348.

[86] Mich.Syr., IV, 391, 403–4 (trans. II, 381, 402–3); *Chron.1234*, 223.16–30, 230.17–29 (trans.124, 133–4).

Nile valley. The hypothesis advanced above that Persian authority reached deep into provincial society is borne out by this small collection of documentary material.[87]

Persian authority was exercised in traditional ways within the established framework of provincial and local government. Every effort was made to ensure continuity of administrative practice. A striking example is provided by the policy adopted towards Jerusalem after the city was reoccupied for a second time in the course of 616. It might have been expected that the Persians would allow free Jewish movement into the holy city, given that Jews had proved more welcoming than Christians when they first entered Palestine and that it was an appeal from the Jews with established residence in city which had led to their initial intervention in 614. They did nothing of the kind, but rather issued a general order forbidding Jewish immigration into the city. Stability was evidently reckoned to depend on maintaining the existing balance between Christian and Jews in the city. A change of policy ran the danger of causing widespread and deep resentment among Christians in Palestine and farther afield. The Sasanian government was well aware that it must respect Christian sensibilities, not least because of large and influential Christian constituencies in Mesopotamia. The equally important Babylonian Jewish community might be vociferous in its complaints, but it would not forget that many Jews in Palestine owed their lives to the Persians.[88]

Few, if any innovations were made to monetary and fiscal practice. Naturally Persian silver drachms percolated in considerable quantities into the occupied territories now that they were integral parts of the Sasanian economic zone. Although there is very limited evidence of their use in everyday cash transactions, they left a durable mark on the coin stock in the long run. Five silver hoards concealed in Syria and northern Mesopotamia at times of crisis in the middle of the eighth and the early ninth century contain large numbers of drachms of Khusro II.[89] The presence in each of these hoards of a large number coins minted in the first decade of his reign is a clear pointer to their arrival during the period

---

[87] Perikhanjan, 'Pekhlevskijskie papirusy', 88–9 (P 13); *P Oxy* LV 3797 (with comment of J. R. Rea (77–8)); D. Weber, 'Ein bisher unbekannter Titel aus spätsassanidischer Zeit?', in R. E. Emmerick and D. Weber, eds., *Corolla Iranica: Papers in Honour of Prof. Dr David Neal Mackenzie on the Occasion of His 65th Birthday on April 8th, 1991* (Frankfurt am Main, 1991), 228–35, at 228–32; Gariboldi, 'Social Conditions in Egypt', 341–8; Sänger, 'Administration', 654–63.

[88] Ps.S, 117.2–20, with *Hist.Com.*, n.35.

[89] Everyday use: Bijovsky, *Gold Coin and Small Change*, 307–9. Drachms in hoards: M. Abu-l-Faraj al-Ush, *The Silver Hoard of Damascus* (Damascus, 1972)—1,309 drachms out of 3,819 coins, the latest of 748/9; M. Abu-l-Faraj al-Ush, *Trésor de monnaies d'argent trouvé à Umm-Hajarah* (Damascus, 1972)—155 drachms out of 408, the latest of 808/9; R. Gyselen and A. Nègre, 'Un Trésor de Gazīra (Haute Mésopotamie): Monnaies d'argent sasanides et islamiques enfouies au début du IIIe siècle de l'hégire/IXe siècle de notre ère', *RN* 6 ser., 24 (1982), 170–205—436 drachms out of 2,820, the latest of 820/1; R. Gyselen and L. Kalus, *Deux Trésors monétaires des premiers temps de l'Islam* (Paris, 1983)—Bab Tuma, 712 drachms out of 854 coins, the latest dated 747/8, and Qamisliyya, 255 drachms out of 1519, the latest of 815/6.

of Persian occupation. For the working of taxation within the traditional bounds of the Sasanian Empire led to the de facto recall of those early issues and their recoining for reissue as salaries, pay, and other state expenditure by the end of Khusro's reign. Hence the virtual absence of these early issues of Khusro II from hoards concealed in Khuzistan and elsewhere inside the empire.[90]

The circulating medium of the occupied territories remained almost entirely Roman, consisting of a large stock of gold solidi (and its fractions) and copper coins (chiefly dodecanummia in Egypt and folles elsewhere) minted in the past.[91] Money thus continued to convey traditional Roman and Christian messages to the provincials. The attitude of the Persian authorities was complaisant. Since there was no immediate need to top up the plentiful inherited coin stock (and new Constantinopolitan issues, both gold and copper, percolated into the Levant, it being impossible to seal the land and sea frontiers), they refrained from minting coins of their own with new legends and images.[92] The only official new issues datable to the period of the occupation were struck at Alexandria, probably because of a well-documented outflow of coins to Palestine.[93] The weight standard was that customary in Egypt—12-nummia or 6-nummia copper coins of the usual thick, stubby shape. The types were distinctive: on the obverse of the 12-nummia coins, a facing beardless bust wearing cuirass and crown surmounted by a cross, placed between a crescent and a star, and on the reverse, a long cross on globe; a palm tree and no legend on the very small 6-nummia pieces. It is intriguing to see the Persian authorities issuing coins with crosses—an action

---

[90] The proportion of drachms from years 1–10 is as follows: Damascus 33 per cent; Umm-Hajarah 17 per cent; Bab Tuma 29 per cent; Qamisliyya 31 per cent; Jazira 42 per cent. This contrasts with their virtual absence in five substantial hoards, all probably concealed on Sasanian territory before the Muslim conquest: Susa I: A. de La Fuye et al., *Mémoires de la mission archéologique de Perse*, 25 (1934), 68–76, 84–7; Seleucia: H. Göbl, 'Die Sasanidische Münzfund von Seleukia (Veh-Ardašer) 1967', *Mesopotamia*, 8–9 (1973–4), 229–60; Susa II: R. Gyselen, 'Note de métrologie sassanide: les drahms de Khusrō II', *Revue Belge de Numismatique*, 135 (1989), 5–23; Basel: R. Gyselen, 'Un Trésor de monnaies sassanides tardives', *RN* 6 ser., 32 (1990), 212–31; Quetta: H. M. Malek, 'A Seventh-Century Hoard of Sasanian Drachms', *Iran*, 31 (1993), 77–93.

[91] The best evidence of coins in use comes from hoards concealed at times of heightened anxiety, either during the Heraclian revolution or at the approach of Persian armies. Apart from a few unusual cases of recently acquired coins (91 solidi of Phocas found at Bat Galim, Haifa, or the 264 freshly minted solidi of the Jerusalem Giv'ati Hoard), hoards both of gold and copper coins consist predominantly of sixth-century issues, for example Afrus, Syria (29 solidi, Justinian-Phocas), Alexandria-Chatby 1903 (concealed after Heraclius' accession—well over half the 191 gold coins date from the sixth century, with a handful from the fourth), Cyrrhus (402 folles and 98 fractions, Anastasius-Maurice, plus one follis of Phocas (603–4), with a peak of 200 from the reign of Justin II), Hama (230 folles and 338 half-folles, from Anastasius to Phocas, again with a peak under Justin II), Antinoe I 1914 (1 copper coin of Constantius II, 1 6-nummi of Justinian, 108 12-nummi from Justin I to Heraclius (613–18)), and Egypt 1975 (118 12-nummi and 7 6-nummi, from Justin I to Heraclius)— H.-C. Noeske, *Münzfunde aus Ägypten I: Die Münzfunde des ägyptischen Pilgerzentrums Abu Mina und die Vergleichsfunde aus den Dioecesen Aegyptus und Oriens vom 4.-8. Jh. n. Chr*, 3 vols (Berlin, 2000), II, 210–12, 359–60, 418, 453–68, 480–1, 486, Bijovsky, *Gold Coin and Small Change*, 414–15, 426, 467–8.

[92] Bijovsky, *Gold Coin and Small Change*, 379–81, 383–4, 418–20.

[93] Bijovsky, *Gold Coin and Small Change*, 388–92, 416.

which clearly signalled their readiness to respect the Christian faith of their new Egyptian subjects. Both types may have been issued originally as a fractional coinage for use by Persian forces serving Egypt, but the twelve-nummia pieces proved popular and were put into general circulation.[94]

Taxes, though, continued to be paid in gold and copper by Roman provincials. Some of the gold was forwarded to the central authorities, but what was retained for local administration in the occupied territories (predominantly solidi and folles rather than their fractions, together with dodecanummia and hexanummia in Egypt) was, it appears, simply recycled by the authorities rather than being reminted. An old coin stock, if carefully husbanded, could continue to oil the machinery of government for several years after the last substantial new issue.[95] There was, therefore, no financial problem in managing the occupied Roman provinces without much fresh minting.[96] The devising of a new coin, especially a high-value Persian equivalent of the Roman solidus, would also have posed a difficult dilemma. The Sasanian government would have had to decide whether or not to adhere to tradition and thereby to display to its new as to its old subjects of all faiths the state's Zoroastrian core, with the attendant risk of rousing Christian opposition.

Local elites were handled carefully. Obviously, potential opposition had to be quashed at the outset. But, even in the case of the Edessan notable deported after the city's capitulation, there was no move to seize his assets. He was well treated during his period of detention, and, after a while, his loyalty being assured, was allowed to return home. The story that his widowed mother was deported, kept in squalor, and never released because of a slighting remark overheard by Khusro when he was a fugitive in 590 looks like pure fantasy. All that had gone missing during his absence was the family plate which his mother had buried and which was only located two centuries later.[97] Even when the death of Apion III (at about the time of the fall of Alexandria) and the disappearance of the heir (unidentified, presumably a refugee in Constantinople) left a wealthy Egyptian estate ownerless, it was not expropriated but left as a going concern, run by the managerial staff. It looks as if the Persian regime was anxious to avoid antagonizing local vested interests throughout the conquered territories and did what it could to cultivate notables and secure their willing collaboration in the localities.[98]

---

[94] J. R. Phillips, 'The Byzantine Bronze Coins of Alexandria in the Seventh Century', *NC* 7.ser., 11 (1962), 225–41. Phillips makes the plausible suggestion that the beardless figure represents Maurice's eldest son Theodosius, in whose name Khusro II had originally declared war.
[95] *P. Oxy.* LI 3637, lines 17–19 for the dispatch of gold to the king of kings.
[96] Gariboldi, 'Social Conditions in Egypt', 340–2.
[97] Mich.Syr., V, 403–4 (trans. II, 402–3); *Chron.1234*, 223.16–30, 230.17–29 (trans.124, 133–4).
[98] *P Oxy* LVIII 3959, 3960 and LXVIII 4703. J. Banaji, *Agrarian Change in Late Antiquity: Gold, Labour, and Aristocratic Dominance* (Oxford, 2001), 149–59, 182–5; Gariboldi, 'Social Conditions in Egypt', 339–40.

There is no evidence to hand of social dislocation, only of elites maintaining their status and, we may infer, continuing to play an active part in local government. Thus, for example, the same family remained dominant in the small town of Nessana in southern Palestine at the end as it had been at the beginning of the seventh century.[99] In Caesarea of Palestine relations between local notables and Persian authorities remained good to the end. The most influential local postholder, the *kommerkiarios*, was able to secure the temporary release of a notorious Zoroastrian apostate from prison to attend the liturgy in the cathedral on the Feast of the Elevation of the Cross on 14 September 627. He took him home to dine after the service.[100] The four leading families of Edessa remained on good terms with all but one of the governors appointed to the city. At the end of the war, the last governor did his utmost to delay implementation of an order to deport the city's population. It was not surprising, then, that the notables of the city were in a weak position when the Emperor Heraclius visited the city in 630, so much so that they felt unable to voice their opposition to his decision to transfer the cathedral and all the endowments which they had given it from Monophysite to Chalcedonian control.[101]

Measures were taken to win support or, at the very least, to avoid antagonizing the local population. Persian troops seem to have been kept for the most part under strict discipline. Archaeological investigation reveals that most cities survived the initial invasion and subsequent occupation relatively unscathed.[102] Allegations of wanton destruction of buildings and atrocities (directed primarily at monks) should largely be discounted, unless they can be corroborated, as in the cases of Jerusalem and the environs of Alexandria (the pilgrimage centre of St Menas and the nearby town on the far side of Lake Mareotis were severely damaged).[103] They were the two cities far removed from the militarized frontier zone which, rather than capitulating swiftly to superior Persian forces, fought hard and were taken by storm. It is true that there is no evidence about measures taken to repair the damage at Alexandria once the fighting was over. Too much, though, should not be made of this silence, since there is virtually no documentary evidence about Alexandria, and the extant narrative sources, exiguous and highly tendentious as they are, cannot compensate for the long gap in John of Nikiu's

---

[99] C. J. Kraemer, *Excavations at Nessana*, III *Non-Literary Papyri* (Princeton, NJ, 1958), 6–8, 132–41 (nos. 44–7), 149–50 (no. 53), 156–74 (nos.56–9), 198 (no.68), 202–3 (no.70), 209–11 (no.74), 215–25 (nos.76–7).

[100] *V.Anast*, cc.29–30.

[101] Mich.Syr., IV, 403–4, 408–9 (trans. II, 402–3, 411–12); *Chron.1234*, 230.17–231.13, 236.20–9 (trans. 133–5, 140–1).

[102] A. Walmsley, *Early Islamic Syria: An Archaeological Assessment* (London, 2007), 45–7.

[103] Jerusalem: see Chapter 3.3. Allegations about massacres of monks in Egypt: *Hist.Patr.Alex.*, 485.1–5, 486.4–7. Fire damage at St Menas: P. Grossmann, *Abū Mīnā*, I *Die Gruftkirche und die Gruft* (Mainz, 1989), 182–5. The only other area known to have suffered was a stretch of the coast between Tyre and Acre where several churches were destroyed: see Russell, 'The Persian Invasions of Syria/Palestine and Asia Minor', 47–8.

coverage. Jerusalem, on the other hand, is known to have benefited from a large relief programme after the siege in 614. The Persian authorities allowed in aid from Roman-held Egypt. The mission organized by the patriarchate of Alexandria seems to have been free to make its own assessments of need and to distribute food, clothing, and cash as it saw fit. Two years later, when direct rule was introduced in Palestine, a large reconstruction programme was launched. Funds were sought from Christian communities, but it is likely that the main cost was borne by the Persians. The work on the main churches in and around the holy city was well publicized. It could be announced by the acting head of the Jerusalem patriarchate that 'there is peace in this city of God and its surroundings', God having 'made our opponents friendly'.

There was one large and influential constituency which the Persians set out to cultivate. Monophysite Christians, who were in a numerical ascendancy in Syria and Egypt, may have remained loyal to the Roman Empire (after all, it was impossible to imagine a world without it, and it was generally thought to have the divine imprimatur) and may have been ready to fight and die in its defence, but they had long felt aggrieved at imperial policy which backed the rival Chalcedonian confession and imposed an official Chalcedonian episcopate on them. A dissident, shadow hierarchy had been created, but the official episcopate kept control of most churches and most church property.[104] Several years earlier, during the first attritional phase of the war, before, possibly well before 609, Khusro II had abandoned the traditional policy of favouring the Nestorian church against other Christian confessions inside the empire, taking account probably of the rapidly growing strength of Persian Monophysites.[105] This new neutral stance towards the confessions led naturally to the abandonment of the Romans' pro-Chalcedonian policy. Deprived of official backing and expelled from churches appropriated under Maurice, the Chalcedonian hierarchy saw their grip weakened, especially in northern Mesopotamia and Syria, where Monophysites were in a great majority (unlike Palestine, where Chalcedonians were predominant). Monophysite bishops could be appointed freely and Monophysite congregations, with the backing of local notables, were able to take over church assets from Chalcedonians. At a stroke, the Persians gained considerable popularity in large swathes of the former Roman Middle East. Their only error was to condone what looks like an attempt by the Metropolitan of Mosul to extend his authority over key sees in northern Mesopotamia and Osrhoene. The bishops whom he parachuted into the great sees of Amida, Constantia, and

---

[104] L. Pietri, ed., *Histoire du christianisme des origines à nos jours*, III *Les Églises d'Orient et d'Occident* (Paris, 1998), 399–409, 423–6, 457–81; Whitby, *Emperor Maurice*, 213–15.
[105] Flusin, *Saint Anastase*, II, 106–18; Payne, *State of Mixture*, 184–8.

Edessa were rejected by the local faithful, who continued to accept the authority of the patriarch of Antioch.[106]

It would have been completely out of keeping with these conciliatory policies for the new Persian regime to try to extract as much money and materiel as possible from their newly acquired subjects. The last thing the provincial authorities or central government should have contemplated was a ratcheting up of taxation. It is equally unlikely that they would have been ready to lower the burden while the war was still being fought.

The fragmentary documentary record from Egypt under Persian occupation provides some suggestive evidence about the tax paid in gold—but nothing, alas, about payments in grain, the *embole* (likely to have been reduced, Persian forces based in the Levant generating less demand than Constantinople). A small dossier of three documents from Oxyrhynchus provides figures for the amount of gold paid in the 623-4 fiscal year by Oxyrhynchus and the neighbouring city of Cynopolis on the opposite bank of the Nile. A fourth document provides a point of comparison before the Persian conquest. A local official, Marinus, was responsible for forwarding to the Persian authorities revenue raised in cash from the two cities. Marinus dealt directly with a Persian official, Razbana, who was answerable in turn to the senior postholder whom we have already encountered, Shahranalyozan. The tax was paid in three instalments, between October and May. Figures are given for two instalments in 623-4. An initial payment of 3,962 solidi made in October 623 was 2,016 short of the required total of 5,978 solidi. Razbana demanded the balance owing and received it nearly three weeks later.[107] Payment of 5,040 solidi towards the third instalment is acknowledged in a receipt dated April-May 624 and issued in the name of Shahranalyozan.[108]

This documentation is not unproblematic. Lacking an official receipt for the first payment, we cannot be sure whether it was made on behalf of one city or both. If it came from only one, the total sum paid in the first instalment would have amounted to around 10,000 solidi rather than a little under 6,000. Then there is the puzzling discrepancy between the amount owing on the first instalment in October, which is divided equally between the two cities, and the imbalance in their contributions to the down payment on the third instalment in April-May—Oxyrhynchus put in four times as much as Cynopolis. If that imbalance was to be redressed in a later payment, Cynopolis contributing much more than Oxyrhynchus, the third instalment would also have amounted to 10,000. If the larger figures for individual instalments are taken to be more likely, then the two cities were paying roughly a quarter more in cash in the 623-4

---

[106] Cyriacus of Amida, *Translation of the Relics of James*, ed. and trans. E. W. Brooks, PO 19.2, 268-73, at 269.2-6; Mich.Syr., IV, 389-91 (trans. II, 379-81), Chron.1234, 224.27-225.9 (trans. 125-6).
[107] P Oxy LI 3637, XVI 1843.
[108] P Oxy LV 3797.

financial year (some 30,000 solidi as opposed to 24,500) than they had before the arrival of the Persians. If the lower is to be preferred, their tax liability was reduced by about a quarter (to approximately 18,000 solidi).

All that can be said is that there was a significant but moderate variation in the taxes raised in cash from two cities in the middle Nile valley in one year of the Persian occupation, and that taxation in kind is likely to have been reduced. Generalization is, of course, perilous. But the signs are that the Persians refrained from squeezing their new subjects too hard.

All in all, the documentary record suggests that Egypt suffered from no general ill effects during the occupation. The presence of the Persians is rarely mentioned. A few cases of maltreatment of provincials are picked up in the papyrological record, most probably occurring at the outset of the occupation.[109] One act of resistance in middle Egypt is documented, but may have involved no more than a small group of conspirators. They caused fire damage in an unnamed city (perhaps burning an administrative building) and then went into hiding in the countryside. The Sasanian authorities were prepared to negotiate with them through an intermediary, probably a bishop. In his letter urging them to respond, he stressed that no one had been killed so far.[110]

There was no perceptible change in the tempo of life under the occupation which might be attributable to the Persians. Great affairs of state, high politics, and warfare made little impact on society at large at that time or for well over a millennium to come until the mechanization of warfare and tightening of communications brought about by the Industrial Revolution. Only on rare occasions, when the fighting was concentrated in a small area or when systematic degradation of whole regions of an enemy state became a strategic aim, did war really impinge on everyday life in the localities. This did not happen in Egypt, where it was the expectation of Persian attack which caused damage in the form of serious inflation between 614 and 618.[111] Senior managers of the estate of Apion III centred on Oxyrhynchus continued to exchange business letters, as in the past. One dossier of correspondence involving the chief factor, Victor, and the bursar, George, contains items dated to 611, 612, and 618 and is likely to have extended later. The bursar authorized payments; the factor issued receipts. Issues of all sorts were dealt with—tax matters, crimes, procurement of equipment (two new boats, for example), personnel matters (for example, the use of armed retainers as messengers), and the problem of work left unfinished by bricklayers.[112] The estate remained highly productive. The production of thirteen or fourteen vineyards came to the equivalent of 214,000 bottles of wine in 621.[113] The keeper

---

[109] Foss, 'Persians in the Roman Near East', 167; Gariboldi, 'Social Conditions in Egypt', 338–9.
[110] *Ägyptische Urkunden aus den Staatlichen Museen Berlin: Koptische Urkunden*, III (Berlin, 1968), no.338.
[111] See p. 128 above.
[112] *P Oxy* I 152–3, XVI 1844–61, 1864, 1904, 1936–7, 2010–11, 2033, LVIII 3954, 3957.
[113] *P Oxy* LVIII 3960 (n. 82 of this chapter).

of the stable received deliveries of everything that he needed (some ready cash, wine, oil, eggs, and sheep, as well as fodder) and worried about the possibility of fraudulent orders being issued in future. Unusual items, 70 pounds of Nile fish or 28 bunches of asparagus, were specially acknowledged.[114]

Far to the south, a small community of eremitic monks living outside Thebes continued to exchange notes on practical matters (the linen cloth, shrouds, bandages, and leather binding which they made) and to respond to the pleas for prayers, spiritual advice, and practical matters which they received from the laity. A collection of over 500 papyri and ostraca, most written in Coptic, dating from the early seventh century, contains only three references to Persians, only one of which is tinged by apprehension (a plaintive letter in the course of which the writer asks what to do now that the Persians are coming south). Without the evidence of the Pahlavi papyri, we would be hard put to document the Persian presence. Apart from the handful of Greek and Coptic documents already mentioned, there is an interesting document which throws light on the purchase of manufactured goods—a receipt dated 8 November of the fourteenth indiction (625) from fourteen villagers in the district of Hermopolis acknowledging the payment by the Lord Firuz Khusro of 36 solidi for the transport of 1,980 loads of linen cloth due for delivery within a fortnight.[115]

The best evidence for general social and economic conditions in the seventh century comes from archaeological investigations carried out on the territories of the modern states of Jordan and Israel. The quantity and quality of knowledge accumulated there is superior to that obtained from regions lying farther north (in Lebanon, Syria, and Turkey). It can be supplemented by a small dossier of papyri from Nessana in southern Palestine. The considerable advances made in classifying and dating ceramic evidence in the recent past have transformed historical understanding. It is now plain that the Persian and Arab conquests neither dislocated nor transformed the societies and economies of the Roman Levant. It is true that general economic growth halted in the second half of the sixth century, primarily under the impact of the initial pandemic of bubonic plague and its subsequent recurrences. A late antique boom fuelled by pilgrimage to the Holy Land, thriving east Mediterranean commerce, and increasingly active overland trade with Arabia had affected the whole Levant from the coast to the edge of the desert, from long-established cities to marginal country in their hinterlands. Its acme was over, but there was no vertiginous drop when the seventh century set in.[116]

---

[114] *P Oxy* XVI 1857, 1861–2.
[115] J. Krall, *Corpus Papyrorum Raineri*, II *Koptische Texte* (Vienna, 1895), 18–23 (no.5) (cf. Gariboldi, 'Social Conditions in Egypt', 339).
[116] J. Johns, 'The *Longue Durée*: State and Settlement Strategies in Southern Transjordan across the Islamic Centuries', in E. L. Rogan and T. Tell, eds., *Village, Steppe and State: The Social Origins of Modern Jordan* (London, 1994), 1–31, at 4–10, 13–14. See also B. de Vries, *Umm el-Jimal: A Frontier*

The larger economic story can be followed, in miniature, in the ceramic evidence, as well as, at an intermediate level, in the fabric of the cities which studded the Levant, especially those of the prosperous desert frontage. At Pella, for example, an important city of the Decapolis (in northern Jordan), there was no sudden break in the finds either of amphorae, cooking vessels, or tableware corresponding to the Sasanian (or Arab) conquest. Change was gradual, both in terms of types of ware and the shape of individual types, and it continued steadily through the seventh century and beyond. Sources of supply also changed, wares manufactured at Jerash, another city of the Decapolis, coming to the fore in the seventh century, while imports from the Mediterranean tailed off. It seems reasonable to extrapolate from the principal phenomena discernible at Pella, the ceramic finds from which have been subjected to meticulous scrutiny, and to envisage economic stability at the local level in much of the Levant but a gradual narrowing of horizons which led, probably by the end of the century, to a general decoupling of the region from the Mediterranean. Reorientation was only to be expected in an era when the main political and economic centres were to be found in the interior and far to the south.[117]

Most cities survived relatively unscathed and reasonably prosperous. In an exceptional case such as Apamea, which had suffered gravely when sacked by the Persians in 573, there may have been an exodus of notable families. The city may have become shabbier. Aristocratic residences may have been put to other uses. But an effort was made to uphold civic standards.[118] Elsewhere, the grand public buildings (above all churches and associated structures) and monumental thoroughfares were better maintained and there is little evidence of governing elites' leaving. The examples of Jerash, Bostra, Scythopolis, Philadelphia, and Epiphania may be cited, while at Pella a large improvement scheme, which involved remodelling the area around the cathedral, was carried out between 580 and 659-60.[119] There was plenty of building activity in the early decades of the seventh century across the Hauran and the Balqa. Those two areas, however, were as exceptional as Apamea, but to their benefit, as they were particularly fertile and under the special protection of the important Ghassan tribe and its clients.[120]

Town and Its Landscape in Northern Jordan, I *Fieldwork 1972-1981*, JRA, suppl. ser.26 (Portsmouth, RI, 1998), 91-127, 229-41.

[117] P. Watson, 'Change in Foreign and Regional Economic Links with Pella in the Seventh Century A.D.: The Ceramic Evidence', in P. Canivet and J.-P. Rey-Coquais, eds., *La Syrie de Byzance à l'Islam: VIIe-VIIIe siècles* (Damascus, 1992), 233-48; Walmsley, *Early Islamic Syria*, 49-59.

[118] C. Foss, 'Syria in Transition, A.D. 550-750: An Archaeological Approach', DOP 51 (1997), 189-269, at 205-26.

[119] A. G. Walmsley, 'The Social and Economic Regime at Fihl (Pella) and Neighbouring Centres between the 7th and 9th Centuries', in Canivet and Rey-Coquais, *La Syrie*, 249-61; Foss, 'Syria in Transition', 230-2, 237-45; Y. Tsafrir and G. Foerster, 'Urbanism at Scythopolis-Bet Shean in the Fourth to Seventh Centuries', DOP 51 (1997), 85-146, at 135-46; Walmsley, *Early Islamic Syria*, 83-7.

[120] Foss, 'Syria in Transition', 245-58; Walmsley, *Early Islamic Syria*, 41-5; A. Michel, 'Le Devenir des lieux de culte chrétiens sur le territoire jordanien entre le VIIe et le IXe siècle: Un État de la

There is admittedly a general tailing-off in the epigraphic record of new construction elsewhere, especially in northern Syria in the early seventh century. Although it is questionable how much should be read into this silence, it probably marks the start of a period of stagnation which would shade into gentle decline after the middle of the eighth century, when the political centre of the caliphate moved east.[121]

The important point, though, is that there was no hiatus during the period of Persian occupation. The orthogonal armature characteristic of Roman cities was everywhere in evidence when the Arabs arrived and was subsequently respected when they put up new buildings and laid out new towns.[122] Cities had not suffered serious damage, either materially or socially, during the period of Persian occupation. They emerged from it as viable social and economic entities. Evidence that the wider economy was not seriously damaged comes from marginal lands, where the inhabitants were dependent on active interchange with nearby cities. The survival through the seventh century of large, well-built villages on the relatively inhospitable limestone massif of northern Syria, demonstrates that war and occupation did not have a devastating impact on former Roman provinces. In their case, decline was very gradual, the *coup de grâce* being delivered in the first half of the tenth century by the truncated and brutalized remnant of the Roman Empire which had survived and was then temporarily in the ascendant. Byzantine forces all too successfully pursued a strategy designed to destroy agricultural infrastructure and drive away existing rural populations.[123]

Cautious, prudent, and anxious to avoid innovation though they were, the Persians, nonetheless, did introduce one major reform. It has long been known, but its significance has not been fully appreciated. The date is uncertain but the bare outline of events is reasonably clear. The story is told in the *Khuzistan Chronicle* and reappears in a longer, much-embellished form in early Islamic historical tradition.[124] It is a tale of intrigue in high places. Two strong characters, Khusro himself and al-Nuʿman, his Arab client king, are pitted against each other. Both are driven by emotion—resentment at real or imagined slights—and both pursue their aims with deliberate cunning. In the Syrian version, Khusro bears a grudge because al-Nuʿman would not accompany him when he was fleeing to the

---

question', in A. Borrut et al., *Le Proche-Orient de Justinien aux Abbasides: Peuplement et dynamiques spatiales*, Bibliothèque de l'Antiquité Tardive 19 (Turnhout, 2011), 233–69, at 235–9.

[121] P.-L. Gatier, 'Inscriptions grecques, mosaïques et églises des débuts de l'époque islamique du Proche-Orient (VIIe–VIIIe siècles)', in Borrut, *Proche-Orient*, 7–28, at 26–8. Cf. F. R. Trombley, 'War and Society in Rural Syria c. 502–613 A.D.: Observations on the Epigraphy', BMGS 21 (1997), 154–209, at 177–82, 190–8, who infers serious demographic decline and attributes it to warfare (unlike Foss, 'Persians in the Roman Near East', 159).

[122] Walmsley, *Early Islamic Syria*, 83–95.

[123] A.-M. Eddé and J.-P. Sodini, 'Les Villages de Syrie du Nord du VIIe au XIIIe siècle', in C. Morrisson, ed., *Les Villages dans l'Empire byzantin: IVe–XVe siècle* (Paris, 2005), 465–83.

[124] *Khuz.Chron.*, 19.22–20.17 (trans. Greatrex and Lieu, 231–2); Tab., 1015.17–1037.18.

Romans in 590 and refused his requests for a horse and for one of his daughters as a wife (the latter in offensive terms). Later, it is al-Nu'man's turn to take offence when he is given scraps of hay at a dinner. The Arab version goes back to the circumstances of al-Nu'man's appointment (a famous Arab poet of the day, who was highly regarded by Khusro, backed him), describes al-Nu'man's subsequent imprisonment and execution of the poet (behind which lay devious machinations), and homes in on the critical factor, his insulting refusal to allow one of his daughters to marry Khusro. In both versions, relations break down. Al-Nu'man reluctantly goes to the court at Ctesiphon, where he is arrested. He dies in prison, either poisoned (Syrian version) or victim of plague (Arab version). Arab tribes who are clients of the Lakhm turn against the Persians in both versions, either before al-Nu'man's arrest (Syrian version) or afterwards (Arab version). In the latter version they win a victory over a Persian force and a new set of Arab auxiliaries. It may have been no more than a minor skirmish, but the Battle of Dhu Qar is picked out in Islamic historical tradition as a turning point in Arab-Persian relations.[125]

This everyday tale of intrigue in high places begins to take on extraordinary significance if one pauses and reflects. Behind the gossipy story retailed both in Mesopotamia and in Arabia lies an important policy decision of Khusro's, namely to dismantle a system of client management which had served the Sasanians well. Since the late third century, members of the leading Nasrid clan of the Lakhm had been chosen to police the desert for the Sasanians and, at times of crisis, had played an important part in imperial politics. Nasrid rulers ranked high in the hierarchy of the Sasanian court and were regarded as key loyalist supporters of the Sasanian dynasty. They were designated kings and deputed to manage the affairs of north-eastern Arabia.[126] They were thus made responsible for the security of the Sasanians' Mesopotamian heartlands. From their court at Hira on the edge of the alluvium, not far from the future site of Kufa, they established a complex nexus of ties with Beduin of all sorts.[127]

Money undoubtedly changed hands. Honours were distributed. The court at Hira probably aped that at Ctesiphon, tribal chiefs receiving ranks in accordance with their status. Additional leverage was gained if their sons were in attendance and grants of land had been made. Commercial agreements were made with distant tribes, but those nearer at hand were organized into a tribal confederation

---

[125] Elements of both versions are combined in *Seert Chron.*, 539.8–540.2: an intrigue leads to Nu'man's poisoning; this triggers unrest among all the Arabs, who rebel against both empires and grow in power.

[126] G. Fisher, *Between Empires: Arabs, Romans, and Sasanians in Late Antiquity* (Oxford, 2011), 91–5.

[127] F. M. Donner, 'The Bakr B. Wa'il Tribes and Politics in Northeastern Arabia on the Eve of Islam', *Studia Islamica*, 51 (1980), 5–38; D. Genequand, 'The Archaeological Evidence for the Jafnids and the Nasrids', in G. Fisher, ed., *Arabs and Empires before Islam* (Oxford, 2015), 172–213, at 207–12.

controlled by the Lakhm.[128] There must have been many changes to its shape and membership over the centuries, but in its final form (the Bakr b. Wa'il confederation) it can be observed thanks to information conserved in early Islamic genealogies and tales of tribal warfare. The Banu Shayban, the most powerful of the seven tribes in the confederation, were managed via their leading clan, the Banu Hammam, with whom the Nasrids established close ties. Special favour was also shown to the leaders of another tribe, the Banu Duhl. Patronage of this sort took place within a system of checks and balances. A grouping of four lesser tribes acted as a southern counterweight to the potentially dominant Banu Shayban in the north as well as a defensive coalition against regional rivals.[129]

The Lakhm achieved immense prestige in pre-Islamic Arabia. This rested above all on their military power. Their army, comprising regular Persian units, an armed retinue of their own, and contingents from subordinate tribes (the core coming from the Bakr b. Wa'il at the beginning of the seventh century), was able to project their influence into central Arabia, where it met that of the south Arabian kingdom of Himyar.[130] In the north they were clearly superior to the Romans' Arab clients, as they showed unequivocally at the beginning of the sixth century, when fighting broke out between the great powers. They were able to strike west into Roman territory virtually at will in 502–4, and again in 529 after the failure of Justinian's grand eastern offensive in 528. Justinian's only recourse was to replace the traditional Roman system of multiple client management with a monarchical system aping that of the Persians. Previously independent tribes under phylarchs were subordinated to the Ghassan, and the title of king was granted to the head of the leading Jafnid clan.[131] While the Ghassan were able to match the Lakhm until the 570s, Persian influence was steadily extended and intensified, principally through the agency of the Lakhm, elsewhere in the Arabian peninsula, especially in the south. Quite naturally, Hira achieved the position of pre-eminent cultural centre of Arabia. It was surely through Lakhm (and Ghassan) sponsorship that Arabic consolidated its mastery over other branches of ancient Arabian, north and south, and that pre-Islamic poetry reached its acme and helped to foster Arab pride in the desert and past warlike feats of the tribes.[132]

---

[128] M. J. Kister, 'Al-Hira: Some Notes on Its Relations with Arabia', *Arabica*, 15 (1968), 143–69, at 149–65.

[129] Donner, 'Bakr b. Wa'il', 16–28.

[130] Kister, 'Al-Hira', 165–9; Robin, 'Royaume Hujride', 674–95.

[131] Fisher, *Between Empires*, 95–9; P. Edwell et al., 'Arabs in the Conflict between Rome and Persia, AD 491–630', in Fisher, *Arabs and Empires*, 214–75, at 221–7, 230–4.

[132] R. G. Hoyland, *Arabia and the Arabs: From the Bronze Age to the Coming of Islam* (London, 2001), 240–3; M. C. A. Macdonald, 'Ancient Arabia and the Written Word', in M. C. A. Macdonald, ed., *The Development of Arabic as a Written Language*, Supplement to the Proceedings of the Seminar for Arabian Studies 40 (Oxford, 2010), 5–27.

The deposition of al-Nuʿman was, therefore, an act fraught with significance. It signalled the end of the long-standing special relationship with the Nasrids. It was only to be expected that there would be repercussions, as there were, repercussions which resulted eventually in rebellion. It is unlikely that such an act was a mere spasm, purely emotional, without political calculation. But before attempting to seek out other, supplementary reasons, a date of some sort needs to be put upon the act. All that can be said for sure is that it post-dated Khusro's flight to the Romans in 590 and predated the Muslim conquests, when the new Arab clients were in charge of the desert frontage of Mesopotamia. Time has to be allowed, on the one hand, for resentments to fester and for plans of revenge to mature, and, on the other, for the usurping tribes to consolidate their authority over the Beduin of the north-east. We are still left with a wide opening, say, from late in the peace of 591–602 to the middle of the second phase of the war. The opening can be narrowed to the first phase of the war if we turn to Islamic sources. Al-Tabari, the most authoritative of Abbasid historians, took pains to correlate the different categories of historical material he collected about the last era of pre-Islamic history with events in Mecca and Medina. He gives two conflicting dates for the death of al-Nuʿman, Khusro's fifteenth year (604–5) and one year, eight months (around 608) before the start of Muhammad's mission, which he places in Khusro's twentieth year (609–10). The battle of Dhu Qar is dated later, since Muhammad was already preaching when he reported that the Arabs had received satisfaction from the Persians.[133]

There may be a spurious precision in these dates, which, in any case, conflict, unless it is al-Nuʿman's death which is placed in 608, three or four years after his arrest and incarceration. It would then have taken five years or more, from his deposition in 604–5 for opposition to the Sasanians to develop into an uprising. The two events, though, are concertinaed together in an early ninth century Syrian chronicle which dates serious fighting between Persians and Arabs to 604–5.[134] Given that there is nothing to gainsay a rough dating of the fall (and subsequent death) of al-Nuʿman and the consequent dissolution of the Lakhm nexus of alliances given by al-Tabari and backed by the Syrian source, this episode, which had a profound effect on the political configuration of the northern half of Arabia, may provisionally be placed in the first phase of the war.

That being so, a rational explanation grounded in high policy can be suggested for Khusro's move against the Lakhm. For after the opening round of fighting had demonstrated Persian military superiority in the field and had inflicted serious damage on Roman forces in both major arenas of war, south and north of the Armenian Taurus, there was every prospect that Khusro's forces would advance

---

[133] Tab., 1009.4–5, 1031.2–4, 1038.8–14.
[134] *Chronicon anonymum ad annum 819 pertinens*, ed. A. Barsaum, CSCO, Scriptores Syri 36 (Paris, 1920), 10.26–7, trans. J.-B. Chabot, CSCO 56 (Louvain, 1937), 7.

into Roman Mesopotamia and might even push west and south of the Euphrates into Syria. If he was confident of making gains, as he surely was, he had to plan ahead, and if he planned ahead, he could not but realize that the monarchical system used by his predecessors to manage the relatively narrow desert frontage of Mesopotamia could not be extended indefinitely north and west. The many different sorts of ties which had held the Lakhm nexus of clients and allies together would stretch and break if more and more tribes of north-west Arabia were incorporated. Moreover, many generations of rivalry between the Lakhm and the Arab clients of the Romans would have made it virtually impossible to subordinate the latter to the former.

Khusro, therefore, had no option but to replace the Sasanians' traditional bilateral arrangement with a multilateral one. It would not be feasible to manage northern and western as well as the eastern Arabia from a single peripheral centre. The large and powerful tribes sustained by the comparatively rich and extensive grazing in the north-west of the peninsula would have to be treated respectfully and cultivated assiduously. This required a system on the old Roman model under which the desert frontage was divided up into sectors, each managed by a phylarch or designated Arab client (leader of a powerful local tribe) and watched over by a nearby army commander. There was no alternative if peace were to be maintained in the desert and the wealthy lands surrounding it were to be kept secure from Beduin raiding.[135]

It is hard to say which tribes were, in the event, picked out to manage the desert approaches to the lands conquered in the second phase of the war. As has already been seen, there is a general dearth of information from Roman sources about conditions in the occupied territories. All that can be stated with confidence is that there was a short period after the fall of Jerusalem in 614 in which Palestine suffered from Beduin raiding, but that soon, from 616, order was restored when the Persians imposed direct rule and monks were able to repopulate monasteries in the Judaean desert which they had been forced to abandon.[136] Early Islamic historical tradition is more forthcoming, but the careful disentangling and analysis of material transmitted about the Bakr b. Wa'il tribes carried out by Donner have not been replicated for the tribes of the north and west.

The new arrangements can only be observed at either end of the Fertile Crescent. In place of the dethroned Lakhm kings of Hira, Iyas b. Qabisa of the Banu Tayyi' was appointed chief local client and put in charge of Hira. He it was who commanded the mixed force of regular Sasanian troops and Beduin from the B. Iyad, B. al-Namir b. al-Qasit, B. Taghlib, and B. Tami as well as his own tribe, who fought at Dhu Qar. Despite that defeat, Iyas succeeded in restoring a

---

[135] W. Liebeschuetz, 'The Defences of Syria in the Sixth Century', in C. B. Rüger, ed., *Studien zu den Militärgrenzen Roms II* (Cologne, 1977), 487–99, at 495.

[136] Flusin, *Saint Anastase*, II, 177–80.

stable system of management into which substantial elements of the Bakr b. Wa'il were reintegrated. It was eventually destabilized and demolished in the first stage of Islamic expansion.[137] Far to the west, fronting Palestine, the Ghassan re-emerged as an important force among the Beduin after a period of obscurity following the dissolution of their client network in the course of Justin II's Persian war. They loom large in the poetry which is embedded in accounts of the Prophet's life. They were later to be portrayed as forming a key component of the Roman forces which faced the Muslims at Yarmuk.[138] Sponsorship by the Sasanian authorities provides the most likely explanation for their return to prominence. They dominated the Hauran plain and were probably allocated a large sector to the south of the Jebel Druze.

The evidence, such as it is, thus suggests that the Persians reinstated the system of multiple phylarchates upon which the Romans had traditionally relied to manage neighbouring Beduin tribes. The details of the system are not recoverable as of now. We do not know how many phylarchates were set up or which tribes, besides the group headed by Iyas b. Qabisa and the Ghassan, were given the managing role within each sector. We can only speculate that the long desert frontage of the Fertile Crescent was divided up into comparatively large segments, so that the Sasanian authorities would be dealing with a smaller rather than larger number of tribal leaders. The managerial task would thereby be made somewhat easier for them, and the prestige of their designated clients would be raised well above that of other tribes within their sectors, which would make them relatively immune to challenge. What is clear, though, is that the new system worked well. The tribes of northern Arabia were effectively managed. Beduin raiding was brought to an end in Palestine by 616. Order was reimposed on eastern Arabia after a short period of turbulence following the suppression of Lakhm kingship. Persian authority was firmly impressed, either by direct rule or through client rulers, on the whole periphery of Arabia, from Yemen to Oman, up the Gulf, and in a great northern arc running round to the Negev. Persian power was projected throughout the peninsula. Only one region in the west lay for the moment beyond their effective reach—the Hijaz. It looked likely that before long the whole of Arabia would be incorporated loosely within a greatly enlarged Sasanian Empire.[139]

In sum, the Persians kept their military presence in the occupied territories as discreet as possible, co-opted local leaderships into their administration, and

---

[137] Donner, 'Bakr B. Wa'il', 28–37.
[138] Ibn Ishaq, *Kitab Sirat Rasul Allah*, ed. F. Wüstenfeld, 2 vols. (Göttingen, 1858–60), 519.4, 527.19, 613.14, 624.12, 843.14, trans. A. Guillaume, *The Life of Muhammad* (Oxford, 1955), 342, 350, 405, 415, 568; Abi al-Abbas Ahmad b. Yahya b. Jabir al-Baladhuri, *Kitab Futuh al-Buldan*, ed. M. J. de Goeje, *Liber expugnationis regionum* (Leiden, 1866), 135.1–7, 136.5–21, trans. P. K. Hitti, *The Origins of the Islamic State*, I (Beirut, 1966), 207, 208–10.
[139] P. Crone, *Meccan Trade and the Rise of Islam* (Oxford, 1987), 245–50.

sought to win over the Roman provincials by adopting a relaxed attitude to the competing Christian confessions and by refraining from taxing them too heavily. A key element in their political strategy was preservation of the administrative status quo in the lands which they conquered. Reforms were all too likely to antagonize their new subjects. It was in their interest to make the transition from the old to the new political authority as smooth as possible, and to avoid doing unnecessary harm to existing political or economic structures. The only major change which they introduced (reorganization of the Arab client system) had entirely beneficial effects on the settled peoples of the whole region.

The extant evidence, patchy though it is, suggests that these conciliatory policies worked, that crises in relations were confined to specific localities and had special local causes, and that the Persians were careful not to flaunt their military power. There seems to have been no armed resistance, and virtually no overt dissidence. The natural leaders of opposition, city notables, collaborated, principally because their valuable suburban properties, with well-appointed villas, gardens, and orchards, were being held hostage for them, but also because there could be no question in their minds about the return before too long of Roman forces. An empire which had presided over the whole Mediterranean world for six centuries, in effect since time immemorial, could not conceivably cease to exist.

The only discernible evidence of dissidence comes in the form of Roman bronze coins (folles) minted in relatively small quantities during the Persian occupation. They were dated by regnal years of Heraclius and bore many different mint marks, all spurious. There is no question of their being official Sasanian issues, given the small numbers struck (they formed in aggregate no more than 0.4 per cent of the Syrian coin stock in 630), the several types issued, and the varying quality of the workmanship. The mint, which was operating at or close to Emesa and which seems to have carried on the traditions of the Antioch mint, was, it may be inferred, clandestine. Variations in quality between different issues can then be explained as caused by circumstance, as the danger of detection rose and fell. Interspersed among imitations of old types of Justin II, Maurice, and Phocas, which would not arouse suspicion, it minted local copies of current official Roman coins bearing the images of Heraclius and his son, Heraclius the New Constantine.[140] It may have been simply a money-making venture, a scheme to insert forged specie into the coin stock and to profit from its spending power. But the inclusion of imitations of current Roman coins with images of the reigning emperor and his designated heir points rather to a political aim, an effort by dissident elements in Syria to remind their fellow provincials of their rightful ruler, of their Roman allegiances. The dates, given in regnal years of Heraclius,

---

[140] H. Pottier, *Le Monnayage de la Syrie sous l'occupation perse (610–630)*, Cahiers Ernest-Babelon 9 (Paris, 2004).

when these loyalist issues were slipped into the circulating medium correspond to times of heightened tension—614, the year of the sack of Jerusalem, 618, when preparations were under way for the invasion of Egypt, and 622-4, when the assault on Asia Minor began in earnest. This suggests that the minting and circulation of the coins were more than a gesture of defiance. The clandestine group was trying to foment sedition when emotions were roused.[141]

Any such hopes were vain. The Persian occupation seems to have been accepted as a brute fact by the great majority of the population. As for the longer-term integration of Roman provincial elites into the upper echelons of the Sasanian government and society, a few very tentative suggestions may be made. Patronage has always been a powerful weapon in building up political support. Systematic discrimination in the allocation of local posts could be used to build up a loyalist constituency among provincial notables. At a higher level, members of magnate families could be offered careers in royal service which might take them to distant reaches of the empire. There were fifth-century Armenian precedents for this. A cadre of middle-ranking administrators of assured loyalty could also be built up on the model of the cadets gathered by Khusro I at his court, who were then introduced into public service as a check on entrenched local elites. Military garrisons would probably evolve into permanent colonies and gradually embed themselves in local society, disseminating Persian culture, promoting (discreetly) Zoroastrian beliefs, and, in due course, absorbing some elements of the local population. Recruitment into the Sasanian army and service in distant places might also prove a powerful Iranizing agent. By such methods, one great empire could hope to absorb much of the territory and in due course to win over the governing elites of another, especially if it was widely, though vaguely known that a remote ancestor of that empire had once ruled over those same territories. Ideological adaptation to a new world order was much easier if it simply involved the substitution of one empire for another than if an imperial system was dismantled and its constituent peoples were left to fend for themselves in a world of flux.

5.3 The Sasanian Empire

The Sasanian Empire suffered from the geopolitical disadvantage of all continental powers: it was exposed to attack from all sides. There were refractory highlanders in Transcaucasia and the Caucasus mountains in the north-west. In the far south-east equally refractory tribesmen were to be found in the wild, desiccated country of Sistan, Zabulistan, and Makran. The empire's political and commercial

---

[141] Pottier, *Monnayage*, 56 (table VIII).

heartland in Mesopotamia abutted directly onto what was virtually a continent in its own right, the Arabian peninsula, over which power could be projected but where it was hard to establish any sort of durable control. The greatest danger traditionally came from the rival antecedent great power to the west, but, with the rapid expansion of the Turkish khaganate in the third quarter of the sixth century, it was to the east and the north that the regimes of Khusro I Anushirwan, Hormizd IV, and Khusro II Parvez had increasingly to look. The decision taken by Khusro II in winter 615–16 to break once and for all with the familiar binary system in western Eurasia made good sense in this context, fraught though it was with risk.

It was an empire which had to be geared for fighting, with a flexible and responsive military system capable of deploying forces on different fronts as external circumstances changed. There was an inherent militarism dating back to the early third century, when the founder of the Sasanian dynasty, Ardashir I, imposed his authority by force on larger and larger swathes of territory in successive aggressive campaigns. The natural reservoirs of fighting manpower in the two great mountain chains of the Elburz and Zagros were effectively tapped to sustain a large standing army on a par with that of the Romans and with the same three principal components—regional field forces (four, each under its own *spahbed*, since the army reforms of Khusro I), frontier garrisons manning linear defences and great cities with hardened defences, and guards regiments stationed in the metropolitan area and at other nodal points.[142] The empire was Iranian, Iran forming its ideological and military heartland, the base from which Sasanian authority was projected over large stretches of the surrounding world. Iranians, speakers of Pahlavi (Middle Persian), predominantly Zoroastrian in faith (Christianity and Judaism having made but limited inroads), settled in cities, towns, and villages, and relying on stock-raising, agriculture, and trade for their livelihood, were conscious of their distinctiveness, of their special civilizing mission on earth. Generations of government propaganda had helped to impress this notion of common national character and imperial destiny over highlanders and lowlanders from Khurasan and Fars in the east and south to Media and Adurbadagan in the west and north.[143] The leaders of society in the localities, a large class roughly approximating to country gentry, and the aristocracy, the greatest of whom looked for preferment to the royal court, were thoroughly militarized. Command, feats of valour, service on distant fronts—these were the stuff of their lives.[144]

---

[142] J. Howard-Johnston, 'The Late Sasanian Army', in T. Bernheimer and A. Silverstein, ed., *Late Antiquity: Eastern Perspectives* (Exeter, 2012), 87–127, at 87–108.
[143] G. Gnoli, *The Idea of Iran: An Essay on its Origins* (Rome, 1989).
[144] A. Christensen, *L'Iran sous les Sassanides* (Copenhagen, 1944), 103–13; Wiesehöfer, *Ancient Persia*, 171–4, 197–9.

There was not too much difficulty, then, in keeping up the military effort demanded by Khusro II's extended war of revenge and conquest—despite long tours of duty on distant fronts, a steady stream of casualties, the disruption of trade inevitably caused when men were called away from their normal lives and the military had prior claim on resources, and the virtual closure of trans-Asian trade routes to Persian merchants because of fraught relations with the Turks.[145] The Sasanian Empire was used to prolonged periods of conflict. Stamina was culturally programmed in after whole decades or more of commitment to warfare against the Romans in the third, fourth, and sixth centuries. In Khusro II's case, the sustaining of the war effort was particularly impressive, since it was not as if the opening of the war followed on a period of peace. He had had to fight for his throne, as little more than a boy, and then to engage in a long civil war after freeing himself from the tutelage of his maternal uncles.[146] Four years into the war, he called on yet more of his subjects to serve in the armed forces. A recruiting campaign boosted fighting manpower to a level, possibly unprecedented, which enabled the high command to launch and sustain simultaneous offensives on both western fronts. Potential crises were surmounted, notably, in 613, when Heraclius mobilized all available resources for his attack from west and south on the Persian salient in northern Syria, and in 616, when it was necessary to deploy substantial forces in the east to restore Sasanian prestige after the Turks' intervention in 615, at the same time as taking direct control of Palestine. There is no evidence of opposition to the war, even at the nascent stage of a susurration of doubt.

The reason is obvious. Apart from a reverse on the Armenian front in the first year and the encirclement of Shahen's army in Caesarea in 611–12, victory had followed victory, and Roman forces had been so bludgeoned that they had lost their customary assurance in the field by the early 620s. A concerted effort involving both lengthy exercises and morale-boosting speeches would be necessary before they could engage the Persians with any confidence in 622, nine years after Heraclius' enforced withdrawal from the region of Antioch and Cilicia. Each victory led to an advance, gradual and painful in a first attritional phase. But after the vital breakthrough in 610, Persian forces were able to move forward with long strides, taking control of several Roman provinces at a time, as they occupied successively northern Syria, Cilicia, southern Syria, Palestine, and the great prize, Egypt. Highly productive commercial and industrial cities in both the Levant and Egypt were thus brought under the sway of a well-developed, multi-tiered administrative system, not to mention the naturally irrigated agricultural

---

[145] Movses Daskhurants'i (or Kałankatuats'i), ed. V. Arak'eljan, *Movses Kałankatuats'i: Patmut'iwn Ałuanits'* (Erevan, 1983), 145.4–1,7, trans. C. J. F. Dowsett, *Moses Dasxuranc'i's History of the Caucasian Albanians* (London, 1961), trans. 89–90—cited henceforth as MD.

[146] Ps.S., 75–80, 94–5, 96–8, 99, with *Hist.Com.*, nn.10–11, 18–19. Cf. J. Howard-Johnston, 'Khosrow II', c, https://iranicaonline.org/articles/khosrow-ii, accessed 26 October 2020.

heartland of the Roman Empire in Egypt. The Sasanian tax base was thus greatly enlarged in the second phase of the war.

The cost of victory and expansion was undoubtedly high, but was, it appears, borne by the exchequer without strain. The sorts of taxpayer complaints which surfaced in the late 620s, chiefly about harsh measures taken against those in arrears, were not being voiced. Inevitably expenditure rose significantly in the critical five years between Heraclius' counterattack (613) and a year of apparent calm (618) when the Persians were planning and preparing for the invasion of Egypt in 619. In addition to the two great efforts required to hang onto the north Syrian salient and to launch a large-scale punitive operation into central Asia in 616, Persian forces were consolidating their position in former Roman territory in western Armenia, north Mesopotamia, and Syria, as well as launching diversionary attacks in force into Asia Minor (615 and 617). Tax revenues rose. An increase of a little over 40 per cent is reported in a later Arab source.[147] Some of the increase probably came from additional demands placed on Persian taxpayers in the first half of the war. Most, though, is probably to be accounted for by the tax revenues appropriated from the Romans. It would not be surprising if regions as extensive and well developed as those which had been conquered—the western half of Transcaucasia, northern Mesopotamia, Syria, Palestine, and Egypt—yielded revenue approaching half that extracted from the Sasanian Empire.

The additional revenue from the conquered territories came to the exchequer in the form of the gold solidi in which Romans customarily paid their taxes. The conversion of the gold into silver was presumably handled by money changers and bullion traders—but of them, of the processes involved, and of the places, whether inside or outside the empire (in India, say), where the exchanges were made, we know nothing. All we can say is that the gold was used to fund an increase in expenditure and, over the five years from 613 to 618, an increase in the volume of new drachms issued by the more than thirty mints in operation. There were fluctuations in coin production from year to year, but the general trend was upwards, steeply upwards. This can be gauged from an increase in the number of coins per regnal year present in five hoards buried just before or just after the end of the war—on the assumption that such evidently emergency hoards were representative of coins in circulation at the time of their burial in the localities where they were found (Susa in Khuzistan in two cases, Seleucia in one, and probably highland Iran in the remaining two, which have no recorded provenances).[148] Admittedly, not all government expenditure was made in new drachms. It was probably often convenient simply to recycle rather than recoin

---

[147] Ibn Khordadhbeh, *Kitab al-masalik wa'l- mamalik*, ed. and trans. M. J. de Goeje, *Bibliotheca geographorum arabicorum*, VI (Leiden, 1889), 15.6–9 (text) and 12 (trans.).

[148] Late Sasanian hoards: Susa I: La Fuye, *Mémoires de la mission*, 68–76, 84–7; Seleucia: Göbl, 'Die Sasanidische Münzfund'; Susa II: Gyselen, 'Note de métrologie sassanide'; Basel: Gyselen, 'Un Trésor de monnaies sassanides tardives'; Quetta: Malek, 'A Seventh-Century Hoard'.

drachms received in taxation, and the ratio between new and old coins in government spending may have varied from year to year and region to region. But a steep rise in the amount of new coin issued may surely be taken as good corroborative evidence that spending was rising.

There was a tripling on average in the number of drachms per year in all five of the hoards concealed at the end of the war, between regnal year 24 (613–14) and year 28 (617–18) or 29 (618–19).[149] Six later hoards, three of them very large, buried in the first century of Islamic rule, all but one of them in Syria, contain statistically significant numbers of Sasanian drachms.[150] They document an even greater increase in numbers of drachms (well over a quadrupling on average) from year 24 to a peak in year 27 in one case and year 28 in the remaining five.[151] There was no question, of course, of a tripling or quadrupling in the size of the Sasanian budget. It looks as if the years in which more money was being pumped into the economy for the war effort were years in which a concerted effort was made to recoin as much as possible of the old drachms received in taxation—presumably as a demonstration that the regime was, if anything, raising its monetary standards as it pursued its victorious war.

Like its Roman counterpart, the Sasanian Empire was managed effectively from the centre, as can be demonstrated from the high purity and uniform design of the drachms issued from its many mints.[152] There was a tiered administrative system in which the military and the judicial, fiscal, and civil authorities exercised separately delegated powers, not necessarily at the same level, and were severally accountable to the centre. The highest tier was military. Since the reorganization of the army instituted by Khusro I Anushirwan, Sasanian territory was divided into four great commands—Khurasan (East), Nemroz (South), Khwararan (West), and Adurbadagan (North)—each with its own commanding general, a *spahbed*, equivalent to a Roman *magister militum*. Several clay sealings imprinted with the images, names, and titles of *spahbeds* have survived from the later sixth

---

[149] Susa I: 41 (year 24)–111 (year 28). Seleucia: 6 (year 24)–18 (year 29). Susa II: 37 (year 24)–103 (year 28). Basel: 5 (year 24)–26 (year 29). Quetta: 4 (year 24)–22 (year 28).

[150] Syria: al-Ush, *Silver Hoard of Damascus*; Gyselen and Kalus, *Deux Trésors monétaires*; al-Ush, *Trésor de monnaies d'argent trouvé à Umm-Hajarah*. Jazira: Gyselen and Nègre, 'Un trésor de Gazīra'. Babylon: H. Simon, 'Die sāsānidischen Münzen des Fundes von Babylon: Ein Teil des bei Koldeweys Ausgrabungen im Jahre 1900 gefundenen Münzschatzes', Acta Iranica, 3 ser.,12, Textes et mémoires 5, Varia 1976 (Tehran-Liège, 1977), 149–337.

[151] Damascus: 17 (year 24)–69 (year 28). Bāb Tūmā: 6 (year 23)–30 (year 28). Umm-Hajarah: 4 (year 24)–8 (year 27). Qamišliyya: 2 (year 24)–16 (year 28). Babylon: 3 (year 23)–16 (year 25), 16 (year 28). Jazira: 2 (year 24)–18 (year 28).

[152] *Sylloge Nummorum Sasanidarum: Paris-Berlin-Wien*: M. Alram, R. Gyselen et al., I *Ardashir I.—Shapur I.*, Öst. Ak. Wiss., Phil.-hist. Kl., Denkschrift 317 (Vienna, 2003); M. Alram, R. Gyselen, et al., II *Ohrmazd II.—Ohrmazd II.*, Öst. Ak. Wiss., Phil.-hist. Kl., Denkschrift 422 (Vienna, 2012); N. Schindel et al., III.1–2 *Shapur II.—Kawad I./2. Regierung*, Öst. Ak. Wiss., Phil.-hist. Kl., Denkschrift 325 (Vienna, 2004). Cf. J. Howard-Johnston, 'The Sasanian State: The Evidence of Coinage and Military Construction', in R. Payne and M. Soroush, eds., *The Archaeology of Sasanian Politics*, Journal of Ancient History 2.2 (2014), 144–81, at 157–62.

and early seventh century (Figure 6).[153] The iconography is uniform. The *spahbed* is shown in full armour, riding an armoured horse and holding a lance, with a sheathed sword at his side. An emblem on the helmet (three crescents supine) indicates his rank, which is also stated in words. The inscription details the particular command held and the military post traditionally associated with each command—Parthian *aspbed* (Master of Horse—East), Persian *aspbed* (South),[154] *hazarbed* (Commander of a Thousand—West), and *aspbed* of the Empire (North).

The commands were defined in terms of subordinated civil provinces, which are listed in the Armenian geography of Ananias of Shirak written not long after the Arab conquest of Mesopotamia and Iran. The principle underlying the division was that of allocating roughly equal resources, human and material, to each of the commands. Because of the unequal geographical distribution of resources—concentrated in the west, in Media, Adurbadagan, and Transcaucasia north of the Zagros and Armenian Taurus, in Khuzistan and Mesopotamia to the south—the eastern command (out to the Oxus) and the southern (out to the Indus) were far larger than the northern and western, with twenty-six and nineteen provinces respectively.[155] It was almost as if the system of commands had been devised with a view to the incorporation of the adjoining Roman territories. Only with the inclusion of western Armenia and the whole of Asia Minor would the Adurbadagan command (with fourteen provinces) match Khurasan in size. The same was true for the western command (with eight provinces), which would only balance the southern in terms of territory with the inclusion of Syria, Palestine, and Egypt. Thereafter, Asia Minor and Egypt would act as two great outer bastions for this greatly enlarged Sasanian Empire.[156] The distance to the Bosporus (the natural frontier in the west) and the southern limit of Egypt on the upper Nile was no greater than to the Oxus and the Indus in the east and south-east, and the well-developed system of Roman roads would aid communications. So control could be exerted as effectively over the distant western as over the distant eastern reaches of the empire from the imperial capital in Mesopotamia.

---

[153] R. Gyselen, *The Four Generals of the Sasanian Empire: Some Sigillographic Evidence* (Rome, 2001); R. Gyselen, *La Géographie administrative de l'empire sassanide: Les Témoignages épigraphiques en moyen-perse*, Res Orientales 25 (Bures-sur-Yvette, 2019).

[154] Omitted in the case of one of the three attested postholders (Pirag)—Gyselen, *Four Generals*, 40–1.

[155] Ananias of Shirak, *Geography*, ed. A. Soukry, *Géographie de Moïse de Corène* (Venice, 1881), reproduced in facsimile as *Ashkharhatsoyts (AŠXARHAC'OYC'), the Seventh Century Geography Attributed to Ananias of Shirak*, ed. R. H. Hewsen (Delmar, NY, 1994), 40. Translation and commentary in R. H. Hewsen, *The Geography of Ananias of Širak (AŠXARHAC'OYC'): The Long and Short Recensions*, Beihefte zum Tübinger Atlas des vorderen Orients B.77 (Wiesbaden, 1992), 72, 226–34.

[156] But see p. 180 below for an alternative scenario.

The quadripartite army command was well suited for the task of defending individual frontiers, but when offensive action on a large scale was planned, as it was for the final great push from 622 (and in several previous campaigns), it would be necessary either to reinforce the army of the command most directly involved with units seconded from other commands or to involve a second whole army under its *spahbed*. There would be no difficulty in coordinating operations: the *shahanshah* would take personal charge or he would appoint a commander-in-chief of his choice or he would dispatch the armies, each under its own *spahbed*, against different targets. But, whatever the case, an assembly ground was needed to which designated units from different commands could be directed and where they could be melded into a cohesive, responsive, adaptable fighting force—open terrain, accessible from all four commands and safely withdrawn from frontier regions.

Such an assembly ground can be identified on the basis of oblique indications given in the *Geography* of Ananias of Shirak. The territorial commands of the four *spahbeds* converged on Media at the western end of the Iranian plateau, where extensive and lush grazing grounds in the region of modern Sultaniye abut onto a zone of rolling hills and high plains. Each of the four commands had its own presence in this region: the South had a subdivision centred on Ispahan; the West's consisted of the hill country to the south of Hamadan (May or Mad); the North had the district of Rayy (on the outskirts of modern Tehran); the most surprising association, though, was that of the subdivision of Hamadan with the East. This meant that North and East, as it were, leapfrogged over each other. Each had a bridgehead in the other's territory, and their two bridgeheads marched with the subdivisions of Mad and Isfahan to the south. Since all these military districts adjoined each other, together they could act as the arena for the mobilization of a composite army, drawing on more than one regional command. Media, together with the adjoining fertile margins of the plateau, thus constituted the military fulcrum of the Sasanian Empire, the designated zone for the assembly and mobilization of grand armies.

The military achievements of the late Sasanian army are partly to be explained by the ideological commitment of the troops and by the generalship of its commanders. But they would have been unattainable but for the development of a flexible, regionally structured and centrally controlled organization which facilitated both independent action by regional armies and their amalgamation into larger grand armies for major offensives. As a result, the performance of the army at the end of antiquity was very impressive. Particularly striking was its ability to sustain a rolling offensive in the west, led by Shahen, *spahbed* of Adurbadagan, and Shahrbaraz, *spahbed* of the West, and then to redeploy their armies for a joint attack on Egypt in 619, despite a sudden heavy call on resources in the east occasioned by the serious defeat inflicted by the Turks on the regional army of the East commanded by Smbat Bagratuni in 615 and their subsequent raid deep into the interior of Iran.[157]

Relations with city notables in the former Roman provinces would undoubtedly have changed in the long run, as some were drawn into higher levels of the administration and the pressures to assimilate became harder to resist. Remembered *Romanitas* would have slowly receded into the past, the world view of *Eranshahr* increasingly suffusing the thoughts of former Roman provincials. Similarly, the command structure inherited from the sixth century overarching the whole administrative system of the Sasanian Empire would very probably have had to be adapted for the greater security of the enlarged empire. Instead of a single imperial rival, Khusro's successors would have had to cope with a whole variety of adversaries in the west—(1) the North African rump of the Roman Empire with dependencies to the north in Sicily, the Balearic islands, Sardinia, Corsica, and southern Italy, (2) Berbers, who had proved remarkably successful in resisting Roman culture, and who might, if united, constitute a formidable fighting force, (3) initially small Germanic states, their whole being committed to warfare, growing steadily in size and power as they were Romanized and forcibly amalgamated, and (4) a Turkish khaganate able to harness and direct its Germanic, Slav, and sub-Roman client peoples in central, eastern, and south-eastern Europe. It might make sense to extend the Adurbadagan command to the empire's new western limit (probably on the Bosporus), thereby uniting Transcaucasia and transforming it into the organizing centre of the command. But the resource-rich and commercially well-developed regions bordering on the Mediterranean, Cilicia, Syria, Palestine, and Egypt (probably with Pentapolis as its western outlier), would have to be secured against whatever threats might materialize, not least from the open, easily traversed waste tracts of sea and desert to the west and south-east. This could best be achieved by the creation of a new western command covering the annexed provinces south of the Taurus and constituting a new outer shield for the inner lands of Mesopotamia and Khuzistan. The army of the old western command would have then taken on the role of a central reserve analogous to the praesental armies of the Roman Empire.

The prospects of victory, of the utter destruction of Roman rule in the Middle East, looked very good in the early 620s. A final push, for which the Sasanian Empire was well organized, should succeed in overrunning Asia Minor, defeating whatever forces the brigand emperor Heraclius might put into the field, and, with Avar help, taking out the nerve centre of empire in Constantinople. The morale of Khusro's armies was high. The heterogeneous peoples of his empire remained committed to his grand enterprise. Overweening as it might have seemed in the abstract, his ambition was carrying his people along with him. There was, as has

---

[157] Ps.S., 101.26–103.13, with *Hist.Com.*, n.21.

already been observed, no trace of dissent until a much later and grimmer stage in the war.[158] Not that Khusro left such matters to chance. Just as he had to fend off Roman propaganda designed to stir up the feelings of his Christian subjects by actions calculated to demonstrate fairness towards the different confessions found among his subjects—hence the maintenance of the status quo in Jerusalem, the dispatch of Monophysite bishops to Syrian sees, and the transfer of the most precious of all Christian relics, the fragments of the True Cross, into Nestorian care in Mesopotamia—so too he had to do what he could to bolster support for the war among the opinion-forming classes of his empire, from the great men of his court to officialdom throughout the empire and army officers. There was only one important constituency of whose support he was assured—the Babylonian Jewish community—after Shahrbaraz had intervened swiftly and decisively to halt the pogrom in Jerusalem in 614.

With no indigenous Iranian written sources transmitted to us, save through intermediary Christian texts—hence no Iranian equivalent of Strategius' officially sponsored Jerusalem laments—we look elsewhere for evidence of Khusro's methods for informing and cultivating public opinion. The only extant official communications available for study are the messages conveyed by images and legends on coins—not the regular issues with their familiar iconography and minimal legends, but special ceremonial issues produced for distribution to leading elements at the centre and elsewhere. There were numerous occasions in the course of the war, both before and after 621, calling for such issues, with victory either in prospect or achieved. Coins issued on the eve of an important campaign served both to state the king's confidence in the outcome and to perform the vital function of co-opting the opinion-forming and governing classes into the royal military venture. Those issued after the winning of victory were similarly political acts designed both to disseminate good news and to strengthen the standing of the king. Both types were culling prestige at home from success abroad.

There are two distinct types of gold ceremonial issues, the second of which has a silver analogue and a silver variant. The gold coins are of two denominations, dinars and one and a half dinars. The silver are all drachms of conventional weight. All are dated. The first type is confined to dinars and seems to have been inspired by a special issue of Khusro I Anushirwan at a time of acute crisis in his forty-fourth regnal year (573–4). The type can probably be categorized as referring forward to future victory, since the wings of Verethragna, the god of victory, have been removed from the sides of Khusro's crown (Figure 7). Khusro himself

---

[158] *Contra* K. Mosig-Walburg, 'Sonderprägungen Khusros II. (590–628): Innenpolitische Propaganda vor dem Hintergrund des Krieges gegen Byzanz', in R. Gyselen, ed., *Sources pour l'histoire et la géographie du monde iranien (224–710)*, Res Orientales 18 (Bures-sur-Yvette, 2009), 185–208, at 188–9, 198–206.

(bearded) appears on both sides of the coin: a frontal rather than the usual profile bust on the obverse; a full-length figure, likewise looking out from the reverse, with his hand resting on the hilt of a long sword with its point on the ground. The legends credit him with increasing *khwarrah* (royal glory) and, on the reverse, with freeing the world from fear. There are only minor variations between issues, which date from years 13 (602–3), 33 (622–3), and 34 (623–4). They look like ceremonial coins issued on the eve of major campaigns, namely the opening offensive against the Romans (603) and the beginning of the final phase of the war, the planned conquest of Asia Minor (622–4). The coins seem to downplay Khusro's role as the agent of the gods: as well as doing without the wings of Verethragna, he, a mere human being, replaces the fire altar with attendants which is customary on the reverse. The long sword points surely to the human feats of valour which are expected.[159]

The second type, by contrast, stresses Khusro's divine empowerment and devotion to the true faith. It is found on one and half dinars, dinars, and drachms issued in year 21 (610–11), the year when his forces crossed the Euphrates and reached the Mediterranean beyond Antioch, thereby cutting the Roman Empire in two. It probably marked the victorious conclusion of the first phase of the western war (Figure 8). On the obverse, there is a profile bust of Khusro (bearded) wearing his usual crown with the wings of victory. The reverse shows a frontal bust of a beardless man whose head and hair are haloed in flames. The legend announces Khusro's success—'Khusro, King of Kings, has increased *khwarrah*' (obv) and 'has increased Iran, well-omened' (rev).[160] The reappearance of the title King of Kings on a coin for the first time since the fifth century signals the extraordinary success which Khusro had achieved by the summer of 610, with the incorporation of all Roman territory east of the Euphrates. While the identity of the flame-haloed figure on the reverse is disputed, there can be little doubt that the flames which rise vertically are those of the sacred fire, normally represented in miniature on top of a fire altar on the reverse of the drachm. The placing of a bust in the fire had a precedent, in the reverse type of drachms issued by Ohrmazd II and his successors down to Yazdgerd I, where a minuscule bust can be seen inside the flames on top of the altar.[161] Flames and figure, enlarged on Khusro II's special issue and detached from the altar, may have carried a second meaning,

---

[159] K. Mosig-Walburg, 'Sonderprägungen des Xusrō II. vom Typ Gölb V/6 und VI/7', *Iranica Antiqua*, 28 (1993), 169–91, at 169–77, 184–90.

[160] M. Malek, 'The Sasanian King Khusrau II (AD 590/1–628) and Anahita', *Name-ye Iran-e Bastan*, 2 (2003), 23–43; R. Gyselen, 'New Evidence for Sasanian Numismatics: The Collection of Ahmad Saeedi', in R. Gyselen, ed., *Contributions à l'histoire et la géographie historique de l'empire sassanide*, Res Orientales 16 (Bures-sur-Yvette, 2004), 49–140, at 64–5; Mosig-Walburg, 'Sonderprägungen Khusros II.' (2009), 189–94.

[161] *Syll.Num.Sas.*, II, 362–7, III.1, 89, 215–19, 250–1, 268–9, 288–91, 321–5. The small bust moved to the front of the altar on the reverse of Wahram V Gor's drachms before disappearing after his reign (*Syll.Num.Sas*, III.1, 347–50).

representing the radiating light or glory (*khwarrah*) of a divinely appointed and divinely guided King of Kings.[162]

While the first type was probably intended to rouse patriotic feelings on the eve of major offensives (and to enhance the governing elite's sense of involvement in the war), the second conveyed a simple triumphalist message which was well worth broadcasting to the population at large through the main circulating medium, the silver drachm. This may explain why drachms of a variant of the second type, in which Khusro's bust is turned from the right to face forward, were issued, again probably to members of the governing apparatus, at three later stages of the war—in year 23 (612–13), when the Persians were consolidating their hold on northern Syria, in years 26–8 (615–18), when the whole of the Roman Levant had been conquered, and in years 36–7 (625–7), when the final supreme effort was being made to capture Constantinople in conjunction with the Avars in Europe and thus to decapitate what was left of the Roman Empire. As well as the shift to a frontal bust on the obverse, there was an alteration to the legend on the reverse from the year 26. Instead of being given the epithet 'well-omened', Khusro is described as 'of the good religion'.[163] Despite this additional emphasis on his Zoroastrian faith, there was hubris in these last two issues. Khusro was announcing victories before they had been won, assuming that Constantinople could not possibly hold out.

As has been suggested, the intended audience for these claims was in the first instance the officials and officers to whom they were given, doubtless on ceremonial occasions, in different parts of the empire. Thereafter, they would percolate into the general currency. Their initial distribution may have been served two specific purposes, besides giving a general boost to Khusro's reputation—(1) to enhance the prestige of the regime among the provincial elites living in the farther reaches of the empire, far removed from the theatres of war, and (2) to crack down on opposition to war when it was voiced later, in 627. It is probably more than chance that a direct imitation of this second triumphalist issue was minted by the ruler of Zabulistan at the beginning of the eighth century.[164]

It was Khusro's hubris which ultimately brought him down. That is the principal theme brought out in all the sources which drew on versions of the *Khwadaynamag*. He assumed an increasingly arrogant posture towards his subjects, even the greatest of his subjects. He was accused of breaking the compact between king and aristocracy upon which the whole hereditary social order was

---

[162] Cf. R. Gyselen, 'Un Dieu nimbé de flammes d'époque sassanide', *Iranica Antiqua*, 35 (2000), 291–314. For *khwarrah* and its representation, see T. Daryaee, 'The Use of Religio-Political Propaganda on the Coinage of Xusrō II', *American Journal of Numismatics*, ser.2, 9 (1997), 41–53, at 46–9.
[163] Gyselen, 'Un Dieu nimbé de flammes', 309–10; Gyselen, 'New Evidence', 64–5; Mosig-Walburg, 'Sonderprägungen Khusros II.' (2009), 190–1, 193–4.
[164] Gyselen, 'Un Dieu nimbé de flammes', 298–301.

based.[165] Apart from the list of charges brought against him and a few specific cases of maltreatment of the great, the clearest evidence of hubris is provided by the arrangements put in train in the 620s before the expected victorious end of the war for the celebration and commemoration of his victories. Projects were approved, commissions were given out, and work was well in hand when, in 627, the wheel of fortune turned and they were abruptly abandoned. Four have left behind durable material remains, and these give us some idea of the grandiose scale of the programme. All four were monumental reliefs designed to impress the majesty and achievements of Khusro II on his subjects, his successors, their subjects, and all others who passed by for the foreseeable future. The very choice of medium, panels of rock carved to display an ideologically charged scene, was significant. Khusro II was reviving a tradition of the early Sasanian kings who had built up the empire and had won notable victories over the Romans.[166] After a gap of at least two hundred years, he was showing that his achievements surpassed theirs. The scale of his planned memorials made this very plain.

Three of the projected reliefs were located in Media. Because of its proximity to the governing centre in Mesopotamia, Media had long usurped the position of Persia as the Iranian heartland of the empire. It was to Media that the court moved in the summer months. It was in its mountains and valleys, rather than those around Bishapur or Ardashir-khwarrah, that the king went hunting. We have also seen how Media and adjoining regions of western Iran had become the military centre of the empire where forces from the four commands were mobilized. Media now took on an additional role, as an ideological centre where the king displayed his majesty and his might to the world. The area chosen by Khusro was the large interior basin of Media, now dominated by Kermanshah. It is centred on the plain north of the confluence of the Qara Su and Gamas-i Ab rivers, athwart one of the two main roads crossing the Zagros, roughly halfway between Qasr-i Shirin on the edge of the Mesopotamian alluvium, site of a fine late Sasanian pleasure palace (also unfinished), and Hamadan on the edge of the open, rolling uplands of Media. It was the Median equivalent to the Marvdasht in Persia, a fertile basin on the east side of the main Zagros range, where lay Istakhr, the ruins of Persepolis, and Naqsh-i Rustam.

The best known of Khusro's projects was nearly finished when he fell from power. It is to be found at Taq-i Bustan, ten kilometres or so north-east of modern Kermanshah (Figures 9–14).[167] The site, a low cliff fronted by a pool (now a rectangular boating lake in a public park, in Sasanian times probably the focal point of a walled *paradeisos*), had already been chosen by Shapur II for reliefs

---

[165] MD, 145.3–17 (trans. 89–90); Tab., 1047.5–8.
[166] G. Herrmann and V. S. Curtis, 'Sasanian Rock Reliefs', https://iranicaonline.org/articles/sasanian-rock-reliefs, accessed 26 October 2020.
[167] S. Fukai, K. Horiuchi, K. Tanabe, and M. Domyo, *Taq-i Bustan*, I-IV (Tokyo 1969–84).

depicting the investiture of his brother Ardashir II and the designation of his son Shapur III as his next successor but one. It had the attributes of a sacred site, three of the four vital elements coming together (air, earth in the form of living rock, and water). A small figure trampled beneath the feet of Shapur II and Ardashir II is recognizable as a Roman emperor—either Julian, whose expedition into Mesopotamia ended in catastrophe and his own death, or his short-lived successor, Jovian, who had to agree a humiliating peace.[168] Khusro could show here that he had capped the achievements of Julian's victor.

A large round-headed recess was excavated in the cliff face. Reliefs were then carved on the three walls of this *ayvān* (a vaulted hall open on one side) cut into the living rock. The images on the back wall were placed in two tiers which are linked together by thin framing bands on either side. Khusro himself stands between female and male figures in the upper panel. He is identifiable by the crown which he wears, crenellated, winged, and surmounted by a large crescent supporting a *korymbos* (ball of royal hair). His companions are divine figures, Anahita to his right pouring water from a jug and holding out a wreath and Ohrmazd to his left wearing a long beard and handing over a wreath which Khusro reaches for with his right hand. It is plainly a scene of investiture. Below, Khusro's warlike prowess is represented by his *fravashi* (guardian spirit) armed from head to toe and mounted on an armoured charger. The crown and *korymbos* on the rider's head together with a symbol of kingship branded on the horse's rump establish the connection with the figure of Khusro portrayed above.[169]

The style and character of the two-tiered relief of Khusro II and his *fravashi* differ markedly from those of early Sasanian reliefs. This is not surprising, given that Khusro was reviving a long defunct art form. The figures in the upper tier are stocky and curvacious. There is nothing elegant about their poses or gestures. Khusro himself stands in full frontal pose, with his right arm thrust awkwardly across his chest to hold the wreath held out by Ohrmazd, while his left hand rests on the hilt of a long sword. The relief is very deep, but the sculptural effort has been put into intricate surface decoration rather than modelling forms. The impression is very much one of stucco work transposed into stone carving.

No less innovative within the context of Sasanian monumental reliefs were the scenes depicted on the side walls: to the left, a boar hunt takes place in marshland, the animals being driven inwards by riders mounted on elephants, past the king who is dressed in a magnificent silk kaftan decorated with senmurv motifs (a mythical flying creature) and who stands up in a boat to shoot with his bow; to the right, the prey are deer, the setting is an enclosed hunting park, and the hunt

---

[168] Fukai et al., *Taq-i Bustan*, IV, 143–60. Neil McLynn has suggested the identification of the emperor as Jovian (personal communication).
[169] Fukai et al., *Taq-i Bustan*, IV, 41–142; H. von Gall, 'Entwicklung und Gestalt des Thrones im vorislamischen Iran', *AMI* n.s.4 (1971), 207–235, at 230–233.

itself (dominated by the king who is centre stage, mounted, and holding a mace) is bracketed between the initial drive and the final removal of dead animals. The representation of both hunting scenes is schematic and stylized, with aerial and earthbound views combined in the deer hunt. The contrast in both scale and movement could not be greater with the paired scenes on the rear wall of the *ayvan*. There is also another striking difference. The relief is very shallow, unprecedentedly shallow for monumental stone carving. Novel too was the choice of hunting as a theme. It was normally reserved for silver and gold plate and, in highly stylized form, for silks. Khusro II's glory (*khwarrah*) was deliberately being made manifest in a non-ceremonial, non-military context.[170]

The Taq-i Bustan project was not quite complete when Khusro fell from power. Work was finished on the deep reliefs displaying Khusro's majesty and might, as also on the boar hunt. The detailing of armour and arms, of royal insignia, and above all of dress makes this plain. So precise is the depiction of the patterns on fabrics that historians of silk weaving regard the Taq-i Bustan reliefs as one of their best sources of information. The deer hunt, however, is unfinished. The basic layout has been done. Animal and human participants are outlined. But the surfaces within most outlined shapes are still flat and plain. The final phase of fine decorative carving had scarcely begun when work stopped. It is clear then that this was a project of Khusro's last years. Much effort, financial and artistic, was invested in it, but it was not brought to completion.

The range of hills behind Taq-i Bustan bounds the interior basin of Media on the north. Fifty kilometres to the east, it ends in a high cliff at Bisutun. This too was (and is) a numinous spot, where earth, sky, and water meet. An abundant spring feeds a pool which stands immediately below the cliff. The road running east to Nihavand leaves the plain and climbs the first of the low passes which it has to cross. It was here, high up on the beetling cliff above the pool, that Darius had broadcast, both in word and image, his unification of Iran, his conquest of Media, and his swift suppression of those who had rebelled against him.[171] None of Khusro's Sasanian predecessors had made use of the site to advertise themselves, despite its strategic position. Khusro, though, set about appropriating it and commissioning works which would relegate Darius' relief to a supporting role. The Taq-i Bustan complex was dwarfed by what he planned for Bisutun.

The Bisutun scheme was abandoned at a much earlier stage, but the material remains testify to its grandiose character. Already some 40,000 cubic metres of rock had been cut from the cliff face when worked stopped. Apart from the detritus of rock splinters liberally scattered below, most of this material was carved into dressed stone blocks for use in the various structures planned for the

---

[170] P. O. Harper, 'La Vaisselle en métal', in *Splendeur des Sassanides: L'Empire perse entre Rome et la Chine (224–642)* (Brussels, 1993), 95–108.
[171] Wiesehöfer, *Ancient Persia*, 13–21.

site. As well as this mass of basic building components, three loose capitals with elaborate decoration were found. They are now displayed in the park at Taq-i Bustan. The sculpted capitals establish a connection between the planned works at Bisutun and Khusro II. Two faces are decorated with abstract ornament, but two have busts—on one a female figure, probably the goddess Anahita who appears in the investiture scene at Taq-i Bustan, and on the other a Sasanian king, identifiable by his crown as Khusro II.[172]

Traces of several distinct projects have been detected.[173] A new access road from the east was being built with a bridge over the Gamas-i Ab aligned on the centre of the planned relief. A walled embankment constructed from ashlar blocks cut on the site was built on the west side of the river and may have been intended to form the outer wall of a projected palace. Beyond, a stupendous monument was planned. A terrace some 36 metres high and 198 or more metres long was in process of construction in front of the cliff. Eight courses of a retaining wall up to 15 metres thick are still in place. When completed, the terrace would have projected 130 metres from the cliff, where a gigantic relief panel was being prepared (Figure 15). Only the central third was finished. On either side, the quarrying work was halted in mid-process: stonecutters placed at 1.5 metre intervals on the stepped facade of the cliff were hewing out short vertical shafts from which a mass of building blocks was being extracted; the shafts themselves were then knocked together to form a single plane; progress was from top to bottom, the ledges which acted as working platforms being gradually lowered; layer by layer the cliff was being stripped until it would present a smooth surface. The projected relief panel was the largest in the whole Near East, 183 metres wide and a maximum of 37.8 metres high. It sweeps across the base of the cliff like the widest of cinemascope screens, reducing Darius' relief some 350 metres away and high up on the cliff to relative insignificance.[174]

The main task for masons and sculptors at work on the site was the carving of the relief panel.[175] The gist of the message which Khusro wished to convey is plain: victory in war, subjection of once proud opponents, annexation of extensive territories and wealthy cities. To judge by the evidence of Taq-i Bustan, it is unlikely that he would have revived the iconography of triumph of early Sasanian

---

[172] H. Luschey, 'Zur Datierung des sasanidischen Kapitelle aus Bisutun und des Monuments von Taq-i-Bostan', *AMI* 1 (1968), 129–42.

[173] H. Luschey, 'Bisutun, ii Archaeology', *Encyclopaedia Iranica*, IV (London and New York, 1990), 291–9, at 293–6.

[174] W. Salzmann, 'Die "Felsarbeitung und Terrasse des Farbad" in Bisutun: Ein spätsasanidisches Monument', *Archäologischer Anzeiger*, 91 (1976), 110–34.

[175] Salzmann, 'Die "Felsarbeitung und Terrasse des Farbad"', 128–33 suggests that a gigantic *ayvān*, 33 metres high and 35 metres wide, was to be cut in the centre. This seems improbable, given the scale and breadth of the panel. It was surely designed to accommodate a single sweeping scene. A second suggestion (133–4) that it might have been intended to accommodate Khusro II's tomb is equally implausible, given the Zoroastrian prohibition on burial of the dead.

reliefs, and the style would have been very different. If inspiration was to be sought from the past, one suspects that Achaemenid monuments would have been chosen—perhaps a scene in which two processions of subject peoples and leaders converged on Khusro and attendants in the centre. Or Khusro might have chosen Roman triumphalist iconography to commemorate his annihilation of the Roman Empire.

The effect on the visitor would have been stupefying. With carving as deep as that at Taq-i Bustan but on a much larger scale, the scene displayed would have been visible at a considerable distance on the new road. As the visitor came nearer, more and more of the relief would have been concealed by its fronting terrace, until at 150 metres nothing would have been visible. He would then have climbed up one of two flights of steps to the top of the terrace to be confronted by colossal figures from close at hand.

There is no explicit evidence that two other equally blank rock screens were commissioned by Khusro, apart from their size and their unfinished condition. However, it is hard to conceive of alternative circumstances in which projects might have been conceived on a grand scale and then abruptly abandoned. Attribution of both to Khusro is reasonably secure. At Harsin, 34 kilometres to the south-east of Bisutun, on the northern edge of the interior basin of Media, the rock panel was designed as the focal point of another royal complex. Here too was that combination of cliff, springhead at its base, and sky which made a site numinous or at least very attractive in Sasanian eyes. Khusro, apparently the first king to appreciate the potential of the site, planned a development which included a terrace fronting the relief panel, a pool fed by the spring, and a palatial residence.[176]

Although on a considerably smaller scale than that at Bisutun, the Harsin development was still impressive. The panel, which was still being excavated from three working platforms at different heights when work stopped, measures 50.75 metres by a maximum of 10 metres. The terrace in front, partly rock-cut, partly of masonry construction, projected up to 8 metres. The pool, a round rock-cut basin, 4.10 metres in diameter and 0.72 metres deep, lay below the east end of the terrace, to which steps gave access. A fluted column rising from the centre of the basin added a Roman touch. The palace lay some distance away. Foundations had been laid and water piped in when the project was abandoned. A fort was later built on the site, probably soon after the Arab conquest, but vestiges of the

---

[176] D. Huff, 'Harsin', *AMI* 18 (1985), 15–44 unhesitatingly dates the Harsin project to the later Sasanian period, but attributes its non-completion to its scale. The implication is that money ran out or interest waned. He does, however, note the parallels with Taq-i Bustan and Bisutun, but refrains from drawing the obvious conclusion.

planned palace (including broken pillars and plain capitals) were still visible when Rawlinson visited Harsin in 1836.[177]

Work was more advanced at Harsin, on both the relief panel and the palace, than at Bisutun. As for the fourth project, far away in the heart of Persia proper, it is hard to say how much progress had been made. For a huge blank relief panel which was being prepared at Naqsh-i Rustam has not been studied with the care and attention given to Bisutun and Harsin. Viewed from a distance, it seems ready for carving. It cannot be dated after the Sasanian period, since no figural reliefs were to be carved until the handful commissioned by the Qajars in the nineteenth century. It is unlikely to have been prepared in the early phase of Sasanian history when monumental reliefs were regularly used to display royal glory to contemporaries and posterity, since a prepared surface left blank by one king would surely have been exploited soon by a successor. It should, therefore, probably be attributed to Khusro II, the one late Sasanian king who revived monumental relief carving. Certainly, it shares two key characteristics, grandeur of conception and failure of execution, with the Median projects, two of which are known to have been commissioned by him.

Naqsh-i Rustam is the name given to the cliff at the western end of a range of low hills jutting into the plain of Persepolis and visible in the distance from the ruins of the Achaemenid capital. The tombs of four Achaemenid kings are carved high in the cliff, looking out towards a mysterious square tower known as the Cube of Zoroaster with carefully spaced rectangular panels inset on each of its sides. It was evidently a spot held in awe in both Achaemenid and Sasanian times. There was a small spring of fresh water nearby, in a low natural recess, called Naqsh-i Rajab, on the far side of the road connecting Persepolis to Istakhr (3 kilometres to the east), but Naqsh-i Rustam itself is waterless. It was surely the presence of monuments from a distant imperial past which led the first Sasanian kings to appropriate the whole site and use it to display their glory. It also lay conveniently close to Istakhr, where Ardashir I's grandfather had served as a priest in the temple of Anahita. Ardashir and his successors carved a series of monumental reliefs along the base of the cliff. Shapur I even went so far as to inscribe a trilingual record of his achievement on the exterior of the Cube of Zoroaster.[178]

The blank panel at Naqsh-i Rustam provides perhaps the most striking testimony to Khusro's confidence in victory and high appreciation of what he had

---

[177] See H. C. Rawlinson, 'Notes on a March from Zoháb . . .', *Journal of the Royal Geographical Society*, 9 (1839), 26–116, at 110–111, for traces of the foundations of a palace beneath what appears to be a late Sasanian or early Islamic fort in the modern village, together with several broken pillars, plain capitals, and the remains of a well-engineered aqueduct bringing water from a springhead about half a mile away. By the second half of the twentieth century there was no trace of the palace or its water supply system (Huff, 'Harsin', 40–1).

[178] Wiesehöfer, *Ancient Persia*, 27–8, 154–5, 159–61.

achieved by the early or middle 620s (Figures 16 and 17). He set out to do more than emulate the greatest of his predecessors. The early Sasanian reliefs are monumental but not overwhelming. Situated at the base of the cliff, they could be viewed from close at hand. Short labelling inscriptions in small letters were legible. The manner of displaying royal glory varied from ruler to ruler. There are scenes of investiture (Ardashir I and Narseh), of triumph (Shapur I), of king and courtiers (Bahram II), and of combat (Bahram II and Hormizd II).[179] What Khusro had in mind cannot be known, but it was intended to surpass everything put up by his predecessors. The true measure of his ambition, as of his hubris, is the scale of the relief which he had prepared to commemorate his final victory. Its dimensions have not been measured precisely, but it is much the largest at Naqsh-i Rustam (and perhaps the second largest, after that at Bisutun, in the Middle East).[180]

As the last successful Sasanian ruler, Khusro was to loom large in historical traditions about the recent and remote past handed down to writers at work in the medieval heyday of Islam. He acquired the stature of a mythical hero, a fearless warrior who fought steadfastly to recover his throne and to suppress rebels, a faithful lover who surmounted all difficulties in his pursuit of Shirin, a ruler who conquered much of the world and acquired immense riches. But with success came arrogance, and this is the trait highlighted by sources written closer to the events and picked up in later Islamic chronicles. Khusro was accused of overweening pride, of discarding the traditional restraining conventions of the Sasanian monarchy, of transforming his rule into high-handed autocracy. The monuments which he planned to commemorate his achievements are the durable, visible manifestations of his arrogance.

[179] L. Vanden Berghe, 'La Sculpture', in *Splendeur des Sassanides*, 71–88.
[180] This carefully prepared panel, which bears a small Islamic inscription dated 1821, has not been subjected to close scrutiny, nor have its measurements been taken. Its position at the base of the cliff, to the right (east) of the extant series of early Sasanian reliefs, is marked on the panoramic photograph (at no.17) published by E. F. Schmidt, *Persepolis*, III *The Royal Tombs and Other Monuments* (Chicago 1970), and on the ground plan (at no.21) drawn by G. Gropp, 'Urartäische Miszellen', *AMI* 22 (1989), 103–124, at 117. It is larger than any of the early Sasanian reliefs, but does not have the awe-inspiring dimensions of the Bisutun panel. I am grateful to Pierfrancesco Callieri for showing me a slide which confirms my observation that the panel was ready for carving.

6
Opening of the Battle for Survival

The battle for Asia Minor began in 622. As spring drew near, a Persian expeditionary force was poised to attack from its winter quarters in the Pontic region. Its base was almost certainly within easy striking distance of the chief cities in north-east Asia Minor (Satala, Nicopolis, Neocaesarea, and Sebastea), perhaps in the relatively secluded plain of Ereza (modern Erzincan). There was plenty of pasture there for the cavalry's horses, since it had been spared from urbanization by the Romans because of its religious importance to the Armenians. It was conveniently placed inside Persian-held territory, and off the main east-west road.[1]

The war was quickening again after the ominous lull when the Persians were consolidating their hold on Egypt. The opening engagements might have a critical bearing on the outcome of the whole conflict. They would determine whether the Persians could sustain an offensive momentum and, if so, what the pace of their advance would be. A campaign of conquest would differ from their earlier forays into Asia Minor in 615 and 617, when the prime objective had been immaterial gain (the demoralization of a weakened and defeated adversary) in the hope that this might lead to a general collapse of resistance. Now the Persians would move forward more cautiously, seizing and securing hold of Asia Minor piece by piece, just as they had done in Armenia, northern Mesopotamia, Syria, and Palestine in previous campaigns. For the Romans, it was the opening of the last act in the war. If the advance could not be halted that year or in the very near future, all would be lost. For the empire's hold on its Balkan and western provinces was steadily weakening, and there were formidable predators waiting to pounce if the news from the east were to become yet worse.

There was no question but that Heraclius must take personal command of defensive operations. He received conflicting advice, but does not seem to have hesitated.[2] The closer the war drew to his capital and the grimmer the future looked, the more urgent was it for the Roman emperor to plunge into the fray himself, to invest all his mental and physical energy into the struggle for survival, and by his presence and example to give added inspiration to his men. The defeat

---

[1] Geo.Pis., *Expeditio Persica*, ed. and trans. Pertusi, *Giorgio di Pisidia*, 84–136, at ii.256–8. A. Bryer and D. Winfield, *The Byzantine Monuments and Topography of the Pontos*, DO Studies 20 (Washington DC, 1985), I, 32–3.

[2] Geo.Pis., *Expeditio*, i, 112–23.

of 613, terrible in its consequences, for which he as supreme commander must have had to shoulder responsibility was now to be pushed aside. All his intelligence, all his strategic and tactical acumen, all his skills of man-management, all his diplomatic subtlety would be required, if the fortunes of the Romans were to be revived.

6.1 Heraclius Takes Command in Asia Minor in 622

The *Expeditio Persica* commissioned from George of Pisidia by Heraclius on his return to Constantinople in summer 622 is our sole first-hand source about the campaign. The thick historiographical fog which has largely obscured our vision since Heraclius' seizure of power at last begins to thin. With each passing year until the end of the fighting, more can be seen and more can be made of what can be seen. But the principal phenomena of 622 are still hard to make out, so opaque and allusive are most of George's words.

There is not much help to hand. Theophanes supplies a date for the campaign by placing his notice about it in the year 621–2.[3] The notice, a long one, makes extensive use of the poem and appears to add a fair amount of additional matter which latter-day historians have been tempted to use in reconstructing events.[4] However, his dating must be approached with scepticism, and little trust should be placed in his interpretation of the material extracted from George which forms the main body of his notice (demonstrably wrong, as it is, at several points). Such additional items of information as he supplies or appears to supply should also be viewed with the utmost suspicion, since they may well be nothing more than inferences and surmises of his own.

Somehow history has to be teased out of our only authoritative source, the *Expeditio Persica*. All sorts of difficulties are encountered. It is a panegyrical work. Attention is focused on Heraclius, as first he seeks to transform attitudes and improve fighting capability and then directs operations. George does not give a connected narrative of events, although he can do so, as he shows in his account of the siege of Constantinople in 626. Instead, shafts of light are directed at a small number of isolated episodes. They are picked out and presented as scenes which both illustrate Heraclius' involvement in the hardships and dangers of campaign and demonstrate the crucial importance of his intellectual contribution to the conduct of the war. His men are given new heart by the example he sets of level-headed, resolute action in crises and by his rousing speeches. Their performance

---

[3] Theoph., 302.31–306.8.
[4] For example, Stratos, *Byzantium in the Seventh Century*, I, 135–44, and, with considerable reservations, N. Oikonomides, 'A Chronological Note on the First Persian Campaign of Heraclius (622)', *BMGS* 1 (1975), 1–9.

is improved by intensive training under his direction and by his devising of intelligent plans of action once operations have begun. Heraclius is *the teacher of armed words, the general of wise counsels.* His reason is *like a deep spring which divides into many channels* to cope with manifold problems. *He is the general, tactical instructor, planner to whom everyone looks. His clear mind encompasses the whole earth like Ocean, watering everything, yet never depleted. His clear mind is a fire of reasoned thoughts which makes everything white and soothes everyone, without burning them.*[5]

Ideas and images cascade out of the poet's imagination. It is a glittering display of verbal virtuosity and intellectual ingenuity. There is unceasing wordplay, a rapid flow of paradoxical juxtapositions. Ideas and images are stretched and pulled in unusual directions. Conceits are devised and drawn out, sometimes entwined with each other. There are flashes of colour as a theological point or a jibe at Zoroastrianism tumbles down in the main flow, catches and refracts the light. Similes of all sorts, some recurring, glint below the surface of the panegyric, crowding together in places, sliding sinuously over each other, like fish of many colours moving about and feeding in a pool. It is no easy task to catch the humdrum phenomena of military history here.[6]

There are very few indications of time in the *Expeditio Persica*. Heraclius leaves Constantinople on Easter Monday. Later, a full moon forces the Persian general to defer a night attack. There are also references to a six-day delay before the news of the outcome of one action reaches the Persian general, and to fifteen days of skirmishing before a larger engagement between the two armies.[7] Nothing is said which helps us to identify the year. A fair amount of guesswork is needed to estimate the length of the campaign. A phrase which used to be taken literally as referring to a lunar eclipse in the middle of operations has been reinterpreted more convincingly in the light of its immediate context in the poem as a figure of speech referring to the gradual waning of the full moon.[8]

The campaign cannot be dated later than 622, since Heraclius stayed in Constantinople to deal with western affairs in 623 and was engaged in bold offensive operations on Sasanian territory from 624 to early 628, with but one break from the middle of 626 to the middle of 627. Nor can it be dated any earlier, since it is bracketed with Heraclius' two counteroffensives (624–6 and 627–8) in the Official History which George was commissioned to write after the end of the war, and George likens Heraclius' six years of labour in the field before he returned

---

[5] Geo.Pis., *Expeditio*, i.35, ii.42–51, iii.220–4, 374.

[6] Cf. J. Trilling, 'Myth and Metaphor at the Byzantine Court: A Literary Approach to the David Plates', *Byz*.48 (1978), 249–63, at 255. 258–61, and Mary Whitby, 'A New Image for a New Age: George of Pisidia on the Emperor Heraclius', in E. Dąbrowa, ed., *The Roman and Byzantine Army in the East* (Cracow, 1994), 197–225.

[7] Geo.Pis., *Expeditio*, i.132–8, 154–6, ii, 286–8, 361–75, iii.13–16.

[8] Geo.Pis., *Expeditio*, iii.1–6. Cf. C. Zuckerman, 'The Reign of Constantine V in the Miracles of St. Theodore the Recruit (BHG 1764)', *REB* 46 (1988), 191–210, at 209–10.

to Constantinople in the seventh to God's fashioning of the universe in six days and resting on the seventh.[9] The six years would then run from spring 622, when Heraclius left for Bithynia, to spring 628, when operations had ceased and news came of the deposition and execution of Khusro II.

One fixed point can be established. Heraclius left Constantinople on 5 April 622 (Easter falling on 4 April). Thenceforth, we must travel in the poem, *a small, slow-moving craft crossing the measureless sea of Heraclius' achievements*, as the poet puts it in fawning mode.[10] The first scene occurs in what is clearly marked out as a digression.[11] It is an episode plucked out of context, another sea journey at another time which was not as swift and easy as this crossing to the port of Pylae, on the south side of the gulf of Nicomedia (modern Yalova).[12] A contrary wind has risen. The various ships carrying the emperor and his entourage of courtiers and guards have difficulty rounding the point of Hieria. One ship runs aground. Waves break onto a rocky shore. Echoes of their booming are *spat* back by the rocks along with *sparks* of water. The emperor hears a cry of distress and springs into action. He takes charge of the rescue operation. Even the court eunuchs join in. The efforts of emperor, men, and eunuchs are successful. The stricken vessel is hauled and pushed off. The emperor has shown concern for his men, courage, and resourcefulness. He has *cut* the thrust of the waves and emptied the wind of force, by the exercise of reason.[13]

George now brings the first canto to a close with an extraordinary turn. A stone hits Heraclius' big toe, the envious Devil's revenge for the saving of the ship. Blood spurts out, *baptizing* the earth and dubbing Heraclius *martyr*. The injury is Heraclius' *stigmata*. George then prays that the Logos of God protect him and save the whole cosmic ship through him. It is hard to know what to make of this apparent likening of Heraclius' minor mishap to the Passion of Christ.[14] It is introduced in so few lines, apropos of so trivial an incident, that it is hard to take it completely seriously. It is perhaps best viewed as a daring piece of light flattery by a poet who enjoyed the emperor's confidence and knew that he could go quite far. It is hard to suppose that any of his listeners imagined that he really meant to portray the emperor as the successor as well as the vicegerent of Christ.

The second canto is dominated by Heraclius' preparations for campaign. He landed at Pylae and was met by the army which had already been assembled. Units previously dispersed in different districts had been brought together *like streams on a mountainside*.[15] It was a large polyglot force[16] comprising probably

---

[9] Theoph., 327.24–328.2.   [10] Geo.Pis., *Expeditio*, iii.381–84.
[11] Geo.Pis., *Expeditio*, i.166–9, ii.6–7.   [12] C. Foss, 'Pylai', *ODB*, III, 1760.
[13] Geo.Pis., *Expeditio*, i.170–238.
[14] Geo.Pis., *Expeditio*, i.239–47 and commentary of Trilling, 'Myth and Metaphor', 259–60.
[15] Geo.Pis., *Expeditio*, ii.8–18, 52–6, 66–9. Theoph., 303.10–12 introduces the technical term 'theme' anachronistically at this point. It is the first of many errors.
[16] Geo.Pis., *Expeditio*, ii.163–9.

most of what remained of the old field armies, Praesental, Eastern, and Armenian, as well as whatever troops had been transferred in the past from the Balkans and perhaps some foreign auxiliaries. The only figure that can be put upon it is that given in the *Strategicon* of Maurice, some thirty years earlier, for a large army— some 15–20,000 men.[17]

The preparations involved much staff work, a rousing speech by Heraclius, and training exercises which he organized and supervised. This second scene or set of scenes takes place in the plains of Bithynia, which, shielded by a rampart of mountains from attack by land, formed a huge natural parade ground where the exercises could be held in relative safety.[18] Security was increased by a screen of cavalry units sent out to watch for enemy forays. Some of the enemy did venture across the mountains, either during or after the manoeuvres, but they were intercepted, taken prisoner, and brought to Heraclius.[19] George summarizes the thrust of Heraclius' speech (perhaps made on several occasions to different components of the army). It was preceded by a formal acclamation, during which the standards were lowered, bowing before the emperor like *horizontal flames*. Heraclius sought to raise spirits: he addressed the troops as his brothers and said that they were all serving a higher commander; they would be advancing together against impious enemies as the *plasmata* (creatures) and agents of God.[20]

Then the exercises began, following, it appears, schemes laid down (in words and diagrams) in the *Strategicon* of Maurice.[21] Mock combats were staged between opposing forces. Units closed ranks, until they formed solid lines bristling with weapons. One line would advance, turn, and retreat, while its adversary did the opposite. Simulated hand-to-hand combats took place, both lines pressing against each other. George marvels as he watches in his mind's eye the flux and reflux of the two lines, *their manoeuvres orchestrated by a single commanding intelligence.*[22] George does not say how long they lasted. But several weeks were required at a minimum if the troops were to be steeled in mind and

---

[17] Mauricius, *Strategicon*, ed. G. T. Dennis and trans. (German) E. Gamillscheg, CFHB 17 (Vienna, 1981), trans. (English) G. T. Dennis, *Maurice's Strategikon: Handbook of Byzantine Military Strategy* (Philadelphia, PA, 1984), iii.8.32–6, 10.25–8—cited henceforth as *Strategicon*.

[18] There was no question of marching deep into the interior of Asia Minor to hold the exercises in Cappadocia, as is suggested by Oikonomides, 'Chronological Note', 2–3, 6–7.

[19] Geo.Pis., *Expeditio*, ii.203–38. The exercises were probably still going on when the prisoners arrived, *contra* Theoph., 304.13–18, who supposes that they were over (error 2). George notes that one of the prisoners was an Arab chief who changed sides because he, like the other prisoners, was well treated. Theoph., 304.14–15 misunderstands George, supposing that all the raiders were Arabs (error 3).

[20] Geo.Pis., *Expeditio*, ii.70–119.

[21] Cf. *Strategicon*, iii.5.

[22] Geo.Pis., *Expeditio*, ii.120–202. I am grateful to Mary Whitby for insisting to me that George transports himself in his imagination to the exercises rather than witnessing them in reality. Cf. Mary Whitby, 'Defender of the Cross: George of Pisidia on the Emperor Heraclius and his Deputies', in Mary Whitby, ed., *The Propaganda of Power: The Role of Panegyric in Late Antiquity* (Leiden, 1998), 247–73, at 250, n.21.

body, the fighting units welded together and so accustomed to all manoeuvres that they became almost reflex actions, and the whole army given a tensile strength and power of endurance superior to the enemy's. On the other hand, the exercises could not be prolonged too much, since the interior of Asia Minor had been stripped of most of its defenders and was all too vulnerable to attack for as long as they went on.

It may, therefore, be conjectured that the whole army moved into action by the end of May or the beginning of June at the latest. The Persians had used their relatively free hand in the interior of Asia Minor to blockade an unspecified number of unnamed cities, presumably in or near that part of the Pontic region where the expeditionary army had wintered.[23] The main body of the army was probably committed to the laborious task of forcing them to submit and extending Persian authority into the core of Asia Minor. A subsidiary force was sent forward, probably using the northern support road to make good speed, and seized control of all the routes crossing the mountain ranges between the plateau and Bithynia. The effect was to stop up Heraclius and the whole Roman field army in the plains where they were being trained, and to shield the operations of the blockading forces many hundreds of kilometres to the east.[24]

This advance force was outnumbered by the full Roman field army under Heraclius' command. But it was formidable, nonetheless, and had come prepared to cause maximum damage if ever Heraclius were to break out from Bithynia. With its equipment and provisions transported on pack animals (including camels) rather than wagons, it was not confined to the road network, but was ready to harass the Romans with guerrilla attacks from the higher, rougher ground traditionally favoured by Persian armies.[25] The Persian general, who is called 'the barbarian' by George, has usually been identified as Shahrbaraz, it being assumed that there is a play on words (Sarbaros, the Graecized form of the name, becoming *barbaros*, as happens throughout the *Bellum Avaricum* when there is no doubt that Shahrbaraz was the Persian commander).

Two episodes are picked out by George. In the first (scene 3), a Roman feint succeeds in luring a Persian detachment out of the pass which it is holding. The Romans then seize the pass, march through it, and set off east in the direction of Armenia. It is only six days later, at the end of the day, that the news reaches the Persian general. George now ventures to explore the workings of his mind, portraying him as the very antithesis of Heraclius. His mind is darkened, suffused with anxiety, filled with confused thoughts. He is irresolute. He cannot decide

---

[23] Geo.Pis., *Expeditio*, ii.256–7, iii.300–4.
[24] Geo.Pis., *Expeditio*, ii.256–8. Theophanes is apparently bewildered by these lines of the poem. His version (304.13–20) is a confused concoction: Heraclius arrives in Armenia immediately after the end of the exercises (it is there that a large number of Arab raiders fall into his hands) and then turns back and goes into winter quarters in the Pontic region (errors 4–5).
[25] Incidental references to pack animals and camels: Geo.Pis., *Expeditio*, iii.249–50, 286–7.

whether to turn and hasten after Heraclius or to withdraw along the main diagonal road leading to Cilicia. He worries about the possibility (surely very remote in 622) that Heraclius may push on through Armenia to invade Persia. His thoughts will not stay still, but *rush downhill like an unstable rolling stone, only to be suddenly pulled up before plunging down again*. In the end he is compelled to follow Heraclius, which entails a wearying transverse march across difficult country.[26]

Time has passed when the fourth and last scene opens. Both armies are marching east, the Romans over flat country, the Persians shadowing them from higher, rugged terrain. The Persians have resorted to guerrilla tactics. A night attack has been put off until the moon has waned. Instead, harassing forays are launched by day, but are fielded without difficulty by the Romans. Fifteen days of intermittent skirmishing pass by. Roman morale is high. Troops from crack units vie with each other, inspired by the sight of an emperor at war, *hair plastered in dust, protected from the sun by a coating of sweat, lance replacing sceptre and shield crown, eager to dye the black boots of a soldier red with Persian blood*.[27] The Persians, by contrast, are increasingly downcast: they have not taken up Heraclius' challenge to fight in open country, and for every mile the Romans cover, they have to cover two. A Persian deserter is shocked at their low morale when he returns after fourteen days with the Roman army, and deserts again on the following day.[28]

At last the Persian general prepares for a full engagement. At dawn his army, arrayed in three divisions, bars Heraclius' route to the east. A force of elite troops is concealed in ravines nearby, with orders to launch a surprise attack at the critical moment. Heraclius, however, has got good intelligence and has set a counter-trap.[29] A detachment makes a sortie towards the main Persian army, turns, and hurriedly retreats. The Persian ambush is lured out and sets off in pursuit only to be ambushed itself by elite units of the Roman army. The Persian general now orders the main army forward in support, but its morale is low, and he decides to retreat instead, behind a smokescreen. The retreat becomes disorderly as the troops try to make their way past precipices, through defiles,

---

[26] Geo.Pis., *Expeditio*, ii.259–91, 331–60. Theoph., 304.20–305.1 presents a horribly garbled version: Heraclius slips past the Persian army which had been blockading him during the fictitious winter and invades *Persia*; the Persian general is caught by surprise and dismayed; he now marches with his own army into *Cilicia*, meaning to invade Roman territory from there, but then changes his mind, fearful that Heraclius may invade Persia through Armenia, and follows the Roman army (errors 6–7).

[27] Geo.Pis., *Expeditio*, ii.361–75, iii.13–136. Theoph., 305.1–5 takes George's reference to an eclipse literally and then supposes that it was the eclipse (rather than the illumination cast by the full moon) which caused the Persian commander to abandon a planned night attack (error 8).

[28] Geo.Pis., *Expeditio*, iii.137–77.

[29] Geo.Pis., *Expeditio*, iii.178–206. Theoph., 305.17–24 leaves out the vital element in the Persian dispositions (the ambush), has the Persian army face east, rather than west, and adds that Heraclius arrayed his army in three divisions, like the Persians (errors 9–10).

enveloped in a darkness of their own making. The Romans do not bother to strike camp, but stand and watch as *some leap from rock to rock like wild goats, and others are pressed into an unmoving, tight-knit mass, heaving like a stormy sea.*[30]

How much time elapsed between the end of the training exercises and this victory is hard to say. A little under two months is probably a reasonable guess, which brings us to late July or the beginning of August. News now came of developments in the west which demanded Heraclius' attention. He left the army in the charge of an unnamed general to continue the campaign and hurried back to Constantinople.[31] Nothing is known of the subsequent course of operations in 622, since George halts his narrative with the emperor's departure. He concludes with some general reflections on what had been achieved and a long prayer in which he asks God to guide Heraclius to victory and to protect his offspring.[32]

George's prime concern is to develop his two principal themes, that of Heraclius as a general who plunges into the thick of things and labours with his men (scenes one and four), and that of Heraclius as a general of rare sagacity who can transform a whole army into the pliable instrument of his will (scene two) and then deploy it with scientific skill on the battlefield (scenes three and four). His Persian adversary is deliberately (and probably falsely) presented as his antithesis, deficient in reasoning and resolution. A third subsidiary theme is introduced to explain Heraclius' success in managing his men on exercise: the Holy Ghost is at work, speaking through Heraclius' tongue; Heraclius' mind is thus presented as the instrument through which God is acting on earth and redressing the balance of war.[33] It is a theme which is picked up again in the coda to the poem, George praying that Heraclius' mind and heart be filled with the purifying zeal of Elijah and the piety of Moses, so that he may be victorious as God's lieutenant general on earth.[34]

George discharges his commission from the emperor with extraordinary skill. Heraclius is the prime mover of events. He transforms the attitudes and performance of his men and in a matter of a few months begins to turn the tide of war. Evidently there is some embellishment of the truth. Flattery, sometimes rather gross, is offered up here and there. It is, therefore, only prudent to be on guard as one tries to discern the realities of training and operations in the first half of the campaigning season of 622. Might George have transmuted the Roman

---

[30] Geo.Pis., *Expeditio*, iii.207–19, 225–80. Theoph., 305.24–306.2 again gives an inaccurate version of George's account: the Romans pursue and press the Persians hard; there is no mention of a smokescreen and the confusion which it caused; the Persian camp and baggage are captured by the Romans (errors 11–13).

[31] Geo.Pis., *Expeditio*, iii.305–40. Theoph., 306.7–8 has Heraclius depart at the end of the campaigning season, leaving the army to winter in Armenia (error 14)—so too does M. Hurbanič, 'The Eastern Roman Empire and the Avar Khaganate in the Years 622-624 AD', *Acta Antiqua Ac. Scient. Hungaricae*, 51 (2011), 315–28, at 316–17.

[32] Geo.Pis., *Expeditio*, 385–461. [33] Geo.Pis., *Expeditio*, ii.70–5, 163–76.

[34] Geo.Pis., *Expeditio*, iii.385–427.

phenomena as much as the mental processes of the Persian general? Have humdrum training exercises been turned into something close to a remodelling of the army? Has too much significance been attached to a minor victory in the field, simply because the emperor was in command? Is the poem primarily a work of propaganda, intelligent, ingenious, packed with meaning and allusion, but ultimately serving the Roman cause at the time and seeking to please the emperor of the day?

It is difficult to suppress such doubts if the activities of 622 are viewed in isolation, since there is no other source against which to check George's account. But if they are placed in context, if note is taken of the performance of the Roman field army under Heraclius' command in 624 and the following years, there is nothing implausible in the scenario presented by George. It should also be remembered that he was very far from being a placeman ever anxious to curry favour with the emperor. He shows his independence at several points in the *Expeditio Persica*. Who but a bold and daring spirit would offset the sight of chorus girls cavorting before the Persian king as he goes to war with Heraclius' hopes imagined as virgins dancing chastely in his mind? Who else would liken his generalship, in the phase of skirmishing, to Alexander's, with the difference that there was no risk? Who else would introduce the obvious comparison with Herakles, but with the caveat (expressed in a roundabout way) that the hydra which Heraclius confronts had lost none of its heads? While he was ready to flatter, George was his own man and, if need be, could be daringly outspoken, exercising a *parrhesia* at times almost as startling as that of the most uncompromising of holy men.[35]

His assessment of the results of the campaign should, therefore, be taken seriously. He reckoned, in his ruminations on the campaign, that it brought three notable immediate gains. Roman morale was raised in the preparatory phase. A victory, modest perhaps, but the first for many years against the hitherto invincible Persians, gave an additional boost and, no less important, began to undermine Persian confidence. That same victory also had an important strategic effect: the blockade of the Roman cities well to the east was lifted when the main Persian army lost its forward shield; with this, the Persian offensive lost momentum and may even have been halted for a year.[36] More significant, though, was the enhancement of Roman fighting capability brought about by the battle training instituted by Heraclius. Stamina, morale, discipline, tactical flexibility, and cohesion were lifted to a new level. Not only could Heraclius face the Persians in open, frontal combat, but he could also take a calculated risk and enter the open space between two enemy armies. Relying on superior speed of movement and an initial element of surprise, he sought to counter superior numbers by

---

[35] Geo.Pis., *Expeditio*, ii.240-8, iii.48-9, 350-4.   [36] Geo.Pis., *Expeditio*, iii.300-4.

taking on the enemy in detail. This was a radical break with past Roman practice, the first, but by no mean the last, bold initiative which Heraclius would take.

What Heraclius said to his men was no less important. Their cause was a high one. They were not just the defenders of what remained of a once great empire. They were the earthly champions of the true religion. Their mission was to halt the advance of an evil empire which threatened the good order of the cosmos by venerating created things above the Creator and by defiling the proper places of His worship. The cause was holy and the ultimate direction of operations came from God Himself. Words of this sort were likely to make a strong impression in the grim circumstances of 622, encouraging the troops and giving an additional religious impetus to their actions. Perhaps it was not the first occasion that attempts were made to activate the troops' Christian beliefs as an additional motivating force; certainly it was not the last. But it marked a significant stage in the ideological escalation of the war and, by hardening Roman resolve, increased the chances of ultimate victory.

6.2 Crisis in the Balkans

George of Pisidia merely alludes to the crisis in the west. He does not describe it. To have explained why the emperor was so concerned would have been to distract attention from the subject matter of the *Expeditio Persica* and to detract from the emperor's (limited) achievements on the campaign. Nor is there information in any other extant metropolitan source which might help to define the nature of the crisis. So we have to resort to circumstantial evidence.

The crisis was evidently serious. Why else would Heraclius suddenly give up his directing role in the field just when the Persians had been forced onto the defensive? Here was an opportunity, with the strategic initiative temporarily in Roman hands, to clear Persian forces from the northern and eastern fringes of the Anatolian plateau and to begin stopping up the main natural routes of invasion— (1) the northern support road past Satala and Nicopolis, (2) the southern road leading from Persian-held Melitene through the Anti-Taurus towards Caesarea, and (3) the Cilician Gates.[37] Some of these aims, if indeed they were the aims of the campaign, may have been achieved, despite Heraclius' departure. But only the gravest of crises would have led him to forgo the chance to boost his prestige by claiming the credit for himself.

---

[37] D. H. French, 'The Roman Road-System of Asia Minor', in H. Temporini, ed., *Aufstieg und Niedergang der römischen Welt*, II.7.2 (Berlin, 1980), 698–729, at 704–14; T. B. Mitford, 'Cappadocia and Armenia Minor: Historical Setting of the *Limes*', in Temporini, *Aufstieg und Niedergang*, 1169–1228, at 1183–5, 1206–8.

The ultimate cause of a grave crisis in the west at this time can be identified readily on a priori grounds. There was only one power with the military capability of inflicting serious damage on the empire's main western resource base, the Balkan provinces and the cities there which were still under Roman control. That power was the Avar khaganate centred on the Hungarian plain, which exerted effective authority over a swathe of surrounding territory and extended its influence far beyond. For most of the twenty years since Maurice's grand counteroffensive had come to an abrupt end, the Avars had been at peace with the Roman Empire as a result of the treaty which Phocas had perforce negotiated with them in 603–4.[38] They had gradually recovered from the severe military and political damage inflicted on them by sustained and concentrated Roman military action.

If some value can be attached to the silence of the sources, western as well as Roman, about Avar military activity in this period, they were concentrating on reconstruction and refrained from attacking and antagonizing either their Germanic or their east Roman neighbours. Only one act of aggression is recorded, a foray in considerable force into north-east Italy, datable after 610, perhaps several years later. The attack was strikingly successful. Gisulf II Duke of Friuli was killed. The Lombards were cooped up in a number of strongholds. Cividale, where Gisulf's family and many of his followers took refuge, surrendered without a fight. A large number of prisoners were taken, including Gisulf's wife and four sons. The Avars were serving notice on both the western Slavs and their predatory Germanic neighbours that they were once again a power to be reckoned with. The expedition must also have raised the prestige of the khagan at home and given encouragement to those among the ruling elite who were spoiling for a war of revenge against the Romans.[39]

That war was eventually fought. Its culminating moment was the siege of Constantinople in August 626. But we know that relations between Romans and Avars had broken down rather earlier, because we have evidence of the strenuous diplomatic efforts made by the Romans to patch them up. Two embassies, led respectively by the Patrician Athanasius and the Quaestor Cosmas, prepared the way for a summit meeting between Heraclius and the Avar khagan, which was scheduled to take place, amid much pomp and ceremony, at Heraclea on the Sea of Marmara on Sunday 5 June 623. The crisis which had broken out in the previous summer and had demanded the emperor's attention was evidently being brought to a formal end by the emperor in person. The negotiations carried out by the two named Roman ambassadors probably occupied the intervening months. The seriousness of the problems in 622 is underlined by the time it took

---

[38] Theoph., 292.11–14.
[39] Paul D, iv.37. Cf. W. Pohl, *The Avars: A Steppe Empire in Central Europe, 567–822* (Ithaca, NY, 2018), 283–4.

to negotiate a solution and by the solemnity and grandeur of the planned peacemaking ceremony involving the two heads of state.[40]

What, though, happened in 622? No clue to an answer is given by any of the sources which report the subsequent negotiations. The answer, however, stares us in the face if we turn to a provincial Balkan source, the *Miracula Sancti Demetrii*. This contains an account, rather florid in places, with a marked tendency to exaggerate, of a long siege of Thessalonica, the second-ranking city of the Balkans, by a large Avar army led by the khagan in person (ii.2). It is rather thin on hard military detail, concentrating rather on the general threat to the city (hence a long catalogue of the hardware deployed against it) and on the figure of the archbishop, John. He is portrayed as giving vital moral support to the defenders when they were disheartened at the sight of the army arrayed against them and plays the role of chief intercessor with the city's guardian saint, St Demetrius. In spite of the wordy rhetoric and evident tendentiousness of the account, it is made plain that the siege was the longest and most serious crisis of the city's existence.

There is no explicit indication of the date. But circumstantial evidence—namely inclusion of the siege narrative in the second collection of miracles stories—helps to narrow the period within which to locate it. It clearly took place after the latest datable episode covered in the first collection (i.10, dealing with rising social tension in the city in 608) and after completion of work on that first collection by its author, Archbishop John—a few years later probably, so early in Heraclius' reign. There is thus a fairly secure *terminus post quem* at the beginning of Heraclius reign (October 610).[41] There was also no question of the Avars mounting the expedition after 626 (when they entered a period of prolonged and profound internal crisis), and they were precluded from doing so in the two previous years under the terms of the treaty which they eventually agreed with Heraclius late in 623 or early in 624. The attack on Thessalonica can then be located confidently in the period 610–22 and should surely be identified with the crisis which demanded Heraclius' personal attention in the middle of summer 622 and led to several rounds of negotiations with the Avars over the following year and a half.

There is no contrary evidence, either literary or archaeological, strong enough to overturn this powerful circumstantial argument. The only other source to mention a renewal of warfare in the Balkans is the chronicle of Isidore of Seville. He first became aware of serious disturbances in the Balkans *after* completing the chronicle in Heraclius' fifth regnal year (614–15). In a postscript added to a copy made *eleven years later*, he summarized Roman losses by the beginning of Heraclius' sixteenth regnal year (October 625): besides the Persians' conquest of 'Syria, Egypt, and very many provinces', he reported that 'the Slavs took Greece

---

[40] *Chron.Pasch.*, 712.12–21; Nic., c.10.1–15 (L, c.10.1–11). *PLRE* III, Athanasius 10 and Cosmas 20.
[41] Lemerle, *Miracles*, II, 28, 32–4, 40–6, 79–81.

[which in Isidore's usage may encompass Illyricum as well as Greece proper] from the Romans'. The date of resumption of Slav colonization (probably at the instigation of the Avars) can thus be narrowed to the years 615–22, at a time when the Avars were preparing for direct military action. There is no reason, however, to place it earlier rather than later in this period.[42]

The Avars mobilized a large army, both from the peoples inhabiting their core territory (the Hungarian plain) and from their other subject peoples, two of whom are named (Bulgars and Slavs). The process of assembling this force took some two years. The considerable technological resources of the Avar Empire were also brought into play. The army went to war with the materiel for constructing a formidable array of siege engines, including powerful artillery, armoured shelters for sappers, rams, and at least one wooden siegetower higher than the walls of Thessalonica. It advanced swiftly south (therefore, probably causing little damage beyond its immediate line of march and netting few, if any, of the cities it passed) and caught Thessalonica completely unprepared. The armoured cavalry of the vanguard burst into the plain in the middle of the day, when harvesting was in full swing. The harvesters were unable to escape to the city. Those who were not slaughtered there and then were captured along with a large number of livestock and the harvesting equipment.[43]

A few days later, the khagan, who had taken personal command of the expedition, arrived with the main body of the army and invested the city. The defenders' spirits, which had dropped at the appearance of the vanguard, now plummeted at the sight of the besiegers' massed forces and equipment. Even the archbishop found it hard to reassure himself that the city's supernatural protector, St Demetrius, would be able to help them this time. He simply prayed fervently that God would come to the aid of his chosen people and would rescue a latter-day Israel from its Egyptians.[44] Siege operations began and were to last for more than a month. By their actions the Avars demonstrated a firm determination to take the city. Had it fallen, the consequences would have been catastrophic for the Roman position in the Balkans, and the Avars would have acquired a secure base from which to apply military pressure on Constantinople itself.

The account of the siege is rather insubstantial compared to that of several other episodes covered by the *Miracula*. It seems to have been composed over a generation after the event, probably in the 650s, by an author who had no detailed written account to hand.[45] He even seems to have been short of hagiographical material. Thus, although he sets out to glorify the saint and to attribute the city's survival on this and other occasions to his intervention, he seems to have known

---

[42] Isidorus, *Chronica*, 479. [43] *Mir.Dem.*, ii.2.198–200, 203 (pp.185.23–186.6, 186.20–30).
[44] *Mir.Dem.*, ii.2.201–3, 205 (pp.186.7–31, 187.6–18).
[45] Howard-Johnston, *Witnesses*, 152–4. Cf. Lemerle, *Miracles*, II, 83–5, 172–4, who prefers a date of composition in the 680s.

of only four specific incidents, trivial in the context of the siege, which could be construed as examples of supernatural intervention. He notes the human efforts of the defenders and the human help which eventually came from outside, but deliberately leaves them in shadow. The saint and Archbishop John are centre stage.

It is not possible to trace the development of siege operations, as it is in the case of Constantinople four years later. Apart from general references to setbacks suffered by the Avar army, we are only told of two specific military incidents, both involving siege engines: the first was plainly a miracle performed by St Demetrius—when two pieces of artillery were fired at the same time, the smaller but faster Roman projectile (inscribed with the name of St Demetrius) flung back the larger Avar projectile with which it collided in mid-air, and then struck down the artificer and crew of artillerymen who had discharged it; the second, the spontaneous self-destruction of the armoured siege tower as it was being pushed into position, is simply credited to divine intervention.[46] A second intervention by the saint took the form of a prophecy made in a dream to Archbishop John—if all the citizens were to shout '*Kyrie Eleison*' simultaneously, the city would be saved. This they duly did when they felt an earth tremor. A fourth miraculous event, not credited to any specific supernatural agency, boosted the morale of the defenders: they observed that some of the arrows shot at the city embedded themselves in the walls with their iron heads pointing outwards.[47]

The local and imperial authorities were caught completely by surprise. The Prefect of Illyricum was not present at the start of the siege to take charge of the city's defence. A new appointee was on his way to take up the post and only arrived after the siege had begun. But once the news reached Constantinople, the authorities responded swiftly and effectively to the crisis—not that they are given credit (it is reserved for the saint). The news, it may be assumed, was relayed immediately to Heraclius in Asia Minor, and emergency supplies and reinforcements were rushed by sea to Thessalonica. Sometime before the end of the siege (a week, or ten days at the most, one would guess), cargo ships, described as grain carriers (perhaps belonging to the fleet evacuated from Alexandria three years before), began arriving every day, delivering supplies of all sorts. There were so many of them that the harbour and roadstead were constantly full of shipping. They also brought sailors who were adept at the technical side of siege warfare and joined in the city's defence.[48]

Faced by increasingly effective resistance from the city, which could not be blockaded, the khagan indicated that he was ready to lift the siege in return for gifts. When that met with a refusal, he backed his offer with menaces. He issued

---

[46] *Mir.Dem.*, ii.2.206, 211 (pp.187.21–9, 188.30–40).
[47] *Mir.Dem.*, ii.2.204, 207, 208 (pp.186.33–187.5, 187.29–31, 188.3–9).
[48] *Mir.Dem.*, ii.2.209–10 (p.188.10–27).

orders for the burning of all extramural churches and suburban villas, and warned that he would press on with the siege and call reinforcements to his aid. It is not clear whether or not the orders were carried out, but the threats worked. There was unanimous agreement in the city that a payment should be made to bring about the withdrawal of the Avar forces. The siege was brought to an end after thirty-three days, and those taken prisoner by the Avars were ransomed.[49] The way was opened for negotiations to begin between the imperial authorities and the khagan's court in the following months. Heraclius, who had probably been unable to affect events at Thessalonica (the siege ending, it may be supposed, not long after his return to Constantinople), took charge of the diplomatic effort. Peace had to the restored in Europe if his counteroffensive in the east was to have any chance of success.

Before we turn to the denouement of the negotiations in the following summer, we should first place the Avar attack of 622 in context and, in doing so, search for its cause or causes. The crucial question is whether or not the Persians, who were the chief beneficiaries of the siege of Thessalonica and who were to profit as much or more from Heraclius' continuing absorption in western affairs in 623, incited the Avars to go to war with the Romans in 622. While it was possible for the Persians to make contact with the Avars, as they may well have done in the late 570s,[50] there is no evidence of collusion between the two, in particular no hint in the works of authors with access to inside information. As for the *Miracula*, it is Slavs, not Persians, who are presented as the initiators of events in 622. It is reported that two years earlier they had made their own unsuccessful attempt on the city by land and by sea, after a phase of widespread sea raiding in the Aegean and Adriatic. On that occasion there had been no ships to guard the harbour, and various defensive measures had to be improvised at the last moment. The city's patron saint was made directly responsible for the failure of the naval assault which then led to the collapse of the whole siege. The miracle story focuses on the Slavs' initial hesitation, which allowed the defenders to introduce countermeasures, on the disorderly naval attack which led to collisions and capsizes, and on the effectiveness of the improvised defences. The Slavs then withdrew, in the process losing many of the prisoners and some of the booty which they had taken.[51] The response of the Slavs, who are portrayed as independent players in Balkan affairs, was to appeal for help to the khagan of the Avars. An embassy taking all manner of presents was sent to induce him to intervene. The Avars were told of the wealth of Thessalonica, which was theirs for the taking, since it was the only Balkan city still in Roman hands and was stuffed with

---

[49] *Mir.Dem.*, ii.2.212–14 (p.189.4–19).

[50] Hence, perhaps, the sudden about-turn in Avar foreign policy in 579, when they unilaterally broke the peace and made a surprise attack in massive force on Sirmium (Menander Protector, ed. and trans. R. C. Blockley, *The History of Menander the Guardsman* (Liverpool, 1985), fr.25.1–13).

[51] *Mir.Dem.*, ii.1, 2.196 (pp.175–9, 185.4–12).

refugees from the cities which had fallen. The khagan is said to have agreed with enthusiasm and to have begun mobilizing his subjects.[52]

This is history of a very basic, naive sort. It fitted the scenario conjured up in the *Miracula* of a city isolated in a sea of Slavs and exposed to attack from different quarters, which made the role of its supernatural protector in assuring its survival all the more striking. In reality, however, there is clear evidence, from several sources, of the subordination of Slav tribes to the Avars.[53] The Slav attack on Thessalonica in 620 and the sea raids which preceded it were, in all likelihood, planned and directed by the Avars. It should cause no surprise that they chose initially to act through Slav clients. There was much to be gained from concealed aggression of this sort. Apparently uncoordinated local attacks on Roman centres of population in the interior and on the coasts might cause cumulatively severe damage before the Romans realized what was happening and responded. If they protested, the Avars could disclaim responsibility and thereby gain more time. Eventually, they could declare war and escalate the fighting as and when they chose. An appeal for help from their Slav clients could then be invoked to justify violation of their treaty agreement with the Romans. The Avars were employing a familiar diplomatic device (used a few years earlier, in 615, by the Turks, who justified an unprovoked attack across the Oxus and into Persian territory as a response to an urgent plea for help from their Kushan clients).[54] Certainly, contemporaries such as George of Pisidia and Theodore Syncellus were not deceived. They had no doubt that the Avars were the prime movers and associated the renewal of their past aggression with the accession of a new khagan.[55]

It was surely the increasingly parlous condition of the Roman Empire in the second decade of the seventh century which induced the khagan to act. The news of successive disasters in the Middle East—the Persian crossing of the Euphrates in 610, victory over the full Roman field army commanded by the emperor in person near Antioch in 613, the fall of Jerusalem in 614—news which we know circulated widely, assuredly reached the Avars. Like other great nomad powers, they had the diplomatic wherewithal to observe events at a distance, but it appears that they remained reluctant to tangle again with the Roman Empire, engaged though it might be in a war in the east, unless there were unequivocal signs that it was permanently weakened as a military power and that victory could be assured.

---

[52] *Mir.Dem.*, ii.2.197–8 (p.185.12–26).
[53] To the evidence of effective Avar command and control over Slavs at the sieges of Thessalonica in 623 and Constantinople in 626 may be added the clear statements of Archbishop John (*Mir.Dem.*, i.13.117 (p.134.14–16)) and Fredegar (ed. and trans. J. M. Wallace-Hadrill, *The Fourth Book of the Chronicle of Fredegar with Its Continuations* (Edinburgh, 1960), 40.1–10 (iv.48)).
[54] Ps.S, 101.26–102.5. See Chapter 5.
[55] Geo.Pis., *Bellum Avaricum*, ed. and trans. Pertusi, *Giorgio di Pisidia*, 176–200, at lines 67–112; Theodorus Syncellus, *Homily* I, ed. L. Sternbach, *Analecta Avarica*, Rozprawy Akademii Umiejętności, Wydział Filologiczny, ser.2, 15 (Cracow, 1900), 298–320, at 301.13–30—cited henceforth as Theod. Sync., *Hom.* I.

It was the next series of damaging blows struck by the Persians which convinced them that there was nothing to lose and much to gain by going to war. What could Heraclius do in the Balkans if a Persian army was able to advance within sight of his capital in 615, if Asia Minor could be transected by two raiding armies in 617, if Alexandria could be captured and Egypt opened up to occupation in 619? It was only a matter of time before the Persians would be able to dismember what remained of the empire in the east. It was when the risks of war were reduced to an absolute minimum that a reluctance rooted in grim memories of the damage suffered at the hands of Roman armies in the 590s and in awareness of Avar isolation amid potentially hostile great powers (Merovingian to the west, Roman to the south, and, most dangerous of all, Turkish to the east) was finally overcome.

6.3 The Avar Surprise

The immediate crisis was probably over within a few weeks of Heraclius' return to Constantinople. The principal task facing Heraclius was to turn a brief armistice into a longer-lasting peace and thus to close down the second front which had opened up. There is no information about the substantive discussions or the chief issues raised. But somehow—probably with a mixture of inducements and threats backed by armed force—Heraclius coaxed the Avars into negotiating and managed eventually to agree a deal. There were three rounds of negotiations, all probably closely supervised by Heraclius. The detailed provisions of a new Roman-Avar treaty were probably hammered out by the second embassy, which was led by the senior law officer, the Quaestor Cosmas. The final round, in which the first Roman ambassador, the Patrician Athanasius, took part as well as Cosmas, probably finalized the terms of the treaty and made the arrangements for a summit meeting at which the two rulers would sign it.[56]

The summit was scheduled for early June and would take place just outside the Long Wall guarding the land approach to Constantinople, at Heraclea (ancient Perinthus, renamed in honour of Diocletian, who was styled Herculius). Apart from the aptness of its name, Heraclea had, in its hippodrome (probably attached to the Tetrarchic palace), a convenient and appropriately grand setting for the summit meeting.[57]

---

[56] Nic., c.10.1-11 (L, c.10.1-7, 11-12); Theod. Sync., *Hom.* I, 301.30-4 and *Homily* II, 593-4, ed. C. Loparev, 'Staroe svidetelstvo o polozhenii rizy Bogorodnitsy vo Vlakherniakh . . .', *VV* 2 (1895), 581-628, at 592-612, trans. Averil Cameron, 'The Virgin's Robe: An Episode in the History of Early Seventh-Century Constantinople', *Byz.* 49 (1979), 42-56, repr. in Cameron, *Continuity and Change in Sixth-Century Byzantium* (London, 1981), no.XVII, at 593-4 (trans. 49); Theoph., 301.26-8 (misplaced).

[57] A. Külzer, *Ostthrakien (Eurōpē)*, TIB 12 (Vienna, 2008), 405-6.

The preparations for the meeting and the unexpected events which ensued are described from three points of view in three extant sources. The *Chronicon Paschale*, as usual, represents the court view, which reached the anonymous author in the form of official communiqués. Rather more of the action is reported, at one point with a critical tinge, by Nicephorus, who, here as elsewhere, probably draws on the lost second continuation of the chronicle of John of Antioch (which also provided material for Theophanes' short misdated notice). Finally, in a homily probably written after the end of the war, Theodore Syncellus, a senior member of the capital's clergy, focused on the fate of a precious relic, a fragment of the Virgin's Robe which was conserved in a reliquary in a large circular or octagonal shrine standing next to the church of the Mother of God at Blachernae. The three main descriptions, though succinct, are graphic.[58]

A large crowd of interested onlookers left Constantinople when they heard that the signing ceremony at Heraclea was to include racing in the hippodrome. The official party accompanying the emperor comprised representatives of several strata of metropolitan society—office holders, men of property, and clergy, together with artisans and members of the circus factions. The equipment needed for chariot racing had been sent ahead to Heraclea. Court dress was made ready, as it was to be worn during the ceremony. Heraclius went to Selymbria and awaited the khagan's arrival. He came three days later to Heraclea with a large entourage. On the morning of Sunday 5 June, Heraclius and his party came through the Long Wall and began making their way to Heraclea.[59]

Then Heraclius realized that something was wrong. A large Avar ambush was concealed in the wooded hills just outside the Long Wall. A trap was about to be sprung. The concealed force was to prevent the emperor and his party retreating behind the Long Wall, while the khagan and the troops in his entourage advanced against him from Heraclea. Heraclius hastily changed into ordinary clothes, hid the crown under his arm, and raced back to the city. Meanwhile the khagan gave an evidently prearranged signal with his whip and the troops with him rushed the Long Wall, broke through, and raided the whole area up to the land walls in the course of the day. A large number of prisoners and animals of all sorts were seized, together with the racing equipment, the court dress, and the emperor's own robes.[60]

---

[58] Sources: Howard-Johnston, *Witnesses*, 50 (*Chron.Pasch.*), 146–8 (Theodore Syncellus), 248–50 (second continuation of John of Antioch); A. Wenger, *L'Assomption de la T. S. Vierge dans la tradition byzantine du VIe au Xe siècle: Études et documents* (Paris, 1955), 114–24 (Theodore Syncellus). Date: *Chron.Pasch.*, 712.12–13 (Sunday 5 June 623); Isidorus iunior, *Chronica*, 490.3–5 (fourteenth regnal year of Heraclius (October 623–October 624), fortieth of Frankish King Chlothar's (623–4)). Theoph., 301.25–302.4 transfers it arbitrarily to an otherwise blank year entry for 619. Cf. Gerland, 'Die persische Feldzüge', 333–7, Pohl, *Avars*, 290–2, and Whitby and Whitby, *Chronicon Paschale*, n.451 and appendix 4. *Contra* N. H. Baynes, 'The Date of the Avar Surprise', *BZ* 21 (1912), 110–28.

[59] *Chron.Pasch.*, 712.12–21; Nic., c.10.11–18 (L, c.10.7–11, 12–16).

[60] *Chron.Pasch.*, 712.21–713.8; Nic., c.10.18–37 (L, c.10.16–31); Theoph., 301.31–302.3.

The Avars advanced swiftly along the main road, the easternmost section of the Via Egnatia, to the Hebdomon and the Golden Gate. From there they set about ravaging the whole built-up penumbra of the city, along the length of the land walls to Blachernae (Figure 1), then up to the head of the Golden Horn, where a bridge over the river Barbyssus gave them access to Sycae (modern Galata) and the Bosporus shore.[61] There was very little that the Roman authorities could do to prevent them taking rich pickings from suburban properties, above all from well-endowed extramural churches. There was just time to send a squad to the most venerated of the churches at Blachernae, that dedicated to the Mother of God, who had become the city's chief supernatural patron.[62] Their orders were to strip out all the gold and silver fittings and revetment from the church and the adjacent shrine. This they did in great haste, using picks, axes, and other crude instruments, and then, on their own initiative, hacked out, from its gold and silver casing, the marble reliquary which held, in an inner container, a precious piece of the woollen clothing once worn by the Mother of God. They took the small inner casket into the city and handed it over to the patriarch, but not before taking a look inside and snipping off part of the purple silk wrapping which they mistook for the relic itself.[63]

Theodore Syncellus, who describes this incident without mentioning the punishment, human or divine, which should have befallen these presumptuous soldiers, focuses on the mood in the city when the Avars were swarming like locusts outside. He may well have exaggerated the anxiety of the citizens and the urgency of their prayers for rhetorical effect, but the crisis was real enough. He presents the emperor as taking the lead. After first returning to the palace, he went to the church of the Mother of God, known as Jerusalem, which was inside the Golden Gate. There, he was joined by the patriarch in a vigil of prayer which lasted day and night for the duration of the crisis. Similar vigils were held throughout the city in the Mother of God's other churches, attended, says Theodore, by the whole population, men, women, and children who made tearful pleas for help. Outside, the Avars were causing extensive damage, which included, as anticipated by the authorities, robbing churches of their valuables. Two are singled out, the church of St Cosmas and St Damian on the Golden Horn close to Blachernae and that of the Archangel at Promotus on the Bosporus. Both lost

---

[61] *Chron.Pasch.*, 713.5–10; Nic., c.10.30–4 (L, c.10.24–7); Theod.Sync., *Hom.* II, 594 (trans. Cameron, 'Virgin's Robe', 49). Golden Gate: C. Mango, 'The Triumphal Way of Constantinople and the Golden Gate', *DOP* 54 (2000), 173–88, at 179–86. Hebdomon: A. van Millingen, *Byzantine Constantinople: The Walls of the City and Adjoining Historical Sites* (London, 1899), 316–41. Barbyssos bridge: C. Mango, 'The Fourteenth Region of Constantinople', in O. Feld and U. Peschlow, eds., *Studien zur spätantiken und byzantinischen Kunst, Friedrich Wilhelm Deichmann gewidmet* (Mainz, 1986), 1–5, at 2 (map) and 4.

[62] C. Mango, 'The Origins of the Blachernae Shrine at Constantinople', in *Acta XIII Congressus Internationalis Archaeologiae Christianae* (Vatican and Split, 1998), II, 61–76, at 62–5, 67–70.

[63] Theod.Sync., *Hom.* II, 595–8 (trans. Cameron, 'Virgin's Robe', 50–1).

their *ciboria* and other portable treasures, and, in the case of the latter, the whole altar.[64]

It is possible that the attack lasted little more than a day and a night, since Theodore Syncellus may give a misleading impression of the length of the vigils held in the city.[65] The khagan, who did not himself venture inside the Long Wall (where, if things had gone wrong, he might have been trapped in turn), could only count on a short period of grace before the Roman troops in and near the capital organized a counterattack (and there were probably other forces to be reckoned with stationed farther afield in Thrace, if, as is possible, troops had been transferred from Asia Minor the previous winter). In any case, the crisis was soon over. Avar troops withdrew, rejoined the khagan, and marched north with their animate and inanimate booty to their territory beyond the Danube without encountering any opposition.[66] They may have failed in their attempted *coup de main* against Heraclius—and coup it was, flouting as it did all the norms of diplomacy—but they had compensation in the form of a large haul of booty and prisoners. A terrible shock had been given to the Roman governing elite. Valuable suburban properties had been ransacked. Those who had gone out in the official imperial party were all probably captured. Much imperial paraphernalia had been plundered. But there was the consolation that the emperor had escaped and that some precious objects had been saved—the crown which the emperor himself had carried back and that cherished relic which established a direct physical link with the city's leading heavenly champion and which was kept safe in the treasury of St Sophia for the duration of the war. The episode was subsequently commemorated annually by a special service of thanksgiving on 5 June, in the course of which the clergy processed from St Sophia to the Golden Gate and on to the Hebdomon.[67]

Very little is reported in the extant sources of what was going on in the east in 623. Roman authors kept their eyes fixed on the dramatic events involving the emperor and the capital. Of the non-Roman sources, only the West Syrian historical tradition which originated with Theophilus of Edessa in the middle of the eighth century has anything to say. A notice, best preserved in the *Chronicle to 1234*, is all too brief: 'Shahrbaraz captured Ancyra in Galatia and also many

---

[64] Theod.Sync., *Hom.* II, 594–5 (trans. Cameron, 'Virgin's Robe', 49–50); *Chron.Pasch.*, 713.9–13. SS Cosmas and Damian: R. Janin, *La Géographie ecclésiastique de l'empire byzantin*, I *Le Siège de Constantinople et le patriarcat œcuménique*, 3 *Les Églises et les monastères* (Paris, 1969), 286–9. Archangel of Promotus, identifiable as St Michael of Anaplous, allegedly founded by Constantine I, on Cape Akıntıburnu between Arnavutköy and Bebek: Janin, *Géographie ecclésiastique*, 338–40, 445.

[65] Both the *Chronicon Paschale* and Nicephorus give the clear impression that the attack was swiftly over. See Theod. Sync., *Hom.* II, 594 (trans. Cameron, 'Virgin's Robe', 49–50) for the opposite impression.

[66] *Chron.Pasch.*, 713.2–3, 13–14; Theod.Sync., *Hom.* I, 301.34–7; Nic., c.10.37–41 (L, c.10.31–4), who gives an absurdly inflated figure of 270,000 men and women taken off into captivity. Theoph., 302.3–4 adds that the Avars devastated many villages of Thrace during their return march.

[67] Baynes, 'Avar Surprise', 122–5; J. Mateos, *Le Typicon de la Grande Église*, I (Rome, 1962), 306–7.

islands in the sea and carried out much killing.'[68] So, according to this source, Shahrbaraz remained in command of the Persian forces massed against Asia Minor, despite his relative lack of success in 622, and there was a marked escalation in the fighting, a new naval front being opened up. The sea and land offensives were, one may presume, coordinated. Striking successes were achieved. Besides those attributed to Shahrbaraz, Slav sea raiders were credited with attacks on Crete and other islands.[69] The islands of the Aegean which now formed an important component of the rump Roman state were being subjected to raids from the east as well as the north. The next logical step for the Persians would be to occupy them permanently, beginning with Rhodes (taken apparently late in 623).[70] At the same time Persian land forces pushed deep into Asia Minor and seized Ancyra, the most important city of the north-west quadrant of the plateau.[71] Although they did not garrison and hold it through the following winter, they had opened the way for a new advance over the mountains of the north-west into the Marmara coastlands where Heraclius had trained his troops in 622. A grand offensive by land and sea was gathering way against a steadily weakening Roman Empire.

The continuing absence of Heraclius (and probably of a considerable number of troops transferred to Thrace to put some military sinew into his diplomacy) cannot but have undermined Roman defences in the east. The news of the Avars' repudiation of peace, of Heraclius' narrow escape, and of the attack on Constantinople must have struck a second serious blow at morale. The Avars thus undoubtedly made a significant indirect contribution to Persian success in 623. It may well have been a contribution specifically requested by the Persians. For the khagan's behaviour is hard to explain without the intervention of an extraneous factor. His treacherous abuse of the conventions of diplomacy was likely to damage Avar interests in the long run, whether or not he succeeded in seizing Heraclius. For it could not but engender deep suspicion on the Roman side which would make it difficult to conduct diplomacy in future. Bitterness and rancour, on the part either of Heraclius or of those left in charge of Roman affairs (had the coup succeeded), would also have injected a new non-rational, souring element into negotiations, if any were ever again to be held between the two sides.

It is hard to envisage the khagan disregarding diplomatic convention so flagrantly unless he had been pressed to do so by a third party and that third party had both provided him with moral justification and convinced him that it was

---

[68] *Chron.1234*, 230.7-9 (trans. Hoyland, 66).   [69] *Chron.724*, 147.1-4 (trans. Palmer, 18).
[70] Persian conquest of Rhodes: reported alongside Heraclius' invasion of Persian territory, in the year entry following 622-3, i.e. October 623-September 624, in *Chron.724*, 147.5-7 (trans. Palmer, 18), but with the an error in the Seleucid date (934 instead of 935); placed 'at the end of the year', in this case probably the calendar year in which Ancyra was captured (i.e. after the end of Seleucid year 934 on 30 September 623), by Agapius, 451.7 (trans. Hoyland, 66).
[71] Mitchell, *Anatolia*, II, 74, 84-95, 120.

bound to work to his advantage. The third party to hand, the Sasanian Empire, stood to benefit militarily in the months immediately following the incident, when the Romans would have to maintain, if not reinforce, their forces in Thrace. The Persians could also deploy persuasive arguments in support of a scheme to seize Heraclius under the cover of negotiations. For there was no question of his being recognized by them as a head of state. Khusro had never acknowledged the legitimacy of his regime and had refused to engage in any sort of diplomatic dialogue, save for a fleeting moment of hesitation in 615–16. He might well have characterized his Roman antagonist as a mere brigand leader, in the way he was supposed to have done in a spurious letter given much publicity in the weeks before Heraclius set off on campaign in 624.[72] The Persians then had arguments which could overcome the moral scruples of the khagan and were also in a position to assure him that the final destruction of the Roman Empire was imminent and would be hastened if the Avars were to cooperate actively with the Persians.

The Avar surprise attack of 5 June 623 thus provides the first positive—though circumstantial—evidence of collusion between the two enemies of the Romans. Their active cooperation was, of course, to become very plain three years later, when they combined to attack the metropolitan area from east and west.[73] On both occasions, the Persians, the more powerful of the two, may be presumed to have taken the lead, first instigating the attempt on Heraclius and then planning the joint offensive of 626. Enhanced confidence on the part of the Avars, assured of future assistance from Persian forces, would also help explain their deliberate despoiling and desecration of churches in the environs of Constantinople during the attack on the city in 623—which was in marked contrast to the restraint they had shown a year earlier before Thessalonica, when they did not threaten to damage the extramural churches until a late stage in the siege. There was more than a tinge of religious antagonism to the great power conflict. The Avars may have been urged to demonstrate once again the powerlessness of the Christian God to protect his own or may simply have ceased to be concerned by likely Roman reactions.[74]

The future looked grimmer than ever for the Romans in the middle of June, when the Avars were marching north through Thrace and Persian offensives were gathering way in the east by land and sea. The peace negotiated by Phocas with the Avars, which had become increasingly precarious in recent years, had broken down definitively. Heraclius' attempt to renew it had ended in conspicuous and nearly disastrous failure. The Romans were now caught between two powerful adversaries without the resources to fight on two fronts at once. Defeat was inevitable unless something could be done to limit the military demands of the secondary northern front which had just opened up. Heraclius had no choice but

---

[72] Ps.S., 123, 15–33, with *Hist.Com.*, n.38.   [73] See Chapter 8.3.
[74] But see Pohl, *Avars*, 293–4, who highlights the khagan's need to assert himself vis-à-vis his Slav clients by achieving a striking success.

to reopen negotiations with the Avars. Desperate efforts must be made to close down the northern front, even if only for a short time. The flouting of diplomatic norms must be ignored and some sort of a deal agreed, whatever the cost.

Eventually a new agreement was reached, on terms as humiliating in their way as those offered to the Persians by the Senate in 615. Heraclius, who assuredly stayed put in Constantinople after his narrow escape, must have been involved at every stage of the negotiations, his sanction being needed for the renewal of contact and for the terms finally agreed. These involved annual payments of 200,000 solidi, a sum only extracted once before from the Romans, by Attila at the acme of his power, and the handing-over of three highly placed hostages—Heraclius' illegitimate son John Atalarich, his nephew Stephen, and another John, the illegitimate son of the Patrician Bonus.[75] Some of the lightweight (20- carat) solidi specially minted for the tribute (eight *officinae* were put to work) percolated into the lands surrounding the khaganate. They are the last Roman coins to be found in quantity in the north—from Russia and eastern Europe to south Germany, the Rhineland, Frisia, and England. One formed the centrepiece of the garnet filigree Wilton Cross (made probably between 635 and 638) which was found in Norfolk not far from Sutton Hoo.[76]

The Avars thus gained a substantial contribution to the cost of mounting a future attack in massive force from their intended victims, and a period of guaranteed peace in which to mobilize their forces. For the function of the hostages whom they had obtained was to prevent the Romans taking any action to interfere with their preparations and to leave the decision on the timing of the future war entirely to them.

All that the Romans gained in return was a brief interlude of peace in Europe, of indefinite length, in which their forces could be concentrated in the east and improvements made to the fixed defences of the capital and other likely Avar targets. From the moment the deal was struck, at the latest in the course of winter 623-4, Heraclius had to make the most of the breathing space which he had gained. He had to inflict as much damage as he could on the Persians and to cause as much disruption as possible to their own offensive preparations. But more, much more was needed. He would have to make contact with the Turks, who were able to draw on the resources of a transcontinental empire and who were long-standing adversaries of the Avars. If only they could be drawn into the war on the Roman side, there might be a genuine hope of surviving the coming crisis, when Persians and Avars would be launching simultaneous offensives against what remained of the Roman Empire.

---

[75] Nic., c.13.1-9 (terms). Theod.Sync., *Hom.* I, 301.37-302.8, reports, doubtless with rhetorical exaggeration, that the khagan had originally demanded half the city's wealth and subsequently received a great deal.

[76] M. M. Archibald, 'The Wilton Cross Coin Pendant: Numismatic Aspects and Implications', in A. Reynolds and L. Webster, eds., *Early Medieval Art and Archaeology in the Northern World* (Leiden, 2013), 51-71.

7
Heraclius' First Counteroffensive

The price paid for peace, ephemeral as it turned out to be, was very high, symbolically as well as monetarily. The dispatch of such high-ranking hostages to a foreign court was an extraordinary act of political obeisance. It did, however, free Heraclius to immerse himself in forward planning. That winter, he directed the staff work which devised the strategy for the next two campaigning seasons, when Roman forces were to be concentrated against the eastern adversary.

First, there was a round of research into military science involving extensive reading of classical tactical manuals. The accumulated experience of the Graeco-Roman world was being scoured for ideas on future strategy and tactics. This was perhaps the key phase in the war, when Heraclius and his staff consciously strove to detach themselves from the immediate concerns of the present and, taking inherited military knowledge in all its variety as their starting point, conceived new types and combinations of action which might disconcert and disorder the enemy. Subsequent events make it clear that they succeeded in breaking free of conventional wisdom and acquired the intellectual capability to out-think the Persians (and, indeed, most of their Greek and Roman predecessors).

Then the detailed planning began, in which all manner of formations and manoeuvres were devised. Much paperwork was generated, including, it appears, diagrammatic representations of tactics. To judge by its outcome in the field, this prolonged round of planning resulted in six key decisions: (i) to move onto the offensive, which would entail cutting loose from Roman-controlled territory and thereby severing communications with the governing centre of what remained of the empire; (ii) to keep the supreme command in the field in Heraclius' hands, from which it followed that he must temporarily set aside his governmental functions; (iii) to make maximum use of deception to weaken the enemy at intended points of attack; (iv) to use black propaganda to increase the commitment of the field army and such auxiliaries as it might gather on campaign; (v) to stretch the conventional campaigning season at either end and thereby to test the endurance and spirit of the enemy to the limit; and (vi) to bring the Turks into the war on the Roman side.

George of Pisidia devotes a fair amount of space to this process of planning, naturally giving all the credit to Heraclius. But what he stresses above all is where it took place—not, as one might have expected, in the comfort of Constantinople but in its European suburbs (behind the protective screen of the Long Wall). His explanation is not the obvious one—that Heraclius went to join his staff in their winter quarters with the army rather than installing them in the palace and thereby perhaps softening their temperament—but that he was anxious to avoid distraction from the affairs of the city and to conceal his plans from the spies who might lurk concealed in the city crowd. George then goes on to admit that security could not be guaranteed even outside the city, that there was loose talk and information was spread abroad, but that Heraclius did not take severe action against offenders. The suspicion arises that the whole planning exercise was itself part of a deception project: the presence of the emperor with a substantial force in Europe was calculated to mislead the Persians into thinking that Heraclius was planning a campaign of revenge against the Avars or, once they got wind of the agreement which he had made with them, that he intended to take advantage of it to impose Roman authority on the Slavs settling in the Balkans; at the same time there was an ostensible tightening of security around his headquarters, which would have had the incidental effect of enhancing the value of such information as was allowed to leak out (which, it may be conjectured, indicated that Roman eyes were set on the Balkans).[1]

Heraclius returned to Constantinople before the end of winter. It was there that he announced that he had received an extraordinarily offensive diplomatic note from the Persian king. The text is reproduced, apparently in full, in the *History of Khosrov* (some phrases which have dropped out of the seventeenth century manuscript can be restored with the help of Thomas Artsruni's version). Khusro styles himself 'Lord and King of all the earth'. He dismisses Heraclius disdainfully as his 'senseless and insignificant servant' with empty pretensions to independent political power. He is accused of appropriating treasure which belonged properly to Khusro and of collecting together a troublesome 'army of brigands'. Then he turns his attention to the Christian God, whom he dismisses as an impotent divinity. No help from him can be expected by the Romans. There follows a roll call of Roman possessions which God failed to save—Caesarea, Antioch, Tarsus, Amasya (a mistake for Emesa), Jerusalem, Alexandria, and, finally, the Thebaid (in Upper Egypt). What prospect was there, then, that Constantinople alone might not be erased by the conqueror of the sea and the dry land? Nonetheless, he is ready to forgive Heraclius all his trespasses and makes an offer, modelled on that of Sennacherib in Isaiah 36.16–17: 'Arise, take your wife and children and come here. I shall give you estates, vineyards and olive-trees whereby you may make a living. And we shall look upon you with friendship.' He ends with an anti-Christian flourish:

that Christ who was not able to save himself from the Jews—but they killed him by hanging him on a cross—how can the same save you from my hands? For if

---

[1] Geo.Pis., *Heraclias*, ed. and trans. Pertusi, *Giorgio di Pisidia*, 240–61, at ii.98–143.

you descend into the depths of the sea, I shall stretch out my hand and seize you. And then you will see me in a manner you will not desire.

With its clear reminiscence of Psalms 138.7–10, this last passage had blasphemous undertones for a Christian reader, Khusro apparently likening his earthly reach to that of the God of the Old Testament.[2]

The diplomatic note cannot have been genuine. There was no reason for the Persians, poised as they were to overrun Asia Minor after the successful invasion of 623, to abandon their long-standing refusal to engage in any sort of diplomatic dialogue with what they regarded as the illegitimate regime of Heraclius. The absence of references to Zoroastrian belief (apart from a mention of Ahuramazda in Khusro's titulature) and the citations of Scripture betray a Christian hand at work. Similarly, the Persian successes which are picked out are those likely to have been etched most deeply on the Roman consciousness: the list features episodes of minor significance from the Persian perspective but menacing in their implications for the Romans (the temporary seizure of Caesarea of Cappadocia, the capture of Emesa, the first city (after Zenobia) to fall beyond the Euphrates, and, the most recent success, the occupation of the Thebaid), while nothing is said about strategically more important gains such as the recovery of western Iberia and Persarmenia, the conquest of Roman Armenia, Osrhoene, and Mesopotamia, or the capture of Damascus, which sealed the fate of Palestine. Finally, so strident is its anti-Christian tone, so offensive its attitude to emperor and empire, that it was calculated to outrage Christian opinion, to stiffen rather than soften the resolve of the beleaguered Romans. There was also a real danger of it souring relations between Khusro's government and the powerful Christian communities of Mesopotamia and the occupied territories, were news of its content to leak out.

The Persian diplomatic note is undoubtedly spurious. Who then concocted it? Not the author of the *History of Khosrov*, for he was an admirably modest historian who sought simply to preserve for posterity material which he judged to be of historical value with a minimum of clearly demarcated editorial commentary. The omission of any Persian gains in Transcaucasia also argues strongly against his involvement. The answer surely is that the note was composed by those whose interests it served, and they are immediately identifiable as the Roman authorities. The document is surely black propaganda which was devised during Heraclius' planning sessions with his staff and issued after his return to Constantinople. It cannot be proved beyond all doubt that it was a Roman fabrication, but the proposition receives strong corroboration from the strenuous efforts made by Heraclius to broadcast its contents to his subjects. His own

---

[2] Ps.S., 123.15–33; TA, 91.23–92.17.

behaviour, both in Constantinople and on his way to join the army in Asia Minor, was carefully choreographed as a response to this blast of blasphemy and anti-Roman abuse. The diplomatic note was thus given yet greater publicity and simultaneously used to heighten Roman religious and patriotic feeling. If deception was a vital *offensive* weapon of intellectual warfare designed to weaken the enemy, disinformation of a different sort, blackening the enemy, was its *defensive* counterpart, intended to strengthen Roman resistance at a dark time by raising and solidifying morale at all levels, both in governing circles and in society at large, among both civilians and soldiers.

Heraclius first ordered the note to be read 'to the patriarch and the magnates'. One may perhaps envisage its declamation to a large assembly in the palace comprising both the upper echelons of the Constantinopolitan clergy headed by the patriarch and the full court arrayed in hierarchical order. After this first oral publication to the controllers of the apparatus of government, lay and clerical, the note was carried—in perhaps the grandest and gravest rogation ceremony of all time—by the assembled dignitaries to the great church nearby (Figure 18). There it was laid before the altar, while clergy and court 'fell on their faces to the ground before the Lord and wept bitterly, so that he might see the insults which his enemies had inflicted upon him.' Fabrication though it was, those pleading for God to intervene in earthly affairs surely believed that it did represent the real attitudes and intentions of the Persians and that it could therefore be shown to the all-knowing Almighty.[3]

7.1 Heraclius' Opening Moves

Heraclius demonstrated by his actions that he spurned the comfortable retirement offered to him and his family. He left Constantinople on 25 March 624, the feast of the Annunciation, *with his whole family*, the children of his first marriage (Heraclius Constantine and Epiphania Eudocia) and his new wife, Martina. A lapidary notice in the *Chronicon Paschale* probably reproduces the court circular subsequently issued about this first ceremonial stage in his march to war, which lasted three weeks or so. With its aid, it becomes possible to make sense of what has been garbled both in the *History of Khosrov* and in Theophanes' chronicle. The anonymous Armenian author has conflated Heraclius' departure in 624 with that in 622, has him celebrate Easter in Constantinople rather than later in Bithynia, and has plumped for the intervening year, 623, while all of Heraclius' campaigns from 624 have been pulled back a year by Theophanes, who thus manages to fill the 623 year entry after emptying it of the Avar surprise.

---

[3] Ps.S., 124.1–5.

Theophanes also dates Heraclius' departure from Constantinople to 15 March, ten days too early.[4]

The imperial family sailed across the Bosporus to Chalcedon and journeyed overland to Nicomedia. They do not seem to have lodged in the city but to have stayed nearby—perhaps under canvas to signal the whole family's participation in the coming campaign. There they celebrated Easter, which fell on 15 April that year, after which the two children were sent back to Constantinople, Heraclius Constantine to act as the nominal head of the government, as he had in 622. Martina accompanied Heraclius on the second, more military stage of his march to war. They travelled south-east to Cappadocia to join the field army at Caesarea. The leisurely pace adopted so far—Heraclius must have spent well over a month in transit—was perhaps dictated as much by the time it took to transfer troops back from Europe and to mobilize the forces stationed in Asia Minor as by the need to present his journey as a deliberate, solemn, stately progress.[5]

At Caesarea he immediately signalled that he was committing himself wholeheartedly to the war by pitching his tent in the middle of the army's camp. He convened a meeting of all the troops, had the Persian note read out, and declared that his journey to join them for the coming campaign was his reply to Khusro's offer. The official version of these events, which has percolated through to us via the text of the *History of Khosrov*, reports that this broadcasting of the note to the whole army had the desired effect. Shock at the contents was combined with an enthusiastic welcome for the emperor who had come to lead them into battle. Several military assemblies of this sort would be held in the course of the following two years' campaigning. Their prime function was to raise or sustain the morale of the troops, however grim the circumstances, morale being yet more important that training or numbers in determining the final outcome. On this occasion, the troops are said to have wished him victory and said 'Wherever you may go, we are with you to stand and die. May all your enemies become dust beneath your feet, as the Lord our God obliterates them from the face of the earth and removes the insults paid him by men.'[6]

Before we start tracking Heraclius as he marched rapidly across Transcaucasia towards the core territories of the Sasanian Empire, we need to cast a glance at the instrument of war which he had fashioned, to gauge the strength and composition of the field army under his command, and also to scan the horizon for any complementary diplomatic initiative which he might have taken. It is also vital to take account of Persian military dispositions and plans on the eve of the campaigning season. They were surely proposing to follow up the successes achieved by their invasion of Asia Minor and their naval offensive in 623.

---

[4] *Chron.Pasch.*, 713.19–714.8; ps.S., 124.6–13, with *Hist.Com.*, n.38; Theoph., 306.19–21, with Howard-Johnston, *Witnesses*, 281–2.

[5] Journey to Caesarea: ps.S., 124.13–15.   [6] Ps.S., 124.15–22.

The single most important source of information is a lost work which I have called the Official History of Heraclius' Persian campaigns. It was commissioned by Heraclius from George of Pisidia and was based largely on Heraclius' dispatches from the field. George added short passages in verse to highlight Heraclius' personal contribution to ultimate victory. Although it has not survived, it was used extensively by Theophanes for his account of both of Heraclius' counteroffensive campaigns.[7] It is, alas, uninformative about the army which he led to war. Much can be learned about Heraclius or, at any rate, about the image which he wished to project from what George himself says about the emperor. But the dispatches, which were originally intended to keep up the spirits of those who received them at home, are not concerned to delineate the main features of the field army nor to describe the humdrum processes involved in campaigning (the organization of camps, the order of march, the commissariat, the equipment carried, the nature of the baggage train). Good news was needed. Victories, great hauls of itemized booty, raiding marches across enemy territory, manoeuvres which outwitted the enemy—such was the stuff of the imperial dispatches, which might occasionally give incidental information about the size of enemy forces encountered. So there is much that we will never know about the instrument of war which Heraclius directed with devastating effect against his hitherto victorious adversary.

Still, some educated guesses can be made. First, about the army's size. Its strength lay first and foremost in its morale and motivation (carefully nurtured by the emperor and imperial propaganda) and, second, in the high degree of stamina and skill induced by intensive training, which gave it an unusual degree of tactical flexibility and strategic mobility. Manoeuvrability was the key to its success, and this precluded very large numbers. There was no question of Heraclius setting off from Caesarea with the 120,000 men which he is given in the *History of Khosrov*.[8] It is very rare indeed to find armies approaching 100,000 in strength before the early modern period in western Eurasia, and a huge resource base was needed to produce them—the east Roman Empire at the height of its economic prosperity in 503–4, the Caliphate in its early Abbasid heyday (782), the whole of fractious western Europe at the time of the First Crusade. Forces of this order of magnitude could be deployed against Heraclius by the Persians, able as they were to draw on the combined resources of the two empires (credible figures are given for two individual armies by the Official History, 40,000 with Khusro in 624 and 30,000 commanded by Shahen in 625), as also by the Avars, who fielded a polyglot army of some 80,000 men drawn from a wide range of nomad and sedentary subjects for their grand assault on Constantinople in 626. But Heraclius had to make do

---

[7] See Appendix 3.   [8] Ps.S., 124.22–3.

with a far smaller force, one large enough to confront Persian armies of 30,000 or so in open battle but small enough to be guaranteed to outmarch and outmanoeuvre them (and to avoid serious commissariat problems on campaign). I would put its strength at between 15,000 and 20,000 men, which is the figure given by the *Strategicon* of Maurice for a large army.[9]

Any suggestions about the composition of Heraclius' army must be even more conjectural. For no information at all can be extracted from the Official History about the balance of infantry to cavalry. Heraclius' army was, I am sure, a mixed army, even though infantry are only specifically mentioned on one occasion, the siege of Tiflis in 627.[10] For how else could the entrenchments of camps be dug? How else could siege engines be constructed, deployed, and operated? How else could the army's supply train be supervised or the perimeter of camps be secured or safe passage be guaranteed through defiles and over passes? On the battlefield too, a cavalry force, however large or well trained, needed the infantry's tenacious grip of terrain and the solidity of an infantry line as an ultimate human redoubt. Compelled to guess, I would put the ratio of infantry to cavalry at 2:1, since that is the ratio which seems to be envisaged in a section tacked onto the *Strategicon* about joint infantry-cavalry operations and it reappears in later Byzantine military manuals.[11]

As for the army's operation in the field, we can only assume that well-tried Roman military traditions were kept up. It is likely that marching camps continued to be constructed, that iron rations for a month or so were carried for emergencies, and that there were specialized corps to deal with the wounded, to look after baggage animals and cavalry remounts, to site and lay out camps, etc. But there is one innovation of which we can be sure, even though there is no direct evidence for it: the manoeuvrability which Heraclius sought could only be achieved if the army jettisoned its traditional wagon train and, transferring its baggage to pack animals, cut loose from smooth or reasonably smooth surfaced roads.

Military action was, of course, not the only means of attack available to Heraclius. Propaganda probably continued to be directed at the Christian subjects of the Persians, on the lines developed since the fall of Jerusalem in 614. After nearly ten years in which it seemed to have had little effect on the behaviour of former Roman provincials in the occupied territories of the Near East, it was now probably targeted mainly at Transcaucasia. It was perhaps more realistic to hope that outraged Christian sensibilities might lead to collective action on the part of the traditionally refractory peoples of the region than of the citizens of the ordered, highly urbanized provinces of the south. While there might be little chance of prompting armed risings of whole peoples, given the overwhelming military power of the expanded Sasanian Empire and the rivalries endemic within

---

[9] *Strategicon*, iii.8.32-6, 10.25-8.   [10] MD, 139.3-4 (trans. Dowsett, 85).
[11] *Strategicon*, xii.8.33-4 and 9.4-6 (24,000 infantry treated as normal), 13.3-7 (12,000 or more regarded as a large cavalry force).

each indigenous people, it was not unreasonable to hope that individuals, activated by their consciences, would volunteer in considerable numbers to join the Roman expeditionary force and might in aggregate add appreciably to its strength.

A third weapon, diplomacy, was as valuable as direct military action. An ally with military resources at least commensurate with either of the imperial powers in the era of equilibrium before the Roman Middle East was overrun was needed to redress the military balance. Without military assistance on a formidable scale (or a general rising in the occupied territories), there was no hope of reversing the Persian gains of the previous two decades, save by a long war of attrition for which the resources were not available. Heraclius and his elite force might scamper about and bewilder the Persian forces deployed against them for a while, but in the end they would either be trapped and annihilated or would lose their effective striking power through weariness and gradual attrition. Hence Heraclius did not neglect diplomacy when he set off to war. His eyes were set on the third great power of western Eurasia, the nomadic confederation of the Turks who controlled the steppes from the inner Asian frontiers of China to the Black Sea. They had the military resources which could bring about a rapid reversal in the fortunes of war, if only they could be induced to breach Sasanian frontier defences and intervene in force on the Roman side.

Heraclius took the first, formal step towards forming an alliance with the Turks probably early in 624, before he left Constantinople (rather than at the end of the year, when he took up winter quarters in Caucasian Albania). The journey being long and hazardous, it was better for the ambassador whom he dispatched (we only know his Christian name, Andrew) to set off in spring and sail to a Turkish-held port on the Black Sea and then continue his journey overland under Turkish protection than to make a difficult winter crossing of the Caucasus and hope to make contact with the Turkish authorities in the steppes beyond. Andrew brought with him a promise of 'innumerable and countless treasures' if the Turks were to intervene. This message, backed by the alluring prospect of pillaging the lands of the Persian king, was to find a ready hearing when Andrew reached the *yabghu khagan*, deputy to the King of the North (almost certainly Tong, western khagan). On his return with representatives of the khagan, an agreement was sealed between the two powers, and the Turks undertook to attack across the Caucasus. The date given in the *History to 682*, Khusro's thirty-sixth regnal year, which began in June 625, was probably that of the crucial second stage in negotiations back in the west. Given the distances to be covered by the embassies (and the need for the Turks to report back what had been agreed), it would not be surprising if two years passed between the initial dispatch of Andrew and the Turkish attack (securely dated to 626).[12]

---

[12] MD, 141.5–142.7 (trans. Dowsett, 87).

So much, then, for the actions, military and diplomatic, initiated by Heraclius in 624. They were each crucial to the success of his enterprise. Without an effective fighting force under his command, he could not expect to be able to direct Turkish actions so as to serve Roman interests, but without Turkish intervention he could do no more than stave off inevitable defeat for a while. An alliance with the Turks had a potential added bonus in the effect which it might have on the Avars in Europe. They would be more inclined to observe their agreement with the Romans if there was a possibility of a punitive attack by their great eastern neighbours.

What, then, of Khusro? What were his plans for 624? Where were his forces concentrated? What might have happened, had Heraclius not entered the fray with his mobile force of highly trained soldiers ready to make ultra-intelligent use of intelligence, true and false? These questions are virtually impossible to answer for lack of Persian sources of information which might have provided some insight into the planning process on their side. Nor is it possible to reconstruct Khusro's aims and objectives from the actions of his forces, since whatever his plans were, they were disrupted from the start by Heraclius' attack and subsequently amounted to no more than a series of improvised and ineffective defensive measures.

There is, however, one precious piece of information provided by the Official History. Khusro is reported to have been at Ganzak in Atropatene in summer 624 with a large army, said to number 40,000 men.[13] This figure, possibly somewhat inflated but representing Roman intelligence estimates of Persian strength (it derives ultimately from a dispatch of Heraclius'), indicates that a large expeditionary force had been mobilized, presumably under the command of Khusro, who was at hand. It follows, both from the size of the army and from Khusro's presence, that the campaign in prospect was of exceptional importance, since Khusro had been careful to distance himself from military action in all theatres of war for nearly twenty years (his prestige could not be dented if he could choose whether or not to shoulder responsibility for the outcome of campaigns).[14] He had only taken personal command of armies in the field on two previous occasions, both of critical importance: in 591, his claim to the throne of his ancestors was at stake, and he had to submit himself to the rigours and risks of a campaign if he was to gain widespread support in Persia; then, twelve years later, at the start of his war to avenge Maurice, he needed to establish that he was the manager of military events, that he deserved the credit for whatever successes might be achieved by Persian armies—this required his taking direct control of the opening operations in the southern, Mesopotamian theatre (the risks attached

---

[13] Theoph., 307.23–5.
[14] Cf. Michael Whitby, 'The Persian King at War', in Dąbrowa, *Roman and Byzantine Army*, 227–63.

were not great, given that he had the active support of the Roman commander-in-chief in the region).[15]

It looks as if Khusro was embarking, in 624, on a campaign intended to be the pendant to that against Dara in 603–4 in circumstances which were no less favourable (the military weakness of the truncated Roman Empire having been amply displayed in 623). The large army under his command was expected to bring or help to bring the war which he had personally inaugurated to a victorious close. Asia Minor would be overrun and Constantinople would be besieged. The capital was bound to fall once it was isolated from former Roman territory. Khusro himself would thus be able to preside over the final liquidation of the Roman Empire. There was no question, though, of his taking the lead in the conquest of Asia Minor, since his army had not moved out of its base at Ganzak by the time of the summer solstice (21 June).[16] Ganzak would also have been a surprising choice of base, given the many alternatives firmly held by the Persians much closer to Roman territory. It follows, surely, that another attack was planned from another direction by another large Persian army, that under Shahrbaraz's command, which had been operating in Asia Minor in 623 and which was based in the northern Levant. It is inconceivable that Shahrbaraz, who continued to hold the southern command until the end of the war, was not expected to play a major part in the final Persian offensive, especially as he could use as his springboard the fertile plain of Cilicia which had been firmly under Persian control since 613. In this scenario, the role of Khusro's army was first to impress Persian authority deeply on the whole of Transcaucasia, then to follow up the initial advance of Shahrbaraz over Asia Minor, and, in due course, to receive the formal surrender of the last Roman emperor.

This final phase of the war was probably scheduled to last two campaigning seasons. Given his late start, it may be conjectured that Khusro planned to do no more than march to the eastern edge of Asia Minor in 624, while, ahead of him, Shahrbaraz thrust into the interior, defeated whatever defensive forces might be fielded by the Romans, seized the cities controlling access to the north-west, and prepared to advance on Constantinople. Established in secure winter quarters, perhaps in the plain of Melitene or in Cappadocia, where supplies were relatively plentiful, Khusro's army, by its mere presence, would consolidate the gains made by Shahrbaraz and undercut the Romans' will to fight on. The critical stage would come in 625, when Persian forces would need both to impose their authority throughout Asia Minor and force Constantinople to capitulate.

Whatever the plans of Khusro and his high command for 624 and 625, however ambitious or cautious, nothing came of them in the end. For Heraclius did the unexpected. Instead of remaining on the defensive, as he had since his

---

[15] 591: Sim., v.3–11. 603: ps.S., 107.1–19.   [16] Theoph., 307.21–5.

unsuccessful expedition to Antioch in 613, and confronting the main invasion force commanded by Shahrbaraz, he cast aside prudence, moved suddenly onto the offensive, and marched swiftly towards Atropatene. In doing so, he achieved complete strategic surprise and succeeded in bewildering, disordering, and destroying Khusro's army before it left its base at Ganzak. He then made good use of the strategic initiative which he had seized to cause as much material damage as possible both to an important component of the Persian Empire and to Khusro's prestige.

We leave the realm of inference and speculation once Heraclius leaves Caesarea at the start of the campaigning season in late April or early May 624 and the military action begins. We can piece together the main features of the two campaigns which followed from the important Armenian sources, the *History of Khosrov* and the *History to 682*, which provide complementary accounts, from the celebration of Heraclius' achievements written by George of Pisidia soon after the end of the war (the *Heraclias*), of which, alas, only two cantos have survived, and, most useful of all, the material excerpted by Theophanes from George of Pisidia's Official History.[17]

7.2 Invasion of Persian Territory

The physical mobilization of the men summoned to arms by Heraclius, likened by George of Pisidia to *the drawing together of particles of gold by quicksilver*,[18] was complemented in the psychological sphere by his well-judged use of black propaganda to strengthen their commitment to the Roman cause. Caesarea, the chosen assembly place, was not only convenient in terms of terrain (its plain was open but shielded from attack by the Taurus and Anti-Taurus ranges) and the availability of supplies, but it also served a strategic purpose. Once the Persians got wind of Roman movements, it would no longer be possible to pretend that a European campaign was being planned for 624, but the choice of a forward base of operations in southern Asia Minor was calculated to give the impression that Heraclius intended to take the field against Shahrbaraz's forces in Cilicia and northern Syria. Shahrbaraz would have to take measures to cope *both* with a Roman pre-emptive thrust into the occupied territories *and* with the great enhancement of Asia Minor defences which a large field army would bring about. That would inevitably delay the start of his own campaign and allay any anxiety in the army being mobilized far away to the north-east in Atropatene.

---

[17] My reconstruction accords in all essentials with that of Gerland, 'Die persischen Feldzüge', 348–62.

[18] Geo.Pis., *Heraclias*, ii.153–9.

Figure 15. Bisutun: blank screen prepared for Khusro II monumental relief. Author's photograph.

Figure 16. Naqsh-i Rustam: general view. Author's photograph.

Figure 17. Naqsh-i Rustam: blank screen. Author's photograph.

Figure 18. Constantinople: St. Sophia. Library of Congress Prints & Photographs Division, LC-DIG-ppmsca-03035.

Figure 19. Takht-i Sulaiman: defences. Author's photograph.

Figure 20. Takht-i Sulaiman: lake. Author's photograph.

Figure 21. David Plates: David's first audience with Saul. The Metropolitan Museum of Art, New York. 17.190.397. Gift of J. Pierpont Morgan, 1917.

Figure 22. David Plates: David and Goliath. The Metropolitan Museum of Art, New York. 17.190.396. Gift of J. Pierpont Morgan, 1917.

Heraclius' real plan of campaign was quite different, and when he put it into action, he achieved complete strategic surprise. Martina, not subsequently mentioned as accompanying her husband on campaign in any reputable source, was sent back to Constantinople, probably in the charge of Anianus (deputy to the Magister Officiorum and regent Bonus), who had accompanied her to Caesarea.[19] Heraclius then set off north-east at high speed (*like a fast running breeze*), to pick up the main northern road leading from Asia Minor into Armenia. He marched east along the upper Euphrates valley, aiming initially for Theodosiopolis. He forded the river, sped past the city, crossed the watershed beyond, and entered the traditional Persian sector of Armenia. Caught by surprise, their defences ill-organized, several important cities were exposed to attack as he passed by. No opposition was encountered in the field. Dvin, the administrative and military capital of Persarmenia, saw its territory ravaged, as did Nakhchawan, which commands the strategic passage where the Araxes pushes its way around the southern outliers of Karabakh.[20] After this, the route of invasion turned south into Atropatene and the core territories of the Sasanian Empire.[21]

At this psychologically important moment (not long before the summer solstice), Heraclius addressed another formal assembly of his troops. The gist of his speech is presented in verse form by George of Pisidia in the Official History. A fair amount of it is reproduced reasonably faithfully (much of the metre has been preserved) by Theophanes. By taking personal command of operations, Heraclius had cast aside the traditional aloofness of an emperor. His role on campaign was to lead by example and to share the hardships and dangers with his men. He stressed his solidarity with them by addressing them as his brothers. He reminded them of the causes for which they were fighting—their faith (Khusro had insulted God), their fellow Christians who had suffered terrible ills, and the independence of the Roman state. References to the impiety and brutality of the enemy were included to fire them with anger. They were reminded that there was no alternative to fighting vigorously, since escape was impossible now that they were deep in Persian-controlled territory. He concluded on a more optimistic note, observing that 'danger is not without reward but opens the way to eternal life' (a phrase resonant with meaning, indicating that salvation was on offer to all his fellow combatants) and that God would aid them and would destroy their enemies. The response was enthusiastic and reaches us again with vestiges of the verse in which George expressed it: Heraclius' words had indeed encouraged and

---

[19] Anianus: *Chron.Pasch.*, 714.5–7.
[20] For Karabakh (ancient Utik' and Arts'akh), see R. H. Hewsen, *Armenia: A Historical Atlas* (Chicago, 2001), 90 (map 69, B5–6, C5–6) and 100–3.
[21] Geo.Pis., *Heraclias*, ii.160–6; ps.S., 124.23–6; TA, 92.30–2.

given wings to his men, had sharpened and animated their swords; they promised to obey all his commands.[22]

Heraclius marched south, keeping to the west of Lake Urmia and setting fire to the towns and villages he passed. The town of Urmia was attacked. There was much killing and taking of prisoners. Heraclius' objective was Ganzak, where his intelligence placed Khusro and his army. An advance foray of Arab troops made the first contact with elements of Khusro's army, called by Theophanes a watch or guard. They were apparently a detachment of considerable size under the command of a general. With the advantage of surprise, the Arabs won an easy victory, in the course of which the Persian troops were either killed or captured. The prisoners included the general in command. News of the defeat seems to have induced panic in Khusro's headquarters. He immediately left Ganzak, abandoned his army, and fled south-east towards Media. There is no record of any organized resistance from the army itself. The surprise achieved by Heraclius was so complete that a single small shock shattered it as a fighting force, and relentless subsequent harrying prevented it from regrouping. The only countermeasure taken by Khusro was desperate: he ordered crops to be burned throughout the region, to deprive the Roman army of supplies. Even this proved counterproductive, since it probably encouraged Heraclius to push on yet deeper into Persian territory.[23]

Heraclius advanced to Ganzak, took control of the town, and at last allowed his army a brief rest in its suburbs. He now gained more intelligence, from Persian fugitives, of the route taken by Khusro. He had fled first to a great fire temple at Thebarmais (called the Gate of Ardashir by George of Pisidia in the *Heraclias*, after its original founder) to remove the treasure deposited there and some of the sacred fire. His plan was to take both south across the mountains to his palace at Dastagerd. Heraclius set off in pursuit. Thebarmais, which is securely identified with the site now known as Takht-i Sulaiman ('Throne of Solomon'), lay a hundred kilometres as the crow flies to the south-east of Ganzak, at the head of a high, remote valley in the mountains of eastern Atropatene. The ruins of the temple complex and its precinct have been excavated (Figures 19 and 20). In the middle of the building complex stood the main sanctuary with the sacred flame of Adur Gushnasp, one of three great fires venerated by the Zoroastrians. Its altar stood beneath a dome supported by arches resting on four massive piers which were themselves surrounded by a square ambulatory. Two columned halls, four minor sanctuaries, and an archive room have also been identified. This temple complex was approached from the main gateway in the north by a processional way crossing a pillared courtyard, while to its south a huge ceremonial *iwan* looked out over a much larger courtyard enclosing a circular volcanic lake from

---

[22] Summer solstice: Theoph., 307.21–3. Heraclius' speech and the response: Theoph., 307.1–19.
[23] Theoph., 307.19–21 and 23–9, 308.1–3; ps.S, 124.25–6; TA, 92.32–3.

which came a steady flow of warm, mineral-rich water. The whole precinct was well fortified, its thick mudbrick wall faced with an outer masonry skin and strengthened with numerous round buttresses.[24]

When Heraclius reached Thebarmais, he prepared to lay siege to it. But the mere sight of his army exercising, of the encircling siege wall under construction, and of the various machines which he was deploying led the defenders to surrender unconditionally. Their lives were spared, but the temple complex was savaged. Ten years on, Heraclius was taking revenge for the sack of Jerusalem and the various acts of sacrilege which the Persians were alleged to have committed there. He put out the sacred flame of Adur Gushnasp (thereby rededicating to God a part of his Creation which Zoroastrians wrongly took to be divine) and deliberately polluted the waters of the lake enclosed within the temple precinct by throwing in corpses (presumably of those killed during the preliminary siege operations). Then he turned fire into a weapon against the fire worshippers. He burned down the whole temple complex, in the process incinerating the documents kept in the archive room but hardening and preserving the clay seals (nearly 300 of them) which authenticated them.[25]

The destruction of Thebarmais did not take long. The site was compact, and the buildings formed a single intercommunicating complex in which fire unaided could do its work. Soon Heraclius and his men were back on the trail of Khusro, who had gone south over the uplands of Media to the Zagros mountains. They did not give up the pursuit until they had followed him into the passes linking southern Media to Mesopotamia. By that stage they had created a long swathe of destruction through the countryside and had attacked the towns in their path, including the regional capital Hamadan. It is impossible to be sure which route Khusro took, but the safest ran due south from Thebarmais to the plain of modern Kermanshah, where it turned west along a series of valleys connected by relatively easy passes to enter the upper Diyala plain at Qasr-i Shirin. It would have taken Khusro past the great cliff at Bisutun and the sacred lake at Taq-i Bustan.[26]

With Khusro's army dispersed and Khusro himself sent scurrying ignominiously for safety, Heraclius could now set about the systematic devastation of Media and Atropatene, both probably left largely unscathed during his hurried outward march. The only constraint was time (the invasion of Atropatene and pursuit of Khusro having probably taken to the end of July). He had three months

---

[24] Theoph., 307.31–308.7; Geo.Pis., *Heraclias*, ii.167–203. K. Schippmann, *Die iranischen Feuerheiligtümer* (Berlin, 1971), 309–57; R. Naumann, *Die Ruinen von Tacht-e Suleiman und Zendan-e Suleiman* (Berlin, 1977); D. Huff, 'The Functional Layout of the Fire Sanctuary at Takht-i Sulaimān', in D. Kennet and P. Luft, eds., *Current Research in Sasanian Archaeology, Art and History*, BAR Int. Ser. 1810 (Oxford, 2008), 1–13.

[25] Geo.Pis., *Heraclias*, ii.204–30; ps.S, 124.26–7; TA, 92.32–5, 93.2–3; Theoph., 308.7–9. R. Göbl, *Die Tonbullen vom Tacht-e Suleiman und seiner Umgebung* (Wiesbaden, 1968).

[26] Theoph., 308.9–12; TA, 92.33. Cf. Naval Intelligence Division, *Persia*, Geographical Handbook Series B.R. 525 (Oxford, 1945), 59–63.

to find appropriate winter-quarters where his men could rest, sheltered from the worst of the weather and safe from attack. The decision on where to go had probably already been taken, perhaps during the original planning of the campaign, although the formal announcement to an army assembly was only made at the approach of winter, in a ceremony staged to demonstrate that the plan was sanctioned by God. The winter quarters designate lay due north of Atropatene, in the lowlands of the Kur valley in Caucasian Albania, where the formidable mountains of Karabakh would act as a natural southern shield. The Romans, therefore, would be retracing their steps from the southern border of Media, where they halted their pursuit of Khusro. Raiding forays could to be dispatched on either side of the main army's line of march to widen the swathe of destruction during a comparatively leisurely withdrawal.

In this second, more relaxed phase of the campaign Heraclius inflicted severe damage on an important resource base of the Sasanian Empire. The *History to 682*, which alone distinguished this phase clearly from that of the initial pursuit, reports that he plundered, ruined, and enslaved the whole land. The *History of Khosrov*, in a passage only preserved in Thomas Artsruni's version, notes that he slaughtered all the Persian soldiers whom he encountered, but goes too far in supposing that civilians were put to the sword indiscriminately along with their livestock. More credence should be given to Theophanes' statement that a great many prisoners were captured and taken away, although not to his figure (50,000). Theophanes confirms that many cities and rural districts were devastated. The area affected extended from Gayshawan on the southern edge of Media, a district of fortified summer residences where the court could pass the summer months in a comparatively cool and healthy climate, through the provinces of Hamadan and Media to Atropatene. It comprised the mountains and enclosed basins of the northern Zagros, the open hill country of southern and western Media (where the only serious impediments to military movement were deep-cut river valleys), and the rich alluvial plains of the Urmia basin.[27]

Heraclius could not have expected to achieve more in the course of a single campaign. Khusro's prestige must have plummeted among his magnates, the military, and his subjects at large when he took to headlong flight and the great army he was leading dissolved. The destruction of one of the three premier fire temples must have sounded a grim warning to the whole secular and priestly apparatus of government. The material damage too was not to be discounted, in both economic and political terms. Heraclius had succeeded in demonstrating that a heavy price would have to be paid if Khusro's ambitions were to be realized in full.

---

[27] MD, 131.20–132.4 (trans. Dowsett, 79); TA, 92.35–93.6; Theoph., 308.11–12, 17–18, 22. W. B. Fisher, ed., *Cambridge History of Iran*, I *The Land of Iran* (Cambridge, 1968), 8–14. Cf. Nav.Int. Div., *Persia*, 50–1, 54–6.

With winter now approaching, he held a formal assembly of the army to discuss the next move. George of Pisidia may have allowed himself some licence to embellish on reality in the set-piece description which he wrote in verse and included in the Official History. He has two options put forward, one realistic (to march north to Albania), the other absurdly ambitious but pointing forward to Heraclius' boldest move of all, made in the very different circumstances of autumn 627 (to attack Khusro in person, which would have involved crossing the Zagros and entering the metropolitan region of the Sasanian Empire). The decision was remitted to God. The troops whom Heraclius had previously designated God's creatures (*plasmata*) fasted for three days. Then Heraclius consulted the Gospels and took his instructions from the first passage which he read. This directed the army north, to Albania.[28]

Very little is known about this final phase of the 624 campaign. The ultimate destination was the valley of the river Terter, upstream from P'artaw, the regional capital.[29] Nothing is reported about the route taken by the army. There were two alternatives north of the Araxes: either to make straight for P'artaw across the difficult terrain of Karabakh, where even small forces might launch effective guerrilla attacks, or to play safe and skirt the mountains, first marching east down the Araxes valley and then swinging north and eventually north-west. Had the decision rested with anyone other than Heraclius, one would have little hesitation in assuming that the easier, safer alternative was chosen. Heraclius, however, was a commander of rare boldness who, confident in the superior mobility and fighting skill of his men, was ready to step beyond the bounds of normal military prudence, whether by stretching the campaigning season well into winter or by cutting across hazardous mountain ranges. I incline, then, to think that Heraclius took the shorter route, even though the large number of prisoners being taken north inevitably slowed the army's progress and restricted its manoeuvrability. The very act of venturing into Karabakh would demonstrate that there was no district, however well defended, which could escape attack. In the event, attacks were launched by Persian forces, perhaps elements of the Khusro's expeditionary army which had eventually managed to regroup, more probably local troops based in Karabakh and Albania, and severe winter weather further hampered the army's movements. But the army seems to have reached the comparative safety of the P'artaw region without serious mishap.[30]

In the course of this march north, Heraclius sent letters to the princes and leaders of the three main component parts of Transcaucasia—Albania, Iberia, and Armenia—demanding that they attend on him in person and serve him with

---

[28] Theoph., 308.12–16. Cf. MD, 132.4–5 (trans. Dowsett, 79).
[29] J. A. Manandjan, 'Marshruty persidskikh pokhodov imperatora Iraklija', VV 3 (1950),133–53, at 139 and map 3.
[30] Theoph., 308.17–21; MD, 132.21–133.1 (trans. Dowsett, 80).

their forces. Failure to do so, he warned them, would be construed as an unchristian act and would result in assaults on their strongholds and the conquest of their lands. The only reactions reported were those of different sections of the population of Pʻartaw. Those who belonged to the Persian-sponsored ruling elite made no attempt to hold the city against the Roman field army. They were allowed by the Persian authorities to abandon the city and to disperse to various secure places of refuge. Many other inhabitants of the city, Christian, Jewish, and pagan, all classified as skilled, stayed put, pleading incapacity and infirmity. They then surrendered, sending a rising star in the local church, a certain Zacharias, to negotiate terms with the Romans. It is likely that they agreed to help provision and re-equip the army. Heraclius thus not only eliminated the only serious potential local threat to his forces, but gained an invaluable additional resource (the administrative and commercial capability of the city) for organizing the commissariat that winter, and for obtaining materiel from its workshops.[31]

The burden of supporting the Roman army through the winter was not going to strain the resources of Pʻartaw and the central section of the Kur plain. The large number of prisoners who had been uprooted from the cities and villages of Media and Atropatene and brought with the army were quite another matter— apart from the deleterious effect on military efficiency which prosaic guard duties might have on many of the troops. Heraclius had no choice but to let them go after his arrival in Albania. Their release is glossed in the Official History, which probably picks up the line spun in Heraclius' original dispatch, as an act of Christian charity which evoked the gratitude of the prisoners. They are said to have prayed that Heraclius rescue Persia and kill Khusro, the destroyer of the *kosmos* (as in much of the speech, direct or indirect, preserved in Theophanes' version, the verse is still detectable). Some hard-headed military calculation probably lay behind this advertised act of generosity. The prisoners could have been freed much earlier, before the army left Atropatene, before the onset of winter. But then they might have been able to make their way home without requiring much assistance from the Persian authorities (local judges and guardians of the poor) in Karabakh, Atropatene, and Media and without putting much strain on the economies of those regions. By detaining them for as long as he did, Heraclius not only halted agricultural and craft production in the districts he had raided for a longer period (in effect, excising a year's harvest), but also extended economic disruption to other areas. The death rate among the returning prisoners was also likely to be higher, and this, though carefully masked behind the spin-doctoring, was probably intended, since it would cause longer-term economic damage.[32]

---

[31] MD, 132.4–21 (trans. Dowsett, 79–80).
[32] Theoph., 308.21–5.

For the Roman troops, the winter passed uneventfully. They changed camp once, when the first site, at the village of Kałankatuk', was churned up into a quagmire. But the move was a short one, to the neighbouring village of Diwtakan.[33] Reinforcements came in answer to the general call to arms issued by Heraclius. The northern auxiliaries were numerous enough to exercise a significant influence in a debate about strategy early in the 625 campaign. Three contingents—the Laz, Abasgians, and Iberians—are picked out because of their vociferousness, and two (the Laz and Abasgians) feature again at a later stage, when they left the army and returned home. The Iberians presumably showed more determination and continued to serve with Heraclius.[34] What, though, of the Albanians and Armenians to whom Heraclius had also directed his appeal? Surely they had been affected by the propaganda disseminated over the previous decade which had blackened the Persians as anti-Christian zealots responsible for all manner of outrages? Surely those princes and local lords who were not enmeshed in the Persian administration were susceptible to the call to fight with their fellow Christians? And even if their religious sentiments were not roused, surely some rallied with contingents of their followers simply to spite local rivals who were supporting the Persians?

The extant sources do not enable us to answer these questions. Theophanes' source, the Official History, is concerned to trace the progress of the army and to highlight the personal contribution of the emperor to its ultimate success. References to non-Roman troops are incidental and very occasional. The author of the *History of Khosrov*, who might be expected to stress the role of Armenians in the achievement of victory, seems to have been striving to keep his text within manageable bounds. He has condensed his Heraclius-focused source rather ferociously, squeezing out any mention of the winter spent in Albania and thus conflating the very different campaigns of 624 and 625.[35] His editorial policy in this section thus precluded the introduction of supplementary material about Armenian attitudes and behaviour, while the occasion for doing so, Heraclius' call to arms, disappeared with the excision of winter 624–5 from his truncated account. Finally, the *History to 682* shows little sympathy for the Roman cause, which was before long to result in the invasion and occupation of Albania by the Turks. It is no surprise then to find that he maintains a discreet silence about any

---

[33] MD, 132.21–133.3.   [34] Theoph., 309.13–15, 310.21–3.
[35] Ps.S., 124.28–125.11 leaps abruptly from the destruction of the Adur Gushnasp fire temple to Khusro's countermeasures in the course of the following winter and the initial operations of Persian armies against Heraclius in spring 625. C. Zuckerman, 'Heraclius in 625', *REB* 60 (2002), 189–97, follows the chronology implied by the *History of Khosrov*, despite the contrary evidence of the two fuller sources, the Official History (via Theophanes) and the *History to 682*. Kaegi, *Heraclius*, 122–32 and W. Seibt, '...Zog Herakleios 625 wirklich in das "Land der Hunnen"?', in K. Belke et al., eds., *Byzantina Mediterranea* (Vienna, 2007), 589–96 accept the Zuckerman chronology, which squeezes all the operations of 625 into the preceding winter months and leaves Heraclius and his army underemployed in the following campaigning season.

Albanian contingents which might have joined the Roman expeditionary force and manages to summarize the operations of 625 in five sentences.[36]

So there is no reason to read too much into the silence of the sources. It can be argued on circumstantial evidence that Heraclius' call to arms was answered in Armenia and, probably to a lesser extent, in Albania, as well as in Iberia and the lands fronting the Black Sea (perhaps still under Roman control, even at this late stage of the war). The silence of the Official History can be explained: the Armenians in particular were perhaps less hesitant in their commitment than the Laz, Abasgians, and Iberians; they were perhaps ready, like the Roman troops, to follow wherever Heraclius led, and neither opposed his initial plan of campaign in 625 nor tried to leave the army in the autumn. A substantial Transcaucasian *host* can be envisaged, consisting of a multitude of small noble-led contingents, all probably mounted. In addition, the very plan of campaign adopted by Heraclius, directed as it was into the north, surely bespeaks confidence in the level of local support which would be forthcoming in Transcaucasia. The intense interest shown by Armenian historians in his counteroffensives is explicable as a later reflection of a contemporary concern and commitment.

Nonetheless, the silence is disturbing. The only reference to Armenian troops in Byzantine service comes towards the end of the *Chronicon Paschale*'s account of the siege of Constantinople in 626, when they are reported to have butchered the Slavs who swam ashore after the sinking of their ships in the Golden Horn.[37] While these Armenians could have been detached from the expeditionary army when Heraclius rushed reinforcements to the city just before the siege began, it is equally likely that they were regular troops recruited long before and stationed in the capital. Such positive information as is given by the Official History suggests that Armenians were also backing the Persian side: many Armenians *from the former Roman sector* joined Shahrbaraz's army as it followed Heraclius west in late autumn 625; two years later, Armenians troops were serving with the Persians until a late stage in Heraclius' triumphant advance towards Ctesiphon.[38] A scenario quite contrary to that sketched above may therefore be conjured up according to which the traditionally fissiparous Armenians, torn between their traditional cultural and political ties to Iran and the new faith which linked them to the Roman Empire, had swung almost en masse to the Persian side, as victory had followed victory and the Sasanian Empire seemed set to absorb all the territory of its once-great rival. Despite all the propaganda pumped out over previous years, the most perhaps that Heraclius could expect in the short term was the neutrality of the northern Christians as he campaigned in Transcaucasia, clinging perhaps to the forlorn hope that military success might eventually detach

---

[36] MD, 133.4–11 (trans. Dowsett, 81). [37] *Chron.Pasch.*, 724.11–15.
[38] Theoph., 311.10–12, 320.26–7.

some northern Christians from their allegiance to the Persians or, in a yet more distant future, might set in train a general rising in Transcaucasia.

The question should, therefore, be left open. Denied the chance to poll Armenian (and Albanian) opinion by a dearth of trustworthy contemporary material, we should perhaps refrain from conjecturing what Heraclius' realistic expectations might have been when he issued his call to arms and what scale of response it might have evoked. In which case, we must leave it uncertain as to whether he was going to have to face the Persian forces massing against him that winter with the lean force he had brought from Caesarea, swift-moving, responsive to his touch, capable of applying intense force to specific isolated targets, or whether substantial, well-motivated northern contingents had arrived and added greatly to his military musculature.

7.3 The Persian Hunt for Heraclius

Persian preparations for a counterattack in overwhelming force began well before the start of winter. For it was in midsummer, after his grand army had broken up, that Khusro sent a first urgent appeal for help to Shahrbaraz, commander-in-chief in the west. It could not be answered instantaneously. For it took time to reorganize the military administration of Syria, Palestine, and Egypt so as to ensure that Persian control would not be challenged when the forces of occupation were reduced. It also inevitably took time to withdraw the field component in the army of occupation from forward positions threatening Asia Minor. So it was probably not before late August or early September that Shahrbaraz was able to march east with a large army more than capable of confronting Heraclius' on its own. His route took him across the Euphrates and south of the Tur Abdin to Nisibis, a great city which, in the past, had doubled as the main Persian base on the old frontier in northern Mesopotamia.[39]

Nisibis had lost its traditional military role with the disappearance of the frontier, but assuredly contained extensive barracks which could accommodate much of Shahrbaraz's army in comfort. It was also a convenient platform from which to monitor what was going on in the interior of the Sasanian Empire and to exercise an influence on the outcome of the campaign. For Heraclius was likely to adopt one of two courses of action: if he took the safer option of withdrawing west through Armenia after doing as much damage as possible to Atropatene and Media, Shahrbaraz could march north, crossing the Armenian Taurus by the Bitlis pass, so as to intercept the Roman army in western Armenia (whichever route was chosen, whether the southern along the Arsanias valley, or the northern

---

[39] Theoph., 306.27–8; ps.S, 124.28–9, 125.1–2; MD, 131.8–19 (trans. Dowsett, 79).

down the Euphrates); if Heraclius was bolder and took advantage of the temporary dislocation of the defences of the metropolitan region to cross the Zagros, Shahrbaraz could march rapidly south and trap the Roman army in lower Mesopotamia. In the event, with Heraclius unexpectedly withdrawing north beyond Karabakh, Shahrbaraz's army had no influence on the course of operations in 624, but at least had procured decent quarters in which to pass the winter.

In the meantime Khusro had deputed his other senior general, Shahen, to mobilize a second field army from within the Sasanian Empire. While there were not the competing demands of internal security which affected Shahrbaraz, Shahen had the additional task of training troops who had probably not seen action for some time. His army, its strength put by the *History of Khosrov* at 30,000 men, was only battle-ready in spring 625.[40] A third army, designated the 'New Army' and commanded by Sharaplakan, was the first to enter the fray. Before the end of winter it took up a position in the Karabakh highlands, barring the direct route south. It appears to have been composed of guards units named after Persian kings (Peroz and Khusro, presumably Khusro I Anushirwan) and provincial forces under a local governor, Granikn Salar, who enjoyed royal favour.[41]

The Persian plan was to confine the Roman expeditionary army to Transcaucasia by blocking all egresses from it and then to engage it in a coordinated operation involving all three armies. Shahraplakan's initial task was to prevent Heraclius repeating his southern thrust into Atropatene and Media.[42] Shahrbaraz was ordered across Armenia to the region of Gardman (north-east of Lake Sevan), from where he could command and interdict the easiest line of retreat for the Romans through Iberia to Lazica and the Black Sea coast.[43] He would also be able to double back and intercept the Romans in the unlikely event that they reached the Araxes valley and took the northern route through Armenia which they had used in their initial attack in 624 (up the Araxes valley, then down that of the upper Euphrates). Finally, Shahen's army was deployed south of the Armenian Taurus, based probably at the provincial capital of Arzanene, where it could take over one of the strategic functions previously performed by Shahrbaraz's force at Nisibis, namely to strike north across the Armenian Taurus and block the southern route west.[44] That route ran from the Araxes valley at Nakhchawan across Bagrewand and the linked plains of modern Patnos and

---

[40] Theoph., 306.28–307.1; ps.S, 125.8–9.
[41] Theoph., 308.27–309.3; MD, 133.3–8 (trans. Dowsett, 81). Ps.S., 124.29–31 mentions what sounds like the same scratch force, but mistakes Shahen for Sharaplakan as its commander.
[42] Theoph., 309.3–4.
[43] Ps.S., 125.1–8. Heraclius' position in Albania is wrongly given as P'aytakaran (towards which he marched in late summer 625) instead of P'artaw, near which he wintered in 624-5.
[44] Ps.S., 125.8–11.

Manzikert to the yet larger plain of Taron. From there, relatively easy routes ran west on both flanks of the Armenian Taurus.[45]

The supreme command seems to have been given to Shahen. He is called 'general of [the] Persians' by Theophanes. He commanded what was probably the largest army, with 30,000 men. When he and his troops, the last to join the campaign, were approaching the area of fighting, both the other generals were eager to bring Heraclius to battle before he arrived lest he appropriate the credit for the victory. At a later stage in the campaign, when the action shifted back to Albania, it was he, accompanied by Shahrbaraz, who led the Persian forces against Heraclius. He was perhaps deliberately kept out of the initial operations so as to be able to give strategic guidance to the campaign.[46]

However, things did not go according to plan. Heraclius was not deterred from renewing his offensive by Sharaplakan in Karabakh. He decided to march at high speed around the mountains through open plains, rich in pasture—clearly those of the lower Kur and lower Araxes rivers. He encouraged his men by telling them that the strain of trying to outmarch them in difficult terrain would be worse for the Persians, in particular that it would exhaust and disable their mounts. In the event, the Romans, despite the much greater distance they had to cover, were the first to reach the Araxes valley south of Karabakh. Heraclius' plan was to make another swift thrust into Persian territory in the hope of taking Khusro once again by surprise and giving the Persian body politic another disorienting shock. But when he aired the plan, probably at a meeting of senior officers, there was concerted opposition led by the Laz, Abasgian, and Iberian auxiliaries. It was an occasion which provided George of Pisidia with the materials for the first of the set-piece debates with which he punctuated the Official History's narrative of the 625 campaign. Heraclius bowed to the collective will, which was, in effect, insisting that the army abandon the offensive and withdraw to Roman territory. The decision, the Official History noted, resulted in grave difficulties.[47]

So, instead of turning south, Heraclius probably continued west and northwest up the Araxes valley, only to learn that Shahrbaraz's army was advancing against him, having presumably retraced its steps around the northern end of Lake Sevan and reached the Araxes plain in the vicinity of Dvin. The news that they were now caught between two Persian armies shook the army and made it once again a pliant instrument in Heraclius' hands (a change of mood highlighted in what was probably the second of George's set-piece debates). Operations now began in earnest.[48]

Heraclius turned back to deal with Shahraplakan's pursuing army, which had been keeping its distance in the expectation of joining forces soon with Shahrbaraz's larger army. Before this could happen, Heraclius harried it

---

[45] H. F. B. Lynch, *Armenia: Travels and Studies*, 2 vols. (London, 1901), II, 391–402.
[46] Theoph., 309.31–310.3, 310.23–4.   [47] Theoph., 309.4–15.   [48] Theoph., 309.16–25.

mercilessly day and night until its morale broke. Then came another change in the Roman direction of movement. They marched 'with all speed against Khusro', a phrase which clearly indicates that they struck south across the Araxes into Atropatene, belatedly implementing Heraclius' original plan of campaign. Shahrbaraz was now able to link up with Shahraplakan, and their united forces set off in pursuit of the Romans. Heraclius brought disinformation into play, conveying it to the Persian high command by means of two supposed deserters who convinced them that the Romans had lost their nerve and were fleeing. News also came of Shahen's approach with a third army. Determined to seize the victory dangling before them, Shahrbaraz and Shahraplakan pushed on. At dusk one day they camped within striking distance of the Roman army, intending to attack at dawn the next day.[49]

Heraclius, who may perhaps have allowed them to catch up and who certainly anticipated their plan, now removed his troops from the target area. They marched right through the night and reached a plain rich in pasture. Here, well away from their pursuers, they established a camp and, at their leisure, prepared for battle, taking up a solid defensive position based on a wooded hill. The poison of disinformation took effect on the Persians when they realized that their adversary had slipped away. Confident that it was flight driven by fear, they set off in pursuit and did not maintain proper discipline on the march. Their ranks were disordered when they reached the plain where the Roman army was waiting, arrayed for battle in a carefully prepared position. In the ensuing battle the Romans seem to have won an easy victory which they followed up with their customary hard pursuit. Heavy casualties were inflicted on the Persians in the ravines through which they were driven. This determined effort to exploit victory to the utmost and to inflict as much damage as possible on the enemy army had not ended when the third Persian army, commanded by Shahen, came on the scene. It too was engaged by the Romans, suffered heavy losses, and was relentlessly pursued until it was dispersed and disabled as a fighting force.[50]

Complicated and varied though Heraclius' movements may have been, bewildering though they have proved to many commentators, it is possible to track them across a landscape where the principal natural features have remained unchanged. A rough location can be proposed with reasonable confidence for the two major battles (south of the Araxes, somewhere in Atropatene). Since there is no indication that Heraclius had pushed deep into Persian territory nor that much time had elapsed from the moment when he turned south, they should probably be placed in northern Atropatene. The plains of Her and Zarewand should be strong candidates for the site of the first battle against Shahrbaraz and Shahraplakan. Shahen's march from the northern outlet of the Bitlis pass, skirting

---

[49] Theoph., 309.25–310.5.   [50] Theoph., 310.6–17.

the formidable mountains immediately to the north-east of Lake Van, would have brought him into the plain of Kogovit within easy reach of northern Atropatene. The second battle may then be placed somewhere in the hill country separating Kogovit from Her. This incidentally is probably the battle singled out in the *History of Khosrov* (it is fought against the army which, at the outset of the campaign, was 'behind' Heraclius and that army was Shahen's).[51]

The first phase of the campaign was now over. As in 624, victory secured freedom of movement for Heraclius, while the disordered and dispersed units of the three Persian armies were reformed and their discipline and morale were restored in preparation for further encounters with the Romans. Theophanes leaves us in the dark about the use to which Heraclius put this temporary freedom, since he leaps on to his withdrawal from Persian territory. We can only resort to conjecture about the operations of the period when he held the strategic initiative. If one of his objectives remained the inflicting of as much damage as possible on Persian material resources and on the prestige of Khusro's regime, the obvious course of action was to resume the raiding activity of the previous year and to direct it at regions hitherto unaffected. This was a strategic opportunity which Heraclius surely did not forgo. What, then, were the obvious regions to target? Not the impenetrable and relatively unrewarding mountains of Vaspurakan to the west of Lake Urmia. Not the west shore of the lake nor the plains and hills of southern Atropatene and southern Media which had been attacked in 624. Not distant Mesopotamia, since it was far too hazardous to cross the Zagros with a potentially formidable adversary to the rear. There was only one set of convenient and naturally rich target areas, *to the east of Lake Urmia*—the alluvial plains of modern Tabriz and Maragha on the northern and southern flanks of Mount Sahand, and a series of large inland basins stretching east as far as modern Ardabil. Heraclius, it may be postulated, turned east after routing the three armies deployed against him and extended the swathe of devastation over much of Atropatene.[52]

Indirect corroboration is provided from what is reported of his subsequent movements in what should be classified as the third phase of the campaign, the initial stage of his withdrawal. Theophanes reports that he marched towards the territory of the Huns and their highlands across rugged, difficult terrain.[53] Mention of the Huns, who controlled the eastern half of the steppes immediately north of the Caucasus and whose power lapped against that of the Persians at the Caspian Gates, shows that Heraclius' route ran north, as in 624, but farther to the east.[54] The difficult country en route may then be identified with the mountains

---

[51] Ps.S., 125.12–14. Cf. Nav.Int.Div., *Persia*, 49–50.   [52] Cf. Nav.Int.Div., *Persia*, 52.
[53] Theoph., 310.19–20.
[54] Hewsen, *The Geography of Ananias of Širak*, 57 (c.5.18 end) and 123 (n.107). Zuckerman, 'Heraclius in 625', 192–3 emends 'land of the Huns' (Οὔννων) to 'land of Siwnik' (Σύννων), as suggested

which separate the interior plains of northern Atropatene and Media from the conjoined valleys of the lower Araxes and lower Kur. Such a line of march would have brought the Romans to P'aytakaran, the principal city of eastern Albania. P'aytakaran is indeed named in the third passage which appears to deal with this episode—a notice in the *History of Khosrov* according to which Heraclius 'returned through the difficult terrain of Media and reached P'aytakaran'.[55] Two distinct episodes seem to have been amalgamated in this notice: Heraclius' withdrawal to the vicinity of P'artaw in the middle Kur valley in 624 (the prisoners of war taken north that year are mentioned) and a second march north in 625 to P'aytakaran in the lower Kur valley in 625. The resulting hybrid has been placed in the wrong year, in 624, *before* rather than after the coordinated Persian attack of spring 625. There can be little doubt, though, that the line of march which is reported belongs to the later episode, when Heraclius is known to have been aiming for the region of the Caspian Gates.

It is not hard to detect the motives for this move, which was taking the Roman army farther and farther away from the comparative safety of Asia Minor. The vital clue lies in the reference to the Huns. They had been incorporated in the Turkish khaganate in the 560s.[56] Like the ubiquitous Sogdian merchants whose trading network spread throughout the Turkish Empire, the North Caucasus Huns were potential intermediaries through whom diplomatic communications with the great power of the north might be channelled. They may even have taken the initiative, acting on behalf of their Turkish overlords and raising the possibility of a grand Turkish-Roman alliance. For a Hun embassy arrived in Constantinople in the early 620s, ostensibly with a religious purpose (the Hun ruler and other leaders were baptized during their visit), but their arrival may have prompted Heraclius to send an ambassador of his own directly to the governing centre of the western half of the Turkish khaganate (as he did early in 624).[57]

In marching north, into eastern Albania, aiming for Hun territory, Heraclius was surely looking for an answer from the Turks to the proposal which he had transmitted through his ambassador Andrew. This is more than empty hypothesis. For the *History to 682* reports that Andrew returned in the second half of 625 *through the Caspian Gates*.[58] This means that an overland route was chosen for the return journey of the embassy when it was accompanied by emissaries of the *yabghu khagan*, the deputy to the supreme khagan (namely the senior eastern *yabghu khagan*, Illig). The only conceivable reason for this choice of a slower and

---

by Manandjan, 'Marshruty',141; Seibt, 'Herakleios 625', locates the battles of 625 in Siwnik' and suggests (595–6) an alternative emendation, Apahounik'.

[55] Ps.S., 125.2–5.
[56] P. B. Golden, *An Introduction to the History of the Turkish Peoples: Ethnogenesis and State-Formation in Medieval and Early Modern Eurasia and the Middle East* (Wiesbaden, 1992), 106–8. Hewsen, *Geography of Ananias*, 57 (c.5.18 end) and 123 (n.107).
[57] Nic., c.9.   [58] MD, 141.20–2 (trans. Dowsett, 87).

more hazardous route was Heraclius' presence in eastern Transcaucasia. A rendezvous at or near P'aytakaran may have been planned from the first, or the Huns may have monitored events south of the Caucasus and kept the *yabghu khagan* informed of Heraclius' movements. In any event, when the *yabghu khagan* sent a reply to his fellow ruler, he directed it not over the steppes to the Taman peninsula, say, and then by sea to Constantinople, but across the heavily fortified Caucasus frontier of the Sasanian Empire to Albania.

The diplomats, Roman and Turkish, were given a powerful escort of a thousand or so mounted archers. These sliced their way through the fortifications of the Caspian Gates. Persian forces were taken by surprise. Neither garrison troops nor field units succeeded in barring their way. They then swept down to the river Kur. At which point something has gone wrong in the *History to 682*. The late seventh-century editor has assumed that Heraclius was in Constantinople, the natural venue for negotiations involving the Roman emperor. This was easy to do, as the military operations undertaken after the winter of 624–5 spent near P'artaw (which placed Heraclius in Transcaucasia in 625) and the return of Andrew with a Turkish embassy (dated to Khusro's thirty-sixth regnal year (June 625–June 626)) are covered separately. So the ambassadors and their nomad escort speed up the Kur and over the difficult country of Iberia and Lazica, take ship across the Black Sea, and meet Heraclius in Constantinople. Unless the whole journey to Constantinople has been invented, there were, it appears, two rounds of negotiation, the first with Heraclius in the field (to seal the offensive alliance?) and the second with the regents in Constantinople (to devise a detailed plan for coordinated action in 626?). According to the *History to 682*, the message was that the *yabghu khagan* welcomed the Roman proposal, would join in the war on the Roman side, and intended to take personal command of his forces. The agreement was sealed with oaths, each side swearing according to their own religion. The embassy then returned home. Secrecy was preserved. While the Persians must have suspected that something was afoot, they did not anticipate the attack of 626 and took no countermeasures.[59]

While the Romans were raiding Atropatene, Shahen and Shahrbaraz reassembled the dispersed remnants of the three defeated Persian armies. The third general, Shahraplakan, had been killed in the first of the set-piece battles.[60] The Persian troops were reorganized into a single fighting force, under the joint command of Shahen and Shahrbaraz. Once discipline and morale were restored, they followed Heraclius north.[61] It is difficult to say, for lack of evidence, at what stage they caught up. There are three possible alternatives: they may have closed

---

[59] MD, 141.10–142.7 (trans. Dowsett, 87).
[60] His death is only reported in the ninth-century Latin translation of Theophanes in Anastasius bibliothecarius, *Historia Tripartita*, ed. C. de Boor, *Theophanis chronographia*, II (Leipzig, 1885), 192.16–17.
[61] Theoph., 310.17–21.

in during the march north, or during the negotiations (for which the Roman army probably slowed down, if not halting altogether), or during a subsequent march west some distance up the Kur. As it is, neither Theophanes nor the *History of Khosrov* refers to the diplomatic activity of 625 in the course of their military narratives. If it featured in the Official History, Theophanes has excised it, while the Armenian historian, who alludes to negotiations with the Turks in his preface, seems to have cut it out from the final version of his text.

However, the Persian and Roman armies unquestionably came within striking distance of each other at some stage when they were still in Albania. Persian morale rose when two contingents of auxiliaries, the Laz and Abasgians, split off and made for home. Shahen, together with Shahrbaraz, now marched purposefully against the Romans, ready for a full engagement.[62] Heraclius too prepared for an orthodox battle by haranguing the assembled troops. Theophanes' version of the speech he gave is worth quoting in full. It captures the gist of the verse summary included by George of Pisidia in the Official History (phrases in iambics cluster in the Theophanes' prose). George's summary may be assumed to have been faithful to the original speech, not least because Heraclius was commissioning the work.

It was a dark hour for the Romans who had hitherto been able to choose the ground and the time for the engagements they had fought. Hitherto they had not had to confront the Persian forces massed against them as a single fighting unit. They were undoubtedly outnumbered, and their morale must have dipped when the Laz and Abasgians abandoned them and marched west. Heraclius appealed once again to their Christian faith, both to boost their confidence in the outcome of the battle and to heighten their individual commitment:

> Be not disturbed, O brethren, by the multitude of the enemy. For when God wills it, one man will rout thousands. So let us sacrifice ourselves to God for the salvation of our brethren. *Let us seize the crown of martyrdom* that a future age may praise us and that God may grant us our recompense.[63]

By a strange coincidence, a Christian Roman emperor was enunciating a doctrine which has an uncanny resemblance to Islamic jihad at the very time when, according to later, widely disseminated and widely accepted Muslim traditions, Muhammad was beginning to formulate it. The circumstances were similar. Both were monotheist leaders whose outnumbered followers needed to be fortified

---

[62] Theoph., 310.21–4.
[63] Theoph., 310.25–311.2 (my italics).

psychologically if a long defensive war against greatly superior adversaries was to be sustained.[64]

Whatever the roots of jihad, it is not difficult to identify the source of Heraclius' inspiration. It lay in Transcaucasia, in Armenia. For when Armenian insurgents took up arms against the Sasanian authorities in 450–1 and 482–4, as much to defend their aristocratic *amour propre* as their Christian faith, it soon became plain that both rebellions were doomed enterprises, and all but the most intransigent and committed dropped away. Whatever the original motivation of the hard core among the 450–1 rebels, it was retrospectively transmuted by the clergy into Christian fervour, and their deaths were equated with martyrdom. A generation later, when once again Armenian forces took up arms against the imperial Persian power, this notion that death in battle against non-Christians was tantamount to martyrdom was taking firm hold.[65] Like the Catholicos John and Vahan Mamikonean, the rebel leader, in the early 480s, Heraclius needed to transform the faith of his troops into an energizing force which would push aside rational calculation of outcomes and make his men fight with unbreakable determination. Circumstance perhaps drove him to develop a similar line of argument, but he may also have deliberately picked a theme which he knew would resonate with such northern auxiliaries as had remained firm. That he or his historian, George, was aware of the Armenian notion of military martyrdom is indicated by a telltale expression which has made its way into Theophanes' text: Heraclius is said to have drawn up the army for battle with *a radiant countenance*—a clear reminiscence, surely intentional on George's part, of that shining radiance which, according to Łazar P'arpets'i, marked out the faces of Armenians chosen for a martyr's death.[66]

The two armies faced each other in full battle array only a short distance apart for a whole day, from dawn to dusk. There was no fighting. Without exchanging a blow or submitting themselves to the hazard of orthodox, full-frontal combat, the Romans won another victory, entirely psychological this time. For all their superiority in numbers and Shahēn's determined, confident drive towards battle, the Persians dared not begin an engagement. When evening came, the Romans moved off, followed but not harried by the Persians. They were now setting off on the long march back to Asia Minor. Winter had come. A Persian attempt to speed ahead and cut them off ended in near disaster in marshy country. Well before they reached the district of P'artaw, the Romans turned south-west and cut directly through the mountainous canton of Cłukk' (the south-eastern segment of Karabakh) to the plain of Nakhchawan—a bold move bespeaking extraordinary

---

[64] R. Firestone, *Jihad: The Origin of Holy War in Islam* (Oxford, 1999), 47–65, 111–14, 127–34.
[65] Łazar P'arpets'i, *Patmut'iwn Hayots'*, ed. G. Ter-Mkrtch'ean and S. Malkhasean (Tbilisi, 1904), 60–73, 126–7, 128–30, 133–5, 144–5, 150–3, trans., R. W. Thomson, *The History of Łazar P'arpec'i* (Atlanta, GA, 1991).
[66] Łazar, 70, 134; Theoph., 311.2–4.

confidence in their ability to push aside local opposition in forbidding terrain when winter added to the risks. It can have done nothing to repair the morale of their pursuers.[67]

They forded the Araxes not far from Nakhchawan and then gained a clear day's lead by preventing the Persians from following suit immediately. This was probably achieved by a rearguard which held the right bank for a day and then caught up with the main army. They marched west to the plain of Bagrewand, where the Arsanias gathers its headwaters, then on to Apachounis farther down the Arsanias valley (with two large plains, those of modern Patnos and Manzikert). The Persian army followed, now under the sole command of Shahrbaraz. Shahen seems to have left, presumably on orders from Khusro, when the army reached the Araxes. He may have taken some troops with him. Certainly, the advance became more cautious as Shahrbaraz traversed the traditional Persian sector of Armenia in Heraclius' tracks, and Armenian volunteers were welcomed in large numbers. He pushed west and established himself in the district of Aliovit centred on the plain of Arčeš at the north-east angle of Lake Van. Apachounis seems to have formed a no-man's-land between the two armies, since Shahrbaraz was able, later, to station a forward unit there (at Ali).[68]

The village of Hrčmunk', where the Romans had set up their winter quarters, evidently lay farther west, almost certainly in the fertile plain of Taron (modern Muş), which commanded the northern outlet of the Bitlis pass and the lower valley of the river Arsanias. There, the necessary provisions could be obtained for winter, the plain of Taron being one of the two largest in the former Roman sector of Armenia, while control of the pass gave the Romans a choice of two routes for the continuation of their march west in the spring. They could either cross the Taurus to the upper Tigris basin and then aim for northern Syria and Cilicia or they could remain north of the mountains and aim directly for eastern Asia Minor beyond the Persian-held base of Melitene.

Winter did not prevent the two armies sparring. Shahrbaraz planned to attack the Romans with an elite force of 6,000 men (the figure given in the *History of Khosrov* may well be inflated) which he assembled at Arčeš. Heraclius got wind of this and made a pre-emptive strike with a carefully chosen body of cavalry (whose numbers are absurdly exaggerated in the Armenian account—to 20,000). A forward detachment of the Persian army sent to Ali was taken out in a swift night attack which achieved complete surprise. A single survivor brought the news to Shahrbaraz, whose initial angry incredulity soon vanished when the Romans attacked Arčeš from three sides (the fourth fronted the lake). He managed to

---

[67] Theoph., 311.4–9; ps.S, 125.14–15 (a notice which marks a leap forward of several months from one of the decisive battles fought earlier in 625 reported in the previous sentence (125.12–14)).

[68] Theoph., 311.9–12; ps.S., 125.16–23. Geography and extant monuments: T. A. Sinclair, *Eastern Turkey: An Architectural and Archaeological Survey*, 4 vols. (London, 1987–90), I, 271–96; Hewsen, *Armenia*, 90 (map 69, C4 and D4).

escape on horseback. His troops and headquarters staff fought as best they could, but were forced up onto the rooftops when the Romans set fire to the town. Casualties were high. Many perished in the fire; others were killed trying to escape from burning buildings. Those who survived were taken prisoner, along with a rich haul of booty.[69]

Much, perhaps rather too much, was made of this episode in the Official History, upon which both Theophanes and the Armenian history can be seen to be drawing. The narrative was lively: it included a vignette on Shahrbaraz's reception of the unwelcome messenger and gave a graphic account of the fighting; much play was made of Shahrbaraz's ignominious flight, naked and unshod according to Theophanes, on a sorry horse according to the *History of Khosrov*; he was said to have left his wives behind; pieces of his ceremonial equipment and dress uniform which were captured were carefully itemized.[70] But for all the propagandistic tone, surely an integral part of Heraclius' dispatch at the time, which had to buoy up spirits at home, we need not doubt that the victory was psychologically significant for both sides and that it led to a Persian withdrawal.[71]

Heraclius' successful attack on Shahrbaraz's headquarters and the retreat of the Persians are the last episodes of the 624–5 campaigns to be recorded. Nothing more is heard of either side until March 626, when winter was easing its grip on the mountains and elevated tablelands of Armenia. This pause between operations provides an opportunity to take stock of the Roman army's achievements over the two years of Heraclius' first counteroffensive.

It owed much of its success to its own capabilities—to skilful handling of weapons, to the flexibility and tensile strength of its constituent fighting units, above all to the powers of endurance instilled by intensive training and honed in field operations. This was an army which did not shy away from combat with considerably superior enemy forces in the open. Normally, though, it was able to avoid the risks inherent in such battles. For the Romans could, when they chose, accelerate with forced marches to a pace which the Persians could not match. Superior strategic mobility was the key to their success: it helped them to surprise and rout Khusro's expeditionary army without a fight in 624; it enabled them to pick off one by one the three armies deployed against them in 625; finally, it virtually guaranteed their safety as they marched home in late autumn and early winter that year, since both they and the Persians knew that they could always quicken their pace if the Persians drew too close.

The exemplary stamina of the Romans, both mental and physical, gave them two other advantages not normally enjoyed by the field armies of organized states. They were ready and able to continue operations beyond the end of the

---

[69] Theoph., 311.12–312.8; ps.S., 125.21–126.7.
[70] Theoph., 311.22–4, 312.1–3; ps.S., 126.3–5.   [71] Theoph., 312.6.

conventional campaigning season in both 624 and 625. Neither freezing weather (in 625) nor the prospect of snowfalls (as happened later, on the even more spectacular campaign of winter 627–8) was allowed to halt their movements. They were also undaunted by mountainous terrain, where their marching columns might be more vulnerable to guerrilla attacks. On three occasions during the counteroffensive of 624–5, as we have seen, they chose direct lines of march which took them through formidable highlands—on their first march north to P'artaw (through Karabakh), on their second march north to P'aytakaran over the mountains of northern Media, and on their final march west (across the southeastern segment of Karabakh).

Heraclius' contribution is probably only slightly overstated in the Official History. A prime task was to maintain morale at a high level. His speeches to meetings of officers and assemblies of troops were designed to enhance the natural commitment of soldiers on campaign to their cause by presenting that cause as religious as well as political and by giving each of them a strong personal incentive to fight to the last. His object was to infuse them with strong, religiously tinged emotion, as well as to rouse straightforward human anger by stressing all manner of atrocities committed by the enemy. His own presence, sharing their dangers and hardships, his leadership, and his actions also helped to keep up their spirits.[72] Even more important, though, was the strategic direction of the campaigns exercised by Heraclius with the advice of a council of senior officers. Much of the credit for the decisiveness, imagination, and boldness of Roman actions should be given to him, as also for the extraordinarily effective use made of deception.

But we should not forget the gruesome business of fighting itself, where another key to Roman success is to be found. Battles were not fought for their own sake. The object was not to demonstrate Roman superiority. They were not mere tests of courage and manhood. Some thirty years earlier the Emperor Maurice had reminded his generals in the field that the aim was to win at minimal risk and minimal cost.[73] Engagements were, therefore, only to be fought when the enemy had been manoeuvred into a losing position. The battle itself was but a transition between a phase of ordered movement of two opposing forces and a phase in which the defeated side, disordered, dispersing in flight, was an easy prey for the victors. The prime duty of the victorious Roman commander was to extract every possible military advantage from the second phase. A relentless pursuit was to be sustained. As many as possible of the enemy troops were to be hunted down and killed. As much damage as possible was to be inflicted on their fighting capability by diminishing their numbers and by scattering such units as still functioned far and wide. Regular references to the dispersal and prolonged

---

[72] Cf. Geo.Pis., *Expeditio*, iii.81–130.
[73] Mauricius, *Strategicon*, vii.A proem and 12, vii.B 12, ix.1.

pursuit of defeated Persian forces indicate that Heraclius was following these precepts and was seeking, at every available opportunity, to chip away at Persian fighting strength as well as Persian morale.

Heraclius' first counteroffensive was remarkably successful. Not only had he kept the Roman expeditionary force in being and reminded the Christians of Transcaucasia of Roman power, but he had also managed to cause extensive damage to a significant part of the Persian economy, had inflicted serious losses on Persian field forces, and had negotiated an alliance with the Turks. However, the Persians had achieved their main strategic objective, albeit at a heavy cost. Depleted in numbers they might be, mauled and disheartened, nonetheless they could still call on far superior military resources, and this eventually told on the Romans. At the onset of winter in 625, Heraclius had no choice but to retreat west. The *History to 682* gives but a short summary of the operations of 625, but the second of the sentences which is devoted to it catches the essence of the campaign: 'for although heavy blows struck the Persian forces, nevertheless they dislodged him [Heraclius], drove him out, and threw him back to his own country, and then occupied the cities which they had removed from him by force'.[74]

Shahen and Shahrbaraz did indeed succeed in expelling Heraclius from Transcaucasia, once they had combined forces and recovered from their initial defeats. As the Romans were driven farther and farther away from the frontiers of Persian territory proper (Atropatene and Media), the constraints on the Persian high command gradually eased. They regained the strategic initiative. They could begin planning and preparing for a new grand assault on the truncated Roman Empire in 626. That was why Shahen relinquished his directing role early in winter, when the Romans had been seen across the Arsanias and were hastening to leave the old Persian sector of Armenia. He was assigned the task of raising a large new army from all sections of the population of the Sasanian Empire.[75] Things would be looking grim for the Romans once spring came. Two great Persian armies would be poised to invade Asia Minor, while the Avars would be mobilizing their subject peoples for a direct grand assault on Constantinople itself.

Heraclius would need to show extraordinary fortitude if the east Roman Empire were to survive the gathering crisis. He would need once again to use every intellectual resource to deceive and distract his enemies. Above all, he would need to do the unexpected.

---

[74] MD, 133.9–11 (my translation).   [75] Theoph., 315.2–5.

8
Climax of the War

Apart from Heraclius' pre-emptive counterstrike against Shahrbaraz's headquarters, the winter of 625–6 was without incident. Shahrbaraz did not organize a reprisal commando raid, despite his need for a success which he, like Heraclius, might dress up as a major victory. His forward units, still stationed in the plain of Arčeš at the north-east angle of Lake Van, were within easy striking distance of the plain of Taron, where the whole of Heraclius' army was spending the winter. But the open, treeless country separating the two armies, its contours smoothed out by congealed lava flows spewed out in the deep geological past from the great volcanos hemming in Lake Van, was forbidding in the depths of the Armenian winter. Seldom, even by day, would the temperature rise above freezing in so exposed and elevated a region (the average height of western Armenia is 1,500 metres). Bitter winds would periodically rake the open landscape, sweeping over its thick covering of snow and forming deep drifts. Movement by small parties or larger predatory forces would be extremely hazardous. Winter, indeed, was the chief fracturing agent in Armenian history—months of isolation enforced on individual localities in a regular annual rhythm were the primary cause of Armenian particularism. The armies of the two great powers were being subjected to the same overwhelming natural forces.[1]

But there was no general seizing-up of Persian war preparations. Shahen, who seems to have left the united Persian forces pursuing Heraclius when they reached the Araxes and to have handed over the supreme command to Shahrbaraz, probably oversaw the new round of recruiting ordered by Khusro throughout the Sasanian Empire. Certainly it was he who later took charge of the new troops raised. It was a strenuous recruiting campaign, which, according to Theophanes (not drawing on the Official History in this case), affected foreigners (*xenoi*), citizens or townsmen (*politai*) and household retainers or slaves (*oiketai*).[2] It is tempting to speculate about each of these components: the foreigners could comprise Turkish federates settled on the steppe frontages of Iran by Khuso I,[3] as well as Iberians, Albanians, Armenians, and other small Transcaucasian peoples, not to mention Beduin tribesmen within the Sasanian sphere of influence; the cities

---

[1] For first-hand experience of winter 1876–7 in eastern Anatolia and western Armenia, see F. Burnaby, *On Horseback through Asia Minor* (London, 1898), 226–81. Statistics as of 1942: Naval Intelligence Division, *Geographical Handbook Series: Turkey*, 2 vols. (Oxford, 1942–3), I, 195–227.

[2] Theoph., 315.2–5.   [3] Cf. Rubin, 'The Reforms of Khusro Anūshirwān', 279–84.

The Last Great War of Antiquity. James Howard-Johnston, Oxford University (2021). © James Howard-Johnston.
DOI: 10.1093/oso/9780198830191.003.0009

which had developed into an important component of society in Iran proper as well as Mesopotamia in Late Antiquity were perhaps being required for the first time to supply fighting manpower, while aristocratic households were no longer exempt from the demands of war. Temptation, however, should probably be resisted. Too much should not be read into the language used by Theophanes. The phrasing and hence the categorizing may well be his. A similar classification of Romans surfaces in George of Pisidia's poem about the Avar siege of Constantinople in 626: he has Constantinopolitans, both citizens (*politai*) and foreigners (*xenoi*) respond with alacrity, like servants or slaves (*oiketai*), to instructions sent by Heraclius.[4] It is not inconceivable that Theophanes' phrasing is an unconscious reminiscence of the poet's language, since, as will be argued below (pp. 263–4), he probably knew and used the poem.

There is nothing implausible, however, in the implication that the Persian authorities put great effort into recruiting for the final phase of the war. A first grand offensive against Asia Minor, over which Khusro himself was to have exercised the supreme command, had ended in shambles when Heraclius launched his swift, unexpected, devastating counterattack in 624. But strategic control had eventually been wrested back, admittedly at considerable cost, in the complex operations of 625. By winter 625–6 Heraclius was boxed in, with little alternative but to withdraw west, shadowed by Shahrbaraz's army. Shahen's role was not so much to manage the recruiting drive (that was a task for provincial administrations throughout the empire) as to transform a mass of recruits into an effective fighting force. The process of recruitment was probably largely over when he took charge, having been initiated probably in the previous summer, as soon as the scale of Persian losses became known and the Roman expeditionary force had demonstrated its capability. He needed a hard core of experienced troops around which to organize his new army. These he received in large numbers (Theophanes gives the grossly inflated figure of 50,000 men), in the form of troops transferred from Shahrbaraz's command.[5] The new recruits were presumably subjected to intensive drilling and training exercises to prepare them for combat. By spring 626 they were ready for action and Shahen followed Shahrbaraz into Asia Minor, taking the direct northerly route through Armenia.

Meanwhile, in Europe, the Avars had been preparing for war on the grandest possible scale. Theodore Syncellus, an eyewitness of their attack on Constantinople in the summer of 626 who went on a delegation from the city to the khagan in the middle of the siege, claims that the khagan began to mobilize when he learned that Heraclius had set off on his campaign against the Persians (in 624). Contingents were raised from all the peoples under his control, those of the west and the north, as numerous as the sands of the seashore. The necessary materiel

---

[4] Geo.Pis., *Bellum Av.*, 293–301.   [5] Theoph., 315.4–6.

was assembled—weapons and armour, siege engines of all sorts, and shipping. As we have seen, there was nothing in the terms of the one-sided agreement reached after shock of the Avar attack in 623 to preclude the Avars from preparing at leisure to renew the war, and such was the scale on which they planned to do so, calling on the manpower of the full range of their subject peoples, deploying an impressive range of weaponry against the Roman capital, that they surely needed two years to do so.[6]

It is likely that Persians and Avars were in diplomatic contact and were coordinating their plans by 625, if not from the first, in summer 624. The initiative probably lay with the Persians, as it had probably done in 623. For they had every incentive to bring the European adversary of the Romans into play, with Heraclius on the rampage in their territory, in the hope that a renewed crisis in the west would once again pull him back to his capital. Besides which, their own deferred invasion of Asia Minor would be greatly aided if the Avars were advancing at the same time on Constantinople. In the course of 625, with a new recruiting drive under way and in the expectation of being able to execute the long-delayed attack on the last remaining Asian bastion of Roman power in massive force in 626, the Persians probably agreed a plan of joint action with the Avars.

The authorities and people of Constantinople could not but be aware of what was in store for them. Anxiety deepened as winter set in. A short, moving, masterly poem of George of Pisidia's captures the mood of the time. No aspersion, of course, could be cast on the competence of Bonus, the lay regent appointed to run affairs during Heraclius' absence (so George includes an ingenious conceit on the superiority of spiritual harmony, as between emperor and regent, over mere emotional love). The city was likened to a small child who might exasperate a parent (there had presumably been opposition, some of it perhaps too vociferous, to Heraclius' departure in 624) but who retains the parent's love. Heraclius' personal involvement in campaigning is praised, as it had to be (in language reminiscent, at one point, of the Saviour's sacrifice), with an extended medical metaphor. There are blunt appeals for him to return backed by the most persuasive tongues, those of his children.[7]

From his winter quarters in the plain of Taron, Heraclius was probably able to communicate with Constantinople, although there were human as well as natural hazards to be circumvented (Melitene and its hinterlands on both banks of the Euphrates were in Persian hands).[8] It is, therefore, more than possible that the regents sent him a report on the state of affairs at Constantinople and on what

---

[6] Geo.Pis., *Bellum Av.*, 197–201; Theod.Sync., *Hom.* I, 302.9–27; Theoph., 315.7–11; Nic., c.13.19–20.

[7] Geo.Pis., *In Bonum patricium*, ed. and trans. Pertusi, *Giorgio di Pisidia*, 163–70.

[8] Ps.S., 113.26–7, with *Hist.Com.*, n.32.

they knew of Avar preparations. This hypothetical report may or may not have been accompanied by a diplomatically phrased request for his return. It is unlikely, though, that George's poem was also sent. The emperor was invoked in the second person, but only after an initial address to Bonus. There is nothing to suggest that the poem was meant specially for his eyes. Rather, it reads like a public appeal to the absent emperor, the prime object being to assuage the anxieties of Constantinopolitans by reminding them of what the emperor had done and could do. What might have seemed injudicious in a direct appeal to the emperor, an incidental reference to George's familiar theme of heroic labour as atonement for sins (which could be taken to allude to Heraclius' recent marriage to his niece),[9] makes much better sense in this context. George would then be acting as the emperor's moral advocate in his capital.

Constantinople was in need of additional human and material defences and naturally looked to the emperor, as well as the regents, to provide them. Nothing would do more to improve the chances of successful resistance than the presence of the emperor himself. George assuredly spoke for all. Heraclius evidently recognized the perilous position of the capital, as he made military plans for the next campaigning season. There was no question of him disconcerting his adversaries by turning back and ravaging previously unscathed Persian territory. The alternatives canvassed in what the Official History presented as a single debate did not include a counter-thrust south-east into Mesopotamia or a march north along the relatively easy corridor skirting the eastern flank of the spreading mass of the Bingöl Dağ, which led into the heart of Persian Armenia and beyond into Iberia, where Heraclius might make contact with the Turkish invasion force expected in the summer. It was understood that emperor and army must march back to Roman territory. The only question was which route to take, the direct one down the Arsanias valley, where supplies would be scanty, or a longer, initially more difficult route via the plains south of the Armenian Taurus, where provisions would be readily available.[10]

The Persians were in a strong position. Not only was Heraclius' location known, but his general line of action (retreat westward) was predictable. Two armies were available for deployment against the Roman field army and its imperial commander. In contrast to 625, the fighting would take place on Roman territory. The two prime objectives of the Persians, the destruction of Roman military power and the conquest of what remained of the Roman Empire, could be pursued simultaneously. The forces involved were also much larger, since Persian strength had been increased after the recruiting drive and the Avars could bring to bear an army which, at a strength estimated by the Romans as 80,000 men, almost certainly surpassed the combined total of the

---

[9] Geo.Pis., *In Bonum*, 160–1.   [10] Theoph., 312.19–25.

forces fielded by the Persians in 625.[11] Finally, the hardened troops of Shahrbaraz were poised menacingly close to Heraclius' winter quarters in Taron. They would be able to pursue him closely, ready to attack if at any point his line of retreat was blocked.

The Persians did not, however, plan to take more than a symbolic part in the coming siege of Constantinople. Of this we can be certain. For they did not mobilize by sea. They did not assemble a fleet of transport vessels at their forward naval base in Rhodes (captured in 623) for dispatch north through the Aegean under strong naval escort. And without such a fleet, there was no possibility of Persian land forces making any significant contribution to siege operations against Constantinople. This was a decision voluntarily taken rather than forced on the Persian high command. For by no means all the seamen and ships would have fled from the ports of the Roman Levant at the approach of Persian forces. The high command would have had little difficulty in gathering a fleet which could hold its own against such naval forces as could be deployed in defence of Constantinople. Nor was any great leap of ideological imagination required for Persians to conceive of launching a naval offensive. The Sasanian Empire, it must be remembered, was a great maritime power which exercised a dominating influence on the commerce and commercial politics of the Indian Ocean.[12]

Two reasons for this decision may be surmised. First and foremost, the Avars were capable of taking Constantinople on their own. They had little need of reinforcements or additional siege equipment from the Persians. Drawing on all their subject peoples, they were able to mobilize an army as large as any fielded by either of the great sedentary empires in late antiquity, while their siege technology, which included Chinese lever artillery, was as advanced as that of the Persians and Romans.[13] Second, the Persians had no interest in extending their sphere of operations into Europe. The ambitious war aims which Khusro had formulated ten years before, on the occasion of receiving the Roman Senate's grovelling plea for peace in the winter of 615–16, would be achieved once Asia Minor was in Persian hands and the Roman field army had been destroyed. The Roman Empire would have ceased to exist. The Avars could be left to mop up in Europe and to do what they would with Constantinople. A future partition of Roman territory along these lines, giving a free hand to the Avars in Europe, was probably agreed when the two sides were planning their joint offensive. This was clearly implied by the khagan in the course of a final round of negotiations with a deputation from Constantinople, when he advised the defenders of Constantinople to aban-

---

[11] Geo.Pis., *Bellum Av.*, 217–19.
[12] Cf. J.-F. Salles, 'Fines Indiae, Ardh el-Hind. Recherches sur le devenir de la mer Erythrée', in E. Dąbrowa, ed., *The Roman and Byzantine Army in the East* (Cracow, 1994), 165–87, at 175–84; J. Howard-Johnston, 'The India Trade in Late Antiquity', in E. W. Sauer, ed., *Sasanian Persia between Rome and the Steppes of Eurasia* (Edinburgh, 2017).
[13] Chevedden et al., 'The Traction Trebuchet'.

don the city and their properties to him and to cross over the Bosporus to Shahrbaraz.[14]

The principal assignment of the two Persian armies deployed in Asia Minor was to destroy Roman military power. Once that was achieved, Persian forces would have little difficulty in occupying Asia Minor and snuffing out any local resistance. Their strategy was to drive Heraclius westward, deeper and deeper into Asia Minor, where his freedom of manoeuvre would be restricted by the surrounding seas and it would be easier than in 625 to concentrate both Persian forces against him. The most likely scenario was one in which Heraclius rushed to the defence of his threatened capital. Closely pursued by Shahrbaraz and his battle-hardened troops, he would not have the time to ferry more than a small proportion of his forces across the Bosporus. The main body would be left trapped with the sea at their back, weakened in numbers and morale, as a relatively easy prey for Shahrbaraz and, when he arrived, Shahen. Constantinople might or might not weather the Avar storm. Even if it did, though, Heraclius would be unable to carry on the war with the Persians, and it would not be long before the Avars overwhelmed the inadequate forces defending his Balkan possessions and closed in again on his isolated capital. Were he to survive that long, his only course would be to flee, discredited, an emperor only in name, to what remained of his central Mediterranean possessions.

8.1 Pursuit of Heraclius

It is now time to leave these interconnected conjectures and return to the document-based narrative which Theophanes extracted from George of Pisidia's Official History of Heraclius' Persian campaigns. Not that I apologize for including such conjectures in a work of history. For the historian's task is not simply that of documenting what happened but of understanding and explaining it, and a crucial part of the explanation can only be obtained by setting contingent outcomes against what was planned or is likely to have been planned by the principal active historical agents. Some account must be taken of mental as well as material circumstances, of attitudes and ideals as well as physical environments, if structures (social, economic, institutional) are being investigated. If fast-moving processes are being examined, with a variety of dynamic forces in play, it is yet more important to attend to the contributions, rational and irrational, of the human mind. In the case of warfare on the grand scale, with a number of distinct belligerent parties involved, it is essential to follow the shafts of intention emanating from each of those parties and, a much more delicate task, to trace out the

---

[14] *Chron.Pasch.*, 721.14–21; Theod.Sync., *Hom.* I, 306.36–307.1. Cf. Nic., c.13.11–13 (division of operational spheres in 626).

predictions of each party about the intentions of the others. The narrative of events then becomes a narrative of conflicting intentions, the denouement of which depends as much on the intelligence of individual parties as on the brute force which they can marshal. The greatest generals, like the greatest financiers in the modern world, understand the workings of the minds of their opponents and then move onto a higher, more detached plane. Their plans become meta-plans which anticipate and exploit the surmised intentions of their opponents. Surprise or shock become devastating weapons of war, and can offset greatly superior material resources.

What, then, was planned by Heraclius at the approach of spring 626? The prospect was bleak. Somehow he had to keep his army in being, to reinforce the defences of Constantinople, and to impede the Persian takeover of Asia Minor. These three tasks were surely beyond the capacity of a single small army, even under a commander of genius. The only gleam of hope was faint and remote. The Turkish attack on Transcaucasia planned for the summer would have no effect on operations far to the west that year.

Heraclius had little choice but to continue his withdrawal west as soon as movement became possible. The only issue which he debated with his staff was whether to stay north or to cut south of the Armenian Taurus.[15] Of the superiority of the northern route, designated the route to Tarantum, there could be no doubt, despite a shortage of supplies. It was much the shorter of the two. The first section, between the north-west edge of the plain of Taron and Anzitene, could be crossed in swift marches, easy hill passages separating a series of plains in the valley of the river Arsanias. There were only two natural obstacles to be surmounted, the Euphrates separating Anzitene from Melitene, and the subsequent ascent to the Anatolian plateau. The obvious route beyond the plain of Melitene, that of the long-established southern support road through the Anti-Taurus, was not considered, presumably because the eastern stages, where it cut through rugged country to reach the inner basin around Arabissus, were under the firm control of the units garrisoning Melitene (captured by Shahen in 617). Instead, debate focused on an unpaved route well to the north which, in its first stage, followed where it could, and circumvented where it had to, the narrow valley and gorges carved out by the river Tohma.[16]

Tarantum (modern Darende), which commanded the north-west end of this difficult section, was probably singled out as the most forward Roman-held position on this route. The fortifications (of which very little survives) on a massive rock which forms a natural citadel above the modern settlement were probably refurbished in the course of the war, when its eastern counterparts in or near the

---

[15] Theoph., 312.19–25.
[16] Nav.Int.Div., *Turkey*, I, 282–5; F. Hild, *Das byzantinische Strassensystem in Kappadokien*, TIB 2, Österr. Ak. Wiss., Phil.-hist. Kl., Denkschriften 131 (Vienna,1977), 84–103.

Arsanias valley, at Mazgırt, Palu, and Bağın (refortified probably in the run-up to Justin II's war) had fallen into Persian hands.[17] The easier second stage of the ascent was overseen by a late Roman fortress known as Şerefiye on the edge of the open Uzun Yayla. It was a purpose-built cavalry base set in a plain with abundant pasture and with a ready supply of water in the stream which transects the site, its function being to back Tarantum and secure the eastern approaches to Cappadocia.[18]

The Tarantum route was plainly preferable. The return march would be swift and relatively safe (the chief impediment being the Persian garrison, doubtlessly reinforced, at Melitene). However, Heraclius, with the full agreement of his staff, chose the more circuitous and undoubtedly more hazardous southern alternative. The main reason, according to the Official History, was a comparative abundance of provisions, but two important subsidiary considerations probably influenced the decision. There were many more natural obstacles to be surmounted on the southern Syrian route. The army would have to cross two difficult passes gouged out of the eastern and western ends of the range of mountains extending from Lake Van to Rough Cilicia. The rich plains to the south of the mountains, where supplies were plentiful, were transected by five major rivers—Nymphius (modern Batman Su), Tigris, Euphrates, Pyramus (Ceyhan), and Sarus (Seyhan). At each river there was a danger that Heraclius' army might be halted and caught by Shahrbaraz's larger pursuing force. The Syrian route was undoubtedly the more dangerous, but that was precisely its attraction for Heraclius, since it would lead Shahrbaraz to exclude it as a possible line of Roman retreat. By taking it, Heraclius would once again surprise and disconcert his opponent, gaining a valuable head start while Shahrbaraz rejigged his plans and regrouped his men.

A second subsidiary consideration probably carried more weight. If Roman authority were ever to be restored to the occupied Roman Levant, the empire must continue to exist in the minds of former provincials, many of whom had now been subjected to Persian rule for well over a decade. They must be convinced that there was a real prospect of Roman forces driving out the intrusive foreign power within the foreseeable future. While ideological inertia ensured that attachment to a Roman, Christian empire remained strong and Roman propaganda sought to intensify it, nothing would do more to turn such attachment into an active, corrosive agent in the occupied Roman Levant than the reappearance of the Roman emperor at the head of a victorious Roman army. The

---

[17] Taranton, also spelled Taranta: F. Hild and M. Restle, *Kappadokien (Kappadokia, Charsianon, Sebasteia und Lykandos)*, TIB 2, Österr. Ak. Wiss., Phil.-hist. Kl., Denkschriften 149 (Vienna, 1981), 290–1; Sinclair, *Eastern Turkey*, II, 499–504. Eastern counterparts: J. Howard-Johnston, 'Procopius, Roman Defences North of the Taurus and the New Fortress of Citharizon', in D. H. French and C. S. Lightfoot, eds., *The Eastern Frontier of the Roman Empire*, BAR Int. Ser. 553 (Oxford, 1989), 203–29, at 221–3 and 227 (n.27), repr. in Howard-Johnston, *East Rome*, no.II.

[18] Sinclair, *Eastern Turkey*, II, 456–9. Cf. Howard-Johnston, 'Military Infrastructure', 8.

process of dismantling Persian rule would then begin where it must begin, in the minds of Roman provincials. Persian authority would still be accepted. Local elites would collaborate, if only to preserve their assets. But they would be waiting, with genuine hope, for the restoration of the familiar Roman order, for the time when they could transfer their loyalty openly. At that moment, Persian authority would become a mere phantasm and almost certainly would fade swiftly away.

Theophanes recycles, in summary form, the Official History's account of Heraclius' march back to Asia Minor. There is one notable gap, where he has dropped material, and a couple of other mistakes, where he has transposed place-names, thereby making a nonsense of two stages in the march.[19] These slips are intelligible on the part of an author who was condensing his source and had no personal knowledge of the geography of northern Syria, a region which had been under Arab rule for a century and a half by the time of writing. If allowance is made for these errors, the opening operations of 626 may be reconstructed as follows.

The Roman army set off on 1 March 626, before winter had loosened its grip. Once again, Heraclius was stretching a campaigning season beyond its natural limit and thereby stealing several marches on a more conventional adversary who was not ready for action so early. He followed the most direct route south-west from Taron over a high, windswept saddle to Bitlis, then down the long narrow cleft cut by the river Bitlis which led to the upper Tigris basin.[20] His troops, already accustomed to winter operations, made their way in good time through the heavy snow filling the pass, and then, crossing the fertile, undulating plain of north Mesoptamia, passed Martyropolis (on the direct route from the southern outlet of the Bitlis pass to Amida, but misplaced by Theophanes after the Tigris) and reached the Tigris, where Amida, the chief city of the region, stood on the opposite bank. Encountering no resistance from the city, they crossed over to the right bank and halted for recuperation after seven days of strenuous marching. Their safety was assured not only by the long head start which they had over their Persian pursuers but also by the river, which sheltered them against attack from the east.[21]

Heraclius had time to compose and send off a dispatch with all his news, which caused much jubilation when it was received in Constantinople.[22] Theophanes' phrase 'all his news' might suggest that this was the first dispatch from the field

---

[19] Gap: Theoph., 313.6 (Heraclius is marching east against Shahrbaraz, crosses the river Nymphius (Batman Su) and then reaches the Euphrates, far to the west). Transpositions: the Tigris is mentioned before Martyropolis, which lay close to the southern outlet of the Bitlis pass (Theoph., 312.22–3); the same mistake occurs when he comes to Cilicia, Adana, which lay on the west bank of the river Sarus, being mentioned before the river (Theoph., 313.13–14).
[20] Nav.Int.Div., *Turkey*, I, 172–4, 188–90.   [21] Theoph., 312.25–9.
[22] Theoph., 312.30–313.2.

which Heraclius had been able to send since his departure from Constantinople. It seems much more likely, though, that it was merely the latest instalment, covering the first stage of his homeward march (and probably his winter exploits against Shahrbaraz). The news that he was returning (together with an itemized account of the haul of booty gathered from Shahrbaraz's headquarters) would be more than enough to explain its effect in Constantinople. We have already found indirect evidence in George of Pisidia's *In Bonum* that Heraclius had been in touch with the Constantinopolitan authorities at some stage in the previous winter—in which case he had surely taken care to slip a messenger across south-west Armenia with an account of the dramatic events of the 625 campaign, probably having done the same for 624 with a dispatch sent across Iberia, Lazica, and the Black Sea, from his winter quarters on the lower Kur. Regular communications feeding the capital and what remained of the empire with news of successes in the field were absolutely vital if morale were to be sustained at home.

Shahrbaraz evidently took some time to mobilize his forces and take up the pursuit. When he did so, Heraclius sprang his second surprise by turning back from his secure position at Amida and preparing to engage the Persian troops beyond the river Nymphius as they emerged from the southern end of the Bitlis Pass. A detachment was sent north to guard the other passes over the Armenian Taurus, so as to prevent the Persians from outflanking Heraclius' main force.[23] Theophanes says nothing about the outcome of these manoeuvres, but jumps to a later episode (still in March), when the Roman army, plainly intact after what had probably been a successful counterattack, reached the Euphrates upstream from Samosata only to find that the bridge of boats which it was planning to use had been removed to the far side on Shahrbaraz's orders. Heraclius managed to find a ford and to convey his army across before the spring flood could bar his passage. His route now took him past Samosata, over the southern outliers of the Anti-Taurus and the plain of Germanicia which they enclose, into the Cilician plain and across the bridges over the rivers Pyramus and Sarus.[24]

Shahrbaraz, after putting the bridge of boats back in place, gradually closed the gap and caught up with the Romans at the Sarus. The Romans, however, had safely crossed to Adana on the far side (mistakenly placed east of the river by Theophanes) and held the bridge over it. There, Heraclius is reported to have rested his men. As at Amida, they were shielded from attack by an impenetrable line of riverine defence. He thus transformed a potential hazard into a Roman asset. He may even have allowed the Persians to catch up (Theophanes' phrasing suggests that he allowed his men plenty of time to rest), planning to surprise the

---

[23] Theoph., 313.2–6.
[24] Theoph., 313.6–14. Route: Nav.Int.Div., *Turkey*, I, 152–4, 156–8, fig.34; F. Hild and H. Hellenkemper, *Kilikien und Isaurien*, TIB 5, Österr. Ak. Wiss., Phil.-hist. Kl., Denkschriften 215 (Vienna, 1990), I, 132–3, II, pl.11, 12, 15, 27. Bridges: Procopius., *De aedificiis*, v.5.4–13.

Persian army with a counterattack as it approached the river. In the event, things nearly went wrong when the Roman troops who sallied out pressed their attack too far and good order was lost, which allowed the Persians to fight their way onto the bridge. Heraclius is portrayed in the Official History as playing a heroic part in the melee that followed, rousing Sharhbaraz's admiration: he strikes a gigantic adversary and flings him into the river, thus instigating a disorderly retreat over the narrow bridge from which other Persians are forced to jump like frogs; he then takes the lead in the fighting, which succeeds in securing once again the eastern end of the bridge for the Romans. Whatever happened in reality has been highly embellished in this scene, one of many in which George turns the spotlight on Heraclius.[25]

The outcome of the fighting, which lasted a whole day, was that desired by Heraclius. Shahrbaraz's army was demoralized and retreated during the night. Heraclius made good use of this psychological advantage and the time which it had gained him. His army marched unimpeded, unharassed, through the most formidable of the natural obstacles on this southern Syrian route, the long passage between vertiginous cliffs known as the Cilician Gates, from which a pass then led over the Taurus.[26] Once he reached its northern end near Podandus, he took the right-hand fork leading towards Caesarea, and beyond to Sebastea in the north-east angle of the Anatolian plateau.[27] By thus veering away from the direct road to Constantinople, he was making another move likely to disconcert Shahrbaraz. Instead of hastening to the defence of his threatened capital, he was remaining in the field and by doing so was posing a dilemma for Shahrbaraz. He could continue his march on Constantinople, but with the risk of harassing attacks from the Heraclius' troops. Or he could hunt down the emperor and the last Roman field army, but at the cost of delaying his scheduled advance on Constantinople. If he chose the former course, Heraclius would gain another welcome respite for his men; if the latter, the threat to Constantinople would be diminished. In the event, Shahrbaraz took the road to Constantinople, and Heraclius stayed put for the moment at Sebastea. It was still early in the campaigning season, probably towards the end of April or the beginning of May.

From Caesarea, where he had probably halted, or possibly as soon as he emerged from the Cilician Gates, Heraclius took action to reinforce Constantinople. He sent off a large swift-moving detachment to boost the number of professional soldiers among the defenders. By accelerating ahead of Shahrbaraz's army, they were able to complete the crossing of the Bosporus unhindered. They brought written instructions from Heraclius: detailed advice was given about strengthening the foundations and outworks of the walls; wicker

---

[25] Theoph., 313.14–314.18.
[26] Nav.Int.Div., *Turkey*, I, 150-2, pl.68 and 70; Hild, *Strassensystem*, 57–9, pl.24 and 26.
[27] Theoph., 314.18-22; ps.S., 126.6-7.

protective screens were to be made for the archers; advice was also given about the construction of artillery and the deployment of the warships which had been built some time before as a precautionary measure. These instructions were probably accompanied by a dispatch bringing the capital up to date about events in the field, from which George of Pisidia later drew his detailed information about operations following the army's departure from Amida.[28]

Although there is nothing to indicate that Heraclius was already aware of Shahen's movements (at this early stage in the campaigning season, Shahen may well have only just assembled his army, probably in Atropatene and, almost certainly, was still far from Roman-held territory), he must surely have suspected that at least one other Persian army would be entering the fray before long. Caesarea was a good base from which to monitor Persian military activity. A watch could be kept on all the principal routes leading from Cilicia, northern Syria, and western Armenia into Asia Minor. When, in due course, intelligence was received that Shahen was taking the northern (Araxes-Euphrates) route through Armenia and would be entering the north-east angle of the Anatolian plateau, Heraclius and his somewhat shrunken force moved north to Sebastea, from where they could, if they dared, intercept Shahen's great army.

8.2 Information, Confusion, and Disinformation in the Chronicle of Theophanes

There we must take leave of Heraclius for the moment, to take stock of the raw materials from which the history of the main part of next two campaigning seasons must be constructed. For our surest guide, the Official History, as retailed in abridged but relatively continuous form by Theophanes, gives out for sixteen months or so—from the point at which Shahrbaraz withdrew temporarily after the battle of the Sarus bridge (probably in the second half of April 626) to September 627, when Heraclius entered Atropatene at the head of his hardened troops. It is only from September 627 that the method used to reconstruct Heraclius' first counteroffensive can be employed once again to establish a solid core of *histoire événementielle*—namely, careful elucidation and analysis of the detailed narrative provided by Theophanes, care being taken to identify geographical slips and unannounced leaps forward through time.

It is hard to say why Theophanes abandoned what was undoubtedly his soundest source once he had Heraclius safely on the last leg of his journey back to Asia Minor. It is conceivable that the Official History itself gave out soon after this point. If so, it must have been narrowly focused on Heraclius' two

---

[28] Geo.Pis., *Bellum Av.*, 266–92. Cf. Theod.Sync., *Hom.* I, 303.33–304.4.

counteroffensives and must have passed over the intervening defensive phase (lasting from late April 626 to summer 627) in complete silence. We would then have to envisage it as comprising two distinct texts, which we might designate *Persian Expeditions* II and III. It is much more likely, though, that Theophanes, whose appetite for the details of military history was limited, sought out the most economical way of dealing with the complex events of 626 and then saved space by skipping over most of the following year's events to home in on the decisive phase of Heraclius' second counteroffensive in autumn and winter 627-8. He may or may not have read or glanced through the intervening section of the Official History. His policy here, as elsewhere (for example in his highly selective use of Procopius' *Wars*), was simply to set aside a rich but voluminous narrative if there was more conveniently packaged material to hand in other available sources.[29] In this case, he may also have been swayed by the combined testimony of two sources, both previously used by him and both much more compact than the Official History. For, as will be suggested below (pp. 262-5), it appears that the second continuation of John of Antioch's chronicle and the chronicle of Theophilus of Edessa each independently presented a scenario quite at odds with that given by the Official History.

Despite the temporary failure of our chief source, much of the military and diplomatic history of 626-7 can be filled in, often in remarkable detail, on the basis of the testimonies of several other sources of demonstrable worth. A contemporary document reproduced and slightly retouched by the *Chronicon Paschale* was almost certainly a report written immediately after the event by the Patriarch Sergius for dispatch to Heraclius. It presents a detailed day-by-day account of the siege of Constantinople and associated diplomatic activity, only marred by a long lacuna covering the three and half days in which the final general assault was prepared and launched. It supplies internally consistent dates which anchor the siege in the ten days between 29 July and 7 August 626. It can be supplemented from two other eyewitness accounts, (1) the long sermon composed by the Syncellus Theodore for delivery, probably soon after the end of the siege, at a service of thanksgiving, and (2) George of Pisidia's narrative poem, the *Bellum Avaricum*, which includes several variations and embellishments on themes introduced by Theodore. A fourth view, dating from half a generation or so later, was provided by the second continuation of John of Antioch, which was recycled by the Patriarch Nicephorus in his *Short History*.[30]

The *History to 682* gives a date, the beginning of Khusro's thirty-seventh regnal year (June 626-June 627), for the first military intervention by the Turks in the

---

[29] Theophanes only makes use of Procopius for a lengthy précis of the Vandal wars (186-216 based on *Bella*, iii-iv) and summaries of two years' campaigning on the eastern front, in 503 and 542 (145-7 and 219-22, based on *Bella*, i.8-9 and ii.20-9). Without pithier material to hand, Theophanes makes more extensive use of the *Historiae* of Theophylact Simocatta for the period 571/2-602/3 (245-91).

[30] *Chron.Pasch.*, 716.9-726.10; Theod.Sync., *Hom.* I; Geo.Pis., *Bellum Av.*; Nic., c.13.

war. It also retails the substance of diplomatic notes exchanged by Turks and Persians almost certainly in summer 626.[31] There follows a blank period of a year or so. The next event to be registered—by the *History to 682*, the *Georgian Chronicles*, Nicephorus (as before, transmitting material from the second continuation of John of Antioch), and Theophanes (in what looks like a highly condensed and isolated extract from the Official History)—was the summit meeting between Heraclius and the *yabghu khagan* of the Turks held outside Tiflis, capital of Iberia.[32] Vital dating information (Khusro's thirty-eighth regnal year, June 627–June 628) is again supplied by the *History to 682*, which, along with the *Georgian Chronicles*, sketches in the military context, a second Turkish invasion of Transcaucasia culminating in a first, unsuccessful siege of Tiflis.[33]

The fullest account of subsequent operations in Heraclius' second counteroffensive is to be found in Theophanes' version of the Official History, which can be supplemented, on some points of detail, by material of Persian origin (deriving from the *Khwadaynamag*) transmitted by a wide variety of eastern sources (Armenian, Syrian, and Arab). Rock-solid dates for the deposition and execution of Khusro II (24 and 28 February 628) are provided by the text of Heraclius' final victory dispatch, which was read out from the ambo in St Sophia and is incorporated whole into the *Chronicon Paschale*. It is then possible confidently to date Heraclius' second counteroffensive, which triggered a political revolution in the Sasanian Empire, to the immediately preceding months (September 627–February 628).[34]

The chronological framework of the turbulent final phase of the war is thus firmly established, as is the outline and, in two cases (the siege of Constantinople and the fall of Khusro), much of the detail of its principal episodes. But there are two important exceptions. None of the sources enumerated above, apart from Theophanes in two passages of unknown provenance, reports the recruiting drive overseen by Shahen or the outcome of his invasion of Asia Minor in 626—although the fate of the Roman Empire hinged on how Heraclius' depleted army fared when it encountered the far larger force commanded by Shahen. Theophanes is also our prime source on Heraclius' movements in the year or so separating his return to Asia Minor in 626 and his reappearance in Iberia in late summer 627. Since Heraclius' supple, innovative strategic thinking had played and would play a decisive part in ensuring the success of his small expeditionary army, and since the alliance which he had negotiated with the Turks depended in large measure on his direct involvement, it is important to try to track his movements through this apparently blank period.

---

[31] MD, 133.16–134.18, 142.8–143.20 (trans. Dowsett, 81–3, 87–8).
[32] MD, 137.20–138.4 (trans. Dowsett, 85); Nic., c.12.19–40; Theoph., 316.4–13.
[33] MD, 135.5–140.14 (trans. Dowsett, 83–6). Cf. *Georgian Chronicles*, 233–4.
[34] See Chapter 9.

Our chief witness, Theophanes, has a most implausible, indeed incredible story to tell: Heraclius, who has been careful to concentrate his small force and use it to deliver separate sharp blows against his adversaries in detail during the 625 campaign, *divides his army in three*, when he reaches the comparative safety of Asia Minor. One part is the detachment which we know, from George of Pisidia, was sent to bolster the defences of Constantinople. The weakened force which he retains is then split into two, the larger portion being assigned to his brother Theodore with orders to engage Shahen, the smaller being taken off by Heraclius, *who sets off there and then for Transcaucasia*. In this scenario, Heraclius is made to commit military suicide by dissipating his limited military resources and is spirited away to Transcaucasia, where he can exercise no direct influence over the outcome of the siege of Constantinople or over the campaign in Asia Minor.[35]

Theophanes has conjured up an extraordinary scenario. It should be rejected out of hand for two main reasons (apart from its intrinsic implausibility). First, we know on the authority of the three extant eyewitness accounts of the siege of Constantinople that Heraclius, although far away, followed events at Constantinople and stayed in touch with the regents. He remained, we may infer, *within relatively easy communicating distance of the city, before, during, and after the siege*. Thus, he was able to send detailed instructions beforehand, and later, in a period of anxious suspense, had no doubt that news of the city's fate would reach him and scanned roads and sea for the messengers who would be bringing it. When eventually he learned that both the city and the peoples entrusted by God to his care were safe, he was able to send a reply, which duly reached the city. The messengers who delivered it could report how the emperor had rushed to a church of the Virgin and Mother of God to pray that the news be good when its arrival was imminent, and how he had knelt down before the army and the people who were with the troops (surely Roman provincials) to thank God and the Virgin when he received it.[36] Second, weak though arguments from silence are, it is surely striking that no Transcaucasian source drops a hint of Heraclius' presence in the region, let alone reports any action, military or diplomatic, of his between late autumn 625 and late summer 627. Heraclius is referred to in the diplomatic interchange between Khusro and the Turkish *shad* who invaded Albania in 626, but as an absent third party.

It may be concluded with a fair degree of confidence that Heraclius continued to direct operations in Asia Minor in the summer of 626. He it was, rather than his brother Theodore (as alleged by Theophanes), who managed to deal with Shahen's army. Although there is no positive corroboration to be had from any of the reputable sources, there is no reason to discard Theophanes' notice about the

---

[35] Theoph., 315.11–16.
[36] Theod.Sync., *Hom.* I, 302.28–30, 303.33–304.4, 319.27–320.9; Geo.Pis., *Bellum Av.*, 266–306.

battle, fought at an unspecified location in Asia Minor, in which a hailstorm helped the Roman forces inflict a crushing defeat on Shahen.[37] For Shahen's army had no influence on events on the Bosporus. There is no hint, in accounts of the siege of Constantinople, of the approach of a second Persian army. They merely report that Heraclius was continuing his strenuous campaigning against Persian forces (Shahen's surely) elsewhere. News of Shahen's defeat might, however, account for Shahrbaraz's early withdrawal very soon after the Avars broke off the siege. As for Shahen himself, he is never heard of again. He plays no part in the operations of 627. Death or disgrace (or both, as alleged by Theophanes) would best account for his disappearance.[38]

Once the Persians had been driven out of Asia Minor, it may be postulated that Heraclius returned to Constantinople. Lack of reported action on his part in the field in the last months of 626 and the first half of 627 is best explained by his presence back in the capital. There, of course, many matters required his attention. Apart from a natural concern to have the regency council account for its actions and to breathe for himself the political atmosphere at home, there were vital diplomatic tasks to be undertaken. Disarray in the Avar Empire caused by the disaster before Constantinople invited the Romans to launch a political counteroffensive and, under its cover, to begin reasserting their authority in the Balkans. Heraclius surely wished to direct this diplomatic activity himself, since it would have a vital bearing on the outcome of the war. It was yet more important for him to take charge of negotiations with the Turks, since it was he who had initiated them and his prestige was likely to carry much weight with them.

Theophanes has deformed history badly in the account which he concocted of the events of 626. It is not only that he spirits Heraclius away from Asia Minor and transfers the credit for the crucial victory won over Shahen to his brother. Much else has gone wrong, horribly wrong.

The first of these other mistakes results from Theophanes' improvised solution to a problem of his own making. Since the whole of Heraclius' first counteroffensive has been pushed one year too early, it has been disconnected by a full year from the events of summer 626. On Theophanes' chronology, Heraclius completes his withdrawal in *spring 625*. But the date of the siege of Constantinople was well known (surely impressed on the collective Constantinopolitan memory and recorded in church documents). Theophanes then has to bridge a gap of some fourteen months between Heraclius' return (by the end of April 625) and the appearance of the Avar vanguard before the city (the end of June 626). He does so by the simple but arbitrary expedient of *sending Heraclius and his whole, undivided army into winter quarters, as soon as he reaches Sebastea* (i.e. at the end of spring).[39]

---

[37] Theoph., 315.16–22.   [38] Theoph., 315.23–6.   [39] Theoph., 314.21–3.

Nothing whatsoever then happens for a year, until Heraclius divides his army in three and goes off to Transcaucasia. A great deal is then packed into 626. *For Theophanes brings forward the start of Heraclius' second counteroffensive by a year.* The main episodes of the two campaigns are interleaved. Shahen's defeat in Asia Minor (626) is followed by Heraclius' meeting with the *yabghu khagan* outside Tiflis (in the second half of 627), which is followed in turn by the Avar siege of Constantinople (626). Heraclius' invasion of Mesopotamia (autumn 627) is then reported, much of it in great detail (taken from the Official History), in the year entry running from September 626 to August 627. Finally, to complete the confusion, Shahrbaraz remains on the Asian shore of the Bosporus in full view of Constantinople *after the end of the siege of Constantinople, until the end of the following winter.*[40] This has the effect of keeping him there until Heraclius threatens the Persian capital (January–February 627, on Theophanes' chronology). Naturally, an urgent summons for the army to return is sent by Khusro, but this is intercepted and doctored so as to alienate the army from Khusro's regime.[41]

We need have little compunction about disregarding Theophanes' assertion about Heraclius' movements in 626, given the other serious errors discernible in the same year entry. The errors are not the product of carelessness. Considerable thought has gone into the concoction which is produced. Theophanes is plainly anxious to make sure that his account reads smoothly, that there are no internal contradictions. But a heavy price is paid for this narrative coherence. He mauls the material provided by his sources. If, as seems probable, the Official History covered Heraclius' actions in the field in 626, he treats its information in the most cavalier manner imaginable—either ignoring it or grossly distorting it. He invents an imaginary winter and then foreshortens the dramatic history of the last two years of the war, in an apparently arbitrary act of extraordinary editorial boldness.

Theophanes was, we know, ready to take editorial initiatives and to rework his source materials, especially if questions of faith were at stake. He could also take considerable liberties with chronology, as, for example, with his uprooting of the surprise Avar attack on Heraclius from its proper place.[42] But the muddle he introduces into his account of the years 626 and 627 is so great that some explanation is required beyond a general propensity to tamper with his sources and to achieve a given level of smooth consistency. It is worth asking whether he may have been led into error by some of the material which reached him, editorial initiatives of his own then playing a secondary role and compounding the mistakes transmitted to him.

All the mistakes of Theophanes' narrative of 626, bar the invented winter and the details of the story of the letter sent to Shahrbaraz, are to be found in the *Short*

---

[40] Theoph., 315.16–316.27.   [41] Theoph., 319.22–5, 323.22–324.16.
[42] Mango and Scott, *Chronicle of Theophanes*, xci–xcv; Howard-Johnston, *Witnesses*, 279–84, 295–306; Avar surprise: see Section 6.3.

History composed some forty years earlier by his contemporary, Nicephorus, in his youth. The events of 626 and 627–8 are interleaved in the same way (although Nicephorus has no knowledge of Shahen's army and its fate). Heraclius is far away, first in Lazica, later in Iberia, while Shahrbaraz remains for a long time on the Bosporus (Khusro duly orders him home, but the letter is intercepted and doctored by the Romans, but in a different way).[43] While there is no evidence that Theophanes was aware of Nicephorus' text, he made use, rather sparing use, of Nicephorus' principal or sole source for the first part of his chronicle. This source, identifiable as a second continuation of the chronicle of John of Antioch, was written in the mid-640s, when memories of the last Roman-Persian war may have been occluded by an immediate past in which the familiar world order had collapsed in the face of Arab attack.[44] At any rate, to judge by the version recycled by Nicephorus, the anonymous author was responsible for the foreshortening of the final climactic phase of the war which added considerably to its drama. It is, therefore, tempting to suggest that Theophanes' structuring of his material was modelled on that of the continuation, his understanding of the interrelationship between events being shaped by it.

However, there is no clear evidence that he recycled any of the contents of the second continuation of John of Antioch about events of 626–7. To judge by Nicephorus' version, this did not cover the activities of Shahen and diverged in certain key particulars in the accounts which it gave of the summit meeting in Transcaucasia, the siege of Constantinople, and the episode of the letter. It seems, rather, that Theophanes extracted material from other sources and placed it within a framework based on that of the continuation. Although no proof can be offered (mainly because Theophanes has compressed his raw materials into tight summary notices and has intervened editorially), three sources can be identified conjecturally.

Such is the precision of the account of the protocol followed during Heraclius' meeting with the *yabghu khagan* that an ultimate origin in an official source may be postulated. This points towards the use of the Official History, based here, as elsewhere, on a dispatch of Heraclius'. A second contributory source must be found for the notice about the Avar attack on Constantinople, since it definitely lay outside the scope of the Official History, exclusively concerned, as it was, with Heraclius' actions. Theophanes gives only the briefest of summaries of the siege, but includes one telltale phrase—the ships launched by the Avars in the Golden Horn are called *skaphe glypta* (hollow [lit. 'sculpted, carved'] boats). This is reminiscent of George of Pisidia's description of the ships onto which the barbarian embarked Slavs and Bulgars—they were scooped-out boats (*eskyphomena*

---

[43] Nic., cc.12.6–13.42.
[44] Howard-Johnston, *Witnesses*, 248–50, 276–7. But see Mango, *Nikephoros*, 12 and Mango and Scott, *Chronicle of Theophanes*, lxxxi.

skaphe) which he had hollowed out (*glypsas* [lit. 'sculpted, carved']).[45] Tenuous though the connection may be, it is all that we have to go on and suggests that Theophanes reduced George's poem to its bare essentials (attacks from east and west, large numbers of siege engines and ships, a siege lasting ten days, the role of the Mother of God, heavy Avar losses). There is only one error, which may be construed as an inference of Theophanes': George does not explain that the Slav vessels were transported overland, and Theophanes, not unreasonably, assumes that they sailed directly from the Danube.[46]

A third source can be identified with confidence for the notices about Shahrbaraz's stay on the Bosporus (as also for the strength, 40,000 men, put on the Turkish force which accompanied Heraclius on his march to the Zagros in 627).[47] Theophanes' material corresponds closely to that of his principal eastern source, a Greek translation of Theophilus of Edessa's mid-eighth-century chronicle. For Theophilus had Shahrbaraz stay put besieging Constantinople for either nine or twelve months and retailed the anecdote about the letter from Khusro which instructed the second in command of the expeditionary force to arrest and execute Shahrbaraz. In Theophilus' version, as in Theophanes', the Romans intercepted the letter and showed it to Shahrbaraz on a secret visit to Constantinople, after which Shahrbaraz widened the order to include 300 of his senior officers (400 for Theophanes), with predictable results.[48] Both these items of information provided corroboration for two key components of the continuation of John of Antioch's reconstruction—the length of Shahrbaraz's stay on the Bosporus and the interception of Khusro's correspondence with Shahrbaraz. Theophanes probably preferred Theophilus' version of the latter because it was more entertaining than Nicephorus' story that Heraclius substituted an order to stay put on the Bosporus for the original urgent recall.[49]

Theophanes has, however, intervened editorially. Knowing that it was the Avars who besieged Constantinople, he excised Theophilus' report that the Persians crossed the Bosporus and besieged the city from the west. Later, he added his own gloss about Shahrbaraz's loss of favour with Khusro, attributing it to suspicion of disloyalty rather than political criticism.[50] He also had no hesitation in replacing Heraclius (Shahrbaraz's host in Constantinople, according to Theophilus) with his son (Heraclius the New Constantine, constitutional head of the regency government) and the patriarch, since his Heraclius had to be in Transcaucasia at the time of the siege.[51] Finally, since his own reconstruction conflated the events of 626 and 627, he disregarded Theophilus' arrangement of episodes, in which the

---

[45] Theoph., 316.19; Geo.Pis., *Bellum Av.*, 411.   [46] Theoph., 316.16–25
[47] Theoph., 316.13–16 and 25–7, 323.22–324.16.
[48] Agap., 458.7–9, 461.5–462.11, Mich.Syr., 408–9, *Chron.1234*, 231.18–233.4 (trans. Hoyland, 68, 70–2).
[49] Nic., c.12.49–64.   [50] Theoph., 323.22–4.   [51] Theoph., 324.2, 7–8.

second counteroffensive came after the end of the (elongated) siege of Constantinople.

Two passages, both concerning Shahen, remain unattributed. It is hard to conceive of a provenance in the Official History, since the relative chronology of events has been so confused and the role of the protagonist, Heraclius, has been transformed out of all recognition. There are, however, two clues lurking in the vocabulary of the first notice which point in the direction of the Official History. As has already been remarked, the three groups from whom Shahen recruits a new army in Persia, foreigners, citizens and retainers, reappear in the very different context of Constantinople on the eve of the siege in *Bellum Avaricum*. It was suggested above (p. 247) that Theophanes, who probably knew and used the poem, was responsible for the verbal reminiscence, but it is, of course, much more likely that the phrase recurred unconsciously in a work composed by the poet himself. The juxtaposition of *ekloge* (used of the selection of new recruits) and *epiloge* (used of the additional experienced soldiers drafted in from Shahrbaraz's army) is also verbal play characteristic of George.[52] There would be nothing surprising, either, in George making much of supernatural intervention in the form of a discriminating hailstorm which disabled Shahen's army in the decisive battle.[53]

It may, therefore, be postulated, albeit hesitantly, that Theophanes took the material on Shahen, which he remoulded to fit into his own schema, from George of Pisidia's Official History and that here too, as in the case of Theophilus' version of the letter story, he was ready to intervene in an aggressive editorial fashion. Three instances of tampering can be detected. In what looks like a gloss elaborating on the objectives assigned to each of the Persian generals, he has Shahrbaraz charged with organizing a grand western coalition of Avars, Bulgars, Slavs, and Gepids and arranging for it to attack Constantinople. Some two years of diplomatic and military preparation are thus squeezed into a few months, while the Avars are stripped of their hegemony in eastern Europe.[54] Second, he concertinas the opening of Heraclius' second counteroffensive and the siege of Constantinople into a single campaigning season, as required by the chronological framework borrowed from the second continuation of John of Antioch. This in turn forces him into his third, most serious error: he changes the name of the Roman protagonist in Asia Minor in 626, substituting Heraclius' brother, Theodore, because, in his scenario, Heraclius could not have been present at the battle against Shahen. Logic required this change, just as it did in the case of Heraclius' supposed presence in Constantinople during the Avar siege.

This last, longest, and most intricate of historiographical investigations has, I hope, established the worth of the different component parts of Theophanes'

---

[52] Theoph., 315.2–7.   [53] Theoph., 315.16–22.   [54] Theoph., 315.7–11.

entry for 625–6. Substantive history cannot be written if the varying weight-bearing capacity of the source material is not established. Sometimes, as in this case, the task of doing so is laborious and time-consuming. It is, however, unavoidable. For it is only by identifying individual sources with a greater or lesser degree of confidence, by defining as precisely as possible their individual contributions to the extant text, and, above all, by tracking the editorial interventions of the chronicler that a properly nuanced appraisal can be made of the amalgam which he has produced. Inevitably, a great deal of conjecture has been involved. The proposed reconstruction of the editorial process twelve centuries later cannot but be hypothetical. The object, though, has been to provide a logically coherent, intelligible explanation for what we find in the text. The results are not negligible. We have learned a little more about Theophanes' library: he probably owned copies of three works of George of Pisidia, since he appears to make direct use of *Bellum Avaricum* as well as *Expeditio Persica* and the Official History. Editorial mistakes have been identified and can be set aside as historically worthless. On the other hand, now that a respectable provenance in the Official History has been proposed, reasonable confidence may be put in the two notices about Shahen and a gaping hole in our knowledge of a critical phase in the war can be plugged.

The investigation is not quite over. For there is one teasing question which remains unanswered—why did the second continuator of the chronicle of John of Antioch combine the events of 626 and 627 into a single composite and confusing narrative and consequently spirit Heraclius away to Transcaucasia at the time of the siege of Constantinople? The foreshortening may have occurred spontaneously. Much had happened by the time he was writing, some twenty or more years later—the outrush of the Arabs, their successive conquests of Palestine, Syria, northern Mesopotamia, and the heartland of the Sasanian Empire in in Mesopotamia. The pace of change showed no sign of slackening in the 640s, with both Egypt and the Iranian plateau under attack. The familiar world order had been shattered. The closing campaigns of the last war between the traditional rival imperial powers doubtless seemed much more remote than they actually were. Individual memories of the exact order of events may well have been clouded, and the continuator may have allowed two contiguous campaigns to coalesce in his memory.

However, there is some evidence to suggest that the conflation may have been prompted. Heraclius and the Roman authorities have been seen making effective use of disinformation on several occasions. The ultimate survival and revival of the east Roman Empire owed much to the harnessing of intelligence to the war effort. Persian misapprehension of Roman intentions, achieved by strategic deception, greatly aided Heraclius' small expeditionary army during his first counteroffensive. Disinformation could also be used to cause confusion to the enemy, for example to provoke dissension within the Sasanian governing elite or uncertainty in the relations between Persians and Avars. Two specific pieces of disinformation of this latter sort, dating respectively from 626 and 627–8 have left traces in extant sources. It may well be that they succeeded in bewildering and misleading both the second continuator of John of Antioch and, to a lesser extent, Theophilus of Edessa.

The first piece of disinformation is noted in passing, without commentary, in the report on the siege of Constantinople sent by the Patriarch Sergius to Heraclius. In the course of negotiations with the khagan of the Avars, which continued during the first part of the siege, the Roman authorities had evidently let it be known that Heraclius had invaded Persia and that a Roman relief force was approaching Shahrbaraz's army encamped on the Bosporus. Their object was clearly to sow doubt in Avar minds about the reliability of their Persian allies, doubt which three Persian ambassadors tried to allay when they reached the khagan's court. Their categorical denial that there was any truth in either statement was in turn denied by the Roman emissaries whom the khagan had invited to witness his good relations with the Persians. They simply reiterated that a Roman army was at hand and that Heraclius was devastating enemy territory.[55] On both points the Persians were almost certainly right. The core of the continuator's story, namely that Heraclius was away campaigning on Persian territory at the time of the Avar siege of Constantinople, is thus present in the false information fed to the Avars by the Romans. It has mutated somewhat, above all because the continuator has inferred, from Heraclius' absence, that his second counter-offensive had already begun.

There is a second mutant element in the continuator's version of the official disinformation—a letter from Khusro to Shahrbaraz which is tampered with in transit. A similar story, also involving a doctored letter, surfaces in several eastern sources, including the chronicle of Theophilus of Edessa, but is associated with the start of Heraclius' second counteroffensive. The device of the letter enables this second, eastern version to home in both on relations between Khusro and his senior general in the west (alleging that they were strained to breaking point, for reasons which vary from account to account) and, after the letter has reached its destination, on treasonable communication between Shahrbaraz and Heraclius.[56] There is no independent confirmation of either allegation. It may be suspected that both originated in Roman propaganda broadcast at the time when Heraclius' second counteroffensive was under way. For the Romans would be the chief beneficiaries if doubt about the relations between the royal authority and the high command in the west began to spread in Sasanian lands. There would be an even

---

[55] *Chron.Pasch.*, 721.21–722.4.
[56] In addition to the sources cited in n. 48, *Seert Chron.*, 540.3–541.6 (with comments of C. Mango, 'Deux Études sur Byzance et la Perse Sassanide', *TM* 9 (1985), 91–118, at 107–9) and Tab., 1007.16–1009.2 (with comments of J. Howard-Johnston, 'Al-Tabari on the Last Great War of Antiquity', in Howard-Johnston, *East Rome*, no.VI, 12–14).

greater gain, if disinformation helped to bring about in reality the dissension which it invented.

To conclude, the following conjectural series of operations would explain the transmutation of real history into the version which the second continuator of John of Antioch probably transmitted to Theophanes. He accepted the false story that Heraclius was ravaging Persian territory at the time of the Avar siege of Constantinople. He was consequently misled into supposing that the second counteroffensive began a year earlier than in reality and therefore sandwiched his notice about the siege between two dealing with Heraclius' activities in Transcaucasia. He came across a second piece of disinformation, alleging a breakdown in relations between Khusro and Shahrbaraz at the time of the start of Heraclius' second counteroffensive, and incorporated it in a much-modified form which fitted neatly into his foreshortened account of the last two years of fighting.

By this stage, the reader may be losing patience. Conjecture is being stretched, perhaps beyond breaking point, as the search moves on first from extant sources to their sources, then to the sources of those sources. But I am confident that the confusion which mars Byzantine accounts of the events of 626 and 627 ultimately originated in disinformation disseminated by the Roman authorities at the time. It is only over the details of the original form of the story of the letter and over the process of transmission and transformation of black propaganda into seeming history that the legitimate limit of conjecture may have been transgressed.

It is time to return to history. Events will come thick and fast upon us, most of them well documented in more than one source of proven worth. There will be little need and little time for conjectures about plans (liable all too soon to be overtaken by events) or for historiographical probes (the source material being on the whole both voluminous and trustworthy). Battle will be joined around Constantinople, far away in Asia Minor, and yet farther away in Transcaucasia. The Turks will start to exert real influence on the affairs of the southern sedentary world. Grandiose conceptions of their place in the world will add a solemn, disquieting tone to their diplomatic exchanges with Khusro. The war will be approaching its climax, and the whole of eastern Europe, the east Mediterranean, and the Middle East will be drawn in, if only, like the Quraysh of Mecca and the followers of Muhammad at Medina, as a distant audience awed at the scale of the conflict and its dramatic outcome.

8.3 Siege of Constantinople

The khagan of the Avars was able to mobilize a huge host for his expedition against Constantinople. Theodore Syncellus, a privileged eyewitness of the siege who larded his account with Old Testament parallels, took it to be the fulfilment of Ezekiel's prophecy about Gog (38.15–16) 'And thou shalt come from thy place in the north parts, thou, and many people with thee, all of them riding upon horses, a great company, and a mighty army. And thou shalt come up against my people of Israel, as a cloud to cover the land.' In his own day, with the Jews dispersed, Theodore located Israel at Constantinople, which had superseded Jerusalem as the navel of the earth and formed a single congregation worshipping God and the Virgin. Both by virtue of the size of his army and its origin in the north, the khagan could be identified as Gog.[57]

George of Pisidia, who also witnessed events but not from quite so privileged a vantage point, and who liked occasionally to slip mundane details into his poem, noted in passing that the Avar host numbered 80,000. This total receives corroboration from the figure of 30,000 for the Avar vanguard given in the *Chronicon Paschale*, and, like it, was probably the official estimate made by the Roman authorities.[58] An army of this order of magnitude was on a par with the largest forces which the Romans had been able to mobilize in late antiquity, whether for Julian's expedition against Ctesiphon in 363 or for the recapture of Amida in 504. It entailed the mobilization of all the peoples, nomad and sedentary, subjected to Avar authority, among whom Roman writers singled out Bulgars and Gepids (probably as being the most notable of the Turkic and Germanic peoples serving in the army), as well as Slavs, who provided the great mass of foot soldiers and sailors.[59]

Romans and Persians had already had some experience of the organizational capability which Altaic nomad peoples had developed in east central Asia in their dealings with the Chinese. But the logistics effort made by the Avars in 626 surpassed that of their Hunnic and Hephthalite precursors in the west. For their huge host had to be provisioned as well as marshalled, and much equipment was required for effective siege operations. Large quantities of supplies were assembled to feed the army during the siege, when it would be forced to rely mainly on such stocks as it brought along. Key parts for siege engines of the most advanced types—including great assault towers and lever artillery of Chinese design[60]—were prefabricated, so that the structures could be erected swiftly on site. But the boldest initiative of all was the decision to transport a whole fleet of Slav boats *overland*. The wagon train which the Avars assembled to carry all this materiel was perhaps the largest seen in the Balkans until the heyday of the Ottoman

---

[57] Theod.Sync., *Hom.* I, 314.18–318.20.
[58] Geo.Pis., *Bellum Av.*, 217–19; *Chron.Pasch.*, 717.4–5.
[59] *Chron.Pasch.*, 719.10–14, 724.7–18, 725.6–8 (Slavs); Geo.Pis., *Bellum Av.*, 197 (two contemporary names, Slav and Bulgar, and two antiquarian, Hun and Scythian); Nic., c.13.19–20, 30–6 (Slavs); Theoph., 315.9–10 (Bulgars, Slavs, Gepids).
[60] Chevedden et al., 'Traction Trebuchet'.

Empire. It was doubtless broken down into a number of smaller units and rolled slowly but remorselessly along the roads leading into Thrace.[61]

The 14-year-old emperor, Heraclius Constantine, the two regents, and the inner circle of advisers with whom they governed Constantinople and what remained of the empire had every reason to be apprehensive. They could, of course, have confidence in the main land defences, built over ten years in the reign of Theodosius II (408–50), consisting of a main wall 11 metres high and 4.8 metres thick, guarded by 96 polygonal and rectangular towers and fronted by a forewall itself 8 metres high and, at vulnerable places, shielded by an 18-metre-wide ditch (Figure 1).[62] The sea walls were another matter. Built in a hurry in the face of a potential Vandal threat in 439, they were in need of strengthening.[63] The detailed instructions sent by Heraclius for reinforcing the footings of walls and protecting them with outer projections, palisades, and stakes (technical matter neatly incorporated into the *Bellum Avaricum*) almost certainly concerned the sea walls.[64]

Other vital preparations had been made in good time, probably several years earlier. A fleet of small, manoeuvrable vessels (*skaphokaraboi*, later called simply *karaboi*), recently constructed, provided a first line of defence against a repetition of Heraclius' own successful maritime attack on the city.[65] Measures had been taken to secure and stockpile food supplies. The main problem, signalled by the suspension of the free bread dole in 618, was supply, once Egypt was lost to the Persians. It may be conjectured that grain was requisitioned from all the provinces still controlled by the Romans, particularly important contributions probably being made by the immediate Thracian and Bithynian hinterlands of the city and by North Africa, the power base of Heraclius' family. Nonetheless, it remained a cause of serious concern. How else can one explain the authorities' plan to increase the price of bread from 3 to 8 folles per loaf? When the news of this leaked out in May, there was an immediate outcry culminating in two days of demonstrations in St Sophia. The hard core among the demonstrators consisted of troops serving in the palace Scholae who objected to an associated measure, the abolition of their bread dole (they had clearly been exempt from its general abolition in 618). The crowd went so far as to prevent the celebration of the liturgy on the Wednesday of Pentecost (14 May) until the patriarch yielded and

---

[61] Theod.Sync., *Hom.* I, 302.20–5, 306.13–18, 312.31–4; *Chron.Pasch.*, 720.15–721.3.
[62] W. Müller-Wiener, *Bildlexikon zur Topographie Istanbuls* (Tübingen, 1977), 286–96; J. Crow, 'The Infrastructure of a Great City: Earth, Walls and Water in Late Antique Constantinople', in L. Lavan, E. Zanini, and A. Sarantis, eds., *Technology in Transition AD 300–650*, Late Antique Archaeology 4 (Leiden, 2007), 251–85, at 262–8.
[63] *Chron.Pasch.*, 583.3–4; Müller-Wiener, *Bildlexikon*, 308–19.
[64] Geo.Pis., *Bellum Av.*, 266–75.
[65] Geo.Pis., *Bellum Av.*, 276–7; *Chron.Pasch.*, 720.15–721.3, 722.14–19, 723.15–21. Cf. C. Zuckerman, 'Learning from the Enemy and More: Studies in "Dark Centuries" Byzantium', *Millennium*, 2 (2005), 79–135, at 112–13.

promised to do what he could to meet its demands. When the demonstrators returned the next day in larger numbers and resumed their chanting against the official, probably the Prefect of the City charged with implementing the policy, the authorities were forced to back down and to announce that the offending official had been dismissed. The issue must have remained of concern, but it faded in significance once it was plain that the Avars would be attacking that summer. Heraclius did not refer to it in the instructions which he sent to the regents, nor did they take any other action (such as the forced removal of citizens without supplies of their own, as happened before the 717–18 Arab siege). Food stocks were, it appears, large enough to tide the city and the refugees who were likely to come over a siege in the near future.[66]

What was needed above all, as the Avars made their preparations, was trained military personnel. While there was a city militia organized by guild and faction and large enough to man the full circuit of the walls, its weaponry ready for issue in emergencies from local armouries, there was a need for a stiffening of seasoned troops to give the defenders the will and military strength to resist a full-scale siege.[67] The palace guards left behind by Heraclius, such as the Scholae who had been demonstrating, were more decorative than effective. A body of regular soldiers, eventually amounting to several thousand men, was probably gathered bit by bit in winter and spring from every available source. By far the most important of the contingents, though, was that sent in by Heraclius after he crossed the Taurus and entered the interior plateau of Asia Minor. It may only have numbered two or three thousand (since Heraclius needed to husband his resources for his own campaign), but its arrival, perhaps almost a month ahead of Shahrbaraz's large army, must have given a great boost to morale. By early or mid-June, there was a sizable force inside the city. A parade was laid on to impress the ambassador about to be sent to the Avars, who was told, almost certainly with considerable exaggeration, that he was looking at more than 12,000 cavalrymen.[68]

Next to manpower, the authorities needed to draw on the tactical sagacity of the emperor. George of Pisidia describes citizens and strangers, officials and magnates as following whatever instructions he sent with the alacrity of servants. The instructions concerned weaponry great and small—the fleet, artillery (which, in the event, was concentrated on the most threatened section of the land walls), and light protective screens for archers—but there was much other technical, tactical, and strategic advice. The systematic and subtle use of disinformation before, during, and after the siege may well have been one of Heraclius' chief

---

[66] *Chron.Pasch.*, 715.9–716.8.
[67] Cf. Alan Cameron, *Circus Factions: Blues and Greens at Rome and Byzantium* (Oxford, 1976), 105–25.
[68] Geo.Pis., *Bellum Av.*, 280; Theoph., 315.12–13; *Chron.Pasch.*, 718.18–22.

contributions, alongside the heartening effect on the defenders of knowing that he was guiding their efforts.[69]

Morale was, of course, of the utmost importance. Sustaining it was a responsibility which fell chiefly on the patriarch, whose actions and words are recorded by one of his highest-ranking clerical colleagues, the Syncellus Theodore. Sergius heightened the religious feelings of the citizenry and orchestrated public manifestations of faith, which took the form of frequent rogation processions and all-night vigils. He urged them to worship God, to weep before him, and assured them that God who had power over all earthly affairs would be fighting on their side together with the city's special protectress, his Mother. He affixed images of the Virgin Mother holding the Christ Child to each of the gates in the land walls, expressing his confidence that the enemy would be routed at her command. Later, when the full Avar army was parading before the walls, he countered by taking the Acheiropoietos (Not Made by Human Hands) image of Christ on procession and calling on the Lord to scatter his enemies. Later still, at a dark moment when it seemed that the Persians might be able to send reinforcements across the Bosporus, he led the prayers with which the authorities and the whole city appealed to God for deliverance from an impious enemy.[70]

Theodore's text proceeds to tell the story of that deliverance day by day, pressing an unusual amount of military matter into a sermon. There is a vividness about his description of the horrors which would have followed the city's fall that suggests that little time elapsed between the siege and the composition of the sermon. It may be conjectured that he delivered it at the service of thanksgiving held by the patriarch in the Virgin's huge basilica at Blachernae, stripped bare but undamaged, after the end of the siege. If time is allowed for burying the dead and clearing away the worst of the debris of war, the service may be dated roughly a month later, an appropriate occasion being the feast of the Nativity of the Virgin on 8 September (exactly one month after the disappearance of the last Avar troops on 8 August).

The finest of the accounts of the siege, George of Pisidia's *Bellum Avaricum*, assuredly took longer to compose. It is dedicated to the patriarch and was written for recitation at a time when the emperor was away, perhaps the first anniversary of the end of the siege (8 August 627). The many traits which it shares with Theodore's sermon (including three of its major themes—Roman-Avar relations before the siege, the emperor's concern at the prospect of the siege, and the climax of siege operations) are not to be explained as borrowings by the senior church official writing in prose from the work of the poet, his junior (hitherto the consensus of scholarly opinion) but rather as the response of a poet with

---

[69] Theod.Sync., *Hom.* I, 303.33–304.4; Geo.Pis., *Bellum Av.,* 288–306.
[70] Theod.Sync., *Hom.* I, 303.14–32, 304.4–16, 304.40–305.12, 307.14–40.

extraordinary powers of expression to a text which he knew well and from which he extracted much information.[71]

George picks up several of Theodore's images and embellishes them with novel variations of his own: the sand of the seashore to which the numberless Avars are compared is whipped up by a gale and *spat* at the city; plain bees around a honeycomb (the Avars around Constantinople) become bees who tighten the encirclement like a cloud of mosquitos; George transforms a comparison with Scylla and Charybdis into poetry (Scythian-nourishing Scylla seethes and boils on one side, the Charybdis of Persia sends back an answering boom).[72] George can be seen to be capping Theodore's sermon in other ways. When Theodore opens his account of the final day's grand assault with a conventional turn on the sounds of battle, George writes a brief, beautifully phrased account of the ways in which divine justice sought out individual enemy soldiers, a slinger's stone delivering death to one man, an arrow from an unseen archer striking down another in mid-speech, or a stone projectile pushing aside the protective shields to reach its target, the senior officer concealed behind them.[73] There are several other instances where George demonstrates his literary virtuosity at Theodore's expense, amongst them his substitution of a list of recommended building works for Heraclius' prayer for Constantinople (presumably because such technicalities demanded more virtuosity) or characterization of Sergius as 'the general of armed tears', an image which is then elaborated into a long conceit, in place of Theodore's matter-of-fact description of his actions and prayers and a simple comparison with Moses.[74] But the proof of George's dependence on Theodore comes in a mistake which he makes: misled by Theodore's reference to consultations held in Constantinople before an embassy was sent out to the khagan on the fifth day, he supposes wrongly that it was a Roman initiative, whereas, in reality, as we are told by the *Chronicon Paschale*, it was at the khagan's request.[75]

Together with the information provided by Sergius' official report, the evidence provided by Theodore and George enables us to piece together a remarkably detailed account of the joint Avar-Persian attack on Constantinople in 626. There is nothing particularly novel about the narrative presented here, save perhaps for the emphasis on diplomacy (which carried on during the fighting), diplomatic subterfuge, and the vital aspect of morale. It must also be remembered that there were two other events, also occurring in 626, which marked a turning in the tide of war in 626—the defeat of Shahen by Heraclius in north-east Asia Minor and

---

[71] P. Speck, *Zufälliges zum Bellum Avaricum des Georgios Pisides*, Miscellanea Byzantina Monacensia 24 (Munich, 1980), 18–19, 24–6, 50–4.
[72] Theod.Sync., *Hom.* I, 300.18–19, 300.19–20, 304.18–19, 305.19; Geo.Pis., *Bellum Av.*, 172–4, 63–4, 204–6.
[73] Theod.Sync., *Hom.* I, 311.2–4; Geo.Pis., *Bellum Av.*, 417–28.
[74] Theod.Sync., *Hom.* I, 302.28–303.4, 304.4–16; Geo.Pis., *Bellum Av.*, 266–75, 141–64.
[75] Theod.Sync., *Hom.* I, 306.20–5; Geo.Pis., *Bellum Av.*, 311–27; Chron.Pasch., 721.4–10.

the Turkish invasion of Transcaucasia. Although neither of these military episodes was well documented, each was almost as significant as the repulse of the Avars from Constantinople.

The Avar army crossed the Danube and marched south towards Constantinople. Its advance probably triggered large movements of refugees to fortified sites. In the case of those living on the Thracian approaches to the capital, whether inside or outside the Long Wall, the obvious place of refuge was Constantinople, where the authorities had surely taken account of the likely influx of refugees when building up the city's food reserves. Hard evidence of flight by two notables living on either side of the Long Wall is provided by two large hoards of gold coins, one at Akalan, not far from the Black Sea on the Bulgarian side of the modern frontier (421 solidi, 2 hexagrams, and jewellery), the other at Çatalka, 12 km away towards Constantinople (152 solidi). To judge by their age profiles (in the case of Akalan from the 17 solidi and 1 hexagram acquired by the archaeological museum in Sofia), both were concealed in 626. How their owners died is not known—whether caught and killed on their flight or dying subsequently from human or natural causes. But they were not alive long enough to retrieve them.[76]

To keep within reasonable bounds the time spent marshalling the army into marching and bivouac order at the beginning and end of each day, as well as to ease the problem of victualling, it was probably broken up into a number of independent units while it was on the move. One of these acted as the vanguard. With an estimated strength of 30,000, it was a formidable army in its own right, matching the largest force which the Romans could manage as a single fighting unit in the field and easily outnumbering the professional soldiers which the regents had gathered for the defence of the city. The khagan followed, escorted, one may presume, by crack troops and keeping the other component parts of the army within easy communicating distance (and therefore under observation).

Shahrbaraz's army was first to reach the metropolitan area, probably by the middle of June, and established itself in full view of Constantinople, at Chalcedon, across the Bosporus. While waiting for the Avars, the Persians struck the first blow at Roman morale by devastating the Asian suburbs. Villas, palaces, and places of worship were systematically burned. The Avar vanguard reached the outer perimeter of Constantinople's defences, the Long Wall of Thrace, on Sunday 29 June. The khagan, like Heraclius, was directing operations from afar. His orders to seize the Long Wall and occupy the area within were carried out. The Roman cavalry stationed outside the city, presumably in the Hebdomon suburb, withdrew inside the Theodosian walls the same day.[77]

---

[76] C. Morrisson, V. Popović, and V. Ivanišević, eds., *Les Trésors monétaires byzantins des Balkans et d'Asie Mineure (491–713)*, Réalités Byzantines 13 (Paris, 2006), 109, 117–19.

[77] *Chron.Pasch.*, 716.17–717.10.

There followed a period of phoney warfare, with the Avars encamped at Melantias, at a distance of 18–19 Roman miles from the city on the Via Egnatia.[78] At a fairly early stage they established contact with the Persian forces by fire signal from Sycae on the Bosporus. Forays were regularly sent out to prevent anyone from leaving the city or gathering fodder for the animals (including the cavalry's mounts) sheltering behind its walls. There was only one engagement of note, when, ten days into the blockade, a foraging party of soldiers, young retainers, and civilians was intercepted some 10 miles from the city and both sides suffered minor losses. Considerable damage may have been done to ecclesiastical and secular buildings in the European suburbs, if Theodore Syncellus is right to have the Avars emulate the Persians' firing of the Asian suburbs.[79]

Diplomacy was not interrupted by the start of operations. Both Romans and Avars seem to have viewed argumentation, whether aggressive or conciliatory, frank or full of wiles, as complementary to military action. Words, whether part of a genuine negotiating effort or intended to browbeat or to deceive, were auxiliaries to deeds. Both were targeted on the adversary's will. Weaken it and the task ahead would be achieved with less risk and at reduced cost. Diplomacy was a vital weapon of war. It was a weapon that the Romans could wield with rather more dexterity than the Avars, deliberately altering their stance between negotiating rounds and repeatedly insinuating carefully devised pieces of disinformation into the discussions.

The regents had sent off an embassy headed by the Patrician Athanasius, who had previous experience of dealing with the khagan, well before the siege, possibly in the course of the preceding winter. His remit, as he reminded the regents' cabinet on his return, was to be as conciliatory as possible in the hope of averting the threatened attack on the city. The khagan kept him in attendance until he reached the district of Adrianople in Thrace, where he may have paused to make final preparations for the siege. There he released him, demanding yet more concessions from the city and doubtless reckoning that his menacing presence would duly extract them. Athanasius, who had been conciliatory to the end, was sharply criticized on his return for indicating that the new demands would be met. The regents and the inner circle of their advisers adopted a new, intransigent line. Instead of trying to buy off the Avars, they now displayed unruffled confidence in the city's physical and human defences, probably in the hope of deterring the khagan from pressing home his attack. A reply was drafted which invited him to advance right up to the city's walls.

Athanasius, who would be conveying it, was briefed about the measures to strengthen the walls (taken during his absence) and the arrival of regular troops. Then a parade (designated an *armastatio* in Sergius' report) was laid on for his

---

[78] Külzer, *Ostthrakien*, 526–7.
[79] *Chron.Pasch.*, 717.10–718.4; Theod.Sync., *Hom.* I, 304.31–5.

benefit. He was told that the soldiers before him were all cavalrymen and that they amounted to over twelve thousand men. Considerable exaggeration may be suspected, since Heraclius could not have spared more than two or three thousand of his troops and most of them, as well as the other professional soldiers scraped together by the regents, were probably infantry. Athanasius was almost certainly being misled into believing genuinely that the city was better defended than it was, in order to make him a more convincing and effective emissary. He was the unwitting bearer of a first tranche of Roman disinformation to the Avars.[80]

Athanasius' second embassy did not, however, deter the khagan, who continued his advance and closed in on the city with the main army on 29 July. That first day, he drew it up in full battle array before the walls. There was no fighting, just a grand parade designed to undermine the morale of the defenders. The daunting sight impressed itself on Theodore Syncellus, who recalled in the sermon he delivered a month or so later how their armour seemed all the more fearsome as it glittered in the sunlight. The regents prepared their defences. While Bonus marshalled the regular soldiers and city militia, Sergius carried the Acheiropoietos image of Christ along the land walls in the midst of a procession of clergy and displayed it to the Avars and the airborne powers of darkness who were their supernatural backers. Using one of his characteristic conceits, George of Pisidia was later to liken the scene to a trial subverted by the wiles of Sergius, the advocate, who managed to impel the Virgin to suborn the judge (God) with tearful pleas on behalf of her son (threatened via his image).[81]

The unnatural calm continued on the second day. The Avars made preparations for a first general assault, which included deployment of armoured shelters on the approaches to the walls. For their part, the Romans reverted to a softer, more accommodating line. Food was sent out to the khagan at his request, both sides apparently maintaining the fiction that he was a guest and his visit diplomatic rather than military in character. Bonus urged him to accept the tribute owing to him and offered an additional sum as a collection fee (an offer which was not withdrawn when the fighting started). At the same time, an effort was made to undermine his confidence in his Persian allies by feeding him two more pieces of disinformation. He was told that Heraclius had invaded Persian territory and that a Roman army was close at hand. The object presumably was to lead him to think that Shahrbaraz would be forced to leave the Bosporus in the very near future.[82]

Then, on 31 July, the besiegers attacked along the whole length of the Theodosian walls (5.7 km.). The fighting was to continue every day until the end of the siege. The main effort was concentrated against the central section, about a

---

[80] *Chron.Pasch.*, 718.4–719.1.
[81] *Chron.Pasch.*, 719.1–7; Theod.Sync., *Hom.* I, 304.36–305.28; Geo.Pis., *Bellum Av.*, 366–89.
[82] *Chron.Pasch.*, 720.10–13 (tribute and fee), 721.21–722.4 (later defence of Roman disinformation); Theod.Sync., *Hom.* I, 305.28–36 (armoured shelters and food).

kilometre long, where the walls surmounted the highest elevation between the Polyandrion and Romanus Gates and then descended north into the Lycus valley and over the stream to the Pempton Gate. The sector of the fortifications crossed by the Lycus was presumably chosen as a potentially weak point, while the high ground enabled the Avars to command a view right down to the Golden Horn in the north and the Marmara shore in the south. From there, the khagan was well placed to coordinate siege operations, as also to monitor the performance of the different ethnic contingents arrayed against the city. This was particularly important in the case of the Slav units who formed the front line during this first general attack and were evidently viewed as expendable, since they did not have the protective armour worn by the infantry in the second line. The defenders' only recorded success was minor but heartening, won in a sortie from the southern sector near the Virgin's church at Pege.[83]

The khagan's strategy over the next few days was to bring steadily increasing pressure, military and psychological, to bear on the defenders. Already on the evening of 31 July the first siege engines were deployed. A small number of *manganika*, artillery pieces probably of conventional torsion design, accurate, but discharging relatively small projectiles at relatively long intervals, were deployed to give covering fire along the whole front. More armoured shelters also seem to have been put in position. On 1 August, the number and variety of siege engines grew, as a large labour force rapidly constructed machines out of the prefabricated parts which they had brought and timber stripped from buildings in the suburbs. They comprised (1) more *manganika*, arrayed in close order on the high ground facing the central sector of the wall between the Polyandrion and Romanus Gates which was to continue to bear the brunt of Avar attack over the following days, (2) a smaller number of *petrareai* with a protective covering of hide, rope-pulled trebuchets discharging massive missiles at a faster rate of fire, and (3) siege towers, the construction of which was the ultimate test of an army's technological capacity. Eventually a total of twelve siege towers, almost matching the height of the battlements, each with a protective covering of hide, were deployed against the same Polyandrion-Romanus section. Whatever success the defenders had against them (a sailor was commended for devising one effective countermeasure involving a boat slung from a mast and spar), the weight of artillery and siege towers facing them continued to grow right up to the final general assault.[84]

There were two ominous developments. The Slav boats which had been transported were launched on the fourth day of the siege in the shallow waters by the St Callinicus bridge over the river Barbyssus at the head of the Golden Horn. The Roman warships, which had been unable to intervene because of their larger draught, were now compelled to establish a defensive cordon across the Golden

---

[83] Chron.Pasch., 719.7–14; Theod.Sync., *Hom.* I, 305.37–306.12.
[84] Chron.Pasch., 719.14–720.9; Theod.Sync., *Hom.* I, 306.13–18. Cf. Nic., c.13.15–17.

Horn at the level of the Theodosian walls to prevent the enemy from reaching the sea walls.[85] On the following day, Saturday 2 August, envoys from Shahrbaraz also succeeded in slipping across the Bosporus. They strengthened the khagan's resolve to press on with the siege and reassured him of the Persians' commitment by offering to send across a contingent (variously put at one, three, and four thousand men) to take part in the siege. That evening the khagan invited the Romans to send a delegation to attend on him, not to renew negotiations but to show off his three silk-clad Persian visitors as visible evidence of the solidity of the Avar-Persian alliance.[86]

The five-strong Roman delegation headed by the Patrician George included Theodore Syncellus. We, therefore, have two extant insider views of what was to be a defining moment in the diplomatic interplay, the account written for Heraclius by Sergius based on the official report of the envoys and Theodore's version, somewhat embellished, of what the envoys said on their return to the city. The khagan is portrayed by Theodore as a Proteus of dry land, a demon in human form, repulsive in appearance and manners, unclean, uttering unspeakable things. Sergius sticks to sober reporting, noting that the khagan received the Roman embassy in the presence of the three Persians, who were seated. The Romans, by contrast, were kept standing throughout the audience. They were told of Shahrbaraz's promise of aid and of the Persian emissaries' categorical denial of the two most recent pieces of Roman disinformation. All George could do was to reiterate that Heraclius was at that time in Persia, that he was causing extensive damage, and that a (phantom) Roman army was close at hand. He also expressed surprise that one who commanded so great a multitude should be in need of assistance (sarcasm which was missed by the khagan). Confident that Constantinople would soon be his, the khagan issued an ultimatum, demanding that the Romans evacuate the city of their own accord and cede it and their properties to him. In return, he offered to obtain a safe conduct for them from his ally Shahrbaraz. With nothing to negotiate, the Roman delegation asked permission to leave and returned to the city.[87]

That night, the Romans had a stroke of luck when they captured the three Persian envoys as they were sailing back across the Bosporus. They exploited it to the full, but in a particularly barbaric manner The next day, Sunday 3 August (the sixth day of the siege), they sent one of the three Persians to the khagan on a boat, minus his hands but with the head of a second envoy suspended from his neck, while the third was taken by boat and beheaded in full view of the Persian army.

---

[85] *Chron.Pasch.*, 720.15–721.3. The cordon ran diagonally across the Golden Horn, from the church of St Nicholas (in Blachernae) to that of St Conon at Pegae (modern Kasimpasa) much farther down the northern shore (opposite the north end of the old Constantinian walls).
[86] *Chron.Pasch.*, 721.4–6, 10–15 (figure of 3,000 Persians at 721.14–15); Geo.Pis., *Bellum Av.*, 311–347 (figure of 1,000 Persians at line 342). Ps.S, 123.13 for the figure of 4,000.
[87] *Chron.Pasch.*, 721.6–722.14; Theod.Sync., *Hom.* I, 306.20–307.11.

The severed head was then thrown ashore with an attached message announcing that the khagan had agreed a treaty with the Romans and had handed over the envoys sent by the Persians, two of whom had already been beheaded in the city. This was as blatant as any piece of disinformation put out by the Romans and cannot have been expected to do more than induce a momentary doubt about the reliability of the Avars. But even a fleeting stab of doubt, combined with the shock of the gruesome sight, might serve to lower Persian morale—and ratcheting it down was a prime task of the Roman defenders. Meanwhile, some food and wine was sent out to the khagan to indicate that he was not bracketed with the Persian enemy and, it can be inferred, could still take up the offer of additional tribute.[88]

The Avars, not unexpectedly, did not waver. An emissary expressed outrage at the treatment meted out to the khagan's Persian guests. Soon the psychological advantage swung back in their favour. For the boats which the khagan had launched at Chalae (modern Bebek) on the Bosporus in the course of Sunday succeeded in evading the seventy Roman warships sent to blockade them and crossed over to the Persians on the following moonlit night.[89] It was now feasible for the Persians to send troops across, and even a token force would be of great symbolic value. In the event the ferrying operation was a failure. It cannot be followed in detail, since the text of the *Chronicon Paschale* has a lacuna at this point which deprives us of Sergius' authoritative narrative of the events of the next three and a half days, up to and including the final general assault.[90] The only reports we have on the outcome are two problematic passages. A badly misplaced notice in the *History of Khosrov* has a large Persian force sent across, only to be intercepted by a Roman fleet. The Persians troops, all four thousand of them (a figure which is surely inflated), are slaughtered. Theodore Syncellus skirted over the episode of the Persian envoys. Atrocities of the sort that had taken place, however justifiable they might be in the eyes of the regents at the time, had no place in a sermon. As for the plan for ferrying Persian troops across the Bosporus, he confined himself to a single laconic sentence in which he remarked that, in answer to the prayers of the young emperor and the two regents, God prevented the Persians from crossing to the dog (the khagan), setting ambushes and striking down some of those sent between the two tyrants.[91]

The siege was now approaching its climax. There was no let-up in the pressure during the sixth, seventh, and eighth days (Sunday 3–Tuesday 5 August). Preparations were being made for a general assault by land and by sea. Skirmishing and local attacks kept the defenders under pressure and the number of siege engines continued to grow. In a coordinated display of military might, the heavy

---

[88] Chron.Pasch., 722.14–723.15, 724.1–2; Geo.Pis., *Bellum Av.*, 348–65.
[89] Chron.Pasch., 724.2–9; Theod.Sync., *Hom.* I, 307.8–14.
[90] Chron.Pasch., 724.9, between the second and third words.
[91] Ps.S, 123.10–14; Theod.Sync., *Hom.* I, 307.11–14, 308.1–2.

Avar cavalry and the whole Persian army paraded under their respective commanders on both shores of the Bosporus and, as Theodore Syncellus put it, roared like wild beasts against the city.[92] On Wednesday 6 August (the ninth day of the siege), the khagan ordered the assault to begin. His forces attacked along the full length of the land walls without respite for the whole of the day and the following night. Then, on the morning of Thursday 7 August, the front was broadened and the pressure intensified. The Slav fleet, carrying an infantry assault force comprising Bulgars as well as Slavs, sailed from the head of the Golden Horn towards the sea walls on what they took to be the prearranged fire signal from Blachernae, just outside the walls on the Golden Horn. The naval action was planned as a massive diversionary attack to distract and confuse the defenders at the very moment when the land forces were to scale the walls.[93]

Bonus had, however, got wind of the Avar plan and made his dispositions accordingly. He divided his fleet, keeping one squadron at its station close to Blachernae on the southern shore, and moving the second squadron forward (presumably under cover of darkness) to a position opposite on the north shore. The two squadrons were now well placed to sweep out against both flanks of the Slav fleet as it sailed down the Golden Horn to attack the sea walls. He also arranged for the fire signal to be given prematurely, before the direct assault by ladder on the land walls was scheduled to begin—to reverse the intended effect and disconcert the attackers rather than the defenders. Theodore Syncellus alone supplies some details about the naval engagement which was then fought. Numerous and densely packed though the Slav boats were, they were no match for the Roman warships when the trap was sprung. To make doubly sure of victory, the Romans initially gave the impression of yielding at the mere sight of the Slav fleet. The southern force, which had moved out from the Blachernae shore, backed water, apparently on the point of breaking up and opening the way to the land walls. But then, in this slow-moving naval equivalent of a nomad feigned retreat, they halted their withdrawal and counter-attacked. Caught between the two Roman forces, their own formations probably disordered and their boats jostled together into a solid, unmanoeuvrable mass, the Slav fleet was overwhelmed. Almost all the men on board were killed in the bloodbath which followed, turning the Golden Horn into a latter-day Red Sea, stained with the blood of another luckless pharoah's army.[94]

Meanwhile, on land, the final grand assault was making no headway. The defenders fought resolutely, and the piles of Avar dead grew steadily larger. When it came, news of the disaster at sea swung the battle decisively in the Romans' favour, their morale soaring, while that of their opponents plummeted. Down by

---

[92] Theod.Sync., *Hom.* I, 308.2–8, 15–21.
[93] Theod.Sync., *Hom.* I, 308.8–10, 310.37–311.12; Geo.Pis., *Bellum Av.*, 409–12; Nic., c.13.19–26.
[94] Theod.Sync., *Hom.* I, 311.12–37; Geo.Pis., *Bellum Av.*, 440–74; Nic., c.13.19–36.

the southern shore of the Golden Horn, a sortie by Armenian troops resulted in the capture and burning of the wharf of St Nicholas, by Blachernae. Slav survivors from the naval battle swam towards the fire, mistaking the Armenians for Avar troops, and were butchered as they came ashore. Those who arrived behind Avar lines fared no better, being executed on the orders of the khagan, who had watched the naval action from a height close to the shore. Only the few who swam to the opposite shore managed to escape. The khagan returned to his headquarters before the land walls, distraught at the misfortunes by land and sea which messenger after messenger brought him 'in sheaves'. With the high command disoriented, the land assault seems to have petered out, allowing some overenthusiastic Romans to sally out to Bonus' dismay.[95]

The following night (7–8 August) the khagan acknowledged failure and gave the order to withdraw. He had no choice after the heavy losses suffered by his forces and the spiralling descent of their morale. It was also rumoured that the Slavs forced his hand when they finally bridled at the high-handed, callous leadership of the Avars and withdrew of their own accord. The khagan himself blamed dwindling supplies in a message which he sent warning the Romans not to impede his withdrawal. Supplies were indeed decisive in limiting the siege to ten days or so, irrespective of its outcome. So formidable a host, roughly three times the size of the largest army normally fielded by the Romans, could not be provisioned for much longer as a single entity staying put in the same position. Thus, from the first, the khagan had had to reckon on achieving success through a short, steadily escalating siege, either by breaking the defenders' will at an early stage or by delivering, at the climactic moment, through a frontal assault on the grandest imaginable scale, a shock so violent as to overwhelm the defences.[96]

There was no disguising the Avars' failure. It was indeed displayed for Romans and Persians to see. For the khagan gave the order to dismantle and burn all the siege engines which he had deployed against the city. The fires lit up the night sky and blanketed the city and its environs in smoke for much of the following day. By then the great host had disappeared, leaving a cavalry detachment to guard its rear and cause a final round of destruction. After setting fire to the churches of St Nicholas (at Blachernae) and SS Cosmas and Damian farther up the Golden Horn, it too disappeared. Then, at last, the two regents could venture out of the Golden Gate and contemplate the smouldering remains of the Avar siege engines. Before a crowd of onlookers they lifted up their hands to heaven, wept tears of gratitude, and praised God for breaking the enemy with his right hand. Many days were then spent collecting and burying the dead and burning the Slav boats which had not been sunk.[97]

---

[95] *Chron.Pasch.*, 724.9–21; Theod.Sync., *Hom.* I, 311.37–312.27; Geo.Pis., *Bellum Av.*, 475–501.
[96] *Chron.Pasch.*, 724.21–725.15; Theod.Sync., *Hom.* I, 313.5–13; Nic., c.13.36–7.
[97] *Chron.Pasch.*, 725.1–4, 725.15–726.3; Theod.Sync., *Hom.* I, 312.5–7, 312.27–313.4.

A message was sent to the khagan with a fifth piece of disinformation to speed him on his way. Bonus announced that the phantom army had now arrived (an impossibility, since the Persians remained in position, barring access to the city, for some time after the end of the siege). To give added verisimilitude, he named its commander, the emperor's brother Theodore. His supposed arrival enabled Bonus to stand down as a negotiating partner (and thus to withdraw the offers which he had made) on the grounds that his plenipotentiary powers were now revoked. Theodore, he added, and his army were crossing over to Europe and would follow the khagan as far as his own country—an entirely spurious statement about a phantom march by the phantom army. There were no Roman troops to spare for such an operation, the objective of which could be achieved by empty words.[98]

As soon as it was drafted, another message, this time recording events dispassionately and in great detail, was sent off to Heraclius, who was anxiously awaiting it, somewhere within reach of the sea in north-eastern Asia Minor. It was a report on the siege, written by the Patriarch Sergius (hence the attention given to the directing role of the lay regent Bonus and the absence of any reference to the patriarch), with a brief preamble which correctly credited the city's survival to the action of God in his mercy at the instigation of the Virgin Mother, who had interceded on behalf of her servants in the city. When the good news reached him, Heraclius was less discriminating, as he knelt and gave thanks in public. His prayer of gratitude, directed as it was both to God and the Virgin, obscured the distinction between supernatural action (the prerogative of God, lord of creation, both visible and invisible) and intercession by the Virgin as venerated patron of the city. He thanked both for keeping safe the city and peoples entrusted to his care.[99]

Sometime later, the Persians, who had remained powerless spectators throughout the siege, withdrew from the Asian shore of the Bosporus. No reason is given for the time, loosely defined by Theodore Syncellus as several days, which they spent in their positions by Chalcedon after the retreat of the Avars. It is possible that Shahrbaraz was anxious to maintain diplomatic contact with the khagan in the forlorn hope of reinvigorating their alliance and planning some further joint move. Equally, he may have been waiting for intelligence of Shahen's and Heraclius' movements before resuming the hunt for the elusive Roman army. In the event, he set off and disappeared from view. The decisive battle between Heraclius and Shahen evidently took place before he could intervene. When news of Shahen's defeat and death reached him, he probably continued his withdrawal

---

[98] *Chron.Pasch.*, 726.4–10.
[99] *Chron.Pasch.*, 716.9–16 (form of preamble transmitted by the chronicler); Theod.Sync., *Hom.* I, 319.27–320.9.

south-east, to the Middle Eastern provinces which remained firmly under Persian control. He was to stay there for the rest of the war.[100]

Finally, perhaps (as has been suggested above, p. 272) exactly a month after the departure of the last Avar troops, on the feast of the Nativity of the Virgin on 8 September, a formal service of thanksgiving was held by the 'general of armed tears', Sergius, who had managed the city's supernatural defences and sustained the morale of the defenders through the siege. Naturally, it took place at Virgin's premier cult site in Blachernae, close to the watery killing ground where the Avar grand assault had been broken. There, the huge basilica, built by Justin I, which had not been damaged in the last round of Avar destruction on 8 August, could accommodate a large congregation. There, the young emperor and the people of the city gave thanks for their deliverance and listened, I would suggest, to Theodore Syncellus' long sermon, which placed the siege in the larger context of the working out of God's will on earth, arguing that it had been prefigured as well as prophesied in the Old Testament.[101]

Theodore was also deliberately, but cautiously building up the cult of the Virgin as Constantinople's protectress. In his sermon he took the crucial step of attributing supernatural power to her in her own right. She could by the mere exercise of her will, by a simple command or nod, bring about the defeat of the enemy.[102] Naturally, he was careful to attribute the city's deliverance mainly to the action of God, to whom more supplicating prayers are addressed in his account. But he has the young emperor and his siblings direct their prayers to the Virgin alone and has the whole city raise up their hands to God and *ask for the Virgin as champion*.[103] He then singles out three episodes in which the Virgin did intervene as an autonomous supernatural force. She it was who brought victory to a sortie which, on the third day, reached another of her extramural cult sites, Pege, near the Marmara shore. Later, she *summoned up her own strength and force* and singlehandedly won the sea battle. Finally, she was responsible for preventing the Romans from sallying out on the last day, insisting instead that the Avars should burn their own equipment.[104] Three episodes are thus transformed into *miracles worked by the Virgin on behalf of her city*. She is no longer just a highly placed, eloquent advocate of the city in heaven but has become its active protectress on earth, able to intervene with her own supernatural power.

This was not a bold step to take in the circumstances, when popular opinion—including that of the distant emperor—clearly regarded the Virgin as the carrier of formidable power and the city's principal supernatural protector. But it was not

---

[100] Theod.Sync., *Hom.* I, 313.14-27.
[101] *Chron.Pasch.*, 725.20-726.3; Nic., c.13.37-40; Theod.Sync., *Hom.* I.
[102] Theod.Sync., *Hom.* I, 304.10-13, 311.27-8, 312.20.
[103] Theod.Sync., *Hom.* I, 302.31-303.4, 305.7-12, 307.17-38 (prayers to God); 303.10-14 (prayer of imperial young to Theotokos); 304.21-7 (prayer of the city to the Virgin); 303.22-30 (prayer to both).
[104] Theod.Sync., *Hom.* I, 305.38-306.4, 311.17-29, 312.19-22, 28-31.

easy to accommodate within a monotheist framework, and the patriarch had, in his dispatch to the emperor, been careful to circumscribe her power to intercession.[105] The wording and thrust of the syncellus' sermon (surely vetted by the patriarch) reveal that he changed his stance in the following few weeks. At the service of thanksgiving, the church authorities were formally sanctioning the popular view of the Virgin as a semi-divinity. They had been given little choice by the strength of feeling in the jubilant population of the city. A year on, the old and new views coexisted in George of Pisidia's poem—the Virgin is both intercessor and invisible fighter who wields weapons and sinks boats—but opinion has continued to shift and he is ready, at the outset, to credit the deliverance of the city entirely to her.[106]

The attribution of miraculous power on such a scale to the Virgin marked a key stage in the development of her cult. The next task was to protect the chief cult site, Blachernae, from future attack by building an extension to the city's fortifications around it. A start was made after the service of thanksgiving. Then, when the danger of attack was past, the venerated relic of her Robe, which had been rescued in 623, could be reinstalled in the octagonal shrine which stood close by the great basilica at Blachernae. In due course, this happened. Theodore Syncellus was once again called upon to give a sermon. The Virgin's Robe was restored to its proper place in a carefully choreographed ceremony conducted by the patriarch in the presence of Heraclius soon after the end of the war. The cult in its new, enhanced form thus received validation from the heads of church and state and could thenceforth be focused on a material object, a miraculously well-preserved piece of her woollen robe.[107]

8.4 Persian Reverses

Our attention has been caught by one of the climactic events of the war, the fierce Avar assault on Constantinople. But much else was happening in 626. A second Persian field army entered Asia Minor to take part in the conquest of the Romans' one remaining major resource base and the concomitant destruction of the emperor's prestige. Much farther east, a large Turkish army broke into Transcaucasia and, by its depredations, gave an earnest of Turkish determination to strip away Sasanian authority from the region. The source material for these episodes is exiguous by comparison with that for the siege of Constantinople. Nonetheless, we must strive to catch sight of what was going on and to assess its strategic significance.

---

[105] *Chron.Pasch.*, 716.9–16.   [106] Geo.Pis., *Bellum Av.*, 1–9, 380–9, 440–61.
[107] Theod.Sync., *Hom.* II; Nic., c.13.40–1.

Shahen probably invaded Asia Minor a considerable time after Shahrbaraz had followed Heraclius through the Cilician Gates and up onto the plateau at the end of April or the beginning of May. He had had to lick his recruits into fighting shape in exercises conducted probably in Atropatene. He then faced a much longer march to reach Roman territory. His arrival in the north-eastern segment of the plateau within the field of vision of Heraclius's army based at Sebastea should probably be placed two, possibly three months later—so between early July and early August.[108]

Heraclius' smallish expeditionary army had been depleted when reinforcements were rushed off to stiffen the defences of the Constantinople. So there was no question of his engaging Shahen's superior forces in open, orthodox combat. Nor, indeed, could he seize the strategic initiative. He had to wait patiently, concealing his troops in the hills and mountains flanking the river valleys and open terrain through which the Persians were advancing. He could rely on the superior mobility and stamina which his men had demonstrated in the campaigning of the two previous years to keep them out of the enemy's reach until he judged the time right to launch an attack. In effect, he had no choice but to remain on the strategic defensive, looking for any opportunity which might hand him the tactical initiative—perhaps to close in on an enemy detachment which had allowed itself to stray too far from the main force, perhaps to seize on a moment when Shahen's guard was lowered (entering or leaving camp, besieging or despoiling a city), perhaps to lay an ambush in a pass where terrain could act as a powerful Roman ally.

The few sentences into which Theophanes condensed the Official History's account of Roman defensive operations do not bring out their guerrilla character. Heraclius' name has been erased, as we have seen, in an unwarranted editorial intervention on Theophanes' part. However, as has been argued above (p. 265), his brief report on the outcome of the campaign was probably based upon a fuller narrative in the Official History and corresponds to reality. The Roman army in Asia Minor did indeed win a decisive victory. Hence the vanishing of Shahen from the historical record after 626 and a serious loss of Persian fighting manpower which would go some way to explaining an evident shift in the strategic balance in favour of the Romans in the following year.

According to Theophanes, the Persians suffered a crushing defeat, in the course of which a great many of them were slain. Exactly where the fighting took place or how the Romans achieved the victory is not stated. Once the army had broken up, it is hard to envisage many Persians escaping. Some managed to do so, including Shahen, who, Theophanes reports, survived the battle as a broken man and died shortly afterwards. Most surely did not. They were, after all, deep in territory

---

[108] Theoph., 315.2–7.

familiar to their pursuers, and Heraclius had inculcated into his men the crucial importance of extracting every conceivable advantage from victory by prolonged, unrelenting pursuit of the fleeing enemy. It was probably the grave loss of fighting manpower in the course of the flight which prompted Khusro II to have Shahen, one of his two most distinguished generals, disgraced posthumously.

Only one concrete detail about the battle—which, given the numerical weakness of the Romans, may have been drawn out into a series of guerrilla actions gradually disordering the Persian army until eventually it lost its cohesion as a fighting force—is reproduced by Theophanes. At one point, a violent hailstorm disrupted Persian ranks and opened the way for the Romans, who had been unaffected, to rout them. George of Pisidia evidently pointed up this incident in the Official History as a clear demonstration of God's active support for the Christian emperor's war against his impious Zoroastrian foe.[109]

The hailstorm provides a link with a later, quite independent hagiographical text which may well shed additional light on the episode.[110] The context is similar. A Persian army is in northern Asia Minor, in the vicinity of Euchaita, which has the chief shrine of the military martyr St Theodore the Recruit. The Persians are camped outside the city, which seems to have capitulated and to have been despoiled, to judge by the disturbance to the saint's bones in his shrine. A Roman force attacks suddenly and inflicts losses before being driven off. The Persians' angry response is to execute many of the prisoners in their hands and to set fire to the city (including the martyr's church, which has to be reconstructed subsequently by the bishop of the day). They then leave, marching east. After covering some distance, at the foot of Mount Omphalimos (probably modern Bouhale Dağ, some 90 kilometres east of Euchaita) another Roman force attacks and wins a clear victory. The Persians, probably caught strung out in marching order, suffer heavy losses in the engagement, the survivors fleeing east until, another 30 kilometres on, the river Lycus bars their retreat. There, they come under supernatural fire—the hailstorm which is divine revenge for their destruction of the saint's church—and all are killed.[111]

Allowance must be made for transmutation of details in a text as tendentious as the Life of St Theodore, which includes this episode in a small set of his notable posthumous miracles. Allowance must also be made for the additional licence given by time for local sponsors of the saint's cult to rework material in transmission. Much, then, may have changed in the century and a half which elapsed between the last phase of the last Roman-Persian war and the composition of the text, which may have been devised for oral delivery at the annual celebration of

---

[109] Theoph., 315.16–26.
[110] C. Zuckerman, 'The Reign of Constantine V in the Miracles of St. Theodore the Recruit (*BHG* 1764)', *REB* 46 (1988), 191–210, at 206–10. Zuckerman, however, places the episode in 622.
[111] *Vita et miracula S. Theodori Tironis*, ed. H. Delehaye, *Les Légendes grecques des saints militaires* (Paris, 1909), 183–201, at 194.28–196.16, trans. Zuckerman, 'Reign of Constantine V', 202–3, 206.

the saint's feast held at Euchaita. Its composition is probably to be put in the 770s, after a later episode, dated to 753, in which the saint is shown intervening on behalf of his protégés at the time of an Arab raid.[112]

The two accounts tally in essentials. The supernaturally instigated hailstorm plays a vital part in a decisive victory won by Roman over Persian forces in an encounter in northern Asia Minor. A very large number of Persians were killed according to Theophanes. The hagiographical text goes further and has none of the Persians escape. It also supplies precise locations for the encounters and confirms the conjecture that the Romans were forced to adopt guerrilla tactics by presenting the battle as a series of engagements fought in the course of the Persian withdrawal from Euchaita towards the Lycus. It may be suspected that a third encounter, perhaps the decisive one, took place on the river Lycus, the Persians being picked off as they tried to flee or fight their way across. In their determination to allocate as much credit as possible to the saint, the purveyors of the hagiographical tradition may well have allowed the story of the hailstorm to blot out any memory of fighting on the riverbank. This would explain the chief discrepancy between the two accounts, which lies in the placing of the divine intervention before the decisive engagement in Theophanes' version, after it in the sermon. That it is credited to the intercession of different saints, the Mother of God (Theophanes), St Theodore (sermon), should cause little surprise—the local supernatural protector being substituted for the non-local in the local account. Alternatively, it is conceivable that the Official History originally highlighted the role of St Theodore but that Theophanes tampered with the text, transforming the saint into Heraclius' brother Theodore, whom he placed in command of the Roman forces, and crediting the supernatural assistance to the persuasive powers of the Mother of God, who, he knew, saved Constantinople that very same year.

An approximate date for the Roman victory can be fixed from the more voluminous evidence dealing with Constantinople that summer. Neither the Persian nor the Roman army operating in the interior of Asia Minor made any impact on the siege. Nor did news of the outcome of their encounter impinge on either Shahrbaraz or the regents inside the city before 2 August, when delegations from the two sides confronted each other at an audience with the khagan. It is highly unlikely that the Romans would have stuck to their black propaganda line if they had hard news so favourable to their cause to report. The engagements fought in northern Asia Minor must, therefore, be placed in August at the earliest. Two other considerations point to the second half of the month or September as the likely date. Heraclius was unable to return to Constantinople in time to take part in the victory celebration at Blachernae, which, as we have seen, was probably

---

[112] Zuckerman, 'Reign of Constantine V', 193, 203–5.

held on 8 September. From this it may be inferred that the fighting was not over by the end of August. An argument from silence, from the absence of any allusion to Heraclius' victory in the sermon which Theodore Syncellus delivered on that occasion, may suggest further that news of the decisive victory with which the prolonged guerrilla encounter ended had not yet reached Constantinople by the time he spoke, and possibly (since he makes no reference to fighting involving Heraclius) that it had not yet begun.

In Theophanes' account, which combines episodes from two distinct campaigning seasons into a single year entry under 626, Heraclius has been spirited away from the scene of the subtly gained victory over Shahen to Transcaucasia, since he could not be in two places at once and he had to be poised ready to meet the *yabghu khagan* of the Turks at Tiflis in 627.[113] His account of the meeting, based upon the Official History, is prefaced with a summary of Turkish military operations, *which took place in 626*, likewise probably based on the Official History. This can be established by comparing it with the much more detailed account of the *History to 682*. In order to compress two years' worth of Transcaucasian events into one, Theophanes simply juxtaposed the opening military and closing diplomatic episodes, excising everything that happened in between. In doing so he cast aside one of the most interesting and important episodes of the war.

The negotiations conducted, first, at the west Turkish court by Heraclius' emissary Andrew and then by the Turkish embassy which accompanied him back at Heraclius' camp on the lower Kur in the second half of 625 and subsequently in Constantinople had resulted in an alliance and a promise of Turkish military assistance.[114] Acting in accordance with this agreement, the king of the north, the senior eastern khagan (Illig, 621–30), took control of affairs in the west from the junior western khagan, Tong, and dispatched an expeditionary force under the command of a nephew, who held the rank of *shad*, against the Sasanian Empire. The Turks advanced swiftly over Albania and penetrated into Atropatene, killing Christians and non-Christians in large numbers and taking many others prisoner.[115] Theophanes picks out the opening and closing phases of this wide-ranging raiding campaign (described more fully in the *History to 682*), the thrust through the Caspian Gates (heavily fortified), and the devastation of Atropatene, noting the firing of cities and villages as well as the taking of prisoners.[116]

After this impressive demonstration of military power in which considerable economic damage was done to a hitherto untouched region of Sasanian Transcaucasia, the *shad* withdrew from Atropatene, established a camp on the bank of the river Araxes, and sent an embassy to the king of kings. The

---

[113] Theoph., 315.14–16, 316.4–5.   [114] See pp. 238–9.
[115] MD, 142.8–15 (trans. Dowsett, 87–8).   [116] Theoph., 315.26–316.4.

negotiations, together with the operations which had prepared the ground, are placed in Khusro's thirty-seventh regnal year (June 626–June 627).

It is now that the *History to 682* performs an immensely valuable service. It reproduces extracts from the diplomatic note which the Turkish embassy brought with it and from Khusro's reply. The extracts give every appearance of being authentic. The anonymous author of the *History to 682*, who put his text together around the year 682, presumably found them in his principal source for the events of the 620s. This was a local Albanian source which paid close attention to the actions and words of the Catholicos Viroy once he was released from detention in Ctesiphon after the fall of Khusro in February 628. The author was, it may conjectured, a clerical associate of Viroy's. He was a member of the delegation of clergy and notables led by Viroy which presented the formal submission of Albania to the Turkish army later that year. Like his Armenian analogue who wrote the *History of Khosrov*, he probably had access to the archives of the catholicosate, and that is probably where he found copies of the documents.[117]

The Turkish note was an ultimatum. The *shad* announced that the Turks were allied with the Roman emperor and had come to his aid. He issued a series of curt demands: all occupied provinces and cities were to be handed back to the emperor; all Roman prisoners of war were to be released; the True Cross was to be returned; all Persian forces were to be recalled from Roman territory. The consequences would be grim, he warned, if these terms were not met:

> The king of the north and lord of the whole earth, your king and the king of all kings, says as follows: 'I shall set my face against you, governor of Asorestan, and I shall repay you double for the ills you brought upon him. With my sword I shall roam over all your borders, just as you roamed over his borders with your sword. And I shall not leave you be and shall not cease from dealing with you in accordance with the words which I have uttered to you.'[118]

Khusro's initial reaction was one of anger, but this seems soon to have given way to the anxiety which so menacing a note from the great nomad power of the Eurasian steppes was designed to arouse. But he was careful to conceal these emotions under an air of studied calm and haughtiness in the reply which he drafted. At first his tone was respectful and reproachful. He addressed the *yabghu khagan* as 'my brother khagan', thus acknowledging a rough parity of status. He reminded him of the honour and respect in which his ancestors and he had held the khagan's house, as that of a beloved brother. He recalled the marriage alliance which had grafted the two ruling houses together and observed that it was wrong

---

[117] Howard-Johnston, *Witnesses*, 120–2.   [118] MD, 142.16–143.8 (trans. Dowsett, 88).

of the khagan to have cast off these ties at the mere word of his servant, the Roman ruler (called *kt'ricn*, 'disembowelled, castrated', instead of Caesar).[119]

He became more threatening in the second part of the note. This has become detached in the version of the *History to 682* which has reached us—embedded in a universal history focused on Albania written by Movses Daskhurants'i in the tenth century. The copy used by Movses was evidently damaged or disordered.[120] Khusro went on to dismiss Heraclius as a fugitive wandering among the islands of the western sea. He offered to double any offer of gold, silver, jewellery, or cloth made by Heraclius and, finally, issued his own ultimatum. He warned the Turk not to insist that he, Khusro, withdraw his forces from the west or else his wishes might come to pass. For Khusro threatened to recall his great generals from the west, Shahrbaraz, Shahen (as yet undefeated and still in favour), and K'rtikarin (a figure not previously named, probably Shahrbaraz's temporary replacement as commander of Persian forces in the occupied Middle East), along with tens of thousands of elite troops deployed there. He issued his own ultimatum: 'Now behold I shall turn their bridles against the east and I shall arise with all my strength against you, and I shall not leave you be nor give you pause or rest, until I have driven you to the ends of the earth.' For he would have no choice but to keep his massive and invincible forces busy campaigning without interruption in the east once they had been withdrawn from Roman territory in the west.[121]

Khusro's letter was taken back by the Turkish ambassador, a *turakan*. On receiving it, the *shad* withdrew with his army across the Caucasus.[122] This is a sign that autumn was approaching and indicates that the diplomatic activity and the preceding the devastation of Albania and part (presumably the northern sector) of Atropatene had taken several months. It is likely, therefore, that the Turkish campaign had a clear military as well as political purpose. It was intended to cause extensive economic damage to yet another major component of Sasanian Transcaucasia immediately adjoining the zones in Atropatene and Media systematically degraded by Heraclius in 624 and 625. In the north-western territories of the Sasanian Empire, only Iberia, Lazica, and Armenia (away from Heraclius' lines of march) remained unscathed at the end of 626.

This military action also served an ulterior political purpose. It demonstrated, in the most forceful manner possible, Turkish commitment to their new Roman ally, as well as preparing the ground for the ultimatum which was sent to Khusro and which, in an extraordinary display of nomad hauteur, dismissed the Persian king who had achieved more than any of his precursors, save Darius and Xerxes, as a mere governor of Mesopotamia. The Turks, who cannot have expected

---

[119] MD, 143.9–19 (trans. Dowsett, 88). [120] Howard-Johnston, *Witnesses*, 105–13.
[121] MD, 133.16–134.17 (trans. Dowsett, 81–2).
[122] MD, 134.17–18, 143.19–20 (trans. Dowsett, 82, 88).

Khusro meekly to comply with their terms, were issuing a declaration of war. They were making plain, both to Khusro's government and to the Sasanian world at large, their determination to rescue the Roman Empire. They remained in touch with the Roman authorities and, during the campaign or (more probably) the following autumn and winter months, agreed on a joint strategy for 627. Tiflis, the provincial capital of Iberia, was designated the prime target. The campaign was to involve an even more striking public display of the two powers' unity of purpose intended to impress and depress governing circles and local elites throughout the Sasanian Empire.

A year which the Persians had begun with high hopes ended in very sombre fashion. The defeat of Shahen's expeditionary force in Asia Minor was almost as serious a reverse as the failure of the Avars to capture Constantinople (which would have deprived Heraclius of his safest haven and organizing centre). They had failed to trap Heraclius' army and break it as an effective fighting force. They had not managed to strip the emperor of the prestige which he had accumulated in the two previous years of campaigning. They had not embarked on the systematic conquest of Asia Minor. Instead, one of the two armies to which these campaign tasks had been assigned had been eliminated in a brilliantly conducted guerrilla encounter. A grave blow was thereby struck at the overall military position of the Sasanian Empire.

The manpower consequences were serious enough by themselves. Almost all the fighting strength of a field army (say 25–30,000 men) was lost in Asia Minor.[123] But there were several political repercussions. Enthusiasm for the war undoubtedly plummeted as the final victory, so tantalizingly close at the beginning of the year, receded into the distance. Disenchantment surely took hold of the families of the soldiers who had fallen after so many years of campaigning far from home. Opposition could be expected to grow in the occupied territories now that a Roman emperor had not only taken the war to the enemy but had defeated one of the two great conquering generals. Few troops, if any, could be spared from Shahrbaraz's command to meet the new Turkish threat from across the Caucasus and from central Asia. Whatever Khusro might say in his diplomatic note to the Turks, there was no question of his recalling Shahrbaraz and redeploying him and much of the army under his command in Transcaucasia, as had happened at the end of 624. Finally, Khusro's own position was weakened. Shahen's defeat brought into question his whole project of annexing the east Roman Empire. He did not have the resources simultaneously to hold the occupied territories, contain the swift-moving, deadly force commanded by Heraclius, and now cope with the full might of the great power of the north. And yet he

---

[123] Not the grossly inflated figure suggested by Theoph., 315.4–6, who has 50,000 troops transferred from Shahrbaraz's command. Cf. J. Haldon, *Warfare, State and Society in the Byzantine World, 565–1204* (London, 1999), 99–106 who views 20,000 as the upper limit.

could not possibly relinquish all the gains which his forces had made in the west. A policy which had, at great human and financial cost, been driving Iran steadily towards supremacy in the sedentary world of western Eurasia suddenly looked fraught with danger. Doom, it could be argued, was now coming with long strides upon Persia.

9
Heraclius' Second Counteroffensive

The small Roman expeditionary force which Heraclius led deep into Sasanian Transcaucasia in 624 had demonstrated remarkable physical and mental resilience. Apart from a period, in the first part of the 625 campaigning season when the northern auxiliaries, or at least some of them, exercised a restraining influence, the last army which the truncated empire could field had moved with an impudent, bold abandon. Khusro's main invasion force had been surprised and dispersed without a fight in 624. Three Persian armies, each on its own a match for the Romans, had been outmanoeuvred and defeated in detail in the course of the wearing operations of 625. Finally, the delayed Persian invasion of Asia Minor in 626 had gone disastrously wrong when the Romans, pushed onto the defensive, resorted to guerrilla tactics and annihilated one of the two field armies involved.

Heraclius had proved himself to be a commander of genius. False intelligence and deliberately misleading moves had repeatedly deceived and weakened his adversaries. Superior strategic mobility and tactical flexibility had enabled him to choose the time and place for battle. An advantage once gained had been exploited ruthlessly to the full. By late autumn 626 serious damage had been inflicted on the Sasanian Empire. Whole regions of the north-west had been systematically degraded—part of Media, much of Atropatene, and, through the actions of Heraclius' Turkish allies, much of Albania. Yet more important were the cumulative loss of fighting manpower inflicted on the Persians by successive defeats and the political shock induced by the intervention of the Turkish khaganate on the Roman side. Hard fighting lay ahead. The Iranian heartland of the empire was now vulnerable to attack both by Romans and by Turks, from the west (through Armenia), from the north (across the Caucasus), and from central Asia in the east. A long defensive war lay ahead which would be putting yet more strain on the manpower and material resources of the empire.

First, though, winter intervened and brought operations to a halt. The Turkish army commanded by the *shad*, the nephew of the senior eastern khagan, withdrew north of the Caucasus. Persian defences had been tested and found wanting. A great deal of booty—prisoners, livestock, gold and silver vessels, precious cloth—was brought back. An expedition which had acted as both a reconnaissance foray and an armed embassy had established that no serious obstacles would confront an invasion in massive force. The *yabghu khagan*, referred to loosely as the Turks' 'prince and lord' in the *History to 682*, now decided that he would direct operations himself and issued mobilization orders to all his subjects. The range of peoples involved was probably as great, if not greater than that involved in the Avar mobilization against Constantinople a year or more earlier: mountain and plain dwellers, settled and nomadic, islanders and mainlanders, shaven-headed and long-haired are listed. They were to appear ready for action at his signal the following spring.[1]

Heraclius too paused for a while. With both Asia Minor and Constantinople safe from attack that winter, he could allow his men to rest and recuperate. To ease the problem of provisioning, they were divided up and dispersed across western Asia Minor. A chance remark in the *History of Khosrov* tacked onto the end of its account of Shahrbaraz's pursuit of Heraclius in spring 626 gives us this information.[2] Heraclius' own movements in autumn and winter 626–7, which go unreported in the sources, must be inferred from circumstantial evidence. There can be little doubt, though, that he returned to Constantinople as soon as he could after destroying Shahen's army. Apart from the boost to morale which his presence would give to the population of the capital, he needed to assure himself that the administration which he had left in place had performed well during his absence. Changes of senior personnel or of structures might be required, and these he would naturally like to oversee. Not to mention briefings on fiscal matters and on foreign affairs, especially on events in the Balkans and beyond, where Avar hegemony was being challenged. What remained of the Roman Empire could only be managed from Constantinople. Diplomacy too was best conducted from a centrally placed capital city with experienced diplomatic staff to hand.

Heraclius only returned late in the autumn. He was not back in time for the celebration of the city's repulse of the Avars on 8 September. The description given by Theodore Syncellus in his sermon of Heraclius' behaviour and words before and after the arrival of couriers from Constantinople was based on information got from the couriers on their return and what Heraclius himself had written.[3] If, as seems probable, the wearing down and destruction of Shahen's army was not completed until the second half of the month, and if Heraclius then organized the army's dispositions for the following winter before he left, he is unlikely to have reached Constantinople before the middle of October. Of his actions there, apart from those conjectured above, very little can be said. Presumably he, like his men, relaxed after his prolonged exertions. But there were plans to be made for a new campaign in the spring, as well as for a high-level meeting between Heraclius and the Turkish khagan. These had probably been agreed with the *shad* when he was in communicating distance at his camp on the Araxes, at the same time as he was issuing the ultimatum to the Persians and waiting for Khusro's reply.

---

[1] MD, 134.17–135.4 (trans. Dowsett, 82–3). [2] Ps.S., 126.8–10.
[3] Theod.Sync., *Hom.* I, 319.27–320.9.

The only evidence for the operations planned comes from the subsequent actions of the two sides, but since no serious opposition was encountered from the Persians and nothing happened to disrupt arrangements until after the two armies had made their rendezvous, it is reasonable to assume that outcome corresponded to plan up to that point. It follows that the summit meeting was scheduled from the start to take place in Iberia, within sight of Tiflis, as a public demonstration of their unity of purpose. It would be preceded by a renewed Turkish invasion and seizure of Albania, while the Roman army entered and occupied Lazica. Persian and local Iberian forces were thus to be caught in a pincer movement, the Turks moving west up the Kur valley and laying siege to the regional capital Tiflis, the Romans advancing from the west over the formidable Likhi mountain range to join the Turks before Tiflis. Subsequent actions during that campaigning season were probably left for joint decision by the two leaders once they met, but both were committed to a common objective, namely the inflicting of as much economic damage as possible on hitherto untouched regions of the Persian Empire. This would be the most effective way of causing serious damage to Khusro's political standing.

9.1 Turkish-Roman Alliance

The uneven coverage of the principal sources hampers historical reconstruction of events in late 626 and 627 at many turns. The *Chronicon Paschale* is largely silent about the war in the 620s, restricting itself to the siege of Constantinople and the final political denouement in Ctesiphon in early 628. The last episode covered by George of Pisidia's full-bodied poems was the Avar attack on Constantinople. Theophanes' highly condensed version of the Official History commissioned from George has excised most of what was written about the movements of Heraclius and his expeditionary force between spring 626 and summer 627. The second continuation of John of Antioch's chronicle, recycled by the Patriarch Nicephorus, presents a chronologically mauled account of the war and conflates Heraclius' first and second counteroffensives. All later Byzantine accounts derive from Theophanes or Nicephorus or, usually, a combination of the two. Hence the inferences and conjectures to which we have had to resort about the 626 campaign in Asia Minor and about Heraclius' subsequent return to Constantinople.[4]

It is a moot point whether or not the *Khwadaynamag*, dating in its final written form from the reign of Yazdgerd III (632–52), covered the military operations and diplomacy of Heraclius before the sudden materializing of Heraclius and his

---

[4] Howard-Johnston, *Witnesses*, 20–5 (G of P), 54–5 (*Chron.Pasch.*), 248–56 (Nic. and second continuation of JA), 284–8 (Theoph.).

army on Persian territory in autumn 627, poised to attack the metropolitan region. Even if it did, very little of its material percolated into extant sources (Armenian, Syrian, Arab, and Persian).[5] Finally little reliance can be placed on the reconstruction (combining elements of the hypothetical *Khwadaynamag* tradition with Roman material) made by Theophilus of Edessa which was transmitted in its fullest form in the chronicle of Dionysius of Tel-Mahre.[6]

It would have been quite impossible to offer any modern reconstruction of events from late autumn 626 to the end of summer 627 if Movses Daskhurants'i had not recycled, with scarcely any tampering, the *History to 682* which had come into his hands (in an only slightly dishevelled state). That text, the work of an author capable of writing elegantly and movingly, combined material taken from the *Khwadaynamag* (picking up the story when Heraclius was threatening Khusro himself) with a local Albanian source, rich in information which is arranged annalistically under regnal years of Khusro.[7] The local Albanian source (as noted in Chapter 8) supplies good information about Turkish-Persian diplomatic exchanges in 626 and the actions of Turks and Romans within the field of vision of Albania in 627. Its detailed narrative also contains incidental information about Persian dispositions which, pieced together, gives some idea of the defensive preparations put in hand by spring 627.

Khusro had no choice but to adopt a very defensive posture. The losses suffered in 626 and commitments elsewhere left him short of manpower. Those commitments included the defence of the steppe frontier beyond Khurasan (the possibility that the Turks might attack there, as in 615, could not be excluded) as well as the continuing military occupation of the Roman half of the Middle East. Khusro's strategy in Transcaucasia relied in the main on fixed, manmade defences. Generations of investment in military infrastructure had effectually blocked up the long, narrow passage separating the eastern slopes of the Caucasus from the waters of the Caspian Sea. A series of defensive lines had been constructed, of which the most important hinged on the great fortress at Chor ('The Gate') at Derbend. From the fortress a strong wall guarded by forts at regular intervals pushed its way inland over the folds of the mountains.[8] The governor of Albania, Gayshak', who may have been appointed specially to take charge of its defence,

---

[5] Howard-Johnston, *Witnesses*, 345–7, 349–51.Cf. Z. Rubin, 'Ibn al-Muqaffa' and the Account of Sasanian History in the Arabic Codex Sprenger 30', *JSAI* 30 (2005), 52–93, at 83–7.

[6] Howard-Johnston, *Witnesses*, 199–206, 341.

[7] Howard-Johnston, *Witnesses*, 108–113, 121–4.

[8] K. V. Trever, *Ocherki po istorii i kul'ture kavkazkoj Albanii IV v. do N.E.—VII v. N.E.* (Moscow and Leningrad, 1959), 267–87, 346–53; S. Khan Magomedov, *Derbent—Gornaja stena—Auly Tabarasana* (Moscow, 1979), 16–36, 69–127, 207–27; R. H. Hewsen, *Armenia: A Historical Atlas* (Chicago, 2001), 89, 91; M. S. Gadzhiev, *Drevnii gorod Dagestana: Opyt istoriko topograficheskovo i sotsiul'no-ekonomicheskovo analiza* (Moscow, 2002), 42–8; A. A. Aliev, M. S. Gadjiev, M. G. Gaither, P. L. Kohl, R. M. Magomedov, and I. N. Aliev, 'The Ghilghilchay Defensive Long Wall: New Investigations', *Ancient West and East*, 5 (2006), 143–77; M. S. Gadzhiev and S. J. Kasumova, *Srednepersidskie nadpisi Derbenta VI beka* (Moscow, 2006).

looked in the first instance to the garrison of Chor to hold up the Turks. That garrison had surely been reinforced to carry out this formidable task. Forward defence was the only feasible way of protecting the partly fortified settlements of the open country of Albania on both banks of the Kur.[9] No consideration was given to holding the line of the Kur, too easily crossed by a nomad army and presenting far too long a frontage. Instead, Gayshak' decided to concentrate on the defence of the regional capital, Part'aw. For this he secured the agreement of the magnates of the countryside and the inhabitants of the city (represented presumably by the leading notables). The population of the surrounding districts, together with their portable possessions, were evacuated to the city. Nothing is said about the provisioning of the city with its inflated population, but foodstuffs must have been stockpiled to enable it to withstand weeks, if not months, under siege.[10]

No mention is made of any field army assigned to the defence of Albania or of any other part of Transcaucasia in the *History to 682*. But it is inconceivable that Khusro left the whole region without any mobile force capable of bringing relief to a beleaguered garrison or of shadowing and harassing the enemy when the Turks had made their intentions of invading so plain. Such a force did indeed come into view later in the campaign, when Heraclius marched south into Armenia. A Persian army commanded by a certain Rahzadh was monitoring the Romans' movements from a safe distance. Later, Rahzadh set off on a hectic pursuit when he realized belatedly that Heraclius was intending to invade Mesopotamia.[11] While it is unlikely that Rahzadh's army was numerically inferior to Heraclius', both his actions and, much later, his words (repeated pleas to Khusro for reinforcements) reveal him to have been a cautious commander, understandably nervous of tangling with Heraclius. This sensible caution explains why he made no attempt to intervene earlier in the campaigning season when Turks and Romans were coordinating their operations and his army was undoubtedly heavily outnumbered. This in turn explains why his army did not feature in the local Albanian account of the Turkish invasion of Albania and Iberia but was first mentioned when material from the *Khwadaynamag* (about Heraclius' operations in Mesopotamia) was picked up by the *History to 682*. The statement that Rahzadh was only appointed at the last moment to command a scratch force from troops to hand when Heraclius had already crossed the Zagros is a concoction of an intelligent writer who evidently felt the need to link the material from his two sources together and devised his own explanation for Rahzadh's belated appearance in the second of them.[12]

---

[9] K. Alizadeh, 'Borderland Projects of the Sasanian Empire: Intersection of Domestic and Foreign Policies', *Journal of Ancient History*, 2 (2014), 93–115.
[10] MD, 135.8–19 (trans. Dowsett, 83). [11] Ps.S., 126.11–19.
[12] MD, 143.21–144.16 (trans. Dowsett, 88–9).

Finally, when, at a late stage, the Persians got wind of the danger threatening Tiflis, the site of the planned Roman-Turkish rendezvous, a small elite force of 1000 cavalry from Khusro's guards regiments was rushed in to stiffen its defence before it came under attack. Khusro is pictured as sending them off all the way from Ctesiphon in what is a most implausible scenario. It is much more likely that they were serving in Rahzadh's army, which was mainly composed of units previously stationed in the metropolitan region. If so, they were seconded from Rahzadh's army when he realized that Tiflis was the Turks' and the Romans' objective. The officer in command, a certain Sharhapał, was presumably one of his subordinates.[13]

Very little can be said about the movements of Heraclius and his army before they joined the Turks before the walls of Tiflis. Only two items of information have been preserved. Nicephorus, whose account is recycled in later Byzantine sources in varying combinations with material ultimately originating in Theophanes, reports that Heraclius sailed across the Black Sea to take charge of the campaign. There is corroboration from the *History to 682*, which, however, misplaces the sea voyage at the start of the first counteroffensive in 624. Nicephorus defines Heraclius' initial objective as Lazica. The *History to 682* again provides confirmation, as does Theophanes, who, in a passage based on the Official History, reports that Heraclius entered Lazica and spent some time there until news came that the Turks had laid siege to Tiflis.[14]

Some inferences can be drawn from these bald statements of fact. There is nothing to indicate that Heraclius was accompanied other than by his usual entourage on the voyage. Apart from the logistical difficulty of transporting a large military force by sea (and the pointlessness of doing so, given that they were already based in Asia Minor), there was always the risk entailed by voyages across a sea as temperamental as the Black Sea. While a small number of rapid sailing vessels could convey the emperor and his staff in reasonable safety, the same could not be said of a large, cumbersome convoy of transport vessels. It follows that the field army probably reassembled in western Asia Minor and marched overland to a forward position within striking distance of Lazica, where it was joined, probably in late spring or early summer, by Heraclius when the time came to start operations. Two late sources, neither possessing much intrinsic authority, name Trebizond as the port where Heraclius disembarked. Although little weight should be attached to their testimony, it made sense for the army to halt and prepare for the campaign once it had reached Trebizond. For it is from that point that the foothills of the Pontic mountains step back from the sea and leave a wide, flat coastal strip running east towards Lazica which is only reduced to a narrow passage for a short stretch beyond the mouth of the river Çoruh. Trebizond, at the

[13] MD, 138.6–11 (trans. Dowsett, 85).
[14] Nic., c.12.7–14; MD, 130.16–131.4 (trans. Dowsett, 78–9); Theoph., 315.14–16.

head of this natural avenue of invasion but at a relatively safe distance from Lazica, was a convenient forward base.

Once Heraclius had rejoined his troops and satisfied himself that they were ready for another arduous campaign, he set off for Lazica. There is no hint that Lazica was subjected to systematic depredation. It was not in the Roman interest to do so, given that the Laz, like other peoples living in the eastern coastlands of the Black Sea, had long been responsive to Roman influence and had already supplied contingents to serve with the Roman expeditionary force. The ravaging and economic degradation to which Albania, deep in the Persian sphere of Transcaucasia and like Iberia traditionally loyal to the Sasanians, had been subjected by the Turks in 626 was quite inappropriate in the case of Lazica. Heraclius probably limited military operations to expelling the Persian authorities and such Persian forces as were stationed there, and to impressing Roman authority, albeit only temporarily, on the Laz and their neighbours while he waited for news of the Turks.

The Turks launched their attack through the Caspian Gates. So large and fearsome was their army, so intense was their arrow fire, that the Persian garrison at Chor was overwhelmed. The *History to 682* gives a graphic description of their shock at the sight of the nomad enemy and of the carnage which followed the storming of the fortress. Streets and alleyways were littered with the bodies of young men and women, the old, those who were disabled, and mothers now suckling their babies with blood. The Turks swept through the fortress like fire through straw, in one gate, out another, and then continued on their way south. Their objective was now Part'aw.[15]

Gayshak', the Persian governor, the magnates and urban authorities, together with the refugees crowded into the city, watched as they came nearer and nearer in what seems to have been a steady, orderly march, the army being accompanied by a baggage train of wagons and pack animals. Finally, when they were very close to the city (a mere three miles away), nerves broke. The sacking of Chor was an exemplary act of terror which had been acting on the minds of those cooped up in Part'aw. A meeting convened by Gayshak' to boost morale and to plan ahead went disastrously wrong when Gayshak', himself overcome by fear, with his knees knocking together, was unable to utter a word to his frightened audience. The meeting broke up in uproar, as those present (probably the leading elements among the refugees and the city population) complained vociferously about being trapped in the city, ready to be offered up to a bloodthirsty enemy, and then decided to make a bolt for freedom. Abandoning their baggage and portable possessions, ignoring the mass of refugees who could not possibly all escape in

---

[15] MD, 135.20–136.13 (trans. Dowsett, 83–4); cf. Theoph., 315.26–316.4 (anachronistically calling the Turks Khazars).

time, they opened all four gates, rushed out, and aimed for the foothills of the mountains behind the city.[16]

The Turks thus captured Part'aw without any exertion on their part. They chased the fugitives into the hills, catching one party, some of whom were killed, others taken prisoner. But they made no attempt to press on into the rugged terrain of Arts'akh as night fell that day nor on subsequent days. The great majority of the fugitives were thus able to make their way deep into the natural fastness of Arts'akh, where they saw out the Turkish campaign. Most of those who had crowded into Part'aw were probably unable to escape but do not seem to have suffered at Turkish hands. Instant capitulation saved their lives. The Turks took control of the city but probably managed it from the camp which they had established outside on the day of their arrival.[17] From this base, they could also maintain control over the lowlands of Albania and keep watch on the refugees penned up in Arts'akh, thus securing their communications for the second phase of the campaign, the invasion of Iberia. Possession of Part'aw also provided them with an abundant and conveniently placed source of supplies, both for the main body of the army which pushed on west and for the force left behind at Part'aw. The foodstuffs stockpiled in the city for the expected siege were now available for use by the Turks, saving them from some two months' foraging and easing the logistical task of sustaining the expeditionary force as it besieged Tiflis, the capital of Iberia.

If the similes used in the *History to 682* can be trusted, there was now a perceptible quickening in the pace of Turkish movements. Before it had been waves advancing little by little; now it became a rapidly flowing river or torrent. Perhaps—but this is no more than a wild surmise—they had received intelligence that reinforcements were on their way to Tiflis and tried to get there first. In any case, they were soon laying siege to the city after an apparently uneventful march and sent Heraclius the message which he was expecting. At which Heraclius marched swiftly east, confident of an easy passage through the difficult intervening country because Persian forces in the region were penned up in Tiflis.[18]

The Romans were given an impressive ceremonial welcome. The *yabghu khagan* rode out to meet Heraclius. The two rulers embraced, and then, according to the Roman version, the *yabghu khagan* did obeisance. Turkish troops were drawn up to receive the emperor, with their officers at a higher level on natural rock platforms. Both troops and officers then prostrated themselves in honour of the emperor. Theophanes only transmits a condensed and truncated account of the scene as described in the Official History but notes that this form of obeisance was unfamiliar to barbarians. It may be suspected that George did an extended turn about the extraordinary deference shown by the Turks on this occasion,

---

[16] MD, 136.14–137.7 (trans. Dowsett, 84).   [17] MD, 137.8–19 (trans. Dowsett, 84–5).
[18] MD, 137.20–138.2 (trans. Dowsett, 85); Theoph., 316.4–5.

going so far as to liken their prostration to that of courtiers in the Great Palace in Constantinople and to suggest that such a show was without precedent among non-Roman peoples.

The ceremony took place in full view of the defenders of Tiflis. It was a carefully stage-managed display of Roman-Turkish amity intended surely to impress public opinion in Transcaucasia and the Sasanian Empire at large. The *yabghu khagan* then presented his teenage son and was said to have taken pleasure in Heraclius' conversation and to have been impressed by his appearance and good sense. At this point Theophanes cuts short his account of the meeting, forcing us to rely on the less trustworthy but fuller version given by Nicephorus (taken from the second continuation of John of Antioch). Nicephorus muddles some of the details: he transforms the initial embrace of the two rulers (betokening a rough parity in status) into self-abasement on the part of the *yabghu khagan* (he *dismounts* and does obeisance, *before* being allowed to remount and embrace the emperor); he has also somehow confused the presentation of the Turkish ruler's son with his (the ruler's) designation as Heraclius' notional son. But there is nothing obviously awry in his account of other ceremonial aspects of the encounter. He reports that Heraclius crowned the *yabghu khagan* with the crown he was wearing, a signal mark of honour, reciprocating that which he had received at his arrival. The Turkish ruler was being invested with the dignity of a quasi-co-emperor. A feast was then laid on for the Turks with a full display of Roman magnificence, after which all the plate together with the imperial robes and pearl earrings were presented to the *yabghu khagan*. There followed a ceremony in which Heraclius decorated the leading Turkish officers with similar pearl earrings.

The elaborate protocol framed a meeting fraught with military and political significance. The Roman-Turkish alliance was being displayed on Persian territory before Persian spectators on the walls of Tiflis. There was also serious business to be transacted: military plans needed to be made for immediate and longer-term joint action by the allies; and, yet more important, a step was taken which would create a close political connection between the two sides. Heraclius formally agreed to marry his teenage daughter, the Augusta Eudocia, to the *yabghu khagan*. He had a portrait of her with him which he showed to his prospective son-in-law. The marriage was to take place in two years' time.[19]

This dynastic marriage was without precedent in the East Roman world, involving as it did so close a relative of the reigning emperor and creating a familial tie with the very type of the barbarian, a northern nomad. It had doubtless occasioned much debate the previous winter in Constantinople. But any ideological hesitation faded away at the prospect of strengthening the Turkish-Roman

---

[19] MD, 138.2–4 (trans. Dowsett, 85); Theoph., 316.5–13; Nic., c.12.19–40. Cf. C. Zuckerman, 'La Petite Augusta et le Turc: Epiphania-Eudocie sur les monnaies d'Héraclius', *Revue Numismatique*, 150 (1995), 113–26, at 117–18, 121–3.

axis and of impressing its solidity as forcefully as possible on Sasanian opinion. The ceremonial respect shown to the *yabghu khagan* makes sense in this context. It was pointing up the close kinship tie which was being established between the Romans and the Turks and the consequent severing of the connections between the Turkish and Sasanian ruling houses to which Khusro (himself the grandson of a Hephthalite princess) had appealed in his letter to the *shad*.[20] The *yabghu khagan* was crowned qua future husband of the Augusta. The presents which were lavished upon him could be taken to be, indeed perhaps were, partly a down payment on the dowry. No wonder both sides took pleasure in the meeting, as the *History to 682* reports, perhaps catching the tone of a communiqué issued about it.[21]

Turks and Romans then turned their attention to the recalcitrant city before them. The *History to 682*, our sole reliable source for the siege of Tiflis, gives no clue as to its length, but makes it clear that, for a while, the two armies concentrated on capturing the city. Although, as we have seen, nomad forces did not lack technical expertise in siege warfare, it is the Romans who are credited with the construction of the machines deployed against the walls, including artillery pieces capable of discharging large projectiles accurately enough to cause serious damage to the walls and four-wheeled structures (probably mobile armoured shelters for sappers). The Romans also diverted the river with goatskins filled with sand and stones so that it undermined the walls. Breaches were made in the city's defences, but they were swiftly repaired by a garrison whose morale remained high. It was the besiegers who lost heart first, despite their overwhelming superiority. They had incurred heavy casualties among the infantry carrying out the siege operations and they seemed to be making little headway. The two leaders conferred, the Turk agreeing with Heraclius' suggestion that the strong man's house should be plundered when he was tied up (Matt. 12.29). He was referring presumably to the surrounding region, hitherto unaffected by the war. Iberia was an inviting target for raiding, with local forces bottled up in the regional capital. Widespread devastation would serve a double purpose: it would undermine the determination of the defenders, while inflicting serious economic damage on another large component of the Sasanian Empire. Like Albania, which the Turks had ravaged in 626, Iberia had forfeited any claim to be spared by its commitment to the Persian cause.[22]

There is no clear account of that campaign. This third phase of the 627 military operations, following the initial attacks from north and east and the strenuous efforts of both armies to breach the defences of Tiflis over a month or more, has been squeezed out from both extant accounts. The author of the *History to 682* introduces instead an anecdote about the insulting behaviour of the defenders,

---

[20] MD, 143.14–19 (trans. Dowsett, 88).   [21] MD, 138.3–4 (trans. Dowsett, 85).
[22] MD, 138.4–6, 138.11–139.7 (trans. Dowsett, 85–6).

who set up and mocked crude images of the two enemy rulers on the eve of their departure, which, it is implied, takes place at the latest in early summer. He seems to have made two false assumptions: (1) that Heraclius planned to invade Mesopotamia in summer, whereas the beginning of his march south is securely dated to September by Theophanes' version of the Official History, which brings him to the northern edge of the Zagros by 9 October; and (2) that Turks could not cope with hot weather.[23] Theophanes, however, has misapprehensions of his own. He supposes that intensive siege operations against Tiflis lasted all summer so that the joint Roman-Turkish operations could only begin in autumn. He has the two rulers part, as they surely did, at the end of the siege, the khagan returning to his own territory in the north. while Heraclius sets off on his long march south. He knows, from the Official History and from Theophilus of Edessa, that joint operations in the field were carried out, but he has left no time for the raiding of Iberia. So he has a large Turkish force, its strength put at 40,000 men by Theophilus, join the Roman invasion of Mesopotamia in the autumn under Heraclius' command, rather than attack the 'house' (i.e. Iberia) guarded by the garrison of Tiflis. He knows too that there were no Turks involved in operations south of the Zagros. So he has them slip off, first in small groups, then the main body all together, daunted at the prospect of winter and Persian harassment.[24]

In reality the khagan's withdrawal was surely prompted by awareness of the distance separating his army from its base in the steppes and of the danger that his lines of communication might be severed if they were extended farther across a second great mountain range (the Zagros). Much had been achieved by the campaign. Above all, it had demonstrated in the most public manner possible the political solidarity of the two powers and the military threat which that entailed for the Sasanian Empire.

From the moment of their parting, the leading role was to be Heraclius' until the following spring. He told the khagan that he intended to strike at the metropolitan region in Mesopotamia, his hope being to prompt Khusro's subjects into ridding themselves of him. Political revolution ushering in a new, more amenable regime, not outright military victory, was already his aim, according to the *History to 682* (but hindsight may have exercised some influence here). The campaign ahead was fraught with danger and best carried out by a small, swift-moving force familiar with both the terrain and the climate. But Heraclius clearly did not expect to bring down Khusro by a single surgical strike at his capital. The war would last some time yet, and the Turkish alliance would be playing a vital part, first by redressing the military balance which otherwise would favour the Persians, and, second, by adding to the political pressure on Khusro's regime. The

---

[23] MD, 139.7–140.14 (trans. Dowsett, 86); Theoph., 317.11–12, 26–7.
[24] Theoph., 316.13–16, 317.11–16; Agap., 462.12–463.1, Mich.Syr., 409, Chron.1234, 233.4–9 (trans. Hoyland, 74).

khagan was to reappear with his army in 628. Once again the rendezvous was to be Tiflis. The recalcitrant city was going to subjected to a second testing siege.[25]

9.2 Invasion of Mesopotamia

Heraclius is presented as boosting the morale of his men after the departure of the Turks with another of the harangues with which George of Pisidia embellished the Official History. What need have they of human allies, he tells them, when God and His Virgin Mother are on their side and can now demonstrate their ability to help those who put their faith in them. The dramatic scene was probably set outside the walls of Tiflis, trepidation at what the future might hold beginning to suffuse Roman minds until the emperor spoke. As has been noted, it has been misplaced (put much farther south) and misdated (latish in September) by Theophanes, partly misled by the vague notice he found in Theophilus referring to joint operations with the Turks. In reality, from the moment it set off south early in September, the Roman expeditionary force had to rely on its own skills, above all its speed of movement and powers of endurance, and on the intelligence of its commander to achieve its objectives.[26]

Heraclius marched south into Armenia, skirting the western flank of Mount Aragats. He forded the Araxes by the small town of Vardanakert (on the south bank), climbed over the huge western shoulder of Mount Ararat, and entered the province of Gogovit. It is now that the Persian field army commanded by Rahzadh comes into view for the first time.[27] Rahzadh, it seems, was monitoring Heraclius' movements. It may be conjectured that he was doing so from the plain of Dvin, where his troops could be provisioned without difficulty. A ring of mountains to the north would have shielded him from Albania and Iberia while the Turkish and Roman armies were conducting their joint operations. He was also in position to march north if need be, either to the defence of the fugitives holed up in the highlands of Arts'akh, if they came under sustained attack, or to try to relieve Tiflis, if were in imminent danger of falling. He remained at a safe distance from Heraclius as he marched south, with first the mass of Mount Aragats and later the Araxes and Ararat separating him from the Romans.

Rahzadh stayed put. The Romans' direction of march, which took them into Gogovit, from which an easy pass led into the upper basin of the river Arsanias and the natural thoroughfare west down its valley, probably deceived Rahzadh into thinking that Heraclius was doing the sensible thing and was withdrawing towards Roman-held territory in Asia Minor by a circuitous, southern route. But

---

[25] MD, 139.9–17, 140.8–14 (trans. Dowsett, 86).
[26] Theoph., 317.16–21; Agap., 463.8–464.2, *Chron.1234*, 233.28–234.2 (trans. Hoyland, 75–6).
[27] Ps.S., 126.11–15; cf. Theoph., 317.21–4.

instead of turning west in Gogovit, Heraclius continued south-east and entered Atropatene. He did as much damage as he could to the towns and villages in his path without slowing up his march. He passed through the districts of Her and Zarewand, marched down the west side of Lake Urmia, an area not previously subjected to attack, and pushed on into the north-eastern outliers of the Zagros. On 9 October he halted in the district of Chamaitha to rest his army before the arduous crossing of the mountains of Kurdistan.[28]

Chamaitha, which appears in Syriac sources as Hnita, a diocese of the Nestorian Church in the mountainous hinterland of Assyria east of the Great Zab, should almost certainly be identified with the 90-kilometre long valley (at the head of the Lesser Zab) which runs just behind the modern Iranian-Iraqi frontier, from Piranshahr in the north to Sardasht in the south, and to which there is relatively easy access from the south-west corner of Lake Urmia. It was and is the largest of the enclosed upland basins which lurk amid the formidable mountains of Kurdistan and can provide secure shelter for a large number of people as long as such weak points as there are in their mountain peripheries are secured against attack. With abundant provisions to hand, especially pasture for the horses, no better arena could have been found for rest and recuperation. Chamaitha was also conveniently positioned at the head of the two main passes, both practicable for a large force, which led into the mountain basins of the Great and Lesser Zab. As and when he chose, Heraclius could thrust west by one or other of these routes over the main ridges of the north-eastern Zagros, aiming for other enclosed basins rich in agriculture and pasture which could then themselves act as secure bases from which to invade the plains of northern Assyria.[29]

Rahzadh only realized his mistake when Heraclius was already in Atropatene. He set off in pursuit, taking a more easterly route which would ensure that he did not come too close to so dangerous an adversary. He marched down the Araxes plain to Nakhchawan, crossed the river, and, keeping to the east of Lake Urmia, managed to reach Ganzak while the Romans were still encamped in Chamaitha. After a week spent in Chamaitha, during which he doubtless considered his longer-term strategic options and immediate tactics in conjunction with his staff,

---

[28] Theoph., 317.24–7; ps.S., 126.14–16.
[29] Nav.Int.Div., *Persia*, 53–4; J. M. Fiey, *Assyrie chrétienne*, 3 vols. (Beirut, 1965–8), I, 191–2, 198–9, 208–9, 213–14, and map facing p.225, squeezes the diocese of Hnita into the highlands immediately west of Ruwandiz along with two other dioceses Ma'alta and Hewton. It is more likely, though, that the dioceses were strung out over a much larger area and that each was centred on a major upland basin—Ma'alta on the Dasht-i-Harir, a large, wedge-shaped plain west of Ruwandiz, Hewton on plains north and east of Ruwandiz (the Dasht-i-Diana and the enclosed basin of the river Rust), and Hnita (Chamaitha) lying to the east beyond the main range (Naval Intelligence Division, *Iraq and the Persian Gulf*, Geographical Handbook Series B.R.524 (London, 1944), 100 and fig.27). Sim., v.7.10–8.3 mistakenly placed it in the north Assyrian plain not far to the east of Erbil in his highly condensed and confused account of operations against Bahram Chobin in summer 591 (for which, see Whitby, *Emperor Maurice*, 302–3).

Heraclius moved off on 17 October. Rahzadh set off in pursuit once he learned of Heraclius' departure.[30]

A concise but detailed account of the next five months' operations was put together by Heraclius' staff and sent off to Constantinople on 15 March 628.[31] No more authoritative source can be found for a campaign than a document of this sort, based upon the collective observation of a general's staff in the field. Most of Theophanes' extended narrative of the final phase of the campaign is derived indirectly from this penultimate dispatch with which the emperor sought to reassure his subjects at home. Of course, the data packed into it requires interpretation. Reverses would be glossed over, successes written up. The latter-day reader must always beware of tendentiousness in such documents, especially in this case, where two additional layers of interpretation were superimposed on the data: first that of George of Pisidia, who embellished the dispatch with verse passages and sought to highlight the personal contribution of the emperor by word and deed; second that of Theophanes, who had to cut down the lengthy text of George's Official History to a manageable length lest it unbalance his chronicle and did so according to his own rather faulty understanding of events. Nonetheless, there is a plethora of hard data in Theophanes' version about major operations and minor forays, with key dates and toponyms given to fix them in time and place. Considerable space is also given to military and political intelligence (in one case, deliberate disinformation) acquired at different stages of the campaign and to the enumeration of the spoils of war, animate as well as inanimate. Operations can now be observed more closely than before. Aims and objectives can be postulated with greater confidence.

There are, however, gaps in coverage, where Theophanes, anxious to condense his source, resorted to the simple expedient of excising whole blocs of material and substituting short linking passages of his own. The first gap, the longest, extends from 17 October (the end of the week-long halt in Chamaitha) to 1 December, when the army forded the lower reaches of the Great Zab.[32] Two things, though, are very clear. Heraclius' direction of march was from east to west, ending up in the lowlands of northern Assyria, and he did not hurry across the Zagros. It follows that he was not, at this stage, aiming directly for Ctesiphon, nor was he scurrying home by a yet more southerly route. He was taking his time to extend the swathe of destruction to another hitherto untouched and apparently secure region of the Sasanian Empire, but this time one which was menacingly close to its Mesopotamian heartland. Initially his chief targets were probably the upland basins strung out across the northern Zagros. Taken from east to west and given their modern names, they are the large plains of Pizhder and Rania on the upper course of the Lesser Zab (reached from the southern end of Chamaitha)

---

[30] Ps.S., 126.14–21; Theoph., 317.26–9. [31] Chron.Pasch., 729.15–18.
[32] Theoph., 317.32.

and three somewhat smaller plains in the mountain basin of the Great Zab, the natural amphitheatre enclosing the Rust stream and its tributaries (just off the route west from the northern end of Chamaitha), the Dasht-i-Diana immediately north of Ruwandiz, and the Dasht-i-Harir in the highlands farther west (also accessible from the north-west edge of the Rania plain).[33] Theophanes, in his summary, is primarily interested in the effect of this destruction of crops on Rahzadh's pursuing army, forced, he says, like a hungry dog, to feed off Heraclius' scraps and losing many of its animals in the process.[34]

From the Dasht-i-Harir, the most westerly of the upland basins of the Great Zab, an easy route led into the open country of Adiabene (central Assyria) on the left bank of the Tigris. Here were yet more inviting targets, the large, fertile, and interlinked plains of modern Koi Sanjak, Erbil, Kandinawa, and Qaraj which lie between the Lesser and Great Zab.[35] Heraclius probably spent the second half of November causing as much damage as possible to crops, livestock, and settlements in this region, sending out raiding forays in all directions, until Rahzadh's pursuing army drew near enough to intervene, Rahzadh perhaps hoping to trap Heraclius in the north-west corner of Adiabene, in the angle between the Tigris and the Great Zab. At this Heraclius turned north, crossed the Great Zab, which could still be forded without too much risk at several places on its lower reaches at the tail end of the low-water season, and made for the next great plain, that of Nineveh, where he camped threateningly close to the city itself.[36]

Rahzadh had asked for and obtained a promise of reinforcements from Khusro II. A powerful force, three thousand strong, was mobilized from the royal guards regiments and sent north. Rahzadh's orders were to engage the enemy, whatever the cost. His objections (it may be guessed that he recommended a more cautious approach involving patience and calculation) were overruled.[37] So he too crossed the Great Zab by a ford three miles downstream from that used by Heraclius. He was now within striking distance of the Romans, but naturally intended to defer a close encounter until the reinforcements arrived. A foray which he sent out was intercepted and destroyed by a Roman detachment. Among the prisoners who were taken was a *spatharios* of Rahzadh's from whom reliable information was obtained about his plans. Heraclius made good use of it. He knew that Rahzadh would have to follow if he marched north from Nineveh and that this would draw him farther away from the reinforcements which were on their way and would thus delay the conjunction of the two forces. He struck camp and began what looked like a fighting retreat, with the baggage train sent to the front. Rahzadh duly set off in pursuit and Heraclius looked for suitable ground on which to fight

---

[33] Nav.Int.Div., *Iraq*, 100–2, 104–5, 109–11, and figs.26–7.   [34] Theoph., 317.29–32.
[35] Nav.Int.Div., *Iraq*, 89–93 and fig.24.   [36] Theoph., 317.32–318.2; ps.S, 126.21.
[37] Theoph., 318.8–11; MD, 144.4–23 (trans. Dowsett, 89), who thinks that the only Persian army in the field was that sent from Ctesiphon and that Rahzadh, who was given the command, pleaded in vain for reinforcements.

before the guards regiments arrived.[38] He found it in a plain which seems to have been distinct from that of Nineveh and which lay close to a difficult mountain range. The most likely candidate is the small plain of modern Dohuk.[39]

Heraclius had used similar tactics earlier on his first counteroffensive, but against different Persian opponents. Rahzadh, impelled forward by the stern orders of an unbending king, marched straight into the trap. The plain was shrouded in mist, presumably early in the morning, on Saturday 12 December (Theophanes underlines the importance of the battle by giving the date in full). The Persian army was caught completely unawares. The Romans suddenly materialized out of the mist in battle array and attacked in force. The Persians did rather better than their counterparts in 625. They fought hard, took heavy casualties, and stood their ground. Rahzadh and many of his senior officers were killed, but his army did not break up, nor did it withdraw from the battlefield until well after nightfall. Roman losses were light. Much was made of this in Heraclius' dispatch, as of the equipment stripped from the bodies of the slain and the most valuable booty seized, Rahzadh's parade armour. It looks as if Heraclius had taken to care to win the battle at minimum cost and risk to his own army. It was no head-on orthodox engagement but probably involved every form of cunning device which would weaken and disorder an adversary. Heraclius' aim—to judge by the outcome—was to inflict serious damage on Rahzadh's army and to destroy it, temporarily at least, as an effective fighting force. This would mean that the fresh troops on their way from the south would have to rescue what was left of the field army rather than beefing it up ready for battle.[40]

After two months of uninterrupted operations, Heraclius could allow his men to rest and recuperate for a week or so.[41] It was also an opportunity to take stock and to plan ahead. The mauled remnants of Rahzadh's army were skulking nervously in the foothills of a rugged mountain (probably the hills behind al-Qosh composed of contorted limestone strata and crumbling sandstone).[42] Ahead, to the north-west, the Tigris valley offered an ostensibly easy, open route home. There were hazards, though. The major left-bank tributaries of the Tigris formed a series of natural lines of defence, which, even if lightly held by Persian forces, might become serious obstacles. Farther west lay a greater danger, the Persian army of occupation under the command of Shahrbaraz. Doubtless its

---

[38] Theoph., 318.2-15.
[39] Nav.Int.Div., *Iraq*, 96-7 and fig.24. But see Kaegi, *Heraclius*, 160-6, for an alternative site in the plain of Nineveh, well to the east of the city.
[40] Theoph., 318.15-319.22, who highlights the feats of Heraclius and his horse Dorkon; ps.S, 126.21-35, who believes mistakenly that the reinforcements were present at the battle and exaggerates the scale of the slaughter; MD, 145.1-2 (trans. Dowsett, 89), who has Rahzadh's army annihilated 'like dust in a storm'.
[41] The next action recorded, the crossing of the Great Zab, took place on 21 December (Theoph., 319.25-320.6).
[42] Theoph., 319.10-14, with Nav.Int.Div., *Iraq*, 96-7 and fig.24. But see Kaegi, *Heraclius*, 163.

units were scattered across Syria, Palestine, and Egypt, but a field force could be mobilized from among them which would be more than capable of intercepting and harassing a retreating Roman army. To the south, lay the Sasanian capital, the twin cities of Ctesiphon and Veh-Ardashir, relatively defenceless now that the guards regiments were depleted and the only field army within reach had been neutralized. Khusro II's palace at Dastagerd lay on the road to Ctesiphon, and Khusro himself was probably in residence (given his known dislike of Ctesiphon). The Sasanian royal road, the major military artery linking the north-west frontier zone to the metropolitan region, offered an inviting route south. It opened the prospect of causing yet more damage to crops and buildings, this time in the core territories of the empire, almost under the eyes of the governing elite. There was also a chance, remote but not completely unrealistic, of a successful sudden assault on the capital itself. But there were hazards on the way south too. Three great rivers drained the north-eastern Zagros and debouched into the plains of Assyria—the Great and Lesser Zab and the Diyala. Irrigation channels, large and small, posed additional problems in the plains between the Lesser Zab and Diyala rivers and to the south of the latter, which had been transformed into the breadbasket of the metropolitan area by massive investment in infrastructure. There was no question of fording the rivers or spreading out across an irrigated landscape. By late December, river levels were rising because of rain and snowfalls in their catchment areas, and, yet more dangerous, heavy downpours far away in the mountains could bring about sudden rapid increases in flow (thus the Abbasids called the Lesser Zab the 'Mad River' because of its impetuous winter current). Irrigation systems could also be turned into traps by deliberately engineered flooding. The freedom of movement of the Roman army would be severely restricted. It would be confined to the Persian road system and, within it, to such sections as it could reach from bridges under its control.[43]

It comes as no surprise that, faced with this choice, Heraclius opted for attack rather than retreat. He seems to have waited until the guards regiment sent north from Ctesiphon joined the remnants of Rahzadh's army and moved west towards Nineveh. That meant that the main road south was clear and that he would have no difficulty crossing the Great Zab by the bridge at modern Girdmamik. He set off as soon as the intelligence reached him on 21 December and marched along the south-east flank of the al-Qosh hills. There the monks of the monastery of Bar-'Idta feared the worst until the commander of a Roman unit promised the abbot that the monastery would not be touched and stationed three men there to ensure its safety.[44] He crossed the Great Zab and sent a swift-moving detachment to seize the four bridges over the Lesser Zab 48 miles to the south. A great deal hung on the success of this operation. For bridges were easily defensible pinch

---

[43] Nav.Int.Div., *Iraq*, 81–97; R. M. Adams, *Land Behind Baghdad* (Chicago, 1965), 3–12, 69–83.
[44] Theoph., 319.22–320.3.

points on the road system, and they must be controlled if the Roman army were to advance south towards Dastagerd and Ctesiphon. If the operation failed, Heraclius would probably have to turn east, sticking to terrain between the Great and Lesser Zab, and retrace his steps through the mountains.

In the event, the operation was a remarkable success (and was given due space in Heraclius' dispatch). The thousand-strong detachment, commanded by a tourmarch (who is named), reached the Lesser Zab in a forced night march and achieved complete surprise when it attacked, presumably on 22 December. The bridges were seized, and the Persian garrisons in the forts commanding them were taken prisoner, apparently without a fight.[45] The way was now clear to advance into the broad zone of open country on the northern flank of the Jebel Hamrin stretching south-east from Kirkuk to the Diyala, and, if a similar success could be gained on the Diyala and the Ruz canal just beyond, the symbolically important prize of Dastagerd would be within Heraclius' grasp and the capital could be threatened from close at hand. It was vital, though, to maintain momentum and to push on south to deprive the Persians of time to organize their defences.[46] Time was pressing for other reasons, the ever-present danger posed by winter and the possibility that Shahrbaraz might intervene. If he did so and Persian forces regained control of key bridges, the Roman army might find itself trapped, its direct line of retreat to northern Syria cut off. The only alternative route ran north-east across the Zagros to the comparative safety of Atropatene. With every passing week, the perils of venturing into the mountains would grow.

9.3 March on Ctesiphon

Khusro was at his favourite residence, the palace at Dastagerd, when Heraclius defeated Rahzadh's army. He stayed put for ten days. Dastagerd had formidable defences—massive walls of baked brick, 16.60 m. thick, strengthened with closely spaced towers. It was also both safely removed from the fighting and a good vantage point for keeping track of events.[47] But when intelligence was received on 22 December that the Romans had seized the bridges over the Lesser Zab, followed on 23 December by reports that they were on their way south,[48] it induced something close to panic in Khusro (or, at least, that is how Heraclius later portrayed it).

---

[45] Theoph., 320.3–8.
[46] *Contra* Flusin, *Saint Anastase*, II, 271–2, 276, 281, who has Heraclius dawdle and only approach the metropolitan area at the beginning of February.
[47] F. Sarre and E. Herzfeld, *Archäologische Reise im Euphrat- und Tigris-Gebiet*, 4 vols. (Berlin, 1911–20), II, 76–93.
[48] Theoph., 321.15 has Khusro learn (on 23 December) of Heraclius crossing the *Diyala by a bridge* rather than the Great Zab by a ford, misled probably by a reference to his push across the Diyala bridge to the palace of Beklal (*on 1 January*) in the preceding passage of the Official History (Theoph., 320.17–25).

Orders were sent on 22 December to what had been Rahzadh's army, commanding it at all costs to get ahead of the Romans. It was urgently needed to bolster the defences of the metropolitan region.[49] At the same time seventy prisoners were taken out of the prison at Beth Saloe and executed, together with Anastasius, the Persian ex-soldier who had been seeking martyrdom since he confronted the occupying forces in Caesarea of Palestine earlier in the year.[50] On 23 December Khusro made preparations to leave Dastagerd. He had all the treasure there loaded on elephants, camels, and mules ready for transport to Ctesiphon. Further orders were sent to the field army to strip the palace and the houses of ministers of their contents (when they passed by—which would be in a week or so's time).[51]

On the following day (so 24 December), Khusro with his wife and children slipped out through a tunnel made in the walls into the gardens outside. When they were 5 miles away, their departure was made public. The troops there and the court were then instructed to leave for Ctesiphon. Khusro, who was suffering from dysentery, and his family reached Ctesiphon in three days and crossed the pontoon bridge to Veh-Ardashir on the right bank of the Tigris. He stopped there with his wife Shirin and three daughters. The rest of the women and his many other children were sent on to a secure place some 40 miles away.[52] Khusro himself supervised preparations for the capital's defence. He made no attempt to organize a stand either on the river Diyala or the Ruz canal, the next major watercourse to the south and the last obstacle to be crossed before Dastagerd. He proposed, instead, to concentrate all available forces on the Nahrawan canal fronting the capital. For this he needed the battered troops who had served under Rahzadh and the guards regiments sent to their aid. The depleted forces of court and capital must be reinforced. Hence the urgency with which he had summoned

---

[49] Theoph., 320.12–15, 321.13–16.

[50] V.Anast., cc.6–10 (fascination with Christianity, military service, and baptism of Anastasius), 15–23 (arrest, questioning, and imprisonment in Caesarea), and 31–2 (deportation to Beth Saloe) for the principal stages on the road to martyrdom for Anastasius. The date of 22 January given for his execution in the Life (cc.38 and 40) is an evident mistake for 22 December. Contra Flusin, Saint Anastase, II, 259–60, 265–81, the chronology of the Life should yield to that of the document-based account in Theophanes, especially as there were internal inconsistencies (later ironed out) in the original version of the Life's dating—22 January of the first indiction (beginning 1 September 627), seventeenth regnal year of Heraclius (beginning October 626), and fifteenth of Heraclius the new Constantine (beginning 22 January 626). It seems that the Syrian month Kanun II (January) was confused with Kanun (December)—as suggested by T. Nöldeke, Geschichte der Perser und Araber zur Zeit der Sasaniden, aus der arabischer Chronik des Tabari übersetzt (Leiden, 1879), 296, n.1. This would have been an easy mistake to make, (1) if the hagiographer's informant, the monk who followed the saint and witnessed his martyrdom, was a Syriac speaker and (2) if the hagiographer presumed that the arrival of Heraclius at Dastagerd, within striking distance of the capital, ten days after the martyrdom of Anastasius (on 2 January in reality, for him 1 February (V.Anast., c.43)) helped precipitate the coup against Khusro on 24 February.

[51] Theoph., 321.13–21.

[52] Theoph., 322.21–323.22, 325.14–16; Chron.Pasch., 729.21–2. Cf. ps.S, 127.6–7, 12–15, who has Khusro flee to the district of Veh-Kavad to the south of capital, apparently mistaking Veh-Kavad for Veh-Ardashir (on the right bank of the Tigris, opposite Ctesiphon).

them south. It would take them some ten days of forced marches to reach the Nahrawan, and more time would be needed to integrate them effectively into the defences (not to mention much-needed rest). Time was of the essence. Khusro sought to gain an advantage by feeding the Romans misleading intelligence about his intentions. A phantom force would be conjured up on the south bank of the Ruz canal, ready to hold the strategic bridge which gave access to the metropolitan region beyond.[53]

Meanwhile, Heraclius was marching rapidly south through Adiabene. Beyond the Lesser Zab the main road ran south-east up the broad and fertile valley of the modern river Jolak and turned south to Karcha (modern Kirkuk) commanding the fertile, irrigated lands of Beth Garmai. He reached Karcha by the evening of 23 December and camped outside the city on an estate belonging to the family of Yazdin. Yazdin had been Khusro's Christian finance minister and had enjoyed great influence at court up to his death a few years earlier. Yazdin's sons, Shamta and Kortak, the current owners, both remained in favour. Heraclius paused there for two days to rest his men and to celebrate Christmas, a vital liturgical act for troops fighting for Christendom against an evil enemy and one which could not but boost their morale. He may also have taken advantage of the pause to reconnoitre ahead. The pause did, however, enable the remnants of Rahzadh's army to obey Khusro's orders and slip past the Romans, presumably braving the dangers of fording the Lesser Zab and using side roads to the west.[54]

Whether or not Heraclius realized this cannot be determined. For Theophanes excises whatever the Official History had to say about the next stage of his march south. We may presume that the army moved off early on 26 December. There was no pause and surely no time for raiding the countryside on either side of the road until it reached Beklal (modern Jalula) on the far (south) bank of the Diyala, where Theophanes reports that it halted for a day on 1 January. Given that the total distance covered was some 180 kilometres, the army managed to average 30 kilometres a day, a swift but sustainable pace. This is testimony to the urgency behind Heraclius' drive for the metropolitan area. The only Persian installations which were targeted were royal palaces lying directly on the army's route. It was at the first of these, Diz-i-Redan ('Castle of Pages'), in the vicinity of modern Kifri, some 110 kilometres from Kirkuk, that the army comes into view again in Theophanes' narrative. The palace was sacked and burned.[55]

The Persian field army was now a day or so's march ahead. While Heraclius was pushing on towards the next palace, Rousa (unidentified and thus not locatable), the Persians crossed over the Diyala and camped on the far (south) bank. It was natural to expect that they might make a stand there, holding and defending the

---

[53] Theoph., 320.26–321.5 (deception), 324.24–7 (Nahrawan defence).
[54] Theoph., 320.9–17. Flusin, *Saint Anastase*, II, 246–54.
[55] Theoph., 320.17–19. Cf. *Chron.Pasch.*, 729.23–730.1; ps.S., 127.7–9.

strategic bridge over the river. There was no slackening, though, in the pace of the Roman advance. The palace of Rousa was destroyed, and the army advanced rapidly towards the Diyala. At which the Persians, possibly already under orders to fall back on the Nahrawan, abandoned the bridge and continued their withdrawal. The Romans crossed over in their turn and entered the metropolitan region, occupying the palace of Beklal just above the offtake of a major left-bank canal. It was here that Khusro's deception plan was put into action in the hope of slowing their advance. Armenians in Persian service (Theophanes does not say whether they were civilians or soldiers) came forward after darkness fell and volunteered the information that the Persian army, including a force of 200 elephants, was deployed under Khusro's personal command at a place called Barasroth, 5 miles north of Dastagerd. There it was in a strong position, since the only approach was by a narrow bridge over an impassable waterway, through narrow streets between buildings, and over land criss-crossed by irrigation channels.[56]

Faced with this disturbing news, Heraclius responded as he was meant to. After consulting his senior officers, he gave orders to halt at Beklal. An additional inducement was the abundance of edible creatures stocked in enclosures by the palace (ostriches, gazelles, and wild asses reared for their meat) and herded nearby (large numbers of sheep, pigs, and cattle). All of these Heraclius made over to his men, who spent 1 January feasting and praising God. Before the day was out, the Persian deception was exposed. Shepherds and herdsmen brought in for questioning reported Khusro's flight from Dastagerd several days earlier. It could now be confidently inferred that his forces too were falling back on the capital and that every effort was being made to strengthen its defences. Little opposition was to be expected on the next few stages of the march. It was safe, therefore, to split the army and thus extend the swathe of destruction as it entered the metropolitan region.[57]

Heraclius changed his plan of campaign, realizing that there was little chance now of breaching the defences of Ctesiphon. The headlong dash for Ctesiphon gave way to a more measured but equally menacing advance. He turned off the main military highway with half the army and sacked another of Khusro's palaces at Bebdarch before rejoining the other half which had marched directly to Dastagerd. The plunder taken at Dastagerd was magnificent: large pieces of aloe wood, raw silk, cotton shirts, sugar, spices, silver bullion, garments of pure silk, woollen rugs and carpets, Khusro's campaign tents, and 300 captured Roman standards. All of it (except presumably for the Roman standards and the bullion) was burned to avoid burdening the army. We know nothing of the fate of the

---

[56] Theoph., 320.19–321.5. The waterway (called a river by Theophanes, 321.4) was probably the Ruz canal.
[57] Theoph., 321.5–23.

animals and birds which they found at the palace and in its associated hunting park (ostriches, gazelles, wild asses, peacocks, pheasants, lions, and tigers), as Theophanes jumps over it. We may suspect, though, that many were eaten and the rest butchered. Wanton destruction of buildings, valuable commodities, and exotic creatures doubtless impressed upon the Persians the determination and ruthlessness of the Roman army.[58]

More startling was Heraclius' second decision—to make a final attempt to negotiate an end to the war with Khusro. He probably reached Dastagerd after the diversionary raid on Bebdarch by the evening of 3 January. He spent the next three days there. A message was sent to Khusro urging him to make peace. The details of the negotiations are not given by Theophanes, who prefers to insert a chunk of fanciful material about Shahrbaraz taken from his West Syrian source (Theophilus of Edessa) at this point.[59] But he does report that Heraclius sent a letter to Khusro and reproduces fragments of George of Pisidia's poetic rendering of its contents: Heraclius was seeking peace as he hunted Khusro down; it was Khusro who had forced him to devastate Persia; now was the time to cast aside their weapons and to embrace peace—'let us extinguish the fire before it consumes everything'.[60] Similar sentiments were probably expressed in wordier diplomatic language in the original document and were designed to worsen Khusro's predicament. Whatever reply he made, his standing would be gravely damaged. If he agreed to negotiate, he would be committing himself to relinquishing most of the gains which his troops had made at heavy cost. Widespread war-weariness would give way to a surge of anger at the futility of the war, the pointlessness of the sacrifices made. On the other hand, if he refused and resolved to fight on, the future would be bleak, with a triumphant Roman army rampant in Mesopotamia and a new Turkish army poised to invade Transcaucasia in the spring. Gloom and despondency would feed growing popular discontent with the regime.

9.4 Fall of Khusro

Khusro had little choice but to fight on and to hope against hope that the Romans might suffer some setback. He rejected Heraclius' offer and busied himself with defensive preparations, trawling the households of the empire's governing elite, his own staff, and his wives for able-bodied men. Popular opinion now turned sharply against him and emboldened elements in the governing elite to act rather than merely voice their disgruntlement. Rahzadh's defeat and the news that the metropolitan region was exposed to attack marked a turning point in aristocratic attitudes to Khusro's regime and its foreign policy, according to the *History to 682*,

---

[58] Theoph., 321.21–322.14.   [59] Theoph., 323.22–324.16.   [60] Theoph., 324.16–20.

which transmits the fullest and most faithful—although somewhat embellished—version of this episode in Sasanian dynastic history. There were growing murmurs of discontent. Khusro's high-handed methods were resented. Arrests, tortures, executions of leading members of the governing class, not to mention the treasury's appropriation of property broke the traditional compact between monarch and aristocracy. But the war was the prime target of criticism, with its heavy costs in terms of lives lost, long tours of duty far from home, and disruption of commerce.[61]

Now that the Roman emperor was so close, within easy striking distance of the twin capital cities, anxiety amplified discontent. This was probably the time when a disturbing rumour began to circulate. It cast doubt on the loyalty of Shahrbaraz, the supreme commander in the west, who controlled the largest and most experienced body of fighting men in the Sasanian Empire. Either he had aroused suspicion at court or an act of Khusro's had antagonized him. The Roman authorities had got wind of the estrangement and had made a successful approach to Shahrbaraz. He had changed sides and was now backing the Romans.[62] Almost certainly there was not a shred of truth in this story, which surfaces, with minor variations, in East and West Syrian sources and in later derivatives from them, both Arab and Byzantine. It may have grown spontaneously within the beleaguered cities. But it seems more probable that the basic story was planted by the Romans in the final phases of the campaign to sow confusion in Persian minds, perhaps even to conjure up in reality something of the suspicion of Shahrbaraz which was pictured in the fiction. Whatever its origin, the story served Roman interests. Intervention in force by Sharhbaraz, the possibility of which caused some concern to Heraclius, was rendered less likely.

Roman sources present Kavad Shiroe, Khusro's eldest son, as prime mover in the conspiracy which now began to take shape, but this surely reflects the public presentation of events both within the Sasanian Empire and in correspondence with foreign powers. In reality, the key role seems to have been played by a retired senior general whose name, Gourdanaspa, is given by the *Chronicon Paschale*. It was only to be expected that resentment at a disastrously mishandled war should be most acute in military circles and that military men should be readiest to do something about it.[63]

Khusro's prestige continued to decline, and the conspiracy gathered momentum with each passing week in January. There was no respite from military pressure. The expected thrust against the outer defences of the capital duly materialized. The Roman army moved off from Dastagerd across the fertile irrigated alluvium.

---

[61] Theoph., 324.20–7; MD, 145.3–19 (trans. Dowsett, 89); Tab., 1041.1–1043.9.
[62] Theoph., 323.22–324.16; Agap., 462.3–7, Mich.Syr., 409, *Chron.1234*, 232.5–15, 24–30; *Seert Chron.*, 540.9–541.6; Tab., 1008.10–1009.2.
[63] *Chron.Pasch.*, 728.12–19; Theoph., 325.20–326.5; MD, 145.19–146.4 (trans. Dowsett, 90).

316   THE LAST GREAT WAR OF ANTIQUITY

After three days' march (7–9 January), it halted 12 miles from the Nahrawan canal and established a camp. From there the defences of the canal were probed. Apprehension doubtless reached its apogee within the twin cities. But the defences held. The bridges had been cut, and there was no other practicable way of crossing the canal. When this was revealed by reconnaissance, the Roman army began a slow, destructive withdrawal. The next six weeks saw widespread devastation of much of the capital's agricultural hinterland. Citizens and governing elite sheltering behind the Nahrawan were being psychologically bludgeoned by a Roman army with no human enemy to fear, only General Winter.[64]

In the course of January and early February the conspiracy developed two distinct foci. A military grouping was built up by Gourdanaspa. It centred on the court at Ctesiphon, but, to judge by the number of senior commanders whom he succeeded in suborning (twenty-two counts) besides officers and many soldiers, its ramifications extended to the forces guarding the Nahrawan. On the opposite, right bank of the Tigris, a coterie of active participants formed in the highest echelons of the court aristocracy around the former tutor of Kavad Shiroe, who is portrayed in the *History to 682* as the conspiracy's mastermind.[65] Kavad Shiroe himself was living at some distance from the capital.[66] The conspirators included several influential figures of his generation: two sons of Shahrbaraz, one of Yazdin's sons, the son of a certain Aram, and Shiroe's foster brother, who acted as intermediary between the two groups. The messages he carried were oral, save for the formal policy statement which Gourdanaspa had solicited from Kavad Shiroe at an early stage in order to convince potential conspirators of his commitment to their cause. This trusted messenger was the essential link which enabled the two groups to coordinate their actions on the night scheduled for the coup.[67]

Their ultimate aim was clear: to bring the war to an end, to make peace with the emperor of the Romans and with the Turks. They intended to depose Khusro and replace him with his eldest son, Kavad Shiroe, who had expected to inherit the throne but who now feared that his half-brother Merdasan was going to be declared the designated successor. As additional inducements, promises were made, in Kavad Shiroe's formal statement, of pay increases for the army and promotions for the aristocratic participants.[68]

The two sides, military and civilian, once they were assured of a solid core of active supporters, could begin planning the mechanics of a coup. It was vital to

---

[64] Theoph., 324.27–325.8. There are two slips in this passage, both probably attributable to carelessness on Theophanes' part: Khusro orders the Nahrawan bridges to be cut when Heraclius 'crossed' (rather than 'approached') the waterway (324.26); the destructive raiding (from around 10 January to 23 February) is dated to 'the whole month of February' (325.8).
[65] Theoph., 326.7–8; MD, 145.20–3, 146.7–21 (trans. Dowsett, 90). Cf. *Chron.Pasch.*, 728.15–19.
[66] Ps.S., 127.14–15 (at Veh-Kavad) and Tab., 1043.9–12 (at Aqr Babil).
[67] Theoph., 325.20–326.6, 326.12–14.   [68] Theoph., 325.25–326.5.

move swiftly so as to achieve surprise. The pontoon bridge over the Tigris must be seized and held to control communications between the twin cities. The nucleus of those privy to the conspiracy must be enlarged as rapidly as possible. The political equivalent of a shock attack must be made to win mass support. Each move must be meticulously planned and incorporated into a detailed schedule of action. In early February a plan was finalized and a date set for the start of the coup—the night of 23/24 February.[69] The conspirators then took an extraordinary step. They decided to send a deputation to Heraclius and to inform him of what was afoot. They needed to know that the Romans would be ready to negotiate an end to the war with a new Persian regime committed to peace. Heraclius' last-minute overture to Khusro must have given them hope, but they needed an explicit assurance from him. Without a guarantee that the Romans too would be committed to making peace in the near future, much of the rationale of the coup attempt would be lost. For it would only serve to weaken the Sasanian state at a time of grave crisis.

A small deputation of four army officers and two high-ranking civilians set off. It was headed by a *hazarbad* called Gousdanaspa Razei. He was authorized to brief Heraclius in detail about the conspiracy and the planned coup, including its timing, once Heraclius had given the sought-after assurance. A week or so had to be allowed for the mission, given that the Roman army was some 200 kilometres from Ctesiphon. In order to return before the date (23/24 February) scheduled for the coup, it must have set off by 17 February.[70]

From the sudden deceleration in the pace of their advance on 1 January, when they arrived at Beklal, the Romans had spent the whole of January and much of February in methodical destruction of Persian resources—royal palaces, cities, and whole swathes of countryside.[71] Their line of march took them along the main Persian road linking Mesopotamia to Atropatene, over the intensively cultivated Diyala plains. After crossing two passes, the first approached past the rectangular tower at Paikuli commemorating the seizure of power by Narseh in 293, they entered Shahrazur, the largest of the upland basins on the western side of the main spine of the northern Zagros (the conjoined plains of modern Halabja and Sulaimaniya). Despite the advance of winter and the ever-present danger of heavy snowfalls, Heraclius allowed his men to rest before the final difficult stage in his withdrawal, the crossing of the high Zagros. Sheltered by two mountain ranges (the modern Qara Dagh and Baranand Dagh), they were in little danger of attack (in the unlikely event that Shahrbaraz had rushed forces from the west), while the Romans' menacing presence there, still within striking distance of the

---

[69] Theoph., 326.8–12; MD, 146.18–147.2 (trans. Dowsett, 90).
[70] Theoph., 325.10–13. Cf. *Chron.Pasch.*, 731.7–10; MD, 146.13–17 (trans. Dowsett, 90). The emissary (Gousdanaspa Razei, a senior officer) and the main organizer of the coup (Gourdanaspa) are conflated by Theophanes into a composite figure, Goundabousan.
[71] Theophanes, 325.6–9.

capital, would keep the eyes of Khusro's regime looking outwards rather than inwards.[72]

It was during this period of rest in Shahrazur that the Persian deputation was picked up by a Roman foray and brought to Heraclius' headquarters (probably, around 19 February).[73] Heraclius made much of the news which it brought in the next dispatch which he sent home (on 15 March).[74] Here at last was evidence that a strategy long aimed at discrediting Khusro's regime and bringing the war to an end by indirect, political means had born fruit. Naturally, he was discreet about the undertakings which he gave the Persians, but they were evidently satisfied, since they gave him a detailed briefing about the planned coup, thereby committing the fate of the conspirators into his hands. There could be no better gauge of their good faith than to trust his.[75]

The coup went remarkably smoothly. Kavad Shiroe was fetched by a party of great men of state and taken at night into Veh-Ardashir on the east bank of the Tigris.[76] The conspirators from Ctesiphon crossed the bridge to meet him, taking the horses out of the royal stables and across the river. A herald announced the seizure of power by Kavad Shiroe and summoned people to his cause. Prisoners were released from the Fortress of Oblivion and were told that the gates of life had been opened for them by the new king. They mounted horses from the royal stables and rode around, brandishing their chains and denouncing Khusro II. Their main contribution was to heighten the revolutionary atmosphere by their shouting and galloping rather than to give military muscle to the coup. There is no evidence that the conspirators took Heraclius' advice to release and arm Roman prisoners of war.[77]

The noise from Veh-Ardashir alerted the palace guards to what was going on, and many slipped across the bridge to join the rebels. Khusro asked about the clamour and the sound of trumpets. When he learned the truth from his attendants, he tried to escape but found that there were no horses left in the stables. When it was light, the rebels crossed over the river and made for the open

---

[72] Nav.Int.Div., *Iraq*, 97-9 and fig.25.

[73] It may be inferred that Barzan, where Heraclius halted for the week according to Theophanes (325.8-9), was in Shahrazur from Heraclius' own statement, in his final dispatch, that it was from Shahrazur that the army set off to cross the Zagros on 24 February (*Chron.Pasch.*, 732.4-5). This Barzan has not been located. Identifications with modern Bana, in the upland basin of the same name on the far, east side of the Zagros, or modern Barzan, in the narrow valley of the Great Zab where it leads north-west towards the tangled mountains of modern Hakkari, should be rejected.

[74] *Chron.Pasch.*, 730.2-4 (date of dispatch).

[75] Theoph., 325.8-326.20. The words of the leading general and Kavad Shiroe are given in direct speech—presumably taken over from the original text of the Official History. Theophanes has confused the general with the head of the deputation (326.5-12)—another example of careless abridging on his part. He is also misled by his earlier reference to raiding over the whole of February (325.8) into emending the dates of the deputation's arrival and of the planned coup to March (325.8, 326.9).

[76] Tab., 1043.9-12.

[77] *Chron.Pasch.*, 728.12-19; MD, 146.21-147.15 (trans. Dowsett, 90-1); ps.S, 127.21-4. Heraclius' advice: Theoph., 326.20-3.

space in front of the palace, prompting the last of the guards to flee. All Khusro could do was to slip in disguise into the garden beside the palace and hide in woodland. He was found there by a search party, arrested, manacled, and taken off to prison in the new treasury building. Kavad Shiroe was crowned king on the following day, 25 February. Before Khusro's execution on 28 February, there was some sort of arraignment, the charges against him being laid out one by one. Merdasan, his favourite son and chosen successor, was executed, we are told, before his eyes, as were all his other sons. Both Armenian versions of the *Khwadaynamag* attribute the wholesale slaughter to the urging of the nobility.[78]

Meanwhile, Heraclius, who planned his departure to coincide with the coup, broke camp and set off into the Zagros on 24 February. It was already beginning to snow. It took him some sixteen days to cross the mountains to safety in Atropatene. The snow continued to fall but did not build up enough to halt the army's passage. This mid-winter march was perhaps the boldest gamble of all those taken by Heraclius in the course of the war. He was challenging General Winter face to face by extending the campaigning season into March. He was very lucky, as he realized after the event. For heavy snowfalls continued to 30 March and blocked the passes.[79] Had that happened a few days earlier, he would have found himself trapped on the wrong side of the mountains, where pasture and supplies would be hard to come by (after the final phase of depredation in Shahrazur). As it was, he was able to set up camp on 12 March just outside the small city of Ganzak, on its plain to the south of Lake Urmia.[80] The local district governor had taken refuge in a fortress some 40 miles away. That left some three thousand houses which the army could use as stables during the worst of the cold weather, merely keeping one horse per man in the camp outside. There was no shortage of fodder or supplies on this northern side of the Zagros. Ganzak and its district had not been touched during the previous year's campaigning.[81]

This was not necessarily the end of Heraclius' second counteroffensive campaign. Further joint operations with the Turks would have to take place in 628, if the coup failed and Khusro remained determined to fight on. The Turks would need to establish a secure forward base for future operations in Transcaucasia, presumably in Albania, where they had destroyed the local Sasanian administration. Tiflis, it had already been agreed, would be the first target of joint operations, to be followed by a push into Persarmenia. By stripping away Sasanian authority from region after region of the Sasanian north-west, the allies would eventually be able to force the Persians to negotiate a peace settlement, whether or not Khusro was overthrown.

---

[78] *Chron.Pasch.*, 728.19–729.6; Theoph., 326.23–327.10; MD, 147.16–148.24 (trans. Dowsett, 91–2); ps.S., 127.24–35; Tab., 1043.12–1044.2, 1045.9–1060.12.
[79] *Chron.Pasch.*, 731.18–732.6.
[80] *Chron.Pasch.*, 734.2–4: 7 April was the last of twenty-seven days spent at Ganzak.
[81] *Chron.Pasch.*, 732.6–18.

For the moment, though, no news reached the Romans in their relatively comfortable winter quarters. The passes were blocked. Scouting parties were sent out along the two main routes across the mountains. They might be able to pick up information from Shahrazur, the basin of the Lesser Zab, or the plains beyond. Twelve days were to pass before they got hard information from good sources.[82]

---

[82] *Chron.Pasch.*, 730.2–15, 731.10–18.

Figure 23. Mren, relief over north portal: Heraclius, dismounted, outside Jerusalem. After Aṙakʻelyan, Babken. *Haykakan Patkerakantaknerə IV–VII Darerum* [Armenian Sculpted Imagery from the 4th to 7th Centuries]. Erevan: Haykakan SSH Gitutʻyunneri Akademiayi Hratarakčʻutʻyun, 1949.

Figure 24. Jerusalem: Golden Gate. John Theodor/Shutterstock.com.

Figure 25. Joshua Roll (folio VII): two spies report back to Joshua—the Israelites are repulsed from the city of Ai. Biblioteca Apostolica Vaticana, Pal. gr. 431. Pt.B.

Figure 26. Joshua Roll (folio X): Joshua is promised that Ai will fall; denuded of defenders, lured out by a feigned retreat, Ai is taken and fired (above right); the men of Ai are slaughtered in a pincer attack (below right). Biblioteca Apostolica Vaticana, Pal. gr. 431. Pt.B.

Figure 27. Joshua Roll (folio XII): Joshua receives the submission of the Gibeonites. Biblioteca Apostolica Vaticana, Pal. gr. 431. Pt.B.

Figure 28. Joshua Roll (folio XIII): the Amorites are routed and their five kings take refuge in a cave. Biblioteca Apostolica Vaticana, Pal. gr. 431. Pt.B.

Figure 29. Jerusalem: Dome of the Rock. meunierd/ Shutterstock.com.

Figure 30. Coins of Heraclius: solidus (629–31). From DOC II.1, no.27.
© Dumbarton Oaks, Byzantine Collection, Washington, DC.

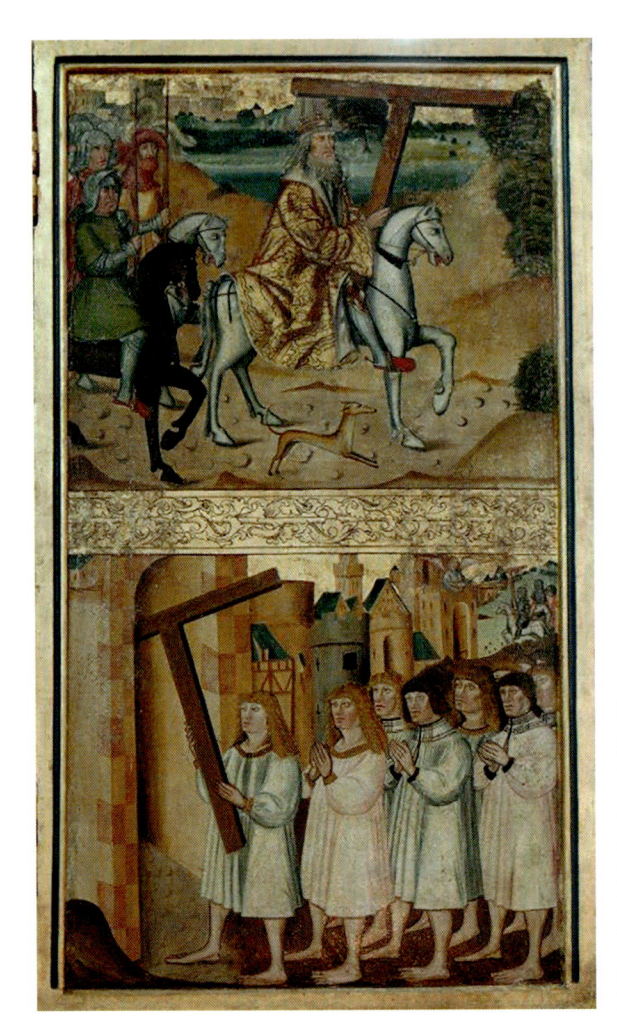

Figure 31. Rostock, Klosterkirche 'Zu den Heiligen Kreuz', Nonnenaltar: thirteenth-century cycle of scenes from the Legenda Aurea: Khusro II captures the True Cross; Heraclius restores the True Cross. Photo Sigrid Mratschek.

Figure 32. Battle of Nineveh, by Piero della Francesca. Photo © Raffaello Bencini / Bridgeman Images.

10
The Difficult Road to Peace

What had happened in Ctesiphon? Had Khusro managed to thwart the conspirators? Would he insist on continuing the war, unwilling to countenance the concessions which the Romans would demand for making peace? Heraclius, his officers, and his men were left in suspense for nearly a fortnight. Heavy snowfalls had blocked the Zagros passes. No one came across the mountains from Mesopotamia bringing news until two men, one Persian, the other Armenian, appeared and were picked up by a Roman picket on 24 March. They had been sent ahead to arrange safe passage for Chosdaï, a senior royal secretary with the rank of Rasnan, whom Kavad Shiroe had sent to Heraclius after his proclamation as king. They delivered a letter from Chosdaï announcing that he was on his way with an official delegation and was bringing written proposals from the new king. He was waiting for a Roman escort at a place called Arman, fearful of proceeding farther after seeing so many corpses (some three thousand, he said) on the road between the Nahrawan canal and Arman.

Heraclius sent off a small party the next day led by two high-ranking military officers. Gousdanaspa Razei, the senior liaison officer sent by the conspirators to Heraclius, was included in the party. Provisions were carried on twenty saddled packhorses, some of which could then become mounts on the return journey. At the same time, arrangements were put in hand for the next phase of diplomacy. One of the two messengers, the Persian, was sent on to take the news of the changed political situation to the district governor in his place of refuge 40 miles away, and to ask him to provide sixty riding animals, so that there might be no delay in the dispatch of the return embassy. As it was, it took several days for the Roman party, aided by men and animals recruited from the garrisons of forts guarding the pass, to make its way across the snow-bound Zagros to the Persian embassy, and several more before the Persians and their escort reached the Roman camp outside Ganzak.[1]

The precise hour (the second) of their arrival, date (3 April), and day of the week (Sunday) were noted down in Heraclius' dispatch. That was the date which marked the end of the fighting for the Roman expeditionary force, the date at which Heraclius and his senior commanders realized that their gambles had paid off and that the putsch had succeeded. The war was at an end. Heraclius and his

---

[1] *Chron.Pasch.*, 730.10–731.18, 732.18–733.3, 733.14–17.

troops gave thanks to God. Within the hour Heraclius received Chosdaï and was given the letter from Kavad Shiroe, together with magnificent presents. Everything that could be done was done to ensure the comfort of the ambassador and his party, which included several persons of distinction.[2]

A war which had lasted a generation and had threatened the existence of the Roman Empire had come to an end.

10.1 First Round of Negotiations

The peace proposals brought by Chosdaï, who is now given his official name and title, Phaiak Rasnan, were carefully thought out. Once Kavad Shiroe had secured his position, he sought formal authorization to negotiate peace from the most important constituency in the Sasanian Empire, the noble estate as represented in a court assembly. This he obtained without difficulty. For it was widespread war-weariness and bitter resentment at many of the measures introduced in order to sustain the war effort that had ensured the success of the palace revolution. In his determination to destroy Roman power and expand his empire, Khusro had broken the social compact which traditionally governed the relations of king and nobility. Peace was the basic aim of the broad coalition which brought about the political revolution. It was backed by a unanimous resolution of the assembly.

It was accepted that most of the immense territorial gains made by Khusro would have to be relinquished. What the precise line of the frontier should be was left vague. Reference was simply made to the boundaries of the Roman Empire. The empire which had for so long cohabited with Iran was given explicit recognition but without a clear definition of its territorial extent. Given the lack of any obvious topographical, ethnic, or cultural line of demarcation south or north of the Armenian Taurus, arguments could be advanced in favour of each of the different frontiers which had divided their territories since the revival of Iranian power in the middle of the third century.[3]

A letter was drafted in Kavad Shiroe's name, of which a mutilated copy survives (on the last damaged folio of the *Chronicon Paschale*). Heraclius appended it to the dispatch which he sent off on 8 April. He was addressed as 'the most clement Roman emperor, our brother'. By using the word *brother* instead of the derogatory language with which Khusro had dismissed him, Shiroe indicated at the outset that he recognized the legitimacy of the Roman Empire and its parity of status. He was restoring at a stroke the binary world order which had prevailed for four centuries. In the body of the letter, which was kept short, he announced his

---

[2] *Chron.Pasch.*, 733.14–21, 734.4–8; ps.S, 128.7–11.
[3] Ps.S., 127.36–128.4.

accession to the throne of his fathers and forefathers through the protection of God. By using the singular and making no reference to the plurality of divine agencies through which, according to Zoroastrian belief, Ohrmazd intervened in earthly affairs, Shiroe was striving his utmost to avoid countenancing the view that the war had been a conflict between two religious systems.[4]

He then went on to outline his proposals, making an oblique allusion to the formal backing which he had obtained. He had it in mind, he said, to release every person of whatever sort held in detention (therefore, prisoners of war as well as political opponents of his father's regime) as an earnest of his determination to do what might be of benefit and service to humanity. He had further considered what he might do for the Persian state as well as humanity in general and had it in mind to 'live in peace and love with you, the emperor of the Romans and our brother, and the Roman state and the remaining nations and other minor rulers (*basiliskoi*) around our state'.[5] The phrasing made it plain that both proposals were conditional on Roman agreement in principle to the renewal of peace. From this point on, we only have the opening few words of each line, so can only follow the gist of what was said. Shiroe introduced his ambassador, invited Heraclius to send a return embassy with his own proposals for peace, and made several references to their brotherhood. Nothing, it should be noted, was said about the geographical delimitation of the state ruled by Heraclius, it being left for Phaiak to convey orally the Persian offer to evacuate Roman territory and for Heraclius to put forward specific proposals in writing in his reply. The letter was accompanied by a solemn oath sealed with salt in the traditional Persian manner.[6]

It did not take Heraclius long to draft his reply. He had achieved his ultimate objective. Khusro had been overthrown and the Roman Empire, which had been reduced to little more than a small, ideologically charged rump, could now be reconstituted in the Middle East. He had had several weeks to consider his future course of action while awaiting news of the planned Ctesiphon coup. Four days later, he was ready to present his proposals, which were to be conveyed in writing to Shiroe. The copy of his reply which, like Shiroe's letter, was appended to his final dispatch, is, alas, very damaged. Only the last few words of each line of the opening section are preserved. Heraclius acknowledged receipt of the letter brought by Phaiak, congratulated Shiroe on his accession (referring both to the role of God and to Shiroe's good fortune), called on God to grant him many years of success and health and a very peaceful tenure of the throne of his fathers, and noted Shiroe's announced intention of working for the good of humanity. At which point, with the opening polite formulae almost disposed of, the fragmentary text breaks off.[7]

---

[4] *Chron.Pasch.*, 735.1–10. [5] *Chron.Pasch.*, 735.10–736.5.
[6] *Chron.Pasch.*, 736.5–25; ps.S., 128.4–7. [7] *Chron.Pasch.*, 733.21–734.2, 737.1–21.

On the analogy with Shiroe's letter, it may be supposed that Heraclius gave a broad outline of his position in the letter, leaving it for his ambassador to present detailed proposals in talks at Ctesiphon. We should, therefore, expect a general statement that Heraclius too was ready to commit himself to peace, together with some indication of what he regarded as an appropriate dividing line between the two states. Shiroe would then be invited, under the terms of his initial offer, to arrange for the evacuation of Persian forces from what was agreed to be Roman territory and to release all Roman prisoners of war. The only trustworthy account of the second stage of negotiations, that of the *History of Khosrov*, does indeed suggest that these were the key issues discussed when the Roman embassy reached Ctesiphon. It also reports that Heraclius responded to Shiroe's offer to release all those held in custody in Persia by ordering the immediate release of 'the multitude of captives' in his hands. This act, a real earnest of his commitment to peace, was assuredly announced in the letter.[8]

There is no hint in the existing fragment that Heraclius, still in a weak military position, designated Shiroe his son, thus claiming superior rather than equal status for the Roman Empire. The assertion that he did so is made by Nicephorus in a summary of the correspondence. But Nicephorus then goes on to strain credulity by having Heraclius regret the forcible deposition of a fellow ruler, even one who had done as much harm as Khusro, and state that he would have restored him to his throne, had not God intervened and punished him. It is inconceivable that any such sentiments could have been expressed by Heraclius and unlikely that they would have done much to smooth relations with Shiroe. These remarks (in direct speech) are a baseless concoction of Nicephorus' or his source's, the second continuator of John of Antioch. One or other of them has also introduced the notion that both rulers used the terms 'unite' and 'union' of future relations between their two states (for which there is no evidence in what remains of either of their letters) and that Heraclius, at this very early stage, demanded the return of the True Cross (for which, again, there is no corroboration). Any summary of diplomatic exchanges presented in the first part of Nicephorus' *Short History*, especially if it includes some direct speech, must be approached with extreme scepticism.[9]

On 8 April the Persian embassy took leave of Heraclius, Phaiak being 'showered with precious treasures'. They were accompanied by a high-ranking civilian official, the *gloriosissimus tabularius* Eustathius. He carried Heraclius' letter and 'magnificent gifts' for presentation to Shiroe. Like Phaiak, he probably travelled with advisers and retainers, and was authorized to represent Heraclius and the Roman state in the second round of negotiations at Ctesiphon.[10] That same day, Heraclius sent off his final dispatch, struck camp, and headed home. According to

---

[8] Ps.S., 128.11–13, 20–1.   [9] Nic., c.15.10–25.
[10] Chron.Pasch., 734.4–9; ps.S., 128.14–17.

the *History of Khosrov*, in a second gesture which underlined his commitment to peace, he gave orders that all the plunder be left behind.[11] This must surely be an exaggeration. One can understand that a great deal of booty which would encumber the army, above all captured livestock and weaponry, could conveniently be discarded. But it is surely inconceivable that the Romans left behind all the spoils of war, the treasures of many sorts gathered from the palaces which they had sacked, not to mention the Roman standards which they had recovered. It would have been madness to try to part ordinary soldiers from the material rewards they had received for hardship and gallantry, and a state which had been forced into desperate financial measures had a pressing need for bullion and other portable precious materials.

The first stage of Heraclius' route took him to Armenia. He was confident that he would encounter no opposition. His march home passed off without incident. An armistice was in force, with both sides committed to peace. His route, it may be conjectured, was that which Rahzadh had expected him to take the previous autumn—below the southern flank of Mount Ararat, across the watershed into the basin of Bagrewand, and then west down the valley of the Arsanias. At a point near the west end of Lake Van, he would, as early in 626, have had a choice between a direct route north of the Taurus (rejected in 626 for lack of supplies) and a more circuitous one to the south.[12]

There was no question this time of his cutting south into the upper Tigris basin or entering any other province currently under Persian control now that negotiations were under way and a voluntary evacuation might be expected before too long. The two medieval Syrian histories which have Heraclius do precisely this are mistaken. The error originated either in their shared source, the ninth-century history of Dionysius of Tel-Mahre, or in Dionysius' source, the eighth-century history of Theophilus of Edessa. One or the other concertinaed two distinct episodes into a single sequence, (1) Heraclius' return march in spring 628 and (2) the reinstatement of Roman administration in the provinces of Mesopotamia and Osrhoene which took place after his visit to Jerusalem in March 630.[13] So Heraclius marches into Syria from winter quarters located either between Assyria and Armenia or in Assyria, where he has concluded peace with Shiroe, sending ahead his brother Theoderic (in fact Theodore) to ensure that Persian units leave in accordance with the terms of the peace treaty. Governors are appointed; garrisons are installed. Persian troops at Edessa, egged on supposedly by local Jews, refuse to leave until a full assault is launched. A pogrom follows which is stopped by an order from Heraclius. Complex negotiations which, in reality, took nearly two years after the initial exchange of embassies have been forgotten. So too the adamant opposition to the initial agreement from

---

[11] Ps.S., 128.12.   [12] *Chron.Pasch.*, 734.13–15; ps.S, 128.16–17. Cf. Theoph., 312.19–25.
[13] See pp. 353–5.

Shahrbaraz, the commander-in-chief of the occupation forces, and the climactic victory celebrations when Heraclius restored the True Cross to Golgotha.[14]

Almost certainly, Heraclius took the northern route, which had the advantage of bringing his men back to Roman-held territory in the shortest possible time. So, on the subsequent stages of his long march home, he probably continued down the Arsanias valley to Anzitene, crossed the Euphrates in the vicinity of Melitene, followed the southern support road through the Anti-Taurus to Caesarea, and, finally, some kilometres farther on, joined the diagonal road which led across Cappadocia and Galatia to Bithynia and the Bosporus. Given the distance to be covered and the likely rate of march of troops hardened over successive campaigning seasons, used to swift movement, and eager to be home, it probably took not much more than a month and a half for Heraclius' victorious army to reach Asia Minor and safety, and three or so weeks more for the emperor and his immediate entourage to travel on to an exultant welcome at Constantinople.[15]

In the meantime, Eustathius carried out his diplomatic mission. The journey to Ctesiphon seems to have been uneventful. Things went well from the first audience, when he handed over the presents sent by Heraclius and Shiroe expressed his pleasure at his arrival. The key issue of frontiers was apparently resolved without difficulty. The language used in the laconic notice in the *History of Khosrov* suggests that some sort of draft treaty document had been prepared by Heraclius including detailed proposals on the frontier question and that it was accompanied by a sworn statement of Heraclius' commitment to peace. The draft seems to have been generally acceptable to Shiroe, who, we are told, 'confirmed the terms of peace and the division of borders', and formally bound himself with a written oath and the customary Persian ritual sealing with salt.[16]

What, though, was the frontier proposed by Heraclius and accepted, with little or no demurral, by Shiroe? On this crucial question, there is no information whatsoever to be gleaned from the sources. So recourse must be had to conjecture. The relatively smooth course of negotiations suggests that both parties were ready to take account of each other's vital interests, that both were ready to compromise because both were whole-heartedly committed to peace. Neither had much

---

[14] Mich.Syr., xi.3 (IV, 409–10, trans. Chabot, II, 409–10); *Chron.1234*, 234.20–236.12 (trans. Palmer, 138–40). *Contra* C. Zuckerman, 'Heraclius and the Return of the True Cross', in C. Zuckerman, ed., *Constructing the Seventh Century*, TM 17 (2013), 197–218, at 211.

[15] Heraclius' small, highly trained force, marching home during an armistice (so without the need to build overnight camps), could surely cover the 30 kilometres per day which would have brought them from Ganzak to Caesarea of Cappadocia (a distance of roughly 1,500 kilometres, 1,000 as the crow flies) by the end of May. From there the emperor and a small entourage could speed off on the main road to Constantinople, arriving well before the end of June, before the ceremonial restoration of the Virgin Mother's Robe at Blachernae on 2 July (p. 333 below). J. Haldon, *Warfare, State and Society in the Byzantine World, 565–1204* (London, 1999), 163–6 for 20–25 kilometres as a rough average for a day's march.

[16] Ps.S., 128.12–13, 18–23.

choice. Shiroe had to bring the fighting with the Romans to an end, not only because he was the candidate of the peace party in a war-weary society but also because all available military resources were needed in the north to face the Turks. Heraclius, for his part, was still faced by the unpleasant reality that the rich Roman Levant and Egypt were in Persian hands and that he was in no position to engage with the occupying forces, superior as they were in numbers, undefeated, and led by Shahrbaraz, a great general with an untarnished reputation.

Both rulers had to make peace and to do so swiftly. This, then, is the context in which Shiroe allowed Heraclius to put forward specific proposals about the frontier. Only one of the several possible lines of demarcation was likely to seem reasonable to both sides—that which had been accepted from the late fourth century and had underpinned the long period of almost uninterrupted peaceful coexistence which lasted to the beginning of the sixth century.[17] Both sides' security needs were met. The Romans had forward defensive zones beyond the Euphrates south and north of the Taurus which provided an effective shield for the rich Mediterranean coastlands and for Asia Minor. Many layers of defence in northern Mesopotamia secured the Persian metropolitan region, while the Persian sector of Transcaucasia formed a deep buffer zone fronting the Iranian plateau. Each side would be in control of at least one direct route across the Armenian Taurus, so that neither had the advantage of inner lines. As for the northern end of the frontier, it is likely that Heraclius insisted on one variation to the 363 frontier, namely control of Lazica (first ceded by the Persians under the terms of the treaty of 562, and probably under renewed Roman control since 627 at the latest), so as to secure Constantinople against the possibility of naval attack.

Substantial concessions would have been required from both sides. The Romans would have to give up the massive gains which they had made in Armenia and Iberia under the terms of their agreement with Khusro in 591, once again giving the Persians control over four-fifths of Transcaucasia. The Persians, though, would have to relinquish much more—all the conquests which they had made south of the Taurus (Egypt, Palestine, Syria, Osrhoene, and Roman Mesopotamia) as well as western Armenia, which traditionally belonged to the Roman sphere. The victories of Khusro, the many gains made at great cost over thirty years of fighting, would thus be reversed at a stroke of the pen. But a settlement on these lines was equitable: it re-established a strategic balance between the two empires and had the backing of history.

At the successful conclusion of negotiations, Shiroe set about fulfilling the terms of the treaty. In Eustathius' presence he issued instructions for a letter to be drafted ordering Shahrbaraz to gather his forces, return to Persian territory, and 'leave the borders of the Romans'. Eustathius was then dismissed and set off to

---

[17] Ps.S., 127.36–128.6, 128.20–5; Mich.Syr., xi.3 (IV, 409), *Chron.1234*, 234.24–30, trans. Hoyland, 78–9.

Constantinople 'laden with treasures'. He would be able to report that he had witnessed the first crucial step in the implementation of the peace agreement, the royal command for the evacuation of Roman territory.[18]

The first step turned out, however, to be the last. Shahrbaraz bluntly refused to obey the order from the new king.[19] The conqueror of the Roman Middle East would not relinquish virtually everything he had gained merely to avoid further bloodshed and expense. The impasse would last for many months. For the moment, though, Shiroe and Eustathius could compliment themselves on the achievement of peace, the Persian high command could begin planning operations against the Turks in Transcaucasia, and Heraclius and his men could march home in peace, confident that the long war was over.

10.2 Celebration of Victory at Constantinople

Heraclius' victory dispatch arrived in Constantinople not much more than a month after it was sent off. Doubtless the news it brought seeped out unofficially and spread across the city almost immediately. The formal proclamation took place at a time and place chosen to emphasize the religious character of the war. The whole dispatch was read out from the ambo in St Sophia on the Sunday of Pentecost (15 May), the feast commemorating the beginning of a new era of guidance by the Holy Spirit.[20] Heraclius addressed his people with the voice of King David. He opened his dispatch with the first three verses of Psalm 100: 'Make a joyful noise unto the Lord, all ye lands. Serve the Lord with gladness: come before his presence with singing. Know ye that the Lord he is God: it is he that hath made us, and not we ourselves: we are his people and the sheep of his pasture.' He continued for a few more lines in this vein, with one modification (God's name is to be praised not because he is good but because Christ is God) and the addition of some fresh psalmic matter composed for the occasion—'Let the heavens be joyful and the earth exult and the sea be glad, all that is in them. And let all us Christians, praising and glorifying, give thanks to the one God, rejoicing with great joy in his holy name.'[21] Psalm 100 was quoted because it stressed God's power over men, while the new passage (with echoes of Psalm 98:4 and 7) implicitly credited God with the creation of three of the four elements venerated by Zoroastrians and spoke to Christians of all denominations.

The exultant preamble was followed by the announcement of the overthrow of:

> the arrogant Khusro, opponent of God. He is fallen and cast down to the depths
> of the earth, and his memory is utterly exterminated from the earth—he who

---

[18] Ps.S., 128.23–6.   [19] Ps.S., 128.25.   [20] Chron.Pasch., 727.7–14.
[21] Chron.Pasch., 727.15–728.4.

was exalted and spoke injustice in arrogance and contempt against our Lord Jesus Christ the true God and his undefiled Mother, our blessed Lady, Mother of God and ever-Virgin Mary.[22]

A brief account was then given of the putsch and of Shiroe's subsequent execution of his father, who thus learned 'that Jesus who was born of Mary, who was crucified by the Jews, as he himself wrote, against whom he blasphemed, is God almighty.'[23] The stress thus shifted to the divinity and omnipotence of God Incarnate. Then, after recapitulating what he had written in his previous dispatch, Heraclius went on to describe how contact was eventually made with the Persian embassy and news was finally obtained of the outcome of the putsch.[24]

It is not hard for us to gauge the strength of the emotions aroused that day in the congregation in St Sophia or the mood of the whole city over the following weeks and months. The war had lasted a generation. Defeat had followed on the heels of defeat. Swathe after swathe of Roman territory had been lost. The great city itself had come under fierce and sustained attack. The Romans had endured a blitz which had lasted nearly thirty years. The exultation of emperor and army undoubtedly pervaded Constantinople and the whole of the rump Roman state. But what form the rejoicing took, how it was expressed in public and in private, in services of thanksgiving, and out on the streets and fora—for this we have virtually no evidence. There are only two contemporary witnesses who can speak to us. Both George of Pisidia and Theophylact Simocatta had lived through the grim war years. Both were writing in the late 620s and reveal something of their reactions and attitudes.

George, though, was a poet of genius. He was not, never had been, representative of his times. Reality was transmuted and transcended in his poetry. The heady excitement of victory can be caught through the poem which he wrote at the time (the *Heraclias*), but there is nothing commonplace to be found there. Obvious themes of imperial propaganda, familiar sentiments are largely disregarded. He was contrary. He might play with a few of the ideas in the air, but would always twist them into new shapes of his own devising. His thinking was governed by his faith. For him the war had always been one of good against evil, of right against wrong belief and practice. Earthly combat was placed in a cosmic setting. The whole past of mankind, historical (as recorded in the Old Testament) and imagined (in the myths transmitted by the Greeks), could be glimpsed in the background behind current events. By introducing a bewildering range of comparisons, sometimes closely intertwined, he gave extraordinary resonance to his celebration of Heraclius' achievement in the war.

---

[22] *Chron.Pasch.*, 728.4–10.   [23] *Chron.Pasch.*, 728.12–729.14.
[24] *Chron.Pasch.*, 729.15–730.21.

The *Heraclias*, as we have it, is incomplete. The overview of Heraclius' career which it presents breaks off early in the account of the 624 campaign, after the symbolically important destruction of the great fire temple at Thebarmais (II, 204–30).[25] The missing third canto would have taken the story on to the final victory. The opening section of the first canto picks up and plays with the genuine and freshly composed psalmic matter at the beginning of Heraclius' dispatch. Its composition is thus anchored in the period of celebration following the announcement of victory. The stars are to rejoice, the air to dance at the news of the fall of Khusro. Creation has not given shelter to its votary. Khusro, who is likened to Xerxes and Balthazar, has been condemned by God. Bloodshed and slaughter have ceased. The four elements venerated by the Persians (earth, fire, water, and air) join heaven and clouds and the whole upper and lower cosmos in applauding, along with the Romans, Khusro's fall. The planets and stars have gone dark for him in Tartarus (I, 1–64).

In this opening flourish, George touches on a central theme of Roman propaganda to which Heraclius alluded in his dispatch: Khusro and his Zoroastrian co-religionaries made a grave error in mistaking created things for divinities and deserved the punishment inflicted by the one true God. He has Heraclius speak with the voice of David, thus apparently inviting comparison with the greatest of Old Testament war heroes and adopting a contemporary theme of praise. For, well before the start of his second counteroffensive, Heraclius had been declared to be a new David by Theodore Syncellus at the ceremony to celebrate the repulse of the Avars from the city.[26] George himself would prove attentive to contemporary image-making when he received the imperial commission to write the history of the war and portrayed Heraclius as the champion of the truncated and beleaguered empire. At the battle of Nineveh he has Heraclius implicitly outdo David, fighting and winning three duels before the main engagement begins.[27] In 630, when Martina bore him a son on 7 November, Heraclius would name him David.[28] There can be no doubt, then, that one of the imperial images projected in the hour of triumph, perhaps the most important, was that of Heraclius as a modern David. It was picked up far away, in East Frankish lands, when news arrived of Heraclius' victory. Heraclius is reported to have fought the champion sent out by Khusro like a New David.[29]

There is not a hint of this in the *Heraclias*. A great deal is packed into the poem. The style is excited, exclamatory. George shifts abruptly from subject to subject. He introduces all manner of images and analogies. Seldom does he allow conceits to unfurl to their full length.[30] A series of invocations—of Homer, Scipio, and

---

[25] See pp. 226–7 above.   [26] Theod.Sync., Hom.I, 320.18–24.   [27] Theoph., 318.16–24.
[28] Theoph., 335.1–2.   [29] Fredegar, iv.64.
[30] Cf. Mary Whitby, 'George of Pisidia's Presentation of the Emperor Heraclius and his Campaigns: Variety and Development', in G. J. Reinink and B. H. Stolte, eds., *The Reign of Heraclius (610–641): Crisis and Confrontation* (Leuven, 2002), 157–73, at 168–71.

Plutarch—are interspersed among several turns on Heraclius' achievements (I, 65–121). These act as the preface to a eulogy of Heraclius as a military commander: he reinvigorated his men 'who were as motionless as stones burdening the earth with their sterile loads'; he returned transformed both physically (he is white-haired and weather-beaten) and morally; ignoring family ties, he boldly attacked and, with Christ's help, pulled down the tall edifice of Khusro's good fortune; he is now applauded like a victorious athlete by the people of earth from the four sides of the theatre of life (I, 129–30, 140–7, 161–81, 207–11). This eulogy, which occupies the rest of the first canto, itself acts as the preface to the main laudatory account of Heraclius' career. The extant part, in the second canto, picks out Heraclius' main achievements, from his overthrow of Phocas to the preparations for his invasion of Persia (his words drawing soldiers to him like splinters of gold out of quicksilver (II, 157–9)) and the opening phase of the campaign. Again, the treatment is allegorical, with images and comparisons tightly compacted together.

Heraclius is compared successively to Heracles, Noah, Scipio, Alexander, the fortunate Athenian general Timotheus, Perseus, Heracles again, Galen, Odysseus (by implication), Perseus again (by implication), and Elijah. Obvious figures for comparison are left aside—not only David and other Old Testament war leaders, but also those imperial predecessors whose exploits could be seen as foreshadowing Heraclius', notably Trajan qua victor over Persia, and Constantine qua champion of Christianity. George prefers to tease out the significance of Heraclius' feats from often unlikely juxtapositions. Even the more conventional comparisons, such as those with Heracles, Scipio, and Alexander, are treated in unusual ways. George is not interested in narratives of combat, in the feats of Heraclius' near homonym as sets of actions (the labours of Heracles paralleling the emperor's endurance and valour on campaign). His concern is with their beneficial outcomes for the world and for Heraclius himself (morally purged by his endeavours). The comparison with Scipio is even more perfunctory: not a word about Scipio as another general who reversed the fortunes of war; instead, a decree that Scipiones should change their name to Heracleiones; this enables George to summarize the phenomena of Heraclius' campaigns as heads of argument to be presented in the main body of an imperial decree (I, 97–109). Finally, George homes in on Plutarch's image of Alexander locked in combat against adverse fortune, rather than the nitty-gritty of victorious warfare, to signal a principal theme of the poem—that the difficulties confronting Heraclius were much more formidable (I, 113–39).

Theophylact Simocatta could write well when he chose. The literary highlights of his history of Maurice's reign are the speeches which point up occasions of particular importance. They are well-wrought, vividly phrased compositions which could not but absorb something of the atmosphere of Simocatta's own times. There seems to be a fleeting allusion to the heavenly rewards awaiting the valiant dead in the exhortation to the troops delivered by Dometianus, the metropolitan bishop of Melitene, when they were about to cross into Persian territory in the campaign to restore Khusro II to the Sasanian throne in the summer of 591: valour, he declares, opens the way to peace, wounds to salvation as well as renown on earth.[31] A short anti-Jewish diatribe which forms an aside in the account of a swift thrust by a small Persian force into Mesopotamia (coordinated with the main operations farther north) was surely prompted by the anti-Semitism which grew in the charged atmosphere at the end of the war.[32] A clearer allusion to celebratory mood comes in an earlier speech of Dometianus', on the occasion of the recovery of Martyropolis at the beginning of 591. The tone is exultant, and there are clear reminiscences of Heraclius' dispatch. Dometianus begins by referring to David and scatters psalmic phrases over his text. He comes close to crowing over the casting down of an arrogant ruler when he speaks in general terms about the humbling of peaks of arrogance, the casting down of dynasts from their thrones, the enslaving of lions, and the strangling of serpents. God's power over earthly affairs is exalted. The fire venerated by Persians is shown to be harmless. For Dometianus, as for Heraclius in 628, the heavens, earth, and plains rejoice at what has happened. There are also traces of influence from the *Heraclias*: apart from whole tone of the speech, an allusion is made to two of Heracles' labours (the Nemean lion and the Hydra), the writing on the wall recurs, and the recovery of Martyropolis is applauded by the neighbouring rivers (standing in for George's spectators of Heraclius' feats). There can be little doubt, then, that the speech was composed after the sudden, near miraculous end of the war in 628, and that the jubilation which Simocatta felt at the time has impressed itself upon his text.[33]

Eventually, a month or so after the arrival of the victory dispatch, Heraclius neared the capital. Almost certainly, he left the main body of his army once it was safe on Roman territory, probably after reaching Caesarea, where it had assembled for the first counteroffensive campaign in 624. With a small mounted escort, he would have made good time. Elaborate preparations were made for his reception. The people of Constantinople, we are told, went out with unrestrained eagerness to meet him at Hieria on the Asian side of the Bosporus. The Patriarch Sergius was there, as was Heraclius' son, Heraclius the New Constantine, nominal head of government during his absence. The ceremony was choreographed for maximum impact. The crowd carried olive branches and lights, and acclaimed the victorious emperor with tears of joy. The young Constantine came forward and did obeisance. Father and son embraced and 'watered the ground with their tears'. At this the crowd sang hymns of gratitude to God and escorted the emperor into the city, dancing with joy. George of Pisidia, from whose

---

[31] Sim., v.4.7.   [32] Sim., v.7.9.
[33] Sim., iv.16.1–26. Cf. Whitby, *Emperor Maurice*, 39–40, 50–1, 334–5.

Official History Theophanes' notice is derived, glossed the ceremony as one celebrating the return of God's earthly vicegerent for a seventh year of rest after six years of military endeavour.[34]

It is hard to imagine that the celebrations halted with Heraclius' entry into the city. If any emperor's military feats merited a formal triumph, Heraclius' did. Triumphal celebrations are reported by Nicephorus, whose report should probably be believed, even though he misplaces Heraclius' return after the restoration of the True Cross to Jerusalem in 630. He refers to the welcoming ceremony described by Theophanes and then goes on to report that Heraclius held races in the hippodrome at which he paraded four captured elephants to the delight of the crowd. The triumphal celebrations lasted for several days (nine all told, according to Eutychius) and involved much distribution of largesse.[35] The financial strains of war were eased, thanks to the spoils of victory, above all the treasure gathered from the royal palaces of Mesopotamia. Another ceremony, of purely religious character, followed hard on the heels of the secular celebrations. A solemn procession led by emperor and patriarch took the precious relic of the Robe of the Virgin Mother back to her sanctuary at Blachernae from which it had been hastily removed at the time of the surprise Avar attack in 623. At Blachernae, in what looks like another stage-managed ceremony, the patriarch opened the reliquary, established with his own eyes that the relic woven of wool was miraculously well preserved (unlike the purple silk cloth in which it was wrapped), announced this to the assembled dignitaries. and reinstalled the relic in its proper place. The ceremony, which is described by Theodore Syncellus, took place on 2 July, the Feast of the Visitation of the Virgin Mother. It marked the moment at which the imperial and ecclesiastical authorities acknowledged publicly that the capital was no longer in danger of attack. The war had ended with Heraclius' return a few days earlier.[36]

The first steps towards commemorating Heraclius' achievements were taken, it may be surmised, soon after the end of the immediate celebrations of victory. An official history was commissioned from George of Pisidia, the obvious candidate after the production of the flattering *Heraclias*. The decision to base it on the emperor's dispatches was probably his. A sense of the structure, principal themes, and tone of the work can be recaptured from the fragments which survive, odd snatches of verse quoted in the tenth-century *Suda*, and some larger chunks incorporated in condensed form in Theophanes' history. In this sponsored work,

---

[34] Theoph., 327.24–328.10.
[35] Nic., c.19.1–6; Eutychius, ed. M. Breydy, *Das Annalenwerk des Eutychios von Alexandrien: Ausgewählte Geschichten und Legenden kompiliert von Sa'id ibn Batriq um 935 AD*, CSCO 471, Scriptores Arabici 44 (Louvain, 1985), 127.4–5, trans. Breydy, *Das Annalenwerk des Eutychios*, CSCO 472, Script.Arab. 45, 107. Cf. Geo.Pis., *Heraclias*, I, 212–18.
[36] Theod.Sync., *Hom*.II, 599–608, trans. 51–4. Cameron, 'Virgin's Robe', 43–4, places the ceremony, implausibly, before the Avar siege in 626.

George wrote to a brief and concentrated, in the conventional manner, on the processes of war—marching and countermarching, tactical ingenuity, feats of valour, inspiring speeches, battle in all its goriness and brutality—rather than on its outcome and cosmic significance. A richly textured military narrative was embellished with vivid scenes presented in verse in which Heraclius featured as the protagonist in word and deed. The climactic scenes were those of his heroic combats in the battle of Nineveh, and his return to Constantinople after he had replicated on earth the feats of God in the week of Creation.[37]

The officially sanctioned image of Heraclius was used to celebrate his victory pictorially, in a set of nine silver plates which illustrate David's rise to prominence in the court of King Saul and centre on his single combat with Goliath (Figures 21 and 22).[38] They were found in a rich hoard, including much gold jewellery, buried on Cyprus in the middle of the seventh century. They are solid, heavy pieces which come in three sizes—one large with the climactic scene of combat, four small, and four intermediate. The scenes have been chased onto their surface by highly skilled craftsmen. Five hallmarking stamps identify the plates as products of imperial workshops and date their production between 613 and 629-30.[39]

There are unequivocal visual references to the contemporary imperial court on the four intermediate plates, each of which represents a key ritual moment in the story of David—his anointing by Samuel, after which he wears a halo, his first audience with King Saul, his arming by Saul, and his marriage to Saul's daughter Michal. Each of these scenes is a tableau of five figures, their movements and gestures frozen in the middle of a ceremony. The ceremonies take place in a Roman palace (sparingly indicated by a portico), where soldiers stand guard in the secular scenes. Saul is portrayed as a Roman ruler. He sits on a cushioned throne when he receives David. He is clad in an imperial chlamys and wears a halo on that occasion and at the wedding of David and Michal, when they join

---

[37] Howard-Johnston, 'Official History'.

[38] The illustrated episodes are taken from I Samuel 16–18. R. E. Leader, 'The David Plates Revisited: Transforming the Secular in Early Byzantium', *Art Bulletin*, 82 (2000), 407–27 prefers to take the pictorial biography of David's youth which culminates in his anointing and heroism in battle as emblematic of the physical and spiritual training appropriate to young men in a Christianized aristocratic world, the increase in his stature in the wedding scene marking his entry into adulthood. She questions the analogy between the contemporary Roman and Old Testament courts, observing that Saul has his chlamys fastened with the crossbow fibula characteristic of high-ranking courtiers rather than the circular fibula with pendant pearls worn by emperors. But it was David, not Saul, who was taken as the model of Christian kingship in Late Antiquity (as Leader shows), and it was David's deeds which prefigured those of Heraclius.

[39] O. M. Dalton, 'A Second Silver Treasure from Cyprus', *Archaeologia*, 60 (1906), 1–24, at 1–13, 23–4 (circumstances of discovery and other items concealed); E. C. Dodd, *Byzantine Silver Stamps*, Dumbarton Oaks Studies 7 (Washington DC, 1961), no.58–66 (stamps and date); K. Weitzmann, ed., *Age of Spirituality* (New York, 1979), 475–83 (the best short description, save for the identification of the covenant of David and Jonathan as the scene depicted on the most problematic of the small plates).

together their right hands in the Roman manner. Saul's wealth is indicated in the exergues below two of the scenes by bags and baskets of coins symbolizing imperial largesse. A clear connection is thus made between the Roman present and the biblical past. The climactic episode in the biblical story is then illustrated on the large plate, the centrepiece of the set, where David, who carries a sceptre, confronts Goliath (upper exergue), fights Goliath between the armies in the main battle scene, and cuts off his head (lower exergue).[40]

There can be little doubt, then, that the David Plates are an allegorical illustration of current events, a visual analogue to the *Heraclias* of George of Pisidia, although the present is viewed not against a backcloth of the biblical past but through a diaphanous biblical curtain. The classical, mythological dimension, so evident in the celebratory verse, is also signalled by the classicizing style of the plates.[41] Anatomical details and robes are, on the whole, well rendered, and the action, which is caught at a particular moment, takes place within an illusionistic space. This classicism is at its strongest in the four small plates: all have a landscape setting (albeit vestigial), save for David's meeting with his brother Eliab, which takes place in a void; great care is taken, as in the larger plates, over the rendering of surface detail; a mythological past is most strongly evoked by two animal combat scenes in which David is caught at the moment of victory overpowering a lion and a bear, reminiscent as they are of Heracles' heroic struggle in the wild.

David's combat with Goliath and the associated scenes which provide a context are illustrated in a way designed to evoke the seventh-century present and a distant past. That present is to be viewed in future through the medium of the biblical past. Time both stands still and is transcended in this visual narrative. Rather than glorying in the victory over Persia as a feat of Roman arms and imperial generalship, whoever commissioned the plates wished to place it within God's grand providential scheme for mankind.

Who, then, did commission them? It seems hard to ignore the scholarly consensus which attributes the commission to Heraclius himself.[42] Who but the emperor could have proposed to efface himself from the commemorative set of plates? More telling still is the marriage scene on the last of the four intermediate plates. A comparison is made between Heraclius' marital life and that, almost as fraught, of his biblical precursor. Heraclius' much criticized second marriage to

---

[40] A. Grabar, *L'Empereur dans l'art byzantin* (Paris, 1936), 95–7; S. H. Wander, 'The Cyprus Plates: The Story of David and Goliath', *Metropolitan Museum Journal*, 8 (1973), 89–104 (full analysis of iconography).

[41] J. Trilling, 'Myth and Metaphor at the Byzantine Court: A Literary Approach to the David Plates', *Byz.*, 48 (1978), 249–63, at 250–5, 260–3; M. Mundell Mango, 'Imperial Art in the Seventh Century', in P. Magdalino, ed., *New Constantines: The Rhythm of Imperial Renewal in Byzantium, 4th–13th Centuries* (Aldershot, 1994), 109–38, at 122–31.

[42] Literature cited in n. 39–41 together with S. Spain Alexander, 'Heraclius, Byzantine Imperial Ideology, and the David Plates', *Speculum*, 52 (1977), 217–37.

his niece Martina, which took place shortly before his first counteroffensive began, is being likened not to David's affair and subsequent second marriage to Bathsheba but to his first licit union with Saul's daughter Michal.[43] The implicit message is the same as that of the *Heraclias*—Heraclius has purged himself of his great sin by his labour on behalf of Creation in his victorious war against Persia.[44] It is hard to envisage anyone but Heraclius daring to include this scene in the commemorative set.

The set of David Plates, which was buried in northern Cyprus, presumably when the island was under threat of imminent Arab attack in the late 640s or early 650s, had evidently been presented to a grandee of the court. It would be hard to explain the presence on the island of the plates if they had been retained in the emperor's possession. But if one set was given out to one grandee, surely it is more likely than not that other sets were made for distribution to other grandees? On this hypothesis, several sets of David Plates would have been commissioned both to commemorate Heraclius' Persian campaign and to reward a small number of very senior figures who had made it possible. Multiple sets of David Plates would have been made to the highest standard of workmanship in the months following Heraclius' return to Constantinople in the second half of June 628 and would have been handed out to those who headed the administration of church and state on grand ceremonial occasions, probably in the palace in Constantinople before Heraclius' departure for the Anti-Taurus in late June 629.

10.3 Second Round of Negotiations

Kavad Shiroe had been swept to power by a sudden surge of opposition to Khusro II's foreign policy. Prolonged military service in remote theatres, heavy taxation, repressive measures taken against the aristocracy, all these concomitants of war had provoked increasing resentment when it became clear that the final victory, so tantalizingly close in the early 620s, had eluded his grasp and when the war seemed set to continue for several more years and on a yet larger scale.[45] Shiroe's first act, as we have seen, was to send a delegation across the Zagros to make peace with Heraclius. He showed thereby that he meant to bring the war to an end forthwith and thus to relieve his subjects as soon as possible of the burdens which it had imposed upon them.

Shiroe probably broadcast his political programme in official communiqués sent out from the capital. He presented himself as a beneficent, merciful ruler, committed to the welfare and happiness of his subjects. To this end he declared that it was his aim (as also stated in his letter to Heraclius) to live at peace with his

---

[43] 1 Sam. 18:20–7 (Michal); 2 Sam. 11:2–12:19 (David's sin).
[44] Geo.Pis., *Heraclias*, I, 140–7.   [45] MD, 145.3–17, trans. Dowsett, 89–90.

fellow kings, thereby enabling the war-weary troops to return home. On the domestic front, he released all political prisoners and announced the abolition of the new charges imposed by his father and, it is said, an empire-wide three-year remission of regular taxes.[46] The two sources which mention the second of these fiscal concessions—the *History to 682* and *Seert Chronicle*—should be handled with care, since almost certainly they drew on the same source, a version of the *Khwadaynamag*, which may have been misled by the phrasing of the communiqués. These doubtless put the best possible construction on the tax concessions on offer. It is highly unlikely, though, that they amounted to a universal remission of all taxes, as both texts state. For there was no question of Khusro's accumulating financial reserves equivalent to three years' revenue in the course of prosecuting war on so grand a scale.

Among the political prisoners who were freed was the senior cleric of Caucasian Albania, the Catholicos Viroy. He had spent twenty-five years in detention, relatively comfortable detention, in Ctesiphon (he had been allowed to keep the emoluments of his see), after being implicated in a rebellion of Albanian magnates. He now hurried north back to his see, presumably once winter released its grip and the roads were passable.[47] Other churches too benefited from the new regime. The Nestorian Church of the East, which had been deprived of its privileged status and prohibited from electing a catholicos since the death of Sabrisho in 609, was authorized at long last to make an appointment. In Armenia, where the catholicosate had been vacant since the death of Komitas, the new governor, Smbat Bagratuni, arranged for an election.[48]

There was, however, a darker side to the new regime. Shiroe, acting supposedly under pressure from the nobility led by Yazdin's son Shamta, had his brothers first mutilated, then put to death to ensure that his position would not be challenged from within the ruling house.[49] News of this doubtless spread unofficially and tempered the joy occasioned by the policies promulgated in his public announcements. All too soon Shahrbaraz's refusal to implement the terms of the peace treaty agreed with the Romans inaugurated a serious political crisis which was to last for many months. Then the crisis worsened. Shiroe died in late summer or early autumn in his summer residence in southern Media after a reign variously put at six, seven, and eight months. There was no difficulty over the succession after the liquidation of all his brothers, but his son Ardashir was only a small boy when he became king. The dynasty's position was inevitably weakened. For the

---

[46] Ps.S., 129.22-3, with TA, 95.35-96.5; MD, 149.1-10, trans. Dowsett, 92; *Khuz.Chron.*, 29.6-7, trans. Greatrex, 236; *Seert Chron.*, 551.7-9, 555.9-11.

[47] MD, 149.18-151.6, trans. Dowsett, 92-4.

[48] Ps.S., 128.36-129.8; *Khuz.Chron.*, 29.14-18, trans. Greatrex, 237; *Seert Chron.*, 551.10-11, 555.2-7 and 11-12.

[49] Ps.S., 127.31-5; MD, 148.21-4, trans. Dowsett, 92; *Khuz.Chron.*, 29.7-9, trans. Greatrex, 236; *Seert Chron.*, 552.1-2; Tab., 1060.15-1061.1.

times demanded strong and shrewd leadership, which a regency government was ill suited to provide.[50]

Heraclius remained determined to bring about peace by diplomatic means. Rather than renewing the war, he sought a new negotiating partner. He stuck to the decision he had made at Ganzak to refrain from exploiting his and the Turks' victory in the field to the full. He took advantage of growing Persian weakness, but made no attempt to exacerbate the internal crisis when he might perhaps have hoped to induce such instability that the rival empire might shake itself to pieces. He maintained his commitment to restoring the binary world order of recent centuries. This conciliatory stance was almost certainly widely known in Constantinople, and affected Theophylact Simocatta, who was in the city and was at work on his history of Maurice's reign. He picked up and reproduced powerful arguments in favour of the international status quo, putting them into the mouth of the young Khusro II's emissary to the Roman court in 590. They were much better suited to the circumstances at the time of writing than to the earlier Persian crisis, when the legitimate heir to the Sasanian throne had taken refuge on Roman soil and was seeking official Roman backing.[51]

Khusro's formal request for aid on that occasion and the debates which it occasioned at the highest level in the Roman government constitute the central, dramatic episode in Theophylact's history. He goes to the trouble of giving a full summary of the written appeal drafted by Khusro (iv.11): the core of his argument, which has its roots in the dualist Zoroastrian world view, is that God has arranged for earthly affairs to be managed by two great powers, analogous to the two heavenly bodies which illuminate the cosmos, and that their task is to combat demonic forces represented by the refractory and warmongering peoples which menace them from without and the ever-present danger of social disorder within; Maurice, who is flatteringly addressed, is entreated to uphold this divinely sanctioned arrangement by restoring the proper hieratic order in Persia. The space given to the exposition in favour of the old order is surely significant and places Theophylact firmly in the peace party.

Khusro's emissary duly arrives at the imperial court, presents the formal appeal, and backs it up with a long speech which may be viewed as a set of variations of Theophylact's on the arguments of the document (iv.13.4–26). Maurice has an opportunity to fight a just war, to gain the respect of the outer peoples, to establish a durable peace. It is in the Romans' interest to restore Khusro, whose moral disposition is superior both to that of his father Hormizd and that of the usurper Bahram. But the central concern of the speech is to counter Roman imperialist

---

[50] *Chron.724*, 147.14–16, trans. Palmer, 18 (7 months); Ps.S., 129.22–5, with TA, 96.3–5 (6 months); MD, 149.10–14, trans. Dowsett, 92 (7 months); *Khuz.Chron.*, 29.18–23, trans. Greatrex, 237 (8 months); *Seert Chron.*, 555.8–9; Tab., 1061.9–10 (8 months).

[51] Whitby, *Emperor Maurice*, 292–304.

ambitions, as if there had been a danger in 590 of elements in the Roman government pressing for the conquest of the Sasanian Empire. The nub of the argument is forcefully put (iv.13.6–12). It is not possible for a single monarchy to run earthly affairs. There are too many problems to be faced. Human nature is too unstable. Just as a flock cannot be managed by a single shepherd's pipe, so the sublunary world cannot be united under a single ruler. *Alexander was an immature stripling, the mere plaything of fortune, when he tried to realize his mad, unreasonable ambition.*

These were not the thoughts, spoken and unspoken, of everyone in Heraclius' court and the higher and lower echelons of the apparatus of government at the time. George of Pisidia was probably not alone in entertaining the dreams of conquest which he voiced at the end of his great religious poem, the *Hexaemeron*. His view was that a single earthly power should replicate the heavenly order. For him, the war had been a religious conflict, and the proper outcome, he indicated, was for Heraclius, as God's agent on earth, to conquer and annex the defeated evil empire. Of course, he went his own way and could be quite unrepresentative in the views which he expressed. But this is unlikely to be true of this passage. For the view which he took of the war had been a principal theme of Roman propaganda. The scenario which he conjured up, that of a Roman emperor setting out to realize the traditional theoretical claim to universal rule, was not beyond the bounds of possibility at the time he was finishing the poem (between 628 and 630).[52]

This was almost certainly a minority view. The more realistic course, that taken by Heraclius, was to recognize the rival empire's existence and parity or near parity of status and to strive to negotiate an enduring peace. Diplomatic devices of all sorts would be used to ensure that the terms were satisfactory, above all on the central issue of the future frontier between the two powers. But a renewal of war aimed at dealing Persian power a fatal blow was out of the question.

Heraclius had to deal with Shahrbaraz, who was plainly the arbiter of Middle Eastern affairs. A treaty could only be enforced if he, with his immense prestige and the large number of troops under his command, was ready to back it. The initiative naturally was taken by Heraclius, the victor in the war. He could and did bring pressure to bear through his Turkish allies but indicated, probably at the very start of negotiations, that he was ready to develop an agreement into a positive alliance. There was thus an inducement and a threat lurking in the background when first he wrote to Shahrbaraz. The course of negotiations cannot be followed, since the most reliable source, the *History of Khosrov*, simply places the terms eventually agreed in a short passage of direct speech from Heraclius at

---

[52] Geo.Pis., *Hexaemeron*, ed. and trans. F. Gonnelli, *Giorgio di Pisidia, Esamerone* (Pisa, 1998), lines 1838–52, with commentary of Mary Whitby, 'The Devil in Disguise: The End of George of Pisidia's *Hexaemeron* Reconsidered', *JHS* 115 (1995), 115–29, at 118–20, 127–9.

the outset.[53] There must have been many exchanges of letters, given that Heraclius would have to settle for less than the generous demarcation of territory offered by Shiroe and that Shahrbaraz would have to relinquish many or most of the conquests which he had made.

The first task was to establish the outline of an agreement. This was achieved by the prospect dangled before Shahrbaraz of his seizing the Sasanian throne. It was there for the taking, Heraclius observed. Shahrbaraz, though, would have to evacuate Egypt and the Roman Levant. Then, the most difficult issue had to be tackled—which of the conquered provinces would Shahrbaraz be allowed to retain, what precise line of frontier would provide the necessary security for the Romans. The final task was to work out the details of the implementation of any agreement reached—the precise sequence of moves by each side and their coordination, culminating in a summit meeting between the two principals.

The Turkish presence in the north cannot but have influenced the course of the negotiations. The Persians were on the defensive. The Iranian plateau was all too vulnerable to attack from the north-west. The peace which the Turks had made with the Tang in 626 was holding. In 628 they were able once again to concentrate their forces in the west. A huge army, under the command of the *yabghu khagan*, reappeared south of the Caucasus, and marched west into Iberia. Tiflis was besieged for a second time. Its defences were weaker than before. The crack troops who had been sent to bolster its defences in 627 had gone. Morale dropped after two months, and the city fell to a general assault. In the sack, many were killed and much plunder was gathered. The Persian commander and an Iberian prince, whom the *yabghu khagan* held responsible for publicly mocking him during the first siege, were blinded, tortured, strangled, flayed, and stuffed before being hung from the walls.[54]

This swift and successful strike deep into Transcaucasia was an impressive demonstration of Turkish military might. Worse was soon to follow. The main Turkish army withdrew with a large amount of booty. A son of the *yabghu khagan*, another *shad*, was deputed to occupy and annex Albania.[55] He was to deal the Sasanian Empire a second more serious blow. A whole region of great strategic importance was to be removed permanently from Sasanian control. The Turks would thus be making a first move towards the dismemberment of the empire.

The *shad* sent an ultimatum to the Albanian authorities demanding formal submission, acknowledgement of Turkish suzerainty, and the opening of cities, fortresses, and markets to Turkish troops. He claimed sovereignty over Albania and expected magnates and local notables to transfer their allegiance from the

---

[53] Ps.S., 129.25–9 (supplemented by TA, 96.7–14). Nic., c.17.1–6, mistakenly has Shahrbaraz initiate the correspondence after giving a very confused account of the political crisis following Shiroe's death (c.16). Cf. Strategius, c.24.3.

[54] MD, 151.13–153.8, trans. Dowsett, 94–5.   [55] MD, 153.9–20, trans. Dowsett, 95.

Sasanians to the *yabghu khagan*. The *marzban* Semavshnasp refused outright, packed up, and left. It fell to the Catholicos Viroy, reinstalled in his see, to handle the crisis on his own. At first he prevaricated, hoping against hope to obtain Persian authorization for a change of allegiance. There was no question, though, of delaying or opposing the carefully planned Turkish takeover. The whole of Albania, provinces and settlements, mountains and plains, river valleys and marshes, had been divided up, and each component part allocated by lot to a military unit. The operation was programmed to begin on a given day at a given hour. Viroy was simply being asked to accept the fait accompli and license the occupation in advance. He was still fobbing off the Turkish emissaries with excuses when they told him that the scheduled day had arrived. That brought negotiations to an abrupt halt. Viroy, accompanied by a small party, fled into the mountain fastness of the district of Arts'akh (in the heart of modern Nagorno-Karabakh). Many others did likewise. The upper echelons of society had probably already withdrawn to safety in the expectation that the Turkish army would return.[56]

A second Turkish delegation headed by a person of high rank who was guardian and tutor to the *shad* tracked Viroy down and reiterated the Turks' demand that Albania submit. Viroy sought and obtained the backing of a representative assembly of the nobility, office holders, clergy, and scribes which he convened in Arts'akh and made arrangements with the utmost care for the formal act of submission. Accompanied by a large deputation, and taking cartloads of precious gifts carefully calibrated to match the dignity of the named recipients, he then made his way to the Turkish camp in the plain of Uti, not far from Part'aw. At its centre was the *shad*'s court, which seems to have taken the form of a series of grand tents. Passing through an outer space where Turkish magnates and nobles were feasting, Viroy and his party made their way past a doorkeeper into an antechamber, preceded by servants who instructed them in the proper etiquette. Only Viroy was admitted into the innermost tent. There he did obeisance, presented the gifts to the *shad* and his magnates, and, after some amicable exchanges, made the act of submission on behalf of all the inhabitants of the land to the *shad* and his father after the *shad* had formally declared that his father had taken over the land as a personal, perpetual inheritance.[57]

Albania was thus removed from Persian control with surgical precision and transformed into a forward base from which the Turks could project their power over Iberia, Armenia, Atropatene, or Media, as they chose. The blow to Persian power and prestige was very damaging. It greatly weakened Shahrbaraz's hand in his negotiations with Heraclius. His political ambitions would be undermined

---

[56] MD, 153.20–157.16, trans. Dowsett, 95–7.
[57] MD, 157.16–162.6, trans. Dowsett, 97–101.

fatally if he did not show himself ready promptly to defend Persian interests in the north. As commander of the Persian army of occupation, he had the military wherewithal to counter the Turkish threat once he reached agreement with Heraclius and could gather his dispersed troops together into a single fighting force. Turkish actions thus greatly increased his incentive to make peace, which entailed moderating his territorial demands and offering terms acceptable to Heraclius.

Heraclius was undoubtedly aware of Turkish plans for 628. He had, after all, agreed a long-term alliance at his summit meeting with the *yabghu khagan* in 627 which was to be sealed by the marriage of his daughter Eudocia to the *yabghu khagan* himself. The two sides stayed in touch, as arrangements needed to be made for the planned marriage. Heraclius assuredly conveyed the news of the startling success of his expedition into Sasanian Mesopotamia as soon as he could to his allies and, it may be conjectured, kept them posted on subsequent political developments. In these circumstances it is more likely than not that there was collusion between Romans and Turks and that renewed military action by the Turks in 628 and, later, in 629 was designed, at least partly, to strengthen Heraclius' bargaining position.

Shahrbaraz *was* rendered more amenable by Turkish actions in the north. An agreement on the terms outlined at the start by Heraclius took shape. Both sides compromised on the crucial frontier question. Heraclius did not insist on a return to the traditional demarcation. It was Shahrbaraz, though, who made the larger concessions. He agreed to evacuate the whole of Egypt, Palestine, Syria, Cilicia, and a great deal of Armenia. He was thus handing over the two great metropoleis of Alexandria and Antioch, Jerusalem, with its venerated Christian sanctuaries, and a multitude of other cities in what were highly urbanized provinces. He may also have been prepared to make a more generous settlement than Shiroe in Armenia, possibly involving a withdrawal to the line of the 591 frontier.[58] Thus, he was ready to relinquish most of the territory conquered in the course of the second phase of the war without a fight. Most, but not quite all. He insisted on retaining Rome's forward military zone shielding Syria. The Euphrates was to be the frontier south of the Taurus.[59] Two Roman provinces, Mesopotamia and Orhoene, two great cities, Amida and Edessa, and many other places of note were to be incorporated permanently into the Sasanian Empire. They were symbolically important gains for Persia which in any other circumstances would have dealt devastating blows to Roman prestige. Shahrbaraz had to keep some of the gains of war if his candidature for the Sasanian throne was not to be irredeemably damaged.

---

[58] TA, 96.14–20; Nic., 17.11–15.
[59] *Chron.724*, 147.22–4, trans. Palmer, 18 (Euphrates as frontier). Cf. *Chron.1234*, 237.29–238.3, trans. Hoyland, 83.

THE DIFFICULT ROAD TO PEACE   343

These were the principal elements in the agreement reached in the course of winter and spring 629 between Heraclius and Shahrbaraz. The new military balance in the north, which favoured the Romans and their Turkish allies, was acknowledged. In the south, Egypt and the Levant were to be evacuated in return for Roman political backing for a bid by Shahrbaraz to seize power in Ctesiphon. The Persians retained an overall strategic advantage now that neither side controlled all the passes over the Armenian Taurus and a single waterway separated what was now a huge Persian salient from northern Syria. But the Roman Empire was to be reconstituted behind the Euphrates.

The agreement was put into effect in a series of orchestrated moves. The first step was to issue orders for evacuation to the units stationed in Egypt. They probably assembled not far from Alexandria, where the headquarters of the army of occupation were located. Shahrbaraz then left the city and withdrew his forces from Egypt in June. A pause probably ensued during which preparations were made for the more difficult task of withdrawing from Palestine and Syria, where Persian units were assuredly more widely dispersed. Troops would have to be pulled back from their bases to local concentration points in a rolling programme beginning in the south and moving north. The order to initiate this second phase of the evacuation was probably delayed until Shahrbaraz gained personal and written assurances of Roman support from Heraclius at the meeting which, they had agreed, should be held to seal their agreement.[60]

Heraclius must have felt a frisson of anxiety as he travelled across Asia Minor for the summit meeting. For he was witnessing what was in effect the start of the remobilization of the Persian army of conquest. Every precaution was taken to secure his safety. The lessons of 623 had been learned. The site was the small city of Arabissus set in the heart of the Anti-Taurus, a massive natural redoubt which was firmly held by the Romans. Access by road from Caesarea was easy for Heraclius. Shahrbaraz had to make his way north along another road cutting through rugged terrain (the two southernmost ridges of the Anti-Taurus) before he entered the secluded plain enclosed within the mountains where Arabissus lay.[61] He came with no more than a small escorting force. The meeting took place in July. Heraclius formally bestowed the Persian throne on Shahrbaraz and his sons. He offered whatever military aid Shahrbaraz thought appropriate (in the event, a small force of trusted imperial bodyguards, of little military but great symbolic importance) and, in exchange, asked for the return of the fragments of the True Cross which Shahrbaraz had taken from Jerusalem fifteen years earlier. The terms of the agreement, which

---

[60] *Chron.724*, 146.28–30, 147.19–21, trans. Palmer, 17–18; Ps.S, 129.29–32; Nic., c.17.5–9.
[61] Nav.Int.Div., *Turkey*, I, 154–9; F. Hild, *Das byzantinische Strassensystem in Kappadokien*, TIB 2 (Vienna, 1977) 85–90; Howard-Johnston, 'Military Infrastructure', 865–7.

naturally also included war reparations, were then confirmed 'in writing, with a seal and with salt'.[62]

The prime purpose of the summit was to demonstrate the common political purpose of the two leaders. The signing of the formal agreement was assuredly accompanied by ceremonial acts designed to impress the importance of the occasion on the public consciousness. According to Nicephorus, Heraclius invested a son of Shahrbaraz with the dignity of patrician and betrothed a daughter to his own young son, Theodosius. There is nothing improbable about this. Honours and a marriage alliance had previously been used to bind the ruling Turkish and Roman houses together. It was in Heraclius' interest to solidify this new alliance in a similar way. Shahrbaraz's son and daughter may have been baptized shortly beforehand, with Heraclius acting as sponsor—hence their Roman, perhaps baptismal, names, Nicetas and Nike. Furthermore, if Nicetas was Shahrbaraz's eldest son or at any rate his designated heir, Heraclius may have been striving to do more than merely reinforce his agreement. He may have been hoping to instal a Christian ruler on the Persian throne and thus to open the way for widespread proselytizing on Persian territory. This tantalizing scenario is, however, highly conjectural, resting, as it does, on a series of bold inferences drawn from the testimony of a source of far from unimpeachable worth.[63]

Be that as it may, Heraclius and Shahrbaraz concluded an agreement which effectively brought the long war to a close. Peace on terms acceptable to both sides was likely to last. Together they arranged for the construction of a church at Arabissus dedicated to Eirene (peace) as an earnest of their commitment and as a memorial of their meeting.[64] Heraclius was, for the moment, director of events in western Eurasia now that he had locked both Turkish and Persian leaders into binding alliances. Shahrbaraz was free to pursue his political ambitions at home and to do what he could to shore up the Persian position in the north. First, though, he would have to organize the evacuation of Persian forces from the many Roman provinces which he had agreed to leave, trying to ensure that the complex process passed off without incident. Heraclius' principal task was first to wait on the edge of the occupied territories while the Persians withdrew and then, once the way was clear—by late autumn perhaps?—to begin the process of reconstruction in the Middle East. Troops must be dispatched to impose Roman authority, communication re-established with city notables, and provincial and regional administrative institutions brought back under Roman control. It is highly unlikely that any significant reforms were introduced at this stage if the

---

[62] *Chron.724*, 147.18–24, trans. Palmer, 18; ps.S, 129.33–130.4 (supplemented by TA, 96.20–9); Nic., c.17.6–16.

[63] Nic., c.17.16–19. Mango, 'Deux Études', 112–14 for the scenario. The conjectures are his, save for that concerning the timing of baptism of Nicetas and Nike.

[64] *Chron.724*, 147.21, trans. Palmer, 18.

takeover was to be swift and smooth—especially on the desert frontage, where it was essential to maintain an effective Beduin shield.[65]

Shahrbaraz's actions are only reported in outline. Well before the withdrawal was complete—he is described as still in control of Palestine—he had to deal with the growing menace of the Turks. They were consolidating their hold on Albania, using the Persian tax system to extract resources from all sectors of the local economy. They also exploited their new position to launch a first attack on Armenia (the eastern, Persian sector, presumably) in summer, probably late summer. In response Shahrbaraz sent a large force of Arab cavalry to engage and destroy them.[66] By this stage the regency regime was probably aware of his political designs and could take a little comfort when news came that the Arab force, far from achieving the easy victory confidently expected of them, had been annihilated by the Turks in a carefully sprung ambush.[67]

Once he had extricated all his troops from the territory he had agreed to return to the Romans and had assembled a powerful field army out of them, Shahrbaraz could begin asserting control over the cities of northern Mesopotamia and moving south towards the metropolitan region. There was resistance from Mehr Adhur Gushnasp, the regent for Ardashir, but a blockade of the capital proved effective, and Shahrbaraz was able to seize control of the government. A purge followed of all those prominent courtiers and army officers whom he distrusted. Some were sent in chains to Heraclius, presumably because he had issued a list of Persians wanted for trial in the empire. The rest were executed. Ardashir remained the figurehead of the new regime. Seizure of the throne by a non-Sasanian, albeit one with the outstanding military record of Shahrbaraz, was not a step lightly to be undertaken.[68]

Shahrbaraz made sure that he fulfilled all his undertakings to Heraclius. In addition to the extraditions demanded by the Romans and the reparations which he had promised, he handed over 'innumerable presents'. The spotlight falls on one item, the True Cross. Its return is represented in most Christian sources as the principal demand made by Heraclius in his negotiations with Shahrbaraz. Roman propaganda had made much of the loss of this most venerated Christian relic in the latter stages of the war. Now, at its end, it was picked out as the main Roman trophy of war, symbolizing a victory which had been won, with divine help, by Heraclius as Christ's vicegerent on earth. It was located after a search and

---

[65] J. Haldon, 'The Reign of Heraclius: A Context for Change?', in Reinink and Stolte, *Reign of Heraclius*, 1–16, at 4–5; W. Brandes, 'Heraclius between Restoration and Reform: Some Remarks on Recent Research', in Reinink and Stolte, *Reign of Heraclius*, 17–40, at 31–4. Cf. O. Schmitt, 'Untersuchungen zur Organisation und zur militärischen Stärke oströmischer Herrschaft im Vorderen Orient zwischen 628 und 633', *BZ* 94 (2001), 197–229, who takes a more pessimistic view.

[66] MD, 166.14–168.17, trans.Dowsett, 104–5.   [67] MD, 168.18–169.12, trans Dowsett, 105–6.

[68] Strategius, c.24.6; ps.S, 130.5–10, with TA, 96.29–33; *Khuz.Chron.*, 29.22–7, trans. Greatrex, 236–7; *Seert Chron.*, 556.1–6 and Tab., 1061.17–1062.14; Theoph., 329.4–5. Cf. Flusin, *Saint Anastase*, II, 296–7, 306–9 and Zuckerman, 'Heraclius and the Return of the Holy Cross', 215.

handed over to a Roman deputation which was to take it back with all due honour to Roman territory. There, at Hierapolis, within easy striking distance of the new frontier on the Euphrates, Heraclius was waiting. Once the Cross was in his hands, he would take it to Palestine and restore it to its proper place on Golgotha, inside the Church of the Holy Sepulchre in Jerusalem, in what was to be a solemn, carefully choreographed ceremony.[69]

The date of the ceremony was carefully chosen. It may cause some surprise that it was not to take place at Easter, which, in 630, fell on 8 April. But Heraclius had picked out a date of yet greater cosmic significance, 21 March.[70] This was the spring equinox, the turning point between the seasons, which was of great significance for Zoroastrians, as it marked the re-emergence of the powers of good after a long seasonal hibernation during which the powers of evil were in the ascendant.[71] But it was much more than a Christian Nawruz. For in the week of Creation, God had fashioned the sun and moon, celestial chronometers for the whole cosmos, on the third day, and the third day was reckoned, according to an authoritative calculation in the *Chronicon Paschale*, to have been Wednesday 21 March. So it was on the anniversary of the beginning of time itself that Heraclius planned to stage his religious celebration of victory, in a year when the key date also fell on the third day of the week.[72]

10.4 Celebration of Victory at Jerusalem

Despite the damage which it suffered at the end of the first great Jewish revolt in 70 AD, despite its position, set well back from the coast, a stiff climb from the rich plain of Sharon, on the edge of the dry Judaean upland, Jerusalem had grown into a great city. It belonged to the leading tier of regional centres in the Middle East.

---

[69] Strategius, c.24.7; ps.S, 130.10–14, supplemented by TA, 96.33–97.3; *Khuz.Chron.*, 30.1–5, trans. Greatrex, 237; *Seert Chron.*, 556.8–10; Nic., c.17. 7–9, 15–16; Agap., 468.3–4, Mich.Syr. xi.7 (IV, 418), *Chron.1234*, 238.7–13, trans. Hoyland, 84–5. The story that Heraclius received the Cross earlier and journeyed with it to and from Constantinople in autumn-winter 629–30 (Flusin, *Saint Anastase*, II, 309–10 and H. A. Klein, *Byzanz, der Westen und das 'wahre' Kreuz: Die Geschichte einer Reliquie und ihrer künstlerischen Fassung in Byzanz und im Abendland* (Wiesbaden, 2004), 41–3; cf. Zuckerman, 'Heraclius and the Return of the Holy Cross', 212–13) looks like a later concoction. It has lodged in Theoph., 328.13–15 (cf. Agap., 468.4–5) and in a garbled account of the war in the lost work of the authentic Sebeos (cf. J.-P. Mahé, 'Critical Remarks on the Newly Edited Excerpts from Sebēos', in T. J. Samuelian and M. E. Stone, eds., *Medieval Armenian Culture* (Chico, CA, 1983), 218–39, at 231–2).

[70] Strategius, c.24.9; *Translatio S. Anastasii*, ed. and trans. Flusin, *Saint Anastase*, I, 98–107, at c.1.1–12. Mango, 'Deux Études', 112–13; Flusin, *St. Anastase*, II, 298–306. Zuckerman, 'Return of Holy Cross', 200–5, 209–10, proposes two ceremonial restorations in Jerusalem, the first in 629 on 21 March, the second on 30 March 630, with a trip to Constantinople in between.

[71] Boyce, *Zoroastrians*, 34.

[72] *Chron.Pasch.*, 3.1–11, 23.15–24.6, 26.19–27.3, trans. J. Beaucamp, R. Bondoux, J. Lefort, M.-F. Rouan, and I. Sorlin, 'Temps et histoire I: Le Prologue de la *Chronique pascale*', *TM* 7 (1979), 223–301, at 229–30, 251–2, 254.

Nonetheless, in human terms it could not match the great metropoleis of the early seventh-century Mediterranean—Constantinople, Antioch, and Alexandria—which, by virtue of their wealth and political dominance, had become the principal cities of the Christian world.[73]

Jerusalem was invested with extraordinary status, however, from its past history. It was the meeting place between the immaterial and material worlds. In the deep past, God had directed his chosen people across the Jordan. He had aided Joshua as he led the army of Israel into their allotted land and conquered it, city by city. He had authorized David to bring the Ark of the Covenant into the city, where later Solomon placed it in the Holy of Holies in the Temple. Jerusalem was thus the central place in his providential scheme for mankind in that early era when the Jews were the instruments for the realizing of his will on earth. Then it provided the setting for the drama which inaugurated the second era of human history. It was there that God incarnate, the single person of Christ, perfect in his divinity and perfect in his humanity, submitted to a human court and was convicted and sentenced to a lingering, painful death by crucifixion. It was there that, by the climactic act of the Resurrection, the godhead enmeshed in the flesh had opened the way to salvation for all mankind.[74]

It was no wonder, then, that the supernatural aura of Jerusalem grew ever stronger and that places associated with the Passion were increasingly venerated, as this new, more complex, proselytizing form of monotheism infiltrated the Roman Empire east and west. So intense was the devotion of Christians to the holy places that a direct link was soon established between them and the imperial authority once Constantine had adopted the new faith. The legend of the discovery of the True Cross by Helena, mother of Constantine, and the dispatch of a fragment to the new imperial city which bore Constantine's name provided the vital connection between the Gospel story and the role of the Christian Roman Empire as the divinely authorized director of earthly affairs.[75]

Jerusalem thus acquired unrivalled status as a sacred place in late antiquity. It was the central point from which the divine debouched into the material world. If, breaking loose from the trammels of chronology, we look ahead for a moment into the third, Islamic era, in which a purer, more austere monotheism was disseminated throughout the world, we will see that Jerusalem's role was yet more elevated, raised up to a cosmic level. A strange rock which wells up from the surface of the Temple Mount was identified as the place where God's feet had

---

[73] J. H. W. G. Liebeschuetz, *Decline and Fall of the Roman City* (Oxford, 2001), 54–63, 295–303; G. Avni, *The Byzantine-Islamic Transition in Palestine: An Archaeological Approach* (Oxford, 2014), 109–25, 138–45.

[74] F. E. Peters, *Jerusalem* (Princeton, NJ, 1985), 1–130; R. L. Wilken, *The Land Called Holy: Palestine in Christian History and Thought* (New Haven, CT, 1993), 1–19, 46–64.

[75] Peters, *Jerusalem*, 131–75; Wilken, *Land Called Holy*, 82–125; Klein, *Byzanz, der Westen und das 'wahre' Kreuz*, 19–27.

rested when he created the whole visible universe. It was also scheduled to be the place where the Last Judgement would take place at the end of time.[76]

How on earth is the modern observer living in an irreligious age to retroject himself into a distant time when such notions about the supernatural role of Jerusalem were deeply embedded in the collective consciousness of Christians, Jews, and, later, Muslims? How is one to breathe something of the charged atmosphere at the end of the greatest war between the Roman and Persian empires, as Heraclius prepared to restore the True Cross to its proper place on Golgotha? No contemporary could deny that God had intervened in human affairs with the most spectacular results. None, however eminent their position in the hierarchies of state or church, could emancipate themselves from the ambient thought-world. But ideas and attitudes surely varied considerably between milieux and individuals. And there is no single source which can be used as an authoritative guide. Thus, we cannot simply extrapolate from the views expressed by George of Pisidia, who wrote a short poem about the restoration of the Cross but did not witness it in person. He may well have been more representative of contemporary views than usual, when, ten days after the ceremony, the news reached Constantinople and the poem began to take shape in his mind. He seems to have been in a state of high excitement, his attention shifting hither and thither (like the eye of a spectator flitting over the procession) as different thoughts came into his head. But even in this comparatively artless poem, written, one suspects, in some haste, he avoids the obvious biblical comparisons of Heraclius with Joshua and David and introduces one with Jason (retrieving the Golden Fleece) which is unlikely to have crossed anyone else's mind.[77]

Still, the imaginative leap must be made. We must strive to view events from within as well as without, with the aid of other extant accounts of the solemn ceremony which celebrated the triumph of the Romans as Christians, as agents of God's will.

Heraclius waited at Hierapolis for the return of the delegation which he had sent to Ctesiphon.[78] This distant heir of Constantine the Great (something advertised by the name which he gave his eldest son)[79] readied himself to receive back the Cross which God, in his anger, had allowed to fall into Persian hands. He had a large military escort representing the army which had, by its endeavours, recovered it. He was also accompanied by dignitaries, who formed a peripatetic

---

[76] J. van Ess, "Abd al-Malik and the Dome of the Rock: An Analysis of Some Texts", in J. Raby and J. Johns, eds., *Bayt al-Maqdis I: 'Abd al-Malik's Jerusalem*, Oxford Studies in Islamic Art 9 (Oxford, 1992), 89–103.

[77] Geo.Pis., *In restitutionem S. Crucis*, ed. and trans. Pertusi, *Giorgio di Pisidia*, 225–30, at lines 21–4.

[78] Mich.Syr., xi.7 (IV, 418), *Chron.1234*, 238.7–13, trans. Hoyland, 84–5.

[79] Heraclius the New Constantine, born 612 (*Chron.Pasch.*, 702.16–18). Cf. J. W. Drijvers, 'Heraclius and the *Restitutio Crucis*: Notes on Symbolism and Ideology', in Reinink and Stolte, *Reign of Heraclius*, 175–90, 181–3.

court. He set off on a solemn progress. Besides the Cross, he was taking back precious vessels belonging to the churches of Jerusalem which had been spirited out the city and kept safe in Constantinople.[80] He had outdone Constantine.[81] He had not merely threatened war but with the boldness of an Alexander had penetrated deep into the interior of the Persian Empire.[82] Both these images were in the air, but Heraclius preferred to portray himself more modestly as Pious Basileus in Christ, stripping off the other titles (Imperator, Augustus) and victory honorifics which exalted Roman imperial power. His authority was shown thus to be derived from God rather than (manipulated) human election.[83] Like an Old Testament king, he had been acting as God's agent in his campaigns. Just as God had encouraged the Israelites by sending down manna, he had given Heraclius' men a sign of his favour on their entry into Persian territory in 624, when they saw what should have been a desiccated landscape bathed in unseasonal dew.[84] Heraclius had campaigned with all the tactical acumen of Joshua, achieving surprise by ambush and forced march, and with the same God-sanctioned ruthlessness in victory. Like Joshua, he had conquered the Holy Land, although, in his case, the fighting had taken place far away.[85] It was, therefore, as much as Old Testament king as Roman emperor that he was going to take the Cross back to Jerusalem.

The instrument of degrading punishment had long since been transformed into the symbol of Christian victory.[86] For contemporary observers the wooden fragments of the original Cross were imbued with awesome supernatural power. When they described it as instrument of Christian victory, they were not simply speaking figuratively. The Cross became the inanimate pendant to Heraclius in the working out of God's will on earth.[87] Sophronius, the future Patriarch of Jerusalem, at the time a monk and refugee in North Africa, described it as destroyer of death and demons, grantor of life to mortals, in the Anacreontic poem which he wrote to celebrate its return. God had allowed the Persians to capture it as they rampaged over Roman territory, but the Cross had killed Khusro, 'the generator of war, the evil king of evil, the cruel persecutor of sweet peace', rolling that perpetrator of universal slaughter easily out of life.[88]

---

[80] Ps.S.,131.9–14, with TA, 97.3–7. Flusin, *Saint Anastase*, II, 310–11.
[81] Geo.Pis., *In restitutionem*, 47–63.
[82] Cf. G. J. Reinink, 'Heraclius, the New Alexander: Apocalyptic Prophecies during the Reign of Heraclius', in Reinink and Stolte, *Reign of Heraclius*, 81–94, at 84–6, 90–1.
[83] I. Shahid, 'The Iranian Factor in Byzantium during the Reign of Heraclius', *DOP* 26 (1972), 293–320; E. S. Chrysos, 'The Title Βασιλεύς in Early Byzantine International Relations', *DOP* 32 (1978), 29–75; O. Kresten, 'Herakleios und der Titel βασιλεύς', in P. Speck, *Varia VII*, Poikila Byzantina 18 (Bonn, 2000), 178–9; C. Zuckerman, 'On the Titles and Office of the Byzantine Βασιλεύς', *TM* 16 (2010), 865–90.
[84] Exodus, 16:4–35; Theoph., 307.21–3.   [85] Joshua, 8:1–29, 10:1–12:24.
[86] Drijvers, 'Heraclius and the *Restitutio Crucis*', 179–80.   [87] V.Anast., cc.6.6–7.5.
[88] Sophronius, *Anacreontica*, 18, ed. and trans. M. Gigante (Rome, 1957).

George of Pisidia touched on this obvious theme. For him too the Cross was laden with power, a Christian analogue to the Ark of the Covenant, which likewise belonged properly to the Holy City. He too saw its removal by Khusro, described as the plaything/sport of error (a deliberate allusion perhaps to Theophylact's phrase about Alexander the Great), as a punishment for sin. But it had been retrieved from the Persian furnace. Its wood had reduced Persian fire to ashes. The spiritual missiles it shot had caused the Romans' enemies to fight each other.[89] The Cross was the most precious, the most powerful of Christian relics. It was universally venerated, and its return to Jerusalem could be universally celebrated by Christians.

Not by Jews, though. It is here that we touch on the grim underside of the celebrations. At each stage of its progress through Roman territory, the Cross was not only reminding Christians of what they had in common but of what the Saviour had suffered at the hands of the Jews. The Cross, as the instrument of crucifixion, could not but rouse anti-Jewish feeling, could not but direct the collective Christian memory back to the ills inflicted on them by the Jews. There had been some active collaboration on the part of the Jews of Palestine at the time of the Persian invasion. But it was Persian intervention to stop the Jerusalem pogrom, the atrocities (much exaggerated but real) committed after the fall of the city, and the unusual licence enjoyed by the Jews of the city over the following two years of indirect Persian rule which had firmly cast the Jews as allies of the Persians. The return of the Cross, which had been torn with their help from the Holy City, was bound to reactivate Christian rancour, to heighten tension wherever Jews and Christians lived side by side, and to lead to violence on a greater or lesser scale.[90]

Heraclius took the inland route through Palestine, crossing Galilee, where, according to a plausible story retailed by Eutychius, he received a warm welcome from the Jews and promised that there would be no reprisals. However, the conversion, under pressure, of a rich Jew in whose house he stayed at Tiberias did not augur well for the future, and, on his arrival at Jerusalem, Heraclius is said to have rescinded his promise when he saw with his own eyes the mass grave of executed Christians at Maqella (or Mamilla), just outside the western wall. That was probably the occasion for his declaration of a three-mile exclusion zone around the city, which is reported by Theophanes, a measure probably analogous to that taken by the Persians in 616 to prevent new immigration by Jews.[91] Unequivocal evidence of anti-Jewish sentiment in high places at this time is provided by two well-placed observers: Sophronius ended his short poem with the wish that Jewish diatribes against the Cross might rebound against their

---

[89] Geo.Pis., *In restitutionem*, 9, 32–4, 58–68, 73–82.
[90] Cf. D. M. Olster, *Roman Defeat, Christian Response, and the Literary Construction of the Jew* (Philadelphia, PA, 1994), 82–4.
[91] Theoph., 328.15–23; Eutychius, 127.10–129.14, trans., 107–9.

heads, while George of Pisidia slipped in an aside calling on them to abandon their misguided ancestral faith.[92]

Only the barest outlines can be recovered of the ceremony which took place at Jerusalem. None of the sound seventh-century sources describes Heraclius' route into and through the city. A later text, the *Reversio Sanctae Crucis*, does not inspire confidence from its impressionistic and grossly distorted account of the war. But the scenario which it paints of the Jerusalem ceremony is not implausible in essentials, for all its miraculous content (the eastern gate, is transformed into a slab of wall at the approach of Heraclius in his worldly finery) and exaggeration about the degree to which Heraclius abases himself (dismounting, stripping off his clothes except for a linen girdle, and walking barefoot) before the gate is reconstituted and Heraclius can proceed. It is a scenario in which Christ's vicegerent on earth rides down the Mount of Olives, dismounts, and discards his imperial robes and shoes, before entering the city as a humble mortal, carrying the Cross *by the gate used by Christ on Palm Sunday*.[93]

This story of the re-enactment of the Gospel episode by the emperor may be *entertained*—not least because it appears to have been carved in relief on the lintel above the north portal of the small church built a few years later (638–40) at Mren in central Armenia. (Figure 23). That is the only plausible interpretation of a scene in which a figure clad in ordinary clothes and followed by a magnificent riderless horse receives a cross from a small kneeling king (Khusro II?), meets a priest swinging a censer, and goes toward a rock from which grows the Tree of Life (symbolizing both the Temple Mount and Calvary?).[94] This ritual self-abasement of the emperor would help explain the construction of the Golden Gate on the east side of the Temple Mount, roughly on the axis of the Holy Sepulchre (Figure 24). It was no ordinary city gate, but a grand double archway leading into a large hall (some 20 by 10 metres) divided lengthwise into two vaulted passages. There was a great deal of decorative carving inside and out—on the broad entablatures, the voussoirs of the arches, and the capitals of pilasters and columns. It was designed to impress, rather than to provide security. Indeed, once built, it constituted a weak point in the defences of the city. Its construction cannot antedate the long war when defensive considerations were prime, both for

---

[92] Sophronius, *Anacreontica*, 18.85–8; Geo.Pis., *In restitutionem*, 25–6. Simocatta wrote a short diatribe at about this time in which he characterizes Jews as wicked and most untrustworthy, trouble-loving and rebellious, very forgetful of friendship, jealous and envious, and immutable and implacable in enmity (*Historiae*, 5.7.6–9).

[93] *Reversio Sanctae Crucis*, cc.15–21, ed. and trans. S. Borgehammer, 'Heraclius Learns Humility: Two Early Latin Accounts Composed for the Celebration of *Exaltatio Crucis*', *Millennium*, 6 (2009), 145–201, at 186–91. Both the substance of the text (picked up in a roughly contemporary sermon) and its composition should probably be placed towards the middle of the eighth century, given the degree of deformation evident in the narrative (*contra* Borgehammer, 'Heraclius Learns Humility', 158–60).

[94] Cf. C. Maranci, *Vigilant Powers: Three Churches of Early Medieval Armenia*, Studies in the Visual Cultures of the Middle Ages 8 (Turnhout, 2015), 67–72.

Romans and Persians. So it may be viewed as a war memorial which commemorated in particular the final solemn victory celebrations, its construction being placed between the end of the war and the coming of the Arabs (in 635), when we know, from a chance reference, that building work was under way on the Temple Mount. Such a date is consistent with the style of its sculptural decoration.[95]

The emotions roused on Wednesday 21 March 630 as the procession made its way into the city before a large crowd of spectators are caught best by the *History of Khosrov*:

> There was no little joy on that day as they entered Jerusalem. There was the sound of weeping and wailing; their tears flowed from the awesome fervour of the emotion of their hearts and from the rending of the entrails of the king, the princes, all the troops, and the inhabitants of the city. No one was able to sing the Lord's chants from the fearful and agonizing emotion of the king and the whole multitude.[96]

The two great poles of the empire had come together. The Cross was in the hands of an emperor who was, for the first time, visiting the holy city. It was an extraordinary conjunction which impressed itself deeply on the collective consciousness. No wonder George of Pisidia invited Constantine to return and to applaud Heraclius, and viewed the Cross as the Ark of the new dispensation.[97]

Heraclius and the dignitaries led the way to the complex of shrines enclosed in the Church of the Holy Sepulchre.[98] It was there, at the protuberant rock identified as Calvary, that a small piece of public theatre was staged (if we can trust the report of it given by Nicephorus). Heraclius handed the reliquary containing the Cross over to Modestus, the senior churchman left in Jerusalem after the deportation of the Patriarch Zacharias in 614. Modestus inspected the seal and declared that it was intact. A hymn of thanksgiving was sung. The Cross was taken out of the reliquary, unlocked by the key which Modestus had kept, restored to its proper place at Calvary, and venerated by all who were there.[99]

---

[95] C. Mango, 'The Temple Mount, A D 614–638', in Raby and Johns, *Bayt al-Maqdis I*, 1–16, at 6–16; M. H. Burgoyne, 'The Gates of the Haram al-Sharif', in Raby and Johns, *Bayt al-Maqdis I*, 105–24, at 106, 111–15. Arab conquest: Howard-Johnston, *Witnesses*, 380–1, 465–7.

[96] Ps.S., 131.15–20, with TA, 97.7–13; Strategius, c.24.8–9.

[97] *Translatio*, c.1; Geo.Pis., *In restitutionem*, 49–63, 73–4. A visit by the last emperor to Jerusalem where he hands his crown back to God was to become a key element in the scenario of the last days presented in the late seventh-century Apocalypse of ps.Methodius—ed. and trans. B. Garstad, *Apocalypse Pseudo-Methodius: An Alexandrian World Chronicle* (Cambridge, MA, 2012), 1–139.

[98] Shalev-Hurvitz, *Holy Sites Encircled*, 55–76.

[99] Strategius, c.24.9; Nic., c.18.8–16, who goes on to report (c.18.16–17), mistakenly, that Heraclius immediately sent the Cross off to Constantinople (cf. also Agap., 468.3–5); *Seert Chron.*, 556.8–10. Cf. P. Booth, *Crisis of Empire: Doctrine and Dissent at the End of Late Antiquity* (Berkeley and Los Angeles, 2014), 159–61.

The solemn, contrite mood which had gripped all participants and spectators at this awesome ceremony probably lightened somewhat when it was over. Heraclius resumed the demeanour of an emperor. Soon afterwards he appointed Modestus patriarch in succession to Zacharias, who had died in exile.[100] He stayed on for a while. He visited the holy places. He returned the church plate which had been kept safe in Constantinople, distributed alms to the poor, and made grants to cover the cost of incense in the city's churches. He showed his regard and respect for the whole body of Palestinian monks, whose ascetic striving and prayers benefited all their fellow men. He was still there when a bishop arrived from Persian Mesopotamia with letters for him and Modestus from the new Nestorian catholicos, Isho'yahb II, of which more in Section 10.5.[101]

10.5 The Final Settlement

The news of the Jerusalem ceremony was swiftly disseminated across the reconstituted empire. It reached Constantinople, presumably in the form of an imperial dispatch, on the Feast of Lazarus (31 March), a mere ten days after the ceremony. In Armenia, the dispatch was welcomed with jubilation. The main body of the reply sent to Heraclius in Jerusalem has not survived, save for its exultant preamble (quoting from Psalm 96:11), which has lodged in the *History of Khosrov*, where it is wrongly associated with correspondence between churchmen about reconstruction in the city much earlier.[102]

Heraclius, as has been already noted, stayed on in the Holy City. There he was well placed to watch over the final stages in the reinstatement of the old systems of provincial administration in the Levant, and its military organization, in particular the garrisoning of bases in or close to the *badiya* with forces large enough to secure imperial authority over the client Arab tribes responsible for policing the desert approaches. There was no need to go north and beef up the Roman military presence in Transcaucasia, since the Turks had vanished like creatures of the night at the first glimmering of dawn.

This sudden dematerializing of a power which had secured firm control over Albania within easy striking distance of Sasanian Atropatene and the principalities of Transcaucasia was ultimately caused by a crisis which flared up in eastern Eurasia, where the balance of power swung decisively away from the Turks. The new Tang dynasty, rapidly building up its power and prestige within China, had been preparing for a second trial of strength (after a first unsuccessful confrontation in 625–6). Under cover of a comprehensive peace treaty negotiated in 626, measures were taken to improve the offensive as well as the defensive

---

[100] Strategius, c.24.10–11; *Translatio*, c.2.3–8.   [101] *Translatio*, cc.1.7–2.8; ps.S, 131.21–3.
[102] Geo.Pis., *In restitutionem*, 104–8; ps.S, 118.8–17, with *Hist.Com.*, n.36.

capability of Chinese forces. In 629 a grand offensive was launched against the Turks, and the strategy, which involved coordinated operations by several independent corps, achieved great success. One of two khagans in contact with China, Tu'li Khagan, asked for asylum. An official announcement estimated that another 1.2 million refugees were likely to arrive from beyond the frontier. This was followed in 630 by a second thrust deep into the steppes which won a decisive victory and succeeded subsequently in capturing the other khagan, Hie-li Khagan, as he tried to escape with a small cavalry escort into the inner steppes. Hie-li was Illig, the senior-ranking Turkish ruler who had intervened in the west between autumn 627 and spring 628.[103]

The effect in Transcaucasia was dramatic. The *shad*, who had been put in charge of this remote province of the Turkish Empire and had to cope with a serious famine, received a despairing message from the *yabghu khagan*. Marauders, he said, had attacked him. The *shad* would not see his face again. He had not fortified himself but had reached out for a kingdom which was not his by rights. He had now fallen from his high position because of pride. He ended by advising the *shad* to withdraw immediately from Transcaucasia before the news reached the surrounding peoples and they tore him to pieces. The *shad* did so and disappeared in the second half of 629, never to be heard of again south of the Caucasus. The Turkish Empire collapsed and the steppes entered a period of turbulence which was to last some fifty years.[104]

In the Sasanian capital, there was a hiatus of two to three months following Shahrbaraz's seizure of power, when his position was that of informal regent. Then, at the end of April 630, he took the final fateful step of seizing the throne and executing the young Ardashir III. The killing of the legitimate Sasanian king cannot but have given a serious shock to a traditional society which viewed the stability of the family in a graded hierarchy as the basis of good order on earth. The reaction was swift and effective, After a mere forty days of supreme power, Shahrbaraz was killed by an assassin on 9 June as he inspected a military parade in Ctesiphon.[105]

His death inaugurated a period of political turbulence. For the moment, though, his regime remained in place, under the rule of Boran, the daughter of Khusro, whom he had married. The disadvantage of her sex was outweighed by her Sasanian blood.[106] Her government, weak and vulnerable to a counter-coup

---

[103] H. J. Wechsler, 'Tai-tsung (reign 626–49)', in D. Twitchett, ed., *The Cambridge History of China*, III *Sui and T'ang China, 589–906*, Part 1 (Cambridge, 1979),188–241, at 220–4. Cf. J. Howard-Johnston, 'World War in Eurasia at the End of Antiquity', in R. Gyselen, ed., *Sasanian Persia and the Tabarestan Archive*, Res Orientales 27 (Bures-sur-Yvette, 2019), 9–28, at 16–17.

[104] MD, 164.3–166.11, 169.16–170.15 (trans. Dowsett, 102–3, 106).

[105] Ps.S., 130.5–7, 15–18; *Khuz.Chron.*, 29.22–30.1, 30.5–10, trans. Greatrex, 237; *Seert Chron.*, 536.1–11; Theoph., 329.4–6, Agap., 467.5–8, Mich.Syr., xi.3 (IV, 410), *Chron.1234*, 237.26–238.7, 238.20–1, trans. Hoyland, 82–3; Tab., 1061.17–1063.17.

[106] Ps.S., 130.18–25; *Khuz.Chron.*, 30.11, trans. Greatrex, 237; *Seert Chron.*, 557.1–3; Theoph., 329.6–8, Agap., 453.4–5, Mich.Syr., xi.3 (IV, 410), *Chron.1234*, 238.21–8, trans. Hoyland, 82–3; Tab., 1064.2–14.

at home, had good cause to be apprehensive about Heraclius' reaction to the murder of his ally, especially if hopes had been entertained that Shahrbaraz's seizure of power might open the way to active Christian proselytizing in Iran. Heraclius increased the pressure by advancing to Constantia well beyond the frontier agreed with Shahrbaraz, ostensibly so as to escort the clerical party returning to Mesopotamia with Bishop Elias.[107] Boran lost no time in doing whatever she could to patch up relations. A deputation of high-ranking clergy headed by the Catholicos Isho'yabh II himself which was about to set off to continue the discussions with the emperor initiated by Bishop Elias in Jerusalem was given the additional task of renewing the peace accord between the great powers.[108]

The deputation travelled north and met Heraclius at Berrhoea (modern Aleppo), like Hierapolis, an important city close to the Euphrates. The main religious business of the meeting (discussed in Chapter 11) took some time to complete, but the political negotiations seem to have gone smoothly. In its urgent quest to renew the peace, Boran's government was ready to concede what both Shiroe and Shahrbaraz had refused, *a return to the frontier of 591*.[109] This meant that the Romans would recover the swathe of territory inside the great curve of the Euphrates (the provinces of Mesopotamia and Osrhoene) which they had held since the end of the second century. More important, though, was the eastward move of the frontier along the Armenian Taurus to Lake Van and over the western half of Transcaucasia. The clear strategic advantage which this gave the Romans (and which Khusro had sought to nullify) was inducement enough. Heraclius agreed to renew the peace and thus finally succeeded in wiping away all the war gains of Khusro.

The great war thus ended in an extraordinary triumph for Christian Roman arms. Heraclius was in command of the Middle East and could watch developments in the surrounding world from a position of unchallenged superiority. The traditional world order had been restored, but with the Sasanian Empire as very much the junior partner of the Roman. Heraclius was once again the superordinate ruler whose hegemony was acknowledged by Germanic kings in the West. He could and did intervene in the affairs of the Balkans, taking advantage of the troubles of the Avar khaganate which followed the failure before Constantinople. He could gaze with equanimity on the far greater turbulence in the nearer reaches of the Eurasian steppes triggered by the Turks' defeats in the east, since the repercussions would have little effect on the Mediterranean world. Finally, he had a unique opportunity with the immense prestige brought by victory to bring harmony to the fractious confessions of Christendom in the Middle East.

---

[107] *Translatio*, c.3.1–2. Cf. Flusin, *Saint Anastase*, II, 319–32, who queries this sequence of events.
[108] Khuz.Chron., 30.12–16; Seert Chron., 557.3–5.
[109] Khuz.Chron., 30.16–17; Seert Chron., 557.8–10, 559.11–560.1; Agap., 453.5.

A new confidence was engendered in Christians by the ceremonial restoration of the True Cross to its proper place in Jerusalem. It was boosted by Modestus' sponsorship of a new cult, that of St Anastasius, the Persian martyr. The Life which he commissioned was completed during his short tenure of the patriarchate (between March and December 630).[110] It provided an additional illustration of the power of the Cross. For it was the news of the arrival of the Cross in Mesopotamia which had set Anastasius on the road to conversion. And it provided an uplifting example for the monks of Palestine and elsewhere. By the death for which he had striven, inspired by voracious reading of the acts of the early Christian martyrs, Anastasius had shown that martyrdom was still within man's reach in that late age.[111] A Life, however, could not by itself create an enduring cult. A shrine was needed to act as a focal point, and that shrine should contain authentic relics for veneration by the faithful. So one of the two monks who had accompanied Anastasius on his journey towards death was sent back to Mesopotamia on an officially sanctioned mission to recover the martyr's body. He travelled out in the party of the Nestorian bishop who had been negotiating with Heraclius and Modestus and, with the backing of the Nestorian catholicos (and some apparently supernatural help), managed to spirit the body out of the monastery where it was already highly venerated, consoling the monks with a small piece of it and thanking the catholicos with another.[112]

Rather more than a year after the return of the Cross, there was much rejoicing when the martyr's body was brought back to Palestine. Large crowds turned out to watch its arrival at the main cities, Tyre and Caesarea, on its circuitous route to Jerusalem. Popular enthusiasm generated a subsidiary cult at Caesarea (paralleling those which sprang up in Mesopotamia). The celebrations reached a climax on 2 November 631, when the procession reached Jerusalem and the martyr's body was installed in the monastery which had sheltered him during his seven years of ascetic striving and earnest study.[113]

Anti-Jewish sentiment was fanned by the religious fervour generated on such occasions. The Jews could not but view the ambient Christian world as increasingly threatening. They were indeed subject to growing pressure to convert. It was reported that the campaign to bring them to the true faith had official sanction from the very apex of the empire. Whether or not this was so—the evidence is unequivocal but indirect—there was no prospect of the imperial government moving to protect its Jewish subjects. Programmed as it was to defend and propagate Christianity, it could not adopt an even-handed policy like that of the Persians. Rabble-rousers were all too likely to cause trouble in the streets, and, in one case at least (North Africa in 632), the local authorities took the lead and

---

[110] Flusin, *Saint Anastase*, II, 191–3.   [111] *V.Anast.*, cc.5–12, 31–8.
[112] *Translatio*, cc.2.8–5.6.   [113] *Translatio*, cc.5.6–6.18.

instituted a campaign of coercion.[114] In Jewish eyes, Heraclius' image darkened and merged with that of the embodiment of evil, Armilus or Hermolaos (a combination of Romulus and Eremolaos, 'Waster of Peoples'), the son of Satan and a stone statue, who would be a fierce, merciless adversary of the Jews on the eve of the last days.[115]

Christians, as Muslims were to do in the near future, had prised the Old Testament away from the Jews' possessive grasp, viewing current events as prefigured, like the Gospel story itself, in the biblical past. The final step in this assault on Judaism would have been for Christians to appropriate the Temple Mount, which had been left derelict throughout late antiquity. If the *Reversio* is to be believed, their first move was to have the Cross carried in procession over it—a ritual act of great importance in which the assembled dignitaries of the Christian empire implicitly laid claim to the site. Next came the construction of the Golden Gate, if it can be securely associated with Heraclius, as well as the contemporary, similarly decorated double gate at the base of the Temple Mount on the south side.[116] It may be possible to discern a third planned move, namely permanent occupation, if we attend carefully to the clues left by an extraordinary artefact of a later age.

The Joshua Roll is an archaizing illuminated manuscript securely dated to the middle of the tenth century (Figures 25–28). Fifteen sheets of parchment were glued together to form a roll, just under 10.5 m. long and approximately 30 cm. high. It presents a continuous picture frieze which illustrates Joshua's campaigns of conquest in the Holy Land (Joshua 1–12, of which the first and last chapters are not covered in the roll which is incomplete). Short excerpts from the biblical text act as captions. The action is set in an illusionistic landscape, sets of episodes being separated by trees, rock formations, steep hillsides, and pieces of classical architecture. Personifications, familiar in Late Antique secular art, materialize from time to time. The Joshua Roll looks out of place in the tenth century: its form, a roll, is classical (as against the medieval codex), and the lines of text run parallel to the main axis of the visual field (as in antiquity), rather than descending

---

[114] Olster, *Roman Defeat, Christian Response*, 84–92; G. Dagron and V. Déroche, 'Juifs et chrétiens dans l'Orient du VIIe siècle', *TM* 11 (1991), 17–273, at 30–8; Drijvers, '*Restitutio Crucis*', 188–90; S. Esders, 'Herakleios, Dagobert und die "beschittenen Völker": Die Umwälzungen des Mittelmeerraums im 7. Jahrhundert in der Chronik des sog. Fredegar', in A. Goltz, H. Leppin, and H. Schlange-Schöningen, eds., *Jenseits der Grenzen: Beiträge zur spätantiken und frühmittelalterlichen Geschichtsschreibung*, Millennium-Studien 25 (Berlin, 2009), 239–311, at 263–72. Evidence: R. Devreesse, 'La Fin inédite d'une lettre de Saint Maxime: Un Baptême forcé de Juifs et de Samaritains à Carthage en 632', *Revue des Sciences Religieuses*, 17 (1937), 25–35; *Doctrina Jacobi nuper baptizati*, ed. and trans. V. Déroche, in Dagron and Déroche, 'Juifs et chrétiens', 47–229, at 70–3; Fredegar, iv.65; Mich.Syr., xi.4 (IV, 413), trans. Chabot, II, 414; *H.Patr.Alex.*, 492.4–7.

[115] I. Levi, 'L'Apocalypse de Zorobabel et le roi de Perse Siroès', *Revue des Études Juives*, 68 (1914), 129–60 (text and translation), 69 (1919), 108–21, 71 (1920), 57–65; W. J. van Bekkum, 'Jewish Messianic Expectations in the Age of Heraclius', in Reinink and Stolte, *Reign of Heraclius*, 81–112, at 103–10.

[116] Mango, 'Temple Mount', 6–16 and Burgoyne, 'Gates', 105–15.

vertically (as in the Middle Ages); style and iconography are equally redolent of late antiquity. It seems virtually certain that it is a tenth-century copy of an earlier illustrated roll, faithful save for a few lacunae in the captions (where the text in the original was illegible) and some parallel pictorial errors (betraying misunderstanding of minor iconographic details).[117]

The motivation behind so extensive an illustration of Joshua's campaigns was surely contemporary relevance. They were taken to prefigure parallel military feats in the Christian era which had a similar result, conquest of the Holy Land. Of the two historical episodes which spring to mind, John Tzimiskes' single swift thrust towards Jerusalem in 975 can be ruled out, because the extant Joshua Roll is a mere facsimile of an earlier roll, although it is possible that Basil the Chamberlain's interest in having it copied was prompted by Tzimiskes' campaign. That leaves Heraclius' Persian campaigns as the likely latter-day analogue to those of Joshua and the religious celebration of victory at Jerusalem as the occasion of its production.[118]

What, though, was the intended function of the original roll? To judge by the extant copy, it was not a finished work but a set of preparatory drawings. The rendering of figures and settings is spare and monochrome. Clothing and equipment are picked out by a limited palette of pale wash colours. It looks like a cartoon for a frieze on a larger, monumental work. There is indeed a sculptural quality to the scenes pictured. A clearer indication of the character of the projected monument is provided by the subject matter, largely military, which parallels the scenes customary on triumphal columns: thus, the army sets out, is harangued by its leader, builds, marches, crosses a river, fights pitched battles, captures cities, takes prisoners, executes some of them, and sacrifices at an altar. Figures grow larger as the roll unfurls. The most important indication, though, is the slope of the ground, detectable under groups of figures in individual scenes—it rises on average at an angle of 9 degrees from lower left to upper right. It seems highly likely, therefore, that the original Joshua Roll was a cartoon for a triumphal column. Given the overall length of the original roll, the frieze with successive sets of scenes would have wound anticlockwise some seven times around the column.[119] Given the need to be visible to the viewer on the ground, the bands of relief sculpture would have had to be much higher than that of the cartoon—say 1.5–2 metres instead of the estimated 25.5cm. That would have given the column a height of 10.5–14 metres.

Triumphal columns were erected by several of Heraclius' predecessors, most recently by Phocas, but they were plain, without narrative friezes.[120] The tradition

---

[117] S. H. Wander, *The Joshua Roll* (Wiesbaden, 2012), 17–82.
[118] Wander, *Joshua Roll*, 93–7, 133–8.   [119] Wander, *Joshua Roll*, 82–9.
[120] C. Mango, 'The Columns of Justinian and His Successors', in C. Mango, *Studies on Constantinople* (Aldershot, 1993), no.X.

of celebrating victory with a historiated column had lapsed since the reign of Marcian, save possibly for the column begun by Justin II (to commemorate his expected victory over Persia in 573?) and demolished by his successor Tiberius. But there was nothing to preclude Heraclius from reviving the tradition to celebrate so glorious and so unexpected a victory. His great adversary, Khusro II, had likewise been ready to delve back into the past and to resuscitate the third- and fourth-century tradition of celebrating and commemorating victories on monumental rock reliefs.

The intended venue for such a column was surely Jerusalem rather than Constantinople, given its biblical subject matter, and given the significance of Jerusalem both during the war and in the peace celebrations. It was to be a permanent memorial to the victory of the Christian empire over the evil empire of Iran, with the same combination of biblical iconography and classical style as was used in the David Plates. As for the specific site selected for its erection, it may be hazarded that it was on the route from the Golden Gate to the Holy Sepulchre, presumably at a high point along the route, *on the Temple Mount*, perhaps where it intersected with that from the southern gate also rebuilt by Heraclius. That was where the statement of Christian victory would be most visible and that was where the beginning of new era of Christian solidarity and dominance could be declared to greatest effect—the inclusiveness of Christianity being signalled by the Old Testament cladding of Christian victory. If ever the authorities of state and church were to be emboldened to embark on a final act in the long process of Christianization in the Middle East, that time came with a surge of Christian confidence at the end of the great war. In any case, there was evidence elsewhere of a new determination to assert the official faith of the Roman Empire. The two most famous pagan temples in the empire, the Pantheon in Rome and the Parthenon in Athens, had recently been appropriated and converted into churches after two centuries of hesitation.[121] The full incorporation of the holiest of Jewish places into the Christian city of Jerusalem marked the beginning of the third and most dramatic push forward by Christendom. The Joshua Column would presumably have been followed by a larger building programme. Discarding hindsight and staring forward into a murky future from the year 630, we might pick out the dim outline of a massive domed structure or a great basilica standing on the Temple Mount, built as a focal point for the whole of Christendom in what was hoped would be a new era of unity (Figure 29).[122]

---

[121] The conversion of the Pantheon is datable to the first years of the pontificate of Boniface III (608–15), since the emperor who authorized it was Phocas (*Lib.Pont.*, 317.2-4, trans. 62)—see R. Krautheimer, *Rome: Profile of a City, 312–1308* (Princeton, NJ, 2000), 72–5. That of the Parthenon is open to debate: the literary and material evidence is inconclusive—see A. Kaldellis, *The Christian Parthenon: Classicism and Pilgrimage in Byzantine Athens* (Cambridge, 2009), 23–35, 40–53, who prefers a late fifth- or sixth-century date.

[122] Cf. Shalev-Hurvitz, *Holy Sites Enclosed*, 299–303, 307–12.

11
Conclusion

No one in the watching world could have predicted the extraordinary reversal of fortunes in the great war in western Eurasia. They *were* watching. It is impossible to say how fast or slowly news travelled in the later 620s, but it certainly travelled. Kings, courts, and senior churchmen in the early Germanic kingdoms of the sub-Roman West were aware of what was going on (although there may have been some distortion of news in the course of transmission, as there certainly was in the versions later written down). Two, the Visigothic rulers, Sisebut and Suinthila, took advantage of Roman preoccupations in the Middle East to attack the imperial enclave in Spain.[1] The khagan of the Avars, better placed to track events, may well have stirred up the Slav tribes and set off a new wave of migration into the southern and western extremities of the Balkans before he was encouraged to intervene directly by the Sasanians. Far to the east, beyond the east Asian limits of Turkish power, the second Tang emperor, Taizong, knew that Illig, the supreme khagan of the Turks, was committed to a distant venture, since he had refrained from invading when he had China at his mercy in 626 and, at the summit meeting of the two rulers on the bridge over the river Wei close to the capital Chang'an, had agreed to halt operations, and had *offered* three thousand horses and ten thousand sheep, an offer changed, at Taizong's request, to the return of Chinese prisoners of war. Taizong, like the minor kings of the far west and the khagan of the Avars, timed his intervention well (in 629), taking advantage of Turkish involvement in Transcaucasia, as well as their troubles nearer at hand.[2]

Nowhere, though, was closer attention paid to what was happening in the Middle East than in the vast land mass to the south, where a new politico-religious power was taking shape around the two poles of Medina and Mecca. The Muslims had been hoping for a Roman revival in the north.[3] It was, after all, the Sasanians who were the principal threat to Arab autonomy. After their imposition of direct rule over Himyar around 571 and their gaining control of the *badiya* together with the Roman Levant in the second phase of the war, they were able to project their power over all of Arabia except for the Hijaz. No wonder Muhammad

---

[1] See pp. 380–1 below.
[2] *Tang-shu*, trans. Liu Mau-Tsai, *Die chinesischen Nachrichten zur Geschichte der Ost-Türken (T'u-Küe)* (Wiesbaden, 1958), 190–2; *Qu Tang-shu*, trans. Mau-Tsai, 139–41; court annals, trans. Mau-Tsai, 237–8. H. J. Wechsler, 'The Founding of the T'ang Dynasty: Kao-Tsu (reign 618–26)', in *Cam.Hist. China*, III.1, 150–87, at 182–7; Wechsler, 'Tai-tsung', 220–4.
[3] Tab., 1005.15–1006.17.

had a sense of deep foreboding early in his mission. No wonder, some fifteen years later, he was ready to contemplate some accommodation with the Qurayshi governing elite of Mecca as the war in the north reached its climax and the *muhajirun,* the small group of faithful who had left Mecca with him, and his Medinan allies, the *ansar,* were coming under increasing military and political pressure. So it was that early in 628, while Heraclius was waiting in Atropatene for news about the outcome of the putsch against Khusro, Muhammad offered a massive concession to the Quraysh of Mecca. He announced a change in the direction of prayer, which was thenceforth to be towards the prime pagan cult site of Arabia, the Ka'ba outside Mecca. This, not unreasonably, disconcerted the faithful but signalled clearly to the Quraysh his desire for a settlement. He followed up words with deeds, setting out for the Little Pilgrimage with a large party of the faithful. Negotiations then took place at Hudaybiya, just outside the sanctuary's territory. The agreement reached ended the conflict and led within two years to a durable union of Medina, the base of the new religion, and Mecca, the most powerful city state of the Hijaz. This in turn led on to their forcible unification of most of Arabia (632-3).[4]

But the greatest impact of the war was on those who had been directly involved—the Sasanian governing elite who had to make concessions almost as great as Muhammad's to secure a lasting peace, the Turks who had exposed themselves dangerously in the east, the Avars who faced growing turbulence within the boundaries of their khaganate after their failure before Constantinople in 626, and the victorious Romans. The scale of the victory celebrations, the emotions they aroused, and the plans for commemoration of what was depicted as a victory of Christianity over an alien faith provided indirect testimony to the profound shock administered to the old imperial order by a war in which so many defeats had come one after another on the Romans. Heraclius and the soldiers who had served with him, taking such risks, enduring so many hardships, and fighting so many battles, returned older, hardened, brutalized perhaps. This was made manifest in the new image of Heraclius stamped on the Roman coinage issued in the three years following his victory (629-31), an image which was, we may be confident, personally approved by the emperor (Figure 30). His bust was on the obverse, to the right of that of his son, Heraclius the New Constantine, as it had been on all coins issued since the coronation of the latter soon after his birth on 22 January 613. But instead of a neat, short beard, Heraclius now sported an immense flowing one and a long moustache—signalling both the passage of time and the ordeals undergone in the course of his Persian campaigns.[5] The new image was also perhaps intended to hint that Heraclius had, at least temporarily,

---

[4] Howard-Johnston, *Witnesses,* 397-8, 445-60, 464-5. For the traditional account of the Hudaybiya episode (and its dating to March 628), see M. Rodinson, *Mohammed* (Harmondsworth, 1971), 249-52.
[5] Grierson, *D.O. Catalogue,* II.1, 218, 223, 254-7 (nos.26-31, pl.VIII-IX).

supplanted the traditionally bearded Sasanian (and Achaemenid) kings of Iran as the pre-eminent ruler in western Eurasia, a claim which was simultaneously subverted by the assumption of the modest title of 'Pious *Basileus* in Christ'.[6]

11.1 Explanations

The reversal of fortunes in the 620s is far harder to explain than Sasanian success in the first two phases of the war. For that, we need only point to Roman divisions, the mobilization of large, perhaps unprecedentedly large Persian forces, the steady shift in the balance of strategic advantage as Persian forces pushed west to the Mediterranean coast, and the contrasting effects of victory and defeat on the two sides. Roman ideological resilience is also explicable. It is attributable partly to a widespread conviction, deeply implanted by six centuries of Roman imperial rule, that the empire was a fixed part of the earthly order and could not be expunged and partly to a belief in *theodicy*, in targeted divine intervention in human affairs, defeat and disaster being used to punish the misdoings, perhaps of the great, perhaps of the mass of the people, perhaps of both. Just as the Israelites had suffered when they offended and angered God, so the Romans were justly punished for their collective sins, and, in due course, *when their sins were thoroughly purged*, the defeats and disasters besetting them would end. Belief in a revival of fortunes was thus virtually ineradicable.[7]

But what of the extraordinary phenomenon of Heraclius' two counteroffensive campaigns? How on earth did the remnants of the defeated field armies and guards regiments gain the confidence not simply to fight but to take the war to the enemy? How are we to explain the victories won by Heraclius and his men over the numerically superior Persian armies deployed against them? And how was it that this small expeditionary force managed, in the end, to bring down the most successful of Sasanian rulers after Ardashir and Shapur I in the third century?

First of all, we must remember that Heraclius and his staff officers were able to draw on the accumulated wisdom of Greek, Hellenistic, and Roman military men. George of Pisidia notes that they did so in planning sessions during winter 621–2. They studied handbooks on warfare (and the diagrams of recommended formations in them).[8] The latest and most relevant was the *Strategicon of Maurice*, so called because it was written in Maurice's reign (582–602), probably before his armies moved on to the offensive against Slavs and Avars in the 590s. It was a

---

[6] See p. 349 above.

[7] This Deuteronomistic theology, which D. Gyllenhaal, 'The New Josiah: Heraclian Ideology and the Deuteronomistic History' (M. Phil., Oxford, 2015), traces back to the reforms of Josiah in the seventh century BC, underlies Theodore Syncellus' homily on the 626 siege. The key role of the king is to act as penitent-in-chief in the campaign to regain God's favour.

[8] Geo.Pis., *Heraclias*, ii.118–21, 133–43.

compendium of useful tactical advice, probably intended in the first instance for reading by senior officers. It grafted new ideas derived mainly from observation of nomad warfare onto inherited Roman traditions, striving to give Roman cavalry formations more of the flexibility and resilience of steppe nomad forces. The central principle, repeatedly stressed, was that the approach to warfare should be cold, calculating, scientific. Emotions and moral considerations should be set aside. They should not be allowed to interfere with the business of destroying the enemy's fighting capability. Battle should only be joined when the enemy was so disordered that he would break at the first direct application of force. The engagement was to be reduced to a *moment*, between the preliminary manoeuvring and skirmishing, on the one hand, and the pursuit of the defeated troops, on the other, a pursuit which was to be pressed relentlessly so as to cause the maximum damage to the enemy's fighting strength.[9]

These theoretical precepts were put into practice in the large-scale exercises held in Bithynia early in the 622 campaigning season. Heraclius subjected his future companions-in-arms to intensive training—in the handling of weapons, in the drawing up and changing of formations whether for the march, skirmishing, battle, or pursuit, and in extended manoeuvres which culminated in mock combats between large forces. The exercises, on which George of Pisidia dwells, were effective.[10] They gave Heraclius' expeditionary force invaluable *tactical flexibility*, as was shown, at the outset, in the guerrilla-style harassing of Shahrbaraz's army in 622. Two years later, the troops who served on the first counteroffensive campaign repeatedly demonstrated their ability to outmarch the Persians. It was this *superior strategic mobility* which enabled them (1) to choose the time and place for battle, as they did in 625, when they took on the three opposing armies in detail, and (2) to achieve tactical surprise on two occasions— in Atropatene in 625, when they accelerated ahead of the pursuing Persian army, giving the impression that they were fleeing, and then halted, drawn up in battle array, ready to engage an enemy quite unprepared for battle, and in the plain of Nineveh in December 627, when they employed a similar manoeuvre before the final decisive battle, although then they turned back to attack the Persians under cover of dawn mist. The exercises also hardened the troops—in body, improving their *stamina* so that they were able to extend the campaigning season deep into the winters of 625–6 and 627–8, and in mind, raising their *morale* and giving them the confidence to face superior Persian forces in open battle.

Heraclius' greatest achievement as a general, however, was his masterly use of intelligence. He was ever alive to the possibility of planting false information in the enemy's mind. It might be conveyed by deserters, by rumours put into

---

[9] *Strategicon*, with P. Rance, *The Roman Art of War in Late Antiquity: The Strategikon of the Emperor Maurice*, 2 vols. (forthcoming).
[10] Geo.Pis., *Expeditio*, ii.120–62.

circulation, by official but covert propaganda, and by deliberately misleading actions. The objectives were to deceive the enemy about Roman intentions, to foster dissension between commanders in the field and the political authorities at home, and, in general, to create uncertainty in the minds of enemy generals and their men. Spurious scenarios might be conjured up, as happened during the siege of Constantinople in August 626. In this case, the broadcasters were the authorities in Constantinople, who announced that a relief army was close at hand and that Heraclius was far away in Transcaucasia. Later, Bonus warned the Avars, as they began to withdraw, that Heraclius' brother was hurrying back and was set on pursuing them.[11] More insidious was the rumour which began to circulate in 627 that Shahrbaraz was at odds with Khusro and had been won over by Heraclius—it was a rumour which managed to embed itself in several of the extant reputable sources.[12] Actions, though, could prove even more effective, as was shown at the beginning of the first counteroffensive campaign in 624, when Heraclius set off down the main diagonal military route to take command of the army assembled at Caesarea in Cappadocia and, by doing so, deceived the Persians into expecting an attack on northern Syria. The *strategic surprise* gained was invaluable and led before long to the disorderly break-up of the invasion army which Khurso was mobilizing in Atropatene. On other occasions there was no need of deception, when Heraclius did the utterly unexpected, as he did three times in the final phase of the second counteroffensive—first striking south across the Zagros, when he was expected to turn west from the Urmia region and march home down the Arsanias valley, next, when he marched on Ctesiphon-Veh Ardashir rather than escaping west after the Battle of Nineveh, and, finally, when he made the perilous winter crossing of the Zagros back to the Urmia region.

A second innovation was half-forced on Heraclius by grim circumstance. It was fraught with significance for the future. He harnessed religion to war *at the level of a whole state*. Small societies alienated from the ambient world, like the Maccabees, might have done so before. Churchmen might have given a religious colouring to conflict at the time or, more probably, in retrospect, as they did in Armenia after two disastrous rebellions of a disaffected faction among the princes in the fifth century.[13] But Heraclius was the first secular leader to pump out stridently Christian propaganda—propaganda being the only effective weapon to hand during the second phase of rapid Persian advance over the Levant. The war was portrayed as that of an evil empire against God's faithful worshippers. Persians were blasphemers who had committed numerous atrocities and had desecrated sacred places and buildings. Later, the fragments of the True Cross,

---

[11] *Chron.Pasch.*, 721.21–722.4, 726.5–9.
[12] Theoph., 323.22–324.16; Agap., 461.5–462.11, Mich.Syr., 408–9, *Chron.1234*, 231.27–233.1, trans. Hoyland, 70–2; *Seert Chron.*, 540.3–541.6; Tab., 1007.16–1009.3.
[13] Łazar P'arpets'i, *Patmut'iwn Hayots'*, ii.32, 38–9, iii.74, 83 (pp.61–2, 69–73, 134–5, 150–3).

uprooted from Jerusalem and taken into captivity, became the focus of this propaganda. This was all in the air when Heraclius was training his troops in 622. They should regard themselves, he said, as God's *plasmata*, his pliable agents on earth.[14] Later, on campaign, he went further and developed a doctrine remarkably similar to that of jihad in its more militant form. He offered his soldiers *direct entry to Paradise* if they died in battle. They would be *martyrs* for their faith.[15] The harangues in which he said so cannot but have intensified their commitment and tightened the close bonds which naturally formed in the course of long, fraught campaigns. They undoubtedly helped to raise and sustain the morale of his men, giving them the strength of will and resilience which they needed far from home on enemy territory.

Finally, Heraclius recognized that warfare should have a clear political objective and that all military actions should be subordinated to it. He did not seek to destroy Sasanian fighting capability in its entirety—a formidable, probably impossible task—let alone conquer the rival empire (unimaginable in the dark days of the war). No, his aim was *regime change*, to encourage and empower opposition to Khusro and eventually to bring him down now that he had set about the complete destruction of the Roman Empire. It was in part to change attitudes in governing and landowning circles that he set about the systematic degradation of Persian resources by dispatching raiding forays as widely as possible over the various regions which he crossed—notably the fertile plains of Transcaucasia, the upland basins of the northern Zagros, upper Mesopotamia, and the Diyala plains. The increasing radius of damage and the consequential effects on the wider economy were intended to soften up minds in governing circles and the aristocracy. The same objective governed his strategy, fraught with danger, on the final phase of the second counteroffensive. He struck south to bring the war home to the population and elites of the economic and political heartland of the empire in Mesopotamia and then advanced on the binary capital city in the hope of precipitating action on the part of the growing opposition to Khusro.

It is natural to assume that Christian propaganda, which became more strident after the sack of Jerusalem, also played a part in beefing up opposition to Khusro. It was, we may suppose, addressed to Christians everywhere—not just Roman subjects in what remained of the empire, but former Roman subjects living in the occupied territories, the Christian peoples of Transcaucasia, and the large and important Christian communities established within the Sasanian Empire. Shared religious beliefs surely offered the beleaguered Roman authorities a valuable instrument for levering their loyalties away from the Sasanian king? But the evidence, such as it is, suggests that the Roman authorities did not make

---

[14] Geo.Pis., *Expeditio*, ii.105–115.   [15] Theoph., 307.11–12, 310.26–311.2.

systematic use of this instrument. We cannot take George of Pisidia's wartime poems, in which he engaged Zoroastrian beliefs and practices in full-frontal combat, as representative of official views. The aim of Roman religious propaganda was mainly defensive, to shore up the morale of Roman citizens and soldiers. It was the survival of a Christian Roman state which was at stake. The holy war which was being fought and which would earn soldiers killed in battle direct entry into Paradise was a *defensive* war for the Asia Minor heartland of the empire. If anything, it was the Persians who were on the offensive in the religious sphere, as on the ground. That at any rate is the picture presented by Roman sources, which have them launch blasphemous attacks on fundamental Christian tenets as well as behaving brutally.

Of course, propaganda broadcast within Roman confines spread farther afield, especially after the True Cross took centre stage. It was news of its captivity which triggered the conversion of St Anastasius the Persian Martyr. Its recovery from captivity loomed large in Transcaucasian minds, to judge by Armenian accounts of the war.[16] But there were no significant political or military effects at the time, no development of resistance on a large scale or of open rebellion in the occupied provinces. Apart from the hints suggested by the activities of a clandestine mint in Syria, there is no evidence of dissidence in the Roman Levant, Egypt, or western Armenia. Urban notables and other local leaders had every incentive to collaborate, so as to secure their vulnerable suburban villas, orchards, and gardens from reprisals, until that moment, which they surely expected, when a counterattack by regular Roman forces would materialize. It is true that Heraclius issued a call to arms when he settled into winter quarters near P'artaw in late 624, but there was no general erosion of loyalty to the Sasanians in Transcaucasia. Iberians and Armenians serving in Persian forces fought on and can be seen to have played a full part in the final engagements in Mesopotamia in late 627.[17]

Christian communities, like the Jews, were firmly embedded in the Sasanian political order. The antagonism which might have been expected to govern relations between monotheists and dualist Zoroastrians had only manifested itself occasionally in the past—as when the Bishop of Seleucia-Ctesiphon refused to cooperate with the secular authorities in collecting taxes (before Shapur II reopened hostilities with the Romans in 338) or when leading Christians were caught up in political purges in the fifth century. As long as Christians did not attack Zoroastrian temples, as long as they refrained from trying to convert members of the elite, they benefited from an official policy of tolerance. For Zoroastrianism, the Good Religion, which was central to the well-being of the

---

[16] *V.Anast.*, cc.6–7; Ps.S, 116.3–6, 129.35–130.1, 131.9–23; MD, 129.7–9, 142.21–143.1, trans. Dowsett, 77, 88.
[17] Theoph., 319.18–19, 320.26–7.

Sasanian Empire, was self-evidently superior to other religions. It was the leading but not exclusive religion of the state. There were to be no attacks on non-believers (*akden*, literally adherents of Bad Religion) since they were capable of doing good work (*xweškarih*) and thus of aiding believers (*wehden*) in the state's principal task, the marshalling of earthly forces in the cosmic battle against evil. In marked contrast to the Christian Roman Empire, there was no crackdown on doctrinal debate within Zoroastrianism, let alone any misguided attempt to underpin political unity with religious unity.[18]

Khusro II, who owed his throne to Roman arms, was ready to act openly as patron and protector of Christians, without in any way modifying his inner commitment to Zoroastrianism or easing the traditional prohibition of conversion to Christianity (as before, only enforced in high-profile cases). He expressed his gratitude to St Sergius, the saint whom he had twice asked for help, by dedicating a bejewelled cross and a large sum of money at his shrine in Rusafa (Sergiopolis). He honoured the ascetic Sabrisho, whom he appointed head of the Church of the East, with a ceremonial welcome on his arrival in the capital. He treated the True Cross, when it was brought in triumph to Ctesiphon, with due reverence. He is even said to have worn a brocade robe decorated with crosses, a gift from the Emperor Maurice, at court banquets.[19] He sponsored the reconstruction of Jerusalem, once Palestine was annexed in 616, and was careful to reinstitute the traditional balance between Jews and Christians in the Holy City by expelling the Jews who had settled in the interregnum (614–16).[20] These actions of his show how far he was ready to go, further than any of his predecessors, in cultivating the loyalty of his Christian subjects.

In one respect, though, Khusro broke completely with tradition early in the war, before Persian forces crossed the Euphrates and entered Syria. The leitmotiv of Sasanian religious policy had been hitherto not simply toleration towards Christians but the bestowal of special favour on the Church of the East, which adhered to the Nestorian confession condemned by both Chalcedonians and Monophysites. It was in effect an established church, its head, the catholicos, being formally appointed by the king and residing in Ctesiphon.[21] Its privileges clearly needed to be reviewed as Persian forces pushed forward and it became increasingly likely that they would penetrate into Roman Levant, where there were virtually no Nestorians. Another factor, the growing strength of the Monophysite episcopate in Mesopotamia, was also bringing the discriminatory policy into question at home.[22]

---

[18] Payne, *State of Mixture*, 27–56, 166–8.
[19] Payne, *State of Mixture*, 2–4, 172–4, 177–80, 190–1.   [20] See pp. 100–1, 122, 157 above.
[21] Payne, *State of Mixture*, 10–14.
[22] J. M. Fiey, *Jalons pour une histoire de l'église en Iraq*, CSCO 310, Subsidia 36 (Louvain, 1970), 120–37; N. Garsoian, *L'Église arménienne et le grand schisme d'Orient*, CSCO 574, Subsidia 100 (Louvain, 1999), 197–207, 237–8, 374–5, 406–9.

So it was that Khusro followed the example of Roman emperors and convened two meetings of the leaders of non-Zoroastrian religious communities. His aim was to defuse tension, to moderate antagonism, and to remain neutral. The first meeting took the form of an officially sponsored disputation, held almost certainly during the catholicosate of Gregory of Pherat (605–9). Representatives of all monotheist faiths were invited, Jews as well as Christians of different denominations. A highly distorted account is given in a hybrid document, partly authentic, partly contaminated with spurious anti-Chalcedonian material, which was produced at an Armenian synod in 648. The names of several key participants—the two leading laymen on the Monophysite side, Smbat Bagratuni and the chief court doctor, Gabriel of Singara (a convert from Nestorianism), and the two most prominent Monophysite churchmen present, Komitas, at the time bishop of the Mamikoneans, and Qamisho, metropolitan bishop in Mesopotamia—recur in a declaration of faith (the text of which has likewise been tampered with) addressed by Komitas to Qamisho together with his suffragan bishops (eight of whom are named) and leading laymen present at court.[23]

The principal result, after the early dismissal of the Jewish representatives, was a decision to remove favoured status from the Nestorians and to adopt an even-handed policy towards the different Christian denominations. It followed that when the Catholicos Gregory died in 609, no successor was appointed. The vacancy lasted for the rest of Khusro's reign.[24] In effect, Khusro was removing a disability from the offshoot of the Armenian and Syrian churches which was spreading Monophysitism within his realm. In the conquered Roman provinces, he tilted in their favour by removing the bar on the appointment of Monophysite bishops to sees where Monophysites were in a large majority, notably in Syria and north Mesopotamia. It was only a slight tilt, though, because he was careful not to disturb the Chalcedonian episcopate in the regions where it was dominant, notably in Palestine. The Monophysites hoped for more. Gabriel of Singara, adamant in his opposition to Nestorians, pressed in vain for Monophysite primacy within the empire. At his insistence, a second, purely Christian meeting was convened in 612 at which Nestorians and Monophysites debated doctrinal matters. This time it is Nestorian sources which claim the victory, but there was no alteration in the policy of neutrality between the confessions on Sasanian soil.[25]

This policy of gentle, unintrusive oversight of traditionally fractious Christian confessions proved remarkably successful. Indeed, it was only the parachuting of

---

[23] Ps.S, 149.18–151.33; *Girk' T'ght'ots'* (*Book of Letters*) (Tiflis, 1901), 212–19, trans. M. van Esbroeck, 'L'Encyclique de Komitas et la réponse de Mar Maroutha (617)', *Oriens Christianus*, 85 (2001), 162–75, at 163–71. Cf. Flusin, *Saint Anastase*, II, 114–18.

[24] *Khuz.Chron.*, 22.4–14 (trans., 233); *Seert Chron.*, 528.6.

[25] *Khuz.Chron.*, 23.1–9 (trans., 233); Babai Magnus, *Historia Georgii presbyteri*, ed. P. Bedjan, *Histoire de Mar-Jabalaha, de trois autres patriarches, d'un prêtre et de deux laïques, nestoriens* (Paris, 1895), 416–571, at 513–16, cited by Payne, *State of Mixture*, 187–8. Cf. Fiey, *Jalons*, 137 and Flusin, *Saint Anastase*, II, 114, n.101.

east Syrian bishops into west Syrian sees which occasioned serious conflict. Within the old boundaries of the Sasanian Empire, Christian communities and their leaders remained well integrated in the social order. Aristocratic Christians naturally conformed to Iranian social norms. They went to the feasts and took their places according to the hierarchy of honour. They arranged, like their Zoroastrian peers, for the secure transmission of their wealth and status down a paternal lineage. If necessary, they resorted to the legal device of replacing a man who died without male heirs with a surrogate, normally chosen from among his close kin (a nephew, say, or a brother). The less worldly clergy railed against such practices, but with little effect, since otherwise Christian notables could not engage successfully in the competition for power, wealth, and status with their Zoroastrian counterparts. The prominence achieved by Yazdin and Smbat Bagratuni in the reign of Khusro II demonstrated that careers were open to talent and that Christians could reach the summit of their professions.[26]

No wonder, then, that Roman Christian propaganda had so little effect and indeed that the Roman authorities did not make any concerted attempt to prise Christians out of the Sasanian social order.

It was an extraneous force, an earthly surrogate for the divine intervention awaited by Roman Christians, which changed the course of the war. Khusro was quite right to recognize that the traditional balance of power had been disturbed by the rise of the Turkish khaganate. This third great Eurasian power was capable of challenging the Sasanians for hegemony in Central Asia and, with or without an alliance with the Romans, of confronting and defeating Sasanian forces in the field. The nightmare which had reared up in the early 570s of a war on two fronts was assuredly in his mind in 615–16, when he made the fateful decision to destroy the Roman Empire. Of all Heraclius' achievements—the damage he caused to Sasanian resources, his denting of the overweening confidence of the Sasanian governing classes, his demonstration that the Roman field army remained a formidable foe—the greatest was to draw out the war, thereby not only intensifying the pressure on the Sasanian body politic but also increasing the chance of reviving the grand Roman-Turkish alliance of 569–73.

Once the Roman embassy dispatched by Heraclius probably from Constantinople early in 624 reached a Turkish power centre in Central Asia (probably the court of the western khagan rather than that of the senior khagan in the east), the countdown began for Turkish intervention on a massive scale. From the Turks' point of view, the opportunity was far too good to miss. The *Yabghu Khagan* Illig, informed of the Roman appeal for help, prepared the ground carefully, advancing in 626 with a large invasion army against northern China and forcing the second Tang emperor, Taizong, who had just seized power,

---

[26] Payne, *State of Mixture*, 108–23, 133–6, 168.

to meet him and to agree a peace treaty. The cost to the Turks of guaranteeing their security in the east was minimal—the repatriation of Chinese prisoners of war.[27] That same year, a small advance force raided Albania, giving the Sasanian authorities a foretaste of what was to come. The ultimatum delivered by the raiders, with its disdainful tone, administered a first great shock to the Sasanians. They were left in no doubt that within a year they would be facing a war on two fronts.

The second, even greater shock came in 627. It was not so much the invasion of Albania in overwhelming force after the Sasanians' Caucasus defences were overrun. Nor was it the subsequent thrust into Iberia up to the walls of Tiflis, the regional capital No, it was *the appearance in this far western theatre of the great khagan (Illig) in person* and his carefully orchestrated summit meeting with the once-derided Roman emperor in full view of the defenders of Tiflis. This very public demonstration of friendship between Romans and Turks, this openly avowed comradeship of emperor and *yabghu khagan*, doomed Khusro. His war was now unwinnable—or, just possibly winnable, but after many, many more years of campaigning on distant fronts. His *xwarrah* (glory), hitherto inflated by each successive victory, was punctured.[28] His position steadily weakened as his *xwarrah* leaked out, in marked contrast to Heraclius' fortune in the bad years (612–21), when an accumulation of defeats undoubtedly diminished his prestige but, at the same time, could be taken as purging Romans of their sins and improving the prospects of future success.

The problems generated by military overstretch were greatly exacerbated once it became clear that the war was far from won. Soldiers and their families were increasingly discontented at long years of service far from home. The population was growing restive at the authoritarian tone of a government wholeheartedly committed to the war effort and inclined to disregard the traditional compact between kings and their great subjects. Last but by no means least, there was resentment on the part of the commercial classes at the economic damage caused by disruption to trade with the steppe and northern worlds and by the irruption of enemy forces into Sasanian lands. Heraclius' bold strike into the metropolitan region simply brought these discontents to a head and precipitated the coup which brought Khusro down. It was the intervention of the Turks, though, which made the coup possible, magnifying political dissidence at the highest level, both in the officer corps and in court circles. The *xwarrah* (glory) which underpinned royal authority had clearly deserted Khusro. Once it was gone, once the virtuous circle in which each victory contributed to glory was broken, the core groups of

---

[27] References in n. 2 of this chapter.
[28] A. Panaino, 'Astral Characters of Kingship in the Sasanian and Byzantine Worlds', in *La Persia e Bisanzio*, 555–94, at 568–72; M. P. Canepa, *The Two Eyes of the Earth: Art and Ritual of Kingship between Rome and Sasanian Iran* (Berkeley, CA, 2009), 100–3, 192–6.

conspirators were able to stage a virtually bloodless putsch and within a few days, to dispose of the great conquering king.

The fall of Khusro did not of itself end the war. Peace could only be brought about by long, fraught negotiations between the belligerents. The strategy adopted by Heraclius (and probably agreed in advance with the Turks) was a classic one: while the Romans ceased fighting and responded warmly to peace overtures from the new Sasanian government, the Turks continued to keep up the military pressure. I suspect that Heraclius had indicated that he would not oppose their seizing of a bridgehead south of the Caucasus, with its core in Albania, from which they could, if they so chose, move west into Iberia and Persarmenia or south into Atropatene and threaten Media. Control of Albania would give them a platform in the far west from which to influence Iranian as well as Transcaucasian affairs, analogous to the territories in Inner Mongolia (North Hedong and Guannei) from which they projected their power into China.[29]

The Turks maintained the pressure in 628 and 629, while Heraclius was negotiating with successive Sasanian regimes. A fine piece of deception—a provocative venture by a Turkish hunting expedition into Tang territory in the middle of the harsh winter of 627–8 which was supposedly led by Illig—secured a further's year's quiet in the east.[30] Illig could stay at the opposite end of the khaganate and renew the siege of Tiflis in spring 628. With its fall, Iberia was removed, like Albania, from Sasanian control, and Illig set off east, leaving a son, who had the title *shad,* to consolidate the Turkish position in Transcaucasia. The news from the north, first of the fall of Tiflis, then of the installation of a Turkish administration in Albania, in firm control of, inter alia, the Sasanian fiscal machine, greatly strengthened Heraclius' negotiating position in 628–9, not so much with the short-lived governments of Kavad Shiroe and of his young son Ardashir, who had little choice but to accept Heraclius' demands, as with Shahrbaraz who had made it plain that he would not easily disgorge the provinces which he had conquered. A Turkish foray into Persarmenia in 629 which inflicted a crushing defeat on an Arab force sent north by Shahrbaraz added to the pressure and, in combination with Heraclius' offer to back his bid for the throne, finally secured Shahrbaraz' agreement to the evacuation of Egypt and the Levant, up to the Euphrates when they met at Arabissus in July 629.

The menacing presence of the Turks in the north thus played an essential part in bringing together the two parties, Roman and Persian. After the Heraclius-Shahrbaraz summit meeting, there was an unstoppable momentum behind the drive to restore the old world order in western Eurasia. Shahrbaraz' seizure of the throne and his assassination forty days later, on 9 June 630, simply weakened

---

[29] J. K. Skaff, *Sui-Tang China and Its Turko-Mongol Neighbours: Culture, Power, and Connections, 580–800* (Oxford, 2012), 48.
[30] *Tang-shu*, trans. Mau-Tsai, 192–3; *Qu Tang-shu*, trans. Mau-Tsai, 142.

the already weak position of the Persians. It triggered a succession crisis, and enabled Heraclius to demand and to obtain from the government of Khusro's daughter Boran a yet more favourable settlement under which the frontier advanced to the line agreed in 591.[31]

It is the automatic inclination of modern historians either to delve down into the *structures* of belligerent powers, looking for weaknesses in the social order or malfunctions in the economy which might explain the defeat of one or other of them, or to stare up, scanning the ideological cloudscapes of their thought-worlds or *imaginaires*, seeking out flaws which might have diminished the resolve of one side or opened up serious fissures in its body politic. Those lines of inquiry, however, whether taken individually or in tandem, cannot explain satisfactorily the final outcome of the last great war of antiquity, Persian defeat and a return to the *status quo ante bellum*. For it was *actions in the political sphere* (which embraces warfare as well as diplomacy, propaganda, and domestic politics), their direction and timing, above all the close alliance of Romans and Turks and the subordination by the Romans of military operations to a defined and consistently maintained political aim—regime change in Ctesiphon-Veh Ardashir—which, at long last, brought the discontent inevitably roused by a long war to a head and led to a sudden volte-face in the stance of the Sasanian government. *Events* on the battlefield, in the diplomatic sphere, in governing circles, and on generals' staffs and *the thoughts and plans of individuals* which determined the actions of large bodies of men were in command of history in this final phase of classical antiquity.

11.2 Consequences

It is a common assumption that both belligerent powers were *exhausted, their vital forces drained*, at the end of the war, and were thus rendered all too vulnerable to any predator which might emerge from the surrounding world—whether the Germanic West, the nomadic north and east, or that desiccated land of quintessential tribal flux to the south. It is an assumption which should be subjected to close critical scrutiny. Exhaustion needs to be defined and its effects tabulated and analysed. Was it a question of depleted manpower or economic trouble on the Roman side? Were the divisions which had opened up in Sasanian governing circles lasting? Did it take time for both powers to revert to peacetime systems of government and to reimpose effective control on peripheral areas? Was there a weakening in the *nerve*, in the ideological drive of either imperial power, which undermined confidence and the ability to meet new challenges from within or without? Or was their fate not in their own hands?

---

[31] See ch. 10.5.

I shall end this history, which has been long in gestation and which seems to have spread itself in the telling, with some remarks about the aftermath of the war, beginning with an examination first of the east Roman Empire in the early 630s. Thanks to an abundance of sources about a key development in the realm of ideas and beliefs, rather more can be said about ideology than about the physical body politic. This will be followed by an inevitably rather cursory examination of the condition of the Sasanian Empire at the end of Khusro II's disastrous war (because of a dearth of sources), before we come face to face with the most extraordinary of all recorded historical phenomena, the rise of Islam and the Arab conquests, which destroyed both great powers, leaving a mere rump of one to survive into the Middle Ages.

Knowing that Roman emperors, unlike their Sasanian counterparts, were constantly striving to underpin imperial rule with religious unity (with a concomitant need to define, condemn, and persecute deviant sects), we should not be surprised that, despite the demands of war, Heraclius took an interest in religious affairs.[32] A new initiative to reconcile the fractious confessions, principally Chalcedonian and different strands of Monophysitism (or Miaphysitism, a neologism which is gaining currency), was launched by Sergius, the Chalcedonian Patriarch of Constantinople (610–38). He hoped to circumvent the problem of how to express the Union of the divine and the human in the incarnate Christ (a problem exacerbated by differences of language) by shifting attention to the *energeia* (energy, drive, operation (akin to an operating system)) deriving from the *thelesis* (will) of Christ.[33] Sergius put out feelers after the imposition of direct Persian rule on Palestine (616) and before the invasion of Egypt (619) to key figures on both sides. Through an intermediary, he sent a small tract (*libellus*) written by Menas, the Patriarch of Constantinople (536–52), which argued for singularity of energy in Christ, to a noted Chalcedonian theologian, Theodore, the Bishop of Pharan in Sinai, the author of a treatise on key Christological terms. He also wrote to a leading Monophysite in Egypt, a certain George (later called Arsas, 'Heretic', in Chalcedonian circles), asking for citations in support of a single energy, indicating at the same time that he intended to start negotiations between the confessions.[34]

---

[32] J. Meyendorff, *Imperial Unity and Christian Divisions: The Church 450-680 AD* (Crestwood, NY, 1989).

[33] I am most grateful to Marek Jankowiak for letting me have a copy of his doctoral thesis, *Essai d'histoire politique du monothélisme à partir de la correspondance entre les empereurs byzantins, les patriarches de Constantinople et les papes de Rome* (Paris and Warsaw, 2009), which presents a detailed and authoritative history of the seventh-century Christological controversy. For want of a published version (much to be lamented), citations are indirect, via P. Booth, *Crisis of Empire: Doctrine and Dissent at the End of Late Antiquity* (Berkeley, CA, 2014), who makes extensive use of the Jankowiak thesis.

[34] *Disputatio cum Pyrrho*, PG 91, 288–353, at 332B–333A. Cf. Booth, *Crisis of Empire*, 191–2, 196–8.

Heraclius took the leading role in the next, less tentative phase, which involved contacting churchmen on both sides of the confessional divide in the north. He acted, in effect, as the patriarch's agent in the field, armed with a letter from him and two Monoenergistic texts, namely the *libellus* of Menas and Theodore of Pharan's reply to Sergius' inquiry. Probably in spring 624 he met Paul the One-Eyed, a leading Monophysite, at Theodosiopolis on his way to invade Atropatene and handed over copies of both texts. Paul proved unamenable, which led Heraclius to issue a warning about him to Arcadius, appointed Archbishop of Constantia in Cyprus soon after April 625. The warning did, of course, bring Arcadius into the discussions, thus opening up another diplomatic front. Later, in autumn 627, when Heraclius was preparing for his second offensive in Lazica, he talked to Cyrus, the Metropolitan Bishop of Phasis, an up-and-coming Chalcedonian figure who would be put in charge of church in Egypt within a very few years. Cyrus, who was unsure whether one should attribute one or two energies to Christ, was urged to write to Sergius.[35] His letter elicited a carefully phrased letter from Sergius in which, citing Cyril of Alexandria and Menas as authorities, he inclined towards the Monoenergistic formula. Cyrus was won over.[36]

Serious negotiations were postponed until the war was over. Heraclius, who stayed on in the Middle East after the Jerusalem ceremony, remained in charge, but doubtless was advised by a team of Chalcedonian theologians. With the arrival in Jerusalem of an emissary (Bishop Elias) from the recently installed Nestorian Catholicos Isho'yahb II (628–46), a whole new vista opened up. Heraclius, it seems, now began to dream of bringing about a general reconciliation of all the disputatious Christian confessions in his role as a latter-day Constantine.[37] The sense of being a uniquely privileged vicegerent of God on earth, instilled by victory against so many odds, was surely reinforced by the solemn ceremony enacted in Jerusalem. He would follow up victory in war with a counteroffensive on the religious plane on an equally ambitious scale.

It is likely that the key Christological issues dividing the Nestorian from the Chalcedonian church were broached in talks with Elias and that the outline of a compromise took shape. That would help to explain the high regard shown for Elias and his designation as 'entirely orthodox' in the short contemporary account

---

[35] *Disp.Pyrrh.*, 332C–333A; text and translation of first letter of Cyrus to Sergius in P. Allen, *Sophronius of Jerusalem and Seventh-Century History: The Synodical Letter and other Documents* (Oxford, 2009), 160–3; first letter of Sergius to Pope Honorius (winter 634–5), in Allen, *Sophronius of Jerusalem*, 182–95, at 182–3. S. Brock, 'A Monothelete Florilegium in Syriac', in S. Brock, *Studies in Syriac Christianity: History, Literature and Theology* (Aldershot, 1992), no.XIV. Cf. Booth, *Crisis of Empire*, 192–4 (*libellus* of Menas), 198–9 (Paul the One-Eyed).

[36] *Disp.Pyrrh.*, 333A; first letter of Sergius to Pope Honorius, 184–5; *Synodicon Vetus*, c.128. Cf. Booth, *Crisis of Empire*, 198–9.

[37] Drijvers, 'Heraclius and the *Restitutio Crucis*', 181–4.

of the repatriation of the relics of St Anastasius.[38] Both sides would then have had time to prepare for a high-level meeting scheduled for later in the year in Berrhoea (modern Aleppo). It took place in the summer after the assassination of Shahrbaraz. The chief negotiator was the Nestorian Catholicos Isho'yahb himself. He was more than competent to take charge of the theological negotiations, since he had written a Christological treatise before his elevation to the catholicosate.[39] Like Heraclius, he came with advisers, a small party of bishops. The two sides reached an agreement, accepting the new Monoenergistic formula and undertaking to refrain from bringing up contentious matters—hence the names of the three great theologians whom Nestorians revered, Diodorus of Tarsus, Theodore of Mopsuestia, and Nestorius would not be read from the diptychs during the liturgy, nor would there be any reference to the Council of Chalcedon or Cyril of Alexandria (the driving force behind the campaign to anathematize Nestorius at Chalcedon). The restoration of communion was made manifest in two joint celebrations of the liturgy, at which Heraclius received the Eucharist from the catholicos.[40]

Later that year, Heraclius turned his attention to the Syrian Monophysites. A dramatic opening move, his offer to attend the liturgy in the cathedral of Edessa, was rebuffed. He followed it up with a proposal for formal negotiations with Athanasius the 'Camel Driver', the Monophysite Patriarch of Antioch. They took place over winter 630–1 at Hierapolis. Athanasius was accompanied by a team of twelve bishops. The negotiations lasted twelve days, but ended in failure. The Monophysite side refused to accept any formula which referred to two natures, however closely bound together they might be by a single will and single energy. Heraclius, by contrast, was ready to entertain the *libellus* produced by Athanasius in the course of the conference, despite its insistence on a single nature and rejection of the Council of Chalcedon. As an earnest of his commitment to church union, he asked to be given the Eucharist by Athanasius and offered him official recognition as Patriarch of Antioch (a see without a Chalcedonian incumbent). The rejection of both offers brought the conference to an end.[41]

The longer-term outcomes of the two sets of negotiations were not, however, that different. For the text of the agreement reached with Isho'yahb evoked a hostile reaction from prominent Nestorian bishops in Mesopotamia. Isho'yahb's argument that concessions had to be made for political reasons to secure peace did not reconcile them to the omission of the names of the three founding fathers

---

[38] *Translatio*, c.2.3–8.
[39] L. R. M. Sako, *Lettre christologique du patriarche syro-oriental Īšōʻahb II de Gdālā (628–646)* (Rome, 1983).
[40] *Seert Chron.*, 557.8–560.6. Cf. Flusin, *Saint Anastase*, II, 323–9; Booth, *Crisis of Empire*, 200–2.
[41] Mich.Syr., xi.3 (408–10), trans. Chabot, 411–12. Cf. Theoph., 329.21–330.5, a tendentious anti-Monothelete account which has the two sides agree. Cf. Booth, *Crisis of Empire*, 202–3.

of their branch of Christianity. Similarly, in his case under pressure from the imperial authorities, Athanasius had difficulty in carrying his own flock with him in his rejection of a compromise with the Chalcedonians. There were many who were ready to be reconciled with the imperial church, among them the traditional hard-core supporters of Monophysitism in the monasteries of Beit Maron, Hierapolis, Emesa, and southern districts in Syria. Athanasius was driven from from his see, taking refuge first in Phoenicia and then across the border in the Sasanian Empire.[42] The same outcome, the winning over a majority and the isolation of a recalcitrant minority, was also achieved in a third round of negotiations with the Armenian catholicos, aided by the application of political pressure. Under instructions from the military commander in the Roman sector of Armenia, Ezr, only appointed to the catholicosate in 630, convened a synod at Theodosiopolis to consider a statement of faith sent by the emperor and the status of the Council of Chalcedon. The synod finally agreed to stop its open opposition to Chalcedon after thirty days. Ezr was then able to go to meet Heraclius in Syria for a concelebration of the liturgy. There was some subsequent opposition led by a certain John Mayrogomets'i, but it was hard for most churchmen to hold out against a compromise which merely affected what was expressed in public. Before long the metropolitans of Albania and Siwnik' came over.[43]

The final and most fraught step in Sergius' and Heraclius' ecumenical drive involved Egypt—fraught because of the ability of patriarchs to call on monasteries to back their doctrinal positions with demonstrations of strength on the streets of Alexandria. There was no question of Heraclius' taking a leading role. Instead, probably in 631, Cyrus, the Bishop of Phasis, was parachuted in and put in charge of negotiations. The officially recognized (Chalcedonian) patriarchal see was left vacant, Cyrus being designated interim holder of the see. It is not known when talks began, what arguments were deployed by the two sides, or what were the principal difficulties encountered. The negotiations may have been spread over a year or more, but in the end they succeeded. An agreed text with nine articles of faith was drafted and promulgated. The document, which has survived, embedded in the acts of the hostile 680–1 council, highlighted the Trinitarian and Christological doctrines held in common (articles 1–5), was careful to target its anathemas at notable Nestorian theologians (articles 8–9), included many deferential references to Cyril, and pointedly avoided any mention of the Council of Chalcedon or of Severus, who, along with Cyril, was one of the two most revered champions of Monophysitism. Cyril's formulation of 'one incarnate nature of God the Word' (used by the Chalcedonian side at Hierapolis) reappeared

---

[42] *Seert Chron.*, 560.2–561.7; Mich.Syr., xi.3 (410), trans. Chabot, 412–13; Booth, *Crisis of Empire*, 203, n.70.

[43] Ps.S, 131.31–132.8, with *Hist.Com.*, n.49; *Narratio de rebus Armeniae*, ed. G. Garitte, CSCO 132, Subsidia 4 (Louvain, 1952), cc.121–43, with commentary at pp.278–311. Cf. Booth, *Crisis of Empire*, 200.

in article 6 and was elaborated in the key article 7, which incorporated the new Monoenergistic doctrine—'that one and the same Christ and Son performed things befitting God and things human by one theandric activity'.[44]

The new union between the imperial and Theodosian parties in the church (the normal designation of Monophysites as Severans was avoided) was publicly marked by concelebrations of the liturgy on 3 June 633. The services involved took place in many churches across Alexandria, since they involved all the clergy and were attended by civilian postholders, army officers, and thousands of ordinary citizens As in Syria, hard-line opponents of the union were isolated when the monks came down on the side of compromise. Benjamin, the Monophysite patriarch, went into hiding, while Cyrus, now recognized by both parties, was appointed to the patriarchal see.[45]

There could have been no more striking finale to Sergius' ecumenical project and Heraclius' efforts to restore the old world order in the Middle East, with Christianity now acting as a bonding agent rather than divider. The ideological grounding of imperial unity was given its missing religious element, while the restoration of communion with the Nestorian church increased the empire's leverage over the Sasanians. When Cyrus' report on these events reached Sergius in Constantinople, Heraclius could be forgiven for looking at the post-war world with a degree of complacency. The future stretched ahead, its waters shimmering in the light of a beneficent sun. Romans would assume their proper place as the senior of the two great powers, Persians being the moon to their sun. There might be some tidal movement, but the violent Turkish storm was over and the waters were calm.

It is harder to gauge the condition of the eastern Roman Empire on the ground in the Middle East. There is little reliable information about provincial administration, military dispositions, and the identities of key individuals in the interlude of three and a half years between the Jerusalem ceremony and the start of a new crisis. Bits and pieces of information may be picked up from Greek, Syriac, and Coptic sources (notably from John of Nikiu's detailed account of Egypt under attack by the Arabs) supplemented by papyri and less trustworthy later Arab sources. On the basis of this limited and fragmentary material, it is perhaps overbold to try to reconstruct a whole administrative system, to outline the military commands put in place, and to define the relations of the military to the civil authorities.[46] Some observations may, however, be made.

Whatever the military command structure and whatever the origin of the troops on the ground, whether seconded from the field forces who had served

---

[44] Text of agreement: Allen, *Sophronius of Jerusalem*, 168–73. Cf. Booth, *Crisis of Empire*, 205–6.
[45] Second letter of Cyrus to Sergius: Allen, *Sophronius of Jerusalem*, 174–7. Hist.Patr., 490–2. Cf. Booth, *Crisis of Empire*, 206–8.
[46] Cf. Schmitt, 'Oströmische Herrschaft'.

with Heraclius, recruited locally by the reinstated Roman authorities, or detached from urban militias (one of the prime functions of the burgeoning towns of the *badiya* was to generate defensive forces), there was to be no difficulty in mobilizing and deploying them when danger materialized in 634 and 635 (the defeats which they suffered are largely attributable to the strength and sagacity, strategic and tactical, of the Arabs). There is no indication of resistance to the restoration of Roman rule after the Persian evacuation, let alone armed uprisings. Urban notables may have been ready to collaborate with the Persians, but undoubtedly did not expect the occupation to last. When the troops marched away, there is every reason to suppose that they resumed their normal role in the management of the localities in tandem with the Roman authorities. As for the framework of imperial government, it is highly unlikely that there was any tampering with provincial boundaries or military commands.[47] The prime concern of the Roman government was to ensure a smooth transition from Persian to Roman rule, just as the Persian occupation authorities had sought to minimize change when they took over. This was of particular importance on the desert frontage of Palestine and Syria, where it seems from the evidence of al-Baladhuri (better informed and more reliable than many of his ninth-tenth century Arab contemporaries) that the Ghassan were retained as Roman clients to guard the desert approaches to Palestine and southern Syria.[48]

The imperial government could not be satisfied with the status quo in the Balkans, which was as integral a part of the eastern empire as the Middle East. The evidence is very poor and fragmentary, but it provides glimpses of Roman diplomacy at work in the 630s. The Unugundurs and their leader Kubrat, who had established relations with the Romans in the 620s, rebelled and expelled the Avars from their lands (probably the nearer reaches of the Pontic steppes, between the Dniepr and the Danube).[49] Around the same time, Bulgars within the core lands of the khaganate rose up and challenged the rule of the Avars only to be worsted in battle and driven out, some 9,000 fleeing to Bavaria (where most were liquidated later on the orders of the Frankish king Dagobert (613–38)) and others to Italy.[50] Dagobert too, on becoming sole ruler in 630, was drawn into the Roman campaign to weaken the Avar khaganate by intervening in the Slav-populated lands west and south of the Carpathian basin. But the alliance foundered when a key ally, the Frank Samo, who had built up a supratribal Slav grouping in Bohemia, was antagonized and Dagobert turned on the Bulgars who had sought asylum.[51]

---

[47] Haldon, 'The *Ajnād* and the "Thematic Myth"', 385, 399–402.
[48] Al-Baladhuri, *Futuh al-Buldan*, ed. M. J. de Goeje (Leiden, 1866), 135.1–138.5, 164.4–13, trans. P. K. Hitti, *The Origins of the Islamic State* (New York, 1916), 207–10, 254. Cf. Donner, *Early Islamic Conquests*, 107–8, 132–3, 148, 154–5.
[49] Nic., cc.9, 22.   [50] Fredegar, iv.72; Paul D, v.29.
[51] Esders, 'Herakleios, Dagobert und die "beschittenen Völker"', 244–5, 299–308.

Two other diplomatic initiatives were more successful. Contact was made with two distant non-Slav peoples, Croats and Serbs, both at the time living north of the Carpathians. The face-saving formula—that they came south as refugees— used in the late official source almost certainly masks the reality of a Roman invitation to intervene in the Balkans. The Croats arrived while fighting was continuing with the Avars. Heraclius welcomed them as clients, deployed them against the Avars in Dalmatia, and, once they had succeeded in driving out the Avars, allowed them to settle there. One of two leaders of the Serbs followed suit, coming south with half the Serb people and offering his services to Heraclius. Once again Heraclius directed these new clients into the Balkans, this time south of Avar-controlled territory. From their base north of Thessalonica, they could be, and probably were, used to stir up the Slav tribes settled in the Macedonian heartland of the Balkans. After some time, their mission having been accomplished, they were allowed to go home, but, on their changing their minds (after crossing the Danube), they were assigned land in Illyricum and on the Dalmatian coast south of the Croats. The Romans thus gained permanent clients through whom to manage the Balkans Slavs and set about strengthening ties with them by sponsoring papal missions.[52] Light is cast on this process of client management by what is recorded of a later episode in the 640s. On this occasion the rebel leader was a Bulgar, Kuber, whom the Avar khagan had put in charge of his sub-Roman subjects. This people (designated a distinct group by the Avars) comprised descendants of Roman prisoners of war who had maintained their Roman identity and Christian faith. Led by Kuber, they rose up with other tribesmen, but were defeated and driven south, where they were welcomed by the Roman authorities and assigned the rich plain of Pelagonia as their settlement area.[53]

The Roman position was much stronger in the central Mediterranean. Its solid base lay in North Africa, where the fertile plains of Proconsularis and Byzacena, the Numidian uplands, and the Mediterranean coast from the Pentapolis to Caesarea and Ceuta were under Roman control. The fortifications funded by successive regimes in the sixth century fixed Roman authority to the terrain and demarcated the developed, directly governed provinces from the penumbra of Roman-influenced territory in the mountains and pre-desert.[54] Participation in the Heraclian revolution had strengthened ties between Berber tribes and Roman authorities. It would take some extraordinary mishap to loosen them and revert

---

[52] Constantinus Porphyrogenitus, *De administrando imperio*, ed. G. Moravcsik, trans. R. J. H. Jenkins, CFHB 1 (Washington DC, 1967), cc.31.3–25, 32.2–29.

[53] *Mir.Dem.*, ii.5.284–8.

[54] D. Pringle, *The Defence of Byzantine Africa from Justinian to the Arab Conquest: An Account of the Military History and Archaeology of the African Provinces in the Sixth and Seventh Centuries*, BAR, Int.Ser.99 (Oxford, 1981).

to the tensions which had governed relations in the late sixth century (to 595).[55] Sicily, which was dominated by large grain-producing estates owned by the papacy and the senatorial aristocracy of Rome, linked North Africa to the southern half of the Italian peninsula, where Roman authority prevailed except in the Lombard dukedom of Benevento.[56] Farther north, the Lombards were careful not to take advantage of Roman distractions in the east so as to break out of the Po valley and the areas west of the Apennines which they controlled. Like the notables in the occupied provinces of the Middle East, they knew that the phase of Roman weakness would not, could not, last. It was important, then, not to outrage governing circles in Constantinople, especially after the territorial concessions agreed under the treaty of 605, which had also granted them an annual subvention of 12,000 solidi.[57] They made no move to exploit political instability in the exarchate between 615 and 618, whether to extend their control west over Liguria, south-west over Tuscany and Umbria, or even over the routes across the Apennines linking the exarchate to Rome. Even when presented with the tempting opportunity of a serious uprising in Ravenna against the authorities (the exarch and judges were killed), seizure of Naples by a rebel, and, finally, assumption of kingship over Roman Italy by the Exarch Eleutherius after he restored order, they refrained from intervening and chipping away at Roman forward defences. It was from a fortress commanding the Tuscan end of an Apennine pass that Roman troops intercepted and killed Eleutherius.[58] The Romans, in contrast, showed no hesitation about taking advantage of Lombard political divisions when trouble broke out in 624–5.[59]

The only significant territorial losses in the west occurred in Spain. The cities which remained under Roman control in the south-eastern enclave conquered by Justinian centred on Nova Carthago (Cartagena) and strung out along the coast past Malaca to the Straits of Gibraltar were taken out in two campaigns, the first under Sisebut in Heraclius' fifth regnal year (614–15), the second in Heraclius' seventeenth regnal year (626–7) under Suinthila. Both acts of aggression by the Visigoths were, it appears, timed to exploit periods of great peril for the empire in the east. Suinthila became the first Visigothic king to bring the whole of Spain under his rule.[60] Damage, of course, was done to Roman prestige in the west, but it did not matter much in the context of the damage done by Persians and Avars

---

[55] Modéran, *Maures*, 668–81.   [56] Guillou, *L'Italia bizantina*, 226–7, 311–13.
[57] Paul D, iv.28. Cf. N. Christie, *The Lombards: The Ancient Langobards* (Oxford, 1995), 83, 89–91.
[58] *Liber Pontificalis*, ed. L. Duchesne, 3 vols. (Paris, 1886–1957), I, 319.2–6, 321.7–9, trans. R. Davis, *The Book of Pontiffs: The Ancient Biographies of the First Ninety Roman Bishops to AD 715*, TTH, Latin Series 5 (Liverpool, 1989), 63. Cf. Christie, *Lombards*, 96.
[59] Fredegar, iv.49–50.
[60] Isidorus, *Chronica*, 415, 416b (pp.479–80) for dating; for more details, see Isidorus, *Historia Gothorum Wandalorum Sueborum*, ed. Mommsen, *Chron.Min.*, II.2, 291–2 (paras 61–2); Fredegar, iv.33. Cf. M. Vallejo Girvés, *Bizancio y la España tardoantigua (ss.V–VIII): Un capítulo de historia mediterránea* (Alcala de Henares, 1993), 287–302, 306–10.

and it did not materially weaken the eastern empire's position in the west. It would take much more than a few years' reverses to undermine the superordinate status of an empire which was clearly part of the divine dispensation on earth. There was also a ready alternative base for the projection of Roman power into the interior of Spain (via the Balearics) and into southern France (via Corsica), namely Sardinia, in particular the fortified towns lining its western coast from Turris Libisonis (modern Portotorres) in the north to Carales (Cagliari) in the south.[61] The island had been swiftly seized after the initial success of Justinian's expedition to North Africa in late 533, and its role as the base for a high-level military and naval command, attested in 687, probably dated from 625–6.[62]

The Roman Empire survived the war to resume its position as a great power commanding the whole Mediterranean, from the waters off Spain and France to the Levant. In the Middle East it recovered the lost provinces, which had not been subject to widespread systematic depredation by the Persians. The only serious damage was that done to Roman authority in the Balkans by the migration, under Avar sponsorship, of Slav tribes deep into the southern half of the peninsula, some even reaching the Peloponnese.[63] The presence of the Slavs greatly attenuated Roman authority and disrupted the functioning of local government in large areas of the interior, but there was no question of the Romans accepting as brute, unalterable fact the presence of large populations unamenable to management in what was an integral part of the empire. There was no official acknowledgement of the new reality. The Praetorian Prefect of Illyricum was still in post, although he was now based in Thessalonica and was little more than a city prefect. When the provincial system was revised, the old civil provinces being amalgamated to form large regional commands, the two created in the Balkans by the early eighth century embraced, at least notionally, the whole of *Thrace* (the eastern neighbour of Illyricum) and the whole of *Hellas* (to the south), while government over northern Illyricum and Dalmatia was deputed to Serbs and Croats.[64] Romans could look forward with confidence to a gradual extension and intensification of

---

[61] P.G. Spanu, *La Sardegna bizantina tra VI e VII secolo* (Oristano, 1998), 173–98; D. Michaelides, P. Pergola and E. Zanini, eds., *The Insular System of the Early Byzantine Mediterranean: Archaeology and History*, BAR, Int.Ser.2523 (Oxford, 2013), 31–45 and 77–85, arts. by M. A. Cau Ontiveros and C. Mas Florit, 'The Early Byzantine Period in the Balearic Islands' and by D. Istria and P. Pergola, 'La Corse byzantine'.

[62] Conquest: Procopius, *Bella*, iv.5.2–4. Justinian II mentions the Sardinian command in his 687 letter to Pope John V about the 681–2 Trullan Council, ed. R. Riedinger, *Acta Conciliorum Oecumenicorum*, ser. 2, II.2 (Berlin, 1992), 886–7.Traces of administration: P. G. Spanu and R. Zucca, *I sigilli bizantini della ΣΑΡΔΗΝΙΑ* (Rome, 2004); S. Cosentino, 'Byzantine Sardinia between West and East: Features of a Regional Culture', *Millennium*, 1 (2004), 329–67, at 337–43.

[63] *DAI*, c.50.6–25.

[64] Praetorian Prefect: *Mir.Dem.*, i.11.96 (p.119.15–24), i.13.128 (p.137.16–19), ii.4.231 (pp.208.8–209.9); cf. Lemerle, *Miracles de saint Démétrius*, II, 76–7. Hellas: Theoph., 368.18–21 (new theme command in existence by 695). Thrace: Theoph., 415.12–15 (first clearly attested as a command in 741).

their influence over the Slavs from the various districts where local authorities or client peoples were firmly established.

The Sasanian Empire was in a sorrier state. Defeat had dealt a shattering blow to the dynasty, which was compounded when Kavad Shiroe ordered a cull of his brothers. In this context it was not unreasonable for an outsider with Roman backing to think of seizing power. Execution of the last Sasanian male heir in the direct line from Khusro II and Kavad Shiroe was, however, too open an affront to a political system governed by lineage and inherited status. Shahrbaraz's reign lasted little more than a month and inaugurated a period of political instability. There being no obvious male heir after the death of young Ardashir, one of Khusro's daughters, Boran, was enthroned.[65] By reverting to Khusro II's coin type, she stressed her dynastic credentials, but, at the same time, according to the late testimony of the Arab historian al-Tabari, embarked on an anti-militaristic programme and remitted the arrears of (war) taxation. There was, it seems, a military reaction which led to her deposition and death after a reign of sixteen months (so towards the end of 631).[66]

There followed a period of heightened crisis, with a rapid succession of rulers. The written sources list them as if they rose to power and ruled in sequence, but it is more likely that they were making rival, overlapping bids for power from different regional bases.[67] There were, we are told, divisions in the armed forces. The near contemporary, who was writing the *History of Khosrov* in Dvin some twenty years later, noted that Shahrbaraz's army based in northern Mesopotamia was at odds with the regional army of Adurbadagan and that in Persia and Khurasan.[68] He, like later historians, was bewildered by the news coming out of Iran and Mesopotamia. He simply named a number of claimants—Khusro (III), Azarmidukht (another of Khusro's daughters), Hormizd (V), and the ultimate victor Yazdgerd (III), to which should be added Peroz (II), named in later sources.[69] Drachms issued in the names of Khusro III, Azarmidukht, and Hormizd V confirm that each of them gained control of the metropolitan region at some point and exercised royal power, if only for a few weeks.[70]

Regional affiliations are given in the *Chronicle of Seert*, which, though put together long after the events, had access to good Sasanian sources. Peroz (II),

---

[65] See Section 10.5.
[66] *Seert Chron.*, 557.1–3, 579.9–10; Tab., 1064.1–14. Contra ps.S, 130.25, who has Boran die after a reign of two years. T. Daryaee, 'The Coinage of Queen Bōrān and Its Significance for Late Sāsānian Imperial Ideology', *Bulletin of the Asia Institute*, n.s.13 (1999), 77–82.
[67] F. de Blois, 'The Persian Calendar', *Iran*, 34 (1996), 39–54, at 39.   [68] Ps.S, 130.29–32.
[69] Ps.S, 130.25–9, with TA, 97–8; Theoph., 329.8, Mich.Syr., xi.3 (410), *Chron.1234*, 238.22–8 (trans. Hoyland, 82–3); *Seert Chron.*, 579.9–580.4; Tab., 1064.15–1067.2.
[70] Drachms were issued in each of their names from the main metropolitan mint (WYHC), as well as nine provincial mints in the case of Hormizd and one or two in those of Azarmidukht and Khusro (personal communication from Susan Tyler-Smith). Drachms of Hormizd are best represented in the hoard evidence—as, for example, in the Basel and Bab Tuma hoards (Gyselen, 'Un Trésor de monnaies sassanides tardives', 213, 231; Gyselen and Kalus, *Deux Trésors monétaires*, 22).

it reports, was the commander of the army of Persia when he rebelled and killed Boran. This was the act which triggered a bout of civil war, pitting the regional armies against each other. The candidates which they put up are listed as Khusro (Meharkhusro), a child, in Khurasan, Azarmidukht in Mesopotamia, and Yazdgerd III in Persia proper.[71] Hormizd V (not mentioned in the chronicle) is reported to have gained the backing of Shahrbaraz's army and to have been acclaimed at Nisibis, within easy striking distance of the metropolitan region.[72] Yazdgerd rose to power far away in the ancient heartland of the Sasanians, where he was proclaimed king by the notables of Stakhr in the year beginning on 16 June 632 (his first regnal year). Given that many months had passed since Boran's death, it looks as if it was a delayed reaction on the part of the power brokers in Fars to the success of rival candidates. They first dealt with young Khusro in Khurasan, then marched on the capital and installed Yazdgerd as king of kings. This rebellion seems to have gathered momentum slowly, since, to judge by the mints issuing drachms, there is no evidence that Yazdgerd gained control of the metropolitan area or the western half of the empire before the Arab invasion of 635-6 (his fourth regnal year) disrupted the minting system.[73]

The written sources for the last phase of Sasanian history were primarily concerned with the rise and fall of Yazdgerd and with the fighting forced on him by the nascent Muslim-Arab power of the south. It looks as if the internal opposition petered out after his enthronement and the sudden materializing of the Arab threat. Yazdgerd is presented as the dominant figure in the last years of Iranian independence.[74] His authority was unquestioned when Arab forces pushed into the Mesopotamian alluvium and put Ctesiphon-Veh Ardashir under siege (in 636). A call for general mobilization was promptly answered, to judge by reports of the response of three Transcaucasian peoples. The leading princes of Armenia, Siwnik', and Albania sent contingents several thousand strong to serve in the field army commanded by Rustam, the *spahbed* of Adurbadagan, which broke the siege of the capital and drove the Arabs back into the desert beyond the Euphrates in 637.[75] If we may generalize from the case of Juansher, the commander of the Albanian contingent, Transcaucasian forces fought on for Yazdgerd after the war turned against him with the defeat of the counteroffensive at Qadisiyya in January 638. Juansher was involved in defensive operations against the advancing Arabs and a botched attempt to evacuate the government and royal treasure from Ctesiphon. It was only after seven years of loyal service in a losing war that he

---

[71] *Seert Chron.*, 579.9–580.2.   [72] TA, 98.
[73] *Khuz.Chron.*, 30.20-1 (trans. Nöldeke, 26); *Seert Chron.*, 580.1-4; Tab., 1067.3-8. S. Tyler-Smith, 'Coinage in the Name of Yazdgerd III (AD 632-651) and the Arab Conquest of Iran', NC 160 (2000), 135-70, at 158-9.
[74] Ps.S, 130.29; *Seert Chron.*, 580.3-4.
[75] Ps.S, 137.5-15; MD, 172.21-174.10, trans. Dowsett, 109-10.

finally withdrew.[76] As for the field army of Adurbadagan, it seems to have remained responsive to royal authority almost to the end. It was only after it was cut off from the eastern enclave still controlled by Yazdgerd and the army of Khusrasan that the Arabs were able to neutralize it and move to drive Yazdgerd into the steppes.[77]

The best gauge of the functioning of the Sasanian state as it approached its death throes was its coinage. In the initial three regnal years of Yazdgerd's reign (from 632-3 to 634-5), before the first inroads made by the Arabs, the drachms issued in his name from nine mints (five in Fars, two in the south-east (Kirman and Sakastan) and two in Khuzistan) were of a uniform type, well engraved and well struck, and of a high standard of purity (over 90 per cent silver).[78] The subsequent breakdown of government and contraction of royal authority can be traced from his sixth regnal year (637-8) as mints ceased production and standards dropped.[79] But this, like the final fraying of Transcaucasian loyalties, had little to do with Khusro II's Roman war and his surgical removal from power. It was an unbroken sequence of Arab victories, after the initial reverse suffered in 637—the battle of Qadisiyya, the renewed invasion of Mesopotamia, the capture of Ctesiphon-Veh Ardashir, the conquest of Khuzistan, the victory of Nihawand which opened the way up onto the Iranian plateau, and subsequent advances north and south-east—which gradually battered the empire to pieces. Admittedly, very little time separated the reunification of the empire by Yazdgerd and the first Arab attack in force, but, once in control of the apparatus of government, he was able to harness the empire's resources for the new war effort. The external threat undoubtedly helped him secure the backing of two important constituencies, the provincial aristocracy and the merchants who commanded the India trade. His *xwarrah* was bright after what was in effect a re-enactment of the feats of Ardashir, the founder of the dynasty. It was inconceivable that a ragged Arab army would prevail and destroy the empire.[80]

The old world order had been restored in the early 630s. Its binary structure gave it much more stability than it had had in the brief era of the troika when Turks commanded the eastern approaches to the Middle East. The Romans were once again masters of the Levant and the Mediterranean, able to project their power north-west over large swathes of Germanic Europe and south-west over the Berbers of North Africa. They were setting about the demanding task of pacifying and Romanizing the large number of Slavs who had settle in the

---

[76] MD, 174.10-175.1, 176.1-20, trans. Dowsett, 110-11, 112-13.
[77] Ps.S, 163.29-164.4, with *Hist.Com.*, n.67.
[78] Tyler-Smith, 'Coinage in the Name of Yazdgerd III', 139-40, 158-9; S. Heidemann, J. Riederer, and D. Weber, 'A Hoard from the Time of Yazdgard III in Kirmān', *Iran*, 52 (2014), 79-124, at 91-2.
[79] Tyler-Smith, 'Coinage in the Name of Yazdgerd III'.
[80] J. Howard-Johnston, 'The India Trade in Late Antiquity', in E. W. Sauer, ed., *Sasanian Persia: Between Rome and the Steppes of Eurasia* (Edinburgh, 2017), 284-304, at 292-8.

Balkans. Victory undoubtedly acted as tonic to the body politic. The Sasanians were recovering from the terrible blow struck by Heraclius and his Turkish allies. Court magnates, government officials, provincial aristocrats and gentry, the mercantile classes of the capital and the provinces—they were all, it seems, rallying round the young king who had seized power and reunited the empire. This was the latest demonstration of the impressive ideological resilience of *Eranshahr*, which had the leading role on earth in the cosmic battle against evil.[81] Greater shocks to the system had been surmounted in past centuries, as in the period of instability between the death of Shapur I (270) and the accession of Shapur II as a minor (309), or the defeat and death of Peroz in the steppes in 484.[82]

The explanation for Arab success is ultimately to be found in Arabia. There were two key moments: (1) the compromise agreement reached at Hudaybiya in 628 which provided the basis for the union of the new faith, with its extraordinary grip on the thoughts and behaviour of the faithful, and the organizational capability of a city state which had achieved a position of economic and political hegemony in the Hijaz;[83] (2) the swift military and political response to the death of the Prophet in June 632, whereby the nascent Islamic state gained control of the Arabian peninsula. The fractious tribes and clans of Arabia were for the first time brought within the ambit of a single political authority which saw itself as the earthly agent of an infinitely remote, infinitely powerful, all-knowing, ahuman divinity, and that authority set about channelling its energies into a series of bold expeditions into the enveloping, more developed world of the Middle East.[84]

Both Romans and Persians fought hard to repel the invaders from the south, but both were defeated in great set-piece confrontations on the battlefield. So it is in the field of military history that we must look for a second-order explanation. It was not as if either of the great powers was unaware of the potential danger posed by Beduin raiders operating on a smaller or larger scale. It had been an important issue in past diplomatic negotiations. The two sides had agreed to recognize each other's spheres of influence in northern Arabia and each had built up networks of Arab clients to shield their fixed defences (the towns of the *badiya* and ducal bases to the rear in the Roman case).[85] The Romans had the harder task, the fertile provinces of northern Mesopotamia, Syria, and Palestine being fronted with the open *badiya*. Whereas the Persians could fall back on the line of the lower Euphrates, there was only a single natural feature on which Roman regional defence might hinge—the Jebel Hawran and the adjoining seas of *harra*

---

[81] Gnoli, *Idea of Iran*, 129–74.   [82] Daryaee, *Sasanian Persia*, 10–13, 15–16, 25–7.
[83] Howard-Johnston, *Witnesses*, 408–14.
[84] F. M. Donner, *The Early Islamic Conquests* (Princeton, NJ, 1981), 82–90.
[85] Fisher, *Between Empires*, 91–9, 116–24.

(lava fields) which thrust out west and east, barring the inviting route north up the *badiya*.[86]

Of course, the Roman Empire was not as strong or as confident in the 630s as it has been under Justinian (527–65), but substantial fighting forces could still be fielded, and, when battle was joined, they fought hard. Muslim success in breaking Roman resistance and taking over the whole Levant in a mere two years (634–6) was a remarkable achievement in its own right. It was then followed, in 636, by the equally impressive feat of a swift advance over the Mesopotamian alluvium and the siege of the twin cities of Ctesiphon-Veh Ardashir.[87] It is tempting to blame Sasanian weakness. But the key factors of Meccan managerial competence and driving Muslim faith should be remembered. Central direction and effective organization of supplies were in evidence. Troops were assembled and transferred east in numbers equal or superior to those which had been engaged in the Levant. They showed their mettle when Sasanian forces mobilized beyond the Zagros, probably in Media, the preferred zone for the assembly and organization of large campaign armies, counter-attacked in force in 637 and drove them out of Mesopotamia. Instead of fleeing deep into Arabia (at which Muslim authority might well have unravelled), they halted and prepared to fight after crossing the Euphrates. A call for the Arabs, a new chosen people, to rally to the Muslim cause appears to have been answered. The victorious Persian army commanded by the *spahbed* of Adurbadagan and including several thousand highlanders from Transcaucasia was comprehensively defeated at Qadisiyya on 6 January 638.[88] The key role of faith in the conquests showed itself in the resilience shown in this first serious crisis to affect the Muslims outside Arabia.

The Muslims then pushed back over the alluvium, renewed the siege of Ctesiphon-Veh Ardashir, frustrated an attempt to evacuate the government and treasury, took control of Khuzistan (except for Shustar), and advanced to the foothills of the Zagros.[89] Having earlier conquered northern Mesopotamia with pincer attacks from west and south (638), they were now (in 640) in control of the whole Fertile Crescent from the borders of Egypt to the Persian Gulf.[90] The foundations were laid for a new world empire which would be built up,

---

[86] M. Sartre, *Bostra: Des origines à l'Islam* (Paris, 1985), 37–42.

[87] *Chron.724*, 148.5–6 (trans. 19); ps.S, 137.5–7; MD, 172.21–173.4 (trans. 109).

[88] Ps.S, 137.7–20; *Khuz.Chron.*, 30.22–9 (trans. 26); MD, 173.4–175.1 (trans. 109–11); Theoph., 341.2–4, Agap., 470.7–471.2, Mich.Syr., xi.6 (416–17), *Chron.1234*, 246.18–247.27 (trans. Hoyland, 104–5, 118); Tab., 2215.3–2346.8, trans. Y. Friedmann, *The Battle of al-Qadisiyyah and the Conquest of Syria and Palestine, H of Tab.* XII (Albany, NY, 1992); Bal., 251.7–262.8 (trans., I, 403–16). Cf. Donner, *Early Islamic Conquests*, 195–209; Kennedy, *Great Arab Conquests*, 107–15.

[89] *Khuz.Chron.*, 35.20–37.14 (trans. 29–31); MD, 176.1–11 (trans. 112); Bal., 262.9–265.1 (trans., I, 417–21). Cf. C. Robinson, 'The Conquest of Khuzistan: A Historiographical Reassessment', *BSOAS* 67 (2004), 14–39.

[90] Theoph., 340.20–6, Agap., 477.3–10, Mich.Syr., xi.7 (420–1), *Chron.1234*, 256.19–257.4 (trans. Hoyland, 120–1). Cf. C. F. Robinson, *Empire and Elites after the Muslim Conquest: The Transformation of Northern Mesopotamia* (Cambridge, 2000), 28–32.

stage by stage, over the next four generations, culminating in the invasion and occupation of much of Spain (711) and the defeat of Tang forces in Central Asia (751)—a world empire which proved capable of surmounting a succession of grave internal conflicts and of imposing its religious culture on the majority of its subject peoples.[91]

The rise of Islam and the destruction of the old empires—the Sasanian expunged, the Roman reduced to a rump state, the Tang permanently weakened after the civil wars triggered by defeat—marked the opening of a new era.[92] While there were filaments of causation running back to the last great war of antiquity—the apocalyptic colouring of the early suras was not unconnected with the convulsions shaking the northern world, and both antecedent great powers had undoubtedly been weakened—it was the strength of Islam as a religious-political system which gave the vital impetus to its expansion and enabled it to overcome the resistance it encountered (notably from the cities and armies of highland Iran between 642 and 652).[93] Even these causal filaments were missing in the case of other major developments in the wider world in this new era—for example, the Khazars' winning the battle for hegemony in the west Eurasian steppes by the early 660s, the Franks' consolidation of their position as the most powerful of Germanic peoples in Europe, rapid economic growth within the huge continental market created by Islam, and the first stirrings in a new maritime market centred on the North Sea and the Baltic.[94] It was a new era. The long war fought by Persians and Romans in the early seventh century was simply the episode which brought the classical period of Middle Eastern, North African, and European history to a close.

---

[91] Kennedy, *Great Arab Conquests*, 139–323.
[92] La Vaissière, *Histoire des marchands sogdiens*, 213–18, 262; M. E. Lewis, *China's Cosmopolitan Empire: The Tang Dynasty* (Cambridge, MA, 2009), 40–4, 58–64.
[93] Kennedy, *Great Arab Conquests*, 169–99.
[94] C. Zuckerman, 'The Khazars and Byzantium—The First Encounter', in P. Golden, ed., *The World of the Khazars* (Leiden, 2007), 399–432, at 417–19, 426–31; E. James, *The Origins of France: From Clovis to the Capetians, 500–1000* (London, 1982), 127–69; C. Wickham, *Framing the Middle Ages: Europe and the Mediterranean 400–800* (Oxford, 2005), 168–203; M. Lombard, *L'Islam dans sa première grandeur (VIII–XIe siècle)* (Paris, 1971); I. N. Wood, *The Merovingian North Sea* (Alingsås, 1983); E. Christiansen, *The Norsemen in the Viking Age* (Oxford, 2002), 70–4.

Afterword

Only the faintest of echoes of a quarter of a century's fighting can now be heard, and then only by those with ears attuned to the Middle East in the pre-Islamic era. Almost immediately afterwards, listeners in Latin Christendom, the farther reaches of North Africa, and the eastern and south-eastern borderlands of Iran would have been transfixed by the sounds of Arab victories and of Arab armies on the march into the fertile lands arching over Arabia. Farther afield—in the forests of the deep north, from which two centuries later the pelts of thousands and thousands of small mammals would be carried south to clothe the rulers, bureaucrats, and merchants of the Caliphate in furs, in the Far East, where China turned in on itself after the first clash with Muslim forces in Central Asia in the middle of the eighth century, and in the Indian subcontinent and its south-east Asian dependencies, a world unto itself until the first Muslim inroads in the eleventh century—the great war at the end of antiquity in the Middle East passed unnoticed and unremarked.

Neither belligerent, though, could forget.

In the Roman successor state, Byzantium, small, wiry, pugnacious, and geared to a guerrilla war of defence, the feats of the great warrior-emperor were remembered and passed on from historian to historian with relatively little garbling. With a single notable exception in the first half of the ninth century (George the Monk), the standards observed in their working lives—most were members of the governing apparatus—were maintained when they looked into the past and set about combining what they could find into versions of their own.[1] But they were hampered, because most of the sources used in this book were unavailable to them. The *Chronicon Paschale* survives in a single Vatican manuscript.[2] Only Theophanes, the tenth-century compiler of a great antiquarian encyclopedia, the *Suda*, and Michael Psellus in the eleventh century seem to have had access to the secular poems of George of Pisidia.[3] As for the histories written in Armenian (invaluable) and Syriac (useful), with a single exception—the lost work of Theophilus of Edessa, which reached Theophanes in an extended Greek translation—the flow was all one way, from Byzantium to what was regarded as its cultural dependencies. So Byzantine historians were left to cut and sew together what they found in the texts of Theophanes and Nicephorus into patchworks of their own. They might give extensive summaries, as did the retired judge George Cedrenus in the early twelfth century and his younger contemporary John Zonaras, another judge who fell out of favour and withdrew to a monastery on the island of St Glyceria in the Sea of Marmara.[4] Or—to cite two more twelfth-century examples—they might be ready to abridge what they read so as to make space for celestial commentary on terrestrial events (in the form of natural disasters) in the case of Michael Glycas, or to home in on two central episodes, Heraclius' invasion and devastation of Persia (which forces *Khusro* to

---

[1] J. Howard-Johnston, *Historical Writing in Byzantium* (Heidelberg, 2014).
[2] G. Mercati, 'A Study of the *Paschal Chronicle*', *JTS* 7 (1905–6), 397–412.
[3] Howard-Johnston, *Witnesses*, 16–27.
[4] Georgius Cedrenus, *Compendium historiarum*, ed. I. Bekker, 2 vols., CSHB (Bonn, 1838–9), I, 712–36; *Ioannis Zonarae epitome historiarum*, xiv.14–16, ed. L. Dindorf, 6 vols. (Leipzig, 1868–75), III, 303–10.

return home) and the Avar siege of Constantinople, in the case of the succinct universal history in verse written by Constantine Manasses.[5]

The *Khwadaynamag* transmitted a rather more shapely version of the past to later generations in the Iranian world. This is to be found in the greatest of Arab universal histories, the *Annals* of al-Tabari (from Tabaristan, d. 923), in an early example of Persianizing history written by al-Dinawari (d. c. 895), and in the *Shahname*, the great verse historical epic completed by Firdawsi in the early eleventh century, which covers the whole past of Iran, legendary and historical, from the beginning of time to the death of Yazdgerd III and the end of the Sasanian Empire in 652.[6] While it did not neglect Khusro's Roman war and its disastrous end, the *Khwadaynamag* was mainly concerned with the internal troubles of the Sasanian Empire, first and foremost the civil war occasioned by the seizure of the throne by a non-Sasanian, the great general Bahram Chobin. A great deal of space is devoted to the ousting of Khusro, the young legitimate ruler, to the battle of words between him and Bahram Chobin, and to his ultimately successful campaign to recover his ancestral throne.[7] There follows Khusro's estrangement from his maternal uncles, the execution of one and the rebellion of the other, Bistam, who holds out for many years in his Elburz stronghold.[8] Victorious, his kingdom reunited and pacified, Khusro can then be portrayed as a great world ruler held in high regard by his subjects, respected by his neighbours, and in command of enormous wealth. The chief effect of the war with the Romans is to turn him into a harsh, demanding despot who alienates his subjects and their leaders by his extortionate taxation and high-handed behaviour. The putsch which deposes him is described and followed by a long trial scene in which a series of charges is laid against him and he attempts to rebut them one by one.[9] The war is there in the background. Khusro's two great generals, Shahrbaraz and Shahen, are named, along with Rahzadh. The suborning of Shahrbaraz by Heraclius—the most fanciful product of Roman propaganda—helps to explain Khusro's defeat.[10] But it is the giant figure of Khusro which stalks across the pages, and it is his confrontations with his internal adversaries which provide the drama.

The central episode in the history of humanity for Muslim historians was, of course, Muhammad's first revelation, his subsequent speech and action as leader of a nascent community of believers, and those of his utterances which came direct from God and formed the suras of the Qur'an. The *hijra*, the emigration of that small band of true believers from their native city of Mecca to Medina, itself the prelude to the beginning of the armed struggle to impose the faith on Mecca, marked the start of a new historical era. The main subjects for Muslim historians were the *sira*, the biography of the Prophet, the *futuh*, the conquests which were the working out of God's will on earth, the *fitna*, the two early fissures in the Muslim community which led to civil war (656–61, 682–92), and the subsequent history of the Caliphate, initially under the Marwanid and Abbasid dynasties. But Muhammad's prophethood needed a context. The past history of mankind had to be sketched in if events following the third and final divine revelation were to make sense. What was put together by the earliest compilers at work on what became canonical history

---

[5] *Michaelis Glycae annales*, ed. I. Bekker, CSHB (Bonn, 1836), 511.18–513.2; *Constantini Manassis breviarium chronicum*, ed. O. Lampsidis, CFHB 36.1 (Athen, 1996), lines 3632–792.

[6] H. Kennedy, ed., *Al-Tabari: A Medieval Historian and his Work* (Princeton, NJ, 2008); Bonner, *Al-Dinawari*; Howard-Johnston, *Witnesses*, 341–53.

[7] Tab., 993–1001; Bonner, *Al-Dinawari*, 117–24, 135–6; J. Mohl, trans., *Le Livre des rois par Abou'lkasim Firdousi*, 7 vols. (Paris, 1876–8), VII, 1–203.

[8] Bonner, *Al-Dinawari*, 124–8, 136; Mohl, *Firdousi*, VII, 203–12.

[9] Tab., 1041–60; Mohl, *Firdousi*, VII, 267–321.

[10] Tab., 1001–9.

drew on the recorded pasts of the three most relevant peoples—the Sasanian past as transmitted by the *Khwadaynamag*, the story of the people privileged to receive God's first revelation as it was told in the Old Testament, and fragments of south Arabian history.[11] The Romans, the main recipients of the second revelation, remained bit-part players, featuring primarily as the Sasanians' adversaries, but they could not but loom large at the end of pre-Islamic antiquity. Heraclius was viewed as the pre-eminent political figure in the wider world of the Middle East in the lifetime of the Prophet. As such, he receives a remarkably favourable press. He represents something close to an ideal monarch in Muslim sources—pious, just, magnanimous, courageous, politically shrewd, and wise. He is given the role of recognizing Muhammad's prophethood. He dreams about him and receives a letter from him inviting him (Heraclius) to convert. He takes the letter seriously. He is minded to submit to the new faith but cannot persuade his subjects to follow suit. He tries and fails to persuade the generals and notables to convert. Eventually he refuses to renounce his kingdom.[12]

This carefully constructed portrait of Heraclius could, I suppose, be viewed as having a grain of truth—a memory of Heraclius' earnest striving to unite all monotheists, whether by persuasion in the case of Christian confessions or by coercion in the case of the Jews. Khusro too changed character in the hands of Persian writers and painters in subsequent centuries. The doughty fighter for his throne who subsequently went to war on behalf of his murdered Roman patron and pursued that war to the bitter end is transformed into a young man who catches sight of Shirin as she bathes naked in a stream and falls in love. A similar *coup de foudre* has earlier affected Shirin when she is shown a picture of Khusro. The love story which follows is long and complicated. All sorts of difficulties arise before and after their first meeting. Both characters have rivals. But eventually they meet again and marry. The story is picked up from their second meeting by Firdawsi. The popularity of his poem ensured that it was widely disseminated. Its full elaboration was the work of the poet Nizami, who wrote a 13,000-line epic *Khusro and Shirin* at the end of the twelfth century. Nizami, whose poem survives in *over 250 manuscripts*, joined Firdawsi in the broadcasting of the romantic tale, which became one of the most popular motifs in Persian and Moghul miniatures.[13]

The effort put into transmuting and disseminating the images of the two great antagonists, Heraclius and Khusro, may perhaps be taken as evidence of a recognition, only half-conscious, of the importance of the struggle between them on the part of the Iranian and wider Islamic worlds. Latin Christendom, as we have seen, was not unaware of the war and its two chief figures at the time. But there too reality was refashioned with time. Instead of love, the True Cross was put at the centre of the story. Khusro became the predator who attacked Jerusalem and carried off the Cross to Ctesiphon, Heraclius the champion, a proto-Crusader, who recovered the Cross and restored it to its proper place on Golgotha. It seems to have been in the west towards the middle of the eighth century that a key episode in the story, the miracle of the Golden Gate, was first described (Heraclius being barred entry to the Temple Mount until he dismounts and sheds his imperial robes). It was picked up and spread in the ninth century by a homily of Hrabranus Maurus (*c.* 776–856), the

---

[11] C. F. Robinson, *Islamic Historiography* (Cambridge, 2003).
[12] N.M. El Cheikh, *Byzantium Viewed by the Arabs* (Cambridge, Mass., 2004), 39–54.
[13] Mohl, *Firdousi*, VII, 240–7; D. Davis., *Sunset of Empire: Stories from the Shahnameh of Firdowsi III* (Washington DC, 2004), 461–88 and (illustrations) 536–7, 539–40, 546, 549; L. Binyon, *The Poems of Nizami* (London, 1928); O. Grabar, *Mostly Miniatures: An Introduction to Persian Painting* (Princeton, NJ, 2000), 45–9, 56–9, 100–111. Cf. W. Baum, *Shirin Christian-Queen-Myth of Love: Historical Reality and Literary Effect* (Piscataway, NJ, 2004), 1–4, 63–83.

Abbot of Fulda and later Archbishop of Mainz, and numerous later works, notably the verse romances of Gautier of Arras (1159-71) and a German contemporary (Otto). But the real boost to the popularity of the legend of the Cross was given by the *Legenda aurea*, a large compendium of miracle stories written between 1261 and 1266 by the Dominican Jacobus de Voragine of which there are *over 800 manuscripts*. He included separate narratives about the Finding and the Exaltation of the Cross, the first describing the search carried out by Helena, the mother of Constantine the Great, with the help of a Jew whose family had kept the secret of its burial down the generations, the second its capture and deportation by Khusro II, who kept it in a fairy-tale tower (made of gold and silver, its interior decorated with jewel-framed images of the sun, moon and stars and watered by artificial rain), Heraclius' war against the Persians, which culminated in a battle on a bridge over the *Danube*, the beheading of Khusro by Heraclius, the baptism of his young son, and the Golden Gate miracle. The *Legenda aurea* spread the story through France, England, the Netherlands, Germany, and Scandinavia.[14]

Artists of many sorts and in many places picked it up. It was depicted in manuscripts (the earliest being the Sacramentary of Mont St Michel of 1066), on altarpieces (notably that of the Hospitalers in Tempziner, Prussia (1411), the Memminger triptych in the church of St Lorenz, Nuremberg (*c.* 1485), and the Nonnenaltar of Rostock (*c.* 1500)) (Figure 31), stained glass windows (as in the City Church of Lübeck, largely destroyed in an air raid in 1942, and the central window in the choir of St Lorenz, Nuremberg) and in monumental frescoes. Agnolo Gaddi combined the story of the discovery and later recovery of the Cross with another legend which established a direct link between the wood of the Cross and the Tree of Life in the Garden of Eden in the cycle which he painted in the chancel of Santa Croce, Florence (1388-93). The grandest depiction, though, was Piero della Francesca's in the church of St Francis at Arezzo (painted 1452-66), which highlights the roles of the Emperor Constantine, who, asleep in his tent, dreams of the Cross before the Battle of the Milvian Bridge, of his mother Helena, who finds it after torturing the Jew with the secret (who was kept at the bottom of a dry well for a week), and of the Emperor Heraclius. For Piero, Heraclius the warrior-emperor overshadows the humbled ruler who brings the Cross back to Jerusalem in the final scene. He wins the Battle of Nineveh and then receives the submission of Khusro, who kneels before his throne (Figure 32).[15]

Much more can be said about the afterlife of the last great war, Khusro, and Heraclius in the medieval West.[16] But the story does not end with the Middle Ages. For an even more fanciful confection was produced in 1647 by the fine playwright Pierre Corneille.[17] Apart from the setting, Constantinople, the war being fought with Persia, the sequence of Roman emperors (Maurice, Phocas, Heraclius), and a small historical nugget (the attempt by the nurse looking after Maurice's sons to substitute her own for Maurice's youngest, before he was killed), *Héraclius* is the creation of Corneille. Heraclius is Maurice's son (the nurse's subterfuge worked), but has been substituted for Phocas' son, Martian, while Phocas was

---

[14] L. Kretzenbacher, *Kreuzholzlegenden zwischen Byzanz und dem Abendlande: Byzantinisch-griechische Kreuzholzlegenden vor und um Basileios Herakleios und ihr Fortleben im lateinischen Westen bis zum Zweiten Vaticanum*, Bayer. Ak. Wiss., Phil.-hist. Kl., Sitzungsberichte 1995, no.3 (Munich, 1995), 34-58; B. Baert, *A Heritage of Holy Wood: The Legend of the True Cross in Text and Image* (Leiden, 2004), 194-210.

[15] F. Schlie, ed., *Die Kunst- und Geschichts-Denkmäler des Grossherzogthums Mecklenburg-Schwerin*, I (Schwerin, 1896), 184-6; Kretzenbacher, *Kreuzholzlegenden*, 68-77; Baert, *Heritage of Holy Wood*, 144-9, 216-47, 263-77, 350-71, 392-3, 399-400.

[16] See the doctoral thesis (nearing completion at Tübingen) of Anastasia Sirotenko, 'The Image of the Emperor Heraclius in the Works of Medieval Authors'.

[17] C. J. Marty-Laveaux, ed., *Œuvres de Pierre Corneille*, 12 vols. (Paris, 1862-8), V, 156-241.

away fighting the Persians for three years. Martian has become the nurse's son, Leontius. Martian is in love with Maurice's daughter Pulcheria, Heraclius with the nurse's daughter Eudoxia. The play's themes are power and incest. The action takes the form of a stately minuet as the main characters confront and berate each other—Pulcheria refusing to unite the legitimate with the usurping dynasty by marrying Phocas' putative son, Heraclius (Act 1), Heraclius and Martian, who have both been told that they are Maurice's surviving son, reluctant to kill Phocas because it will look like parricide or will be dishonourable (Act 2), renunciation of their incestuous love by Martian and Pulcheria, the latter now agreeing to marry Heraclius (her brother in reality) (Act 3), Phocas at a loss as to which of the two young men claiming to be Maurice's son to execute (Act 4), denouement thanks to a note left by Maurice's widow Constantine, who has recently died, and overthrow of Phocas by the crowd assembled to watch the public execution of Heraclius.

Corneille's *Héraclius* is a gripping play. It would make a fine opera. But it has very little to do with historical reality as it may be retrieved from the full range of written and material evidence. Corneille, though, was right about the virtues of Heraclius, whom Phocas praises to Pulcheria in the first act:

Tant de vertus qu'en lui le monde entier admire
Ne l'ont-elles pas fait trop digne de l'empire?
En ai-je eu quelque espoir qu'il n'aye assez rempli?
Et voit-on sous le ciel prince plus accompli?...[18]

---

[18] Marty-Laveaux, *Corneille*, 164–5.

APPENDIX 1

Dramatis Personae

Sasanian Empire. The great continental power of western Eurasia, with territory stretching from the Indus and Oxus rivers in the east to Mesopotamia and Transcaucasia in the west. Two core regions: (1) highland Iran bounded by the great mountain chains of the Elburz in the north and the Zagros in the south, and (2) the fertile, irrigated lowlands of Mesopotamia below the Zagros, Iran being the military and cultural heartland of the empire, Mesopotamia its most urbanized and commercially active component. Commercially dominant in the Indian Ocean. Held together by specialized branches of a complex, tiered governmental system, and by a deep-embedded sense of *Eranshahr* as the divinely sanctioned earthly protagonist of the good. Capital: the twin cities of Ctesiphon and Veh-Ardashir on opposite banks of the Tigris, provisioned from their immediate hinterlands (the Diyala plains and central alluvium) and virtually impregnable once the Nahrawan/Cut of Khusro canal was constructed in the sixth century on the left bank of the Tigris. Army: perhaps 300,000 strong, divided between (1) frontier forces manning the long walls flanking the Caspian Sea and major hard-point bases elsewhere, and (2) field armies under the command of four *spahbeds* (corresponding to the four points of the compass). Religiously pluralist: Zoroastrianism, the established faith of the governing elite, its rites vital to the welfare of crown and empire, dominant on the Iranian plateau; Judaism, with the main concentration of population and rabbis in Babylonia; rival Nestorian and Monophysite Christian confessions, the former well rooted in Mesopotamia, the latter dominant in Transcaucasia and spreading in Mesopotamia; Buddhism, centred on Bactria in the east. Governing principle—lineage: rule by the Sasanian dynasty in partnership with a hereditary aristocracy; legal system geared to the perpetuation of descent; stability of social order assured by inheritance of status and function. King of Kings (*shahanshah*): Khusro II Parvez, born in 570s, crowned as teenager in mid/late summer 590, forced to flee west by rebel Bahram Chobin, reinstalled with Roman military backing in 591.

Roman Empire. The second established great power of western Eurasia: centring on the eastern Mediterranean, with its main resource bases in Egypt, North Africa, the Levant, and Asia Minor; much frayed in the west after the invasions of Franks, Visigoths, Ostrogoths, and Lombards in the fifth and sixth centuries. Highly urbanized, cities and their territories being basic units of government, and city notables collectively forming a counterweight to provincial authorities in the localities. Held together by a ramified administrative system and a conviction of the superiority of Roman civilization (reinforced after the establishment of Christianity under Constantine); key links between centre and periphery—*honorati*, retired civil servants of senatorial status living in their home cities. Industry and commerce well developed, manufactured goods and natural produce being traded around the inland sea, and exported farther afield. Capital: Constantinople, well placed for managing the Mediterranean world but exposed to attack on its promontory and dependent on grain supplies from across the Mediterranean—hence the requirement for strategically located naval forces in late antiquity. Army: commensurate in size with the Sasanian army and likewise divided between frontier and field forces, the former concentrated in fewer bases than in the past and operating in conjunction with city militias, the latter under the command of two exarchs (Africa, Italy) and six *magistri militum* (Illyricum, Thrace, Praesentales (2), Armenia, and Oriens). A single established faith—Christianity as formulated at the Council of Chalcedon (451); Judaism tolerated but subject to controls; repression of deviant Christian confessions and paganism. Lineage and gradations of status important, but more meritocracy than in Sasanian Empire, with respect to monarchy, court, command, and administration—monarchy taking the form of a constitutionally coated military dictatorship. Emperors: Maurice (582–602), ex-general, nominated by his predecessor Tiberius II (578–82); Phocas (602–10), general serving in Balkans, carried to power by mutinous Danube army; Heraclius (610–41), born in 570s, son of one of Maurice's second-rank generals who was appointed governor (exarch) of Africa by Phocas.

Turkish Khaganate. Newcomer among the great powers, in command of the whole sweep of the Eurasian steppes from the river Liao in Manchuria to the hinterland of the Crimea by the 570s. Rise: successful rebellion against Rouran on inner Asian frontiers of China, 546–52; expansion west culminating in destruction of Hephthalite state (with Sasanian support) and annexation of Transoxiana *c.* 563; diplomatic heyday in 560s, playing off rival Northern Zhou and Northern Qi states against each other in the east, and doing the same with Sasanian and Roman empires in the west. Increasing independence of western and eastern wings from 582; western Khagan, Tardu, pre-eminent around 600. A nomadic confederacy incorporating the mercantile elites of Sogdian cities as partners in a joint imperial project. Capitals: in Orkhon valley and on northern flank of Tianshan range. Key characteristics: grand ideology of universal rule; formidable fighting strength of ruling and client nomadic peoples; promotion of Sogdian-managed overland trade between north and south and along the transcontinental routes linking China to the west.

Arabs. No longer politically marginal to the civilized world in the sixth century, with Romans and Persians projecting power and influence deep into the peninsula through rival nexuses of clients in the north and competing for control of Yemen in the south. Long-distance overland trade between South Arabia, the Levant, and Mesopotamia at its acme, the leading role being played by Mecca and other towns in the Hijaz. Nomadic Beduin society pulverized since time immemorial into small extended family groups, but susceptible to political management from above, as shown in the brief heyday of Palmyra (260–72) and in the zones of Roman and Persian control. Cultural centre: the Nasrid court at Hira, capital of the Persians' Lakhm client kingdom. After the definitive Persian conquest of Yemen in 571, only the Hijaz lay beyond the reach of the great powers. Key figure: Muhammad, born in the 570s like Khusro and Heraclius.

Avar Khaganate. A second new nomadic power formed by a people fleeing west from the Turks, probably a remnant of the defeated Rouran. Welcomed initially by the Romans and designated their chief client in the north. Established authority over variegated peoples of east-central Europe, nomadic (e.g. Bulgars) and sedentary (e.g. Gepids and Slavs), with heartland in the Carpathian basin. Lost hard-fought war against Romans, 582–99.

Minor players: Albanians, Iberians, Laz, Abasgians, and Armenians (Transcaucasia); Slavs (Balkans); Lombards (Italy); Visigoths (Spain); Berbers (North Africa).

Bibliography

(1) Sasanian Empire: M. Boyce, *Zoroastrians: Their Religious Beliefs and Practices* (London, 1979); S. Corcoran, 'Observations on the Sasanian Law-Book in the Light of Roman Legal Writing', in A. Rio, ed., *Law, Custom, and Justice in Late Antiquity and the Early*

Middle Ages (London, 2011), 77–113; V. S. Curtis and S. Stewart, eds., *The Idea of Iran,* III *The Sasanian Era* (London, 2008); T. Daryaee, *Sasanian Persia: The Rise and Fall of an Empire* (London, 2009); R. Gyselen, *La Géographie administrative de l'empire sassanide: Les Témoignages épigraphiques en moyen-perse,* Res Orientales 25 (Bures-sur-Yvette, 2019); G. Herrmann, *The Iranian Revival* (Oxford, 1977); J. Howard-Johnston, 'The Two Great Powers in Late Antiquity: A Comparison', in A. Cameron, ed., *The Byzantine and Early Islamic Near East,* III *States, Resources and Armies* (Princeton, NJ, 1995), 157–226, repr. in J. Howard-Johnston, *East Rome, Sasanian Persia and the End of Antiquity: Historiographical and Historical Studies* (Aldershot, 2006), no.I; J. Howard-Johnston, 'The Late Sasanian Army', in T. Bernheimer and A. Silverstein, eds., *Late Antiquity: Eastern Perspectives* (Exeter, 2012), 87–127; R. E. Payne, *A State of Mixture: Christians, Zoroastrians, and Iranian Political Culture in Late Antiquity* (Oakland, CA, 2015); J. Wiesehöfer, *Ancient Persia from 550 BC to 650 AD* (London, 1996), cc.9–11.

(2) Roman Empire: P. Brown, *The Rise of Western Christendom: Triumph and Diversity AD 200–1000* (Oxford, 1996), cc.1–3, 7; A. Cameron, B. Ward-Perkins, and M. Whitby, eds., *CAH* XIV *Late Antiquity: Empire and Successors, AD 425–600* (Cambridge, 2000); G. Dagron, *Emperor and Priest: The Imperial Office in Byzantium* (Cambridge, 2003), cc.1–2, 4; D. M. Gwynn, ed., *A. H. M. Jones and the Later Roman Empire* (Leiden, 2008); A. H. M. Jones, *The Later Roman Empire, 284–602: A Social, Economic and Administrative Survey,* 3 vols. (Oxford, 1964); S. Kingsley and M. Decker, eds., *Economy and Exchange in the East Mediterranean during Late Antiquity* (Oxford, 2001); J. Meyendorff, *Imperial Unity and Christian Divisions: The Church 450–680 AD* (Crestwood, NY, 1989).

(3) Turkish khaganate: T. J. Barfield, *The Perilous Frontier: Nomadic Empires and China* (Oxford, 1989), c.4; E. de la Vaissière, *Histoire des marchands sogdiens* (Paris, 2002); S. Stark, *Die Alttürkenzeit in Mittel- und Zentralasien: Archäologische und historische Studien* (Wiesbaden, 2008).

(4) Arabs: X. de Planhol, *Les Fondements géographiques de l'histoire de l'Islam* (Paris, 1968), 11–35; R. G. Hoyland, *Arabia and the Arabs from the Bronze Age to the Coming of Islam* (London, 2001).

(5) Avar khaganate: C. Bálint, *Die Archäologie der Steppe: Steppenvölker zwischen Volga und Donau vom 6. bis zum 10. Jahrhundert* (Vienna and Cologne, 1989), 145–92; W. Pohl, *The Avars: A Steppe Empire in Central Europe, 567–822* (Ithaca, NY, 2018); M. Whitby, *The Emperor Maurice and His Historian: Theophylact Simocatta on Persian and Balkan Warfare* (Oxford, 1988), cc.3–6.

(6) Minor players: P. M. Barford, *The Early Slavs: Culture and Society in Early Medieval Eastern Europe* (London, 2001), introd. and cc.1–3; M. Brett and E. Fentress, *The Berbers* (Oxford, 1996), cc.1–2; N. Christie, *The Lombards: The Ancient Longobards* (Oxford, 1995); R. Collins, *Visigothic Spain 409–711* (Oxford, 2004), cc.1–3; R. H. Hewsen, *Armenia: Historical Atlas* (Chicago, 2001), 34–91.

APPENDIX 2
Scene

Middle East around the year 600. The old empires had fought four wars in the sixth century, 502–5, 527–32, 540–62, and 572–91, taking the initiative in turn. The Romans had the advantage in the north in Transcaucasia, the Persians in the south in Arabia. The Persians inflicted more damage (especially in their *annus mirabilis* of 540, when city after city submitted in the Roman Levant and Antioch was captured and sacked), but were in the weaker strategic position, caught between Romans and Turks.[1]

There were two main theatres of war, on either side of the mountain spine formed by the north-west Zagros and its continuation south and the west of Lake Van, the Armenian Taurus. **Transcaucasia** acted as a broad causeway, linking the Iranian plateau to the elevated interior of Asia Minor. There were three main routes available for east-west military movement: (1) over the Kur plain to the difficult mountains separating Iberia (capital Tiflis, modern Tblisi) from the open country of Lazica at the east end of the Black Sea; (2) along a natural corridor up the Araxes valley, over a low watershed, and down the valley of the upper Euphrates to the plain of modern Erzincan where the Roman road veered north and ran west to Satala and beyond; (3) along a second natural corridor running through the plains to the north of Lake Urmia, crossing a pass to the south of Mount Ararat into the upper basin of the river Arsanias (Bagrewand) and running west to a Euphrates crossing near Melitene, either down the river valley or over the uplands on its right bank. The northern segment of the **Fertile Crescent**, between the mountains (Zagros and Armenian Taurus) and the Arabian Desert, was the second theatre of war. It formed an attractive arena for open combat between the armies of developed states operating in orthodox fashion. The only natural features which might be exploited were the isolated hills of Singara (to the south-east of the great city of Nisibis) and the Tur Abdin (on the south side of the upper Tigris basin), and the rivers—the Tigris and its left-bank tributaries, the Euphrates as it described a great curve south of the Armenian Taurus and the Khabur, which ran south from the Tur Abdin to the Euphrates. Operations by large regular forces were confined to three main lateral lines of communication where water was plentiful: (1) up the Tigris valley to Amida and passing north of the Tur Abdin; (2) diverging from the Tigris to run west past Nisibis on the south side of the Tur Abdin; and (3) up the narrow strip of well-watered land alongside the Euphrates.[2]

The frontier between the two powers was stabilized from the 380s, when they agreed on a durable peace and presented a common front to the Huns in the steppes. Transcaucasia was demarcated into two spheres of influence, that of the Persians being much the larger,

---

[1] G. Greatrex and S. N. C. Lieu, *The Roman Eastern Frontier and the Persian Wars, Part II AD 363–630: A Narrative Sourcebook* (London, 2002), cc.5–12; J. Howard-Johnston, 'The Sasanians' Strategic Dilemma', in H. Börm and J. Wiesehöfer, eds., *Commutatio et contentio: Studies in the Late Roman, Sasanian and Early Islamic Near East—In Memory of Zeev Rubin* (Düsseldorf, 2010), 37–70.

[2] Whitby, *Emperor Maurice*, 197–202; J. Howard-Johnston, 'Military Infrastructure in the Roman Provinces North and South of the Armenian Taurus in Late Antiquity', in A. Sarantis and N. Christie, eds., *War and Warfare in Late Antiquity*, Late Antique Archaeology 8, 2 vols. (Leiden, 2013), II, 853–91, at 856–61.

comprising Albania, Iberia, and four-fifths of Armenia (up to the Araxes-Euphrates watershed and the plain of Taron, well to the west of Bagrewand). South of the Armenian Taurus, the frontier cut across the basin of the upper Tigris, leaving Amida as the outermost Roman city, skirted the Tur Abdin (Roman), and passed close to Nisibis (Persian) to reach the Euphrates just below Circesium (Roman). It was a thoroughly artificial frontier for most of its length, cutting across both natural corridors over the Armenian highlands and the open plains of the south, and partitioning culturally homogeneous regions into distinct Persian and Roman sectors.[3] It was not fortified in the north until the sixth century, both sides relying mainly on client Armenian leaders to secure the approaches to their own territory, but defensive systems were developed in the south in the course of a century-long arms race and were elaborated when the arms race resumed in the sixth century (new forward bases were constructed on the Roman side of the frontier and the Tur Abdin was turned into a highland redoubt). They effectually congealed the frontier in the Fertile Crescent, creating a formidable manmade barrier and thereby underpinning the peace (the prospect of gain from warfare being much reduced). The only natural divides between the empires lay in the extreme south—the hot desert which separated the metropolitan region of lower Mesopotamia from the prosperous swathe of territory fronting the Mediterranean in southern Syria and Palestine—and the far north—the mountains separating Iberia from Roman Lazica.

Cities close to the frontier—Nisibis, Amida, Dara (a new fortress built right on the frontier after the opening bout of sixth-century warfare), Chlomaron, Martyropolis, Dvin, Theodosiopolis, Tiflis—doubled as military bases. They were fronted or backed by networks of outlier forts—attested in Arzanene and behind Nisibis in the Persian case, in the uplands and valley of the Arsanias in south-west Armenia, the Tur Abdin, and elsewhere on Roman territory—and other fortified cities in zones of deep defence to their rear. The tiered nature of defence is best exemplified along the course of the Euphrates on both sides of the frontier. Waterways provided inner lines of defence: the Euphrates together with the Nahrmalcha and Nahrawan canals around the binary Sasanian capital, with the main left-bank tributaries of the Tigris acting as outer defences; the Euphrates fronting eastern Asia Minor and northern Syria as it cuts its way south across the grain of the mountains on Roman territory and sweeps round behind the frontier zone in Osrhoene and northern Mesopotamia. Not that no precautions were taken farther into the interior. Cities and towns were fortified, and passes were defended. The Romans went so far as to develop networks of fortified centres in eastern Asia Minor after a devastating Hunnic raid in the 515.

The basic principles underlying the frontier defences were the same on both sides: forward orientation, deep defensive zones, concentration of force, and good communications for rapid deployment. Forward orientation is more marked on the Roman side: after the completion of Anastasius' fortification programme in the early years of Justinian's reign, a line of forward bases ran from Palmyra and Circesium in the south to Dara and Martyropolis in northern Mesopotamia and on to Citharizon, Artaleson, and Horonon in Armenia. The Sasanians achieved rather greater concentration of force, relying for forward defence on one major hard-point base in the south—Nisibis, which commanded all three invasion routes from its position in the lee of the eastern Tur Abdin—and another, Dvin, in a large plain on the Araxes immediately to the north-east of Mount Ararat, within striking distance of Bagrewand (the plain drained by the headwaters of the Arsanias) and the

---

[3] Whitby, *Emperor Maurice*, 202–9; R. C. Blockley, *East Roman Foreign Policy: Formation and Conduct from Diocletian to Anastasius* (Leeds, 1992), 42–5, 47–52, 54–9, 60–2.

open country to the north of Lake Urmia. The Romans preferred to have more than one such base. Thus, Dara was backed by Constantia and Theodosiopolis (formerly Resaena), Melitene by Caesarea, and Armenian Theodosiopolis by Satala and Nicopolis. Natural features were exploited by both sides in the north—troops garrisoning Tiflis watched over the passes from Lazica, while Tzanica was turned into a second Roman highland redoubt— and in the far south—a line of forts backed by water defences (principally the Euphrates) secured Persian lower Mesopotamia from desert raiding, while a screen of forts along the Khabur and the fortified cities on the Euphrates performed the same function for Roman north Mesopotamia.[4]

The Romans' principal weakness was to be found far to the rear of the frontier zone on the western margin of the desert. Apart from the Jebel Druze and the adjoining Leja *harra* (lava desert), there was no natural obstacle barring the way to Arab raiders, or indeed to a Persian force bold enough to strike out across the desert from the Euphrates in the vicinity of Anathon, the outermost Persian base. The Romans had to rely on (1) Arab clients no longer managed by a higher supratribal Arab authority (the Ghassan nexus of alliances having been dissolved, for good cause, in the course of the 573-91 war), (2) troops stationed in a few widely separated military bases, and (3) the militias of the towns which had grown up in the *badiya*, the relatively fertile fringe of the desert.[5] The Persian sector of Transcaucasia was left even more exposed by the terms of the agreement negotiated in 590 between the Emperor Maurice and Khusro II, who had fled from the rebel forces of Bahram Chobin and sought asylum with the Romans, substantial territorial concessions being offered in return for Roman political and military support for the recovery of his throne. The Roman frontier advanced east, dangerously close to Tiflis and Dvin, the regional capitals of Iberia and Persarmenia. Farther south, the full length of the Armenian Taurus as far as the contorted mountains of modern Kurdistan to the east and south of Lake Van was taken over by the Romans, which left all three militarily feasible north-south passes in Roman hands and gave Roman forces the significant strategic advantage of inner lines in moving troops between theatres of war.[6]

---

[4] Howard-Johnston, 'Late Sasanian Army', 96–100, 104–8, and 'Military Infrastructure', 861–86.
[5] C. Foss, 'Syria in Transition, A.D. 550–750: An Archaeological Approach', *DOP* 51 (1997), 189–269.
[6] R. W. Thomson and J. Howard-Johnston, *The Armenian History Attributed to Sebeos*, TTH 31, 2 vols. (Liverpool, 1999), II *Historical Commentary*, 170–3 (nn.10–11).

APPENDIX 3

Sources

A connected history of the last great war of antiquity can be pieced together out of the sources which have survived. Information is scantiest for the period following the episode which caught the headlines more than any other, the sack of Jerusalem in 614. Apart from a subsequent vain attempt by the Roman Senate to secure peace on almost any terms in winter 615-16, the coverage is minimal. But a few Persian actions can be glimpsed, and, with a fair amount of conjecture, it is possible to see what use they made of the years 616-21, when they had a free hand and could reshape the Middle East as they chose. As for the first phase of the war, 603-10, the first half of the second (610-15) and the third (622-30), material, some of it of a very high quality, is to be found in Greek, Armenian, and Syrian sources. Distant observers also took an interest in the great struggle in the Middle East. It has left its mark on works written in Latin Christendom—the brief universal history compiled by Isidore, the Bishop of Seville, the chronicle written by Fredegar and his continuator, and Paul the Deacon's history of the Lombards written a century later.[1] News from the north undoubtedly reverberated round the Arab world too, helping to intensify the mood of apocalyptic alarm so evident in the earliest suras of the Qur'an.

The surviving material is very much skewed in favour of the Romans, since the only contemporary Persian account in the officially sponsored *Khwadaynamag* is episodic and, in the form transmitted to us by later Muslim writers, notably al-Dinawari, al-Tabari, and Firdawsi, skips lightly over the whole war. Instead, we have to turn to Armenian and east Syrian sources which were written on Sasanian territory. They pick up bits and pieces of information, some of it official and taken from government communiqués, most unofficial and circulating probably by word of mouth. The Persians themselves could be observed from close quarters once they had taken over whole Roman provinces. Local sources written in Palestine and Egypt are informative. One stands out—the biography of a retired Persian cavalryman who converted to Christianity, joined a monastery in Jerusalem, and, at the end of the war, strove to emulate the earliest Christian heroes and to achieve martyrdom.[2] More might be expected of a local history of Egypt written by John, the Bishop of Nikiu, in the second half of the seventh century, which survives in the form of a seventeenth-century translation of an early Arabic translation of the Coptic original. But, alas, it gives out suddenly at the end of a detailed account of the takeover of Egypt by North African rebels and the expulsion of loyalist forces sent in by the reigning emperor. Papyri, both Greek and Pahlavi, compensate to some extent for this silence, but they only

---

[1] *Continuationes Isidorianae Byzantia Arabica et Hispana*, ed. T. Mommsen, MGH Auct. Ant. XI, Chron. Min. II (Berlin, 1894), 334-68; J. M. Wallace-Hadrill, ed. and trans., *The Fourth Book of the Chronicle of Fredegar* (London, 1960), 51-4 (cc.63-5); *Pauli historia Langobardorum*, iv.36, ed. L. Bethmann and G. Waitz, MGH, Scriptores rerum Langobardicarum et Italicarum saec. VI–IX (Hanover, 1878), 12-187, trans. W. D. Foulke, *Paul the Deacon, History of the Lombards* (Philadelphia, PA, 1907), trans. F. Bougard, *Paul Diacre, Histoire des Lombards* (Turnhout, 1994).

[2] *Vita S. Anastasii*, ed. and trans. B. Flusin, *Saint Anastase le Perse et l'histoire de la Palestine au début du VIIe siècle*, 2 vols. (Paris, 1992), I, 40-91. Cf. Howard-Johnston, *Witnesses*, 169-71.

cast fitful light on some aspects of the occupation regime after the Persian conquest in 619–20.[3]

The quality of much of the material which has survived is remarkably high. The paradoxical reason for this is that classical standards of historical writing were slipping. Less trouble was taken over outward appearances. History was ceasing to be a branch of literature. Rather than being preoccupied with the reworking of raw materials into a smooth, homogeneous whole finished with a veneer of fine writing, historians strove to examine as carefully as possible the data which they could gather about the recent and not so recent past and to see what sense they could make of it. Contemporaries were aware that they were living through strange, troubling times. Muhammad was not alone in sensing that the last days were at hand. Entertainment of the reader, virtuoso displays of rhetoric or erudition, and elegant passages of conventional moralizing gave way to historical truth. The example of church historians, who acted, in effect, as advocates for their confessions, became more influential. Assertions had to be backed by evidence. Key documents were worth quoting in full. Only through careful forensic examination of the phenomena might something of God's providential plan for mankind be discerned.[4]

Classicizing history was still being written—by Theophylact Simocatta, for example, a high-flying lawyer, who wrote a history of the reign of the Emperor Maurice (582–602) in the 620s, as the war approached its denouement. Simocatta prized classical diction and strove to maintain an elevated, if sometimes convoluted style. He included speeches of his own composition (put into the mouths of key figures) and occasional digressions, devices traditionally used to embellish and enliven history. But the literary patina is no longer so thick as to prevent the keen reader from discerning the outlines of a number of contributory sources—notably, a laudatory account of Maurice's rule and sets of campaign narratives which were subsequently written up to promote the careers of two leading generals. He was also ready to incorporate verbatim the texts of important documents, as well as one short, halting speech (the abdication speech of Justin II (567–78)).[5]

Two near contemporaries joined Simocatta in upholding traditional standards, Theodore Syncellus, a high-ranking patriarchal official responsible for liaison between the spiritual and temporal powers in Constantinople, and George of Pisidia, who likewise rose high in patriarchal service but deserves to be known above all as a poet. Two formal speeches of Theodore's are extant, both delivered on grand ceremonial occasions and couched in rich, sonorous prose, full of biblical and other references. They commemorate two Avar attacks on the capital, an opportunistic raid in 623 which led to the sacking of the Church of the Mother of God at Blachernae, and the ten-day siege of the city in 626, which ended in failure (attributed in large part to divine intervention). The historical narrative which forms the core of each speech is accompanied by much celebratory rhetoric.[6] George of Pisidia was a much finer writer than either Simocatta or Theodore. He demon-

---

[3] John of Nikiu, ed. and trans. H. Zotenberg, *Chronique de Jean, évêque de Nikiou* (Paris, 1883). Cf. Howard-Johnston, *Witnesses*, 181–9.

[4] Howard-Johnston, *Witnesses*, 420–34.

[5] Theophylactus Simocatta, *Historiae*, ed. C. de Boor, rev. P. Wirth (Stuttgart, 1972), trans. M. Whitby and M. Whitby, *The History of Theophylact Simocatta* (Oxford, 1986). Cf. Whitby, *Emperor Maurice*.

[6] Theodorus Syncellus, *Homily* I, ed. L. Sternbach, *Analecta Avarica*, Rozprawy Akademii Umiejętności, Wydział Filologiczny, ser.2, 15 (Cracow, 1900), 298–320; *Homily* II, ed. C. Loparev, 'Staroe Svidetelstvo o Polozhenii rizy Bogorodnitsy vo Vlakherniakh…', *Viz.Vrem.* 2 (1895), 581–628, at 592–612, trans. Averil Cameron, 'The Virgin's Robe: An Episode in the History of Early Seventh-Century Constantinople', *Byz.* 49 (1979), 42–56, repr. in Cameron, *Continuity and Change in Sixth-Century Byzantium* (London, 1981), no.XVII, at 48–56.

strates this neatly and conclusively in poems about the 626 Avar siege—in which the images introduced by Theodore in his speech are neatly capped—and in his poems about Heraclius' achievements in the war, for which he finds parallels of many sorts in biblical and classical history, in contrast to Simocatta's single past reference to Alexander the Great. His secular subjects include Heraclius' seizure of power in 610, the military exercises and operations which took place under his command in 622, the great siege of 626, the fall of Khusro in 628, and Heraclius' restoration of the fragments of the True Cross to Jerusalem in March 630. He wrote poetry of many other sorts besides these celebratory works—epigrams, playful pieces, an earnest polemic against the most renowned of Monophysite theologians, Severus of Antioch, a rueful reflection on the vanity of worldly ambition, and a great celebration of the wonders of Creation. He was an adept of the ingenious, long-drawn-out conceit, and was most at home when writing reflective, devotional verse.[7]

All three of these classicizing writers belonged to the governing elite. All were known to the emperor and enjoyed his favour, although there was a hiatus of several years in the case of George (after an injudicious offhand remark caused grave offence). Imperial favour took the form of literary commissions in the cases of Theodore and George, of promotion for Simocatta. Between them, Simocatta, Theodore, and George, each in his own way, allow us to tiptoe into the court, to breathe the atmosphere of the times, and to catch some of the ideas in circulation. Each, of course, had his own particular views which influenced what he picked up and how he expressed it—George, for example, taking a much more hawkish line at the end of the war than Simocatta. But the collective contribution which they, as insiders, make to our understanding is as vital as the information which they convey.[8]

Information about the past comes mainly from observation of *events* by human beings, both individually and collectively—what classicists like to term *autopsy*. This is to be distinguished from scholarly scrutiny of *things*, material remains of the past which have survived into the present—inscriptions, coins, precious and mundane objects (especially ceramics), buildings, and infrastructure. But observations, like the sense data of which they are composed, have to be arranged within some sort of conceptual framework if they are to be understood. Beams of raw data would merely bombard and bewilder the mind. Similarly, the more numerous the first-hand witnesses of events, the more confusing would be the aggregated information gathered if it were not sifted, collated, organized, and interpreted. The observations of a single witness, on the other hand, may make sense but they suffer from the limitations of individual perception, and any narrative built out of them and subsequently transmitted, orally or in writing, is biased because of the vagaries of memory and personal disposition. It follows that the most useful and reliable evidence for a historian is a set of observations based on direct experience which have been arranged in an intelligible pattern by a *competent authority*, itself close to the phenomena covered and familiar with the context. The arrangement and recording of the resulting narrative should be completed soon after the event. For the longer the gap between observation and inscription as narrative on the mind or in writing, the greater the deviation to be expected between actual and recorded experience.

The few historians currently at work on the early seventh century have predecessors in centuries past, right back to those who lived through the great war. The present being a mere point moving through time, contemporaries had to operate as historians if they were to make sense of the world around them. This mattered most for those in positions of power—Roman emperor and Persian king, army commanders and diplomats, all the variegated elements in the governing apparatus of each empire, especially the court at the

---

[7] L. Tartaglia, ed. and trans., *Carmi di Giorgio di Pisidia* (Turin, 1998).
[8] Howard-Johnston, *Witnesses*, 16–35, 142–8.

centre and administrative cadres in the provinces. Governments had to gather reliable information about conditions in the provinces and about the progress of operations in the field. Similarly, those on the periphery, both civilian and military, needed to know what was going at the centre. This absolutely fundamental need for reassurance could only be met through exchange of information between centre and periphery taking the form of the dispatch of regular reports in both directions. Where it was feasible—and it was feasible for both imperial powers with their ramified literate bureaucracies—those reports had to be made in writing. Much more information can be transmitted with far greater accuracy in writing than orally. So the latter-day historian should be alert for any traces left in extant sources of the many official reports written at the time—dispatches from generals in the field or from the ruler himself when he took charge of operations, diplomatic messages exchanged between the great powers, and official news releases designed to keep officialdom and the population at large informed of current events and to discourage the circulation of damaging rumours. It should be recognized that news management was crucial to the whole process of government and that the debris of this mass of communications may still be detectable in the texts which have come down to us.

Ancient historians seldom refer to the written records (*hypomnemata*), whether official or private, which they used. Ammianus Marcellinus, for example, makes but a single passing reference to the archives which led him, a Greek-speaker from Antioch, to spend the second half of his life in Rome.[9] The best evidence for the use of documents and personal papers comes from the late Republic, when the principal actors deployed history, carefully vetted to burnish their reputations, in political combat.[10] Next come the last centuries of antiquity, when, as has already been noted, literary standards dropped and the shadowy outlines of dossiers of documents can be seen below the surface of extant texts—notably Malchus of Philadelphia's account of Roman-Goth relations in the 470s, Menander Protector's largely diplomatic history of the 560s and 570s, and, at one remove, Simocatta's accounts of Balkan military operations.[11] But neither Malchus nor Menander nor any other historian at work in classical antiquity can match the anonymous author of the *Chronicon Paschale* in this respect. He was an official, probably in the middle or nether reaches of the patriarchate in Constantinople, who pieced together a universal history of mankind from the beginning of measurable time to his own day. He shows a keen interest in time, both in calculating its efflux and in recording precise dates for events (giving days of the week and dates in the month for the most important). The last contemporary section of his chronicle covers his lifetime in the early seventh century and ends with the triumphal ceremony staged by Heraclius in Jerusalem on Wednesday 21 March 630. He was the most self-effacing of historians. Apart from a final chronological disquisition and a single short passage of lamentation about the sack of Jerusalem in 614, he wrote nothing of his own about the early seventh century, but simply acted as editor, selecting and arranging primary material in carefully dated year entries. The primary material was all taken from official documents of various sorts—court circulars, government communiqués, a key diplomatic letter addressed by the Senate to Khusro (dating from 615 and quoted in full), a report on the Persian-Avar siege of Constantinople in 626 written for the Emperor Heraclius in the field (with one tantalizing lacuna as the siege approaches its climax), and Heraclius' victory

---

[9] Ammianus Marcellinus, xvi.12.69–70. Cf. A. Momigliano, 'The Lonely Historian Ammianus Marcellinus', in *Essays in Ancient and Modern Historiography* (Oxford, 1977), 127–40.
[10] F. E. Adcock, *Caesar as a Man of Letters* (Cambridge, 1956), 6–18.
[11] P. Heather, *Goths and Romans 332–489* (Oxford, 1991), 233–7; R. C. Blockley, *The History of Menander the Guardsman* (Liverpool, 1985), 18–20; Whitby, *Emperor Maurice*, 94–105.

dispatch sent from Atropatene (quoted in full), to which was attached the text (much damaged in the manuscript) of a letter from Kavad Shiroe, Khusro II's successor.[12]

As a contemporary placed at a good vantage point, the author of the *Chronicon Paschale* knew enough to be able to sort through the documents to which he had access (copies were probably to hand in the patriarchal archives) and to pick out some of particular interest. The authors of the materials which he reproduced required rather more understanding of the affairs with which they dealt to write informative and lucid accounts for dispatch or dissemination. Inside knowledge and expertise were as important as access to a plentiful supply of detailed information. It was the combination of *information* and *inside knowledge* which gave and still gives official records their peculiar value. At each stage of composition understanding can be brought to bear on the information collected— from the level of the *primary report* composed at the front, civil or military, where officialdom or soldiery encounter reality, to that of the *final report* for dispatch elsewhere, composed by higher authority out of primary reports (oral as well as written) received from below. The process of production of the final report involves an organized group accustomed to collective activity, for example, the staff serving a general in the field, the entourage of a ruler, senior officials in a government department, or the staff of a provincial governor. The best evidence available to the historian is the written product of *collective autopsy* by such organized, cohesive, managerial groups.

The competent authorities responsible for reports did, of course, have an interest in improving on historical reality when they accounted for their actions. Success and failure could be glossed—success made to shine brighter, failure underplayed or excused. Vested interests have always exercised pressure on representations of the recent past. Dispatches, reports, and communiqués are all susceptible to deformation. However, it is only when they are issued for general public consumption that massaging of the truth may lead to serious distortion—when governments, for good or bad reasons, want to maintain morale or to motivate their supporters and discourage their opponents. We have to be wary, therefore, of putting too much trust in communiqués if what is reported is likely to have had an effect on the public mood. In the case of the *Chronicon Paschale*, there may well have been some winnowing of the more tendentious public announcements, leaving a residue of court circulars (which, by their very issue, sustained morale, showing as they did that ceremonial life continued as normal at the heart of the divinely sanctioned Christian Roman state) and Heraclius' victory dispatch, which simply retailed news about Khusro's fall received from the Persian authorities and celebrated it. We have to be warier of documents composed with an ulterior purpose—above all, diplomatic documents which both indicate and protect negotiating positions, like the Senate's letter to Khusro in 615, and letters or news releases intended to mislead the enemy (some of which may have misled historians of later generations). At the opposite end of the spectrum come confidential reports, above all, military dispatches from the field, or reports sent to the emperor when he was in the field, such as that underlying the account of the 626 siege in the *Chronicon Paschale*. It would be dangerous in the extreme to attempt to deceive the emperor when the truth might come out at the time (if news seeped through independently) and would be all too likely to be revealed when, in due course, an expeditionary force came home or a tour of duty came to an end.

The *Chronicon Paschale* performs two useful services. First and foremost, it presents a large body of primary material of high quality—gravid with particulars and lucidly

---

[12] *Chronicon Paschale*, ed. L. Dindorf, CSHB (Bonn, 1832), partially trans. M. Whitby and M. Whitby, *Chronicon Paschale 284–628 AD*, TTH 7 (Liverpool, 1989). Cf. Howard-Johnston, *Witnesses*, 37–59.

expressed. The record of actions is detailed. The dating is precise and, where it can be tested, almost always accurate (day of the week and date in the month coinciding in the year which is specified). It can act, therefore, as a gauge of the worth of other sources, as long as there is some overlap in coverage. Second, it supplies vital clues for detecting the presence of documentary and document-based material in other texts. For it reveals their key characteristics, high specific gravity (plentiful precise information about persons, places, dates, and actions), and clear, concise exposition. Material attributable directly or indirectly to documents can then be unearthed from several of the texts discussed below, as well as from Simocatta's history, as has already been noted. The clearest case of all concerns a detailed account of the penultimate phase of Heraclius' second counteroffensive, from the start of his march south over the Zagros on 17 October 627 to the operations in the hinterland of Ctesiphon which helped to precipitate the putsch against Khusro on the night of 23–24 February 628. It is to be found in the early ninth-century *Chronographia* of Theophanes and corresponds to the first part of a dispatch which went on to cover the final phase, Heraclius' withdrawal north to Ganzak in Atropatene (24 February–15 March).[13] Its coverage and content were reported in Heraclius' next dispatch, his final victory message to his subjects sent off on or soon after 8 April, when he received news of the outcome of the conspiracy against Khusro. Other passages which likewise track the movements and actions of the Roman expeditionary army in 624–6 as well as earlier in 627 and which share the same characteristics are to be found in Theophanes' text. Theophanes seems to have found a copy of a collection of Heraclius' war dispatches, possibly free-standing, more probably embedded in an officially sponsored history, and to have made considerable use of them.[14]

Similarly detailed and well-ordered military narratives figure in several other histories written rather closer to the events. The presence of such material is probably best explained by supposing that officially vetted material was put into circulation in the Middle East during and after the war and that it was picked up by authors at work in widely separated localities. A second copy of Heraclius' dispatches or of a work based on them may have reached the Armenian bishop who wrote the *History of Khosrov* (Khusro II) in the 650s.[15] A summary table of episodes in Heraclius' campaigns is given. A number of passages have the telltale characteristics of dispatch-based narratives. He probably found a set in the archives of the catholicosate, along with three documents which he reproduced in full (a fundraising letter from Modestus, the acting head of the Jerusalem church after 614, the polite refusal sent in reply by Kumitas, the catholicos of Armenia at the time, and the statement of faith agreed at the Council of Dvin in 649) and a collection of communiqués about the principal acts of successive of Persian governors and commanders in Armenia.[16] A near contemporary of his, the anonymous author of the second book of the *Miracula S. Demetrii*, in effect a local history of Thessalonica from 610 to the 650s, recycles reports on major crises affecting the city which probably originated with the city

---

[13] Theophanes, *Chronographia*, ed. C. de Boor, 2 vols. (Leipzig, 1883–5), trans. C. Mango and R. Scott, *The Chronicle of Theophanes Confessor: Byzantine and Near Eastern History AD 284–813* (Oxford, 1997). See Theoph., 317.28–323.22, 324.16–326.23 for material from the 15 March dispatch.

[14] Howard-Johnston, *Witnesses*, 284–95.

[15] See Howard-Johnston, *Witnesses*, 71–4 for the identification of the history attributed to Sebeos (*Patmut'iwn Sebeosi*, ed. G. V. Abgaryan (Erevan, 1979), trans. R. W. Thomson, in R. W. Thomson and J. Howard-Johnston, *The Armenian History Attributed to Sebeos*, TTH 31, 2 vols. (Liverpool, 1999), I, hereafter cited as ps.Sebeos) as the *History of Khosrov*.

[16] Howard-Johnston, *Witnesses*, 71–102.

authorities.[17] A generation later, another anonymous author put together a history of Caucasian Albania in the seventh century (*History to the Year 682*), the first part of which includes a detailed account of diplomacy and warfare in the 620s and the impact of events on Albania. The narrative, taken from a well-informed local source, is, in places, as well articulated as a military dispatch. Two diplomatic notes are included, a Turkish ultimatum and Khusro's reply, both of which ring true. It seems likely that the ultimate source or sources used included officially released reports.[18]

All the works which have been considered so far can be tested by reference to the *Chronicon Paschale*. In most cases, there is some overlap in content. Where there is not, we may, taking all due precautions, fall back on internal evidence (tone, coherence, quantity, and plausibility of data), as long as one essential condition is met—that the information provided should both be compatible with and complement what is known from the *Chronicon* and from other sources vetted by reference to the *Chronicon*. A whole array of sources can now be placed in the category of the generally reliable—two Armenian (*History of Khosrov*, *History to the Year 682*), three high-style (the speeches of Theodore Syncellus, the history of Simocatta, and the secular poetry of George of Pisidia), and three local (John of Nikiu's chronicle (Egypt), the Life of St Anastasius (Palestine), and the *Miracula S. Demetrii* (Thessalonica)). A similar procedure can then be applied to other extant sources to identify those which can be tapped safely for information.

The oldest of them was written as a continuation of a universal history written in the early sixth century by John of Antioch. It only survives in fragments, but these fill out at the end into vignettes of high politics in Constantinople in the first decade of the seventh century.[19] Biographies are extant of three saints who were rough contemporaries of Anastasius. The amount of information provided varies, but all seem to be rooted in reality, and may thus be used, like the Life of Anastasius, to document local repercussions of the war and to probe the social order and religious practices of specific localities—Galatia and Bithynia in the case of Theodore of Syceon (died 613), Alexandria in the case of the Chalcedonian patriarch John the Almsgiver (died 619), the hinterland of Jericho in the case of George of Chozeba (died around 620).[20] For Syria and Persian Mesopotamia, we may turn to two Syriac texts. A collection of chronological and historical notes which come down to 724 and were put together in Edessa (the *Chronicle to the Year 724*) includes a set of brief notices of demonstrably high quality about key events in the early seventh century probably taken from an earlier source written in or soon after 636 in the Tur Abdin. The *Khuzistan Chronicle*, which has a later continuation, was written in the 650 by an author with a taste for gossip and colourful detail. He covers roughly the same period as the *History of Khosrov* but from a Mesopotamian viewpoint and more episodically.[21]

---

[17] *Miracula S. Demetrii*, ed. P. Lemerle, *Les Plus Anciens Recueils des miracles de saint Démétrius*, I *Le Texte* (Paris, 1979), with II *Commentaire* (Paris, 1981). Cf. Howard-Johnston, *Witnesses*, 152–4.

[18] See Howard-Johnston, *Witnesses*, 103–128 for the disinterment of the *History to the Year 682* from Movses Daskhurants'i (or Kałankatuats'i), ed. V. Arak'eljan, *Movses Kałankatuats'i: Patmut'iwn Ałuanits'* (Erevan, 1983), trans. C. J. F. Dowsett, *Moses Dasxuranc'i's History of the Caucasian Albanians* (London, 1961).

[19] U. Roberto, ed. and trans., *Ioannis Antiocheni fragmenta ex historia chronica*, Berlin-Brandenburgische Ak. Wiss., Texte und Untersuchungen zur Geschichte der altchristlichen Literatur 154 (Berlin, 2005). Cf. Howard-Johnston, *Witnesses*, 140–2.

[20] *Vita S. Theodori*; H. Delehaye, ' Une Vie inédite de saint Jean l'Aumônier', *An.Boll.* 45 (1927), 5–74 and E. Lappa-Zizicas, 'Un Épitomé de la Vie de S. Jean l'Aumônier par Jean et Sophronios', *An. Boll.* 88 (1970), 265–78; *Vita S. Georgii*. Cf. Howard-Johnston, *Witnesses*, 149–51, 167–9, 179–80.

[21] *Chronicon miscellaneum ad annum Domini 724 pertinens*, ed. E. W. Brooks, CSCO, Scriptores Syri 3, Chronica Minora II (Louvain, 1960), 77–154, partial trans. Palmer, *Seventh Century*, 13–23, 49–50 (cited as *Chron.724*); *Chronicon anonymum*, ed. I. Guidi, CSCO, Scriptores Syri 1, Chronica

Finally, we come to four problematic sources which need to be scrutinized with care before they can be mined safely for useable material. Information about destruction and atrocities following the capture of Jerusalem in 614 is conserved, together with an eyewitness account of the deportations which followed and the texts of two lamentations by the Patriarch Zacharias in what purports to be a sermon given by Strategius, a monk in the famous monastery of St Sabas in the Judaean desert outside Jerusalem. The tone is emotional, the treatment hagiographical. The composite text looks like a deliberately inflammatory piece of writing, a speech act intended to stir up anti-Persian feelings among Christians rather than a historical report. Its composition may be placed within a few months of the events described, since no reference is made to the removal of the True Cross from its hiding place in Jerusalem, of which much was made by the Romans from 615. Given its wide currency—it reached as far afield as Arabia and Transcaucasia— Strategius' text should probably be viewed as the best extant product of the Roman propaganda machine during the war. At the time, words were the most effective weapons left to the Romans, and the sack of Jerusalem was as rich a vein to mine as the Najran martyrdoms in northern Yemen had been a century earlier.[22]

The *Short History* of Nicephorus was written in the 770s, when Nicephorus, a future patriarch of Constantinople, was young and was experimenting with a classicizing style. It was more literary exercise than historical work, since he merely abridged the content and improved the language of three sources which he found for the period he covered (610–769). The first of them, his sole source for the first half of the seventh century, was a second continuation of John of Antioch's chronicle beginning with Heraclius' seizure of power and going down to the political crisis in the early 640s which followed his death. It was also used extensively by John of Nikiu, possibly through an intermediary, and was known to Theophanes. The material on court life, metropolitan history, and diplomatic dealings is of good quality, to judge by episodes for which there is corroboration. The second continuator, at work between the middle 640s and early 650s, seems to have belonged to patriarchal circles and to have been a partisan of the deposed Patriarch Pyrrhus (638–41). He was not so sure of his ground when he dealt with military operations away from the capital. Nicephorus is probably only partly responsible for the mangling of chronology evident in two passages which set the scene for Heraclius' final expedition in the 627–8.[23] A more substantial work, covering the years 590–754, was written by Theophilus of Edessa, an intellectual who rose high in the service of al-Mahdi, caliph 775–85. His text (in Syriac) has not survived, but its content can be reconstituted from what was recycled by four later histories. Theophilus, who could draw on non-Syrian sources (he knew Greek and Arabic), targeted his history mainly on Syria and the world to the south and west of Transcaucasia. Being at the mercy of his sources, he was all too liable

---

Minora I (Paris, 1903), 15–39, trans. T. Nöldeke,' Die von Guidi herausgegebene Syrische Chronik übersetzt und commentiert', *Sitzungsberichte der kais. Ak. Wiss., Phil.-hist. Cl.*, 128 (Vienna, 1893), 1–48, partial trans. Greatrex and Lieu, *Roman Eastern Frontier*, 229–37 (cited as *Khuz.Chron.*). Cf. Howard-Johnston, *Witnesses*, 59–66, 128–35.

[22] G. Garitte, ed. and trans., *La Prise de Jérusalem par les Perses en 614*, CSCO 202–3, Scriptores Iberici 11–2 (Louvain, 1960) and *Expugnationis Hierosolymae AD 614 recensiones Arabicae*, CSCO 340–1 and 347–8, Scriptores Arabici 26–9 (Louvain, 1973–4). Cf. Howard-Johnston, *Witnesses*, 163–7. Najran publicity: J. Beaucamp, F. Briquel-Chatonnet, and C. J. Robin, eds., *Juifs et chrétiens en Arabie aux Ve et VIe siècles: Regards croisés sur les sources* (Paris, 2010).

[23] C. Mango, ed. and trans., *Nikephoros Patriarch of Constantinople, Short History*, CFHB 13 (Washington DC, 1990). Cf. Howard-Johnston, *Witnesses*, 237–67 and C. Zuckerman, 'Heraclius and the Return of the True Cross', in C. Zuckerman, *Constructing the Seventh Century, TM* 17 (2013), 197–218, at 204–9.

to recycle tendentious material, notably Heraclian propaganda blaming Phocas' regime for the Persians' entry into the Roman heartlands and deliberate disinformation put out in 626 to estrange Khusro from the greatest of his generals, Shahrbaraz. Theophilus' useful contributions are limited to a few bits of information about the ill-documented years at the end of the first phase of the war and the beginning of the third. Although uncorroborated, they tally with what is already known.[24]

Theophanes, a grandee who abandoned a career in government service at an early stage for a monastic vocation, continued the universal history written by his mentor, George Syncellus. He started with the accession of Diocletian in 284 and came down to his own time (813). His library included some twenty historical sources from which he extracted his material.[25] His role, as he declared in his preface, was simply that of editor and transmitter. It involved him in selecting and, if necessary, abridging passages for reproduction in his text and then placing them in individual year entries. We have already encountered all six sources he used for the first thirty years of the seventh century—Theophylact Simocatta, the first and second continuations of John of Antioch, Theophilus of Edessa's history in the form of a Greek translation which George Syncellus brought from Palestine, George of Pisidia's poetry, and Heraclius' war dispatches. The quality of the resulting composite history is very uneven. High value can be accorded to dispatch-based passages, very little by contrast to Theophanes' own version of domestic political history under Phocas, to the black propaganda aimed at the Persians which he picked up from Theophilus, or to the tale of Heraclius' and his cousin Nicetas' race for the throne in 610 (a popular story which also reached Nicephorus and Theophilus). The content and some of the phrasing of lost verse readily attributable to George of Pisidia has been transmitted accurately. The verse is so successfully married to the documentary material in Theophanes' text as to suggest that the two came conjoined into his hands. If so, the immediate source may be conjectured to have been a re-edition (probably for publication) of Heraclius' dispatches commissioned from George and embellished with specially composed poetry. Theophanes, however, had considerable difficulty making sense of George's long, artfully composed poem in three cantos on army exercises and subsequent operations in 622. His precis is very misleading in places.

Besides the intricately worked and allusive poetry of George, Theophanes inevitably had difficulty with events which were not tagged with dates in his sources. Because of the annalistic format which he had adopted, such undated events had to be assigned to a specific year. He had to rely on guesswork based partly on his understanding of the context, but guided also by a chronicler's abhorrence of voids. There was also a standing temptation to spread data so as to ensure that something was entered under every year and, in some extreme cases, to resort to arbitrary transfer from one year to another. Chronological displacements of these sorts were facilitated when he found it hard to relate data from one source to data from another. The whole problem was further compounded by distortions already present in Theophilus of Edessa. As a result, Theophanes' chronology of the reign of Phocas goes awry in many places, Heraclius' second marriage to his niece Martina is shifted back ten years to 613, the surprise Avar attack (623) which he just escaped is put in an otherwise blank year (617/18), and his Persian campaigns are brought forward to 623–7. The task of disentangling these several muddles is far from easy.[26]

---

[24] R. G. Hoyland, *Theophilus of Edessa's Chronicle and the Circulation of Historical Knowledge in Late Antiquity and Early Islam*, TTH 57 (Liverpool, 2011); Howard-Johnston, *Witnesses*, 194–236.

[25] Mango and Scott, *Chronicle of Theophanes* xliii–lxiii, lxxiv–xci.

[26] Howard-Johnston, *Witnesses*, 268–312.

There are other sources of information: lives of saints, homilies, histories, including the *Chronicle of Seert*, which looks on the world from the point of view of the Nestorian church in Mesopotamia, and the *History of the Patriarchs of Alexandria*, which does the same from the point of view of the Coptic church, a Christian-Jewish disputation set in Carthage, short poems by Sophronius, who ended his life as patriarch of Jerusalem, and the *Khwadaynamag*, of which the most famous version is the *Shahname* of Firdawsi.[27] But the essential raw material with which the historian of the last great war of antiquity must work is to be found in the sources discussed above. Bias must be identified and countered, above all a pervasive sympathy for the Romans implicit in the great majority of extant sources. One must be on guard against deliberate deception by the authorities at the time. One must move cautiously over the evidence, seeking out secure stepping stones before venturing gingerly onto others. A narrative of events can only be constructed with much extrapolation from what is known. Inferences must be as strong as possible. Conjectures must be kept to a minimum.

---

[27] Howard-Johnston, *Witnesses*, cc.5, 6, and 10. An exemplary exercise in the prising apart and examination of different layers of material in a complex text is that undertaken by Philip Wood, *The Chronicle of Seert: Christian Historical Imagination in Late Antique Iraq* (Oxford, 2013).

Bibliography

1. Primary Sources

Acta conciliorum ecumenicorum, ser. 2, II.1–2 *Concilium universale Constantinopolitani tertium*, ed. R. Riedinger (Berlin, 1990–2).
Agapius, *Kitab al-'Unvan, histoire universelle écrite par Agapius (Mahboub) de Menbidj*, ed. and tr. A. A. Vasiliev, *PO* 7.4 (1911) and 8.3 (1912).
Ägyptische Urkunden aus den Staatlichen Museen Berlin: Koptische Urkunden, ed. H. Satzinger, 3 vols. (Berlin, 1968).
Ammianus Marcellinus, *Historiae*, ed. and trans. É. Galletier, J. Fontaine, M.-A. Marié, and G. Sabbah, 6 vols. (Paris, 1968–99).
Ananias of Širak, *The Geography of Ananias of Širak (AŠXARHAC'OYC'): The Long and Short Recensions*, trans. R. H. Hewsen, Beihefte zum Tübinger Atlas des vorderen Orients B.77 (Wiesbaden, 1992).
Ananias of Širak, *Géographie de Moïse de Corène*, ed. A. Soukry (Venice, 1881), reproduced in facsimile as *Ashkharhatsoyts (AŠXARHAC'OYC'), the Seventh Century Geography Attributed to Ananias of Širak*, ed. R. H. Hewsen (Delmar, NY, 1994).
Anastasius bibliothecarius, *Historia Tripertita*, ed. C. de Boor, *Theophanis chronographia*, II (Leipzig, 1885).
Anthologia Graeca, ed. and trans. R. Aubreton, F. Buffière, G. Soury, and P. Waltz, *Anthologie grecque, 2ème partie, Anthologie de Planude*, 13 vols. (Paris, 1928–2011).
Antiochus monachus S. Sabae, *Epistula ad Eustathium*, PG 89, cols.1421–30.
Babai Magnus, *Historia Georgii presbyteri*, ed. P. Bedjan, *Histoire de Mar-Jabalaha, de trois autres patriarches, d'un prêtre et de deux laïques, Nestoriens* (Paris, 1895).
Al-Baladhuri, *Kitab futuh al-buldan*, ed. M. J. de Goeje, *Liber expugnationis regionum* (Leiden, 1866).
Al-Baladhuri, *The Origins of the Islamic State*, trans. P. K. Hitti, 2 vols. (New York, 1916–24).
Chronica Byzantia-Arabica, recycled in *Chronica Muzarabica*, ed. J. Gil, Corpus Scriptorum Muzarabicorum I (Madrid, 1973).
Chronicon ad annum Christi 1234 pertinens, ed. J. B. Chabot, CSCO, Scriptores Syri, 3.ser., 14 (Paris, 1920), partial trans. A. Palmer, *The Seventh Century in the West-Syrian Chronicles*, TTH 15 (Liverpool, 1993), 111–221.
Chronicon anonymum ad annum 819 pertinens, ed. A. Barsaum, CSCO, Scriptores Syri 36 (Paris, 1920), trans. J.-B. Chabot, CSCO 56 (Louvain, 1937).
Chronicon miscellaneum ad annum Domini 724 pertinens, ed. E. W. Brooks, CSCO, Scriptores Syri 3, Chronica Minora II (Louvain, 1960), 77–154, partial trans. A. Palmer, *The Seventh Century in the West-Syrian Chronicles*, TTH 15 (Liverpool, 1993), 13–23.
Chronicon Paschale, ed. L. Dindorf, CSHB (Bonn, 1832), partial trans. Michael Whitby and Mary Whitby, *Chronicon Paschale 284–628 ad*, TTH 7 (Liverpool, 1989).
Chronique de Josué le Stylite, écrite vers l'an 515, ed. and trans. P. Martin, Abhandlungen für die Kunde des Morgenlandes 6.1 (Leipzig, 1878), trans. F. R. Trombley and J. W. Watt, *The Chronicle of Pseudo-Joshua the Stylite*, TTH 32 (Liverpool, 2000).
Constantini Manassis breviarium chronicum, ed. O. Lampsidis, CFHB 36.1 (Athens, 1996).

Constantinus Porphyrogenitus, *De administrando imperio*, ed. G. Moravcsik, trans. R. J. H. Jenkins, CFHB 1 (Washington DC, 1967).
Continuationes Isidorianae Byzantia Arabica et Hispana, ed. T. Mommsen, MGH Auct. Ant. XI, Chron. Min. II (Berlin, 1894), 334–68.
Corpus inscriptionum Iudaeae/Palaestinae, ed. H. M. Cotton et al., 3 vols. (Berlin, 2010–14).
Cosmas Indicopleustes, *Topographia Christiana*, ed. and trans. W. Wolska-Conus, 3 vols., Sources chrétiennes 141, 159, 197 (Paris, 1968–73).
Cyriacus of Amida, *Translation of the Relics of James*, ed. and trans. E. W. Brooks, PO 19.2 (1926), 268–73.
Disputatio cum Pyrrho, PG 91 (1865), 288–353.
Doctrina Jacobi nuper baptizati, ed. and trans. V. Déroche, TM 11 (1991), 70–229.
Eutychius, *Annals*, ed. and trans. M. Breydy, *Das Annalenwerk des Eutychios von Alexandrien: Ausgewählte Geschichten und Legenden kompiliert von Sa'id ibn Batriq um 935 A.D.*, CSCO 471–2 (Leuven, 1985).
Firdawsi, Shahname, *Le Livre des rois par Abou'lkasim Firdousi*, trans. J. Mohl, 7 vols. (Paris, 1876–8).
Fredegar, *The Fourth Book of the Chronicle of Fredegar with Its Continuations*, ed. and trans. J. M. Wallace-Hadrill (Edinburgh, 1960).
Georgius Cedrenus, *Compendium historiarum*, ed. I. Bekker, 2 vols., CSHB (Bonn, 1838–9).
Georgius Pisides, *Giorgio di Pisidia poemi: I panegirici epici*, ed. and trans. A. Pertusi (Ettal, 1959).
Georgius Pisides, *Carmi di Giorgio di Pisidia*, ed. and trans. L. Tartaglia (Turin, 1998).
Georgius Pisides, *Hexaemeron*, ed. and trans. F. Gonnelli, *Giorgio di Pisidia, Esamerone* (Pisa, 1998).
Girkʻ Tʻghtʻotsʻ (Book of Letters) (Tiflis, 1901).
Grégoire, H., ed., *Recueil des inscriptions grecques chrétiennes d'Asie Mineure*, I (Paris, 1922).
Heraclius, *Die Novellen des Kaisers Herakleios*, ed. and trans. J. Konidaris, Fontes Minores 5.3 (Frankfurt am Main, 1982).
History of Khosrov: see ps.Sebeos.
History of the Patriarchs of the Coptic Church of Alexandria (St. Mark to Benjamin I), ed. and trans. B. Evetts, PO 1.2 and 4, 5.1, 10.5.
History to 682: see Movses Daskhurants'i.
Ibn Ishaq, *Kitab sirat Rasul Allah*, ed. F. Wüstenfeld, 2 vols. (Göttingen, 1858–60).
Ibn Ishaq, *The Life of Muhammad*, trans. A. Guillaume (Oxford, 1955).
Ibn Khordadhbeh, *Kitab al-masalik wa'l- mamalik*, ed. and trans. M. J. de Goeje, *Bibliotheca geographorum arabicorum*, VI (Leiden, 1889).
Ioannes Antiochenus, *Ioannis Antiocheni fragmenta ex historia chronica*, ed. and trans. U. Roberto, Berlin-Brandenburgische Ak. Wiss., Texte und Untersuchungen zur Geschichte der altchristlichen Literatur 154 (Berlin, 2005).
Ioannis Zonarae epitome historiarum, ed. L. Dindorf, 6 vols. (Leipzig, 1868–75).
Isidorus iunior, *Chronica*, ed. T. Mommsen, MGH Auct. Ant. XI, Chron. Min. II.2 (Berlin, 1894), 424–81.
Isidorus iunior, *Historia Gothorum Wandalorum Sueborum*, ed. T. Mommsen, MGH Auct. Ant. XI, Chron. Min. II.2 (Berlin, 1894), 267–303.
John of Nikiu, *Chronique de Jean, évêque de Nikiou*, ed. and trans. H. Zotenberg (Paris, 1883).
Khuzistan Chronicle: *Chronicon anonymum*, ed. I. Guidi, CSCO, Scriptores Syri 1, Chronica Minora I (Paris, 1903), 15–39, trans. T. Nöldeke, 'Die von Guidi herausgegebene Syrische Chronik übersetzt und commentiert', *Sitzungsberichte der kais. Ak. Wiss.,*

Phil.-hist. Cl., 128 (Vienna, 1893), partial trans. G. Greatrex and S. N. C. Lieu, *The Roman Eastern Frontier and the Persian Wars, Part II ad 363–630: A Narrative Sourcebook* (London, 2002), 229–37.
Kraemer, C. J. *Excavations at Nessana*, III *Non-Literary Papyri* (Princeton, NJ, 1958).
Krall, J. *Corpus papyrorum Raineri*, II *Koptische Texte* (Vienna, 1895).
Łazar Pʻarpetsʻi, *Patmutʻiwn Hayotsʻ*, ed. G. Ter-Mkrtchʻean and S. Malkhasean (Tiflis, 1904).
Łazar Pʻarpetsʻi, *The History of Łazar Pʻarpecʻi*, trans. R. W. Thomson (Atlanta, GA, 1991).
Liber Pontificalis, ed. L. Duchesne, 3 vols. (Paris, 1886–1957), partial trans. R. Davis, *The Book of Pontiffs: The Ancient Biographies of the First Ninety Roman Bishops to ad 715*, TTH, Latin Series 5 (Liverpool, 1989).
Mauricius, *Strategicon*, ed. G. T. Dennis and trans. (German) E. Gamillscheg, CFHB 17 (Vienna, 1981).
Mauricius, *Maurice's Strategikon: Handbook of Byzantine Military Strategy*, trans. G. T. Dennis (Philadelphia, PA, 1984).
Menander Protector, *The History of Menander the Guardsman*, ed. and trans. R. C. Blockley (Liverpool, 1985).
Michaelis Glycae annales, ed. I. Bekker, CSHB (Bonn, 1836).
Michael the Syrian, *Chronique de Michel le Syrien, Patriarche Jacobite d'Antioche (1166–1199)*, ed. and trans. J. B. Chabot, 5 vols. (Paris, 1899–1924).
Miracula S. Demetrii, ed. P. Lemerle, *Les Plus Anciens Recueils des miracles de saint Démétrius*, I *Le Texte* (Paris, 1979), II *Commentaire* (Paris, 1981).
Movses Daskhurantsʻi (or Kałankatuatsʻi), *Moses Dasxurancʻiʻs History of the Caucasian Albanians*, trans. C. J. F. Dowsett (London, 1961).
Movses Daskhurantsʻi (or Kałankatuatsʻi), *Movses Kałankatuatsʻi: Patmutʻiwn Ałuanitsʻ*, ed. V. Arakʻeljan (Erevan, 1983).
Narratio de rebus Armeniae, ed. G. Garitte, CSCO 132, Subsidia 4 (Louvain, 1952).
Nicephorus, *Breviarium, Nikephoros Patriarch of Constantinople, Short History*, ed. and trans. C. Mango, CFHB 13 (Washington DC, 1990).
The Oxyrhyncus Papyri, ed. B.P. Grenfell, A.S. Hunt, H.I. Bell, J.R. Rea et al., 82 vols. (London, 1898–2016).
Paul the Deacon, *Pauli historia Langobardorum*, ed. L. Bethmann and G. Waitz (Hanover, 1878).
Paul the Deacon, *Paul the Deacon, History of the Lombards* (Philadelphia, PA, 1907).
Paul the Deacon, *Paul Diacre, Histoire des Lombards*, trans. F. Bougard (Turnhout, 1994).
Perikhanjan, A. G. 'Pekhlevijskie papirusy sobranija GMII imeni A. S. Pushkina', *Vestnik Drevnej Istorii*, 77.3 (1961), 78–93.
Procopius, *Bella*, ed. and trans. H. B. Dewing, 5 vols. (Cambridge, MA, 1914–28).
ps.Methodius, *Apocalypse Pseudo-Methodius: An Alexandrian World Chronicle*, ed. and trans. B. Garstad (Cambridge, MA, 2012), 1–139.
ps.Sebeos: *Patmutʻiwn Sebeosi*, ed. G. V. Abgaryan (Erevan, 1979), trans. R. W. Thomson in R. W. Thomson and J. Howard-Johnston, *The Armenian History Attributed to Sebeos*, TTH 31, 2 vols. (Liverpool, 1999), I *Translation and Notes*, II *Historical Commentary*.
Qu Tang-shu, *Die chinesischen Nachrichten zur Geschichte der Ost-Türken (T'u-Küe)*, trans. Liu Mau-Tsai (Wiesbaden, 1958).
Reversio Sanctae Crucis, ed. and trans. S. Borgehammer, 'Heraclius Learns Humility: Two Early Latin Accounts Composed for the *Exaltatio Crucis*', *Millennium*, 6 (2009), 145–201.
Seert Chronicle, ed. A. Scher, trans. A. Scher, R. Griveau, et al., *Histoire Nestorienne (Chronique de Séert)*, PO 4.3, 5.2, 7.2, 13.4 (1908-19).
Sophronius, *Anacreontica*, ed. M. Gigante (Rome, 1957).

Strategius, ed. and trans. G. Garitte, *La Prise de Jérusalem par les Perses en 614*, CSCO 202–3, Scriptores Iberici 11–2 (Louvain, 1960) and *Expugnationis Hierosolymae A.D. 614 recensiones Arabicae*, CSCO 340–1 and 347–8, Scriptores Arabici 26–9 (Louvain, 1973–4).

Synaxarium ecclesiae Constantinopolitanae, ed. H. Delehaye, *Propylaeum ad Acta Sanctorum Novembris* (Brussels, 1902).

Synodicon vetus, ed. J. M. Duffy and J. B. Parker, *The Synodicon vetus*, CFHB 15 (Washington DC, 1979).

al-Tabari, *Annales quos scripsit Abu Djafar Mohammed ibn Djarir at-Tabari*, ed. M. J. de Goeje et al., 15 vols. (Leiden, 1879–1901), partial trans. C. E. Bosworth, *The Sasanids, the Byzantines, the Lakhmids, and Yemen, The History of al-Tabari* V (Albany, NY, 1999) (pp.813–1072), K. Y. Blankinship, *The Challenge to the Empires, H of Tab.* XI (Albany, NY, 1993) (pp.2016–212), and Y. Friedmann, *The Battle of al-Qadisiyyah and the Conquest of Syria and Palestine, H of Tab.* XII (pp.2212–418) (Albany, NY, 1992).

Tang-shu, trans. Liu Mau-Tsai, *Die chinesischen Nachrichten zur Geschichte der Ost-Türken (T'u-Küe)* (Wiesbaden, 1958).

Theodorus Syncellus, *Homily* I, ed. L. Sternbach, *Analecta Avarica*, Rozprawy Akademii Umiejętności, Wydział Filologiczny, ser. 2, 15 (Cracow, 1900), 298–320.

Theodorus Syncellus, *Homily* II, ed. C. Loparev, 'Staroe svidetelstvo o polozhenii rizy Bogorodnitsy vo Vlakherniakh…', *VV* 2 (1895), 581–628, at 592–612, trans. Averil Cameron, 'The Virgin's Robe: An Episode in the History of Early Seventh-Century Constantinople', *Byz.* 49 (1979), 42–56, repr. in Averil Cameron, *Continuity and Change in Sixth-Century Byzantium* (London, 1981), no.XVII.

Theophanes, *Chronographia*, ed. C. de Boor, 2 vols. (Leipzig, 1883–5).

Theophanes, *The Chronicle of Theophanes Confessor: Byzantine and Near Eastern History ad 284–813*, trans. C. Mango and R. Scott (Oxford, 1997).

Theophilus of Edessa, *Theophilus of Edessa's Chronicle and the Circulation of Historical Knowledge in Late Antiquity and Early Islam*, trans. R. G. Hoyland, TTH 57 (Liverpool, 2011).

Theophylactus Simocatta, *Historiae*, ed. C. de Boor, rev. P. Wirth (Stuttgart, 1972).

Theophylactus Simocatta, *The History of Theophylact Simocatta*, trans. Michael Whitby and Mary Whitby (Oxford, 1986).

T'ovma Artsruni Patmut'iwn Tann Artsruneats', ed. K. Patkanean (St. Petersburg, 1887), 2.3 (89.20–1), trans. R. W. Thomson, *Thomas Artsruni: History of the House of the Artsrunik'* (Detroit, MI, 1985).

Vita et miracula S. Theodori Tironis, ed. H. Delehaye, *Les Légendes grecques des saints militaires* (Paris, 1909).

Vita S. Anastasii, ed. and trans. B. Flusin, *Saint Anastase le Perse et l'histoire de la Palestine au début du VIIe siècle*, I *Les Textes* (Paris, 1992).

Vita S. Georgii, ed. C. Houze, 'Vita S. Georgii Chozebitae…', *An.Boll.* 7 (1888), 97–144, 336–70.

Vita S. Ioannis, ed. H. Delehaye, 'Une Vie inédite de saint Jean l'Aumônier', *An.Boll.* 45 (1927), 5–74.

Vita S. Ioannis *(epitome)*, ed. E. Lappa-Zizicas, 'Un épitomé de la Vie de S. Jean l'Aumônier par Jean et Sophronios', *An.Boll.* 88 (1970), 265–78.

Vita S. Nicolai, ed. and trans. I. Ševčenko and N. P. Ševčenko, *The Life of Saint Nicholas of Sion* (Brookline, MA, 1984).

Vita S. Spyridonis, ed. P. van den Ven, *La Légende de S. Spyridon évêque de Trimithonte*, Bibliothèque du Muséon 33 (Louvain, 1953).

Vita S. Theodori, ed. and trans. A.-J. Festugière, *Vie de Théodore de Sykéôn*, 2 vols. (Brussels, 1970).
Weber, D., ed. and trans., *Ostraca, Papyri und Pergamente*, Corpus Inscriptionum Iranicarum, III Pahlavi Inscriptions, vols. 4 and 5, Text I (London, 1992).
Weber, D., ed. and trans., *Berliner Papyri, Pergamente und Leinenfragmente in mittelpersischer Sprache*, Corpus Inscriptionum Iranicarum, III Pahlavi Inscriptions, vols. 4 and 5, Text II (London, 2003).

2. Modern Works

Abu-l-Faraj al-Ush, M. *The Silver Hoard of Damascus* (Damascus, 1972).
Abu-l-Faraj al-Ush, M. *Trésor de monnaies d'argent trouvé à Umm-Hajarah* (Damascus, 1972).
Adams, R. M. *Land behind Baghdad* (Chicago, 1965).
Adcock, F. E. *Caesar as Man of Letters* (Cambridge, 1956).
Adontz, N. *Armenia in the Period of Justinian* (Lisbon, 1970).
Aliev, A. A., M. S. Gadjiev, M. G. Gaither, P. L. Kohl, R. M. Magomedov, and I. N. Aliev, 'The Ghilghilchay Defensive Long Wall: New Investigations', *Ancient West and East*, 5 (2006), 143–77.
Alizadeh, K. 'Borderland Projects of the Sasanian Empire: Intersection of Domestic and Foreign Policies', *Journal of Ancient History*, 2 (2014), 93–115.
Allen, P. *Sophronius of Jerusalem and Seventh-Century History: The* Synodical Letter *and Other Documents* (Oxford, 2009).
Altheim-Stiehl, R. 'Zur zeitlichen Bestimmung der sasanidischen Eroberung Ägyptens', *ΜΟΥΣΙΚΟΣ ΑΝΗΡ. Festschrift für Max Wegner zum 90. Geburtstag*, ed. O. Brehm and S. Klie (Bonn, 1992), 5–8.
Archibald, M. M. 'The Wilton Cross Coin Pendant: Numismatic Aspects and Implications', in A. Reynolds and L. Webster, eds., *Early Medieval Art and Archaeology in the Northern World* (Leiden, 2013), 51–71.
Arthur, P. 'Hierapolis of Phrygia: The Drawn-Out Demise of an Anatolian City', in N. Christie and A. Augenti, eds., *Urbes Extinctae: Archaeologies of Abandoned Classical Towns* (Farnham, 2012), 275–305.
Avni, G. 'The Persian Conquest of Jerusalem (614 C.E.) - An Archaeological Assessment', *BASOR* 357 (2010), 35–48.
Avni, G. *The Byzantine-Islamic Transition in Palestine: An Archaeological Approach* (Oxford, 2014).
Baert, B. *A Heritage of Holy Wood: The Legend of the True Cross in Text and Image* (Leiden, 2004).
Bagnall, R. S., 'Review of Borkowski, *Inscriptions*', *Bulletin of the American Society of Papyrologists*, 20 (1983), 75–80.
Bálint, C. *Die Archäologie der Steppe: Steppenvölker zwischen Volga und Donau vom 6. bis zum 10. Jahrhundert* (Vienna and Cologne, 1989).
Banaji, J. *Agrarian Change in Late Antiquity: Gold, Labour, and Aristocratic Dominance* (Oxford, 2001).
Barfield, T. J. *The Perilous Frontier: Nomadic Empires and China* (Oxford, 1989).
Barford, P. M. *The Early Slavs: Culture and Society in Early Medieval Eastern Europe* (London, 2001).
Bates, G. E. *Archaeological Exploration of Sardis: Byzantine Coins* (Cambridge, MA, 1971).

Baum, W. *Shirin Christian-Queen-Myth of Love: Historical Reality and Literary Effect* (Piscataway, NJ, 2004).
Baynes, N. H. 'The Date of the Avar Surprise: A Chronological Study', *BZ* 21 (1912), 110–28.
Beaucamp, J., R. Bondoux, J. Lefort, M.-F. Rouan, and I. Sorlin, 'Temps et histoire I: Le prologue de la *Chronique pascale*', *TM* 7 (1979), 223–301.
Beaucamp, J., F. Briquel-Chatonnet, and C. J. Robin, eds., *Juifs et chrétiens en Arabie aux Ve et VIe siècles: Regards croisés sur les sources* (Paris, 2010).
Bendall, S. 'The Byzantine Coinage of the Mint of Jerusalem', *RN* 159 (2003), 307–22.
Ben Slimène Ben Abbès, H. 'La Production de la monnaie d'or en Afrique byzantine', in J. González, P. Ruggeri, C. Vismara, and R. Zucca, eds., *Le ricchezze dell' Africa: Risorse, produzioni, scambi*, Africa Romana 17, 4 vols. (Rome, 2008), II, 1151–64.
Bernheimer, T., and A. Silverstein, eds., *Late Antiquity: Eastern Perspectives* (Exeter, 2012).
Bijovsky, G. 'A Single Die Solidi Hoard of Heraclius from Jerusalem', *TM* 16 (2010), 55–92.
Bijovsky, G. *Gold Coin and Small Change: Monetary Circulation in Fifth–Seventh Century Byzantine Palestine* (Trieste, 2012).
Binyon, L. *The Poems of Nizami* (London, 1928).
Blockley, R. C. *East Roman Foreign Policy: Formation and Conduct from Diocletian to Anastasius* (Leeds, 1992).
Blue, L., and E. Khalil, *A Multidisciplinary Approach to Alexandria's Economic Past: The Lake Mareotis Resarch Project*, BAR, Int. Ser. 2285 (Oxford, 2011).
Bonner, M. R. J. *Al-Dinawari's* Kitab al-Ahbar al-Tiwal: *An Historiographical Study of Sasanian Iran*, Res Orientales 23 (Bures-sur-Yvette, 2015).
Booth, P. 'Shades of Blues and Greens in the *Chronicle* of John of Nikiou', *BZ* 104 (2011), 555–601.
Booth, P. *Crisis of Empire: Doctrine and Dissent at the End of Late Antiquity* (Berkeley, CA, 2014).
Borkowski, Z. *Inscriptions des factions à Alexandrie*, Centre Polonais d'Archéologie Méditerranéenne dans la République Arabe d'Égypte au Caire, Alexandrie II (Warsaw, 1981).
Börm, H., and J. Wiesehöfer, eds., *Commutatio et contentio: Studies in the Late Roman, Sasanian, and Early Islamic Near East, in Memory of Zeev Rubin* (Düsseldorf, 2010).
Borrut, A., et al. *Le Proche-Orient de Justinien aux Abbassides: Peuplement et dynamiques spatiales*, Bibliothèque de l'Antiquité Tardive 19 (Turnhout, 2011).
Boyce, M. *A Persian Stronghold of Zoroastrianism* (Oxford, 1977).
Boyce, M. *Zoroastrians: Their Religious Beliefs and Practices* (London, 1979).
Brandes, W. *Finanzverwaltung in Krisenzeiten: Untersuchungen zur byzantinischen Administration im 6.–9. Jahrhundert*, Forschungen zur byzantinischen Rechtsgeschichte 25 (Frankfurt am Main, 2002).
Brandes, W. 'Heraclius between Restoration and Reform: Some Remarks on Recent Research', in G. J. Reinink and B. H. Stolte, eds., *The Reign of Heraclius (610–641): Crisis and Confrontation* (Leuven, 2002), 17–40.
Brett, M., and E. Fentress, *The Berbers* (Oxford, 1996).
Brock, S. P. 'Christians in the Sasanian Empire: A Case of Divided Loyalties', *Church History*, 18 (1982), 1–19, repr. in S. Brock, *Syriac Perspectives on Late Antiquity* (London, 1984), no. VI.
Brock, S. 'A Monothelete Florilegium in Syriac', in S. Brock, *Studies in Syriac Christianity: History, Literature and Theology* (Aldershot, 1992), no. XIV.
Brown, P. *The World of Late Antiquity: A.D. 150–750* (London, 1971).
Brown, P. R. L. *The Cult of the Saint: Its Rise and Function in Late Antiquity* (Chicago, 1981).
Brown, P. R. L. 'The Rise and Function of the Holy Man in Late Antiquity', in P. R. L. Brown, *Society and the Holy in Late Antiquity* (London, 1982), 103–52.

Brown, P. *The Rise of Western Christendom: Triumph and Diversity ad 200-1000* (Oxford, 1996).
Bryer, A., and D. Winfield. *The Byzantine Monuments and Topography of the Pontos*, DO Studies 20 (Washington DC, 1985).
Burgoyne, M. H. 'The Gates of the Haram al-Sharif', in J. Raby and J. Johns, eds., *Bayt al-Maqdis*, I *'Abd al-Malik's Jerusalem* (Oxford, 1992), I, 105-24.
Burnaby, F. *On Horseback through Asia Minor* (London, 1898).
Butler, A. J. *The Arab Conquest of Egypt and the Last Thirty Years of the Roman Domination*, rev. edn P. M. Fraser (Oxford,1978).
Cameron, Alan. *Circus Factions: Blues and Greens at Rome and Byzantium* (Oxford, 1976).
Cameron, Averil. 'The Virgin's Robe: An Episode in the History of Early Seventh-Century Constantinople', *Byz.* 49 (1979), 42-56, repr. in Averil Cameron, *Continuity and Change in Sixth-Century Byzantium* (London, 1981), no.XVII.
Cameron, Averil, ed., *The Byzantine and Early Islamic Near East*, III *States, Resources and Armies* (Princeton, NJ, 1995).
Cameron, Averil, B. Ward-Perkins, and M. Whitby, eds., *The Cambridge Ancient History* XIV, *Late Antiquity: Empire and Successors, A.D. 425-600* (Cambridge, 2000).
Canepa, M. P. *The Two Eyes of the Earth: Art and Ritual of Kingship between Rome and Sasanian Iran* (Berkeley and Los Angeles, 2009).
Canivet, P., and J.-P. Rey-Coquais, eds., *La Syrie de Byzance à l'Islam: VIIe-VIIIe siècles* (Damascus, 1992).
Carrié, J.-M. 'Jean de Nikiou et sa Chronique: Une Écriture "égyptienne" de l'histoire?', in N. Grimel and M. Baud, ed., *Événement, récit, histoire officielle: L'Écriture de l'histoire dans les monarchies antiques* (Paris, 2003), 155-72.
Cau Ontiveros, M. A., and C. Mas Florit, 'The Early Byzantine Period in the Balearic Islands', in D. Michaelides, P. Pergola, and E. Zanini, eds., *The Insular System of the Early Byzantine Mediterranean: Archaeology and History*, BAR, Int. Ser. 2523 (Oxford, 2013), 31-45.
Chadwick, H. 'John Moschus and His Friend Sophronius the Sophist', *JTS* n.s.25 (1974), 41-74.
Chevedden, P. E., Z. Schiller, S. R. Gilbert, and D. J. Kagay, 'The Traction Trebuchet: A Triumph of Four Civilizations', *Viator*, 31 (2000), 433-86.
Chitty, D. J. *The Desert a City* (London, 1977).
Christensen, A. *L'Iran sous les Sassanides* (Copenhagen, 1944).
Christiansen, E. *The Norsemen in the Viking Age* (Oxford, 2002).
Christie, N. *The Lombards: The Ancient Longobards* (Oxford, 1995).
Chrysos, E. S. 'The Title Βασιλεύς in Early Byzantine International Relations', *DOP* 32 (1978), 29-75.
Claridge, A. *Rome: An Oxford Archaeological Guide* (rev. edn, Oxford, 2010).
Collins, R. *Visigothic Spain 409-711* (Oxford, 2004).
Corcoran, S. 'Observations on the Sasanian Law-Book in the Light of Roman Legal Writing', in A. Rio, ed., *Law, Custom, and Justice in Late Antiquity and the Early Middle Ages* (London, 2011), 77-113.
Cosentino, S. 'Byzantine Sardinia between West and East: Features of a Regional Culture', *Millennium*, 1 (2004), 329-67.
Crone, P. *Meccan Trade and the Rise of Islam* (Oxford, 1987).
Crow, J. 'The Infrastructure of a Great City: Earth, Walls and Water in Late Antique Constantinople', in L. Lavan, E. Zanini, and A. Sarantis, eds., *Technology in Transition A.D. 300-650*, Late Antique Archaeology 4 (Leiden, 2007), 251-85.
Curtis, V. S., and S. Stewart, eds., *The Idea of Iran*, III *The Sasanian Era* (London, 2008).

Dąbrowa, E., ed., *The Roman and Byzantine Army in the East* (Cracow, 1994).

Dagron, G. *Emperor and Priest: The Imperial Office in Byzantium* (Cambridge, 2003).

Dagron, G., and V. Déroche, 'Juifs et Chrétiens dans l'Orient du VIIe siècle', *TM* 11 (1991), 17–273.

Dally, O., and C. Ratté, eds., *Archaeology and the Cities of Asia Minor in Late Antiquity* (Ann Arbor, MI, 2011).

Dalton, O. M. 'A Second Silver Treasure from Cyprus', *Archaeologia*, 60 (1906), 1–24.

Daryaee, T. 'The Use of Religio-Political Propaganda on the Coinage of Xusro II', *American Journal of Numismatics*, ser. 2, 9 (1997), 41–53.

Daryaee, T. 'The Coinage of Queen Boran and Its Significance for Late Sasanian Imperial Ideology', *Bulletin of the Asia Institute*, n.s.13 (1999), 77–82.

Daryaee, T. *Sasanian Persia: The Rise and Fall of an Empire* (London, 2009).

Davis, D. *Sunset of Empire: Stories from the Shahnameh of Firdowsi* III (Washington DC, 2004).

de Blois, F. 'The Persian Calendar', *Iran*, 34 (1996), 39–54.

de Cosson, A. *Mareotis* (London, 1935).

de Menasce, J., 'Recherches de papyrologie pehlevie', *JA* 241 (1953), 185-96.

Devreesse, R. 'La Fin inédite d'une lettre de Saint Maxime: Un Baptême forcé de Juifs et de Samaritains à Carthage en 632', *Revue des Sciences Religieuses*, 17 (1937), 25–35.

de Vries, B. *Umm el-Jimal: A Frontier Town and its Landscape in Northern Jordan*, I *Fieldwork 1972–1981* (Portsmouth, RI, 1998).

Dodd, E. C. *Byzantine Silver Stamps*, D.O. Studies 7 (Washington DC, 1961).

Donner, F. M. 'The Bakr B. Wa'il Tribes and Politics in Northeastern Arabia on the Eve of Islam', *Studia Islamica*, 51 (1980), 5–38.

Donner, F. M. *The Early Islamic Conquests* (Princeton, NJ, 1981).

Drauschke, J. 'Bemerkungen zu den Auswirkungen der Perser- und Arabereinfälle des 7. Jahrhunderts in Kleinasien', in O. Heinrich-Tamaska, ed., *Rauben, Plündern, Morden: Nachweis von Zerstörung und kriegerischer Gewalt im archäologischen Befund* (Hamburg, 2013), 117–59.

Drijvers, J. W. 'Heraclius and the *Restitutio Crucis*: Notes on Symbolism and Ideology', in G. J. Reinink and B. H. Stolte, eds., *The Reign of Heraclius (610–641): Crisis and Confrontation* (Leuven, 2002), 175–96.

Eddé, A.-M., and J.-P. Sodini, 'Les Villages de Syrie du Nord du VIIe au XIIIe siècle', in C. Morrisson, ed., *Les Villages dans l'empire byzantin: IVe–XVe siècle* (Paris, 2005), 465–83.

Edwell, P., et al., 'Arabs in the Conflict between Rome and Persia, AD 491–630', in G. Fisher, ed., *Arabs and Empires before Islam* (Oxford, 2015), 214–75.

El Cheikh, N. M. *Byzantium Viewed by the Arabs* (Cambridge, MA, 2004).

Esders, S. 'Herakleios, Dagobert und die "beschittenen Völker": Die Umwälzungen des Mittelmeerraums im 7. Jahrhundert in der Chronik des sog. Fredegar', in A. Goltz, H. Leppin, and H. Schlange-Schöningen, eds., *Jenseits der Grenzen: Beiträge zur spätantiken und frühmittelalterlichen Geschichtsschreibung*, Millennium-Studien 25 (Berlin, 2009), 239–311.

Fiey, J. M. *Assyrie chrétienne*, 3 vols. (Beirut, 1965–8).

Fiey, J. M. *Jalons pour une histoire de l'église en Iraq*, CSCO 310, Subsidia 36 (Louvain, 1970).

Firestone, R. *Jihad: The Origin of Holy War in Islam* (Oxford, 1999).

Fisher, G. *Between Empires: Arabs, Romans, and Sasanians in Late Antiquity* (Oxford, 2011).

Fisher, G., ed., *Arabs and Empires before Islam* (Oxford, 2015).

Fisher, W. B., ed., *The Cambridge History of Iran*, I *The Land of Iran* (Cambridge, 1968).

Flusin, B. *Saint Anastase le Perse et l'histoire de la Palestine au début du VIIe siècle*, II *Commentaire* (Paris, 1992).

Foss, C. 'The Persians in Asia Minor and the End of Antiquity', *EHR* 90 (1975), 721–47.
Foss, C. *Byzantine and Turkish Sardis* (Cambridge, MA, 1976).
Foss, C. 'Late Antique and Byzantine Ankara', *DOP* 31 (1977), 27–87.
Foss, C. *Ephesus after Antiquity: A Late Antique, Byzantine and Turkish City* (Cambridge, 1979).
Foss, C. 'Pylaï', in A. P. Kazhdan et al., eds. *The Oxford Dictionary of Byzantium*, 3 vols. (New York, 1991), III, 1760.
Foss, C. 'The Lycian Coast in the Byzantine Age', *DOP* 48 (1994), 1–52.
Foss, C. 'Syria in Transition, A.D. 550–750: An Archaeological Approach', *DOP* 51 (1997), 189–269.
Foss, C. 'The Persians in the Roman Near East (602–630 AD)', *JRAS*, ser. 3, 13 (2003), 149–70.
Fowden, G. *Empire to Commonwealth: Consequences of Monotheism in Late Antiquity* (Princeton, NJ, 1993).
French, D. H. 'The Roman Road-System of Asia Minor', in H. Temporini, ed., *Aufstieg und Niedergang der römischen Welt*, II.7.2 (Berlin, 1980), 698–729.
French, D. H., and C. S. Lightfoot, eds., *The Eastern Frontier of the Roman Empire*, BAR, Int. Ser. 553, 2 vols. (Oxford, 1989).
Frend, W. H. C. *The Rise of the Monophysite Movement* (Cambridge, 1972).
Fukai, S., K. Horiuchi, K. Tanabe, and M. Domyo, *Taq-i Bustan*, I–IV (Tokyo 1969–84).
Gadzhiev, M. S. *Drevnii gorod Dagestana: Opyt istoriko-topograficheskovo i sotsial'no-ekonomicheskovo analiza* (Moscow, 2002).
Gadzhiev, M. S., and S. J. Kasumova, *Srednepersidskie nadpisi Derbenta VI beka* (Moscow, 2006).
Gall, H. von 'Entwicklung und Gestalt des Thrones im vorislamischen Iran', *AMI* 4 (1971), 207–35.
Gariboldi, A. 'Social Conditions in Egypt under the Sasanian Occupation (619–629 AD)', *La Parola del Passato: Rivista di Studi Antichi*, 64 (2009), 321–50.
Garsoian, N. *L'Église arménienne et le grand schisme d'Orient*, CSCO 574, Subsidia 100 (Louvain, 1999).
Gascou, J. 'Enaton, the', in A. S. Atiya, ed., *The Coptic Encyclopedia*, 8 vols. (New York, 1991), III, 954–8.
Gascou, J. 'L'Égypte byzantine (284–641)', in C. Morrisson, ed., *Le Monde byzantin*, I *L'Empire romain d'Orient (330–641)* (Paris, 2004), 403–36.
Gatier, P.-L. 'Inscriptions grecques, mosaïques et églises des débuts de l'époque islamique du Proche-Orient (VIIe–VIIIe siècles)', in A. Borrut et al., *Le Proche-Orient de Justinien aux Abbassides: Peuplement et dynamiques spatiales*, Bibliothèque de l'Antiquité Tardive 19 (Turnhout, 2011), 7–28.
Genequand, D. 'The Archaeological Evidence for the Jafnids and the Nasrids', in G. Fisher, ed., *Arabs and Empires before Islam* (Oxford, 2015), 172–213.
Gerland, E. 'Die persischen Feldzüge des Kaisers Herakleios', *BZ* 3 (1894), 330–73.
Gnoli, G. *The Idea of Iran: An Essay on Its Origins*, Serie Orientale Roma 62 (Rome, 1989).
Göbl, H. 'Die Sasanidische Münzfund von Seleukia (Veh-Ardašer) 1967', *Mesopotamia*, 8–9 (1973–4), 229–60.
Göbl, R. *Die Tonbullen vom Tacht-e Suleiman und seiner Umgebung* (Wiesbaden, 1968).
Golden, P. B. *An Introduction to the History of the Turkish Peoples: Ethnogenesis and State-Formation in Medieval and Early Modern Eurasia and the Middle East* (Wiesbaden, 1992).
Golden, P. B. *Central Asia in World History* (Oxford, 2011).
Grabar, A. *L'Empereur dans l'art byzantin* (Paris, 1936).
Grabar, O. *Mostly Miniatures: An Introduction to Persian Painting* (Princeton, NJ, 2000).

Greatrex, G. *Rome and Persia at War, 502–532* (Leeds, 1998).
Greatrex, G., and S. N. C. Lieu, *The Roman Eastern Frontier and the Persian Wars, Part II ad 363–630: A Narrative Sourcebook* (London, 2002).
Grierson, P. 'The Consular Coinage of "Heraclius" and the Revolt against Phocas of 608–610', *NC* ser. 6, 10 (1950), 71–93.
Grierson, P. 'Dated Solidi of Maurice, Phocas, and Heraclius', *NC* ser. 6, 10 (1950), 49–70.
Grierson, P. 'The Isaurian Coins of Heraclius', *NC* ser. 6, 11 (1951), 56–67.
Grierson, P. *Catalogue of the Byzantine Coins in the Dumbarton Oaks Collection and in the Whittemore Collection*, II.1 *Phocas and Heraclius (602–641)* (Washington DC, 1968).
Grierson, P., and M. Blackburn, *Medieval European Coinage*, I *The Early Middle Ages (5th–10th centuries)* (Cambridge, 1986).
Gropp, G. 'Urartäische Miszellen', *AMI* 22 (1989), 103–24.
Grossmann, P. *Abu Mina*, I *Die Gruftkirche und die Gruft* (Mainz, 1989).
Grossmann, P. 'The Pilgrimage Center of Abu Mina', in D. Frankfurter, ed., *Pilgrimage and Holy Space in Late Antique Egypt* (Leiden, 1998), 281–302.
Guéry, R., C. Morrisson, and H. Slim, *Recherches archéologiques franco-tunisiennes à Rougga*, III *Le Trésor de monnaies d'or byzantines*, Collection de l'École Française de Rome 60 (Rome, 1982).
Guillou, A. *L'Italia bizantina dall'invasione longobarda alla caduta di Ravenna*, in P. Delogu, A. Guillou, and G. Ortalli, *Storia d'Italia*, I *Longobardi e Bizantini* (Turin, 1980), 217–338.
Gwynn, D. M., ed., *A. H. M. Jones and the Later Roman Empire* (Leiden, 2008).
Gyllenhaal, D. 'The New Josiah: Heraclian Ideology and the Deuteronomistic History' (M.Phil., Oxford, 2015).
Gyselen, R. *La Géographie administrative de l'empire sassanide: Les Témoignages épigraphiques en moyen-perse*, Res Orientales 25 (Bures-sur-Yvette, 2019).
Gyselen, R. 'Note de métrologie sassanide: Les Drahms de Khusro II', *Revue Belge de Numismatique*, 135 (1989), 5–23.
Gyselen, R. 'Un Trésor de monnaies sassanides tardives', *RN* 6 ser., 32 (1990), 212–31.
Gyselen, R. 'Un Dieu nimbé de flammes d'époque sassanide', *Iranica Antiqua*, 35 (2000), 291–314.
Gyselen, R. *The Four Generals of the Sasanian Empire: Some Sigillographic Evidence* (Rome, 2001).
Gyselen, R. 'New Evidence for Sasanian Numismatics: The Collection of Ahmad Saeedi', in R. Gyselen, ed., *Contributions à l'histoire et la géographie historique de l'empire sassanide*, Res Orientales 16 (Bures-sur-Yvette, 2004), 49–140.
Gyselen, R., and L. Kalus, *Deux Trésors monétaires des premiers temps de l'Islam* (Paris, 1983).
Gyselen, R., and A. Nègre, 'Un Trésor de Gazīra (Haute Mésopotamie): Monnaies d'argent sasanides et islamiques enfouies au début du IIIe siècle de l'hégire/IXe siècle de notre ère', *RN* 6 ser., 24 (1982), 170–205.
Hahn, W. *Moneta imperii Byzantini von Justinus II. bis Phocas (565–610)* (Vienna, 1975).
Haldon, J. F. *Byzantium in the Seventh Century: The Transformation of a Culture* (Cambridge, 1990).
Haldon, J. 'Seventh-Century Continuities: The *Ajnād* and the "Thematic Myth"', in Averil Cameron, ed., *The Byzantine and Early Islamic Near East*, III *States, Resources and Armies* (Princeton, NJ, 1995), 379–423.
Haldon, J. *Warfare, State and Society in the Byzantine World, 565–1204* (London, 1999).

Haldon, J. 'The Reign of Heraclius: A Context for Change?', in G. J. Reinink and B. H. Stolte, eds., *The Reign of Heraclius (610-641): Crisis and Confrontation* (Leuven, 2002), 1-16.

Hall, K. R. *A History of Early Southeast Asia: Maritime Trade and Societal Development* (Lanham, MD, 2011).

Harmatta, J. 'Laisser-passer en Égypte à la fin de l'antiquité', *Studia Aegyptiaca*, 1 (1974), 165-75.

Harmatta, J. 'Two Economic Documents from the Sasanian Age', *Oikumene*, 1 (1976), 225-37.

Harper, P. O. 'La Vaisselle en métal', in L. Vanden Berghe and B. Overlaet, ed., *Splendeur des Sassanides: L'Empire perse entre Rome et la Chine (224-642)* (Brussels, 1993), 95-108.

Hayes, J. W. *Late Roman Pottery* (London, 1972).

Heather, P. *Goths and Romans 332-489* (Oxford, 1991).

Heather, P. *The Goths* (Oxford, 1996).

Heather, P. *Empires and Barbarians: The Fall of Rome and the Birth of Europe* (Oxford, 2010).

Heidemann, S., J. Riederer, and D. Weber, 'A Hoard from the Time of Yazdgard III in Kirman', *Iran*, 52 (2014), 79-124.

Herrmann, G. *The Iranian Revival* (London, 1977).

Herrmann, G., and V. S. Curtis, 'Sasanian Rock Reliefs', https://iranicaonline.org/articles/sasanian-rock-reliefs, accessed 1 November 2020.

Hewsen, R. H. *Armenia: Historical Atlas* (Chicago, 2001).

Hild, F. *Das byzantinische Strassensystem in Kappadokien*, TIB 2, Österr Ak. Wiss., Phil.-hist. Kl., Denkschriften 131 (Vienna, 1977).

Hild, F., and H. Hellenkemper, *Kilikien und Isaurien*, TIB 5, Österr Ak. Wiss., Phil.-hist. Kl., Denkschriften 215 (Vienna, 1990).

Hild, F., and M. Restle, *Kappadokien (Kappadokia, Charsianon, Sebasteia und Lykandos)*, TIB 2, Österr Ak. Wiss., Phil.-hist. Kl., Denkschriften 149 (Vienna, 1981).

Hirschfeld, Y. *The Judean Desert Monasteries in the Byzantine Period* (New Haven, CT, 1992).

Hopwood, K. 'Consent and Control: How the Peace was Kept in Rough Cilicia', in D. H. French and C. S. Lightfoot, eds., *The Eastern Frontier of the Roman Empire*, BAR, Int. Ser. 553, 2 vols. (Oxford, 1989), I, 191-201.

Howard-Johnston, J. 'The Two Great Powers in Late Antiquity: A Comparison', in Averil Cameron, ed., *The Byzantine and Early Islamic Near East*, III States, Resources and Armies (Princeton, NJ, 1995), 157-226, repr. in J. Howard-Johnston, *East Rome, Sasanian Persia and the End of Antiquity: Historiographical and Historical Studies* (Aldershot, 2006), no.I.

Howard-Johnston, J. 'Procopius, Roman Defences North of the Taurus and the New Fortress of Citharizon', in D. H. French and C. S. Lightfoot, eds., *The Eastern Frontier of the Roman Empire*, BAR, Int. Ser. 553, 2 vols. (Oxford, 1989), 203-29, repr. in J. Howard-Johnston, *East Rome, Sasanian Persia and the End of Antiquity: Historiographical and Historical Studies* (Aldershot, 2006), no.II.

Howard-Johnston, J. 'Heraclius' Persian Campaigns and the Revival of the East Roman Empire, 622-630', *War in History*, 6 (1999), 1-44, repr. in J. Howard-Johnston, *East Rome, Sasanian Persia and the End of Antiquity: Historiographical and Historical Studies* (Aldershot, 2006), no.VIII.

Howard-Johnston, J. *East Rome, Sasanian Persia and the End of Antiquity: Historiographical and Historical Studies* (Aldershot, 2006).

Howard-Johnston, J. 'Al-Tabari on the Last Great War of Antiquity', in J. Howard-Johnston, *East Rome, Sasanian Persia and the End of Antiquity: Historiographical and Historical Studies* (Aldershot, 2006), no.VI.

Howard-Johnston, J. *Witnesses to a World Crisis: Historians and Histories of the Middle East in the Seventh Century* (Oxford, 2010).

Howard-Johnston, J. 'The Sasanians' Strategic Dilemma', in H. Börm and J. Wiesehöfer, eds., *Commutatio et contentio: Studies in the Late Roman, Sasanian, and Early Islamic Near East, in Memory of Zeev Rubin* (Düsseldorf, 2010), 37–70.

Howard-Johnston, J. 'The Late Sasanian Army', in T. Bernheimer and A. Silverstein, eds., *Late Antiquity: Eastern Perspectives* (Exeter, 2012), 87–127.

Howard-Johnston, J. 'Military Infrastructure in the Roman Provinces North and South of the Armenian Taurus in Late Antiquity', in A. Sarantis and N. Christie, eds., *War and Warfare in Late Antiquity: Current Perspectives*, Late Antique Archaeology 8.2 (Leiden, 2013), 853–91.

Howard-Johnston, J. *Historical Writing in Byzantium* (Heidelberg, 2014).

Howard-Johnston, J. 'The Sasanian State: The Evidence of Coinage and Military Construction', in R. Payne and M. Soroush, eds., *The Archaeology of Sasanian Politics*, Journal of Ancient History 2.2 (Boston, 2014), 144–81.

Howard-Johnston, J. 'The India Trade in Late Antiquity', in E. W. Sauer, ed., *Sasanian Persia: Between Rome and the Steppes of Eurasia* (Edinburgh, 2017), 284–304.

Howard-Johnston, J., 'World War in Eurasia at the End of Antiquity', in R. Gyselen, ed., *Sasanian Persia and the Tabarestan Archive*, Res Orientales 27 (Bures-sur-Yvette, 2019), 9-28, at 16-17.

Howard-Johnston, J. 'Khosrow II', *Encyclopaedia Iranica*, https://iranicaonline.org/articles/khosrow-ii, accessed 26 October 2020.

Hoyland, R. G. *Arabia and the Arabs from the Bronze Age to the Coming of Islam* (London, 2001).

Hoyland, R. G. *Theophilus of Edessa's Chronicle and the Circulation of Historical Knowledge in Late Antiquity and Early Islam*, TTH 57 (Liverpool, 2011).

Huff, D. 'Harsin', *AMI* 18 (1985), 15–44.

Huff, D. 'The Functional Layout of the Fire Sanctuary at Takht-i Sulaimān', in D. Kennet and P. Luft, eds., *Current Research in Sasanian Archaeology, Art and History*, BAR Int. Ser. 1810 (Oxford, 2008), 1–13.

Humann, C. *Magnesia am Maeander: Bericht über Ergebnisse der Ausgrabungen der Jahre 1891–1893* (Berlin, 1904).

Hurbanič, M. 'The Eastern Roman Empire and the Avar Khaganate in the Years 622–624 AD', *Acta Antiqua Ac. Scient. Hungaricae*, 51 (2011), 315–28.

Huuri, K. *Zur Geschichte des mittelalterlichen Geschützwesens aus orientalischen Quellen*, Studia Orientalia 9.3 (Helsinki, 1941).

Isaac, B. *The Limits of Empire: The Roman Army in the East* (Oxford, 1990).

Istria, D., and P. Pergola, 'La Corse byzantine', in D. Michaelides, P. Pergola, and E. Zanini, eds., *The Insular System of the Early Byzantine Mediterranean: Archaeology and History*, BAR, Int. Ser. 2523 (Oxford, 2013), 77–85.

Izdebski, A. 'A Rural Economy in Transition: Asia Minor from Late Antiquity into the Early Middle Ages', *The Journal of Juristic Papyrology*, Suppl. 18 (Warsaw, 2013).

James, E. *The Origins of France: From Clovis to the Capetians, 500–1000* (London, 1982).

Janin, R. *La Géographie ecclésiastique de l'empire byzantin*, I *Le Siège de Constantinople et le patriarcat oecuménique*, 3 *Les Églises et les monastères* (Paris, 1969).

Jankowiak, M. 'Essai d'histoire politique du monothélisme à partir de la correspondance entre les empereurs byzantins, les patriarches de Constantinople et les papes de Rome' (Ph.D., Paris and Warsaw, 2009).

Jankowiak, M. '*Notitia* I and the Impact of the Arab Invasions on Asia Minor', *Millennium*, 10 (2013), 435–61.

Johns, J. 'The *Longue Durée*: State and Settlement Strategies in Southern Transjordan across the Islamic Centuries', in E. L. Rogan and T. Tell, eds., *Village, Steppe and State: The Social Origins of Modern Jordan* (London, 1994), 1-31.
Jones, A. H. M. *The Later Roman Empire*, 3 vols. (Oxford, 1964).
Jones, A. H. M., J. R. Martindale, and J. Morris, *Prosopography of the Later Roman Empire*, 3 vols. (Cambridge, 1971-92).
Kaegi, W. E. 'New Evidence on the Early Reign of Heraclius', *BZ* 66 (1973), 308-30.
Kaegi, W. E. *Heraclius Emperor of Byzantium* (Cambridge, 2003).
Kalas, G., 'The Divisive Politics of Phocas (602-610) and the Last Imperial Monument of Rome', *AT* 25 (2017).
Kaldellis, A. *The Christian Parthenon: Classicism and Pilgrimage in Byzantine Athens* (Cambridge, 2009).
Kazhdan, A. P., et al., eds. *The Oxford Dictionary of Byzantium*, 3 vols. (New York, 1991).
Kenawi, M. *Alexandria's Hinterland: Archaeology of the Western Nile Delta, Egypt* (Oxford, 2014).
Kennedy, H. *The Great Arab Conquests: How the Spread of Islam Changed the World We Live In* (London, 2007).
Kennedy, H., ed., *Al-Tabari: A Medieval Historian and His Work* (Princeton, NJ, 2008).
Kent, J. P. C., and K. S. Painter, eds., *Wealth of the Roman World ad 300-700* (London, 1977).
Khan Magomedov, S. *Derbent—Gornaja stena—Auly Tabarasana* (Moscow, 1979).
Kim, H. J. *The Huns* (Abingdon, 2016).
Kingsley, S., and M. Decker, eds., *Economy and Exchange in the East Mediterranean during Late Antiquity* (Oxford, 2001).
Kister, M. J. 'Al-Hira: Some Notes on Its Relations with Arabia', *Arabica*, 15 (1968), 143-69.
Klein, H. A. 'Niketas und das wahre Kreuz', *BZ* 94 (2001), 580-7.
Klein, H. A. *Byzanz, der Westen und das "wahre" Kreuz: Die Geschichte einer Reliquie und ihrer künstlerischen Fassung in Byzanz und im Abendland* (Wiesbaden, 2004).
Krautheimer, R. *Rome: Profile of a City, 312-1308* (Princeton, NJ, 1980).
Kresten, O. 'Herakleios und der Titel βασιλεύς', in P. Speck, ed., *Varia VII*, Poikila Byzantina 18 (Bonn, 2000), 178-9.
Kretzenbacher, L. *Kreuzholzlegenden zwischen Byzanz und dem Abendlande: Byzantinisch-griechische Kreuzholzlegenden vor und um Basileios Herakleios und ihr Fortleben im lateinischen Westen bis zum Zweiten Vaticanum*, Bayer. Ak. Wiss., Phil.-hist. Kl., Sitzungsberichte 1995, no.3 (Munich, 1995).
Külzer, A. *Ostthrakien (Europe)*, TIB 12, Österr Ak. Wiss., Phil.-hist. Kl., Denkschriften 369 (Vienna, 2008).
Ladstätter, S. 'Ephesos in byzantinischer Zeit: Das letzte Kapitel der Geschichte einer antiken Grossstadt', in F. Daim and J. Drauschke, eds., *Byzanz: Das Römerreich im Mittelalter* (Mainz, 2010), II.2, 493-519.
La Fuye, A. de, et al. *Mémoires de la mission archéologique de Perse*, 25 (Paris, 1934).
La Vaissière, É. de. *Histoire des marchands sogdiens* (Paris, 2002).
La Vaissière, É. de. 'Oncles et frères: Les Qaghans Ashinas et le vocabulaire turc de la parenté', *Turcica*, 42 (2010), 267-77.
Leader, R. E. 'The David Plates Revisited: Transforming the Secular in Early Byzantium', *Art Bulletin*, 82 (2000), 407-27.
Levi, I. 'L'Apocalypse de Zorobabel et le roi de Perse Siroès', *Revue des Études Juives*, 68 (1914), 129-60, 70 (1919), 108-21, 71, (1920), 57-65.
Lewis, M. E. *China's Cosmopolitan Empire: The Tang Dynasty* (Cambridge, MA, 2009).
Liebeschuetz, W. 'The Defences of Syria in the Sixth Century', in C. B. Rüger, ed., *Studien zu den Militärgrenzen Roms*, II (Cologne, 1977), 487-99.

Liebeschuetz, W. 'The Circus Factions', in *Convegno per Santo Mazzarino* (Rome, 1998), 163–85.
Liebeschuetz, J. H. W. G. *Decline and Fall of the Roman City* (Oxford, 2001).
Liebeschuetz, J. H. W. G. 'The Lower Danube Region under Pressure: From Valens to Heraclius', in A. G. Poulter, ed., *The Transition to Late Antiquity on the Danube and Beyond* (Oxford, 2007), 101–34.
Litinas, N. *Greek Ostraca from Abut Mina* (Berlin, 2008).
Lombard, M. *L'Islam dans sa première grandeur (VIII–XIe siècle)* (Paris, 1971).
Liu Mau-Tsai, *Die chinesischen Nachrichten zur Geschichte der Ost-Türken (T'u-Küe)* (Wiesbaden, 1958).
Luschey, H. 'Zur Datierung des sasanidischen Kapitelle aus Bisutun und des Monuments von Taq-i-Bostan', *AMI* 1 (1968), 129–42.
Luschey, H. 'Bisutun. Geschichte und Forschungsgeschichte', *Archäologischer Anzeiger*, 89 (1974–5), 114–49.
Luschey, H. 'Bisutun, ii Archaeology', *Encyclopaedia Iranica*, IV (London and New York, 1990), 291–9.
Lynch, H. F. B. *Armenia: Travels and Studies*, 2 vols. (London, 1901).
Macdonald, M. C. A. 'Ancient Arabia and the Written Word', in M. C. A. Macdonald, ed., *The Development of Arabic as a Written Language*, Supplement to the Proceedings of the Seminar for Arabian Studies 40 (Oxford, 2010), 5–27.
McKenzie, J. *The Architecture of Alexandria and Egypt c.300 bc to ad 700* (New Haven, CT, 2007).
Magness, J. 'Archaeological Evidence for the Sasanian Persian Invasion of Jerusalem', in K. G. Holum and H. Lapin, eds., *Shaping the Middle East: Jews, Christians, and Muslims in an Age of Transition 400–800 C.E.* (Bethesda, MD, 2011), 85–98.
Mahé, J.-P. 'Critical Remarks on the Newly Edited Excerpts from Sebeos', in T. J. Samuelian and M. E. Stone, eds., *Medieval Armenian Culture* (Chico, CA, 1983), 218–39.
Malek, H. M. 'A Seventh- Century Hoard of Sasanian Drachms', *Iran*, 31 (1993), 77–93.
Malek, M. 'The Sasanian King Khusrau II (AD 590/1–628) and Anahita', *Name-ye Iran-e Bastan*, 2 (2003), 23–43.
Manandjan, J. A. 'Marshruty persidskikh pokhodov imperatora Iraklija', *VV* 3 (1950), 133-53.
Mango, C. 'Deux Études sur Byzance et la Perse sassanide', *TM* 9 (1985), 91–118.
Mango, C. 'Épigrammes honorifiques, statues et portraits à Byzance', *Aphieroma ston Niko Svorono* (Rethymno, 1986), I, 23–35.
Mango, C. 'The Fourteenth Region of Constantinople', in O. Feld and U. Peschlow, eds., *Studien zur spätantiken und byzantinischen Kunst, Friedrich Wilhelm Deichmann gewidmet* (Mainz, 1986), 1–5.
Mango, C. 'The Temple Mount, AD 614–638', in J. Raby and J. Johns, eds., *Bayt al-Maqdis*, I 'Abd al-Malik's Jerusalem (Oxford, 1992), I, 1–16.
Mango, C. 'The Columns of Justinian and His Successors', in C. Mango, *Studies on Constantinople* (Aldershot, 1993), no.X.
Mango, C. 'The Origins of the Blachernae Shrine at Constantinople', in *Acta XIII Congressus Internationalis Archaeologiae Christianae* (Vatican and Split, 1998), II, 61–76.
Mango, C. 'The Triumphal Way of Constantinople and the Golden Gate', *DOP* 54 (2000), 173–88.
Mansfield, S. 'Heraclean Folles of Jerusalem', in A. Oddy, ed., *Coinage and History in the Seventh Century Near East*, 2 (Exeter, 2010), 49–55.
Maranci, C. *Vigilant Powers: Three Churches of Early Medieval Armenia*, Studies in the Visual Cultures of the Middle Ages 8 (Turnhout, 2015).
Marty-Laveaux, C. J., ed., *Œuvres de Pierre Corneille*, 12 vols. (Paris, 1862–8).

Mateos, J. *Le Typicon de la Grande Église*, 2 vols. (Rome, 1962–3).
Matthews, J. *The Roman Empire of Ammianus* (London, 1989).
Meier, M. 'Kaiser Phokas (602–610) as Erinnerungsproblem', *BZ* 107 (2014), 139–74.
Mercati, G. 'A Study of the *Paschal Chronicle*', *JTS* 7 (1905–6), 397–412.
Meyendorff, J. *Imperial Unity and Christian Divisions: The Church 450–680 ad* (Crestwood, NY, 1989).
Michaelides, D., P. Pergola, and E. Zanini, eds., *The Insular System of the Early Byzantine Mediterranean: Archaeology and History*, BAR, Int. Ser. 2523 (Oxford, 2013).
Michel, A. 'Le Devenir des lieux de culte chrétiens sur le territoire jordanien entre le VIIe et le IXe siècle: Un État de la question', in A. Borrut et al., *Le Proche-Orient de Justinien aux Abbassides: Peuplement et dynamiques spatiales*, Bibliothèque de l'Antiquité Tardive 19 (Turnhout, 2011), 233–69.
Mitchell, S. *Anatolia: Land, Men, and Gods*, II *The Rise of the Church* (Oxford, 1993).
Mitford, T. B. 'Cappadocia and Armenia Minor: Historical Setting of the *Limes*', in H. Temporini, ed., *Aufstieg und Niedergang der römischen Welt*, II.7.2 (Berlin, 1980), 1169–228.
Mitford, T.B., *East of Asia Minor: Rome's Hidden Frontier*, 2 vols. (Oxford, 2018).
Modèran, Y. *Les Maures et l'Afrique romaine (IVe–VIIe siècle)*, Bibliothèque des Écoles Françaises d'Athènes et de Rome 314 (Rome, 2003).
Momigliano, A. 'The Lonely Historian Ammianus Marcellinus', in A. Momigliano, *Essays in Ancient and Modern Historiography* (Oxford, 1977), 127-40.
Montinaro, F. 'Les Premiers Commerciaires byzantins', in C. Zuckerman, ed., *Constructing the Seventh Century*, TM 17 (Paris, 2013), 351–538.
Morrisson, C. *Catalogue des monnaies byzantines de la Bibliothèque Nationale*, 2 vols. (Paris, 1970).
Morrisson, C. 'Le Trésor byzantin de Nikertai', *Revue belge de numismatique et de sigillographie*, 118 (1972), 29–91.
Morrisson, C. 'Byzantine Money: Its Production and Circulation', in A. E. Laiou, ed., *The Economic History of Byzantium*, Dumbarton Oaks Studies 39, 3 vols. (Washington DC, 2002), III, 909–66.
Morrisson, C. 'L'Atelier de Carthage et la diffusion de la monnaie frappée dans l'Afrique vandale et byzantine (439–695)', *AT* 11 (2003), 65–84.
Morrisson, C., V. Popović, and V. Ivanišević, eds., *Les Trésors monétaires byzantins des Balkans et d'Asie Mineure (491–713)*, Réalités byzantines 13 (Paris, 2006).
Morrisson, C., and W. Seibt, 'Sceaux des commerciaires byzantins du VIIe siècle trouvés à Carthage', *RN* ser. 6, 24 (1982), 222–41.
Mosig-Walburg, K. 'Sonderprägungen des Xusro II. vom Typ Gölb V/6 und VI/7', *Iranica Antiqua*, 28 (1993), 169–91.
Mosig-Walburg, K. 'Zu einigen Prägungen sasanidischer Herrscher', *Iranica Antiqua*, 32 (1997), 209–32.
Mosig-Walburg, K. 'Sonderprägungen Khusros II. (590–628): Innenpolitische Propaganda vor dem Hintergrund des Krieges gegen Byzanz', in R. Gyselen, ed., *Sources pour l'histoire et la géographie du monde iranien (224–710)*, Res Orientales 18 (Bures-sur-Yvette, 2009), 185–208.
Müller-Wiener, W. 'Die Stadtbefestigungen von Izmir, Sıgacık und Çandarlı', *Ist. Mitt.* 12 (1962), 59–114.
Müller-Wiener, W. *Bildlexikon zur Topographie Istanbuls* (Tübingen, 1977).
Mundell Mango, M. 'Imperial Art in the Seventh Century', in P. Magdalino, ed., *New Constantines: The Rhythm of Imperial Renewal in Byzantium, 4th–13th Centuries* (Aldershot, 1994), 109–38.

Naumann, R. *Die Ruinen von Tacht-e Suleiman und Zendan-e Suleiman* (Berlin, 1977).
Naumann, R., and K. Selahattin, 'Die Agora von Smyrna', in *Kleinasien und Byzanz: Gesammelte Aufsätze zur Altertumskunde und Kunstgeschichte*, Istanbuler Forschungen 17 (Berlin, 1950), 69–114.
Naval Intelligence Division, *Geographical Handbook Series: Turkey*, 2 vols. (Oxford, 1942–3).
Naval Intelligence Division, *Geographical Handbook Series: Iraq and the Persian Gulf* (London, 1944).
Naval Intelligence Division, *Geographical Handbook Series: Persia* (Oxford, 1945).
Niewöhner, P. 'Archäologie und die "Dunklen Jahrhunderte" im byzantinischen Anatolien', in J. Henning, ed., *Post-Roman Towns, Trade and Settlement in Europe and Byzantium*, II *Byzantium, Piska, and the Balkans*, Millennium Studien 5.2 (Berlin, 2007), 119–57.
Niewöhner, P. 'Sind die Mauern die Stadt? Vorbericht über die siedlungsgeschichtlichen Ergebnisse neuer Grabungen im spätantiken und byzantinischen Milet', *Archäologischer Anzeiger* (2008), 181–201.
Niewöhner, P. 'The Riddle of the Market Gate: Miletus and the Character and Date of Earlier Byzantine Fortifications in Anatolia', in O. Dally, and C. Ratté, eds., *Archaeology and the Cities of Asia Minor in Late Antiquity* (Ann Arbor, MI, 2011), 103–22.
Noeske, H.-C. *Münzfunde aus Ägypten I: Die Münzfunde des ägyptischen Pilgerzentrums Abu Mina und die Vergleichsfunde aus den Dioecesen Aegyptus und Oriens vom 4.–8. Jh. n. Chr.*, 3 vols. (Berlin, 2000).
Nöldeke, T. *Geschichte der Perser und Araber zur Zeit der Sasaniden, aus der arabischer Chronik des Tabari übersetzt* (Leiden, 1879).
Noth, A., and L. I. Conrad, *The Early Islamic Historical Tradition: A Source-Critical Study* (Princeton, NJ, 1994).
Oikonomidès, N. *Les Listes de préséance byzantines des IXe et Xe siècles* (Paris, 1972).
Oikonomides, N. 'A Chronological Note on the First Persian Campaign of Heraclius (622)', *BMGS* 1 (1975), 1–9.
Olster, D. M. *The Politics of Usurpation in the Seventh Century: Rhetoric and Revolution in Byzantium* (Amsterdam, 1993).
Olster, D. M. *Roman Defeat, Christian Response, and the Literary Construction of the Jew* (Philadelphia, PA, 1994).
Ovadiah, A. *Corpus of the Byzantine Churches in the Holy Land* (Bonn, 1970).
Panaino, A. 'Astral Characters of Kingship in the Sasanian and Byzantine Worlds', in Gnoli, G., ed., *La Persia e Bisanzio*, Atti dei Convegni Lincei 201 (Rome, 2004), 555–94.
Parrish, D., ed., *Urbanism in Western Asia Minor*, JRA Suppl. Ser. 45 (Portsmouth, RI, 2001).
Patrich, J. *Studies in the Archaeology and History of Caesarea Maritima, Caput Judaeae, Metropolis Palaestinae* (Leiden, 2011).
Payne, R. E. *A State of Mixture: Christians, Zoroastrians, and Iranian Political Culture in Late Antiquity* (Oakland, CA, 2015).
Perikhanjan, A.G., 'Pekhlevijskie papyrusy sobranija GMII imeni A.S. Pushkina', *Vestnik Drevnej Istorii*, 77.3 (1961), 78-93.
Peters, F. E. *Jerusalem* (Princeton, NJ, 1985).
Petersen, L. I. R. *Siege Warfare and Military Organization in the Successor States (400–800 ad): Byzantium, the West and Islam*, History of Warfare 91 (Leiden, 2013).
Pfeilschifter, R. *Der Kaiser und Konstantinopel: Kommunikation und Konfliktaustrag in einer spätantike Metropole*, Millennium-Studien 44 (Berlin, 2013).
Phillips, J. R. 'The Byzantine Bronze Coins of Alexandria in the Seventh Century', *NC* ser. 7, 11 (1962), 225–41.

Pietri, L. ed., *Histoire du Christianisme des origines à nos jours*, III *Les Églises d'Orient et d'Occident* (Paris, 1998).
Planhol, X. de. *Les Fondements géographiques de l'histoire de l'Islam* (Paris, 1968).
Pohl, W., *The Avars: A Steppe Empire in Central Europe, 567-822* (Ithaca, NY, 2018).
Pohl, W. 'A Non-Roman Empire in Central Europe: The Avars', in H.-W. Goetz, J. Jarnut, and W. Pohl, eds., *Regna et Gentes: The Relationship between Late Antique and Early Medieval Peoples and Kingdoms in the Transformation of the Roman World* (Leiden, 2003), 571-95.
Pottier, H. *Le Monnayage de la Syrie sous l'occupation perse (610-630)*, Cahiers Ernest-Babelon 9 (Paris, 2004).
Poulter, A. G., ed., *The Transition to Late Antiquity on the Danube and Beyond* (Oxford, 2007).
Prigent, V. 'Le Rôle des provinces d'Occident dans l'approvisionnement de Constantinople (618-717): Témoignages numismatique et sigillographique', *Mélanges de l'École française de Rome, Moyen Âge*, 118 (2006), 269-99.
Pringle, R. D. *The Defence of Byzantine Africa from Justinian to the Arab Conquest*, BAR Int. Ser. 99 (Oxford, 2001).
Raby, J., and J. Johns, eds., *Bayt al-Maqdis*, I *'Abd al-Malik's Jerusalem* (Oxford, 1992).
Rance, P. *The Roman Art of War in Late Antiquity: The Strategikon of the Emperor Maurice*, 2 vols. (forthcoming).
Ratté, C. 'New Research on the Urban Development of Aphrodisias in Late Antiquity', in D. Parrish, ed., *Urbanism in Western Asia Minor*, JRA Suppl. Ser. 45 (Portsmouth, RI, 2001), 116-47.
Rautman, M. 'Sardis in Late Antiquity', in O. Dally, and C. Ratté, eds., *Archaeology and the Cities of Asia Minor in Late Antiquity* (Ann Arbor, MI, 2011), 1-26.
Rawlinson, H. C. 'Notes on a March from Zoháb...', *Journal of the Royal Geographical Society*, 9 (1839), 26-116.
Reich, R. '"God Knows Their Names": Mass Christian Grave Revealed in Jerusalem', *Biblical Archaeology Review*, 22.2 (1996), 26-33, 60.
Reinink, G. J. 'Heraclius, the New Alexander: Apocalyptic Prophecies during the Reign of Heraclius', in G. J. Reinink and B. H. Stolte, eds., *The Reign of Heraclius (610-641): Crisis and Confrontation* (Leuven, 2002), 81-94.
Reinink, G. J., and B. H. Stolte, eds., *The Reign of Heraclius (610-641): Crisis and Confrontation* (Leuven, 2002).
Rheidt, K. *Die Stadtgrabung*, II *Die byzantinische Wohnstadt*, Altertümer von Pergamon 15.2 (Berlin, 1991).
Rheidt, K. 'In the Shadow of Antiquity: Pergamon and the Byzantine Millennium', in H. Koester, ed., *Pergamon: Citadel of the Gods* (Harrisburg, PA, 1998), 395-423.
Robin, C. J. 'Le Royaume hujride, dit "royaume de Kinda", entre Himyar et Byzance', *CRAI* (1996), 665-714.
Robinson, C. F. *Empire and Elites after the Muslim Conquest: The Transformation of Northern Mesopotamia* (Cambridge, 2000).
Robinson, C. F. *Islamic Historiography* (Cambridge, 2003).
Robinson, C. 'The Conquest of Khuzistan: A Historiographical Reassessment', *BSOAS* 67 (2004), 14-39.
Rodinson, M. *Mohammed* (Harmondsworth, 1971).
Rösch, G. 'Der Aufstand der Herakleioi gegen Phokas (608-610) im Spiegel numismatischer Quellen', *JÖB* 28 (1979), 51-62.
Roueché, C. *Performers and Partisans at Aphrodisias in the Roman and Late Roman Periods*, JRS Monographs 6 (London, 1993).

Rubin, Z. 'The Reforms of Khusro Anushirwan', in Averil Cameron, ed., *The Byzantine and Early Islamic Near East*, III *States, Resources and Armies* (Princeton, NJ, 1995), 227-97.

Rubin, Z. 'Ibn al-Muqaffa' and the Account of Sasanian History in the Arabic Codex Sprenger 30', *Jerusalem Studies in Arabic and Islam*, 30 (2005), 52-93.

Russell, J. 'The Persian Invasions of Syria/Palestine and Asia Minor in the Reign of Heraclius: Archaeological, Numismatic and Epigraphic Evidence', in E. Kountoura-Galake, ed., *The Dark Centuries of Byzantium (7th-9th C.)*, National Hellenic Research Foundation, Institute for Byzantine Research, International Symposium 9 (Athens, 2001), 41-71.

Sako, L. R. M. *Lettre christologique du patriarche syro-oriental Īšōʿahb II de Gdālā (628-646)* (Rome, 1983).

Salles, J.-F. '*Fines Indiae*, Ardh el-Hind. Recherches sur le devenir de la mer Erythrée', in E. Dąbrowa, ed., *The Roman and Byzantine Army in the East* (Cracow, 1994), 165-87.

Salzmann, W. 'Die "Felsabarbeitung und Terrasse des Farhad" in Bisutun: Ein spätsasanidisches Monument', *Archäologischer Anzeiger*, 91 (1976), 110-34.

Sänger, P. 'The Administration of Sasanian Egypt: New Masters and Byzantine Continuity', *GRBS* 51 (2011), 653-65.

Sänger, P., and D. Weber, 'Der Lebensmittelhaushalt des Herrn Saralaneozan/Šahr-Ālānyōzān...', *Archiv für Papyrusforschung*, 58 (2012), 81-96.

Sarantis, A. 'War and Diplomacy in Pannonia and the Northwest Balkans during the Reign of Justinian: The Gepid Threat and Imperial Responses', *DOP* 63 (2009), 15-40.

Sarantis, A. *Justinian's Balkan Wars: Campaigning, Diplomacy and Development in Illyricum, Thrace and the Northern World A.D. 527-65* (Prenton, 2016).

Sarre, F., and E. Herzfeld, *Archäologische Reise im Euphrat- und Tigris-Gebiet*, 4 vols. (Berlin, 1911-20).

Sartre, M. *Bostra: Des origines à l'Islam* (Paris, 1985).

Schippmann, K. *Die iranischen Feuerheiligtümer* (Berlin, 1971).

Schlie, F. ed., *Die Kunst- und Geschichts-Denkmäler des Grossherzogthums Mecklenburg-Schwerin*, I (Schwerin, 1896).

Schmidt, E. F. *Persepolis*, III *The Royal Tombs and Other Monuments* (Chicago 1970).

Schmitt, O. 'Untersuchungen zur Organisation und zur militärischen Stärke oströmischer Herrschaft im Vorderen Orient zwischen 628 und 633', *BZ* 94 (2001), 197-229.

Seibt, W. '...Zog Herakleios 625 wirklich in das "Land der Hunnen"?', in K. Belke et al., eds., *Byzantina Mediterranea* (Vienna, 2007), 589-96.

Shahid, I. 'The Iranian Factor in Byzantium during the Reign of Heraclius', *DOP* 26 (1972), 293-320.

Shaked, S. *Dualism in Transformation: Varieties of Religion in Sasanian Iran* (London, 1994).

Shalev-Hurvitz, V. *Holy Sites Encircled: The Early Byzantine Concentric Churches of Jerusalem* (Oxford, 2015).

Simon, H. 'Die sasanidischen Münzen des Fundes von Babylon: Ein Teil des bei Koldeweys Ausgrabungen im Jahre 1900 gefundenen Münzschatzes', *Acta Iranica*, 3 ser.,12, Textes et mémoires 5, Varia 1976 (Tehran and Liège, 1977), 149-337.

Sinclair, T. A. *Eastern Turkey: An Architectural and Archaeological Survey*, 4 vols. (London, 1987-90).

Singh, U. *A History of Ancient and Early Medieval India: From the Stone Age to the 12th Century* (Delhi, 2009).

Sirotenko, A., *The Image of the Emperor Heraclius in the Works of Medieval Authors* (Ph.D., Tübingen).

Sivan, H. 'Palestine between Byzantium and Persia (CE 614-618)', in Gnoli, G., ed., *La Persia e Bisanzio*, Atti dei Convegni Lincei 201 (Rome, 2004), 77-92.

Skaff, J. K. *Sui-Tang China and Its Turko-Mongol Neighbours: Culture, Power, and Connections, 580–800* (Oxford, 2012).
Sodini, J.-P. 'The Transformation of Cities in Late Antiquity within the Provinces of Macedonia and Epirus', in A. G. Poulter, ed., *The Transition to Late Antiquity on the Danube and Beyond* (Oxford, 2007), 311–36.
Spain Alexander, S. 'Heraclius, Byzantine Imperial Ideology, and the David Plates', *Speculum*, 52 (1977), 217–37.
Spanu, P. G. *La Sardegna bizantina tra VI e VII secolo* (Oristano, 1998).
Spanu, P. G., and R. Zucca, *I sigilli bizantini della ΣΑΡΔΗΝΙΑ* (Rome, 2004).
Speck, P. *Zufälliges zum Bellum Avaricum des Georgios Pisides*, Miscellanea Byzantina Monacensia 24 (Munich, 1980).
Stark, S. *Die Alttürkenzeit in Mittel- und Zentralasien: Archäologische und historische Studien* (Wiesbaden, 2008).
Stein, E. *Histoire du Bas Empire*, 2 vols. (Paris, 1949–59).
Stoyanov, Y. *Defenders and Enemies of the True Cross: The Sasanian Conquest of Jerusalem in 614 and Byzantine Ideology of Anti-Persian Warfare*, Österr. Ak. Wiss., Phil.-hist. Kl., Sitzungsberichte 819 (Vienna, 2011).
Stratos, A. N. *Byzantium in the Seventh Century*, I 602–634 (Amsterdam, 1968).
Sylloge Nummorum Sasanidarum: Paris-Berlin-Wien: M. Alram, R. Gyselen et al., I *Ardashir I.–Shapur I.*, Öst. Ak. Wiss., Phil.-hist. Kl., Denkschrift 317 (Vienna, 2003); M. Alram, R. Gyselen et al., II *Ohrmazd I.–Ohrmazd II.*, Öst. Ak. Wiss., Phil.-hist. Kl., Denkschrift 422 (Vienna, 2012); N. Schindel et al., III.1–2 *Shapur II.–Kawad I./2. Regierung*, Öst. Ak. Wiss., Phil.-hist. Kl., Denkschrift 325 (Vienna, 2004).
Thonemann, P. *The Maeander Valley: A Historical Geography from Antiquity to Byzantium* (Cambridge, 2011).
Timm, S. *Das christlich-koptische Ägypten in arabischer Zeit*, Beihefte zum Tübinger Atlas des vorderen Orients, Reihe B, no.41, 7 vols. (Wiesbaden, 1984–2007).
Trever, K. V. *Ocherki po istorii i kul'ture kavkazkoj Albanii IV v. do N.E.–VII v. N.E.* (Moscow and Leningrad, 1959).
Trilling, J. 'Myth and Metaphor at the Byzantine Court: A Literary Approach to the David Plates', *Byz*.48 (1978), 249–63.
Trombley, F. R. 'War and Society in Rural Syria c.502–613 A.D.: Observations on the Epigraphy', *BMGS* 21 (1997), 154–209.
Trombley, F. R. 'The Coinage of the Seleucia Isauriae and Isaura Mints under Herakleios (ca. 615–619) and Related Issues', in A. Oddy, I. Schulze, and W. Schulze, eds., *Coinage and History in the Seventh Century Near East*, 4 (London, 2015), 251–72.
Tsafrir, Y., and G. Foerster, 'Urbanism at Scythopolis-Bet Shean in the Fourth to Seventh Centuries', *DOP* 51 (1997), 85–146.
Twitchett, D. C., ed., *The Cambridge History of China*, III.1, *Sui and T'ang China, 589–906 ad* (Cambridge, 1979).
Tyler-Smith, S. 'Coinage in the Name of Yazdgerd III (AD 632–651) and the Arab Conquest of Iran', *NC* 160 (2000), 135–70.
Tyler-Smith, S. 'Calendars and Coronations: The Literary and Numismatic Evidence for the Accession of Khusrau II', *BMGS* 28 (2004), 33–65.
Vaag, L. E. 'Phocaean Red Slip Ware: Main and Secondary Productions', in M. Berg Briese and L. E. Vaag, eds., *Trade Relations in the Eastern Mediterranean from the Late Hellenistic Period to Late Antiquity: The Ceramic Evidence* (Odense, 2005), 132–8.
Vallejo Girvés, M. *Bizancio y la España tardoantigua (ss. V–VIII): Un capítulo de historia mediterránea* (Alcala de Henares, 1993).

van Bekkum, W. J. 'Jewish Messianic Expectations in the Age of Heraclius', in G. J. Reinink and B. H. Stolte, eds., *The Reign of Heraclius (610–641): Crisis and Confrontation* (Leuven, 2002), 81–112.

Vanden Berghe, L. 'La Sculpture', in L. Vanden Berghe and B. Overlaet, ed., *Splendeur des Sassanides: L'Empire perse entre Rome et la Chine (224–642)* (Brussels, 1993), 71–88.

Vanden Berghe, L., and B. Overlaet, ed., *Splendeur des Sassanides: L'empire perse entre Rome et la Chine (224–642)* (Brussels, 1993).

van Esbroeck, M. 'L'Encyclique de Komitas et la réponse de Mar Maroutha (617)', *Oriens Christianus*, 85 (2001), 162–75.

van Ess, J. "Abd al-Malik and the Dome of the Rock: An Analysis of Some Texts', in J. Raby and J. Johns, eds., *Bayt al-Maqdis*, I 'Abd al-Malik's Jerusalem (Oxford, 1992), I, 89–103.

van Millingen, A. *Byzantine Constantinople: The Walls of the City and Adjoining Historical Sites* (London, 1899).

Voegtli, H. *Die Fundmünzen aus der Stadtgrabung von Pergamon*, Pergamenische Forschungen 8 (Berlin, 1993).

von Schönborn, C. *Sophrone de Jérusalem: Vie monastique et confession dogmatique* (Paris, 1972).

Walmsley, A. G. 'The Social and Economic Regime at Fihl (Pella) and Neighbouring Centres between the 7th and 9th Centuries', in P. Canivet, and J.-P. Rey-Coquais, eds., *La Syrie de Byzance à l'Islam: VIIe–VIIIe siècles* (Damascus, 1992), 249–61.

Walmsley, A. *Early Islamic Syria: An Archaeological Assessment* (London, 2007).

Wander, S. H. 'The Cyprus Plates: The Story of David and Goliath', *Metropolitan Museum Journal*, 8 (1973), 89–104.

Wander, S. H. *The Joshua Roll* (Wiesbaden, 2012).

Ward-Perkins, B. 'Specialized Production and Exchange', in Averil Cameron, B. Ward-Perkins, and M. Whitby, eds., *The Cambridge Ancient History* XIV, *Late Antiquity: Empire and Successors, A.D. 425–600* (Cambridge, 2000), 346–91.

Watson, P. 'Change in Foreign and Regional Economic Links with Pella in the Seventh Century A.D.: The Ceramic Evidence', in P. Canivet, and J.-P. Rey-Coquais, eds., *La Syrie de Byzance à l'Islam: VIIe–VIIIe siècles* (Damascus, 1992), 233–48.

Weber, D. 'Ein bisher unbekannter Titel aus spätsassanidischer Zeit?', in R. E. Emmerick and D. Weber, eds., *Corolla Iranica: Papers in Honour of Prof. Dr. David Neal Mackenzie on the Occasion of His 65th Birthday on April 8th, 1991* (Frankfurt am Main, 1991), 228–35.

Weber, D. 'The Vienna Collection of Pahlavi Papyri', in B. Palme, ed., *Akten des 23. Internationalen Papyrologenkongresses* (Vienna, 2007), 725–38.

Wechsler, H. J. 'The Founding of the T'ang Dynasty: Kao-Tsu (reign 618–26)', in D. C. Twitchett, ed., *The Cambridge History of China*, III.1, *Sui and T'ang China, 589–906 ad* (Cambridge, 1979), 150–87.

Wechsler, H. J. 'Tai-tsung (reign 626–49) the Consolidator', in D. C. Twitchett, ed., *The Cambridge History of China*, III.1, *Sui and T'ang China, 589–906 ad* (Cambridge, 1979), 188–241.

Weitzmann, K., ed., *Age of Spirituality* (New York, 1979).

Wenger, A. *L'Assomption de la T. S. Vierge dans la tradition byzantine du VIe au Xe siècle: Études et documents* (Paris, 1955).

Whitby, Mary. 'A New Image for a New Age: George of Pisidia on the Emperor Heraclius', in E. Dąbrowa, ed., *The Roman and Byzantine Army in the East* (Cracow, 1994), 197–225.

Whitby, Mary. 'The Devil in Disguise: The End of George of Pisidia's *Hexaemeron* Reconsidered', *JHS* 115 (1995), 115–29.

Whitby, Mary. 'Defender of the Cross: George of Pisidia on the Emperor Heraclius and his Deputies', in Mary Whitby, ed., *The Propaganda of Power: The Role of Panegyric in Late Antiquity* (Leiden, 1998), 247–73.

Whitby, Mary. 'George of Pisidia's Presentation of the Emperor Heraclius and his Campaigns: Variety and Development', in G. J. Reinink and B. H. Stolte, eds., *The Reign of Heraclius (610–641): Crisis and Confrontation* (Leuven, 2002), 157–73.

Whitby, Michael. *The Emperor Maurice and His Historian: Theophylact Simocatta on Persian and Balkan Warfare* (Oxford, 1988).

Whitby, Michael. 'Procopius and the Development of Roman Defences in Upper Mesopotamia', in P. Freeman and D. Kennedy, eds., *The Defence of the Roman and Byzantine East* (Oxford, 1986), 717–35.

Whitby, Michael. 'The Persian King at War', in E. Dąbrowa, ed., *The Roman and Byzantine Army in the East* (Cracow, 1994), 227–63.

Whitby, Michael. 'The Violence of the Circus Factions', in K. Hopwood, ed., *Organised Crime in Antiquity* (London, 1999), 229–53.

Whittow, M. 'Rome and the Jafnids: Writing the History of a Sixth-Century Tribal Dynasty', in J. H. Humphrey, ed., *The Roman and Byzantine Near East*, II *Some Recent Archaeological Research*, JRA Suppl. Ser. 31 (Portsmouth, RI, 1999), 207–24.

Whittow, M. 'Recent Research on the Late-Antique City in Asia Minor: The Second Half of the 6th-C Revisited', in L. Lavan, ed., *Recent Research in Late-Antique Urbanism*, JRA, Suppl. Ser. 42 (Portsmouth, RI, 2001), 137–53.

Wickham, C. *Early Medieval Italy: Central Power and Local Society* (London, 1981).

Wickham, C. *Framing the Middle Ages: Europe and the Mediterranean, 400–800* (Oxford, 2005).

Wiesehöfer, J. *Ancient Persia from 550 bc to 650 ad* (London, 1996).

Wiesehöfer, J. *Iraniens, grecs et romains*, Studia Iranica, Cahier 32 (Paris, 2005).

Wilken, R. L. *The Land Called Holy: Palestine in Christian History and Thought* (New Haven, CT, 1993).

Wilson, P. 'Settlement Connections in the Canopic Region', in D. Robinson and A. Wilson, eds., *Alexandria and the North-Western Delta* (Oxford, 2010), 111–26.

Wilson, P. 'Waterways, Settlements and Shifting Power in the North-Western Nile Delta', *Water History*, 4 (2012), 95–117.

Winlock, H. E., and W. E. Crum, *The Monastery of Epiphanius at Thebes*, 2 vols. (New York, 1926).

Wood, I. N. *The Merovingian North Sea* (Alingsås, 1983).

Wood, P. *The Chronicle of Seert: Christian Historical Imagination in Late Antique Iraq* (Oxford, 2013).

Yannopoulos, P. *L'Hexagramme: Un Monnayage byzantin en argent du VIIe siècle* (Louvain, 1978).

Yarshater, E. 'Iranian Common Beliefs and World-View', in E. Yarshater, ed., *The Cambridge History of Iran*, III.1, *The Seleucid, Parthian and Sasanid Periods* (Cambridge, 1983), 343–58.

Yarshater, E. 'Iranian National History', in E. Yarshater, ed., *The Cambridge History of Iran*, III.1, *The Seleucid, Parthian and Sasanid Periods* (Cambridge, 1983), 359–477.

Zuckerman, C. 'The Reign of Constantine V in the Miracles of St. Theodore the Recruit (BHG 1764)', *REB* 46 (1988), 191–210.

Zuckerman, C. 'La Petite Augusta et le Turc: Epiphania-Eudocie sur les monnaies d'Héraclius', *RN* 150 (1995), 113–26.

Zuckerman, C. 'Le Cirque, l'argent et le peuple: À propos d'une inscription du Bas-Empire', *REB* 58 (2000), 69–96.

Zuckerman, C. 'Heraclius in 625', *REB* 60 (2002), 189-97.
Zuckerman, C. 'Learning from the Enemy and More: Studies in "Dark Centuries" Byzantium', *Millennium*, 2 (2005), 79-135.
Zuckerman, C. 'The Khazars and Byzantium: The First Encounter', in P. Golden, ed., *The World of the Khazars* (Leiden, 2007), 399-432.
Zuckerman, C. 'On the Titles and Office of the Byzantine Βασιλεύς', *TM* 16 (2010), 865-90.
Zuckerman, C. 'Heraclius and the Return of the True Cross', in C. Zuckerman, ed., *Constructing the Seventh Century*, *TM* 17 (Paris, 2013), 197-218.

Index

Abasgians, 231, 232, 235, 240, 396
Achaemenids, 2, 3, 188, 189, 362
Acheiropoietos image, 272, 276
Adiabene, 307, 312
Adurbadagan, 174, 178
    commandery, 177, 178, 179, 180, 382, 383, 384, 386
Aegean, 61, 62, 63, 64, 140, 141, 144, 148, 151, 205, 250
    coastlands, 125, 126, 132, 140, 142–3, 327
    islands, 120, 131, 132, 141, 144, 211
Africa, exarchate, 40–1, 44, 49, 50, 51, 70, 108, 128, 132, 147, 180, 270, 349, 356, 381, 384, 389
    exarch, 37, 40, 70, 146, 396
    local leadership, 38, 70
    rebellion, 36, 44, 48–9, 52, 69, 70, 403
    resources, 103, 128, 132, 137, 151–2, 379–80, 395
Albania, 20, 229, 234, 235, 237, 239, 240, 293, 296, 302, 304, 319, 337, 345, 353, 376, 383, 400, 409
    Heraclius in, 221, 228–31, 235, 238
    Turkish invasion, 231, 260, 288–90, 295, 297, 299–300, 340–1, 370–1
Alexandria, 11, 41, 48, 54, 55, 58, 60, 61, 62, 63, 87, 97, 128, 129, 130, 161, 215, 342, 343, 347, 376, 409
    Bonosus' attack on, 56–9
    circus factions, 11, 57
    grain fleet, 64–5, 145, 151, 204
    Persian capture, 128–31, 135, 151, 152, 159, 207
    Persian occupation, 154–5, 158, 160
    rebel attack on, 38, 41, 49–54
    trade, 140–1, 204
alliances, 10, 123, 169, 289, 378, 401
    against Phocas, 26, 52, 65
    Avar-Persian, 205–6, 278, 282
    Roman-Turkish, 221–2, 238–40, 245, 259, 288, 300–3, 339, 342, 344, 369, 372
Amanus mountains, 62, 86, 124
Amida, 21, 31, 35, 161, 254, 255, 257, 269, 342, 399, 400
Amorium, 74, 138, 143
Ananias of Shirak, 178–9
Anastasius I, 30, 81, 400
Anastasius, patriarch, 37, 78
Anastasius, *syncellus*, 108, 111

St Anastasius the Persian, 96, 109–10, 311, 356, 366, 375, 403, 409
Anatolia, 32, 34, 153
    plateau, 32, 33, 73, 112, 125, 126, 143, 145, 196, 200, 211, 252, 256, 257, 271, 285
Ancyra, 73, 74, 80, 88, 138, 143, 144, 210, 211
annona, 51, 127
Antioch, 21, 32, 36, 45, 46, 48, 49, 62, 79, 85, 86, 100, 124, 127, 128, 134, 172, 175, 182, 206, 215, 224, 342, 347, 399, 406
    civil unrest, 37–8, 44, 46–8, 64, 78
    patriarchate, 162, 375
Anti-Taurus mountains, 124, 125, 126, 145, 147, 200, 252
Apamea, 79, 150, 165
Aphrodisias, 141, 143
apocalypticism, 1, 134, 348, 387, 403
Arabia, 122–3, 134, 164, 167–71, 174, 360–1, 385–6, 389, 396, 399, 410
    province, 91, 93, 97
    South, *see* Himyar
Arabian Desert, 2, 123, 399
Arabissus, 252, 343, 344, 371
Arabs, 144, 155, 226, 345, 360, 396, 403
    clients, 166–70, 172, 353, 371, 385, 401
    conquests, 3, 113, 131, 143, 145, 148, 164, 166, 178, 188, 263, 266, 271, 287, 336, 352, 373, 377–8, 383–6, 389
Aragats, Mount, 25, 27, 110, 304
Ararat, Mount, 27, 304, 325, 399, 400
Araxes, river, 20, 22, 25, 27, 28, 32, 33, 110, 225, 229, 234, 235, 236, 237, 242, 246, 257, 288, 294, 304, 305, 399, 400
Arčeš, 242, 246
Ardashir I, 174, 189, 190, 362, 384
Ardashir II, 185
Ardashir III, 337, 345, 354, 371, 382
Ark of the Covenant, 347, 350
Armenia, 10, 11, 19, 21, 24, 45, 73, 83, 87, 89, 98, 113, 116, 119, 124–5, 191, 196–8, 216, 225, 229, 232, 234, 240, 242–3, 245, 247, 249, 255, 290, 293, 296–7, 304, 325, 337, 341–2, 345, 351, 353, 364, 376, 383, 396, 400
    Persian occupation, 27–36, 87
    western, 34–5, 78, 100, 103, 112, 126–7, 132–3, 176, 178, 233, 246, 257, 327, 366

Armenian Taurus, 19, 20, 22, 23, 28, 33, 35, 100, 124, 126, 169, 178, 233, 234, 249, 252, 255, 322, 327, 343, 355, 399, 400, 401
Armenians, 10, 22, 33, 80, 117, 191, 231–3, 240–1, 246, 396
  elites, 10, 21, 27–8
  in Persian army, 18–19, 118, 313, 366
  in Roman army, 11, 25–7, 79, 232, 242, 281
Arsanias, river, 27, 29, 33, 78, 100, 126, 131, 233, 242, 245, 249, 252, 253, 304, 325, 326, 364, 399, 400, 401
artillery, *see* siege engines
Artsʻakh, 300, 304
Asia Minor, 3, 6, 22, 26, 35, 47, 62, 63, 64, 69, 72, 73, 77, 78, 79, 81, 82, 85, 86, 98, 100, 103, 104, 105, 112, 120, 124, 125, 126, 127, 131, 132, 133, 136, 137, 140, 141, 142, 143, 144, 145, 148, 151, 173, 176, 178, 180, 182, 191, 192, 196, 204, 207, 218, 224, 225, 238, 241, 242, 254, 257, 265, 268, 271, 282, 294, 298, 304, 326, 327, 343, 366, 399, 400, 414
  economy and society, 73, 137–45, 151, 395
  Persian campaigns, 3, 72, 77–82, 86, 98, 100, 103, 105, 112, 124–7, 131–3, 136, 144, 173, 176, 180, 182, 191–2, 196, 198–200, 207, 210–11, 216, 218, 223, 233, 245, 247–8, 250–2, 259–62, 273, 284–7, 291, 293, 295
  urban change, 140–5
Assyria, 289, 305, 306, 307, 309, 325
Astat Yetzayar, 32–3, 35
Athanasius, patriarch, 375–6
Athanasius, patrician, 201, 207, 275–6
Athribis, 49, 54, 55, 57, 60
Atropatene, 20, 26, 222, 224–8, 230, 233–7, 239, 245, 257, 285, 288, 290, 293, 305, 310, 317, 319, 341, 353, 361, 363–4, 371, 374, 407–8
attrition, war of, 28, 36, 71–3, 161, 175, 221
authority, 117, 123, 169
  Avar, 201, 269, 396
  Heraclian rebels', 52–3, 60–1, 63
  Muslim, 385–6
  Persian, 10, 32, 34, 78, 92, 96, 118, 121, 130, 132, 154, 157, 171–2, 174, 196, 223, 254, 267, 284, 319, 370, 383–4
  Phocas', 37, 44, 46
  Roman, 8, 9, 19, 28, 33, 103, 116, 128, 215, 253, 261, 299, 344, 347, 349, 353, 379–81,
auxiliaries, 155, 167, 195, 214, 231–2, 275
  Berber, 50, 55, 57
  Caucasian, 231–2, 235, 240–2, 246, 293, 383

Avars, 2, 4, 8, 10, 35–6, 66, 103, 152, 201–7, 209–13, 215, 219, 222, 245, 247–51, 261, 263–5, 267–9, 271, 273–7, 279, 281–3, 291, 294, 330, 360–2, 364, 378–80, 413
  attack on Constantinople, 2, 4, 129, 148, 149, 183, 201, 247–8, 250, 252, 258–66, 273–84, 291, 294, 295, 330, 355, 361, 364, 390, 404–5, 406, 413
  attack on Thessalonica, 136, 202–6
  khagan, 9, 148, 201–6, 210–12, 247, 250, 267–9, 273–82, 287, 360, 379
  khaganate, 2, 9, 10, 135, 201, 203, 213, 261, 355, 361, 378, 396
  relations with Persians, 180, 183, 205, 212–13, 248–50, 265, 267, 273, 278–80, 282, 413
  relations with Romans, 35–6, 137, 201–2, 207–13, 267, 271–3, 275–6, 278–80, 333, 364, 378–9
  subjects, 9, 101, 201, 203, 206, 219, 245, 269, 294, 378–9, 381

Babylon, 53, 130
Bactria, 118, 395
badiya, 1, 86, 98, 121, 122, 353, 360, 378, 385, 386, 401
Bagrewand, 27, 28, 234, 242, 325, 399, 400
Bahram VI Chobin, 338, 390, 395, 401
Bakr b. Waʾil, 168, 170–1
Balkans, 2, 8–12, 35, 36, 40, 45, 47, 72, 101, 103, 120, 132, 135, 137, 144, 151, 152, 200–5, 207, 215, 251, 261, 269, 294, 355, 360, 378, 379, 381, 385, 396
  Slavic settlement, 8, 101, 135, 215, 379, 381, 384–5
  troops, 9–12, 16–17, 24, 35, 48, 195, 396
Basean, 28, 32, 33
Beduin, 31, 91, 121, 127, 134, 155, 167, 169–71, 246, 345, 385, 396
  raids, 88–9, 91, 94, 97–98, 121–2, 170–1, 385
Beklal, 312–13, 317
Berbers, 41, 50, 55, 57, 70, 132, 180, 379, 384, 396
Berrhoea, 355, 375
Bethlehem, 54, 97
Bisutun, 186–90, 227
Bithynia, 74, 80, 128, 137, 139, 140, 194, 195, 196, 217, 326, 363, 409
Bitlis, 233, 236, 242, 254, 255
Blachernae, 12, 67, 84, 209, 280–1, 284, 287, 333
  Church of the Virgin, 12, 67, 208, 209, 272, 283, 284, 333, 404

Black Sea, 8, 14, 17, 112, 221, 232, 234, 239, 255, 274, 298, 299, 399
Bonosus, 46, 48, 49, 51, 54, 61, 63, 64, 67, 68, 74, 85
  in Egypt, 38, 48, 49, 52–60, 62, 71
Bonus, 225, 248, 249, 276, 280–2, 364
Boran, 354–5, 372, 382–3
Bosporus, 16, 35, 105, 140, 144, 178, 180, 209, 218, 251, 256, 261–4, 267, 272, 274–6, 278, 279, 280, 282, 326, 332
Bostra, 87, 91, 165, 386
bucellarii, 65, 67, 68, 84
Bulgars, 203, 263, 265, 269, 280, 378, 379, 396

Caesarea in Cappadocia, 34, 81–3, 85, 100, 110, 126, 127, 143, 144, 175, 200, 216, 218, 219, 224, 225, 233, 256, 257, 326, 332, 343, 364, 401
Caesarea Palaestina, 54, 62, 83, 92, 93, 96, 100, 121, 154, 155, 160, 215, 311, 356, 379
Calamon, monastery, 91, 97
caliphate, 35, 113, 166, 219, 389, 390
Calvary, 99, 351, 352
Cappadocia, 34, 40, 72, 73, 75, 81, 82, 83, 84, 86, 100, 110, 112, 127, 195, 200, 216, 218, 223, 253, 326, 364
Carpathian basin, 2, 378, 396
Carthage, 42, 70, 132, 146, 147, 412
Caspian Gates, 237–9, 288, 299
Caucasus mountains, 173, 221, 237, 238, 239, 290, 291, 293, 296, 340, 354, 370, 371
cavalry forces, 11, 45, 88, 91, 110, 118, 155, 191, 195, 203, 220, 242, 253, 271, 274, 275, 276, 280, 281, 298, 345, 354, 363, 403
central Asia, 116, 119, 120, 136, 176, 269, 291, 293, 369, 387, 389
Chaireon, 50, 56, 57
Chalcedon, 16, 106, 108, 110, 127, 131, 218, 274, 282
Chalcedonians, 39, 78, 161, 367, 368, 376
Chamaitha, 305–7
Chor, 296, 297, 299
Chosdaï, 321, 322, 323, 324
Choziba, 88, 90–2, 95, 97, 409
Christendom, 30, 98, 312, 355, 359, 389, 391, 403
Christians in Persia, 87, 89, 99, 100, 113–14, 121–2, 157, 161, 216, 365–9, 395
Chronicle of Seert, 337, 382, 412
Chronicon Paschale, 17, 49, 87, 89, 98, 106, 145, 208, 217, 232, 258, 259, 269, 273, 279, 295, 315, 322, 346, 389, 406, 407, 409

Cilicia, 47, 48, 79, 86, 105, 112, 124, 125, 126, 127, 131, 132, 175, 180, 197, 223, 224, 242, 255, 257, 342
  Rough Cilicia, 124, 125, 253
Cilician Gates, 112, 127, 200, 256, 285
Circesium, 31, 400
circus factions, 14, 15, 38, 45–8, 58, 59, 60, 64, 67, 74, 75, 85, 93, 208
  Blues, 15, 16, 38, 43, 45, 47, 48, 51, 53, 54, 55, 57, 58, 60, 63, 64, 67, 69, 93
  Greens, 12, 14, 15, 16, 38, 45, 47, 55, 58, 60, 64, 65, 67–8, 85, 93
Citharizon, 33, 253, 400
civil war, 25, 144, 175, 387
  in Egypt, 59–60, 73
  in Persia, 8, 18, 175, 383–4, 390
clientage, 121, 136, 180, 206, 379, 396, 400
  Arab, 98, 121–3, 165–72, 353, 378, 385, 396, 401
  Roman, 109, 111
  Slav, 136, 206, 382
coinage, 79, 96, 99, 104, 124, 132, 135, 142–4, 146–7, 150, 152, 157–9, 172–3, 176–7, 213, 274, 335, 361, 384, 405
  drachms, 157–8, 176–7, 181–3, 383–4
  folles, 62, 96, 104, 121, 124, 142, 147, 150, 152, 158, 159, 172, 270
  hexagrams, 99, 104, 106, 124, 146, 150, 274
  hoards, 79, 96, 150, 152, 157–8, 176–7, 274, 334
  Khusro's, 181–3
  rebels', 41–2, 62
  reform, 99
  solidi, 10, 24, 42, 55, 62, 94, 96, 104, 124, 128, 135, 146–7, 150, 152, 158–9, 162–4, 176, 213, 274, 380
Comentiolus, 13–14, 17, 79–80, 82
commerce, 119, 136, 153, 173, 174–5, 238, 315, 370, 395, 396
  Arabian, 125, 134, 164, 167, 396
  Asia Minor, 82, 137–42
  Egyptian, 3, 11, 60, 72, 129, 153–4, 155–6, 163–4, 175, 180, 395
  Indian Ocean, 129, 136, 250, 384, 395
  Levantine, 3, 62, 72, 87, 145, 158, 164–6, 175, 180, 327, 396
  Mediterranean, 120, 129, 135, 137, 164, 180
communications, 5, 29, 34, 82, 106, 107, 109, 111, 123, 125, 126, 134, 136, 146, 178, 181, 214, 255, 300, 303, 317, 344, 400, 406, 414
  by water, 11, 63, 65, 399
Constans II, 142, 143, 150
Constantia, 21, 23, 31, 35, 161, 355, 374, 401
Constantine I, 331, 347–9, 352, 374, 392, 395

Constantine Lardys, 11, 15–17, 148
Constantinople, 1, 4, 8, 14, 18, 21, 24, 25, 38, 40, 41, 47, 49, 58, 64, 72, 75, 77, 80, 81, 83, 84, 89, 98, 99, 103, 104, 105, 110, 111, 120, 132, 139, 145, 148, 159, 180, 192, 193, 194, 198, 203–5, 207, 208, 211–18, 221, 223, 225, 232, 238, 239, 251, 254, 255, 256, 287, 288, 294, 301, 306, 326, 327, 334, 336, 338, 347, 348, 349, 353, 359, 369, 377, 380, 392, 395, 409
  authorities, 26, 146, 204, 248, 270, 380
  defences, 71, 129, 131, 249–50, 252, 256–7, 260, 270, 274–6, 283, 285, 287
  food supply, 12, 65, 127–8, 131, 135, 140–1, 145, 151–2, 162, 270, 395
  Golden Gate, 16, 209, 210, 281
  harbours, 67–8, 129
  Heraclius' attack, 61, 63, 65–71, 78
  hippodrome, 12, 14, 41, 67, 68, 69, 85, 333
  Hormisdas quarter, 67, 148
  land walls, 14, 15, 71, 84, 208, 209, 256, 271, 272, 274, 275, 276, 277, 278, 280, 281
  Mese, 14, 16, 68
  mint, 124, 146–7, 150–1
  palaces, 16, 65, 67, 68, 84, 85, 209, 215, 217, 301, 336
  Persian-Avar siege, 2, 4, 129, 148, 149, 183, 201, 247–8, 250, 252, 258–66, 273–84, 291, 294, 295, 330, 355, 361, 364, 390, 404–5, 406, 413
  Phocas' attack, 13–16
  prefect, 68, 108, 111, 148, 271
  sea walls, 67, 129, 270, 278, 280
  Shahen at, 105–7
  St Sophia, 15, 69, 84, 85, 98, 146, 148, 152, 210, 259, 270, 328, 329
  victory celebrations, 328–9, 332
core territories, 9, 379
  Avar, 2, 135, 203, 396
  Persian, 1, 20, 101, 113, 133, 167, 174, 184, 218, 225, 266, 293, 306, 309, 365, 383, 395
  Roman, 137, 144, 176, 366, 411
coronation, 16, 84
  Heraclius, 58, 79
  Heraclius-Constantine, 64, 85, 361
  Theodosius, 23–4
Cosmas, quaestor, 201, 207
Cosmas, son of Samuel, 53, 54, 55, 58
Crimea, 2, 117, 136, 396
Ctesiphon, 18, 21, 22, 26, 95, 100, 118, 121, 156, 167, 269, 289, 298, 317, 324, 326, 337, 343, 348, 354, 365, 367, 372, 391, 395, 408
  Arab conquest, 383–4, 386
  coup in, 316, 318, 321, 323

  Heraclius' advance on, 87, 232, 295, 306, 309–13, 364
  Khusro's flight from, 311–12
Cynopolis, 156, 162
Cyprus, 61–2, 130, 147, 334–6, 374
Cyril of Alexandria, 374–6

Damascus, 83, 86, 87, 91, 92, 94, 95, 157, 158, 165, 177, 216
Danube, 8, 9, 12, 48, 116, 135, 210, 264, 274, 378, 379, 392
Dara, 21–8, 31, 35, 36, 223, 400, 401
Dardanelles, 11, 61, 64, 65
Dastagerd, 226, 309–11, 313–15
David, 328, 330, 331, 332, 334, 335, 347, 348
David Plates, 334–6, 359
deception, see subterfuge
deportation, 34, 89, 95–6, 98, 101, 102, 122, 156, 159, 311, 392
desert fringes, 31, 83, 86, 97, 122–3, 134, 155, 164–5, 169–70, 171, 345, 353, 378, 379, 401
Dhu Qar, Battle of, 167, 169, 170
diplomacy, 3, 4, 6, 9, 116, 136, 192, 210, 218, 239, 258, 268, 273, 294, 295, 321, 340–1, 372, 374, 378, 396, 405, 410, 414
  Persian-Avar, 180, 183, 205, 212–13, 248–50, 265, 267, 273, 278–80, 282, 413
  Persian-Turkish, 117, 259–60, 267, 288–91, 293, 296, 409
  Roman-Avar, 201–2, 205–8, 210–13, 250, 261, 267, 271, 273, 275–6, 278, 378–9
  Roman-Persian, 1, 4, 22, 28, 77, 80–1, 104–12, 113, 117–18, 120, 128, 131, 140, 205, 207–8, 215–17, 250, 314, 321–6, 329, 336–41, 345, 355, 385, 403, 406–7
  Roman-Turkish, 221–2, 238–40, 288–9, 369
disinformation, 14, 215, 217, 236, 266, 267, 268, 271, 275, 276, 278, 279, 282, 306, 411
dissidence, see opposition
Diyala, 227, 309, 310, 311, 312, 313, 317, 365, 395
Domnitziolus, 25, 66, 68, 73, 76, 77
Dragon Canal, 50, 56, 58
Dvin, 10, 20, 22, 110, 225, 235, 304, 382, 400, 401, 408

Easter, 86, 88, 93, 193, 194, 217, 218, 346
Edessa, 21, 23, 24, 31, 35, 154–6, 160, 162, 325, 342, 375, 409
Egypt, 20, 38, 40, 43, 45–7, 78, 79, 82, 93, 97, 100, 103, 104, 112, 121, 123, 150, 202, 207, 266, 270, 309, 327, 373, 374, 376, 395, 403, 409

Arab conquest, 377, 386
Delta, 49, 50, 52, 53, 54, 56, 57, 59, 60, 124, 129, 130, 131, 132
economy, 3, 11, 60, 72, 129, 153–4, 155–6, 163–4, 175, 180, 395
elites, 41, 159–60, 366
Persian conquest, 6, 35, 72, 105, 120, 124, 127–32, 135, 140, 145, 147, 151, 173, 175–6, 179, 414
Persian evacuation, 340, 342–3, 371
Persian occupation, 153–6, 158–64, 178, 180, 191, 233
rebel war for, 38, 41, 44, 48, 49–60, 61–4, 70, 71, 73, 404
Upper, 215
Elburz mountains, 18, 174, 390, 395
Elephantine, 130, 154, 155
embassies, 201, 205, 221, 238, 325
Persian-Turkish, 267, 288–91, 293
Roman-Avar, 201–2, 207, 271, 273, 275–6, 278
Roman-Persian, 22, 77, 80–1, 104, 109, 111–12, 117–18, 140, 321–5, 329
Roman-Turkish, 221–2, 238–9, 288, 369
Emesa, 79, 82, 172, 215, 216, 376
Ennaton, 97, 129
Ephesus, 63, 64, 125, 141, 143
Epiphania, Augusta, 84, 217
Eranshahr, 180, 385, 395
Erzincan, plain of, 33, 191, 399
Euchaita, 143, 286, 287
Eudocia, elder, 40, 84
Eudocia, younger, 301, 342
Euphrates, 19, 21, 23, 24, 28, 29, 30, 31, 33, 34, 35, 36, 37, 47, 76, 79, 83, 84, 100, 112, 124, 126, 170, 216, 233, 248, 252, 253, 254, 255, 257, 326, 355, 371, 383, 385, 386
frontier zone, 30–1, 33–5, 71, 78, 79, 327, 342–3, 346, 400–1
Persian crossing, 72–3, 78, 99, 153, 182, 206, 367
upper, 32, 78, 225, 234, 399
Eustathius, *tabularius*, 324, 326–8
Eutychius, 62, 87, 92, 333, 350
Excubitors, 15, 65, 67, 68
expeditionary forces, 288, 300, 407
Persian, 32, 105, 110, 140, 191, 196, 229, 243, 264, 291
Roman, 8, 12, 35, 51, 71, 234, 407
under Heraclius, 221, 231, 232, 234, 245, 247, 259, 266, 285, 293, 295, 299, 304, 321, 362–3, 408
Ezr, catholicos, 376

Fayyum, 53, 156
Fertile Crescent, 1, 170, 171, 386, 399, 400

field armies, 243
Persian, 23–4, 71, 174, 224, 234, 245, 249, 284, 291, 293, 297, 304, 308, 309, 312, 345, 395
Roman, 9, 22, 26, 35, 48, 70–1, 73, 79, 81, 82, 84, 125, 132, 145, 195, 250, 362, 383–4, 395
under Heraclius, 85, 127, 196, 199, 206, 214, 218–19, 230, 243, 249, 256, 298, 311, 362, 369, 377
financial crisis, 11, 103, 106, 145–8, 152, 325, 333
Franks, 9, 135, 136, 208, 330, 378, 387, 395
frontiers, 115, 130, 178, 179, 239, 245
inner Asian, 2, 18, 116–18, 221, 296, 354, 396
post-war, 322, 326–7, 339–40, 342, 346, 355, 372
pre-war, 28, 36, 233, 355, 372, 401, 591
Roman-Persian, 1, 5, 10, 19–21, 22, 24, 31, 78, 115, 158, 160, 174, 309, 399–400

Galatia, 74–6, 82, 97, 133, 137, 138, 210, 326, 409
Galilee, 87, 92, 93, 100, 350
Ganzak, 222–4, 226, 305, 319, 321, 326, 338, 408
Gayshak', 296, 297, 299
Genikon, 147, 149, 150
George of Choziba, 88, 90–3, 96–7, 409
George of Pisidia, 6, 39, 69–70, 77, 80, 85, 86, 102, 192–6, 198–9, 200, 206, 214–15, 219, 224–6, 228, 235, 240–1, 247–9, 251, 255–7, 258, 260, 263–6, 269, 271–3, 276, 284, 286, 295, 300–1, 304, 306, 314, 329–35, 339, 348, 350–2, 362–3, 366, 373, 389, 404–5, 409, 411, 414
Bellum Avaricum, 196, 258, 265, 266, 270, 272
Expeditio Persica, 191–3, 199, 200, 266
Heraclias, 224, 226, 329, 330, 332–3, 335–6
Official History, 193, 219–20, 222, 224, 225, 229, 230–2, 235, 240, 243–4, 246, 249, 251, 253–4, 256–9, 262–3, 265–6, 285–8, 295, 298, 300, 303–4, 306, 310, 312, 318, 333, 334
Gepids, 137, 265, 269, 396
Germanic peoples, 101, 135, 136, 180, 201, 269, 355, 360, 372, 384, 387
Germanus, 14–16, 17, 21–2, 23
Germia, 74, 75, 138
Ghassanids, 98, 122–3, 165, 168, 171, 378, 401
St Glyceria, 66–7, 389
Gogovit, 304–5
Golden Horn, 17, 84, 209, 232, 263, 277, 278, 280, 281

440 INDEX

Golgotha, 94, 99, 326, 346, 348, 391
Gourdanaspa, 315–16
Great Zab, 305, 306, 307, 308, 309, 310, 318
Greece, 3, 148, 202, 203
guerrilla warfare, 114, 124, 196, 197, 244,
    285–8, 291, 293, 363, 389

Hamadan, 34, 179, 184, 227, 228
Harsin, 188–9
Hebdomon, 15, 17, 67, 81, 139, 209, 210, 274
Hephthalites, *see* Huns
Heraclea, 201, 207, 208
Heraclius, the Elder, 37, 40–1
Heraclius, 4–6, 396, 405
    613 campaign, 85–6, 92, 127, 131, 134,
       175, 176
    622 campaign, 192–8, 200, 204, 211, 414
    624–6 campaign, 124, 217–22, 223–2,
       233–8, 240, 242–4, 245, 246, 247,
       252–7, 260–2, 266, 267, 271, 273, 282,
       285, 288, 290, 366
    627–8 campaign, 258–9, 262, 265–6,
       297–300, 304–8, 309–10, 312–4,
       317–18, 319–20, 390, 408, 410
    administrative reforms, 148–50, 377–8
    as commander, 3, 71, 85–6, 103, 175, 191–3,
       195, 198–200, 214, 225, 236, 240–1,
       244, 248, 256, 259, 285–6, 291, 293–4,
       304, 331, 361, 362–5, 369, 371
    coinage, 42–3, 96, 104, 132, 142–4, 146,
       150–2, 172–3, 361
    coronation, 58, 69
    dispatches, 219, 222, 230, 243, 254, 255, 257,
       259, 263, 306, 308, 310, 318, 321, 322,
       323, 324, 328–30, 332, 333, 353, 406–8,
       409, 411
    family, 39–40, 67, 270
    image, 13, 42–3, 51, 65–6, 69, 84–5, 215–7,
       220, 268, 284, 330–2, 334–6,
       357–8, 391–3
    naval forces, 62–5, 71, 270
    opposition, 79, 83–4, 105
    rebellion, 36–7, 41, 49, 51–2, 54–5, 61–9, 71,
       72–3, 405, 410, 414
    relations with Avars, 201, 202, 205, 207–13,
       261, 379, 413
    relations with Boran, 355
    relations with Khusro, 77, 80–1, 109,
       111–12, 314
    relations with Shahrbaraz, 267, 339–40,
       341–5, 371, 390, 413
    relations with Shahen, 103–4, 106–11, 128
    relations with Shiroe, 317–18, 321–4, 325–8,
       336, 338, 371
    relations with Turks, 221–2, 238–9, 249,
       259, 263, 288, 294–5, 300–3,
       369–71, 413
    religious settlement, 356, 373–7
    restoration of the True Cross, 346, 348–53,
       405, 406
    return to Constantinople, 332–3
Heraclius-Constantine, 64, 83, 84, 152, 172,
    217, 218, 264, 270, 279, 283, 332,
    348, 361
Hierapolis, 141, 144
Hierapolis-Manbij, 24, 78, 346, 348, 355,
    375, 376
Hieria, 194, 332
highland regions, 6, 32, 34, 126, 139, 145, 152,
    176, 234, 237, 244, 304, 307, 387, 395,
    400, 401, 414
highland peoples, 18, 34, 124, 173–4, 386
Hijaz, 134, 171, 360, 361, 385, 396
Himyar, 122, 168, 360, 396
Hira, 123, 167–8, 170, 396
History of Khosrov, 25, 29, 33, 34, 46, 85, 88,
    89, 94, 106, 110, 119, 125, 127, 215,
    216, 217, 218, 219, 224, 228, 231, 234,
    237, 238, 239, 242, 243, 279, 289, 294,
    324, 325, 326, 339, 352, 353, 382,
    408, 409
History to 682, 221, 224, 228, 231, 238, 239,
    245, 258–9, 288–90, 293, 296, 297, 298,
    299, 300, 302, 303, 314, 316, 337
Holy Sepulchre, Church of the, 94, 122, 346,
    351, 352, 359
holy war ideology, 2, 200, 240, 365–6
Hormizd IV, 174, 338
Hormizd V, 382–3
hostage-taking, 10, 69, 172, 213–14
Hudaybiya, 361, 385
Huns, 116, 237, 238, 399
    Hephthalites, 116, 117, 118, 120, 269,
       302, 396

Iberia, 19, 113, 216, 229, 232, 234, 239, 249,
    255, 259, 263, 290, 291, 295, 297, 299, 300,
    302, 303, 304, 327, 340, 341, 370, 371, 399,
    400, 401
Iberians, 231–2, 246, 366, 396
ideology, 2, 3, 5, 81, 113, 119, 200, 253, 372–3,
    396, 413
    Roman, 101–2, 113, 136, 145, 323,
       362, 377
    Sasanian, 113, 173–4, 179, 184, 250, 385
Illig, *yabghu khagan*, 238, 288, 354,
    360, 369–71
Illyricum, 148, 150, 203, 379, 381, 396
    praetorian prefect, 135, 146, 204, 381
India, 4, 136, 176, 250, 384, 412
Indus, river, 178, 395
innovation, 166, 220, 364
    Heraclius, 220, 363–4
    Khusro, 166

intelligence, 20, 118, 122, 222, 282, 300, 310, 312
  Heraclius' use of, 197, 226, 257, 266, 309, 363
Ioannicius, 50, 51, 52, 54–5, 61
Iran, 2, 3, 20, 113–17, 119–20, 174, 176, 178, 180, 182, 184–6, 228, 232, 246, 247, 292, 322, 355, 359, 362, 370, 382–5, 387, 389, 390, 395
Iranian plateau, 19, 179, 266, 327, 340, 384, 395, 399
Isauria, 124–7
Isho'yahb II, 353, 355, 356, 374–5
Isidore of Seville, 38, 46, 87, 202
Islam, 3, 4, 35, 157, 169, 190, 240, 360–1, 373, 412
Ispahan, 118, 179
Italy, 8, 9, 10, 36, 76, 82, 103, 132, 135, 146, 147, 180, 201, 378, 380, 396

Jafnid, 98, 123, 167–8
Jericho, 87, 90, 91, 92, 93, 94, 95, 97, 409
Jerusalem, 46, 54, 91, 92, 96, 99, 100, 102, 130, 157, 160–1, 173, 181, 215, 269, 342, 355, 356, 367, 391, 410
  communal disorder, 46, 54, 93, 95, 97, 100, 121–2, 127, 181, 350
  Golden Gate, 351, 357, 359, 391, 392
  Heraclius' visit, 325, 333, 346, 349–53, 356, 358, 374, 377, 392, 405, 406
  Jews, 37, 87, 89, 93, 95, 97, 100, 121–2, 157, 350, 367
  Mount of Olives, 88, 94, 95, 122, 351
  sack, 2, 4, 46, 87, 89–90, 93–5, 98, 121, 128, 131, 145, 170, 173, 206, 220, 227, 343, 365, 403, 406, 410
  symbolism, 346–8, 359, 365, 410
  Temple Mount, 97, 347, 351, 352, 357, 359, 391
Jews, 39, 47, 64, 94, 230, 269, 325, 329, 347, 348, 351, 356–7, 359, 366, 368, 391, 412
  in Jerusalem, 37, 87, 89, 93, 95, 97, 100, 121–2, 157, 350, 367
  in Palestine, 92, 100, 121, 157, 350
  in Persia, 89, 101–2, 121, 157, 181, 366
John of Nikiu, 13, 38, 43, 44–5, 49, 50, 51, 52, 53, 54, 57, 59, 60, 61, 123, 128, 160, 377, 409, 410
John the Almsgiver, 58, 128, 130, 409
Jordan valley, 87, 90, 347
Joshua, 347–9
Joshua Roll, 357–9
Judaea, 54, 88
Judaean desert, 87
  monks, 88, 94, 98, 121, 170, 410
Julian, 116, 185, 269

Justin I, 30, 150, 283
Justin II, 8, 20, 119, 123, 171, 172, 253, 359, 404
Justinian, 70, 80, 81, 123, 137, 143, 147, 168, 380, 381, 386, 400

Karabakh, 225, 228, 229, 230, 234, 235, 241, 244, 341
Kars, plain of, 25, 26, 27
Kavad I, 116–17
Kavad Shiroe, 117, 315–16, 318–19, 321–9, 336–7, 340, 342, 355, 371, 382, 407
Kayanids, 2, 116
Khurasan, 118, 174, 177, 178, 296, 382, 383
Khusro I Anushirwan, 73, 80, 115, 117, 173, 174, 177, 181, 234
Khusro II Parvez, 31, 36, 151, 161, 175, 233–5, 242, 246, 286, 295–8, 307, 309, 324, 337, 350, 373, 390–3, 395
  as commander, 20, 23–4, 35, 219, 222–4, 226–7, 229, 243, 247, 293, 311, 313, 390
  building projects, 184–90, 359
  coinage, 157–8, 181–3, 382
  fall, 1, 87, 194, 259, 289, 310–9, 323, 330, 336, 361, 365, 370–1, 384, 405, 407, 408
  family, 311, 315–16, 354, 372, 382, 390
  hubris, 183–4, 190
  relations with Arabs, 122–3, 166–71
  relations with Heraclius, 78, 81, 107–12, 117, 212, 216, 314, 317, 322, 406, 407
  relations with Maurice, 16, 17, 18, 20, 22, 106, 109, 401
  relations with Shahrbaraz, 262–4, 267–8, 364, 390, 411
  relations with subjects, 34, 121, 159–66, 180–1, 303, 315, 322, 365, 367–9
  relations with the Turks, 117–18, 174, 260, 289–92, 294, 302, 369–70, 409
  rise to power, 18, 19, 106, 113, 159, 327, 332, 338, 367, 395, 401
  support for Theodosius, 24, 26, 81
  war aims, 2, 20–2, 28, 80, 111–12, 119–21, 223, 228, 250, 291, 355
Khusro III, 382–3
Khuzistan, 88, 158, 166, 176, 178, 180, 384, 386, 409
Khuzistan Chronicle, 88, 166, 409
Khwadaynamag, 2, 115, 183, 259, 295, 296, 297, 319, 337, 390, 391, 403, 412
Kur, river, 20, 228, 230, 235, 237, 238, 239, 255, 288, 295, 297, 399
Kurdistan, 305, 401

Lakhmids, 123, 167, 168, 169, 170, 171, 396
Laz, 73, 231–2, 235, 240, 299, 396

Lazica, 17, 18, 19, 112, 234, 239, 255, 263, 290, 295, 298, 299, 327, 374, 399, 400, 401
Leontius, prefect, 108, 111
Lesser Zab, 305, 306, 309, 310, 312, 320
Levant, 2, 26, 35, 52, 59, 60, 63, 71, 79, 85, 101, 117, 129, 147, 162, 223, 250, 353, 381, 384, 395, 397, 399,
  Arab conquest, 386
  commerce, 3, 62, 72, 87, 145, 158, 164–6, 175, 180, 327, 396
  discontent, 44, 47–8, 61, 366
  Persian conquest, 100, 120, 153, 183, 360, 364, 367
  Persian evacuation, 340, 343, 371
  Persian occupation, 4, 37, 96, 120, 153, 253, 412
local administration
  in Egypt, 40, 51, 131
  occupied territories, 96, 154–7, 159, 171–2, 233, 247, 377
  Persian, 247, 319
  Roman, 34, 137–8, 325, 344, 353
Lombards, 8–10, 24, 36, 103, 132, 135–6, 201, 380, 395, 396, 403
Long Wall, 14, 66, 207, 208, 210, 214, 274, 296
Lycia, 140, 145
Lycus, 141, 277, 286, 287

magister militum, 11, 79, 177
Magnesia-on-the-Maeander, 141, 143
manpower, 3, 6, 59, 103, 126, 144, 145, 153, 174, 175, 247, 248, 271, 285, 286, 291, 293, 296, 372, 414
Manzikert, 234, 242
Mareotis, district, 41, 50, 52, 58
Mareotis, Lake, 50, 57, 58, 129, 160
Marmara, Sea of, 14, 15, 65, 66, 67, 201, 211, 277, 283, 389
Martina, 40, 217, 218, 225, 330, 336, 411
martyrdom, 89, 96, 156, 194, 240–1, 311, 356, 365, 403
Martyropolis, 254, 332, 400
marzban, 96, 154, 155, 341
Maurice, 8–11, 24, 25, 40, 55, 66, 85, 103, 106, 112, 123, 161, 172, 201, 222, 244, 331, 338, 362, 363, 367, 396, 401, 404
  fall, 14–18, 20, 23, 69, 75, 80, 107
  family, 14, 16, 32, 41, 69, 108, 392–3
  opposition to, 11–14, 21
  Strategicon, 195, 220, 362
Mecca, 123, 134, 135, 169, 268, 360, 361, 390, 396
Media, 18, 34, 174, 178, 179, 184, 186, 188, 226, 227, 228, 230, 233, 234, 237, 238, 244, 245, 290, 293, 337, 341, 371, 386
Medina, 123, 135, 169, 268, 360, 361, 390

Mediterranean, 4, 11, 46, 70, 72, 87, 103, 118, 120, 129, 135, 136, 182, 251, 347, 355, 381, 384, 395, 412
  coast, 36, 91, 123, 137, 180, 327, 362, 379, 400
  commerce, 120, 141, 145, 164–5
  eastern, 3, 44, 61, 129, 136, 141, 268, 395
  world, 56, 101, 107, 115, 172, 347, 355
Melitene, 78, 82, 112, 126, 127, 131, 200, 223, 242, 248, 252, 253, 326, 332, 399, 401
Mesopotamia, 20, 23, 29, 30, 31, 34, 37, 73, 96, 98, 100, 113, 122, 123, 167, 169, 170, 174, 178, 180, 184, 185, 216, 227, 234, 237, 247, 249, 290, 321, 325, 327, 332, 333, 353, 355, 356, 365, 375, 382, 383, 395, 396, 400, 401, 409, 412
  Arab conquest, 178, 266, 384, 386
  episcopates, 367–8
  front, 29, 59
  Heraclius' invasion, 262, 297, 303, 305–10, 312–14, 317, 342, 366
  Jews, 89, 101–2, 121, 157, 181, 366
  limes, 22, 26, 28, 30–1, 34, 37, 71, 78, 126, 400
  northern Mesopotamia, 21, 22, 73, 103, 112, 122, 157, 161, 176, 191, 233, 266, 327, 345, 365, 368, 382, 385, 386, 400, 401
  theatre of war, 19, 28, 223
Miletus, 141, 143
military resources, 3, 11, 19, 28, 55, 59, 103, 104, 144, 154, 175, 178, 179, 219, 221, 245, 260, 293, 327, 384
military stamina, 3, 175, 199, 219, 243, 285, 363
military supplies, 5, 59, 105, 127, 129, 131–2, 196, 204, 223, 224, 226, 230, 242, 249, 252, 253, 269, 281, 294, 300, 304, 305, 319, 321, 325, 386, 413
minting, 62, 96, 104, 135, 172–3, 213, 366
  in Carthage, 42, 132, 146
  in Constantinople, 124, 150–1
  in Isauria, 124, 127
  reform, 146–7, 150
  Sasanian, 157–9, 176–7, 183, 383–4
Miracula Sancti Demetrii, 46–7, 62, 202–3, 205–6, 408, 409
mobility, 59, 219–20, 229, 243, 251, 285, 293, 363, 414
mobilization, 6, 11, 19, 21, 35, 55, 82, 90, 93, 95, 105, 124, 127, 175, 179, 184, 203, 213, 218, 222, 224, 234, 247, 250, 255, 268, 269, 274, 293, 294, 307, 309, 362, 367, 383, 386, 414
Modestus, 90, 93, 95, 98, 121, 122, 352, 353, 356, 408
Monoenergism, 374–5, 377

Monophysites, 10, 29–30, 39, 44, 58–9, 78, 101, 102, 113, 128, 129, 160, 161, 181, 367–8, 373–7, 395, 405
morale, 281, 302, 407
  demoralization, 82, 103, 131, 191, 211, 235, 240, 251, 256, 279, 340
  Persian, 28, 180, 197, 218, 237, 239–41, 244, 299
  Roman, 25, 33, 36, 57, 72, 98, 104, 126, 175, 197, 199, 204, 217, 219, 244, 255, 271–4, 276, 280, 283, 294, 304, 312, 363, 365–6
mountain passes, 5, 19, 23, 28, 46, 186, 220, 227, 253, 255, 305, 317, 319, 320, 321, 343, 400, 401, 413
Muhammad, 134, 169, 171, 240, 268, 360, 361, 390, 391, 396, 404
Muslim, 94, 113, 123, 134, 158, 169, 171, 240, 348, 360, 383, 386, 389, 390, 391, 403

Nahrawan, 311, 312, 313, 316, 321, 395, 400
Nakhchawan, 11, 225, 234, 241, 242, 305
Naqsh-i Rustam, 184, 189, 190
Narses, 21, 23, 24, 25, 29, 35
Nasrids, 123, 167–9, 396
Nativity of the Virgin, 272, 283
naval forces, 56, 61–8, 104, 105, 120, 129, 145, 205, 211, 218, 232, 250, 257, 263–4, 269–71, 277, 279–81, 327, 381, 395
negotiations
  Roman-Avar, 201–2, 205, 207–8, 211–13, 250, 267, 278
  Roman-Persian 1, 4, 28, 80–1, 104, 105–12, 120, 128, 131, 140, 205, 207–8, 250, 314, 322–7, 336–41, 345, 355, 371, 385, 403, 413, 414
  theological, 373–6
  with local officials, 50, 52, 92, 121
  with Turks, 221, 239–40, 261, 288–9, 340–1
Nestorians, 30, 99, 102, 111, 113, 161, 181, 367, 368, 375, 376, 395
Nicaea, 17, 139, 140
Nicephorus, patriarch, 61, 106, 111, 208, 258–9, 263, 264, 295, 298, 301, 324, 333, 344, 352, 389, 410, 411
Nicetas, 37, 50, 52, 55–8, 60–1, 64, 82–3, 85, 93–4, 97, 99, 100, 121, 123, 131, 411
Nicomedia, 139, 140, 147, 218
  Gulf of, 16, 139, 194
Nicopolis, 33, 112, 191, 200, 401
Nikiu, 38, 43, 44, 54, 55, 57, 58, 60, 130, 403
Nile, 11, 50, 53, 54, 55, 56, 57, 123, 129, 130, 132, 151, 155, 156, 157, 162, 163, 164, 178
  Canopic, 50, 56
Nineveh, Battle of, 87, 330, 334, 363–4, 392

Nineveh, plain of, 307–9, 363
Nisibis, 20, 24, 233, 234, 383, 399, 400
nomads, 2, 115–17, 119, 206, 219, 221, 239, 269, 280, 289, 290, 294, 297, 299, 301–2, 363, 372, 396
Nu'man, al-, 166, 169
Nymphius, river, 253, 254, 255

Old Testament, 216, 268, 283, 329, 330, 331, 334, 349, 357, 359, 391
Olympius, 108, 111, 148
Onouphis, 38, 49, 54, 55, 58, 60
opposition, 80, 161
  to Heraclius, 53, 62, 67
  to Khusro, 18, 34, 181, 370
  to Maurice, 11–13
  to Persians, 34, 115, 131, 172–3, 366
  to Phocas, 23, 26, 33, 37–8, 41, 44–52, 58, 63–5, 70
Orontes, river, 79, 82, 83, 86, 100
Osrhoene, 31, 154, 161, 216, 325, 327, 355, 400
Oxus, river, 118, 178, 206, 395
Oxyrhynchus, 49, 132, 154, 156, 162, 163

P'artaw, 229, 230, 234, 238, 239, 241, 244, 366
P'aytakaran, 234, 237, 238, 244
Palestine, 58, 63, 83, 93, 122, 123, 124, 131, 134, 158, 160, 170, 171, 176, 178, 180, 266, 346, 356, 368, 378, 385, 400, 403, 409, 411
  civil disorder, 45–7, 49, 73, 132
  Jews, 100, 157, 350
  local authorities, 92
  Persian conquest, 72, 79, 92, 128, 191, 216, 327
  Persian evacuation, 342–3, 345
  Persian occupation, 37, 92, 96, 98–100, 112, 121, 123, 127, 135, 150–1, 155, 161, 164, 175, 233, 309, 367, 373
papyri, 49, 153, 155, 156, 164, 377
Passion, 93, 194, 347
Patnos, 234, 242
Paul of Sebennytos, 56, 57, 58
Pege, 277, 283
Pelusium, 54, 123
Pentapolis, 41, 48, 49, 50, 120, 180, 379
Pentecost, 81, 270, 328
Pergamum, 141, 143
Persarmenia, 10, 19, 20, 22, 110, 216, 225, 319, 371, 401
Persian withdrawal, 324–5, 328, 342–5, 371, 378
Pessinus, 74, 76, 138
Peter, general, 12, 13, 16, 17
Philippicus, 17, 80, 84, 110, 124

Phocas, 12, 18, 40, 43, 57, 77, 78, 107, 358, 392, 393, 396, 411
    coinage, 150, 172
    coronation 15–16, 53
    fall, 65–8, 72, 79–80, 331
    opposition, 21–4, 26, 37–9, 41–2, 44–51, 53, 55, 58–9, 70–1, 75
    propaganda, 13, 29, 35, 39, 69, 411
    reforms, 148–9
    revolt, 13–17, 48
    support, 35–6, 38, 53, 63–4
    treaty with Avars, 101, 103, 135, 201, 212
Phoenicia, 62, 87, 92, 94, 100, 376
plague, 9, 141, 164, 167
Po valley, 103, 380
pogrom, 93, 95, 97, 122, 127, 181, 325, 350
Pontus, 138, 143, 191
praetorian prefecture of the East, 148–50
    prefect, 11, 15, 111, 146–8
prestige, 11, 168, 171, 201, 339, 353
    Heraclius', 82, 85, 101, 200, 261, 284, 291, 355, 370
    Khusro's, 3, 112, 181, 183, 222, 224, 228, 237, 315
    Persian, 26, 116–17, 175, 341
    Roman, 8, 33, 342, 380
Priscus, 11, 39, 43, 65, 67, 68, 69, 82, 83, 84, 85, 110
prisoners of war, 24, 26, 55, 94, 97, 195, 201, 205, 208, 210, 226, 228, 229, 230, 238, 243, 286, 288, 289, 293, 300, 307, 310, 311, 318, 323, 324, 337, 358, 360, 370, 379
Probus, 65, 68
propaganda, 2, 5, 6, 8, 23, 53, 268, 372, 413, 414
    against Heraclius, 44, 49, 122
    against Phocas, 41, 63, 65, 66, 67, 69, 70, 411
    Persian, 20, 29
    Roman, 28, 46, 61, 89, 92, 99, 102, 114, 130, 137, 145, 174, 181, 199, 214, 216, 219–20, 231–2, 243, 253, 267, 287, 329, 345, 364–6, 369, 390, 410
psychological warfare, 33, 48, 224, 241, 277, 316
public opinion, 301
    in Constantinople, 65–6
    Persian, 20, 101, 121, 181, 301
    Roman, 18, 23, 63, 71, 101
Pyramus, river, 253, 255

Qadisiyya, Battle of, 383, 384, 386
Qur'an, 134, 390, 403
Quraysh, 268, 361

Rahzadh, 297, 298, 304, 305, 306, 307, 308, 309, 310, 311, 312, 314, 325, 390

raiding, 14, 58, 73, 80, 118, 145, 400, 401
    Avar, 208–11, 404
    Beduin, 88, 91, 94, 97, 121–2, 170–1, 385, 401
    Persian, 25, 32, 33, 57, 81–2, 101, 118, 125–6, 129, 144, 163, 207
    Roman 219, 228, 230, 237, 239, 290, 293, 302, 307, 312, 314, 365
    sea raids, 144, 205, 206, 211
    Slav 8, 135, 144, 148, 151, 205–6, 211
    Turkish, 2, 118, 180, 288, 299, 302, 340, 370
Ravenna, city, 146, 380
Ravenna, exarchate, 9–10, 147, 380
    exarch, 9–10, 36, 76–7, 146, 380, 396
recruitment, 10, 28, 117, 173, 175, 246, 247, 248, 249, 259
Red Sea, 123, 136, 280
refugees, 26, 79, 92, 93, 94, 97, 128, 206, 271, 274, 299, 300, 354, 379
regency
    Persian, 338, 345
    Roman, 239, 248–9, 260–1, 264, 270–1, 274–6, 279, 281, 287
Rhodes, 140, 211, 250
rioting, 38, 46, 64, 75, 93, 138
    in Constantinople, 11, 15, 45
road system, 22, 23, 32, 33, 73, 74, 87, 100, 105, 112, 126, 139, 140, 154, 178, 184, 186, 187, 188, 189, 191, 196, 197, 200, 209, 220, 225, 252, 256, 260, 270, 309, 310, 311, 312, 313, 317, 321, 326, 337, 343, 356, 399
Roman-Persian world order, 3, 30, 81, 113, 119–20, 173, 174, 263, 266, 322, 338, 355, 371, 377, 384
Rome, 9, 146, 359, 380, 406
Ruz canal, 310, 311, 312, 313

Samosata, 23, 255
Sardis, 125, 141, 142
Sarus, river, 253, 254, 255, 257
Satala, 32, 33, 78, 112, 191, 200, 399, 401
Scholae, 270–1
Sebastea, 191, 256, 257, 261, 285
Sebennytos, 38, 53, 54, 56, 60
sedentary world, 2, 97, 115, 116, 119, 250, 268, 292
Seleucia, 79, 124, 147, 158, 176, 177, 366
Selymbria, 66, 208
Senate, 6, 15, 38, 42, 65, 66, 84, 85, 105, 106, 107, 109, 110, 111, 112, 118, 120, 131, 213, 250, 403, 406, 407, 414
Senitam Khusro, 27, 28
Sergius, patriarch, 69, 77, 84, 258, 267, 272–3, 275–6, 278–9, 282–3, 332, 373–4, 376–7
Sevan, Lake, 234, 235

Severus of Antioch, 376, 405
Shahen Patgosapan, 33, 83, 121, 179, 219, 239–40, 246, 251, 252, 260, 265, 266, 290, 390
  at Chalcedon, 105–11, 128, 131, 140, 144
  defeat and death, 261–3, 265, 273, 282, 285–6, 288, 291, 294
  in Armenia, 34–5, 78–80, 234, 236–7, 241–2, 245
  in Asia Minor, 125–7, 247, 285
  in Caesarea, 81–3, 85, 144, 175
  in Egypt, 129–30, 179
  recruitment, 247, 257, 259, 265
Shahrazur, 317, 318, 319, 320
Shahrbaraz, 31, 85, 97, 105, 179, 245, 257, 282, 287, 290–1, 308, 310, 316, 317, 345, 363, 383, 390, 411
  against Heraclius, 232–7, 239–40, 242–3, 246–7, 250–1, 253, 255–6, 294
  as Khoream Erazman, 29, 30, 31
  at Jerusalem, 87, 92–6, 98–100, 181
  attack on the Levant, 78–80
  coup, 343, 345, 354–5, 382
  death, 354, 375
  in Asia Minor, 125–7, 131, 196, 210–11, 223–4, 247, 285
  in Egypt, 121, 127, 128–30, 179
  recruitment, 246
  relations with Heraclius, 4, 315, 325–6, 337, 339–45, 355, 371, 390, 413
  relations with Khusro, 264, 267–8, 314–15, 364, 411
  relations with Shiroe, 327–8
  siege of Constantinople, 251, 261–5, 267, 271, 274, 276, 278
Shapur I, 31, 189, 190, 362, 385
Shapur II, 184–5, 366, 385
Sharaplakan, 234–5
shipping, 59, 62, 65, 100, 145, 151, 204, 248
Shirin, 190, 311, 391
Sicily, 151, 152, 180, 380
siege engines, 55, 56, 57, 93, 203, 204, 220, 248, 250, 257, 264, 269, 271, 277, 279, 281, 302
  trebuchets, 57, 60, 277
Siwnikʻ, 237, 376, 383
Slavs, 8, 9, 12, 40, 148, 202, 215, 362, 382, 396
  attack on Constantinople, 232, 263–5, 269, 277, 280–1
  attack on Thessalonica, 205–6
  Avar subjects, 2, 9, 135–6, 180, 201, 203, 206, 269, 360, 381, 396
  migration, 101, 360, 381
  raiding, 144, 148, 211
  settlement, 8, 101, 103, 132, 151, 203, 215, 378–9, 381, 384–5
Smbat Bagratuni, 11, 19, 118–19, 180, 337, 368–9

Sogdians, 136, 238, 396
Sophronius, patriarch, 87, 349, 350, 351, 374, 377, 412
spahbeds, 27, 29, 174, 177–9, 383, 386, 395
Spain, 98, 135, 335, 360, 380, 381, 387, 396
spoils of war, 22, 26, 83, 107, 118, 205, 210, 219, 243, 255, 293, 306, 308, 313, 325, 333, 340
St Menas, 129, 160
St Sabas, 88, 89, 91, 94, 97, 410
St Sophia, *see* Constantinople
steppes, 2, 11, 115–18, 221, 237, 239, 246, 289, 296, 303, 354, 355, 378, 384, 385, 387, 396, 399
  world, 2, 11, 115, 370
Strategius, 46, 88–9, 94–5, 99, 181, 410
subterfuge, 129, 214, 215, 244, 245, 266, 273, 293, 304, 313, 364, 371, 392, 407, 412
Sycae, 209, 275
Syria, 21, 34, 82–3, 122, 154, 155, 157, 161, 164, 170, 175–7, 178, 233, 309, 325, 327, 342, 368, 376–8, 400, 409, 410
  Arab conquests, 266
  dissidents, 46, 73, 78, 132, 172, 366
  northern Syria, 78, 79, 86, 105, 112, 126–7, 150, 166, 175–6, 183, 224, 242, 254, 257, 310, 343, 364, 400
  Persian conquest, 31, 36–7, 72, 79, 110, 191, 202, 367
  resources, 103, 150, 176, 180, 385

Tʻeodos Khorkhoruni, 27, 29
Tabari, al-, 116, 117, 123, 169, 267, 311, 382, 390, 403
Tang dynasty, 136, 340, 353, 360, 369, 371, 387
Taposiris, 50, 58, 129
Taq-i Bustan, 184–8
Tarantum, 252, 253
Taron, 33, 234, 242, 246, 248, 250, 252, 254, 400
Taurus mountains, 26, 28, 33, 34, 86, 99, 100, 103, 105, 111, 124, 126, 145, 180, 224, 234, 242, 253, 255, 256, 271, 325, 326, 327, 336, 342, 343, 399
taxation, 11, 151–2, 156, 345, 390
  Persian, 158–9, 162–3, 172, 176–7, 336–7, 366, 390
  Roman, 51, 59, 128, 145–6, 150
Thebaid, 156, 215, 216
Thebarmais, 226, 227, 330
Thebes, 155, 164
Theodore of Syceon, 73–80, 82–3, 85–6, 90, 137–40
Theodore Syncellus, 206, 208–10, 247, 258, 268–9, 272–3, 275–6, 278–80, 282–4, 288, 294, 330, 333, 404–5, 409

Theodosiopolis, 10, 21, 24, 32, 33, 34, 110, 126, 127, 131, 225, 374, 376, 400, 401
Theodosiopolis-Resaena, 31, 35, 401
Theodosius, 12, 14–18, 21, 24, 32
 pretender, 20, 23, 24, 32, 81, 108–9, 111
Theophanes the Confessor, 5, 35, 64, 87, 192, 208, 217, 219, 224–6, 228, 230–1, 234, 237, 239, 240–1, 243, 246–7, 251, 254–5, 257, 258–66, 268, 285–8, 295, 298, 300–1, 303–4, 306–8, 312–14, 333–4, 350, 389, 408, 410–1, 413
Theophilus of Edessa, 35, 64, 210, 258, 264, 265, 267, 296, 303, 304, 314, 325, 389, 410, 411
Thessalonica, 2, 4, 46, 56, 62, 135, 146, 147, 148, 212, 379, 381, 408, 409, 413
 Avar attack, 136, 202–6
Thrace, 11, 13, 107, 128, 137, 210, 211, 212, 270, 274, 275, 381, 396
Tiberias, 92, 350
Tiberius I, 14, 123, 359, 396
Tiflis, 20, 116, 220, 259, 262, 288, 291, 295, 298, 300, 301, 302, 303, 304, 319, 340, 368, 370, 371, 399, 400, 401
Tigris, 30, 253, 254, 307, 308, 310, 311, 316, 317, 318, 395, 399, 400
 upper Tigris, 30, 31, 242, 254, 325, 399, 400
Tong, khan, 118, 221, 288
trade, *see*, commerce
training, 218–19, 243
 Persian, 234, 247, 285
 Roman, 175, 193, 195–6, 198–9, 211, 222, 243., 271, 363, 365, 405, 411
Transcaucasia, 1, 19, 115, 173, 176, 178, 180, 216, 218, 220, 223, 229, 232, 234, 238, 239, 240, 245, 252, 259, 260, 262, 263, 264, 266, 268, 274, 284, 288, 290, 291, 293, 296, 297, 299, 301, 314, 319, 327, 328, 340, 353, 354, 355, 360, 364–6, 371, 386, 395, 396, 399, 401, 410
transport, 5, 56, 79, 100, 151, 156, 164, 196, 264, 269, 311, 413
 by water, 56, 59, 79, 100, 151, 250, 298
treaties, 19, 80, 116, 117, 340, 353, 369–70, 399, 400
 in 1, 314, 316, 319, 322, 325–8, 337, 342–4, 355, 628–30
 Roman-Avar, 8–9, 24, 35, 36, 101, 103, 135, 152, 201, 202, 206, 207, 212–13, 279
 Roman-Lombard, 10, 24, 36, 103, 380
 Roman-Turkish, *see* alliances
tribute payments, 107, 111, 112, 116, 213, 276, 279
True Cross, 2, 39–92, 87, 95, 99, 122, 181, 289, 324, 326, 333, 343, 357, 364, 366, 367, 405, 410
 Restoration, 345–52, 356, 392

Tur Abdin, 24, 29, 30, 31, 35, 233, 399, 400, 409
Turan, 113, 115
Turks, 2, 136, 290, 291, 293, 303–4, 319, 328, 338, 345, 355, 361, 384, 396, 399
 attacks on Persia, 118, 175, 179–80, 206, 231, 258–9, 288–9, 293, 295–300, 302, 340, 342, 370–1
 khagan, 4, 117, 221, 288–90, 293–4, 303, 354, 360, 369–70, 413
 khaganate, 2, 18, 120, 174, 180, 221, 238, 293–4, 369, 371, 396
 relations with China, 136, 340, 353–4, 360, 369–70
 relations with Persians, 19, 117, 175, 259, 268, 289–91, 296, 316, 327, 341
 relations with Romans, 20, 213–14, 221–2, 238, 240, 245, 259, 261, 288–9, 301–2, 342, 369–72
 shad, 260, 288, 289, 290, 293, 294, 302, 340, 341, 354, 371
 yabghu khagan, 221, 238, 239, 259, 262, 263, 288, 289, 293, 300, 301, 302, 340, 341, 342, 354, 370
Tyre, 87, 100, 160, 356

Urmia, 226, 228, 237, 305, 319, 364, 399, 401

Van, Lake, 19, 236, 242, 246, 253, 325, 355, 399, 401
Veh-Ardashir, 95, 364, 372, 383, 384, 386
Via Egnatia, 209, 275
Virgin Mary, 12, 209, 260, 269, 272, 276, 282, 326, 329, 404
 intercession, 67, 264, 282–4, 287, 304
Viroy, catholicos, 289, 337, 341
Visigoths, 135, 136, 360, 380, 395, 396

war-weariness, 35, 221, 314, 322, 327, 337
western Eurasia, 1, 3, 56, 112, 113, 116, 119, 136, 174, 219, 221, 292, 344, 360, 362, 371, 395

Yazdgerd III, 295, 382–4, 390
Yazdin, 122, 369
 family, 312, 316, 337

Zacharias, patriarch, 88, 89, 92, 93, 95, 98, 102, 121, 130, 137, 230, 352, 353, 410
Zagros mountains, 19, 174, 178, 184, 227, 228, 229, 233, 237, 264, 297, 303, 305, 306, 309, 310, 317, 318, 319, 321, 336, 364, 365, 386, 395, 399, 408
Zenobia, 31, 36, 71, 72, 78, 216
Zoroastrianism, 2, 88, 102, 106, 114, 115, 122, 159, 160, 173, 174, 183, 187, 193, 216, 226, 227, 286, 323, 328, 330, 338, 346, 366, 367, 368, 369, 395